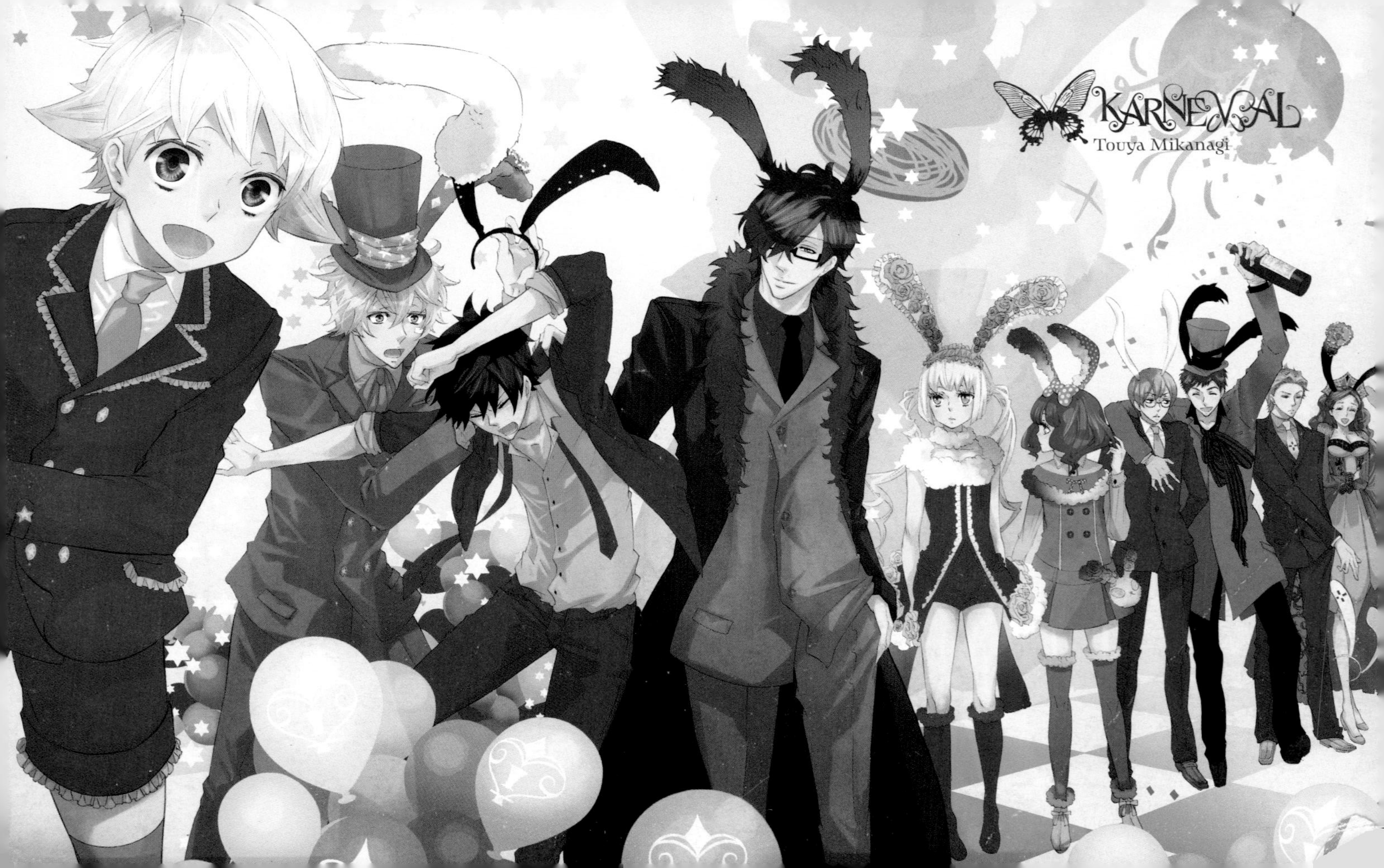
KARNEVAL
Touya Mikanagi

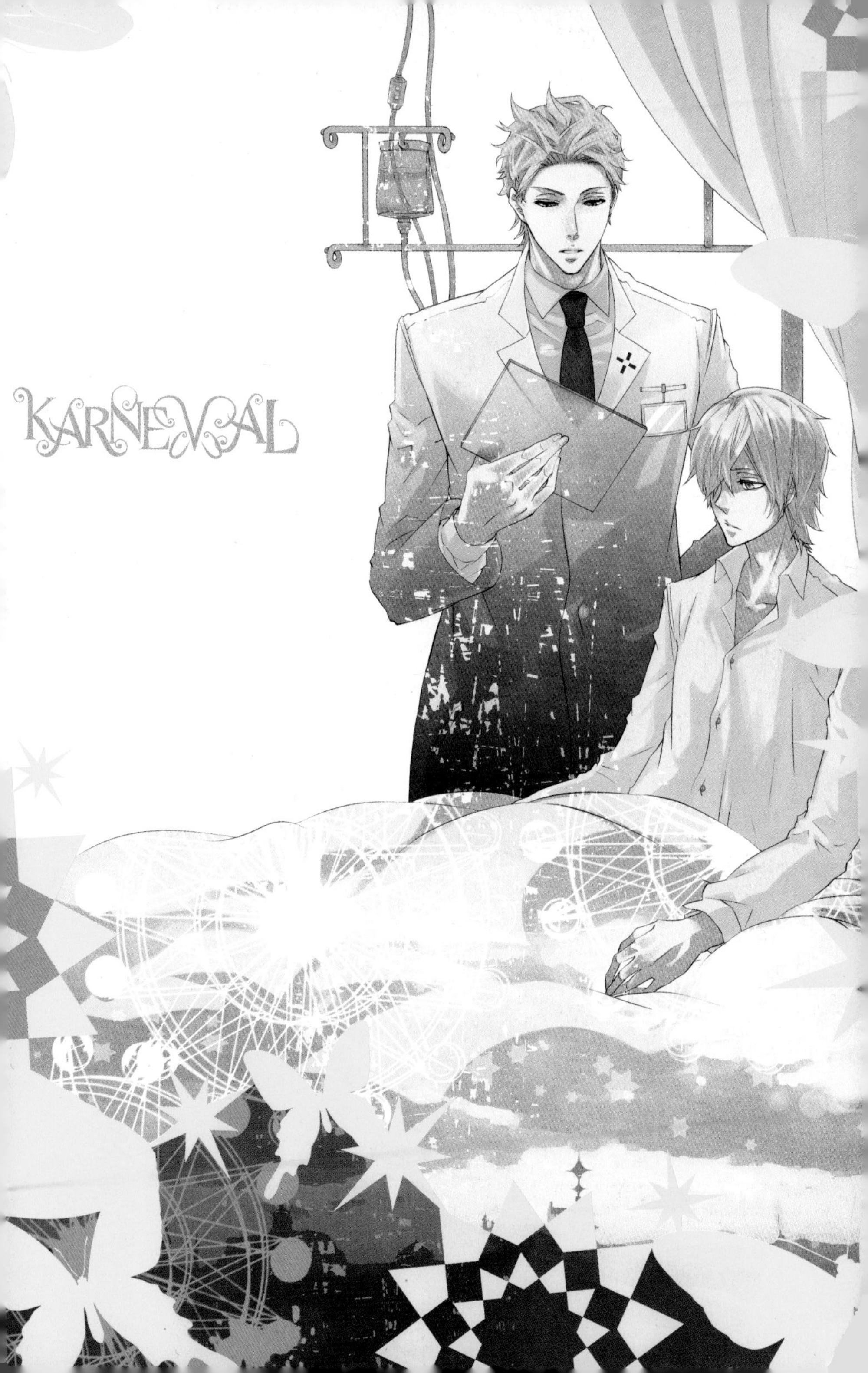
KARNEVAL

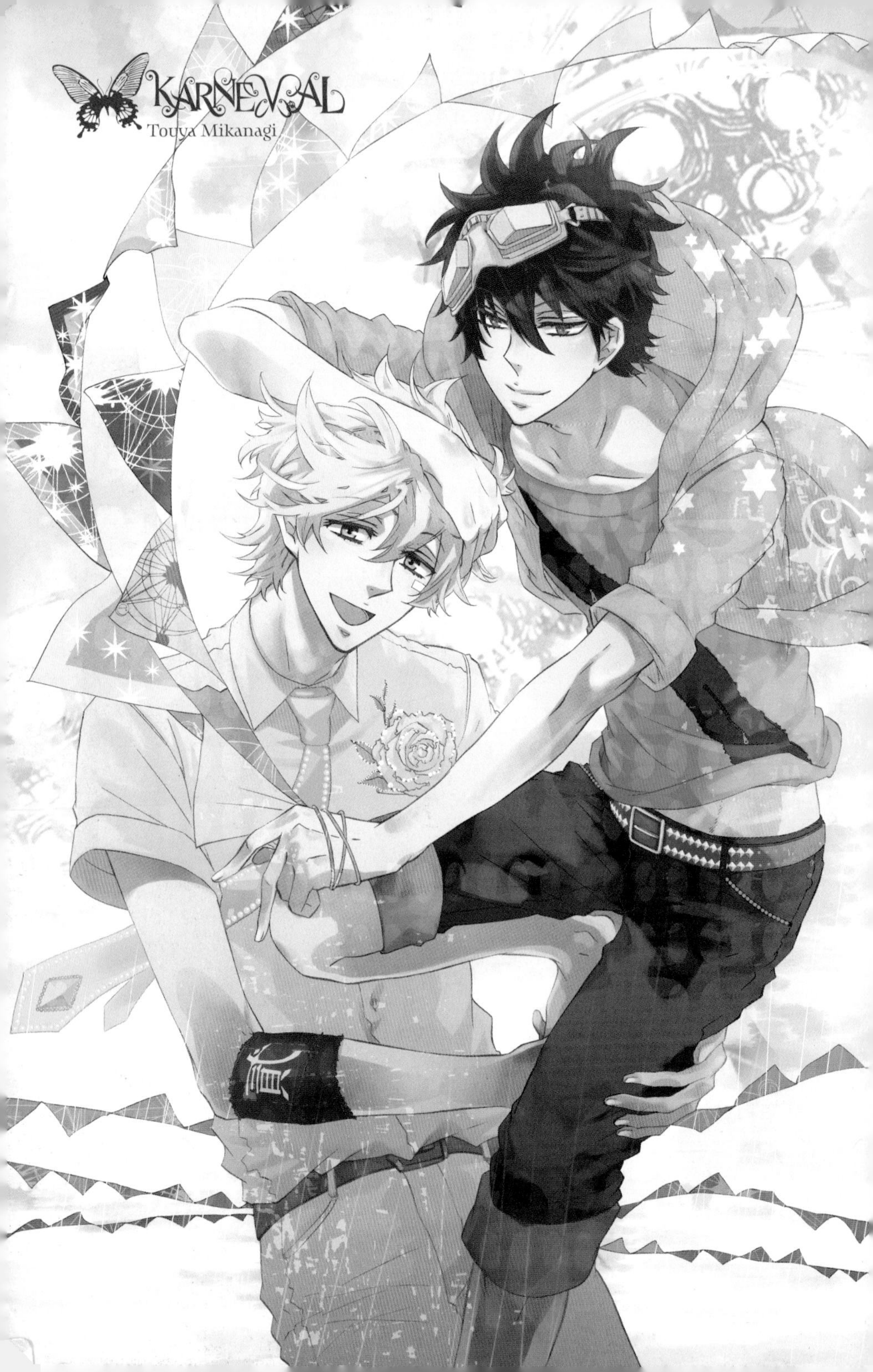
KARNEVAL
Touya Mikanagi

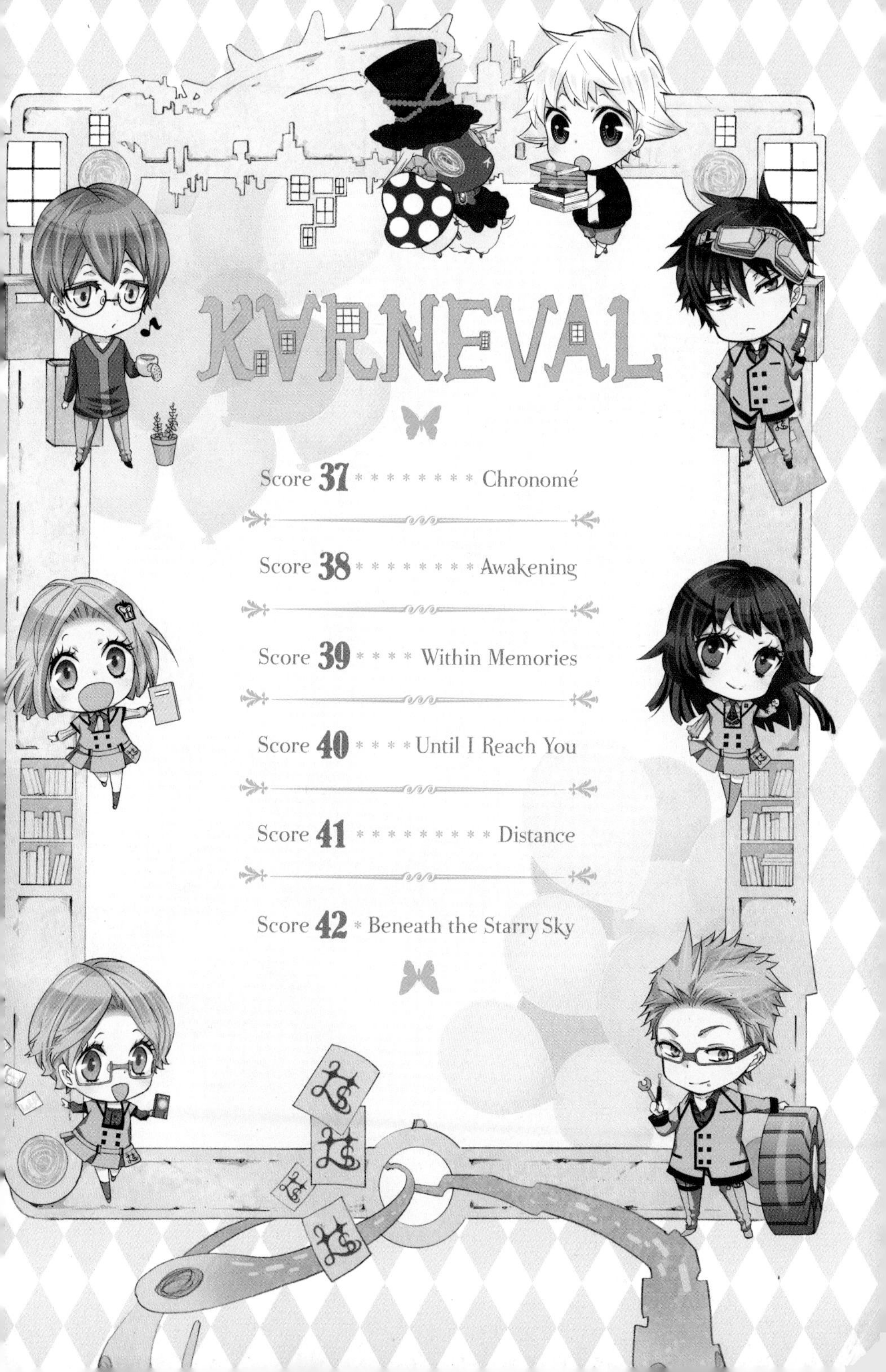

KARNEVAL

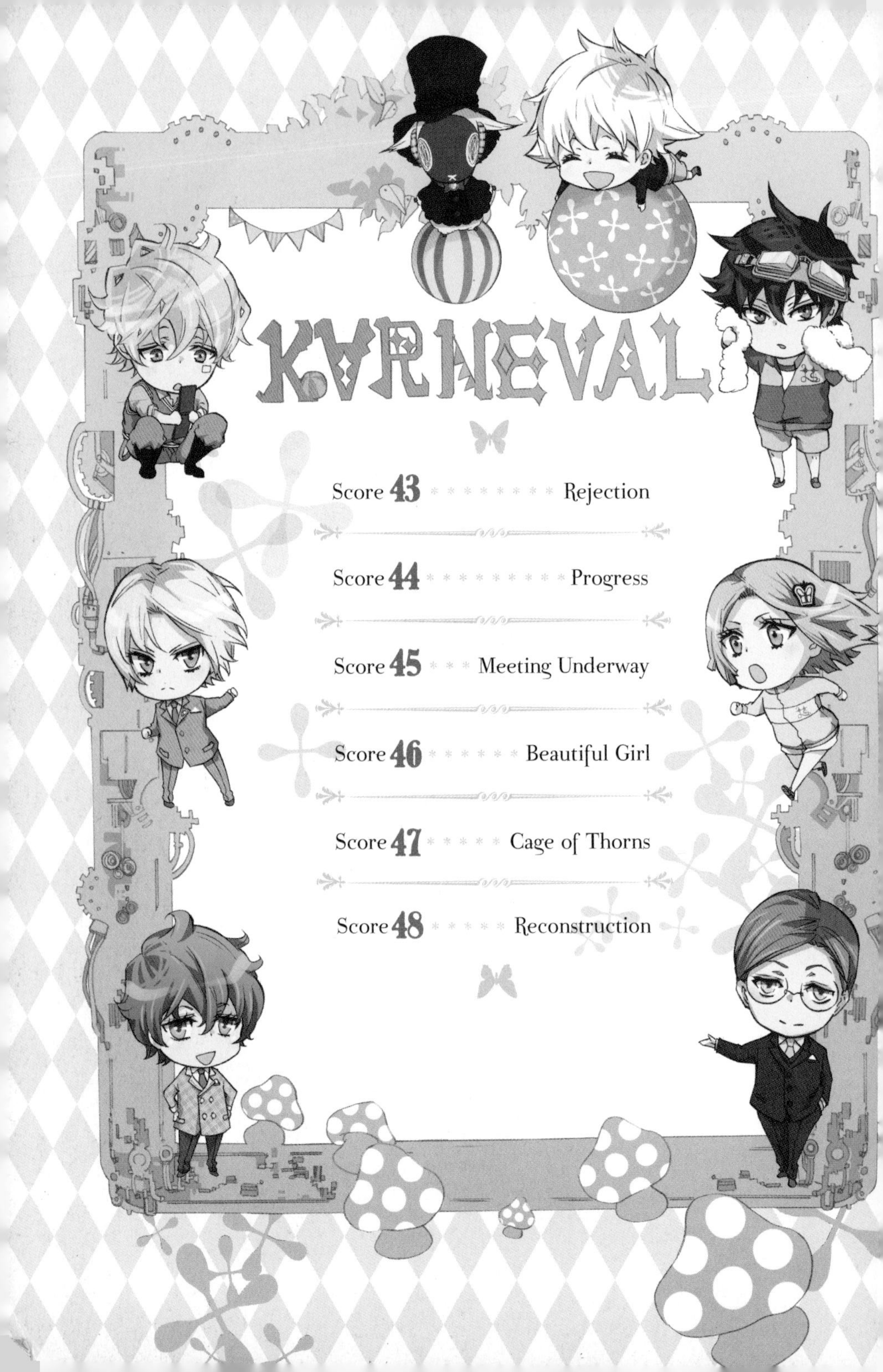
KARNEVAL

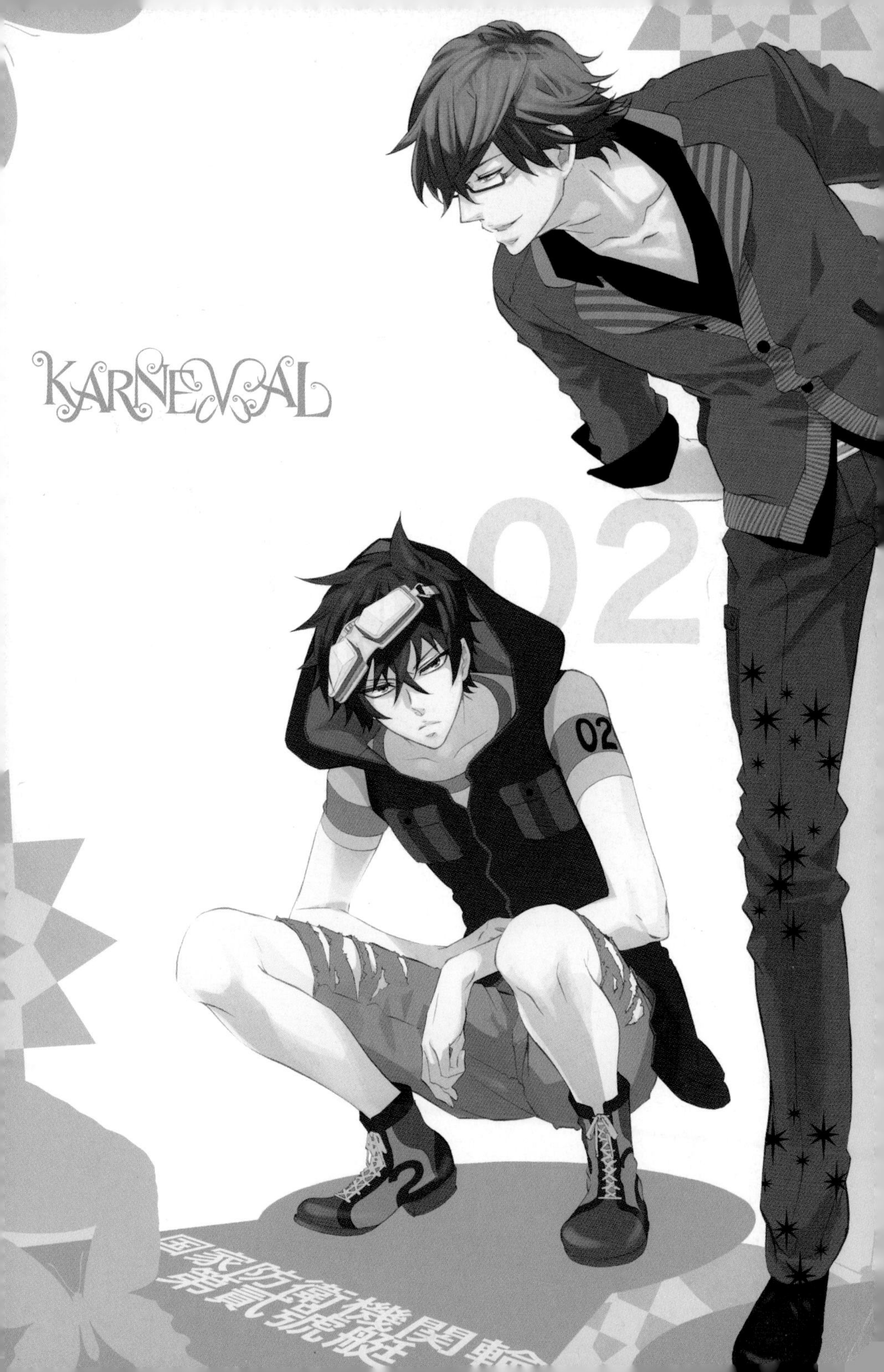
KARNEVAL
02
02
國家防衛機關輪
第貳號艇

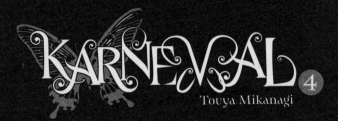

KARNEVAL 4

Touya Mikanagi

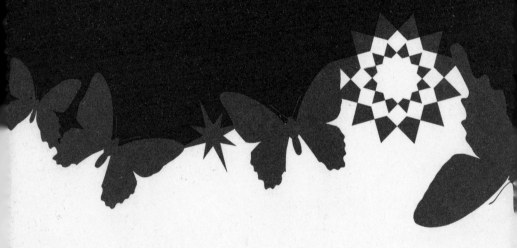

STORY

A YOUNG BOY NAMED NAI JOURNEYS IN SEARCH OF THE MISSING KAROKU, ACCOMPANIED BY GAREKI AND THE AGENTS OF CIRCUS WHOM HE HAS ENCOUNTERED ALONG THE WAY. IN ORDER TO RESCUE KAROKU, THE AGENTS OF CIRCUS COMMENCED AN ATTACK ON THE "SMOKY MANSION" STRONGHOLD. IN THE MIDDLE OF THE BATTLE, A "RAINBOW" AND A SECRET DOOR SUDDENLY APPEARED AS THOUGH RESPONDING TO NAI'S VOICE. IN THE MYSTERIOUS WORLD BEYOND THE SECRET DOOR, NAI AND GAREKI ENCOUNTER TWO KAROKUS. TAKING ADVANTAGE OF THEIR CONFUSION, ONE OF THE KAROKUS SENDS THE PAIR AND HIS UNCONSCIOUS DOUBLE BACK TO THE OUTSIDE WORLD, LEAVING THEM WITH SOME CRYPTIC WORDS. RETURNING TO THE 2ND SHIP, NAI WORRIES FOR THE STILL-UNCONSCIOUS KAROKU. MEANWHILE, HAVING FULLY REALIZED HIS OWN POWERLESSNESS DURING THE BATTLE AT THE SMOKY MANSION, GAREKI CONSULTS WITH HIRATO AND DECIDES TO ATTEND A GOVERNMENTAL SCHOOL...

CHARACTERS OF KARNEVAL

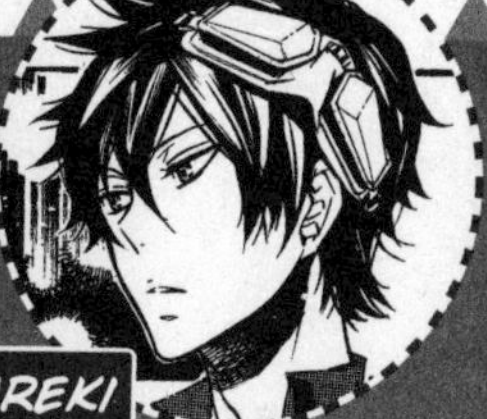

GAREKI

HE MET NAI INSIDE AN EERIE MANSION THAT HE HAD INTENDED TO BURGLARIZE. INTRIGUED BY THE BRACELET NAI CARRIES, HE HAS JOINED FORCES WITH THE BOY.

RESCUED →

← ATTACHED

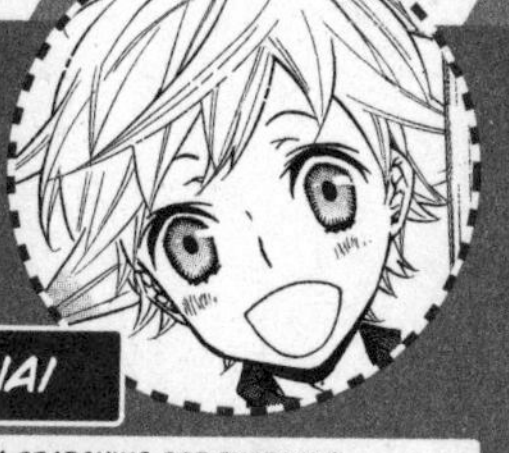

NAI

A BOY SEARCHING FOR "KAROKU" WITH A BRACELET AS HIS ONLY CLUE. THOUGH HIS ABILITY TO SURVIVE ON HIS OWN SEEMS VERY LOW, HE HAS AMAZINGLY SHARP HEARING.

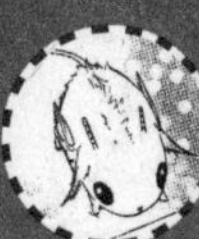

NIJI

THE ANIMAL THAT NAI WAS CREATED FROM. THEY EXIST ONLY IN THE RAINBOW FOREST, A HIGHLY UNUSUAL ECOSYSTEM THAT ALLOWED THE NIJI TO EVOLVE AS THEY DID.

ON THE TRAIL OF

GUARDING

NATIONAL SUPREME DEFENSE FORCE "CIRCUS" 2ND SHIP

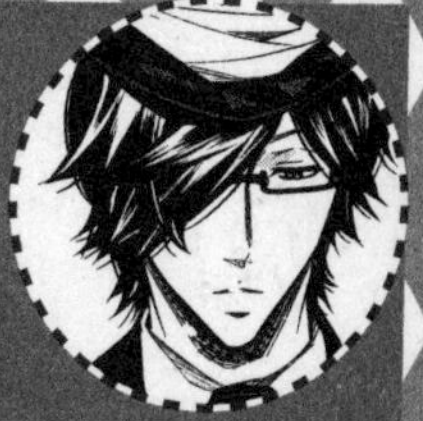

HIRATO

CAPTAIN OF CIRCUS'S 2ND SHIP. NAI (AND GAREKI), WHO BROUGHT THEM A BRACELET BELONGING TO CIRCUS, ARE CURRENTLY UNDER HIS PROTECTION.

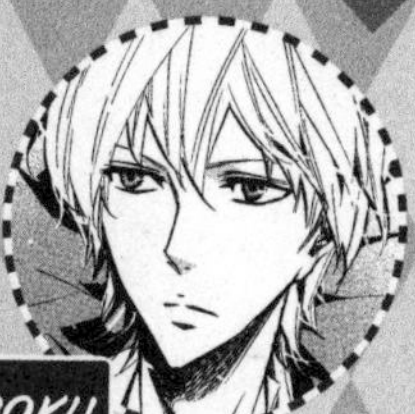

KAROKU

THE PERSON WHO CREATED NAI. HE SEEMS TO BE ABLE TO CONTACT NAI TELEPATHICALLY...

← ? →

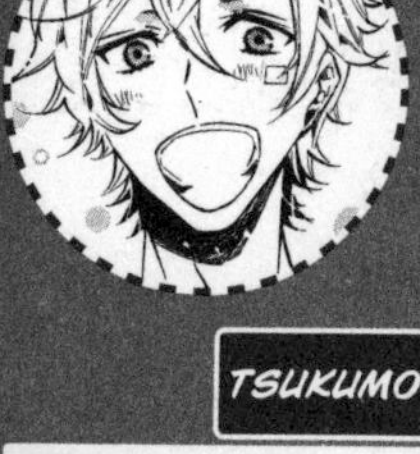

YOGI

CIRCUS'S 2ND SHIP COMBAT SPECIALIST. HE HAS A CHEERFUL, FRIENDLY PERSONALITY. FOR SHOWS, HE WEARS AN ANIMAL MASCOT SUIT.

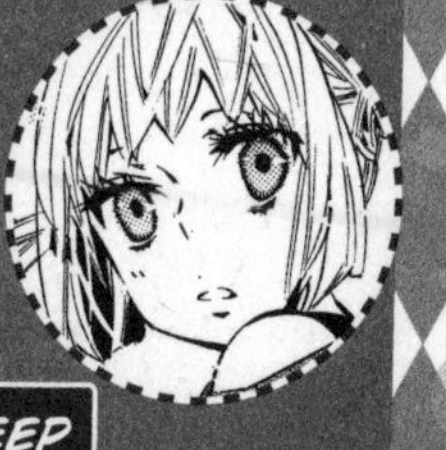

TSUKUMO

CIRCUS'S 2ND SHIP COMBAT SPECIALIST. A BEAUTIFUL GIRL WITH A COOL, SERIOUS PERSONALITY. AS A SHOW PERFORMER, SHE IS VERY POPULAR DUE TO HER DAZZLING ACROBATICS AND BEAUTY.

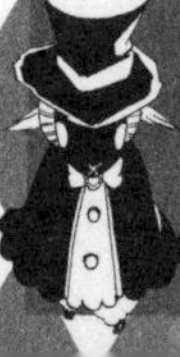

SHEEP

A CIRCUS DEFENSE SYSTEM. DESPITE THEIR CUTE APPEARANCE, THE SHEEP HAVE SOME VERY POWERFUL CAPABILITIES.

Q: WHAT IS CIRCUS?

A: THE EQUIVALENT OF THE REAL-WORLD POLICE. THEY CONDUCT THEIR LARGE-SCALE "OPERATIONS" WITHOUT FOREWARNING TO ENSURE THEIR TARGETS WILL NOT ESCAPE ARREST, UTILIZING COORDINATED, POWERFUL ATTACKS!! AFTER AN OPERATION, CIRCUS PERFORMS A "SHOW" FOR THE PEOPLE OF THE CITY AS AN APOLOGY FOR THE FEAR AND INCONVENIENCE THEIR WORK MAY HAVE CAUSED. IN SHORT, "CIRCUS" IS A CHEERFUL (?) AGENCY THAT CARRIES OUT THEIR MISSION DAY AND NIGHT TO APPREHEND EVIL AND PROTECT THE PEACE OF THE LAND.

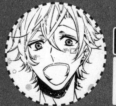

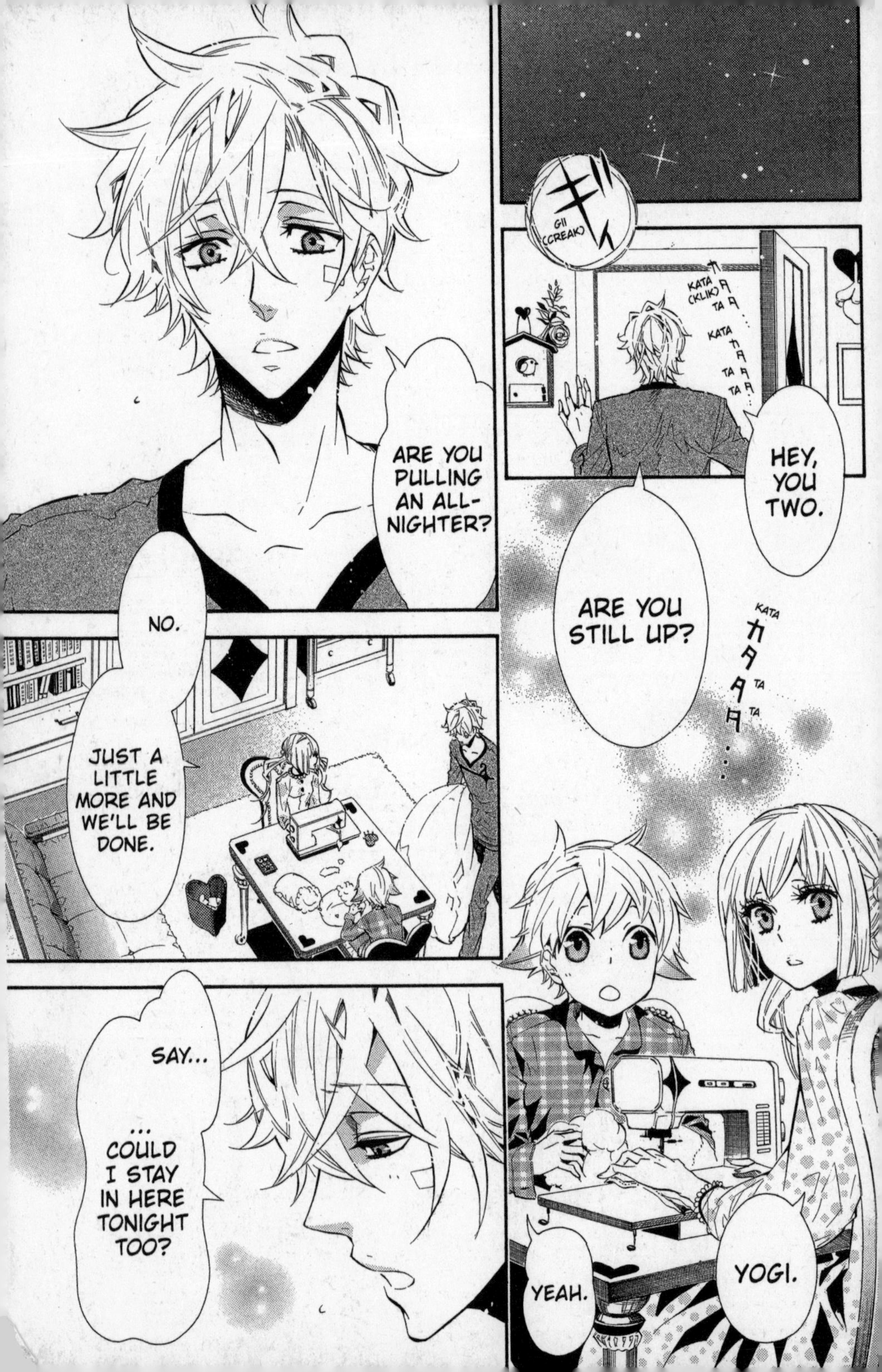
GII (CREAK)
KATA (KLIK) TA TA...
KATA TA TA TA...
HEY, YOU TWO.
ARE YOU STILL UP?
KATA TA TA...
YOGI.
YEAH.
ARE YOU PULLING AN ALL-NIGHTER?
NO.
JUST A LITTLE MORE AND WE'LL BE DONE.
SAY...
...COULD I STAY IN HERE TONIGHT TOO?

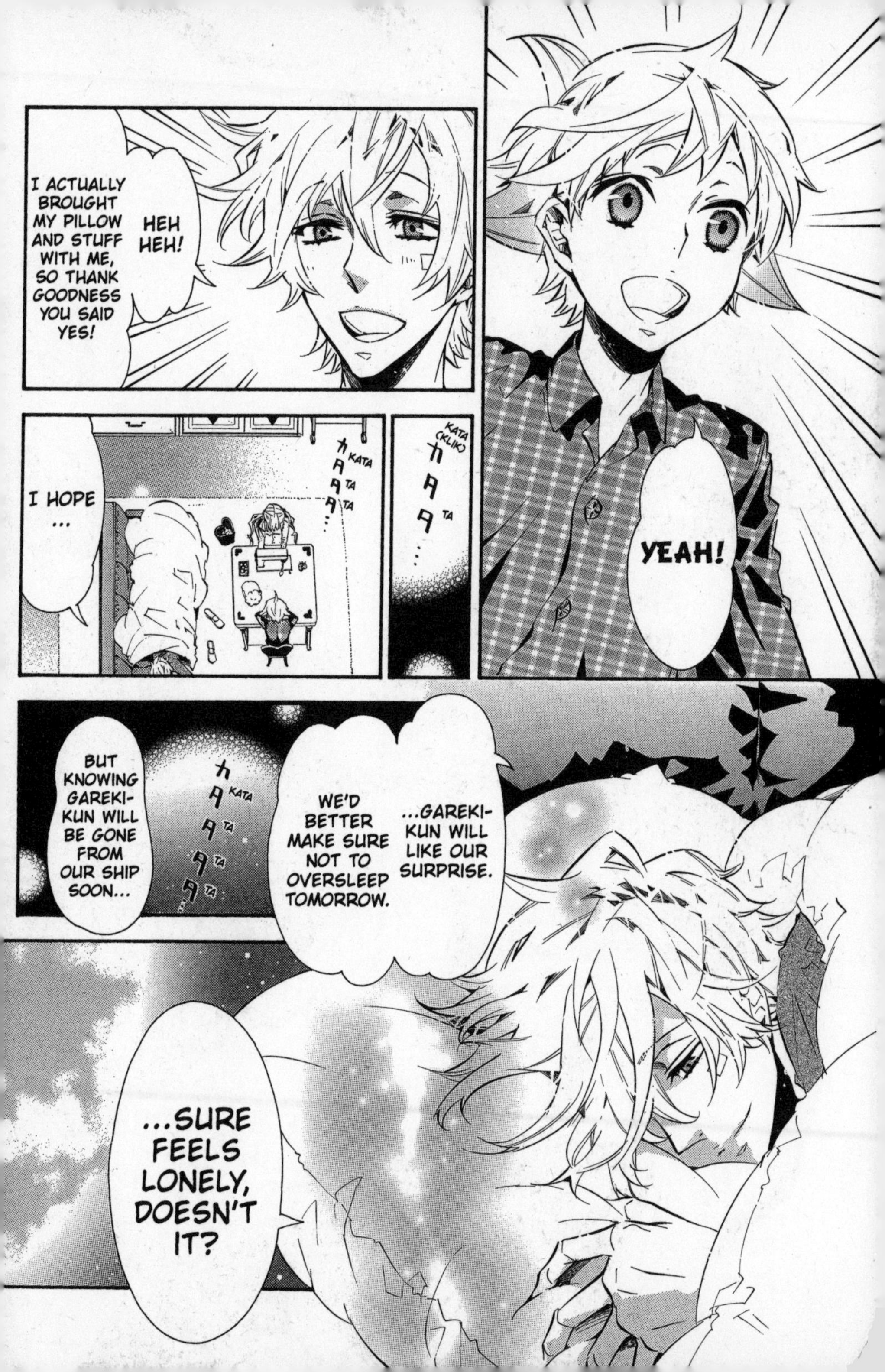
YEAH!
HEH HEH!
I ACTUALLY BROUGHT MY PILLOW AND STUFF WITH ME, SO THANK GOODNESS YOU SAID YES!
カタタ…
KATA (KLIK) TA
カタタタ…
KATA TA TA
I HOPE…
…GAREKI-KUN WILL LIKE OUR SURPRISE.
WE'D BETTER MAKE SURE NOT TO OVERSLEEP TOMORROW.
カタタタタ…
KATA TA TA TA
BUT KNOWING GAREKI-KUN WILL BE GONE FROM OUR SHIP SOON…
…SURE FEELS LONELY, DOESN'T IT?

Score 37: Chronome

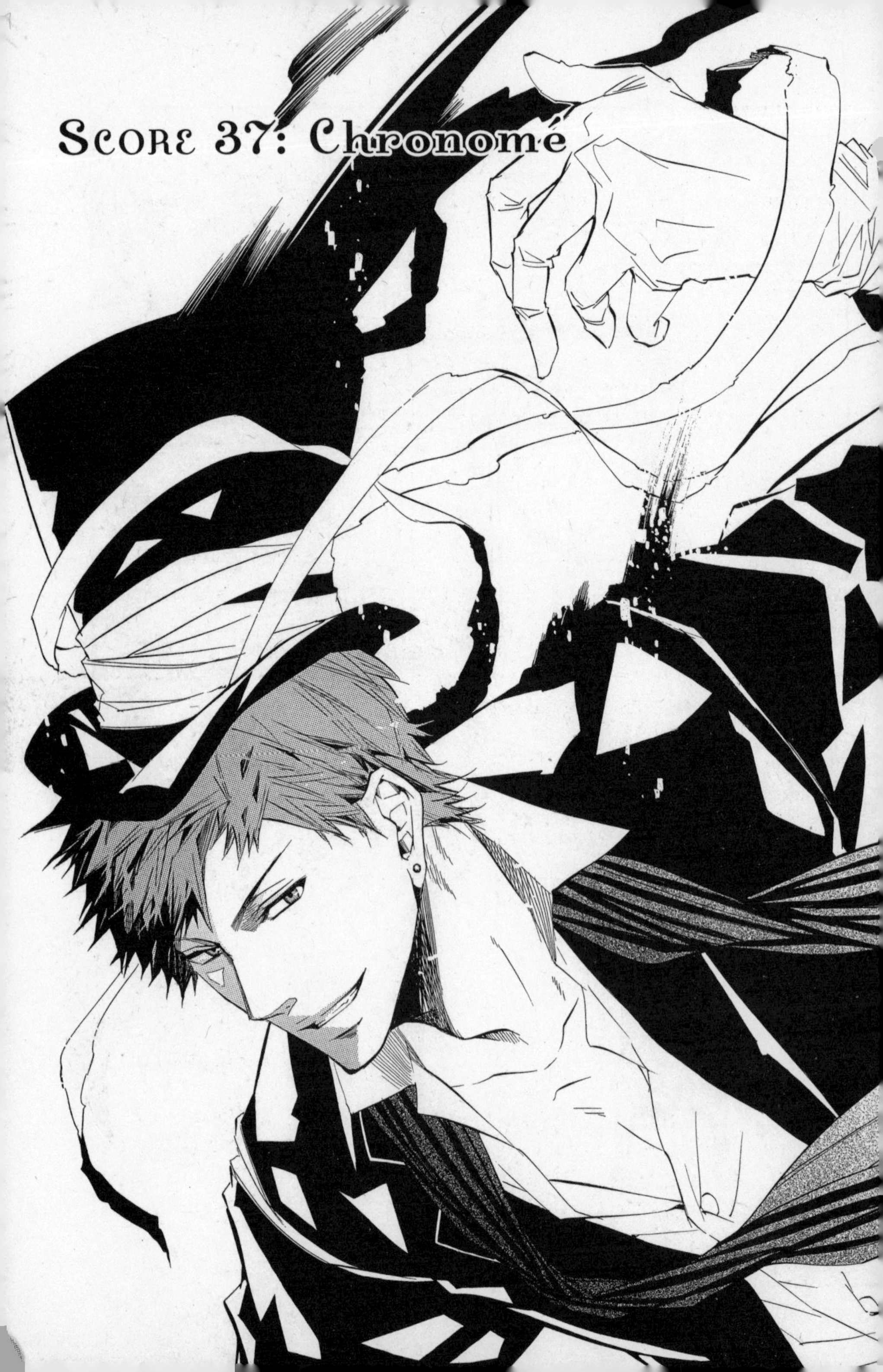

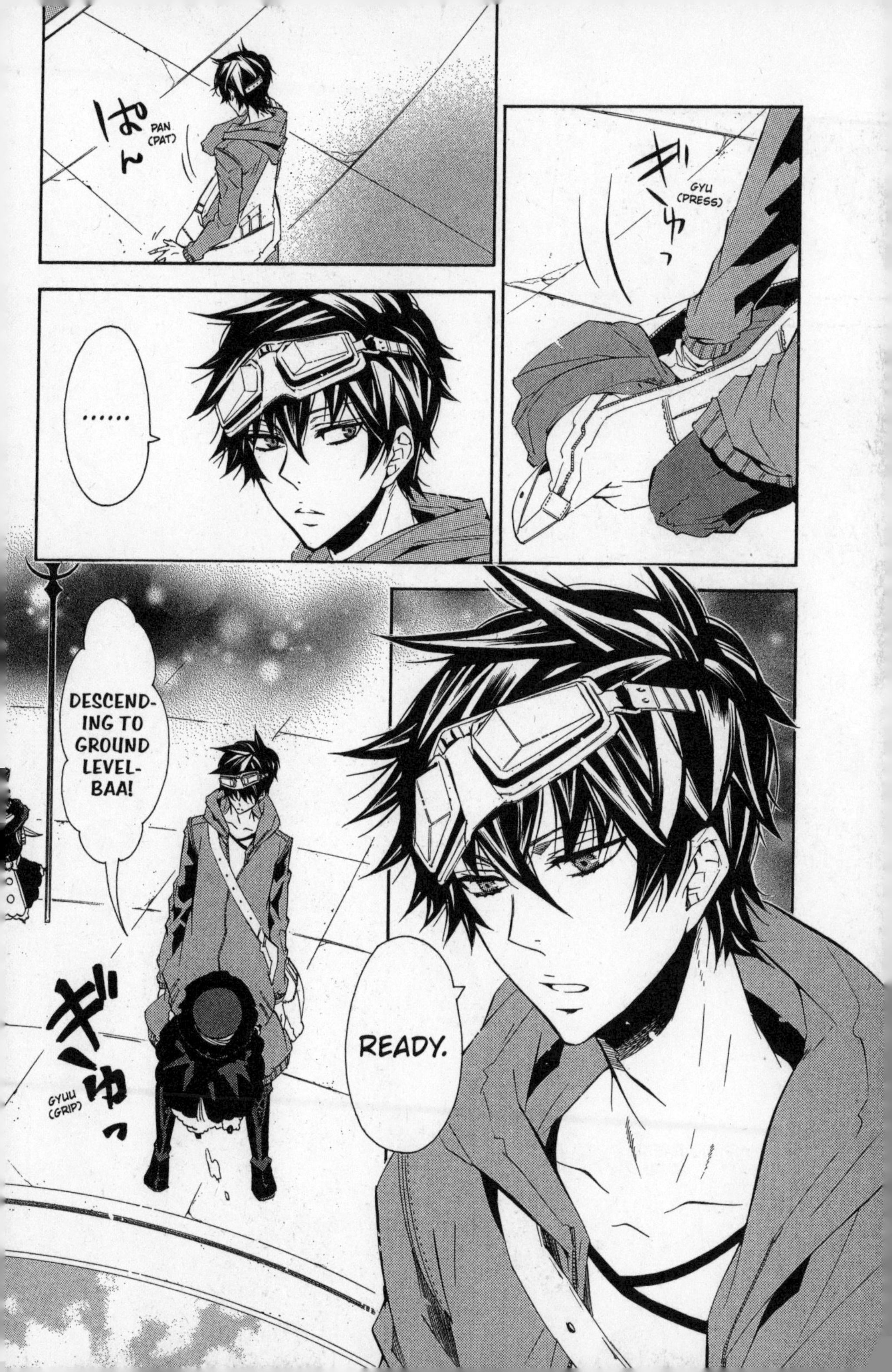
ぎゅっ
GYU (PRESS)
ぱん
PAN (PAT)
......
READY.
DESCENDING-ING TO GROUND LEVEL-BAA!
ぎゅっ
GYUU (GRIP)

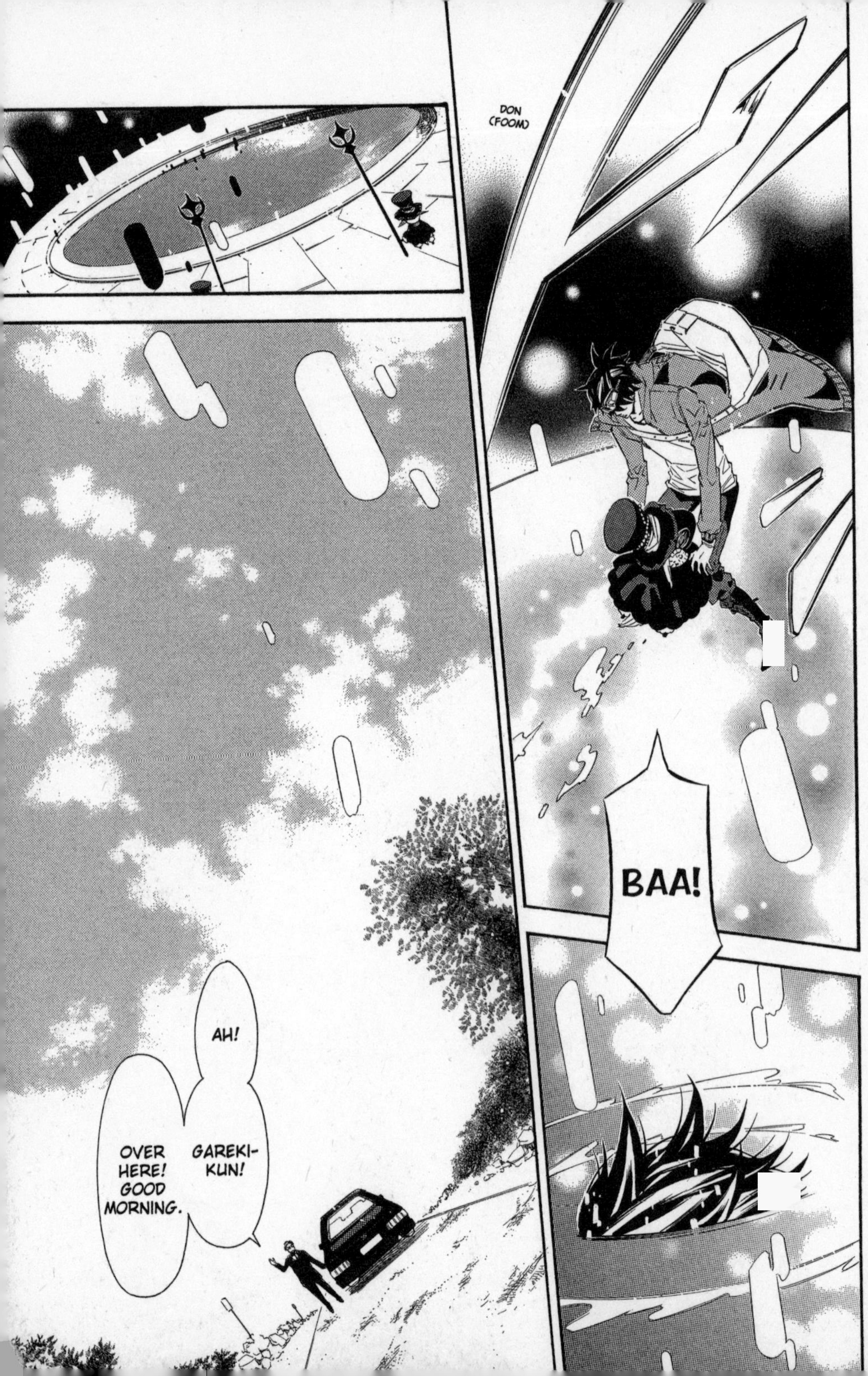
DON (FOOM)
BAA!
AH!
GAREKI-KUN!
OVER HERE! GOOD MORNING.

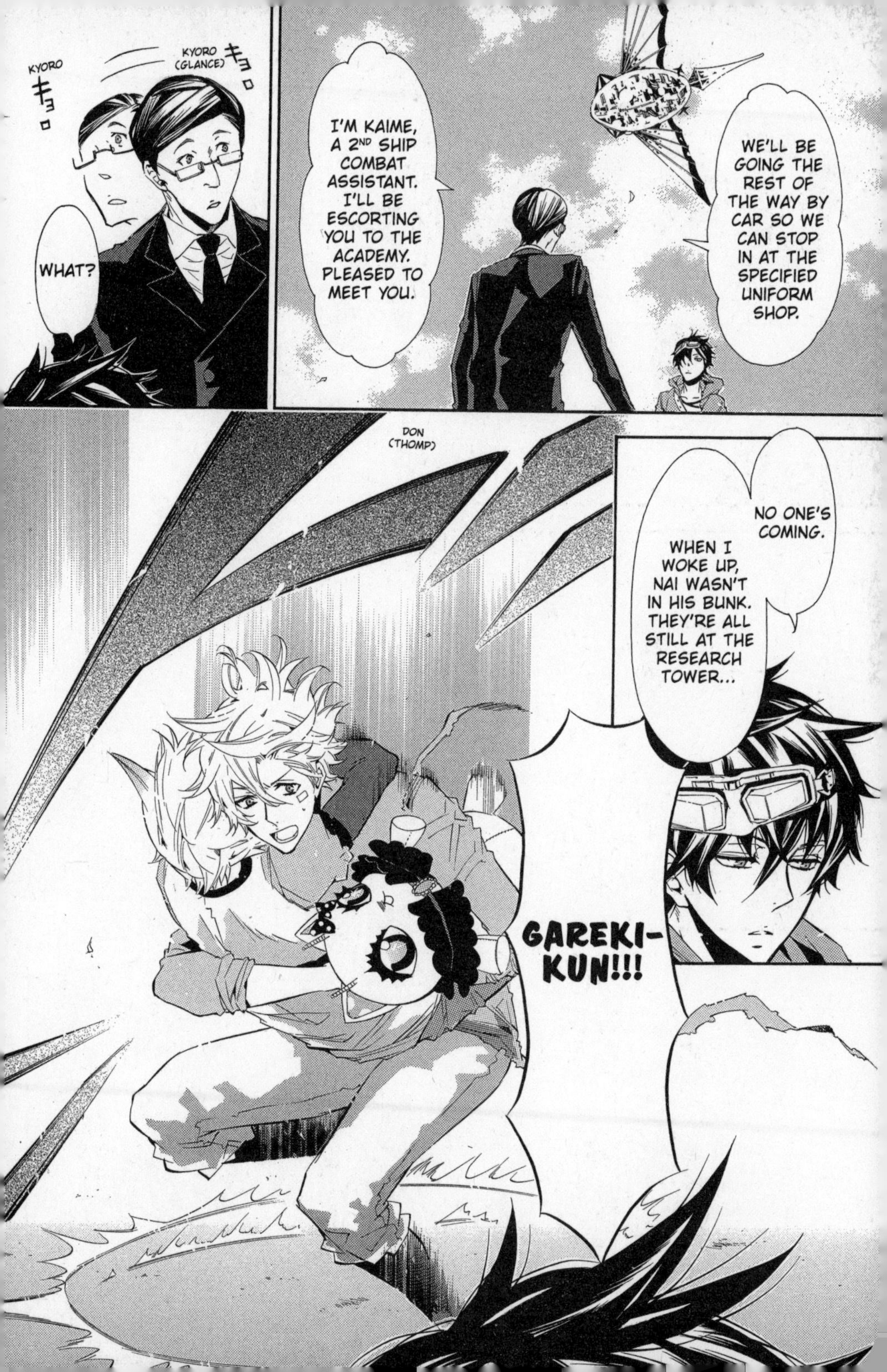
I'M KAIME, A 2ND SHIP COMBAT ASSISTANT. I'LL BE ESCORTING YOU TO THE ACADEMY. PLEASED TO MEET YOU.
WE'LL BE GOING THE REST OF THE WAY BY CAR SO WE CAN STOP IN AT THE SPECIFIED UNIFORM SHOP.
KYORO (GLANCE) キョロ
KYORO キョロ
WHAT?
NO ONE'S COMING.
WHEN I WOKE UP, NAI WASN'T IN HIS BUNK. THEY'RE ALL STILL AT THE RESEARCH TOWER...
DON (THOMP)
GAREKI-KUN!!!

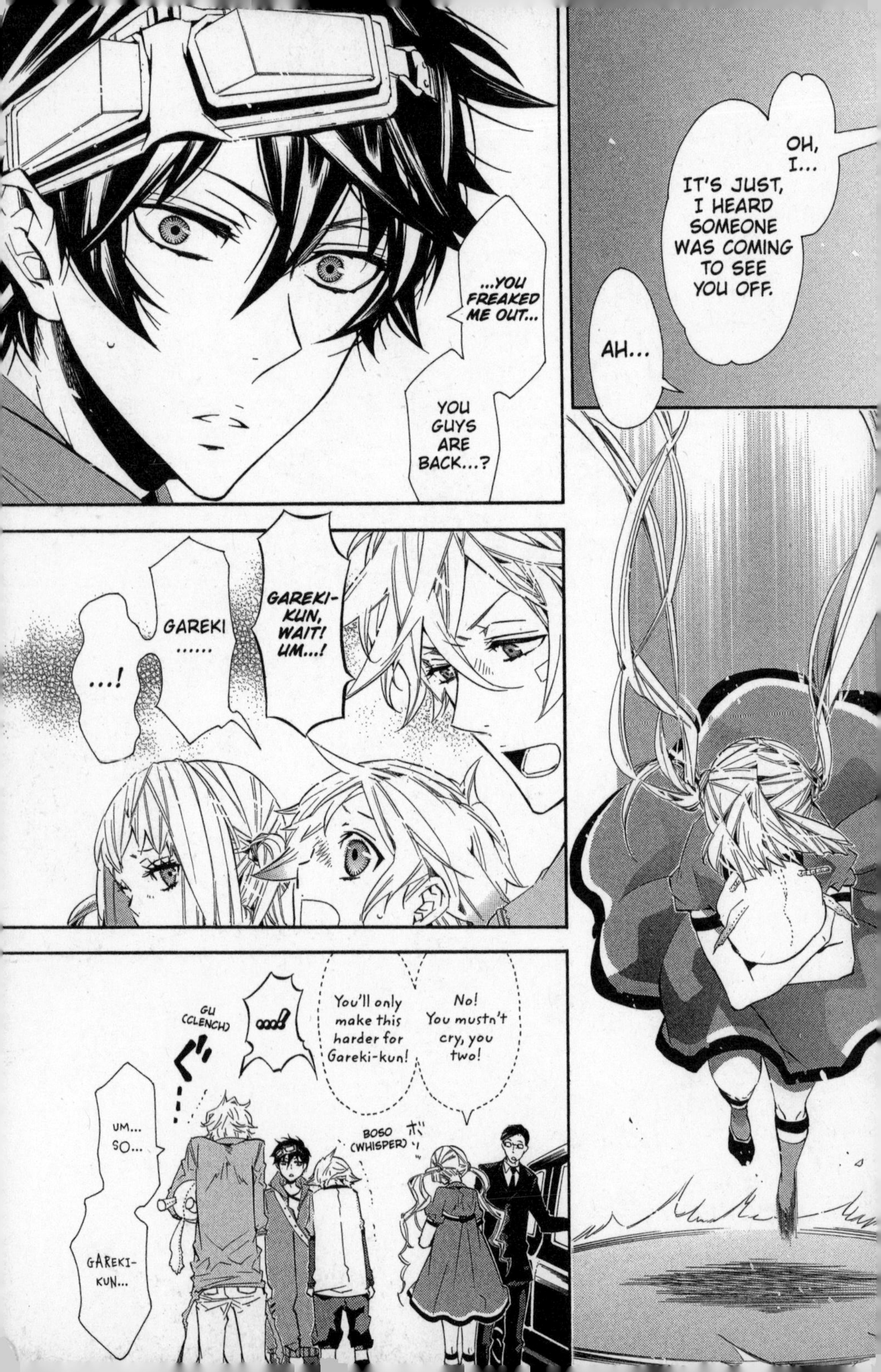
OH, I... IT'S JUST, I HEARD SOMEONE WAS COMING TO SEE YOU OFF.
AH...
...YOU FREAKED ME OUT...
YOU GUYS ARE BACK...?
GAREKI-KUN, WAIT! UM...!
GAREKI......
...!
No! You mustn't cry, you two!
You'll only make this harder for Gareki-kun!
ooo!
GU (CLENCH)
BOSO (WHISPER)
UM... SO...
GAREKI-KUN...

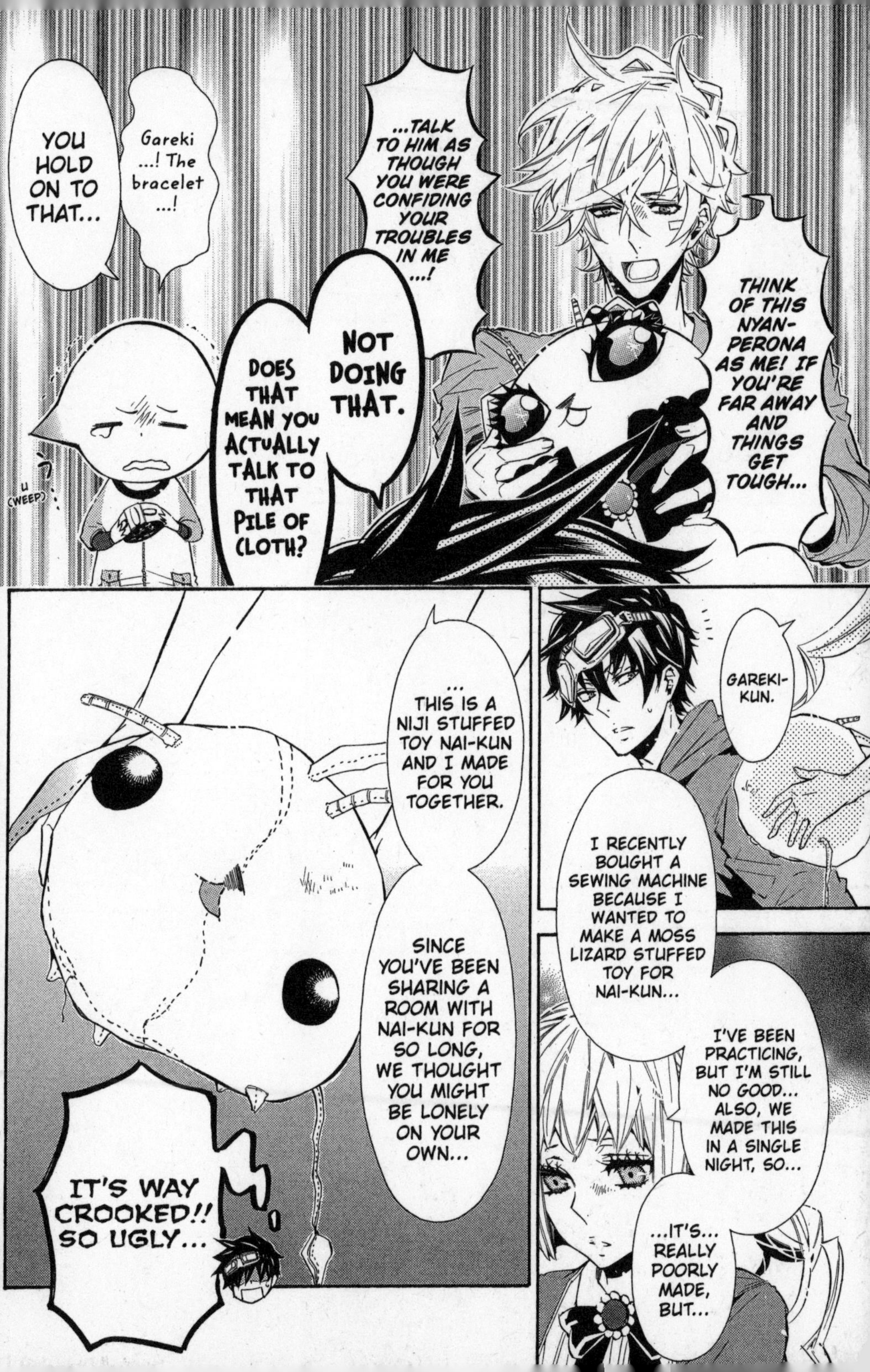
THINK OF THIS NYAN-PERONA AS ME! IF YOU'RE FAR AWAY AND THINGS GET TOUGH...
...TALK TO HIM AS THOUGH YOU WERE CONFIDING YOUR TROUBLES IN ME...!
NOT DOING THAT.
DOES THAT MEAN YOU ACTUALLY TALK TO THAT PILE OF CLOTH?
Gareki...! The bracelet...!
YOU HOLD ON TO THAT...
U (WEEP)
GAREKI-KUN.
I RECENTLY BOUGHT A SEWING MACHINE BECAUSE I WANTED TO MAKE A MOSS LIZARD STUFFED TOY FOR NAI-KUN...
I'VE BEEN PRACTICING, BUT I'M STILL NO GOOD... ALSO, WE MADE THIS IN A SINGLE NIGHT, SO...
...IT'S... REALLY POORLY MADE, BUT...
...THIS IS A NIJI STUFFED TOY NAI-KUN AND I MADE FOR YOU TOGETHER.
SINCE YOU'VE BEEN SHARING A ROOM WITH NAI-KUN FOR SO LONG, WE THOUGHT YOU MIGHT BE LONELY ON YOUR OWN...
IT'S WAY CROOKED!! SO UGLY...

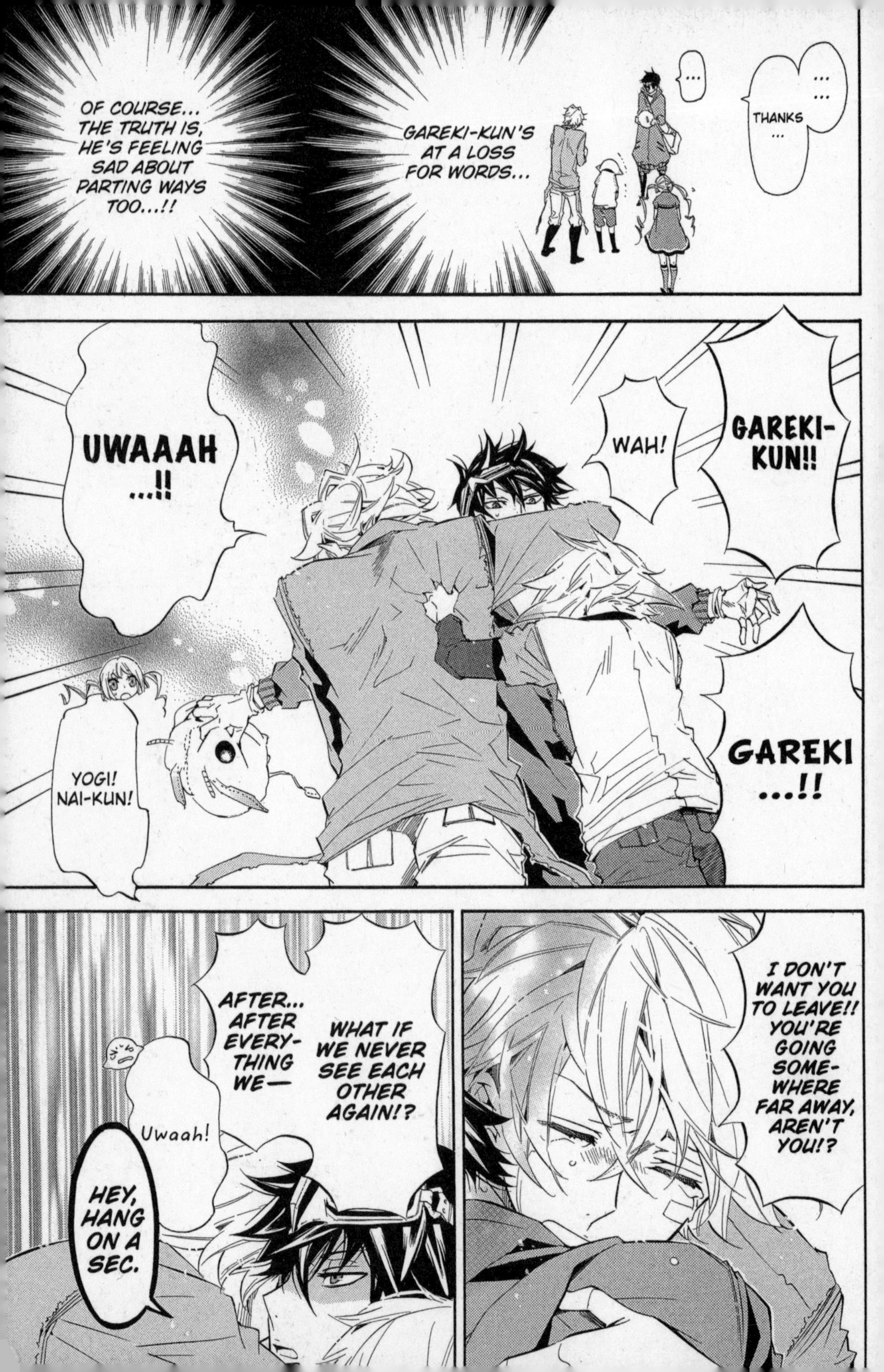

... ... THANKS ...
...
GAREKI-KUN'S AT A LOSS FOR WORDS...
OF COURSE... THE TRUTH IS, HE'S FEELING SAD ABOUT PARTING WAYS TOO...!!
GAREKI-KUN!!
WAH!
UWAAAH ...!!
GAREKI ...!!
YOGI! NAI-KUN!
I DON'T WANT YOU TO LEAVE!! YOU'RE GOING SOMEWHERE FAR AWAY, AREN'T YOU!?
WHAT IF WE NEVER SEE EACH OTHER AGAIN!?
AFTER... AFTER EVERYTHING WE—
Uwaah!
HEY, HANG ON A SEC.

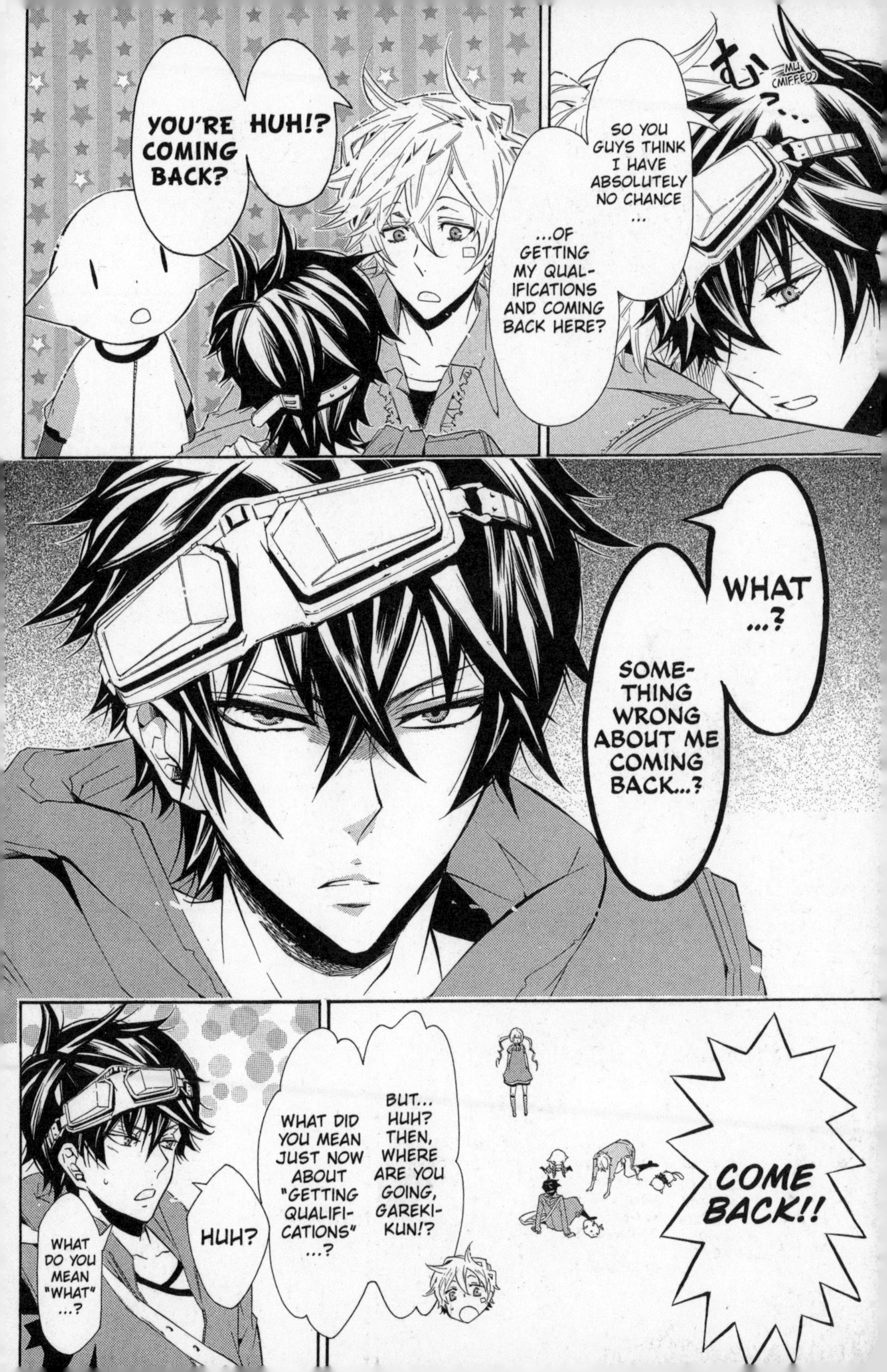
む
MU (MIFFED)
SO YOU GUYS THINK I HAVE ABSOLUTELY NO CHANCE ...
...OF GETTING MY QUALIFICATIONS AND COMING BACK HERE?
HUH!?
YOU'RE COMING BACK?
WHAT ...?
SOMETHING WRONG ABOUT ME COMING BACK...?
COME BACK!!
BUT... HUH? THEN, WHERE ARE YOU GOING, GAREKI-KUN!?
WHAT DID YOU MEAN JUST NOW ABOUT "GETTING QUALIFICATIONS" ...?
HUH?
WHAT DO YOU MEAN "WHAT" ...?

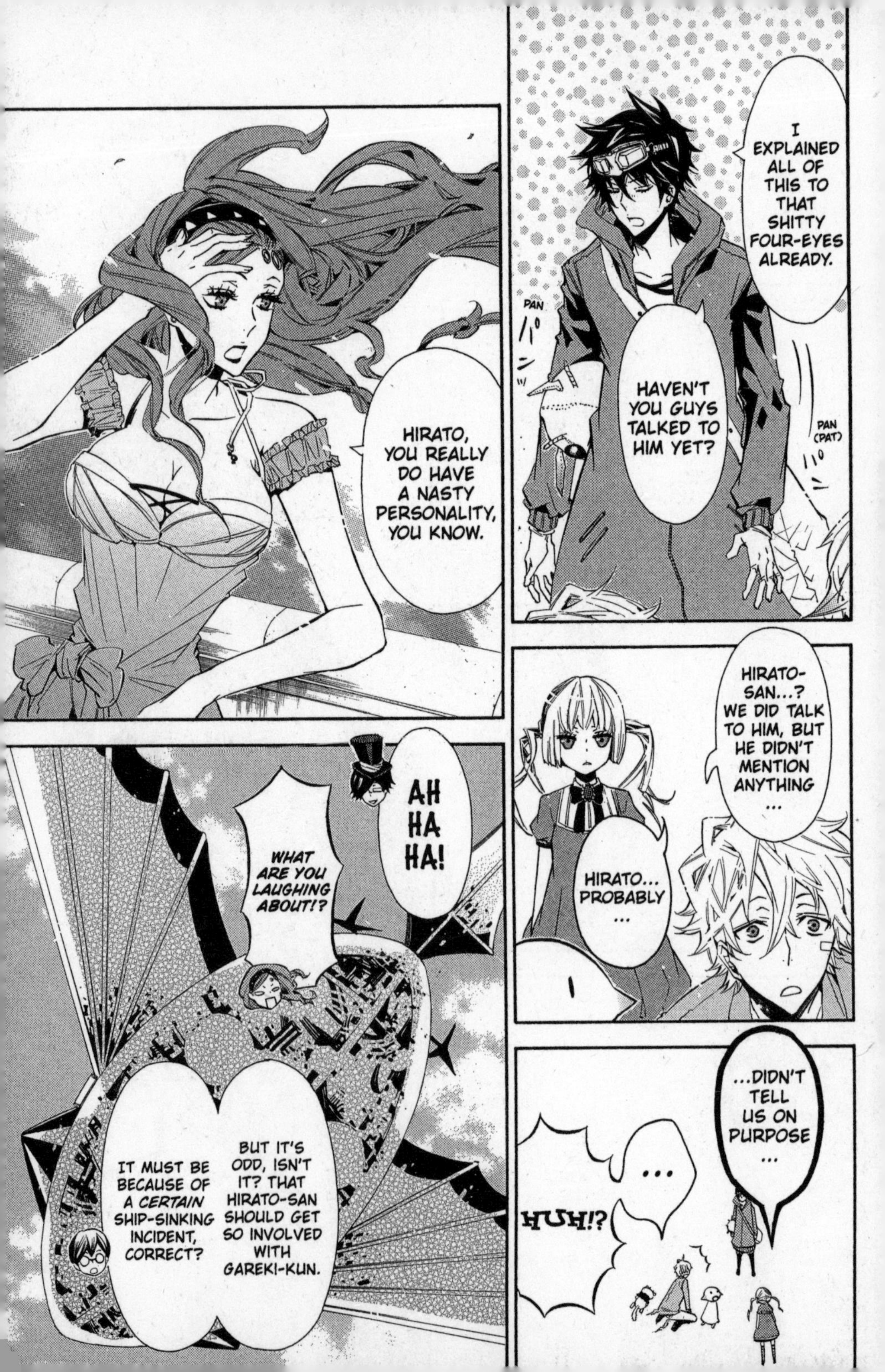
I EXPLAINED ALL OF THIS TO THAT SHITTY FOUR-EYES ALREADY.
PAN (PAT)
HAVEN'T YOU GUYS TALKED TO HIM YET?
PAN
HIRATO, YOU REALLY DO HAVE A NASTY PERSONALITY, YOU KNOW.
HIRATO-SAN...? WE DID TALK TO HIM, BUT HE DIDN'T MENTION ANYTHING...
HIRATO... PROBABLY...
...DIDN'T TELL US ON PURPOSE...
...
HUH!?
AH HA HA!
WHAT ARE YOU LAUGHING ABOUT!?
BUT IT'S ODD, ISN'T IT? THAT HIRATO-SAN SHOULD GET SO INVOLVED WITH GAREKI-KUN.
IT MUST BE BECAUSE OF A *CERTAIN* SHIP-SINKING INCIDENT, CORRECT?

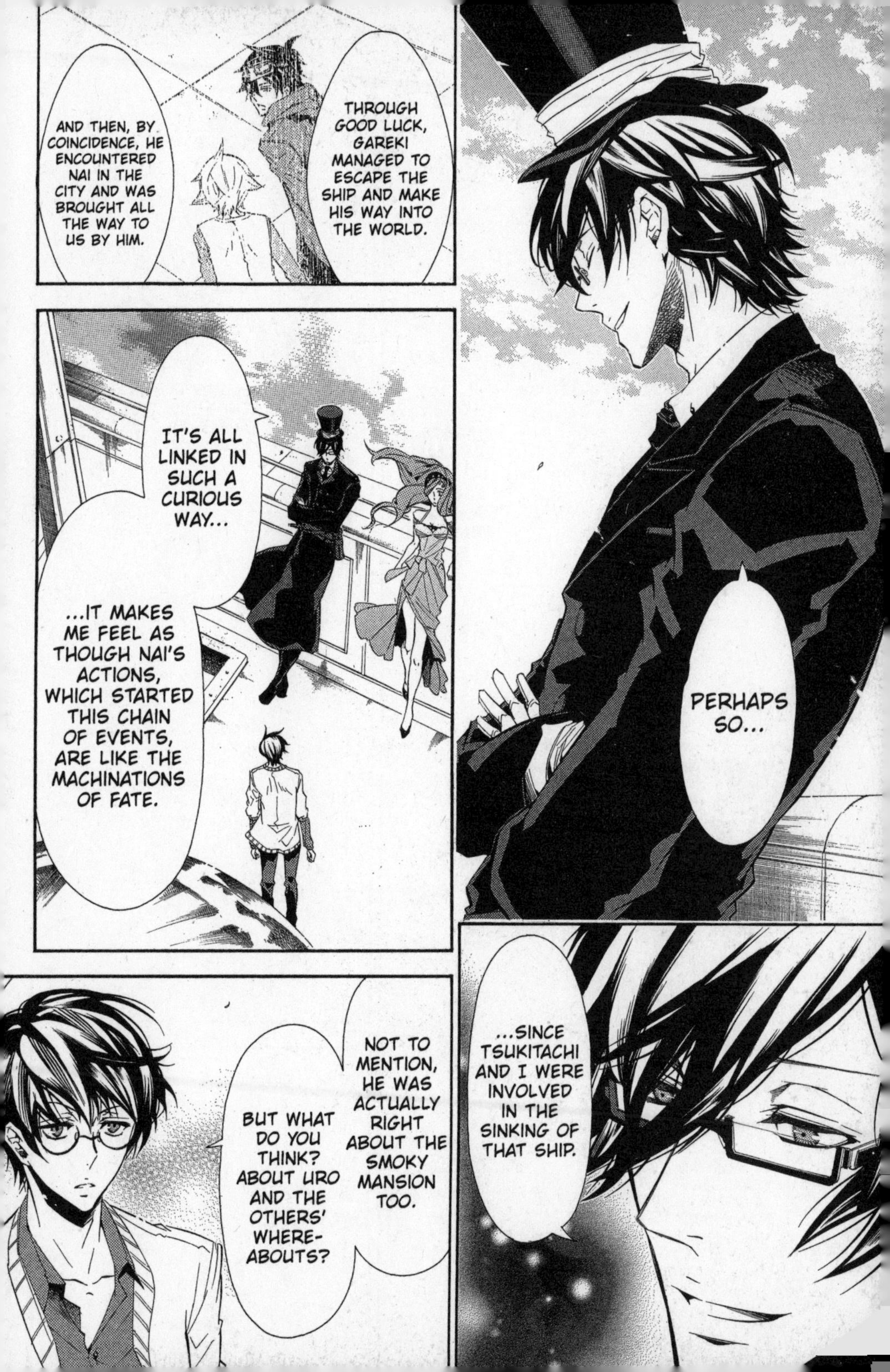
PERHAPS SO...
THROUGH GOOD LUCK, GAREKI MANAGED TO ESCAPE THE SHIP AND MAKE HIS WAY INTO THE WORLD.
AND THEN, BY COINCIDENCE, HE ENCOUNTERED NAI IN THE CITY AND WAS BROUGHT ALL THE WAY TO US BY HIM.
IT'S ALL LINKED IN SUCH A CURIOUS WAY...
...IT MAKES ME FEEL AS THOUGH NAI'S ACTIONS, WHICH STARTED THIS CHAIN OF EVENTS, ARE LIKE THE MACHINATIONS OF FATE.
...SINCE TSUKITACHI AND I WERE INVOLVED IN THE SINKING OF THAT SHIP.
NOT TO MENTION, HE WAS ACTUALLY RIGHT ABOUT THE SMOKY MANSION TOO.
BUT WHAT DO YOU THINK? ABOUT URO AND THE OTHERS' WHERE-ABOUTS?

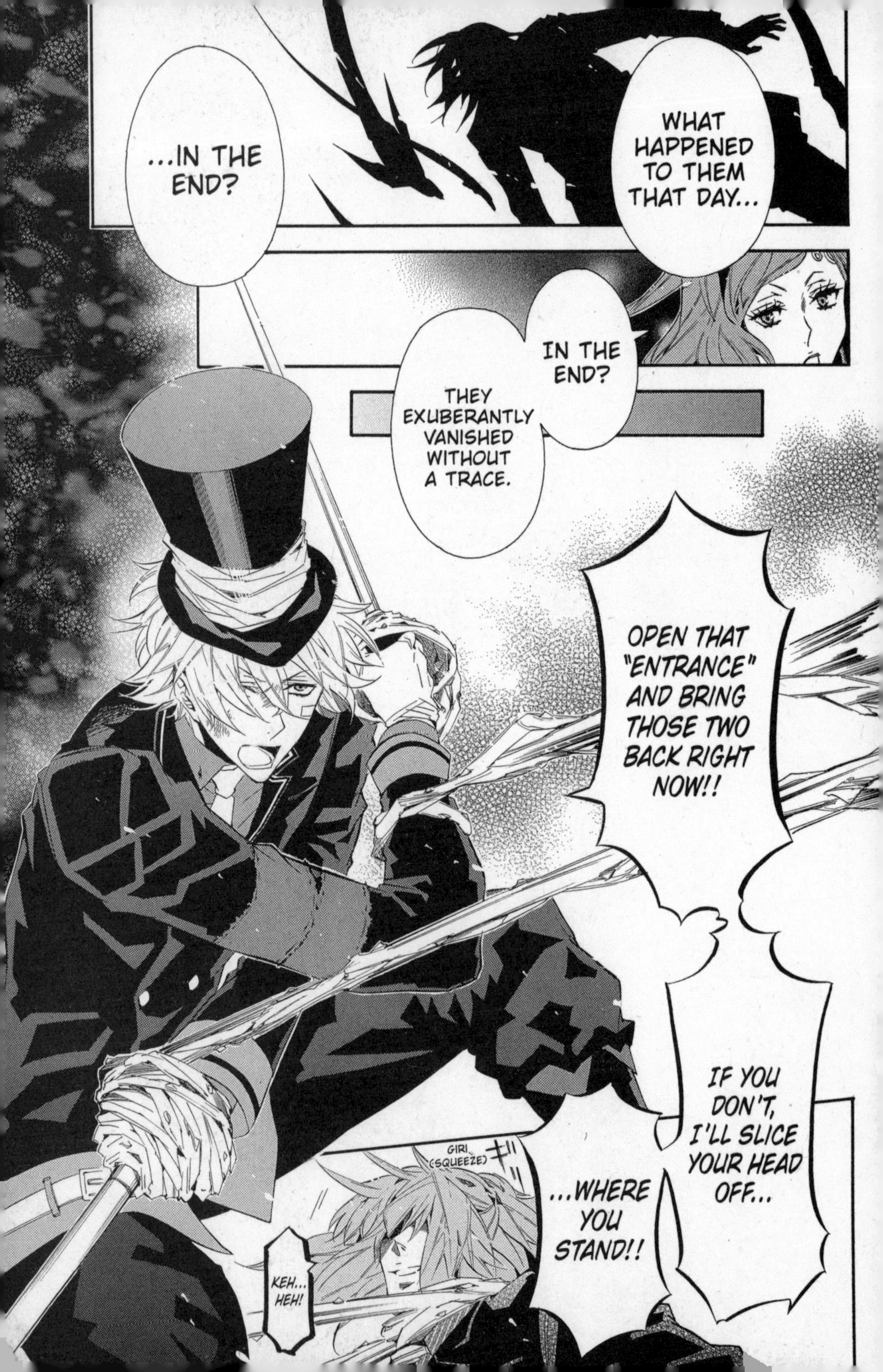
WHAT HAPPENED TO THEM THAT DAY...
...IN THE END?
IN THE END?
THEY EXUBERANTLY VANISHED WITHOUT A TRACE.
OPEN THAT "ENTRANCE" AND BRING THOSE TWO BACK RIGHT NOW!!
IF YOU DON'T, I'LL SLICE YOUR HEAD OFF...
GIRI (SQUEEZE)
...WHERE YOU STAND!!
KEH... HEH!

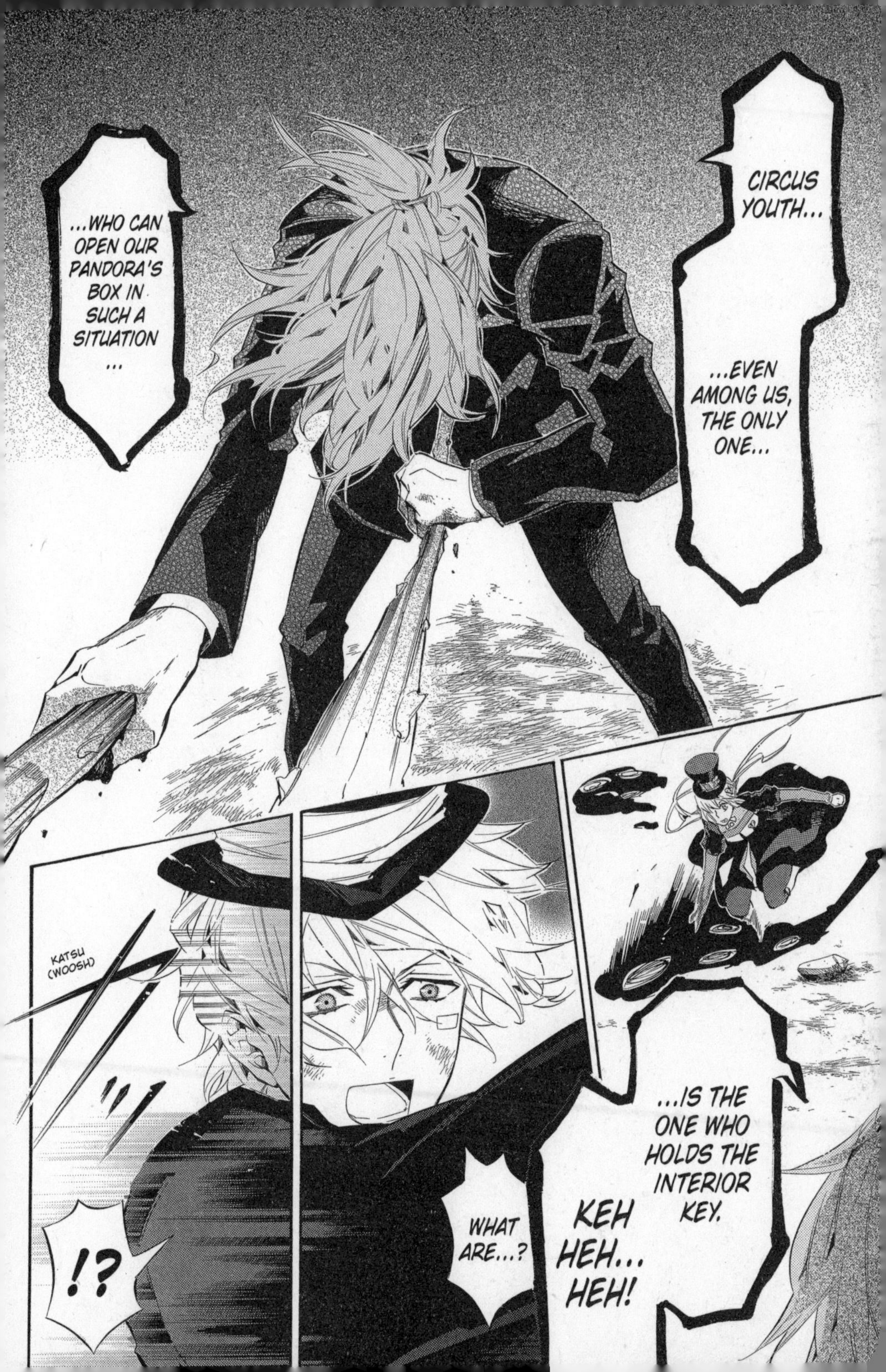
CIRCUS YOUTH...
...EVEN AMONG US, THE ONLY ONE...
...WHO CAN OPEN OUR PANDORA'S BOX IN SUCH A SITUATION...
...IS THE ONE WHO HOLDS THE INTERIOR KEY.
KEH HEH... HEH!
WHAT ARE...?
KATSU (WOOSH)
!?

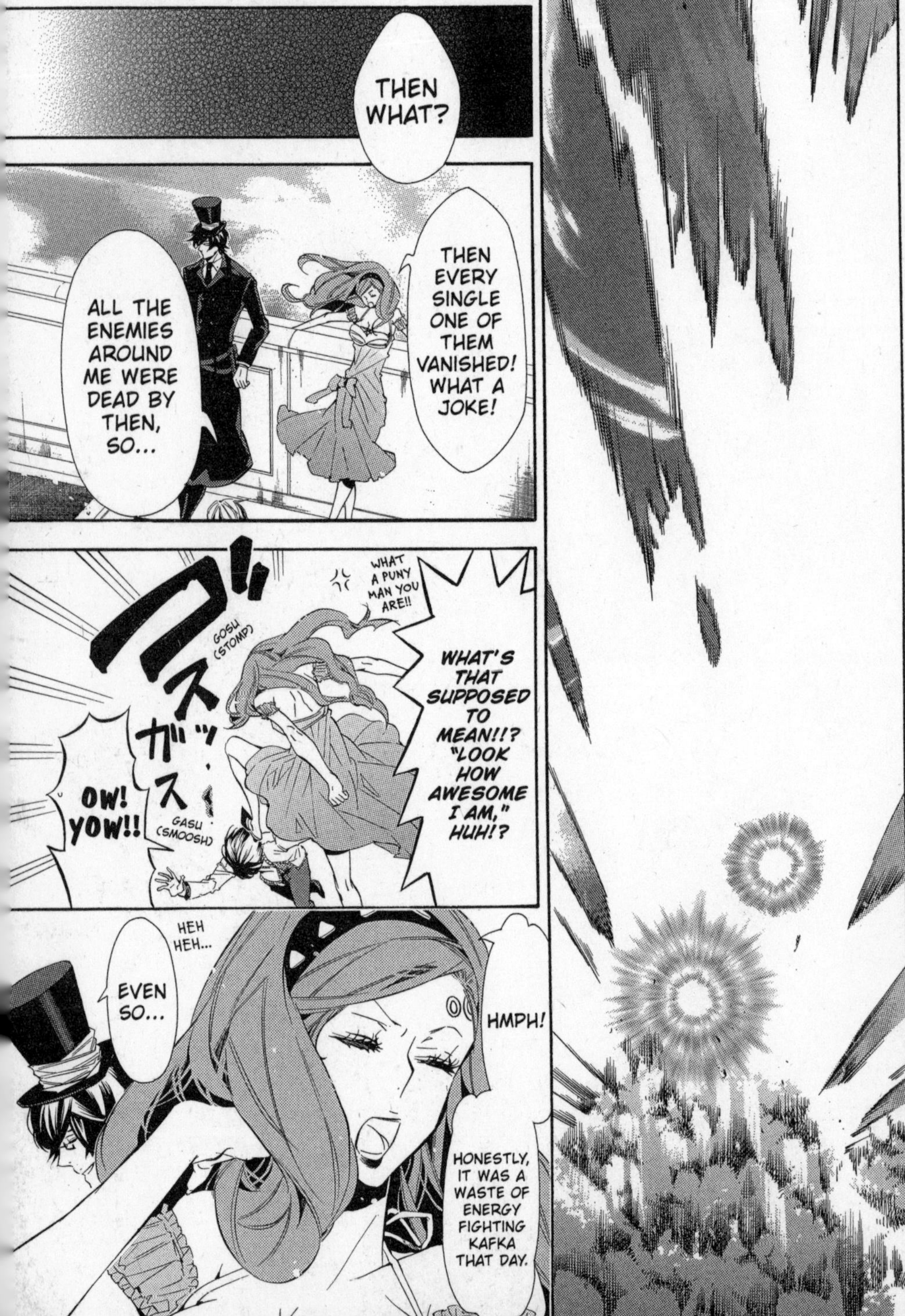

THEN WHAT?
THEN EVERY SINGLE ONE OF THEM VANISHED! WHAT A JOKE!
ALL THE ENEMIES AROUND ME WERE DEAD BY THEN, SO...
WHAT A PUNY MAN YOU ARE!!
WHAT'S THAT SUPPOSED TO MEAN!!? "LOOK HOW AWESOME I AM," HUH!?
GOSU (STOMP)
GASU (SMOOSH)
OW! YOW!!
HMPH!
HONESTLY, IT WAS A WASTE OF ENERGY FIGHTING KAFKA THAT DAY.
HEH HEH...
EVEN SO...

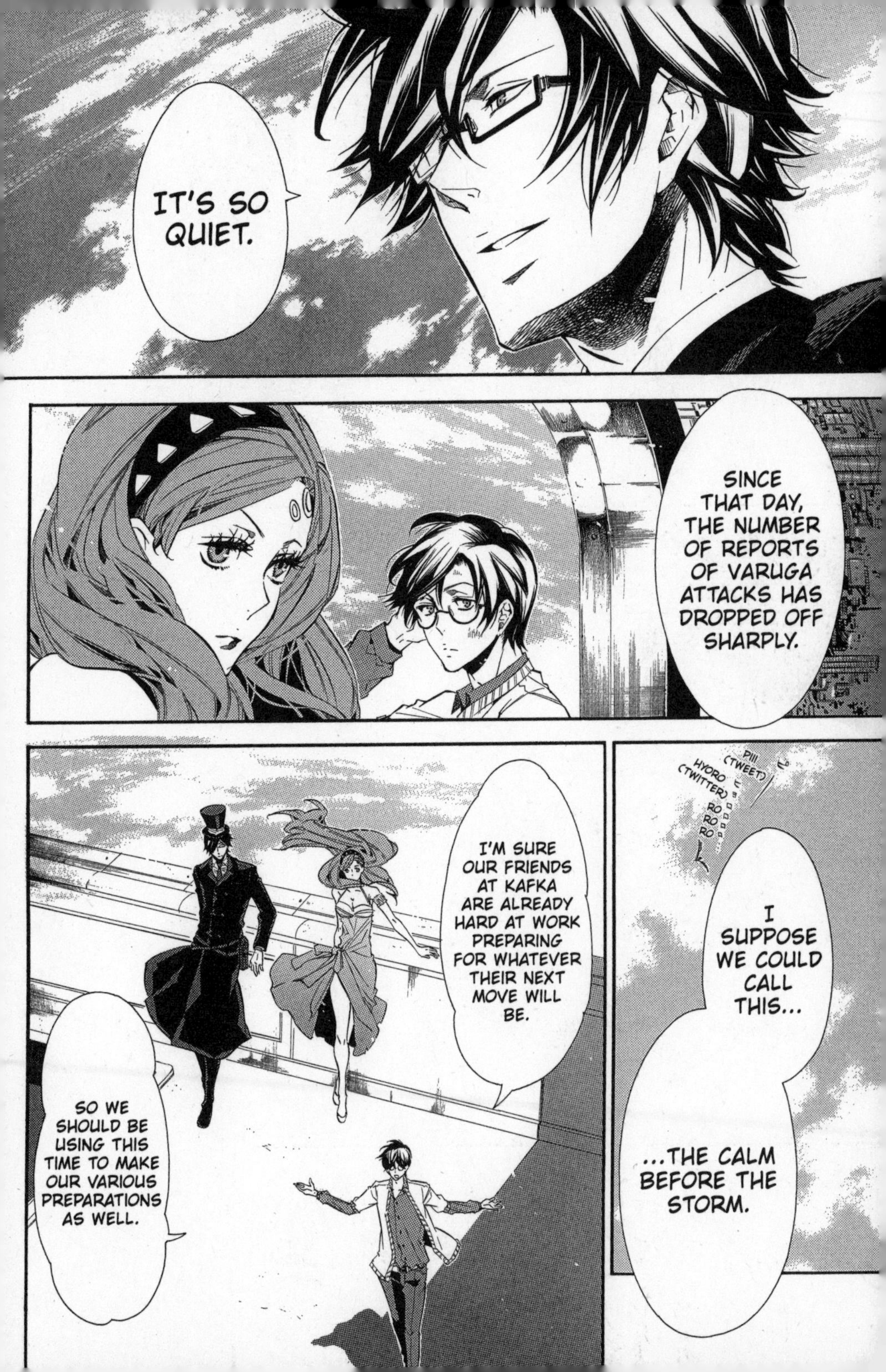
IT'S SO QUIET.
SINCE THAT DAY, THE NUMBER OF REPORTS OF VARUGA ATTACKS HAS DROPPED OFF SHARPLY.
PIII (TWEET)
HYORO (TWITTER)
RO RO RO
I SUPPOSE WE COULD CALL THIS...
...THE CALM BEFORE THE STORM.
I'M SURE OUR FRIENDS AT KAFKA ARE ALREADY HARD AT WORK PREPARING FOR WHATEVER THEIR NEXT MOVE WILL BE.
SO WE SHOULD BE USING THIS TIME TO MAKE OUR VARIOUS PREPARATIONS AS WELL.

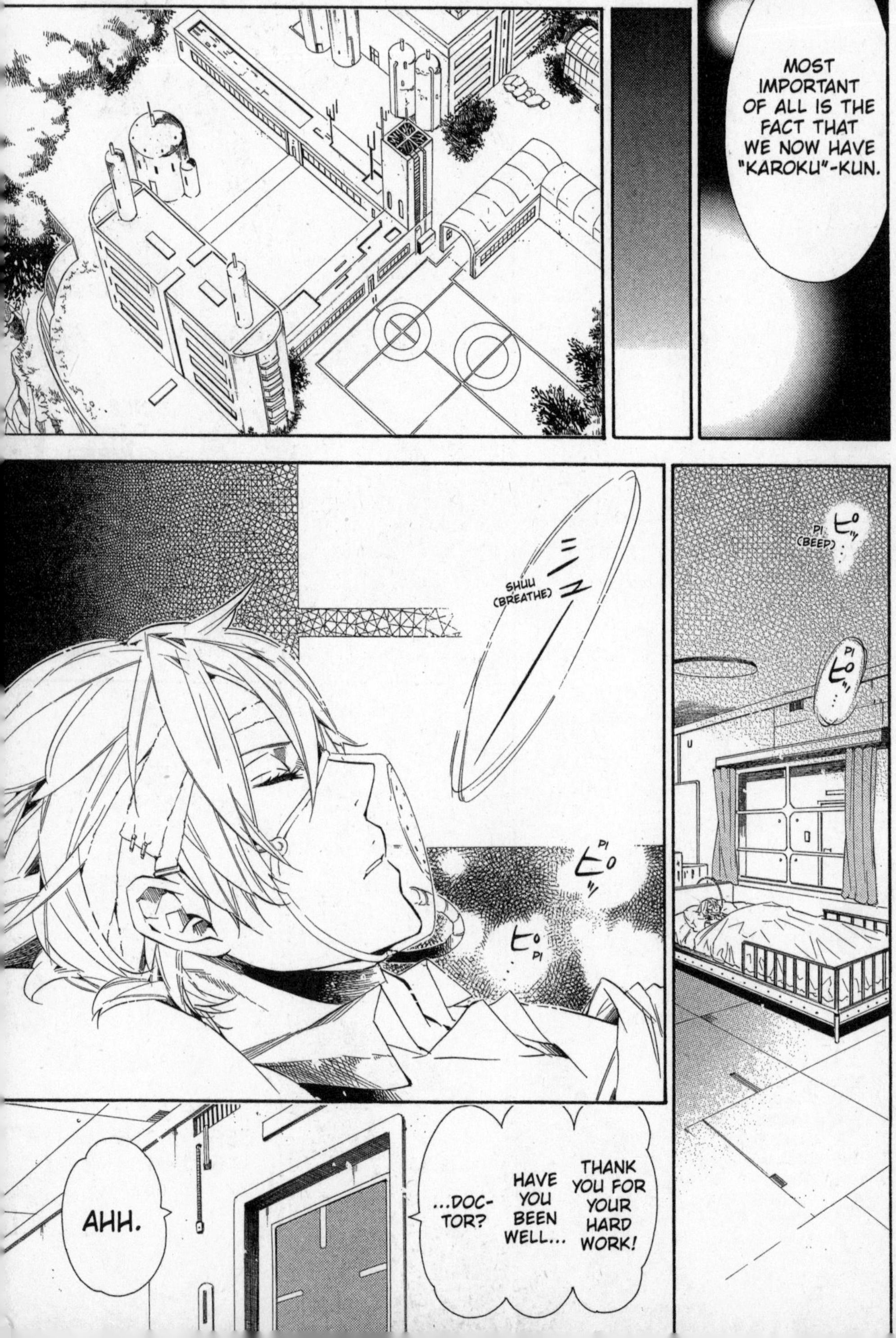
MOST IMPORTANT OF ALL IS THE FACT THAT WE NOW HAVE "KAROKU"-KUN.
PI (BEEP)
PI
SHUU (BREATHE)
PI
PI
THANK YOU FOR YOUR HARD WORK!
HAVE YOU BEEN WELL...
...DOC-TOR?
AHH.

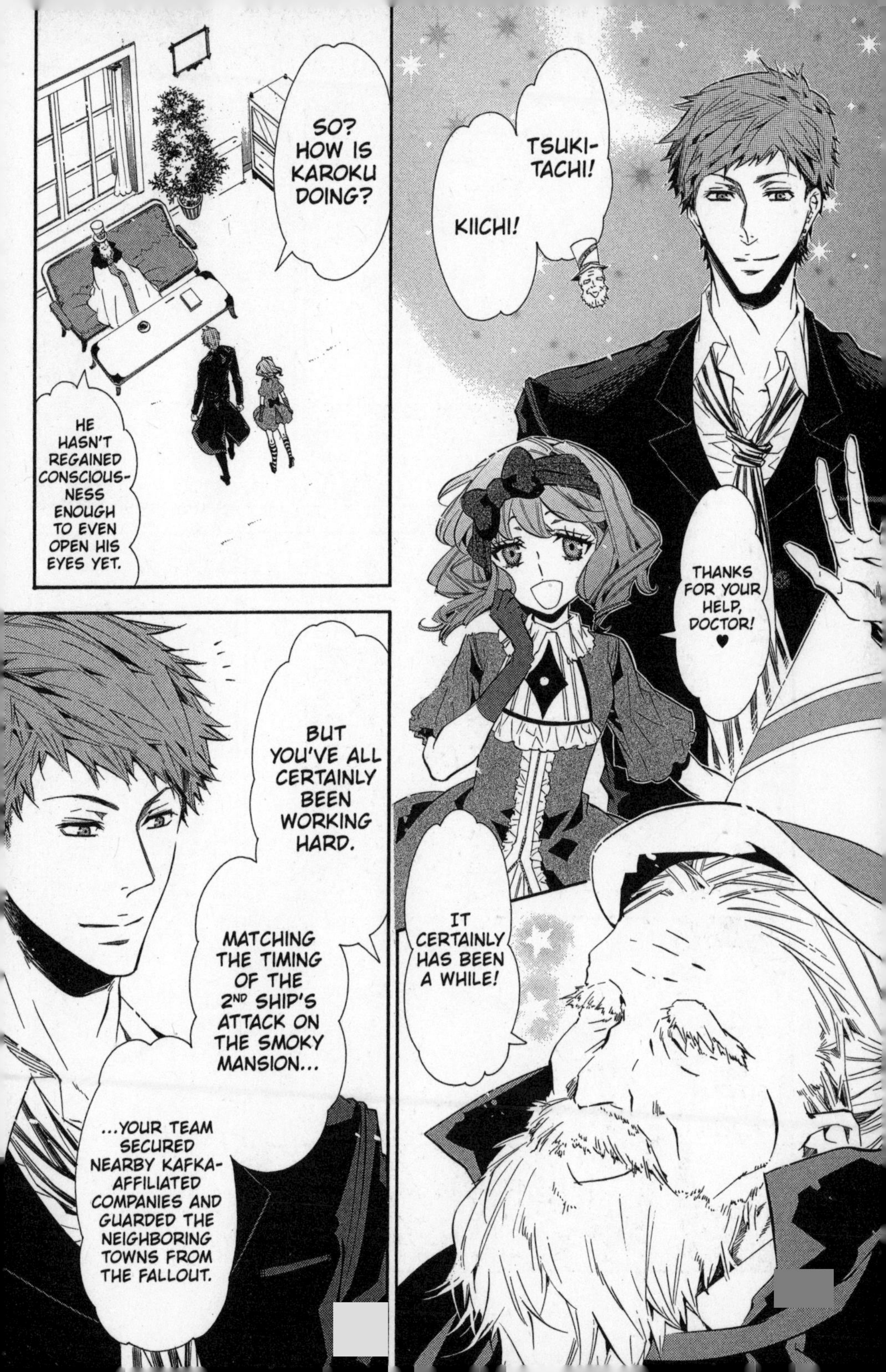
TSUKI-TACHI!
KIICHI!
THANKS FOR YOUR HELP, DOCTOR! ♥
IT CERTAINLY HAS BEEN A WHILE!
SO? HOW IS KAROKU DOING?
HE HASN'T REGAINED CONSCIOUS-NESS ENOUGH TO EVEN OPEN HIS EYES YET.
BUT YOU'VE ALL CERTAINLY BEEN WORKING HARD.
MATCHING THE TIMING OF THE 2ND SHIP'S ATTACK ON THE SMOKY MANSION...
...YOUR TEAM SECURED NEARBY KAFKA-AFFILIATED COMPANIES AND GUARDED THE NEIGHBORING TOWNS FROM THE FALLOUT.

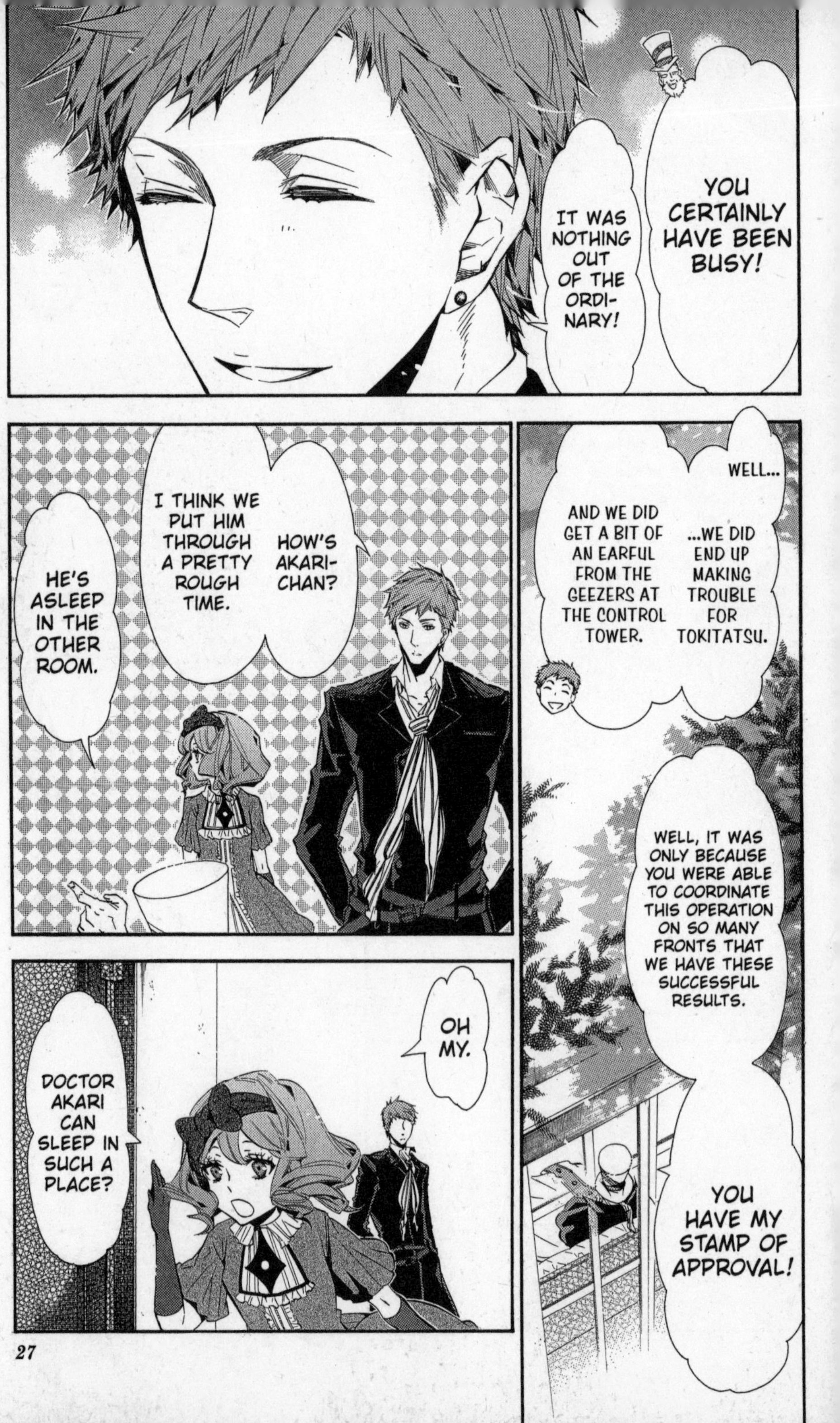
YOU CERTAINLY HAVE BEEN BUSY!
IT WAS NOTHING OUT OF THE ORDI-NARY!
WELL...
...WE DID END UP MAKING TROUBLE FOR TOKITATSU.
AND WE DID GET A BIT OF AN EARFUL FROM THE GEEZERS AT THE CONTROL TOWER.
WELL, IT WAS ONLY BECAUSE YOU WERE ABLE TO COORDINATE THIS OPERATION ON SO MANY FRONTS THAT WE HAVE THESE SUCCESSFUL RESULTS.
YOU HAVE MY STAMP OF APPROVAL!
HOW'S AKARI-CHAN?
I THINK WE PUT HIM THROUGH A PRETTY ROUGH TIME.
HE'S ASLEEP IN THE OTHER ROOM.
OH MY.
DOCTOR AKARI CAN SLEEP IN SUCH A PLACE?

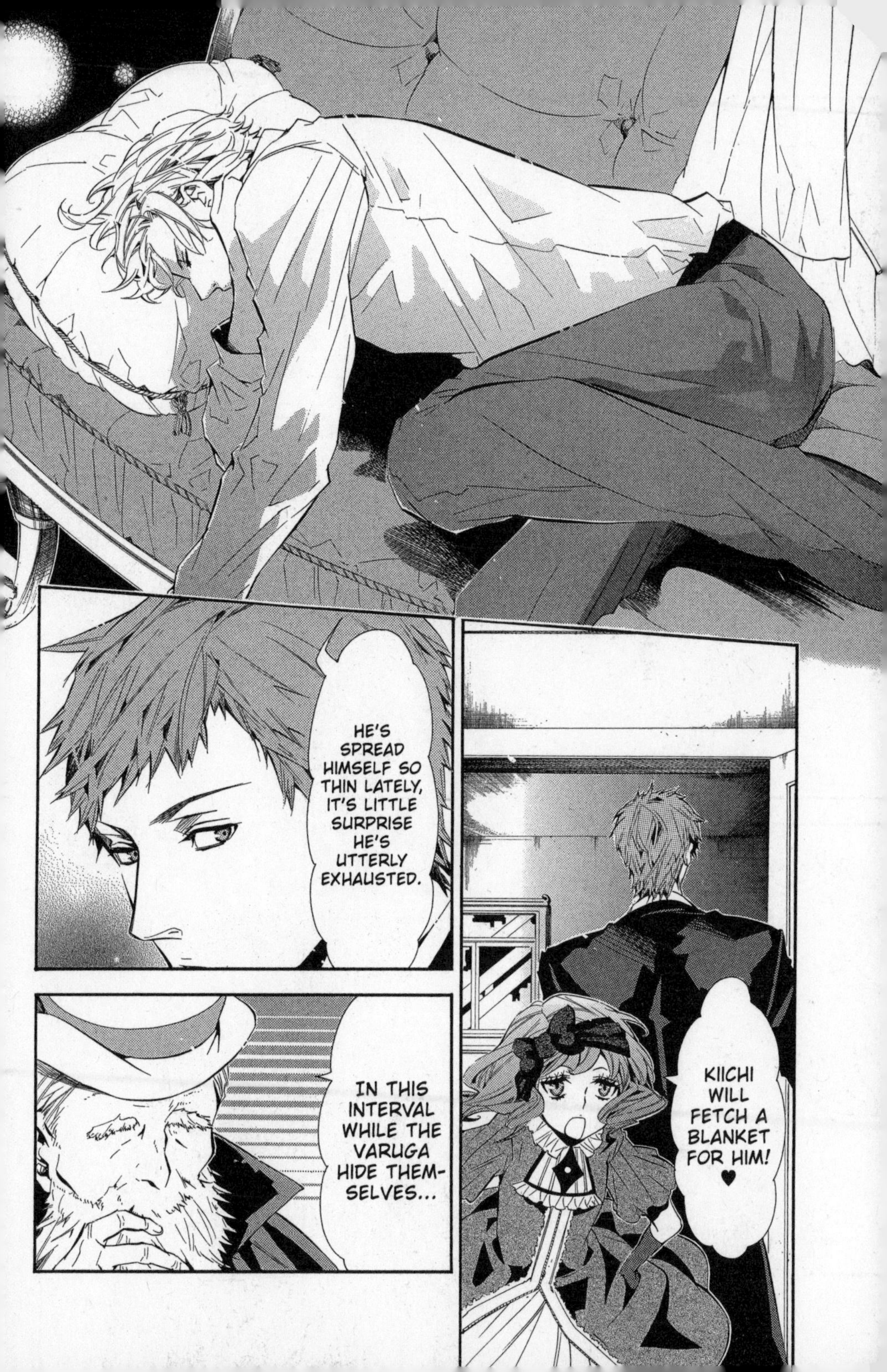
KIICHI WILL FETCH A BLANKET FOR HIM! ♥
HE'S SPREAD HIMSELF SO THIN LATELY, IT'S LITTLE SURPRISE HE'S UTTERLY EXHAUSTED.
IN THIS INTERVAL WHILE THE VARUGA HIDE THEM-SELVES...

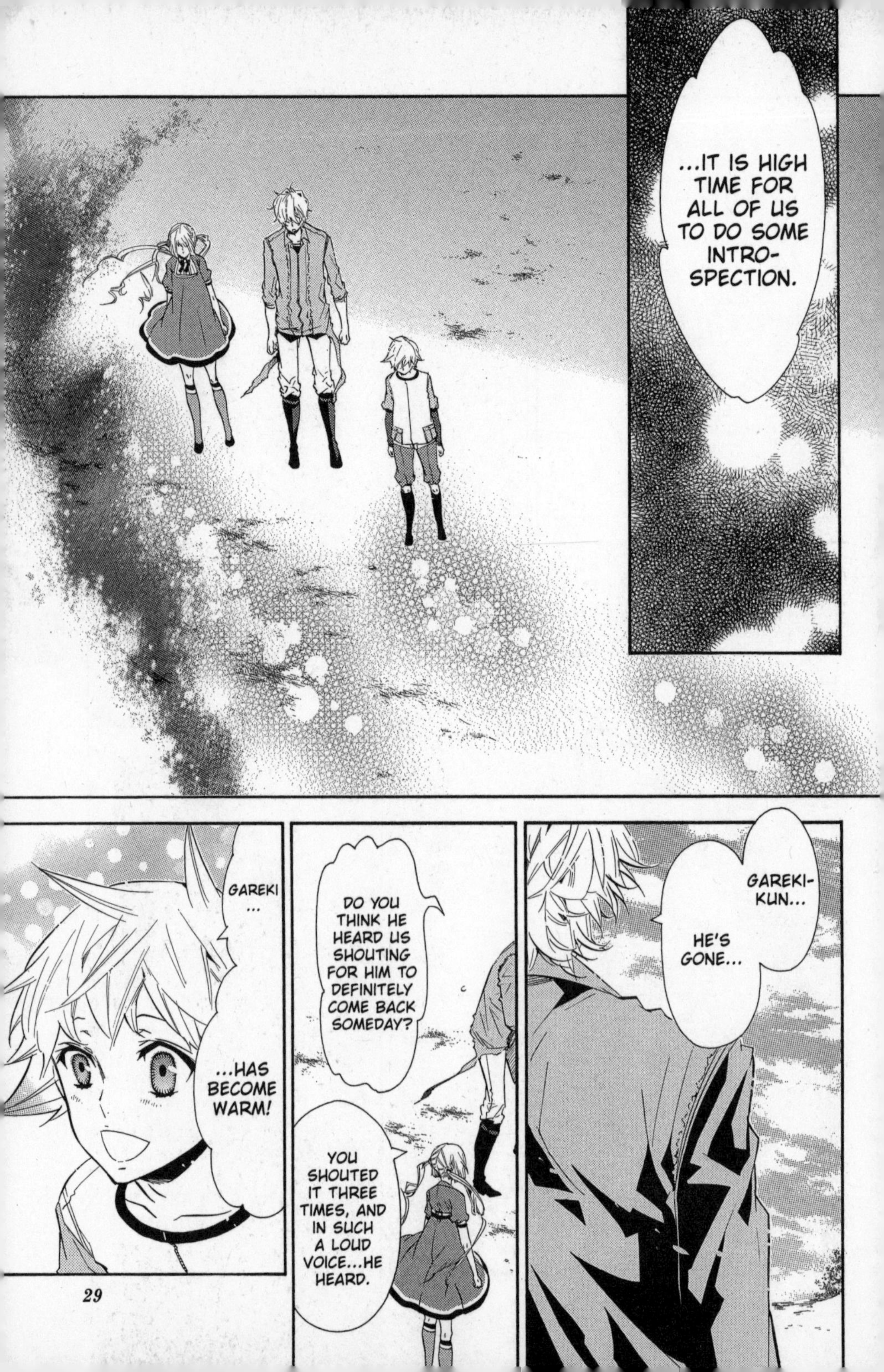
...IT IS HIGH TIME FOR ALL OF US TO DO SOME INTRO-SPECTION.
GAREKI-KUN...
HE'S GONE...
DO YOU THINK HE HEARD US SHOUTING FOR HIM TO DEFINITELY COME BACK SOMEDAY?
YOU SHOUTED IT THREE TIMES, AND IN SUCH A LOUD VOICE...HE HEARD.
GAREKI ...
...HAS BECOME WARM!

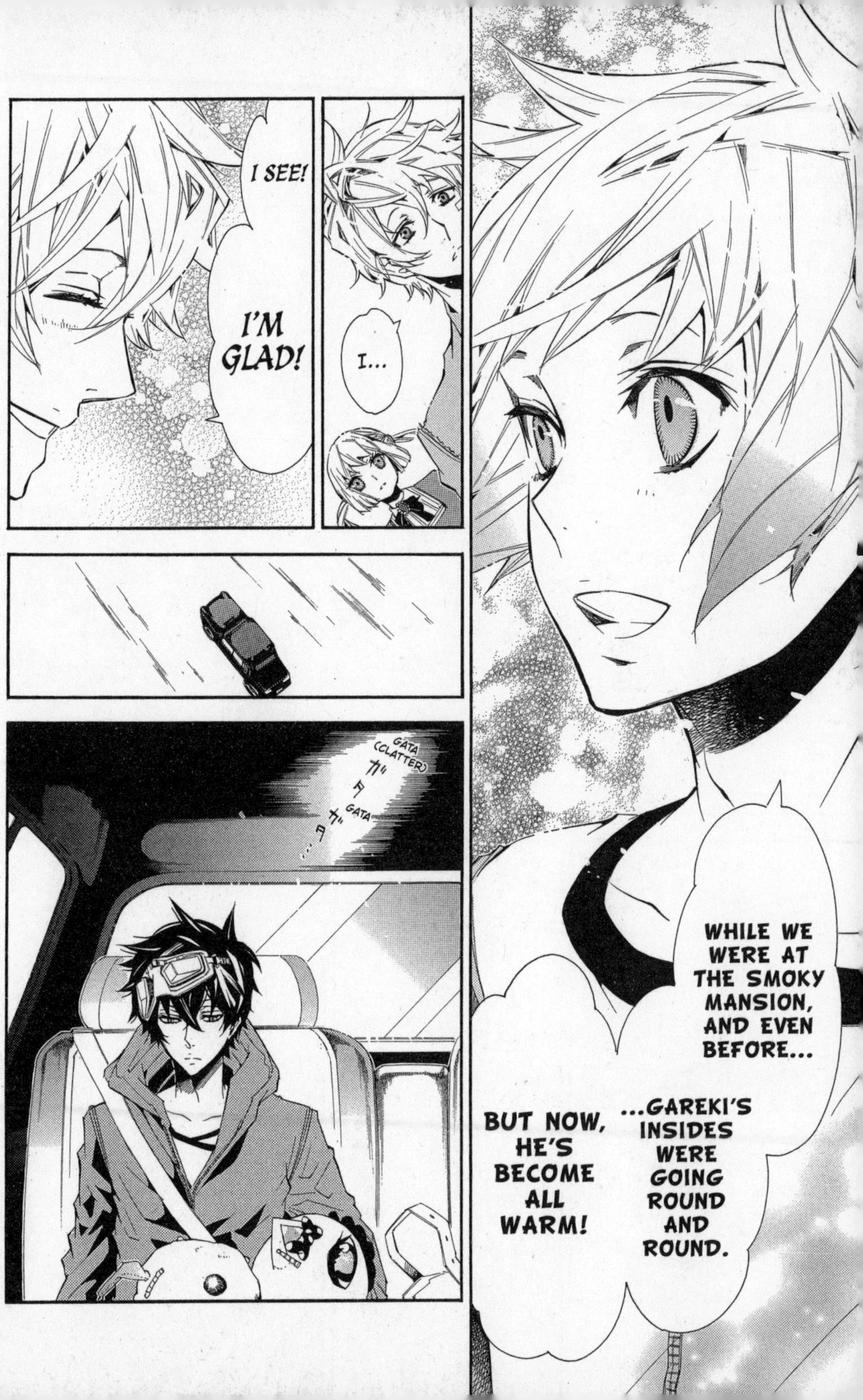
WHILE WE WERE AT THE SMOKY MANSION, AND EVEN BEFORE...
...GAREKI'S INSIDES WERE GOING ROUND AND ROUND.
BUT NOW, HE'S BECOME ALL WARM!
I...
I SEE!
I'M GLAD!
GATA (CLATTER)
ガタ
GATA
ガタ…

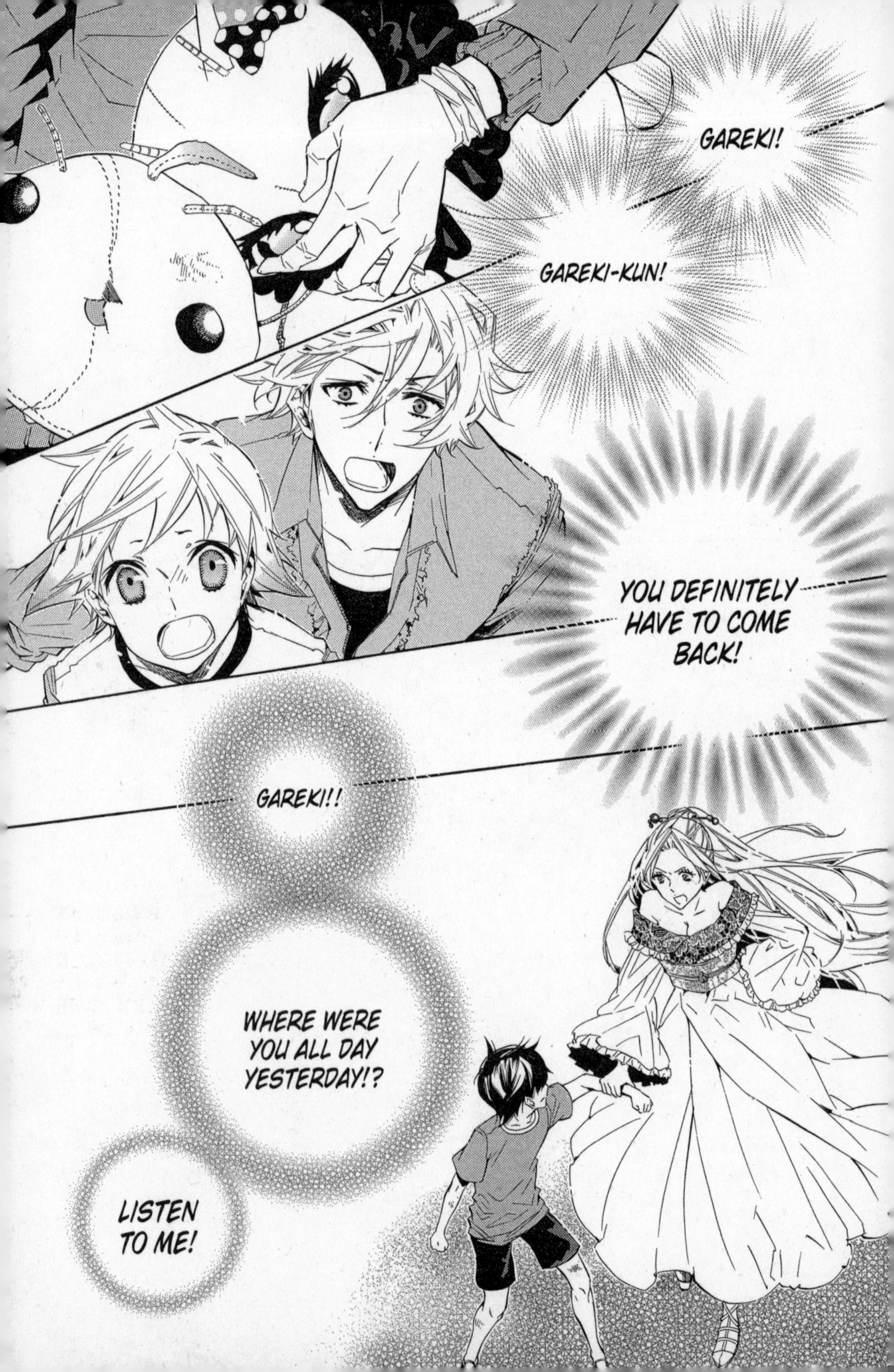
GAREKI!
GAREKI-KUN!
YOU DEFINITELY HAVE TO COME BACK!
GAREKI!!
WHERE WERE YOU ALL DAY YESTERDAY!?
LISTEN TO ME!

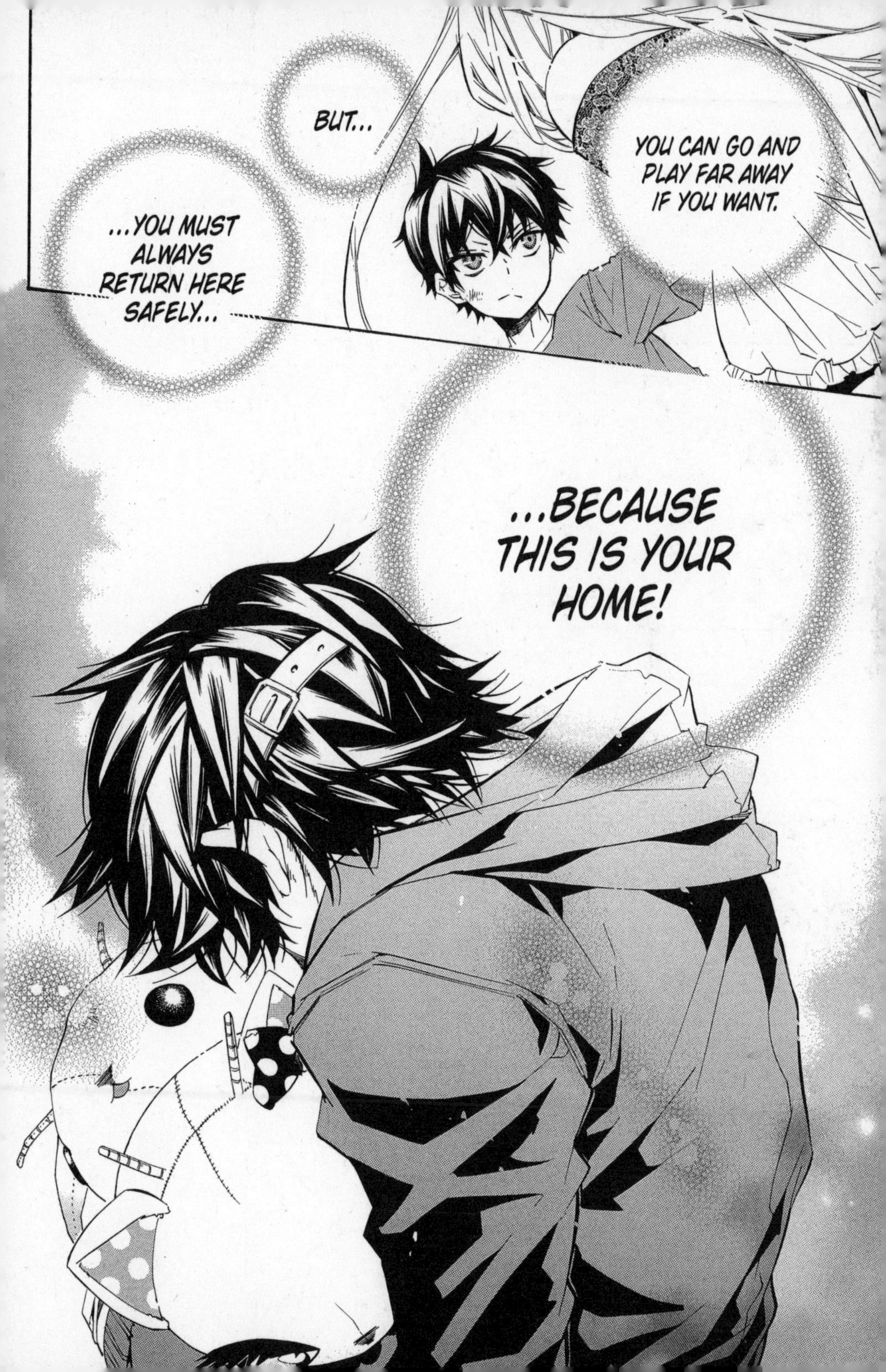
YOU CAN GO AND PLAY FAR AWAY IF YOU WANT.
BUT...
...YOU MUST ALWAYS RETURN HERE SAFELY...
...BECAUSE THIS IS YOUR HOME!

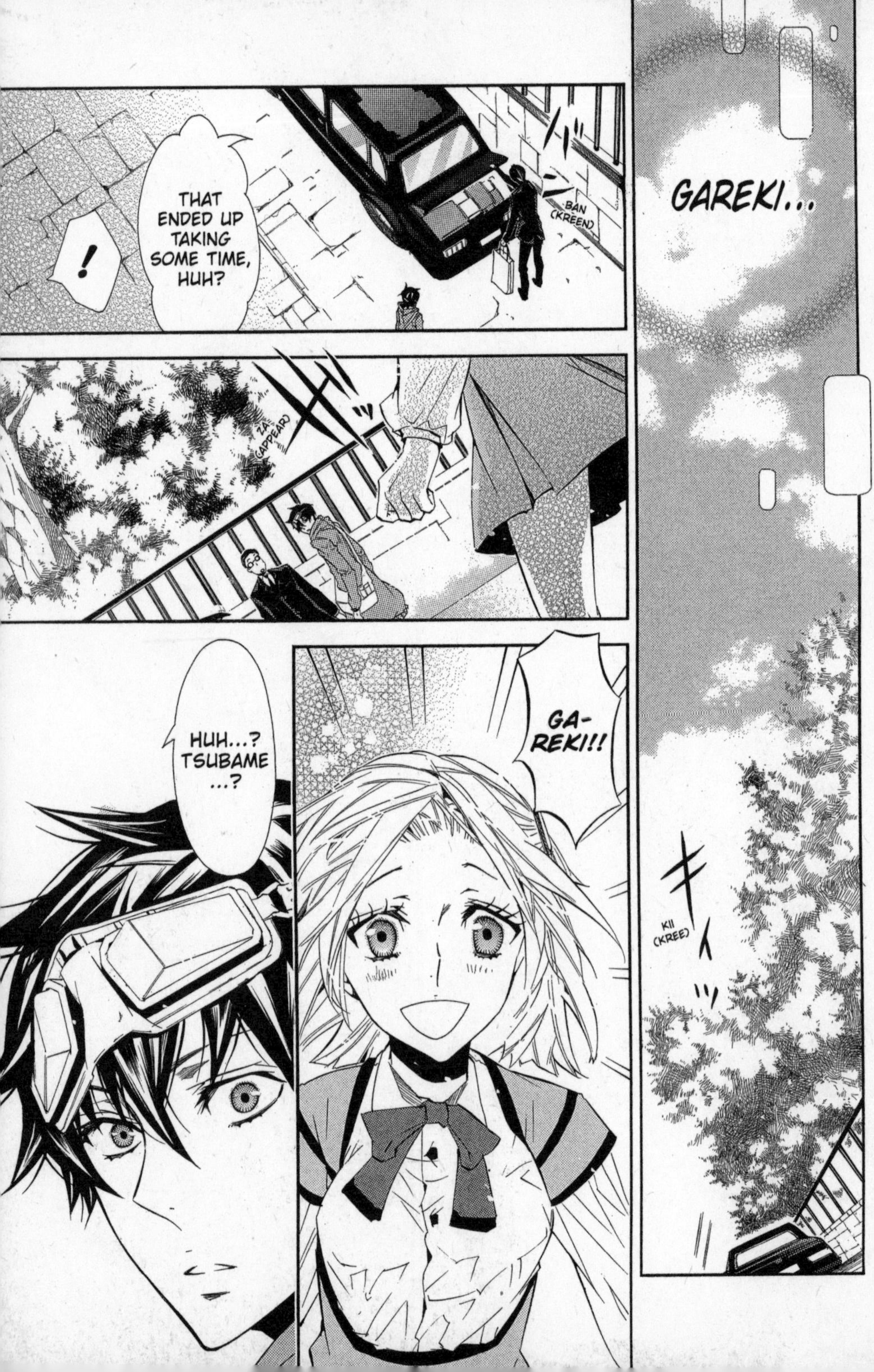
GAREKI...
KII (KREE)
BAN (KREEN)
THAT ENDED UP TAKING SOME TIME, HUH?
!
ZA (APPEAR)
GA-REKI!!
HUH...? TSUBAME ...?

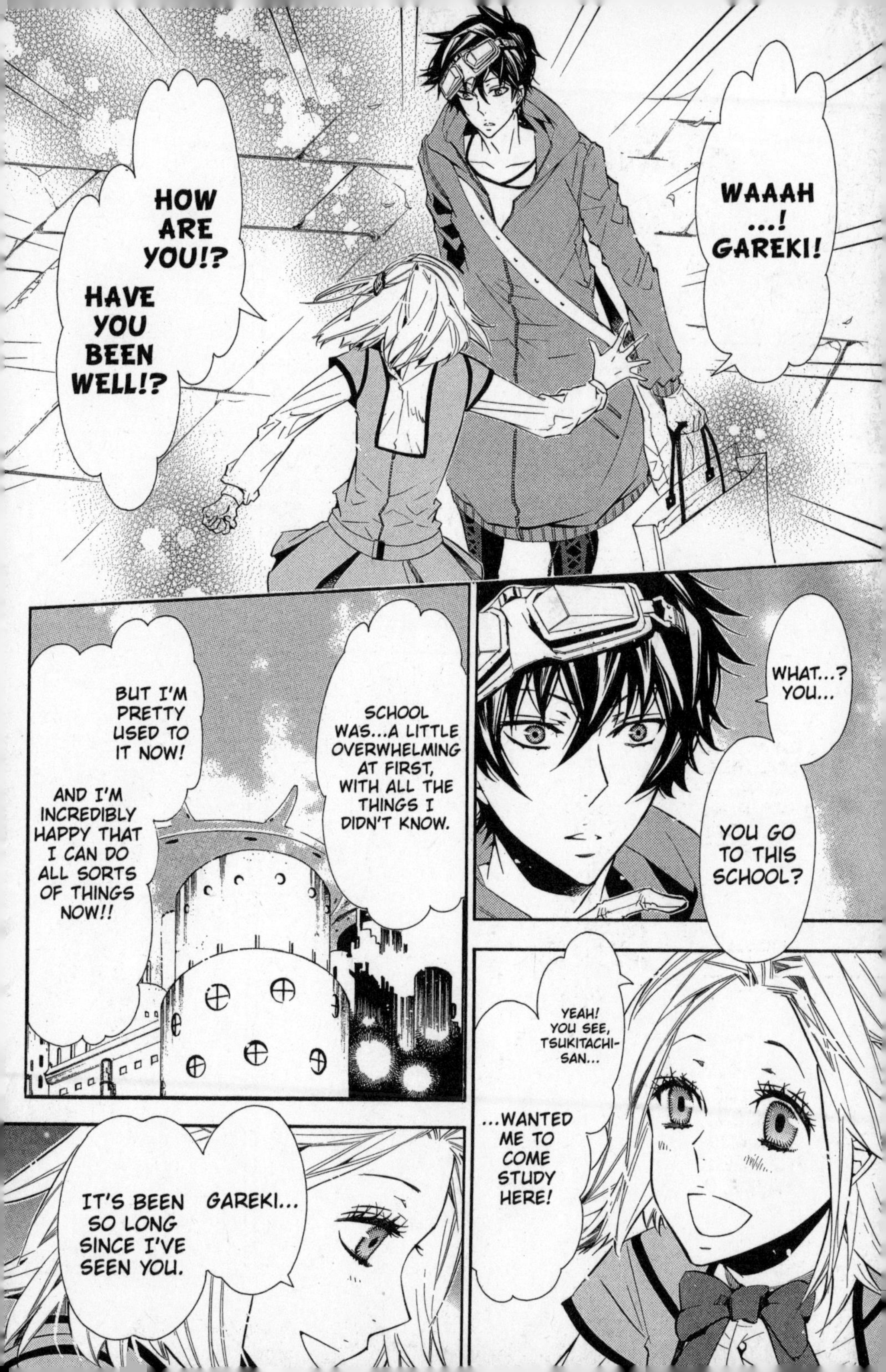
WAAAH ...! GAREKI!
HOW ARE YOU!? HAVE YOU BEEN WELL!?
WHAT...? YOU...
YOU GO TO THIS SCHOOL?
SCHOOL WAS...A LITTLE OVERWHELMING AT FIRST, WITH ALL THE THINGS I DIDN'T KNOW.
BUT I'M PRETTY USED TO IT NOW!
AND I'M INCREDIBLY HAPPY THAT I CAN DO ALL SORTS OF THINGS NOW!!
YEAH! YOU SEE, TSUKITACHI-SAN...
...WANTED ME TO COME STUDY HERE!
GAREKI...
IT'S BEEN SO LONG SINCE I'VE SEEN YOU.

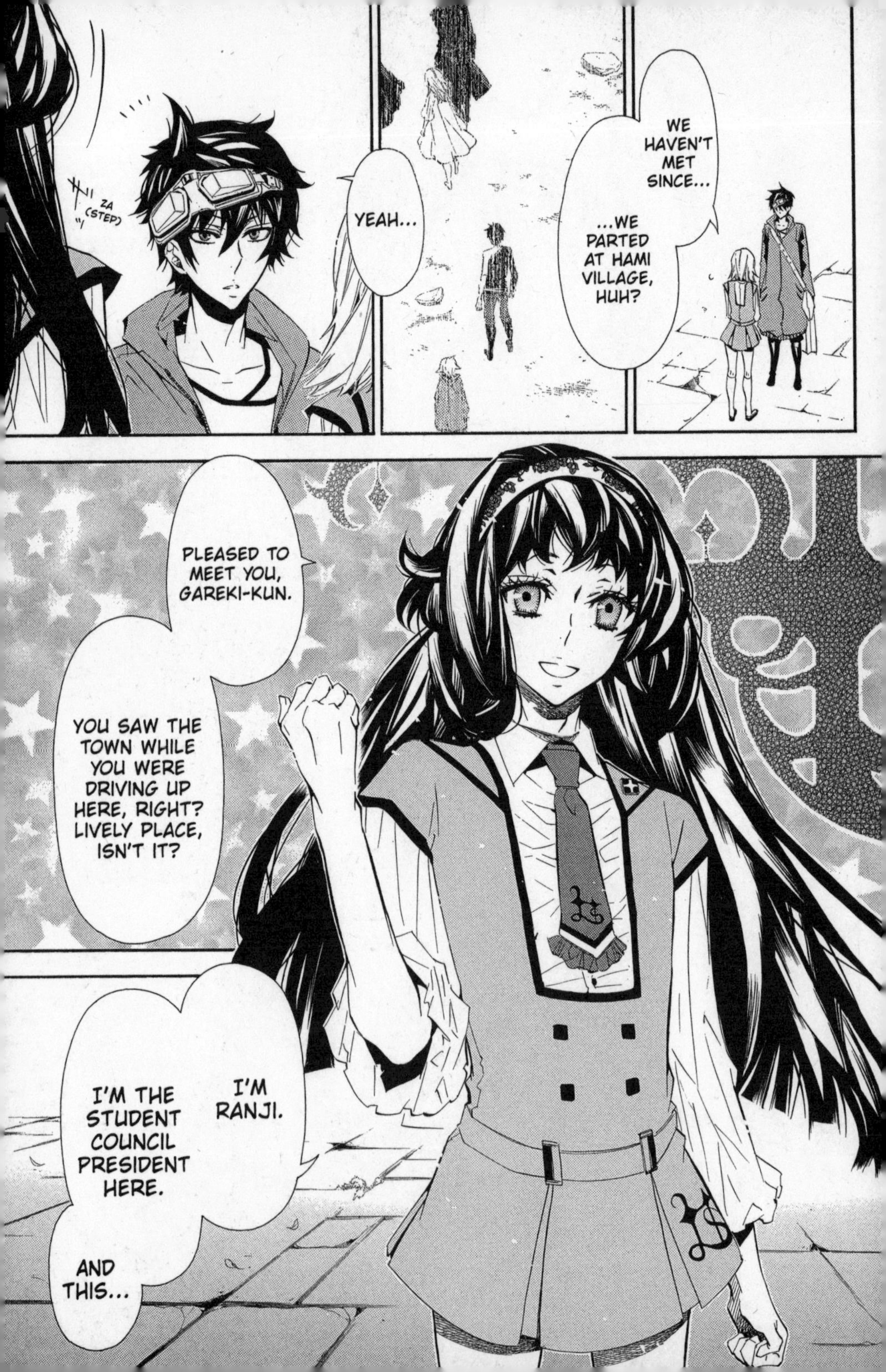
WE HAVEN'T MET SINCE...
...WE PARTED AT HAMI VILLAGE, HUH?
YEAH...
ZA (STEP)
PLEASED TO MEET YOU, GAREKI-KUN.
YOU SAW THE TOWN WHILE YOU WERE DRIVING UP HERE, RIGHT? LIVELY PLACE, ISN'T IT?
I'M RANJI.
I'M THE STUDENT COUNCIL PRESIDENT HERE.
AND THIS...

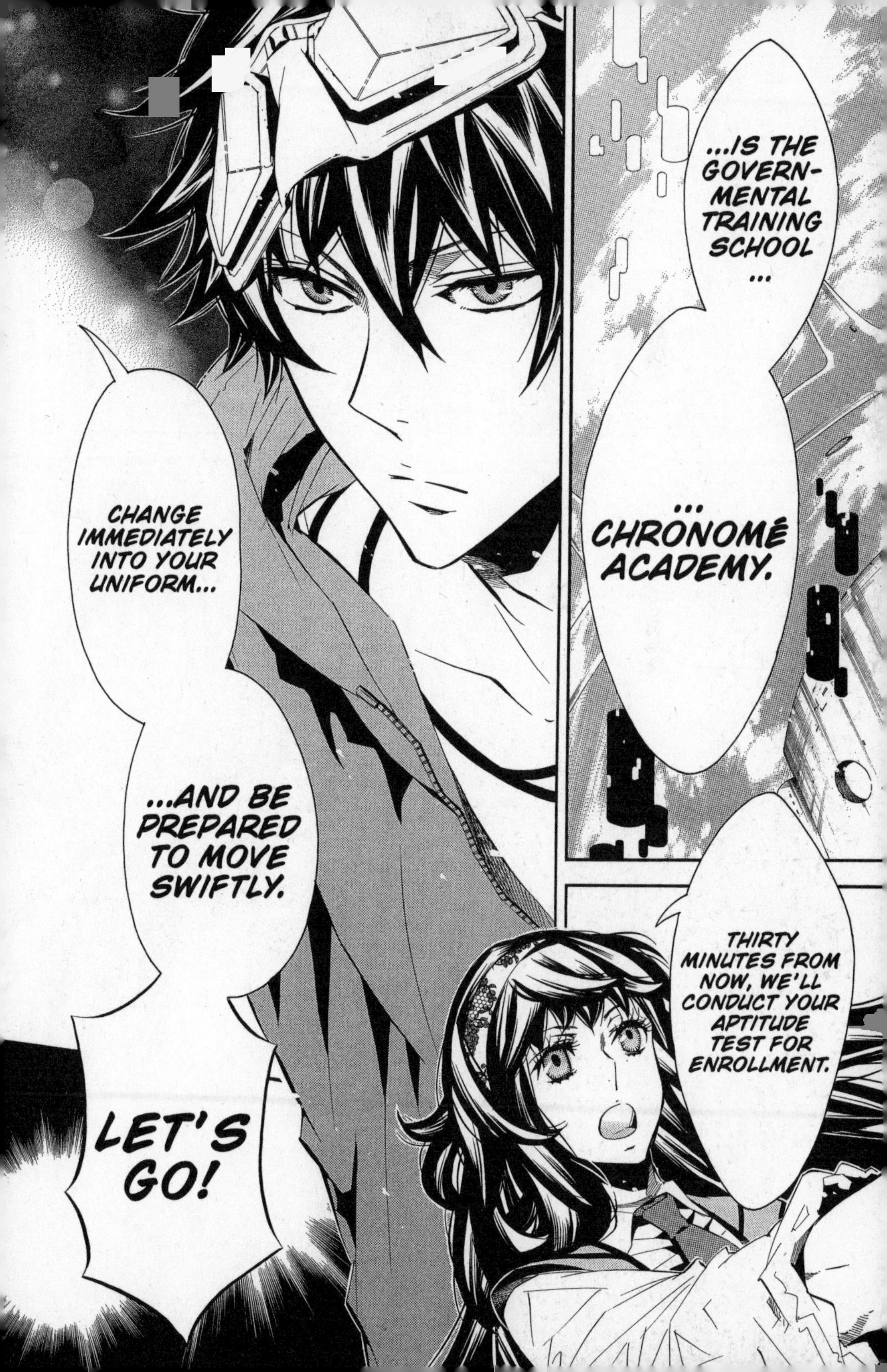
...IS THE GOVERNMENTAL TRAINING SCHOOL...
...CHRÖNOMÉ ACADEMY.
THIRTY MINUTES FROM NOW, WE'LL CONDUCT YOUR APTITUDE TEST FOR ENROLLMENT.
CHANGE IMMEDIATELY INTO YOUR UNIFORM...
...AND BE PREPARED TO MOVE SWIFTLY.
LET'S GO!

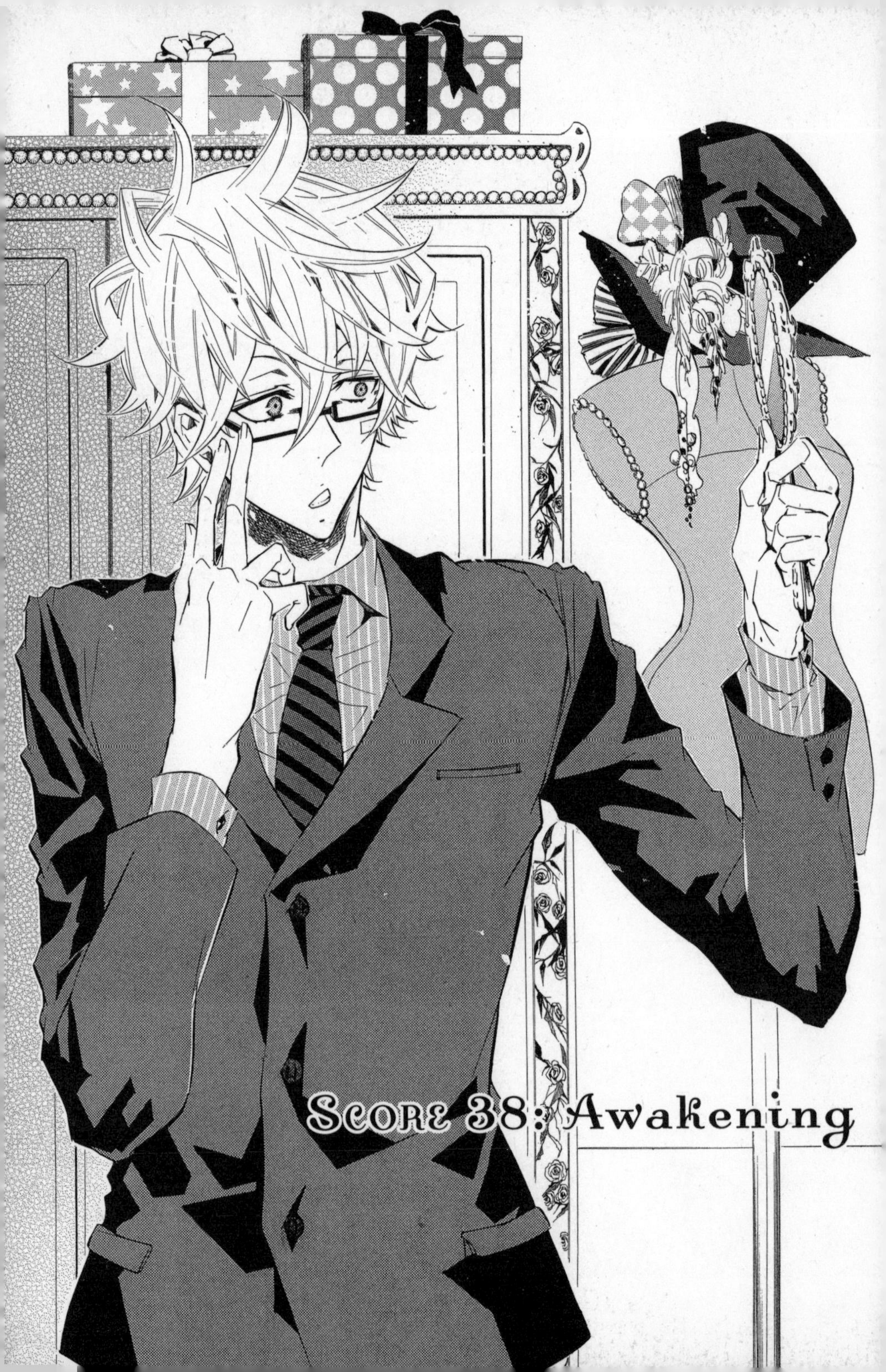
Score 38: Awakening

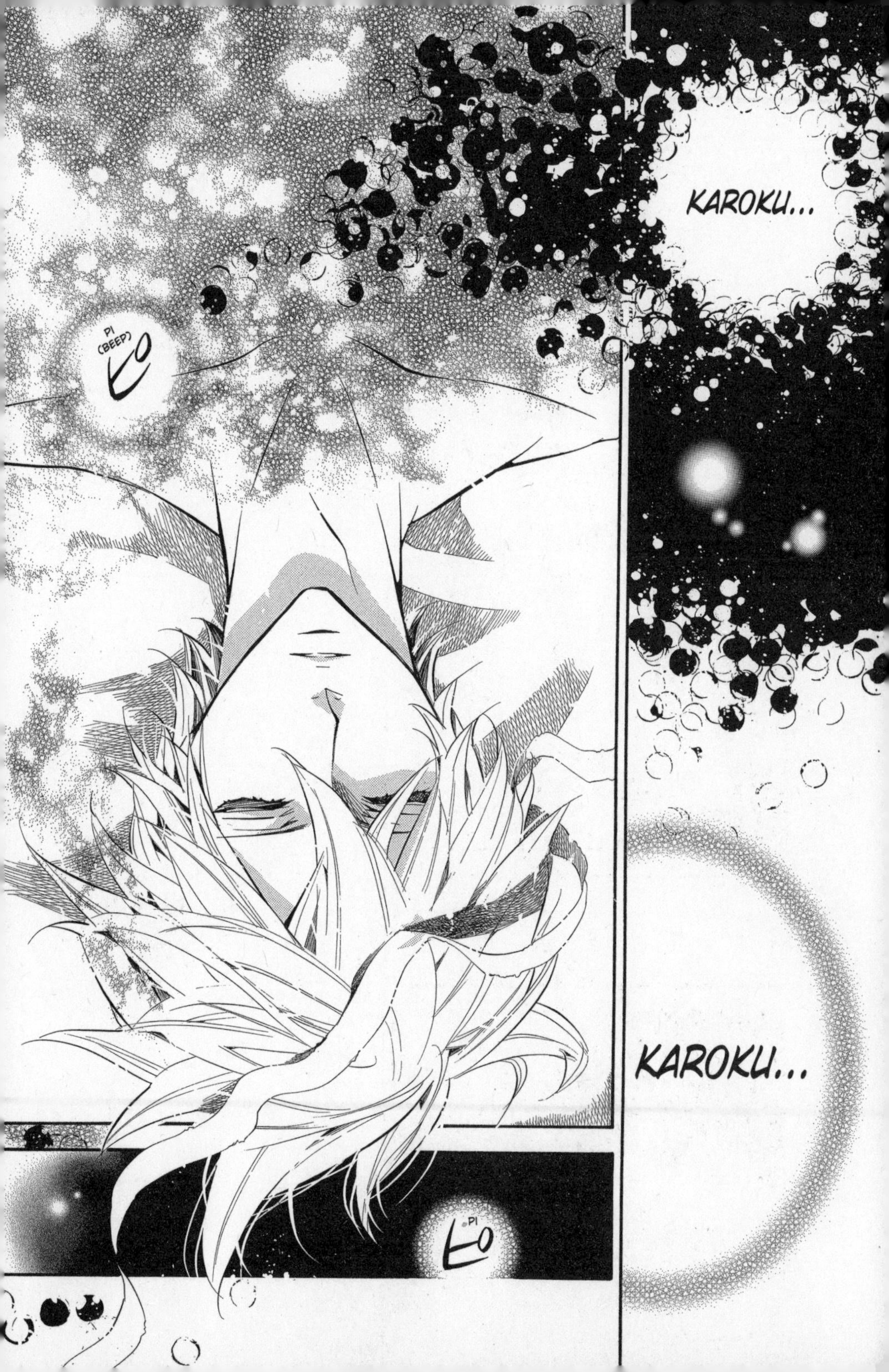
KAROKU...
KAROKU...
PI (BEEP)
ピ
PI
ピ

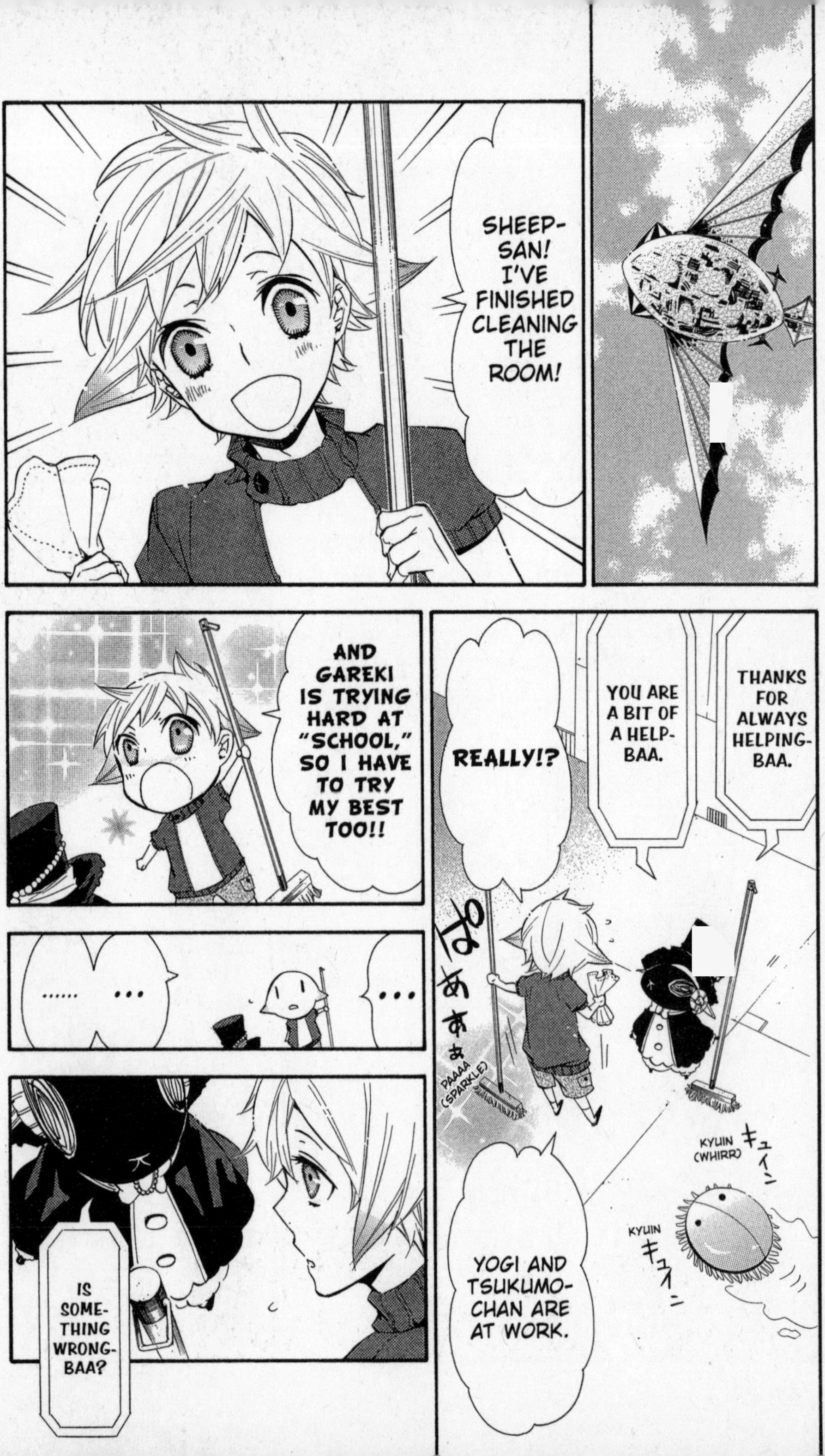
SHEEP-SAN! I'VE FINISHED CLEANING THE ROOM!
THANKS FOR ALWAYS HELPING-BAA.
YOU ARE A BIT OF A HELP-BAA.
REALLY!?
PAAAA (SPARKLE)
KYUIN (WHIRR)
KYUIN
YOGI AND TSUKUMO-CHAN ARE AT WORK.
AND GAREKI IS TRYING HARD AT "SCHOOL," SO I HAVE TO TRY MY BEST TOO!!
...
....
IS SOME-THING WRONG-BAA?

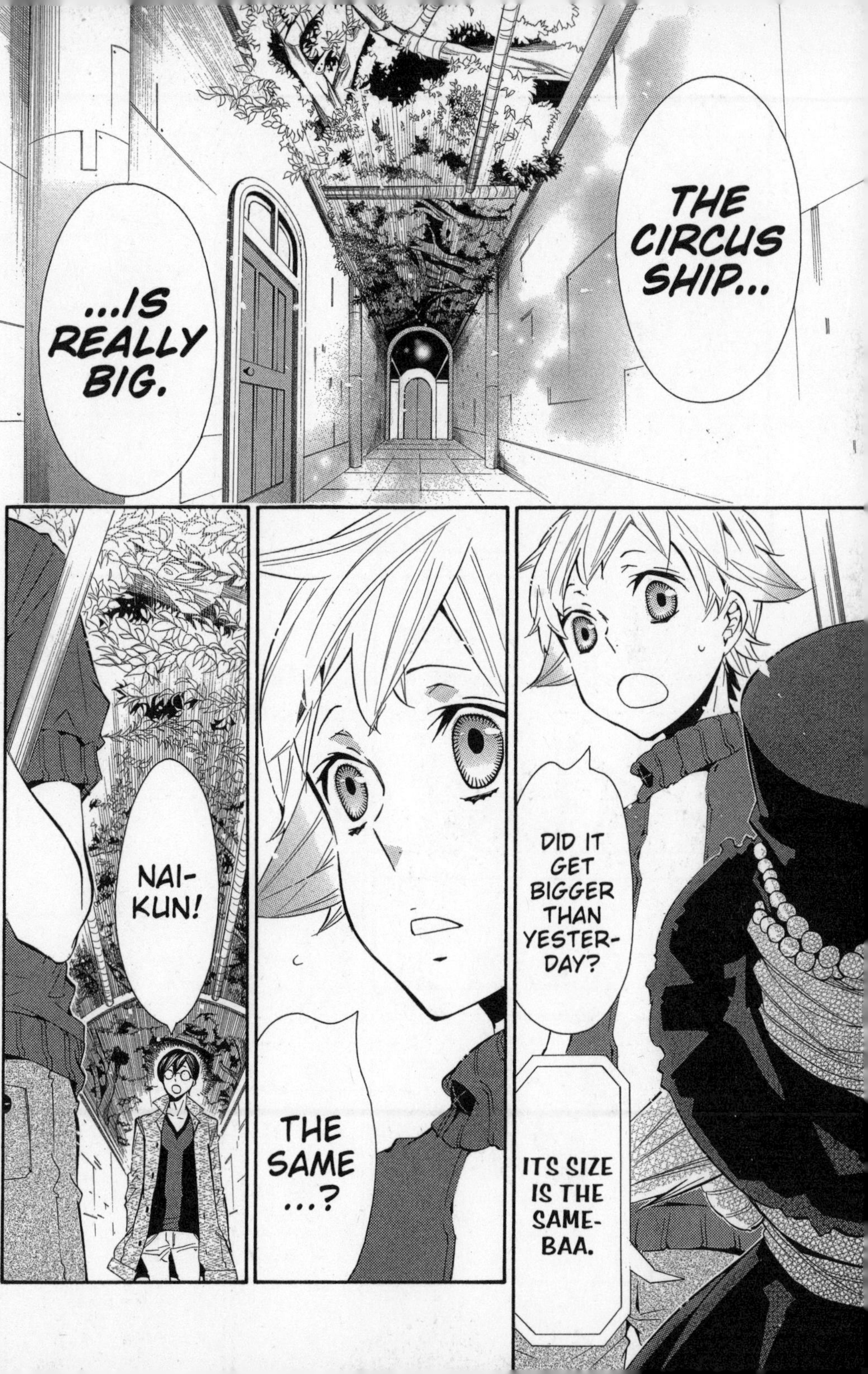
THE CIRCUS SHIP...
...IS REALLY BIG.
DID IT GET BIGGER THAN YESTER-DAY?
ITS SIZE IS THE SAME-BAA.
THE SAME ...?
NAI-KUN!

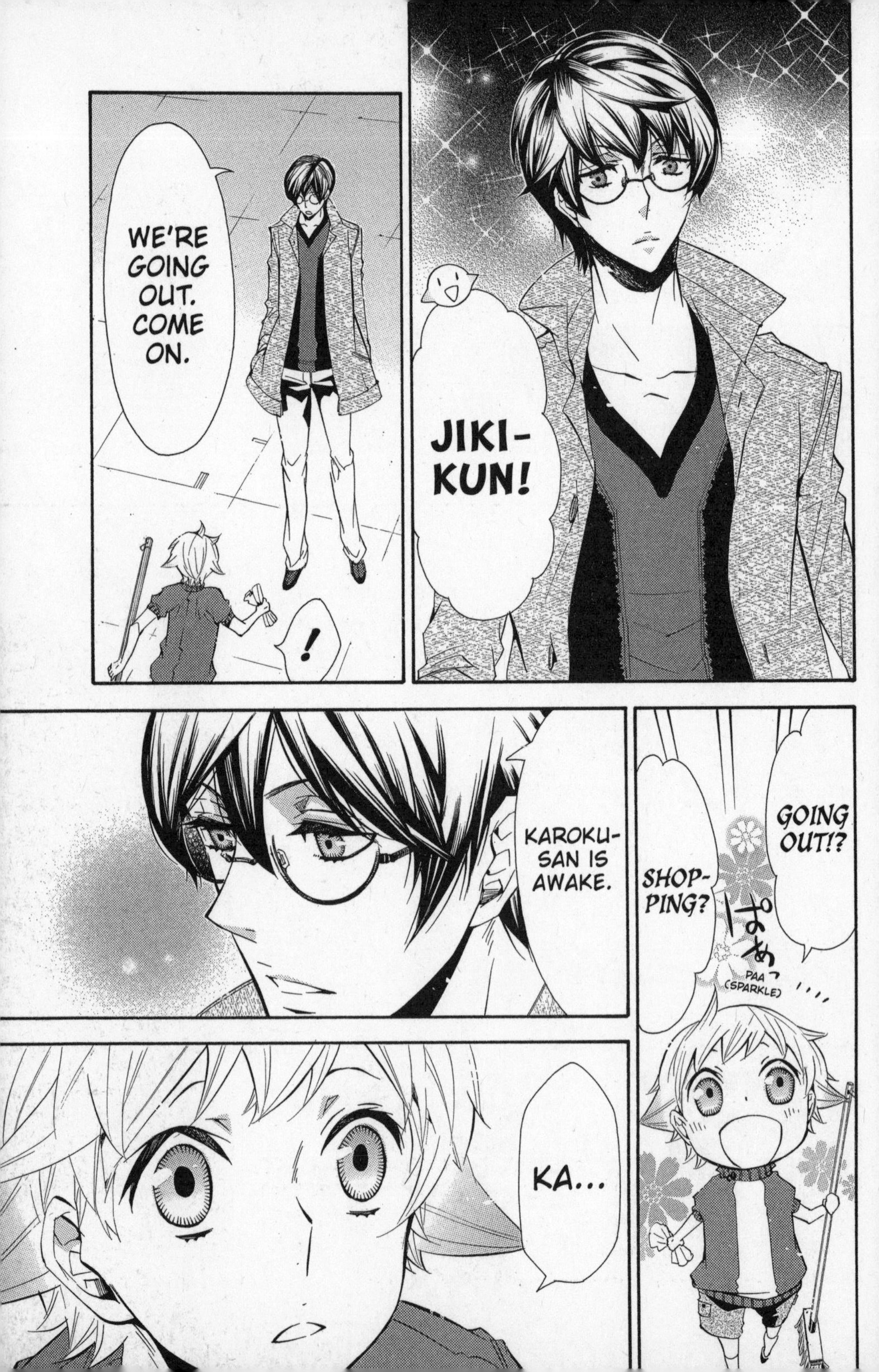
JIKI-KUN!
WE'RE GOING OUT. COME ON.
!
GOING OUT!?
SHOP-PING?
ぱぁっ
PAA (SPARKLE)
KAROKU-SAN IS AWAKE.
KA...

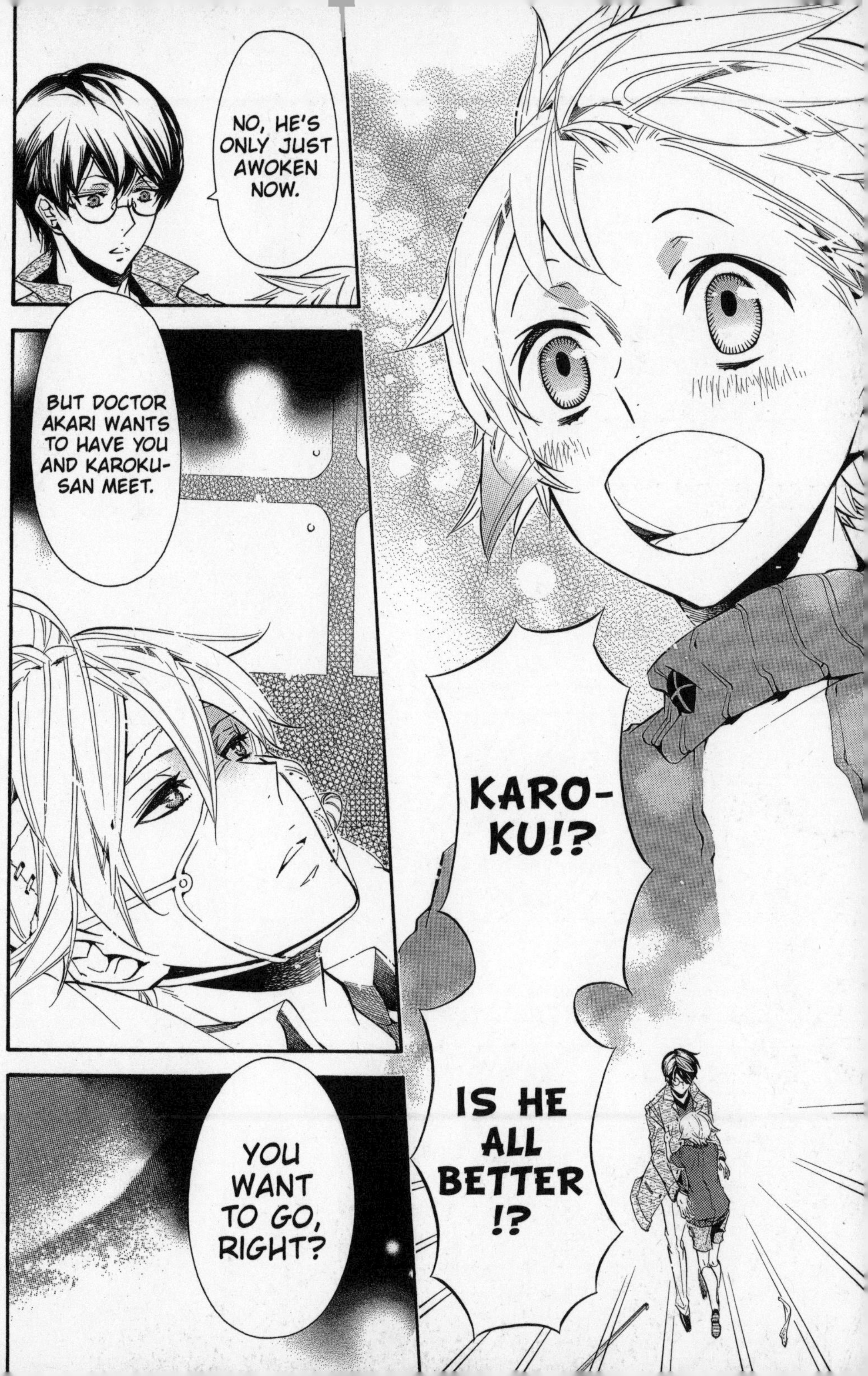
KARO-KU!?
IS HE ALL BETTER!?
NO, HE'S ONLY JUST AWOKEN NOW.
BUT DOCTOR AKARI WANTS TO HAVE YOU AND KAROKU-SAN MEET.
YOU WANT TO GO, RIGHT?

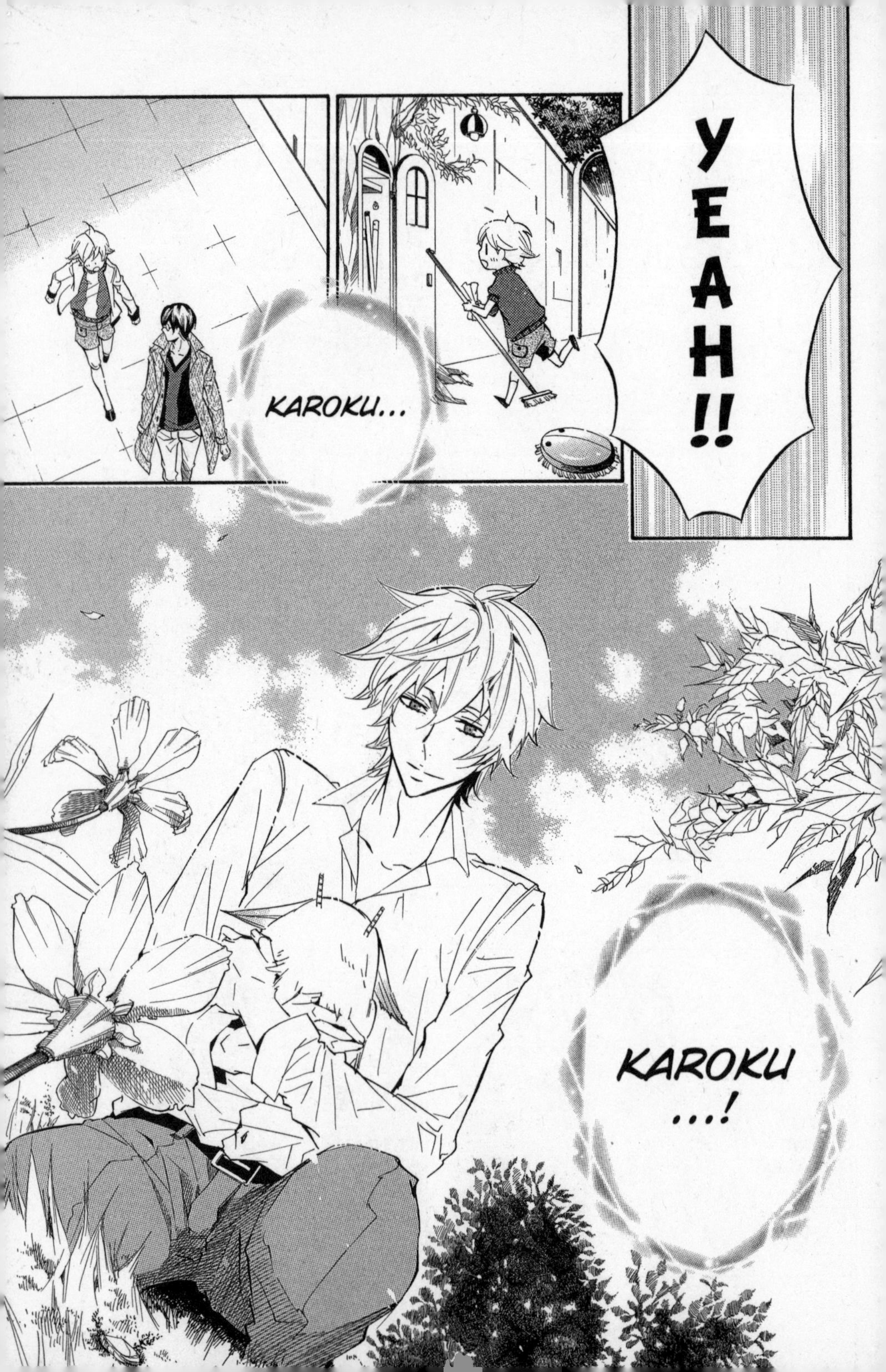
YEAH!!
KAROKU...
KAROKU...!

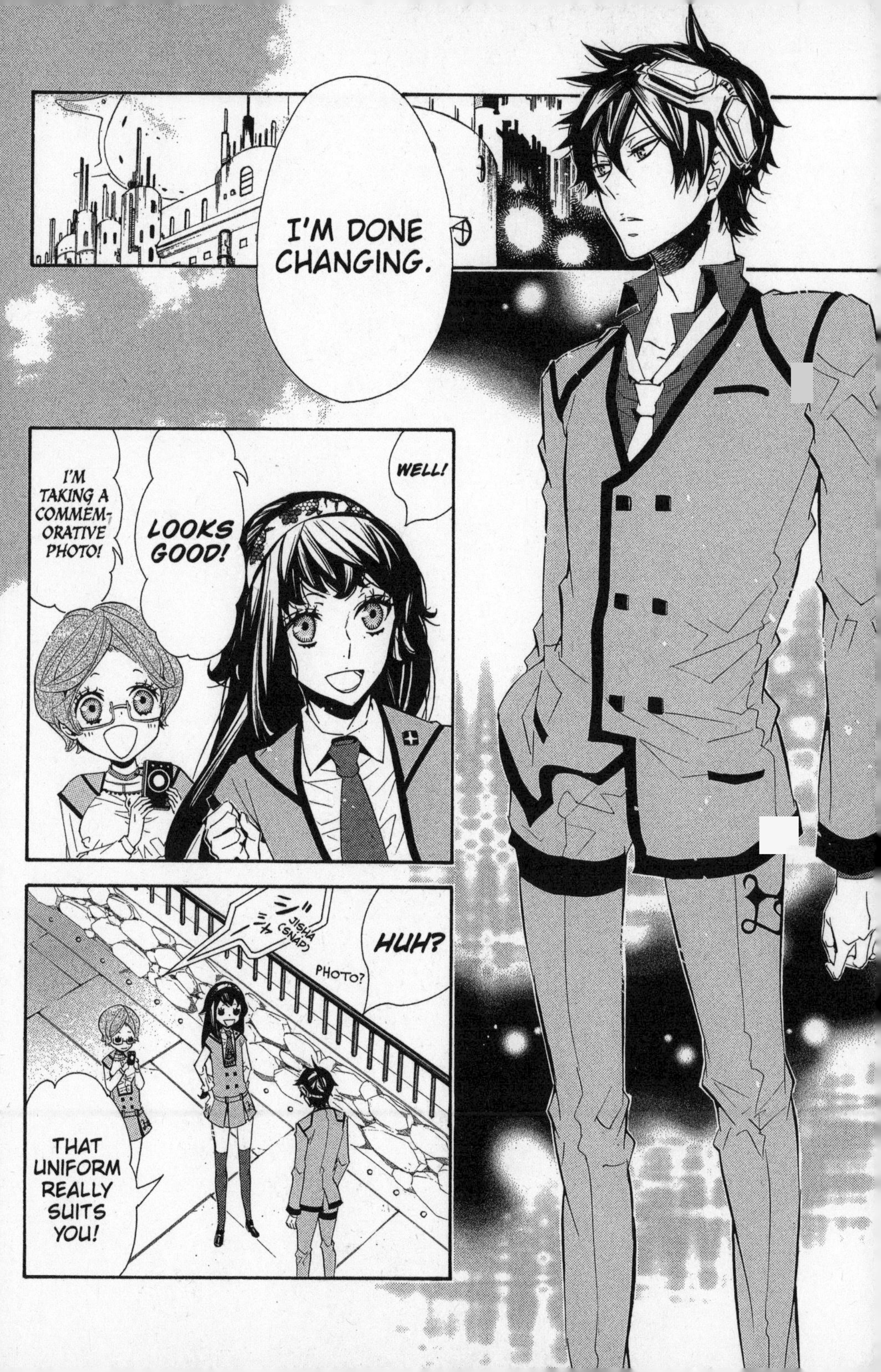
I'M DONE CHANGING.
WELL!
LOOKS GOOD!
I'M TAKING A COMMEMORATIVE PHOTO!
HUH?
PHOTO?
JISHA (SNAP)
THAT UNIFORM REALLY SUITS YOU!

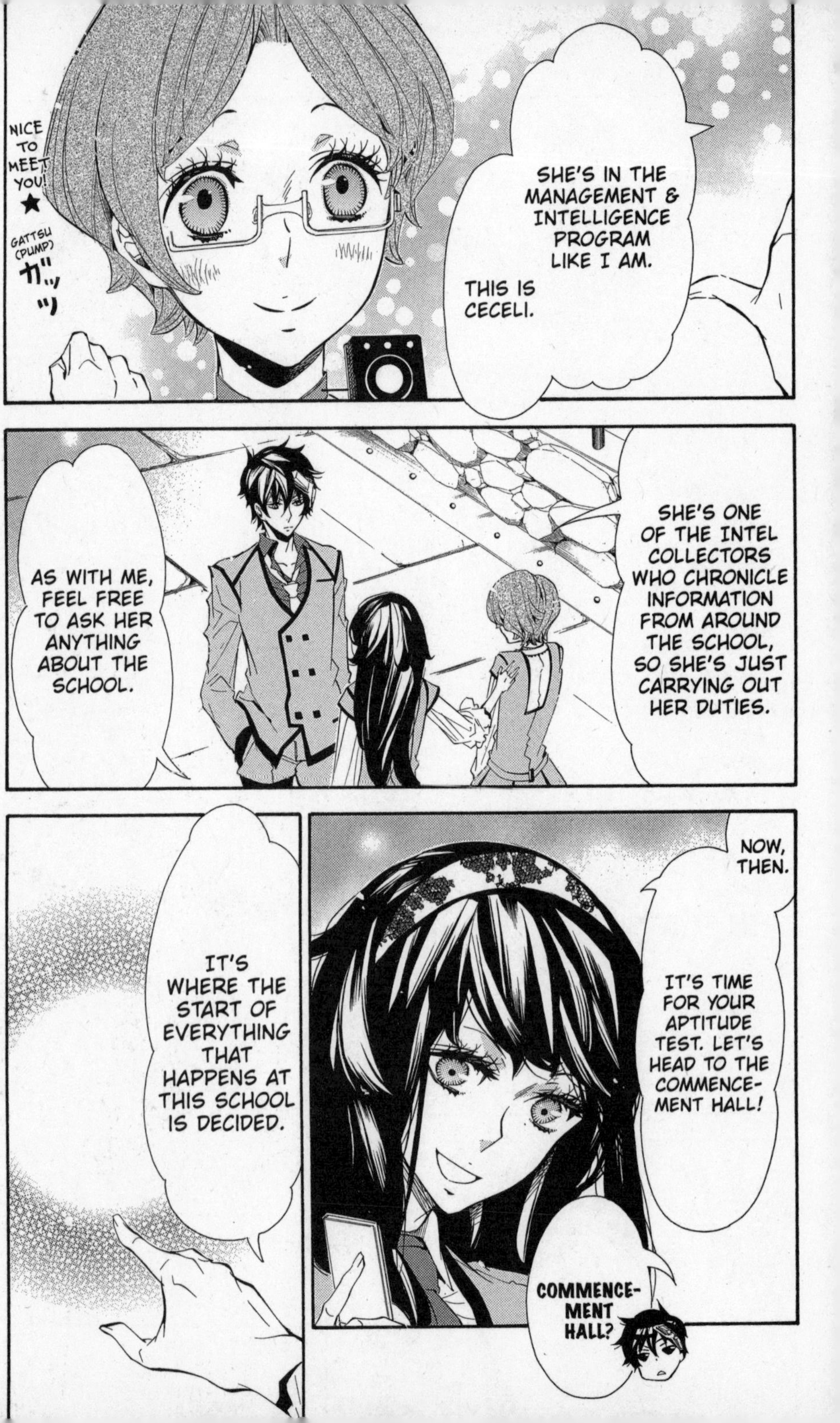
SHE'S IN THE MANAGEMENT & INTELLIGENCE PROGRAM LIKE I AM.
THIS IS CECELI.
NICE TO MEET YOU! ★
GATTSU (PUMP)
ガッツ
SHE'S ONE OF THE INTEL COLLECTORS WHO CHRONICLE INFORMATION FROM AROUND THE SCHOOL, SO SHE'S JUST CARRYING OUT HER DUTIES.
AS WITH ME, FEEL FREE TO ASK HER ANYTHING ABOUT THE SCHOOL.
NOW, THEN.
IT'S TIME FOR YOUR APTITUDE TEST. LET'S HEAD TO THE COMMENCEMENT HALL!
COMMENCEMENT HALL?
IT'S WHERE THE START OF EVERYTHING THAT HAPPENS AT THIS SCHOOL IS DECIDED.

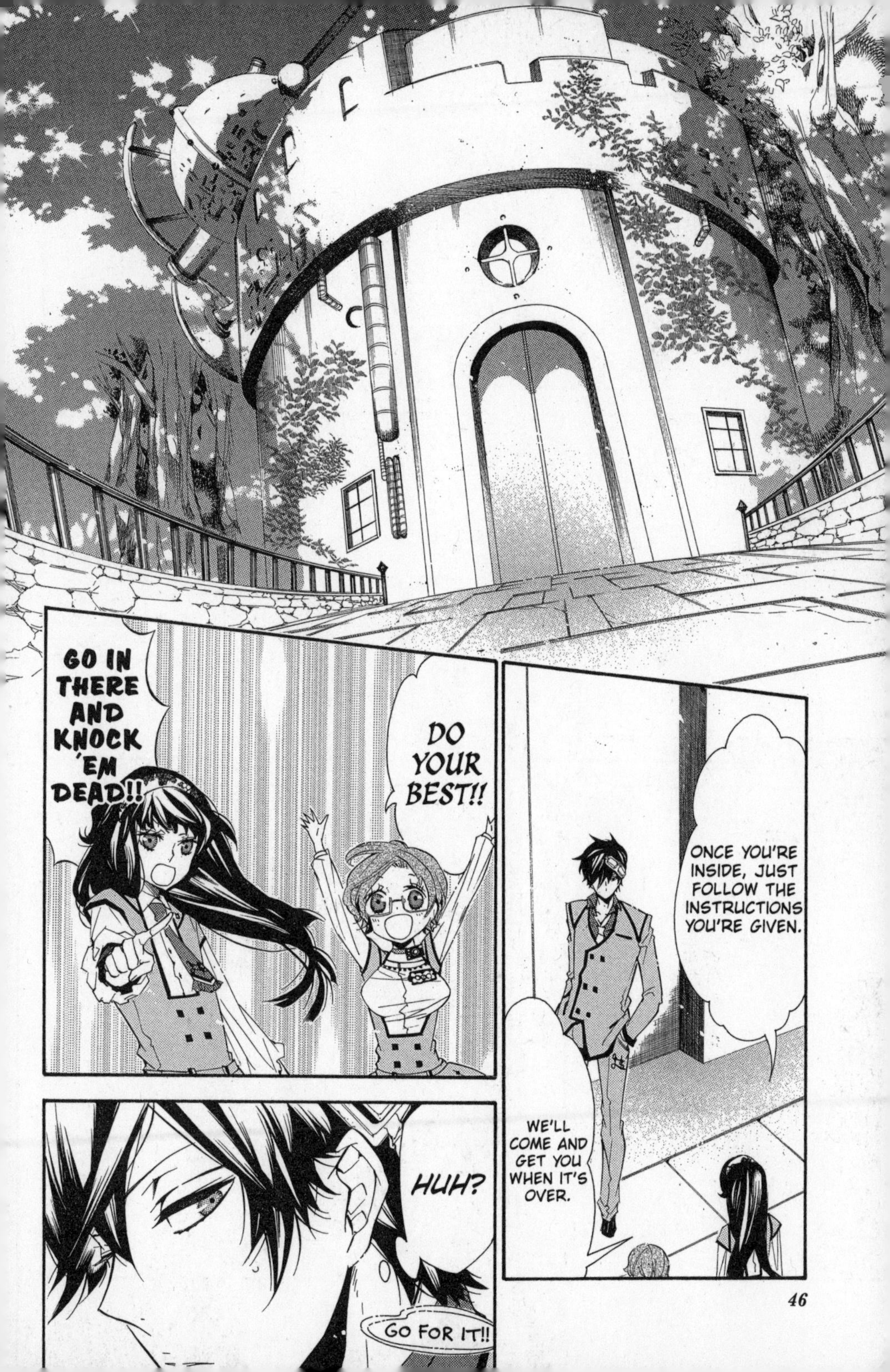
ONCE YOU'RE INSIDE, JUST FOLLOW THE INSTRUCTIONS YOU'RE GIVEN.
WE'LL COME AND GET YOU WHEN IT'S OVER.
DO YOUR BEST!!
GO IN THERE AND KNOCK 'EM DEAD!!
HUH?
GO FOR IT!!

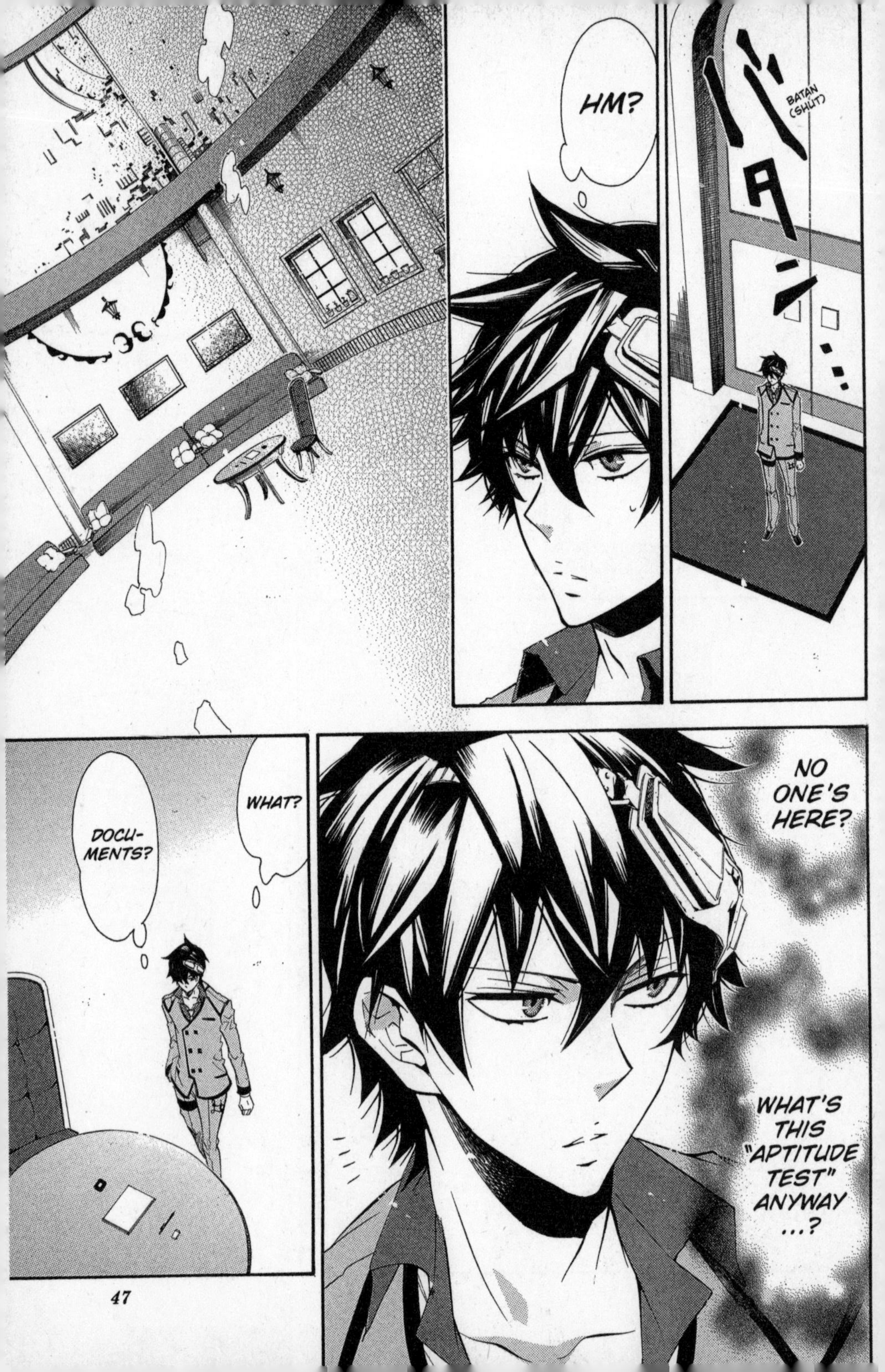
バタン
BATAN (SHUT)
HM?
NO ONE'S HERE?
WHAT'S THIS "APTITUDE TEST" ANYWAY ...?
WHAT?
DOCU-MENTS?

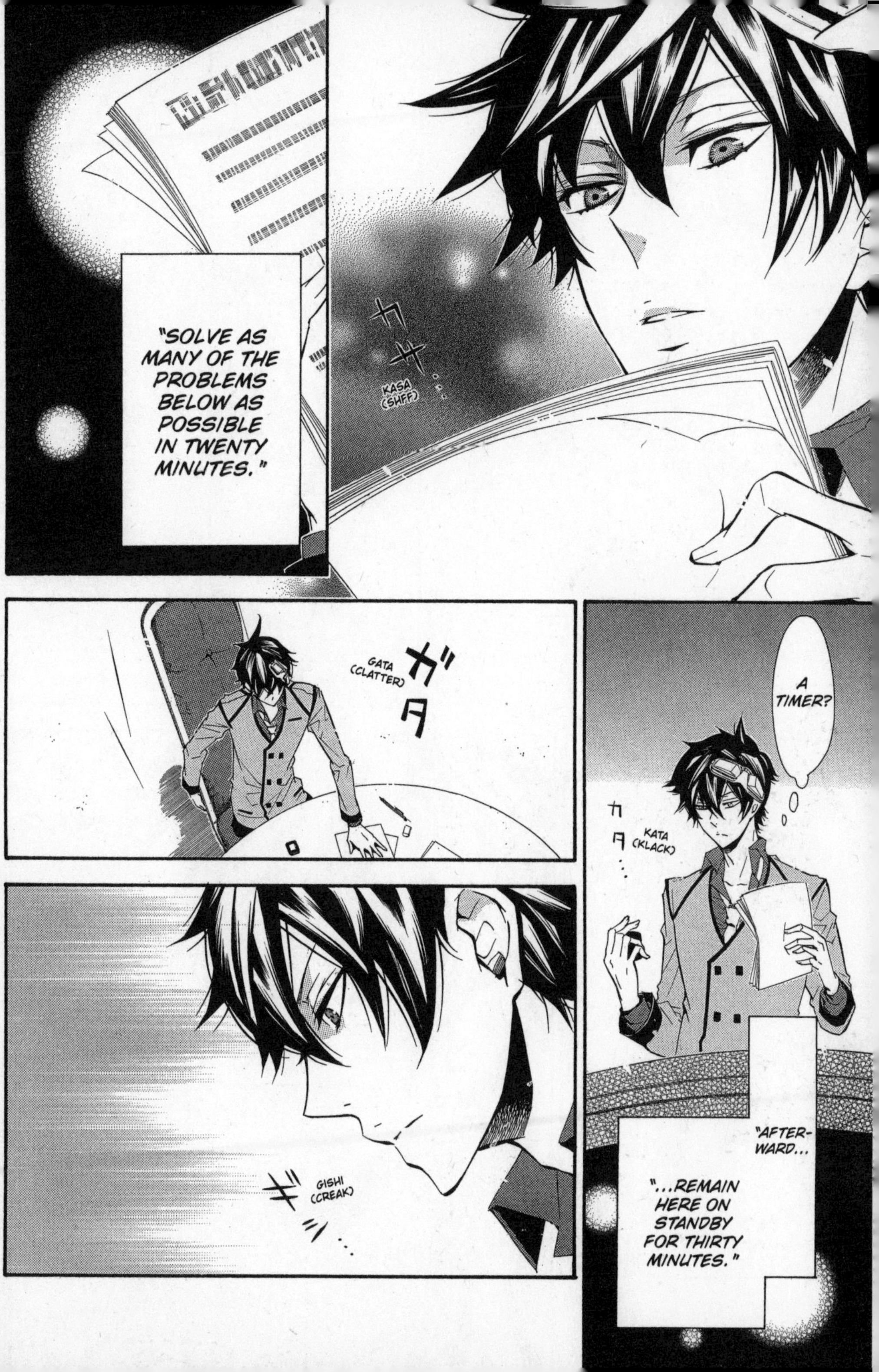

カサ…
KASA (SHFF)
"SOLVE AS MANY OF THE PROBLEMS BELOW AS POSSIBLE IN TWENTY MINUTES."
A TIMER?
カタ…
KATA (KLACK)
"AFTER-WARD…
"…REMAIN HERE ON STANDBY FOR THIRTY MINUTES."
ガタ
GATA (CLATTER)
ギシ…
GISHI (CREAK)

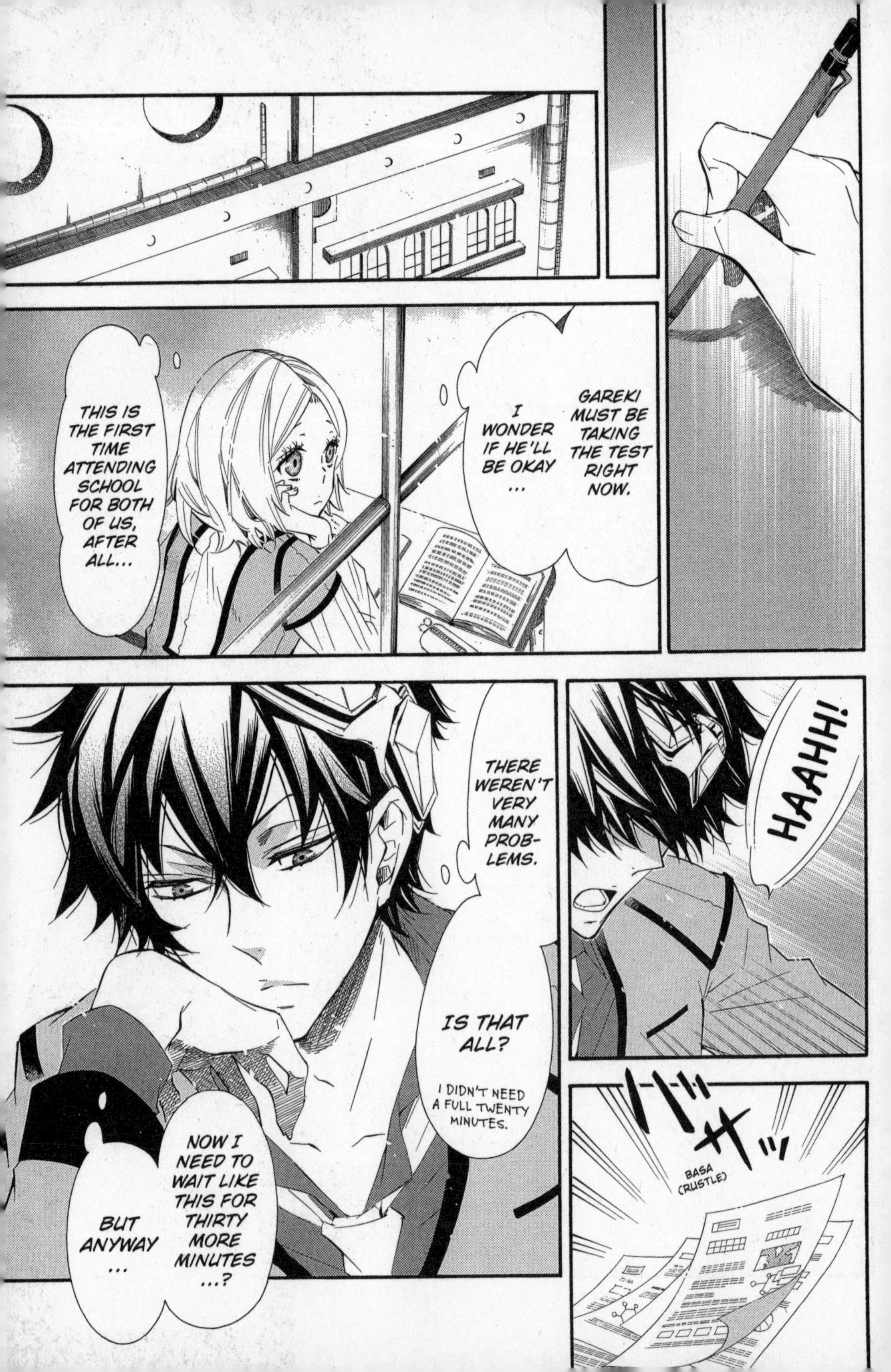
GAREKI MUST BE TAKING THE TEST RIGHT NOW.
I WONDER IF HE'LL BE OKAY ...
THIS IS THE FIRST TIME ATTENDING SCHOOL FOR BOTH OF US, AFTER ALL...
HAAHH!
BASA (RUSTLE)
THERE WEREN'T VERY MANY PROB-LEMS.
IS THAT ALL?
I DIDN'T NEED A FULL TWENTY MINUTES.
NOW I NEED TO WAIT LIKE THIS FOR THIRTY MORE MINUTES ...?
BUT ANYWAY ...

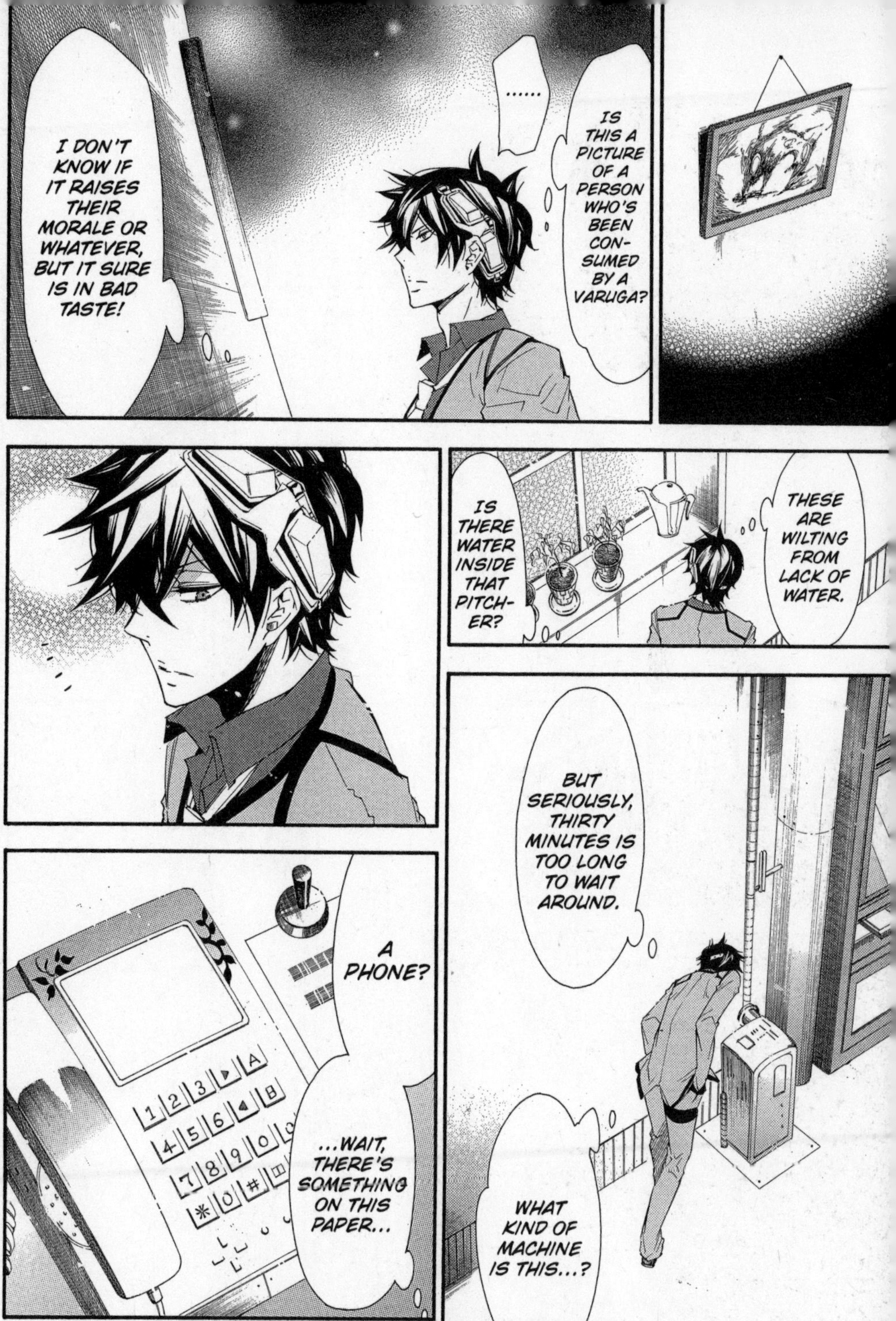
IS THIS A PICTURE OF A PERSON WHO'S BEEN CON-SUMED BY A VARUGA?
......
I DON'T KNOW IF IT RAISES THEIR MORALE OR WHATEVER, BUT IT SURE IS IN BAD TASTE!
THESE ARE WILTING FROM LACK OF WATER.
IS THERE WATER INSIDE THAT PITCH-ER?
BUT SERIOUSLY, THIRTY MINUTES IS TOO LONG TO WAIT AROUND.
WHAT KIND OF MACHINE IS THIS...?
A PHONE?
...WAIT, THERE'S SOMETHING ON THIS PAPER...

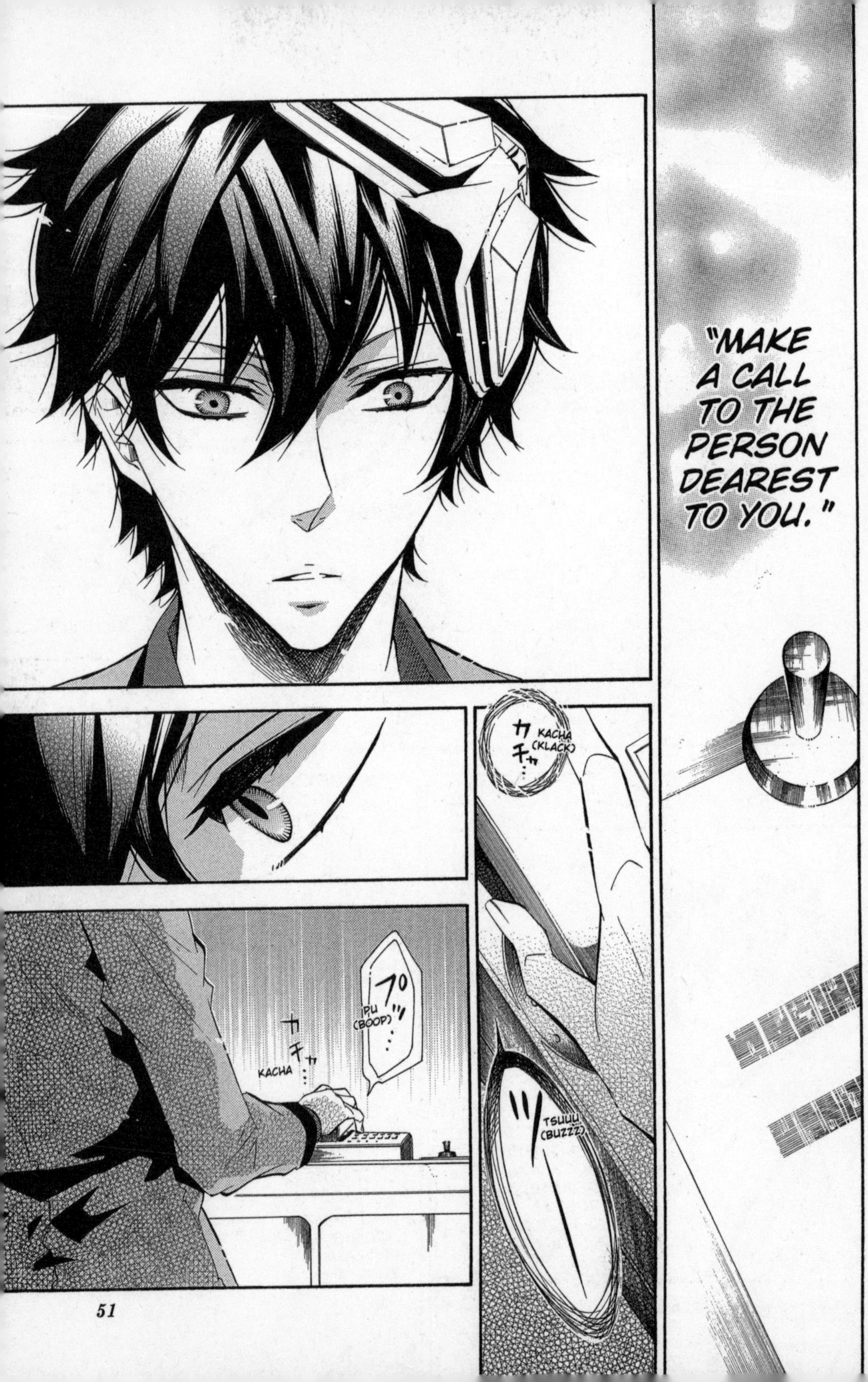
"MAKE A CALL TO THE PERSON DEAREST TO YOU."
カチャ… KACHA (KLACK)
ツ TSUUU (BUZZZ)
カチャ… KACHA
プ… PU (BOOP)

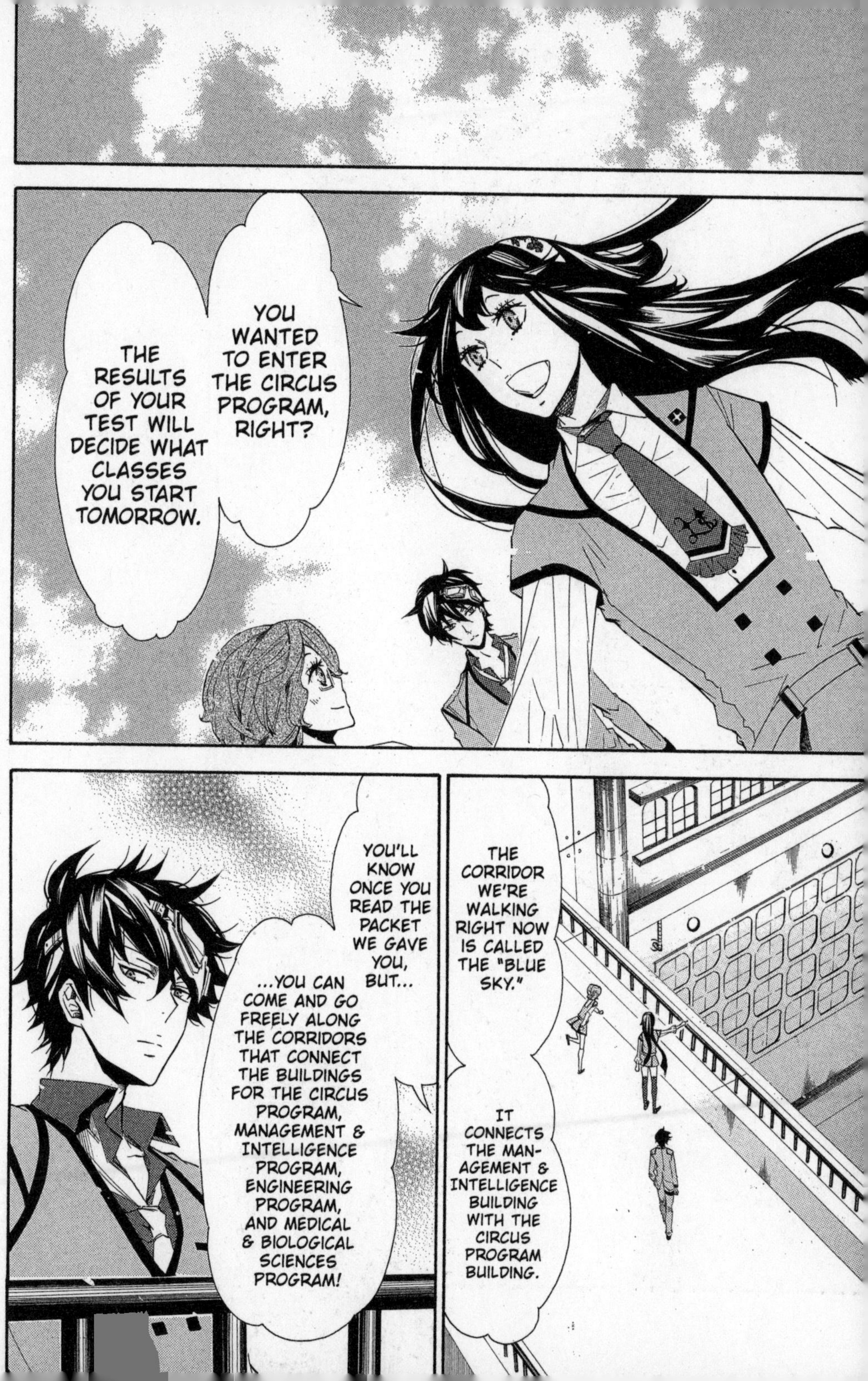
YOU WANTED TO ENTER THE CIRCUS PROGRAM, RIGHT?
THE RESULTS OF YOUR TEST WILL DECIDE WHAT CLASSES YOU START TOMORROW.
THE CORRIDOR WE'RE WALKING RIGHT NOW IS CALLED THE "BLUE SKY."
IT CONNECTS THE MAN-AGEMENT & INTELLIGENCE BUILDING WITH THE CIRCUS PROGRAM BUILDING.
YOU'LL KNOW ONCE YOU READ THE PACKET WE GAVE YOU, BUT...
...YOU CAN COME AND GO FREELY ALONG THE CORRIDORS THAT CONNECT THE BUILDINGS FOR THE CIRCUS PROGRAM, MANAGEMENT & INTELLIGENCE PROGRAM, ENGINEERING PROGRAM, AND MEDICAL & BIOLOGICAL SCIENCES PROGRAM!

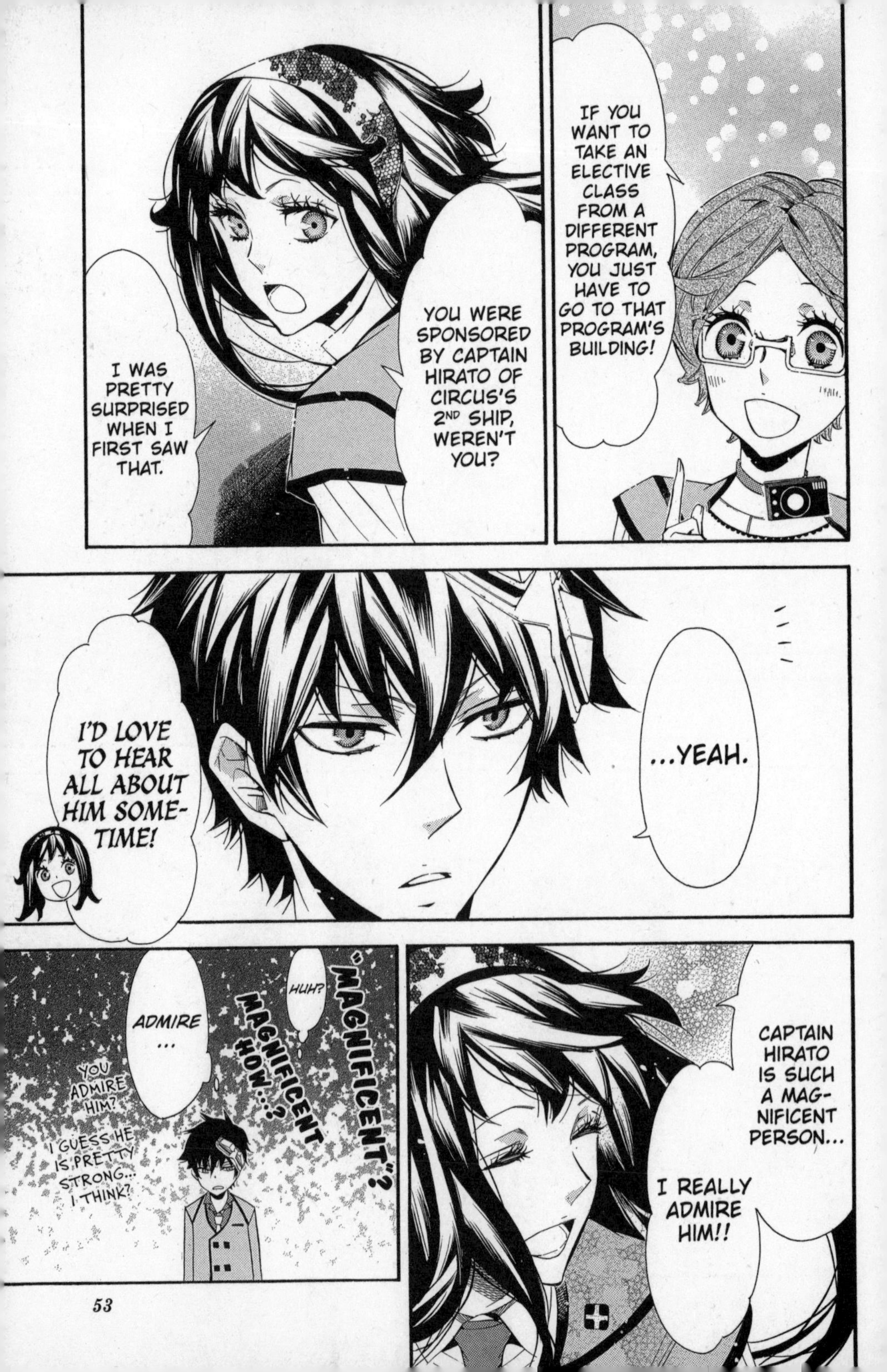
IF YOU WANT TO TAKE AN ELECTIVE CLASS FROM A DIFFERENT PROGRAM, YOU JUST HAVE TO GO TO THAT PROGRAM'S BUILDING!
YOU WERE SPONSORED BY CAPTAIN HIRATO OF CIRCUS'S 2ND SHIP, WEREN'T YOU?
I WAS PRETTY SURPRISED WHEN I FIRST SAW THAT.
...YEAH.
I'D LOVE TO HEAR ALL ABOUT HIM SOME-TIME!
CAPTAIN HIRATO IS SUCH A MAG-NIFICENT PERSON...
I REALLY ADMIRE HIM!!
HUH?
"MAGNIFICENT"? MAGNIFICENT HOW...?
ADMIRE...
YOU ADMIRE HIM?
I GUESS HE IS PRETTY STRONG... I THINK?

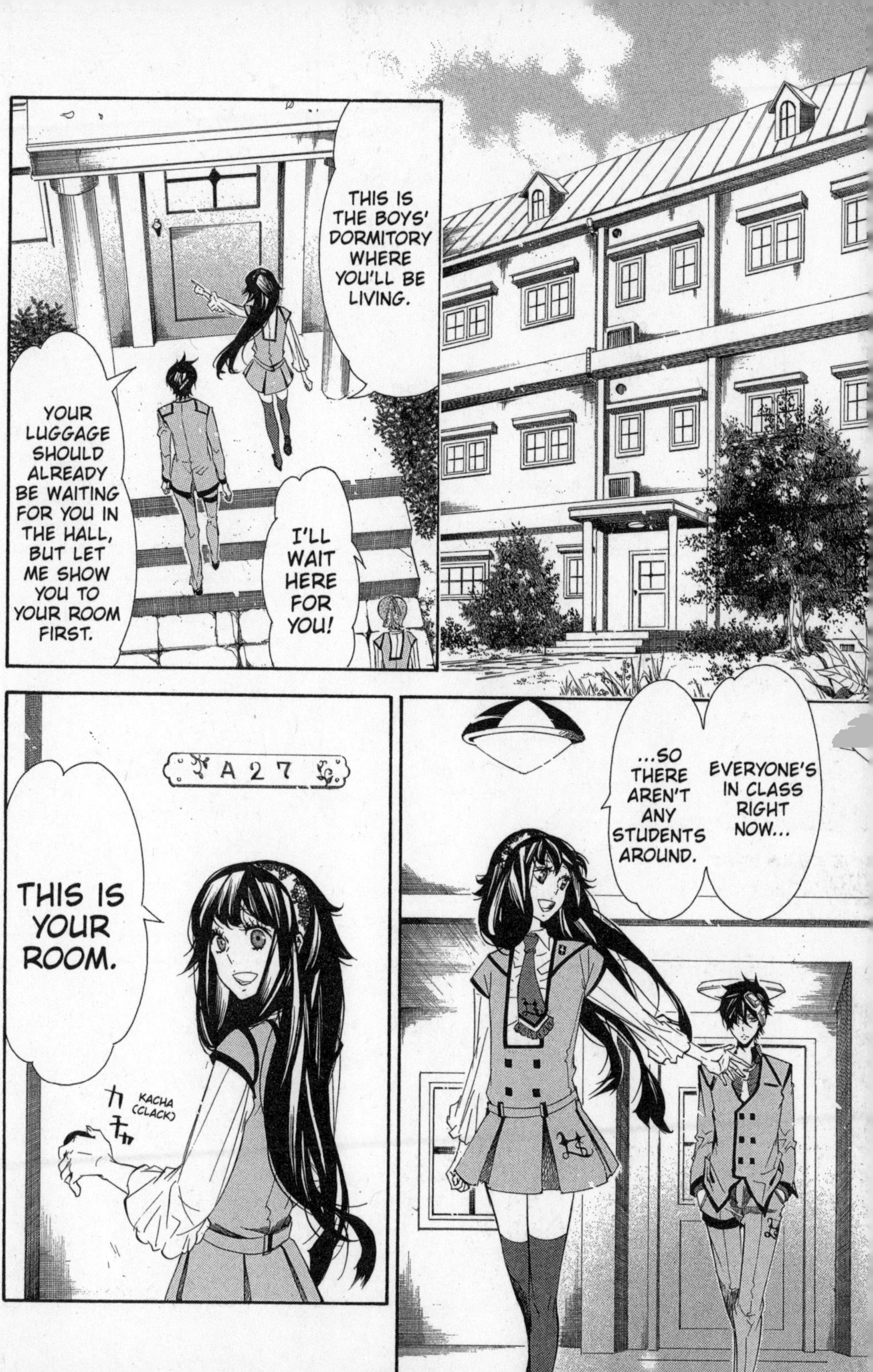
THIS IS THE BOYS' DORMITORY WHERE YOU'LL BE LIVING.
YOUR LUGGAGE SHOULD ALREADY BE WAITING FOR YOU IN THE HALL, BUT LET ME SHOW YOU TO YOUR ROOM FIRST.
I'LL WAIT HERE FOR YOU!
EVERYONE'S IN CLASS RIGHT NOW...
...SO THERE AREN'T ANY STUDENTS AROUND.
A27
THIS IS YOUR ROOM.
カチャ
KACHA (CLACK)

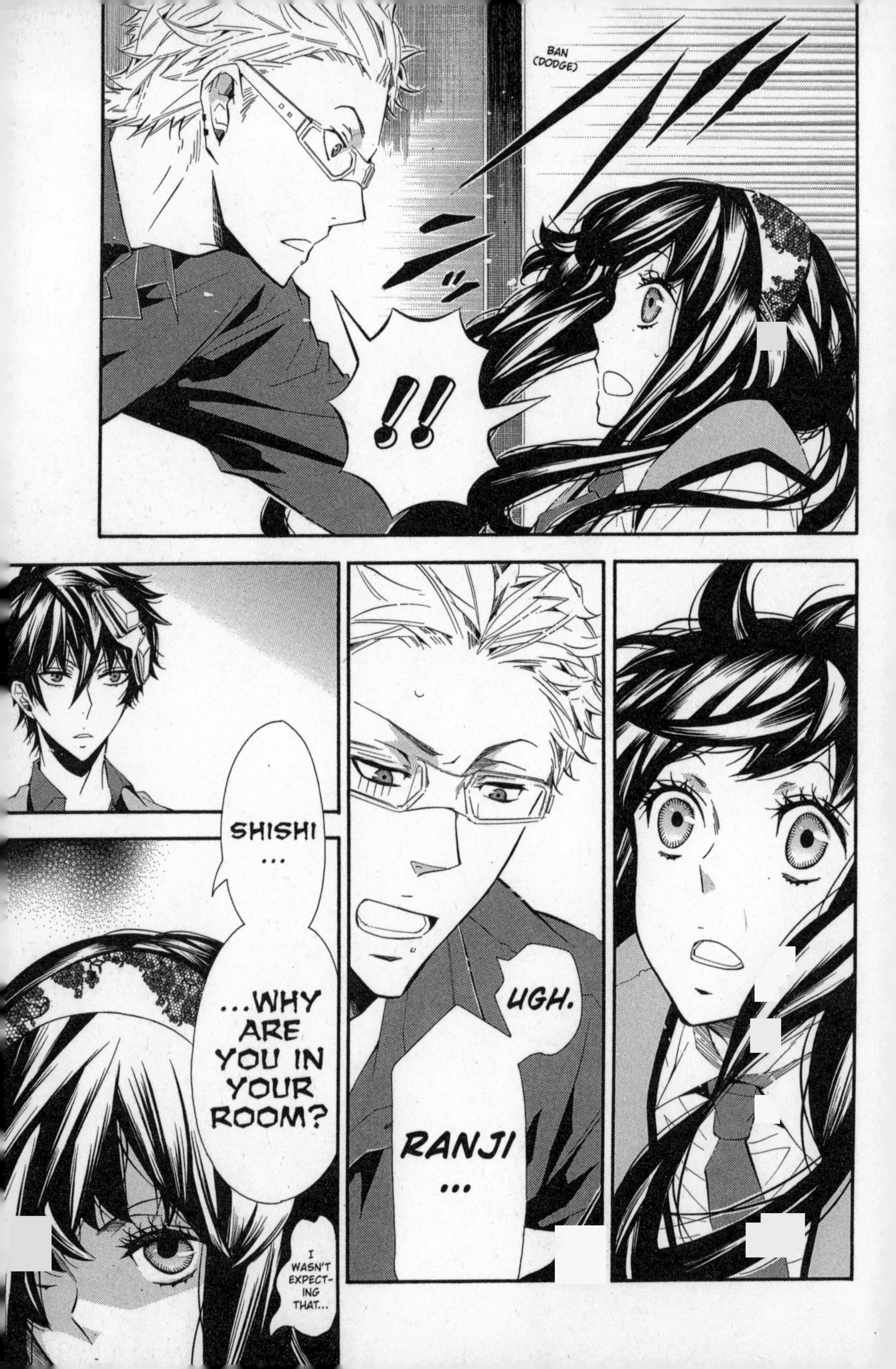
BAN (DODGE)
!!
UGH.
RANJI ...
SHISHI ...
...WHY ARE YOU IN YOUR ROOM?
I WASN'T EXPECTING THAT...

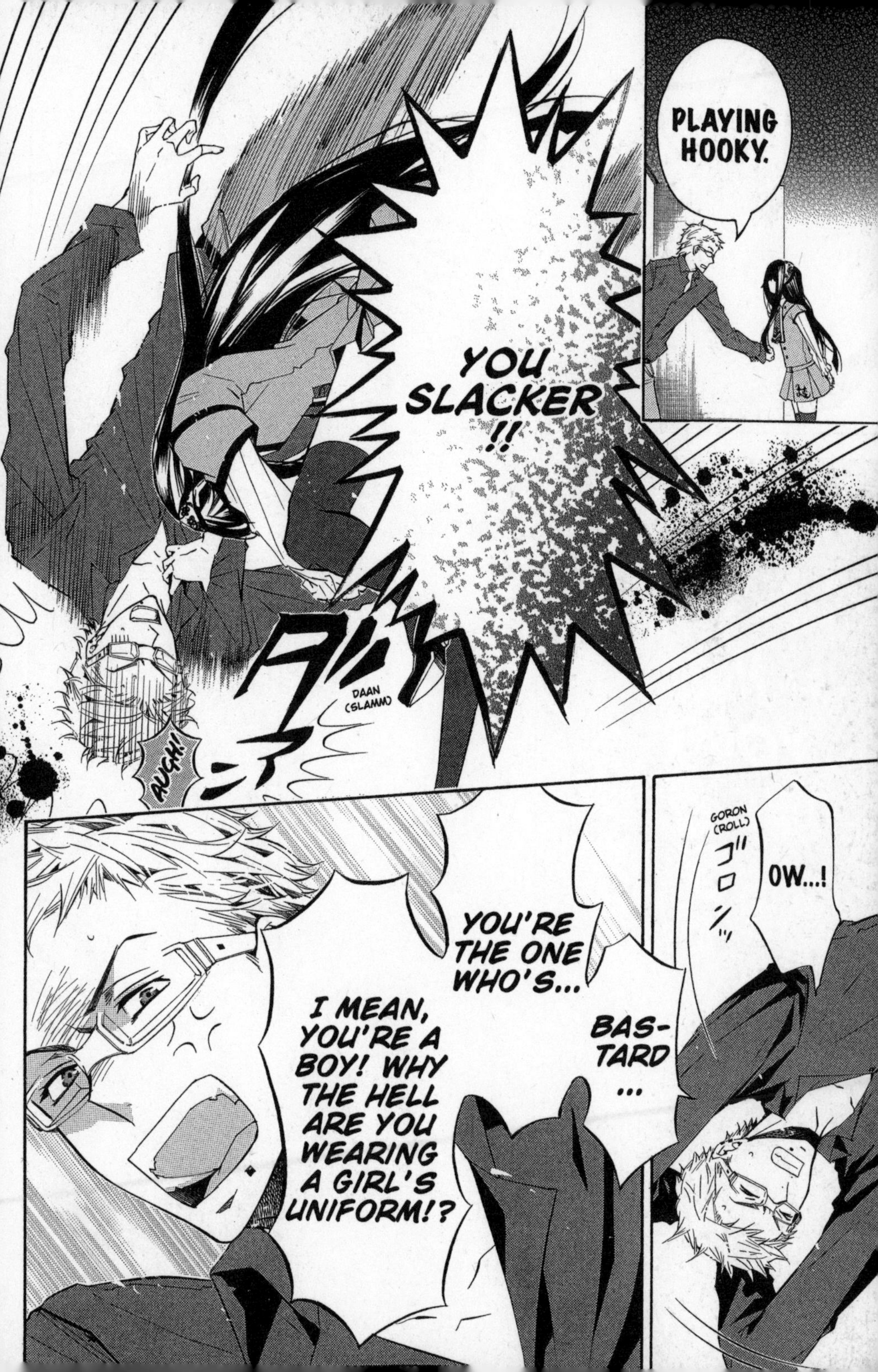
PLAYING HOOKY.
YOU SLACKER!!
DAAN (SLAMM)
AUGH!
GORON (ROLL)
OW...!
BAS-TARD...
YOU'RE THE ONE WHO'S...
I MEAN, YOU'RE A BOY! WHY THE HELL ARE YOU WEARING A GIRL'S UNIFORM!?

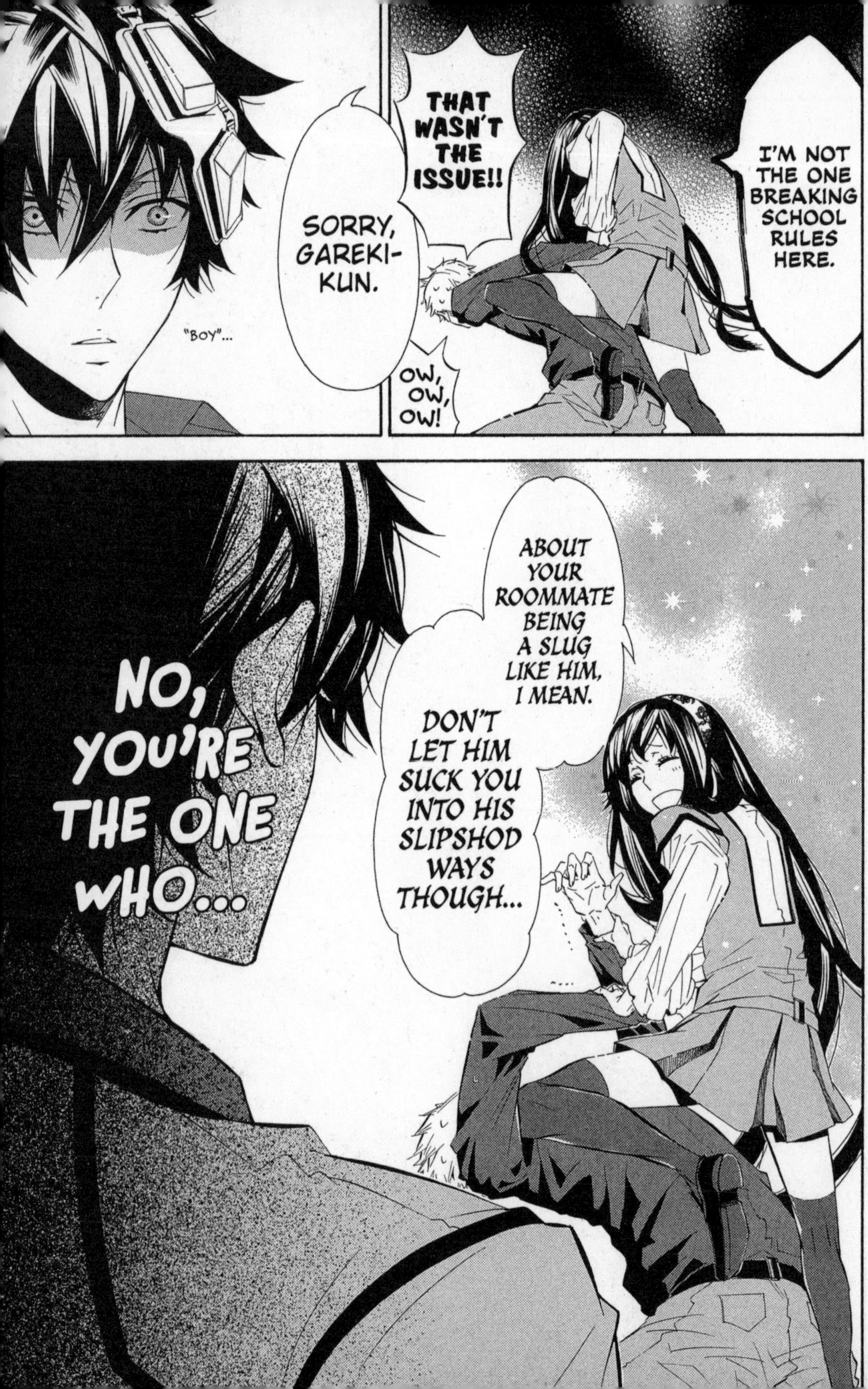
I'M NOT THE ONE BREAKING SCHOOL RULES HERE.
THAT WASN'T THE ISSUE!!
OW, OW, OW!
SORRY, GAREKI-KUN.
"BOY"...
ABOUT YOUR ROOMMATE BEING A SLUG LIKE HIM, I MEAN.
DON'T LET HIM SUCK YOU INTO HIS SLIPSHOD WAYS THOUGH...
NO, YOU'RE THE ONE WHO...

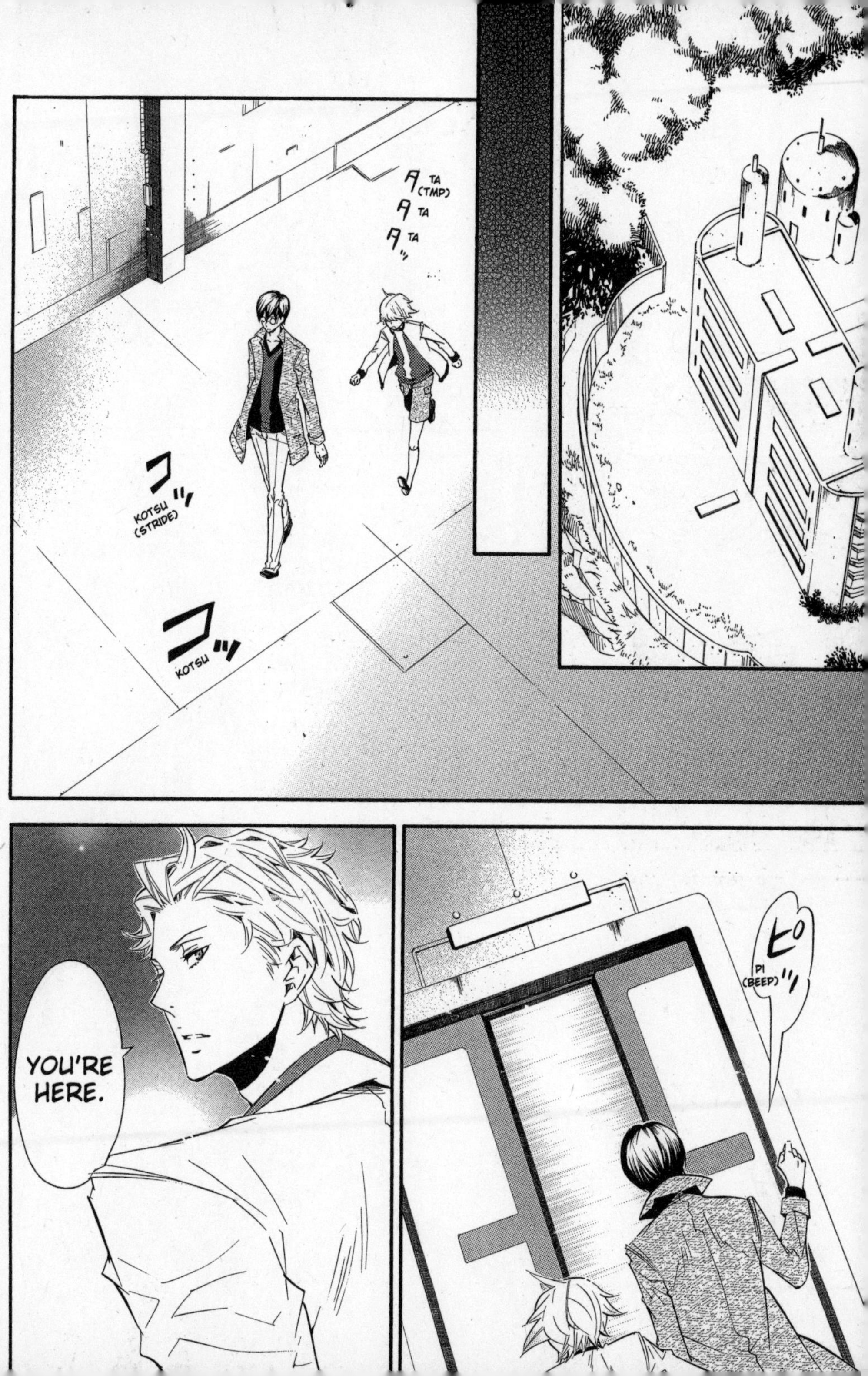
タ TA (TMP)
タ TA
タッ TA
コッ KOTSU (STRIDE)
コッ KOTSU
ピッ PI (BEEP)
YOU'RE HERE.

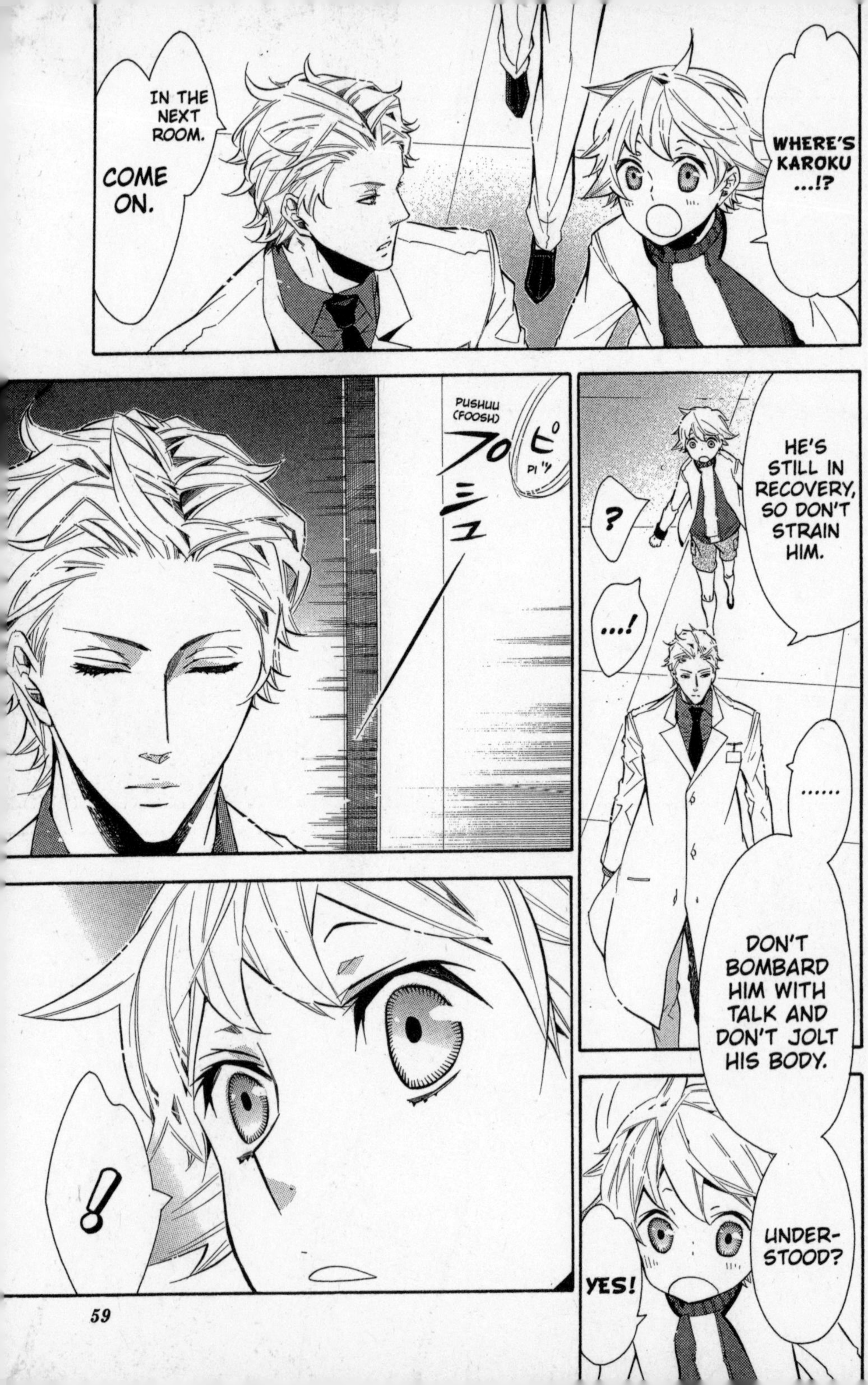

WHERE'S KAROKU ...!?
IN THE NEXT ROOM.
COME ON.
HE'S STILL IN RECOVERY, SO DON'T STRAIN HIM.
?
...!
......
DON'T BOMBARD HIM WITH TALK AND DON'T JOLT HIS BODY.
UNDER-STOOD?
YES!
PI
PUSHUU (FOOSH)
!

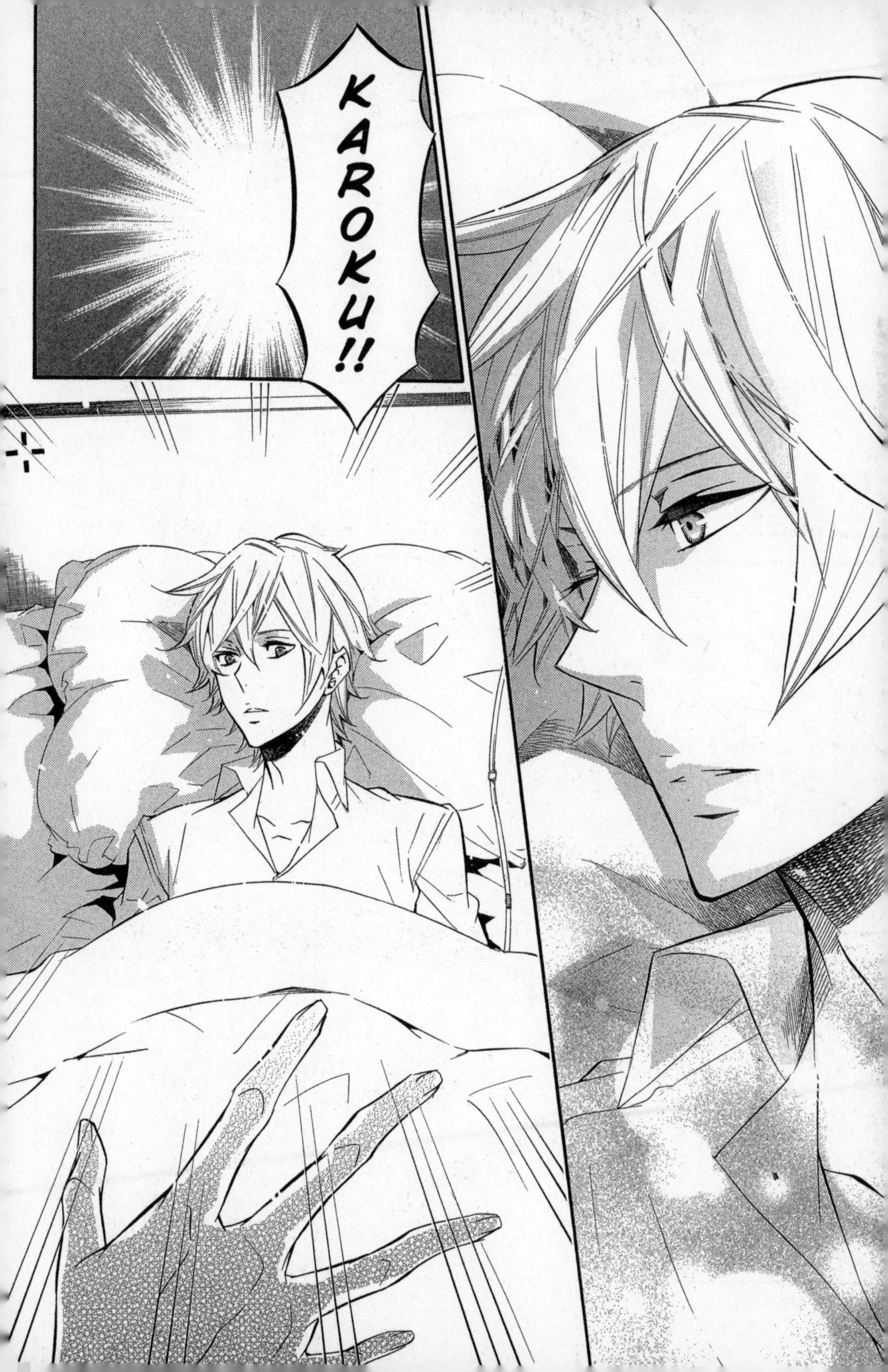
KAROKU!!

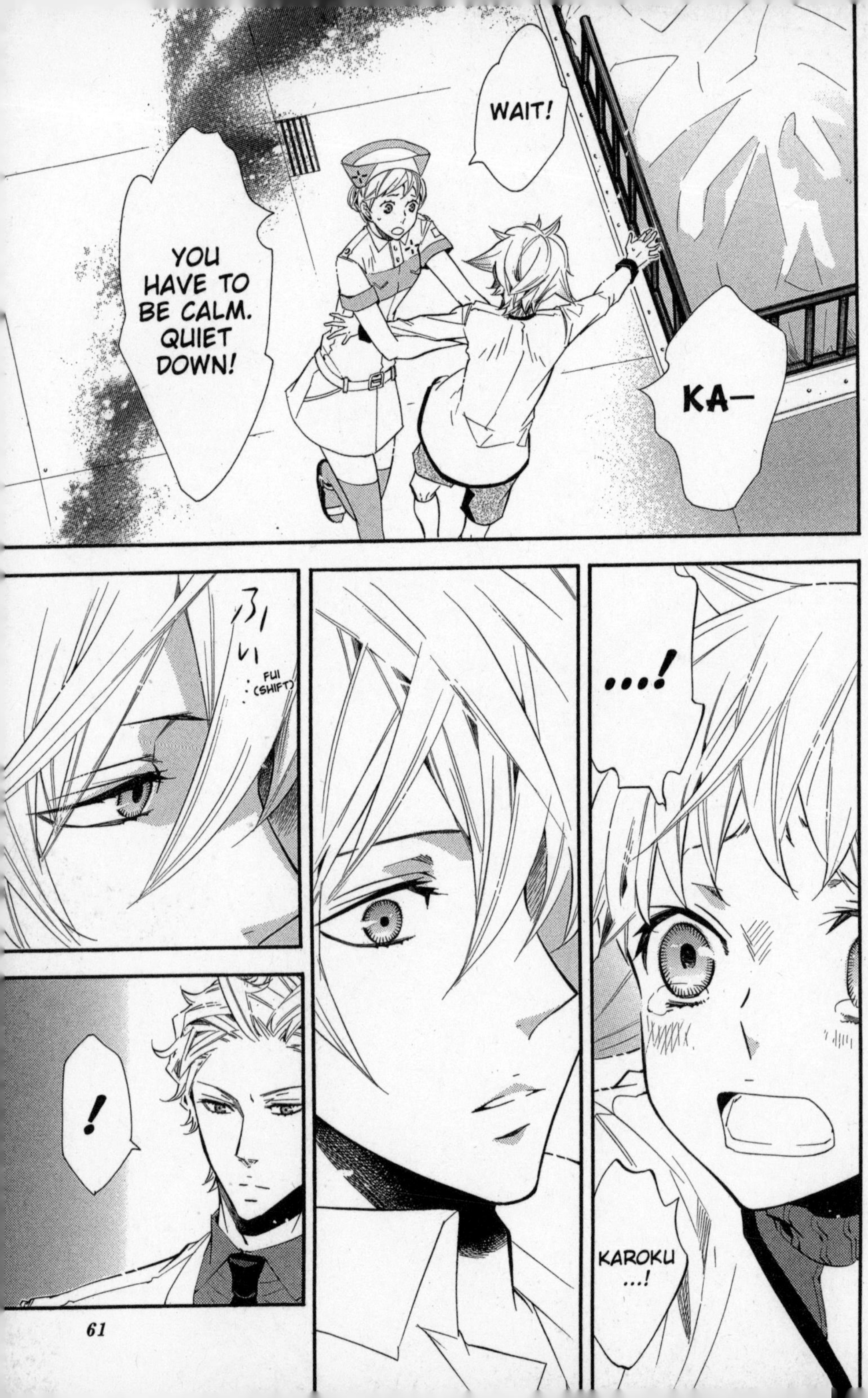
WAIT!
KA—
YOU HAVE TO BE CALM. QUIET DOWN!
...!
KAROKU ...!
ふい
FUI (SHIFT)
!

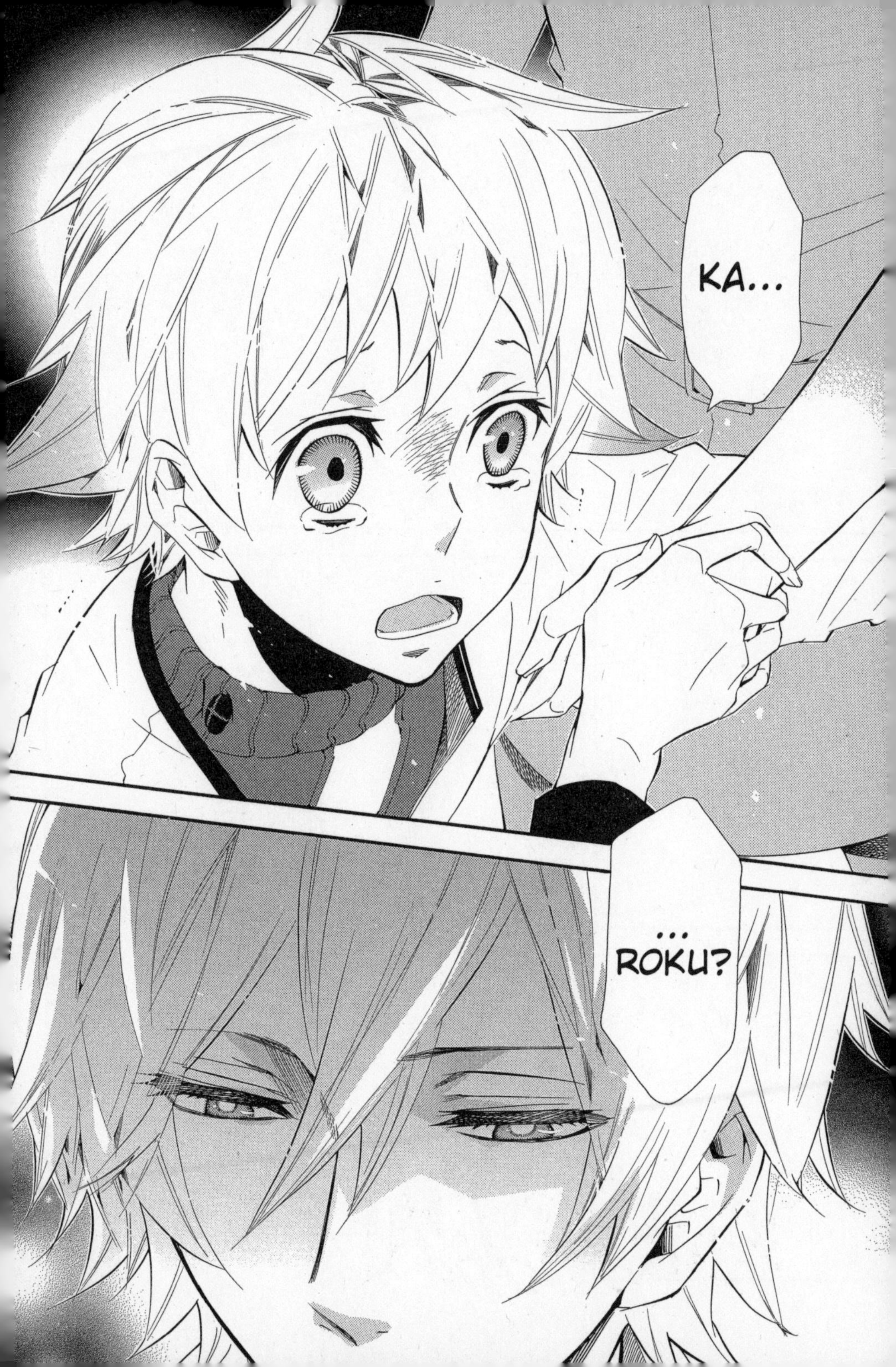
KA...
...ROKU?

KARNEVAL

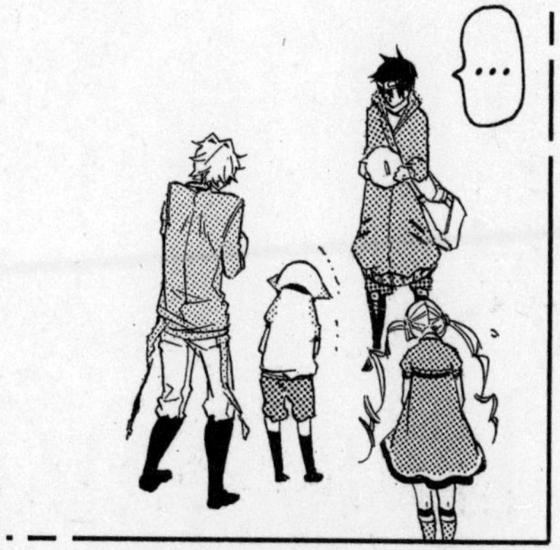
...

KARNEVAL

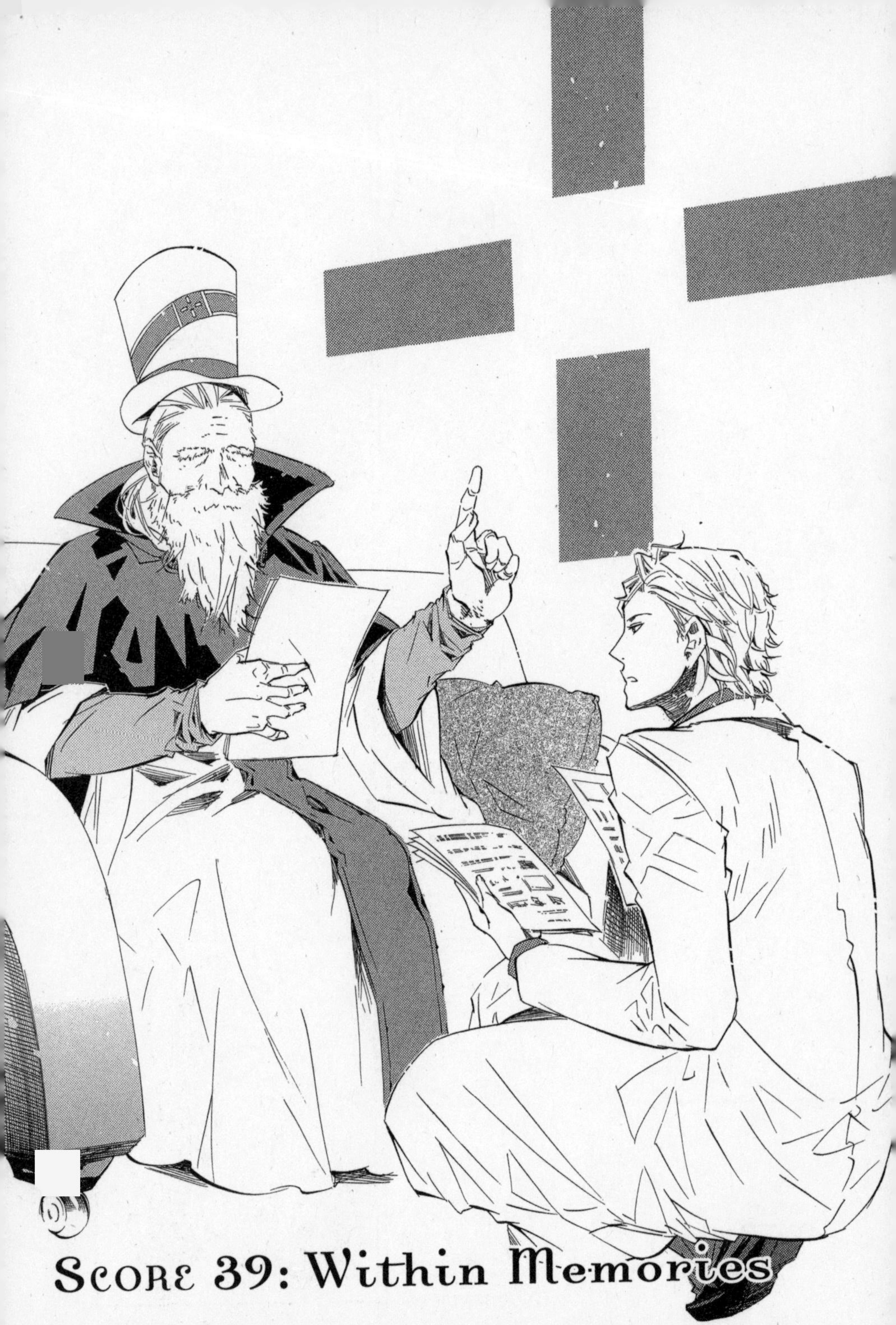

Score 39: Within Memories

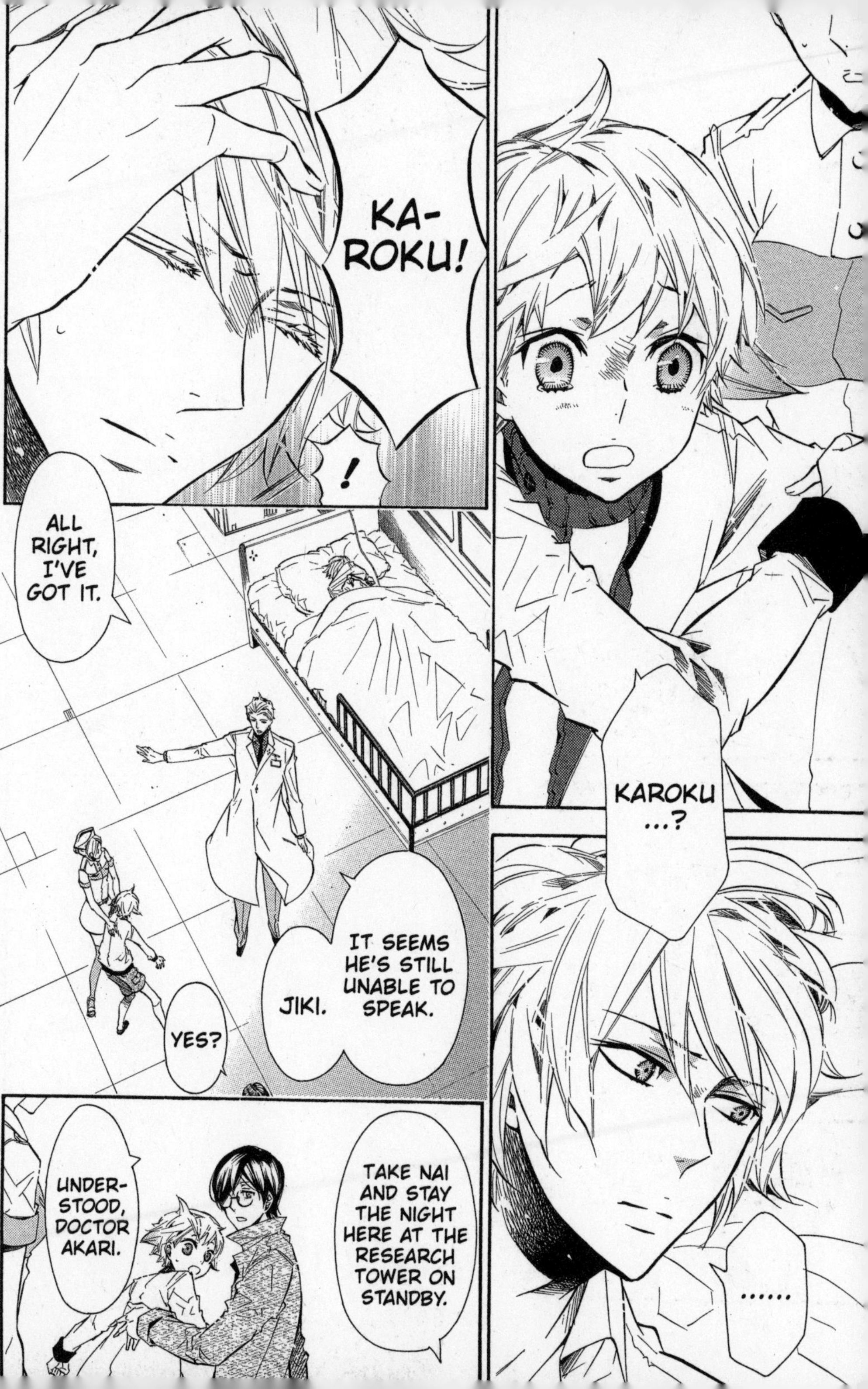
KAROKU ...?
KA-ROKU!
!
ALL RIGHT, I'VE GOT IT.
IT SEEMS HE'S STILL UNABLE TO SPEAK.
JIKI.
YES?
......
TAKE NAI AND STAY THE NIGHT HERE AT THE RESEARCH TOWER ON STANDBY.
UNDER-STOOD, DOCTOR AKARI.

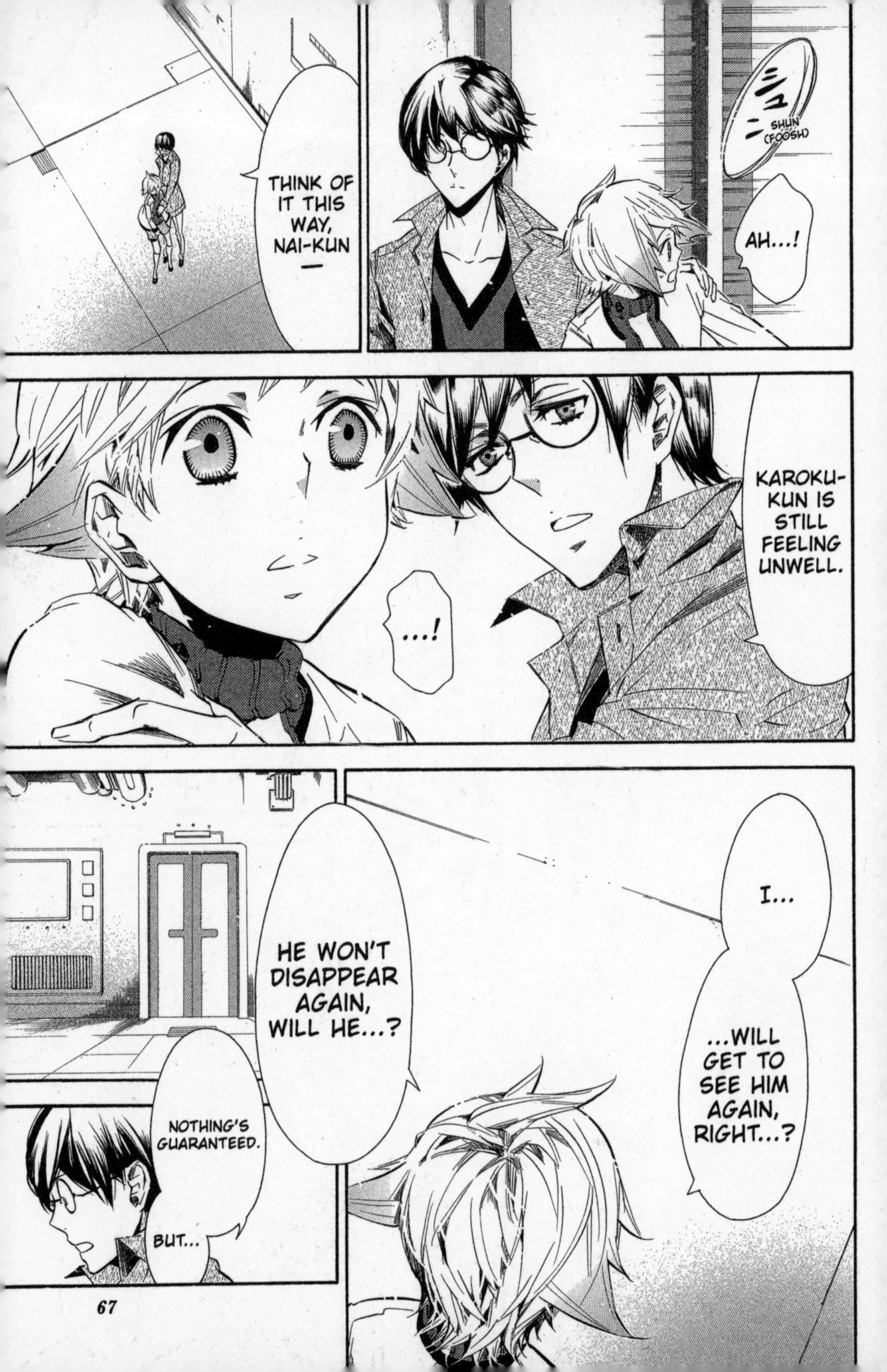
SHUN (FOOSH)
AH...!
THINK OF IT THIS WAY, NAI-KUN —
KAROKU-KUN IS STILL FEELING UNWELL.
...!
I...
...WILL GET TO SEE HIM AGAIN, RIGHT...?
HE WON'T DISAPPEAR AGAIN, WILL HE...?
NOTHING'S GUARANTEED.
BUT...

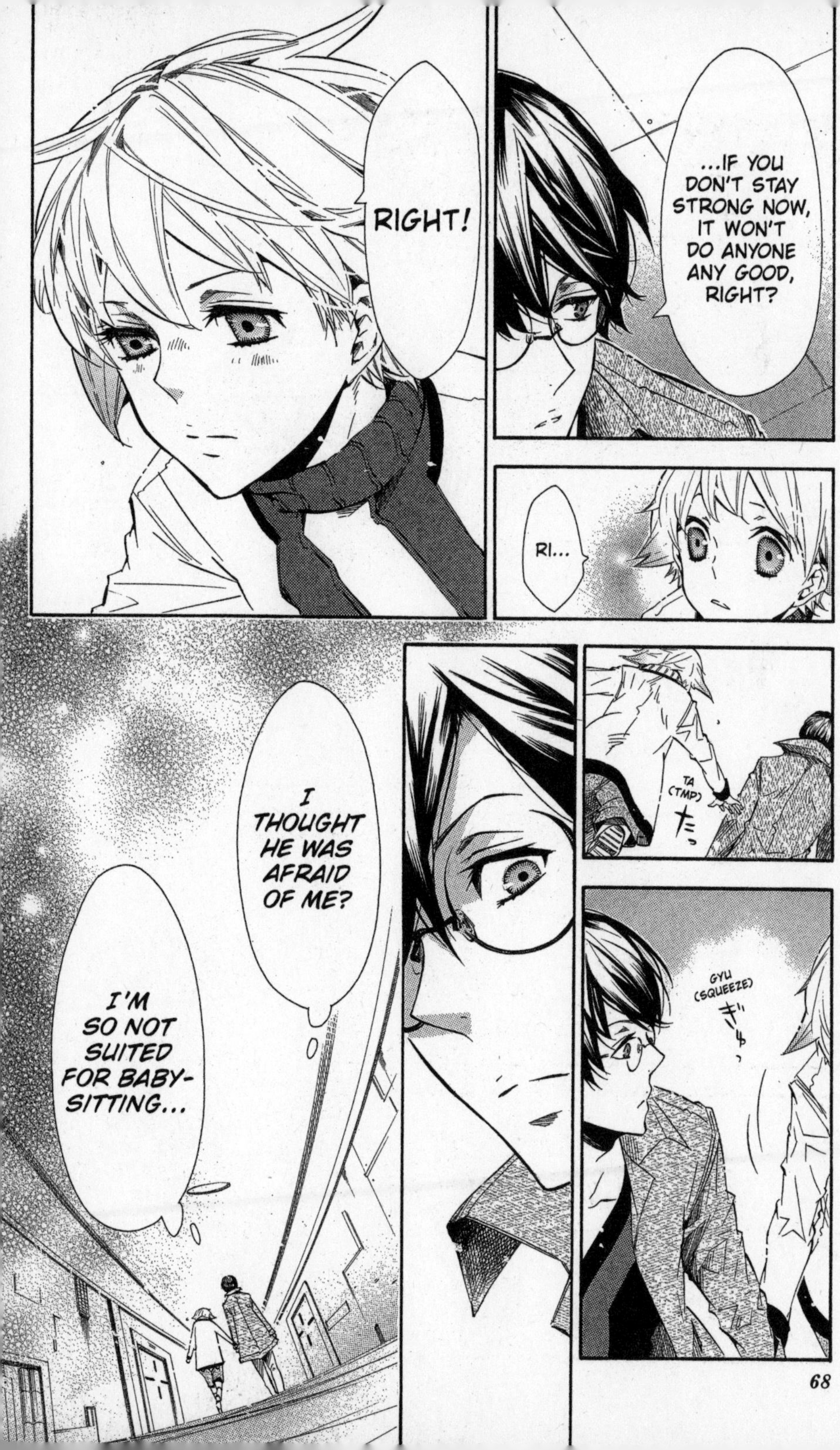
...IF YOU DON'T STAY STRONG NOW, IT WON'T DO ANYONE ANY GOOD, RIGHT?
RI...
RIGHT!
TA (TMP)
GYU (SQUEEZE)
I THOUGHT HE WAS AFRAID OF ME?
I'M SO NOT SUITED FOR BABY-SITTING...

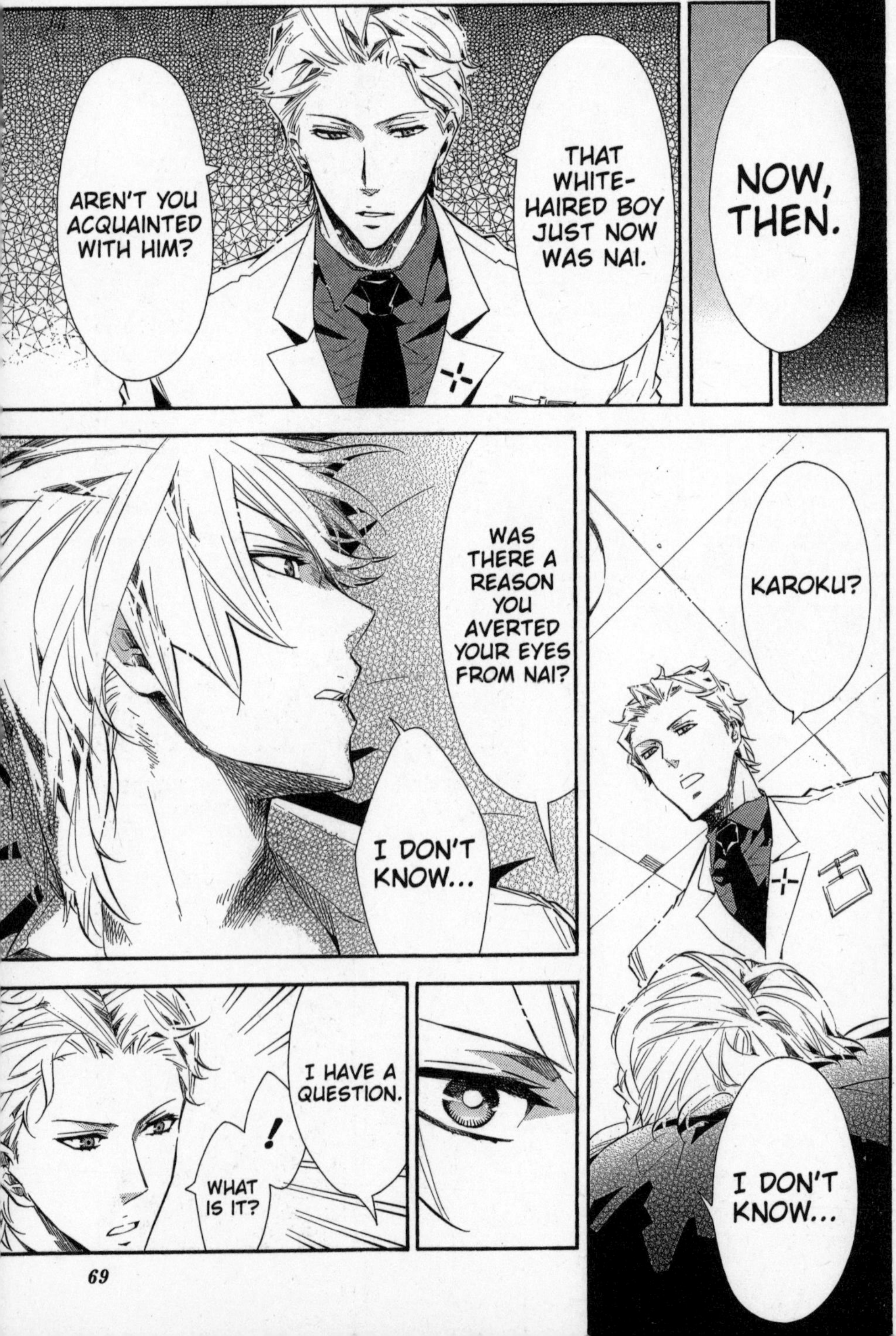
NOW, THEN.
THAT WHITE-HAIRED BOY JUST NOW WAS NAI.
AREN'T YOU ACQUAINTED WITH HIM?
KAROKU?
I DON'T KNOW...
WAS THERE A REASON YOU AVERTED YOUR EYES FROM NAI?
I DON'T KNOW...
I HAVE A QUESTION.
!
WHAT IS IT?

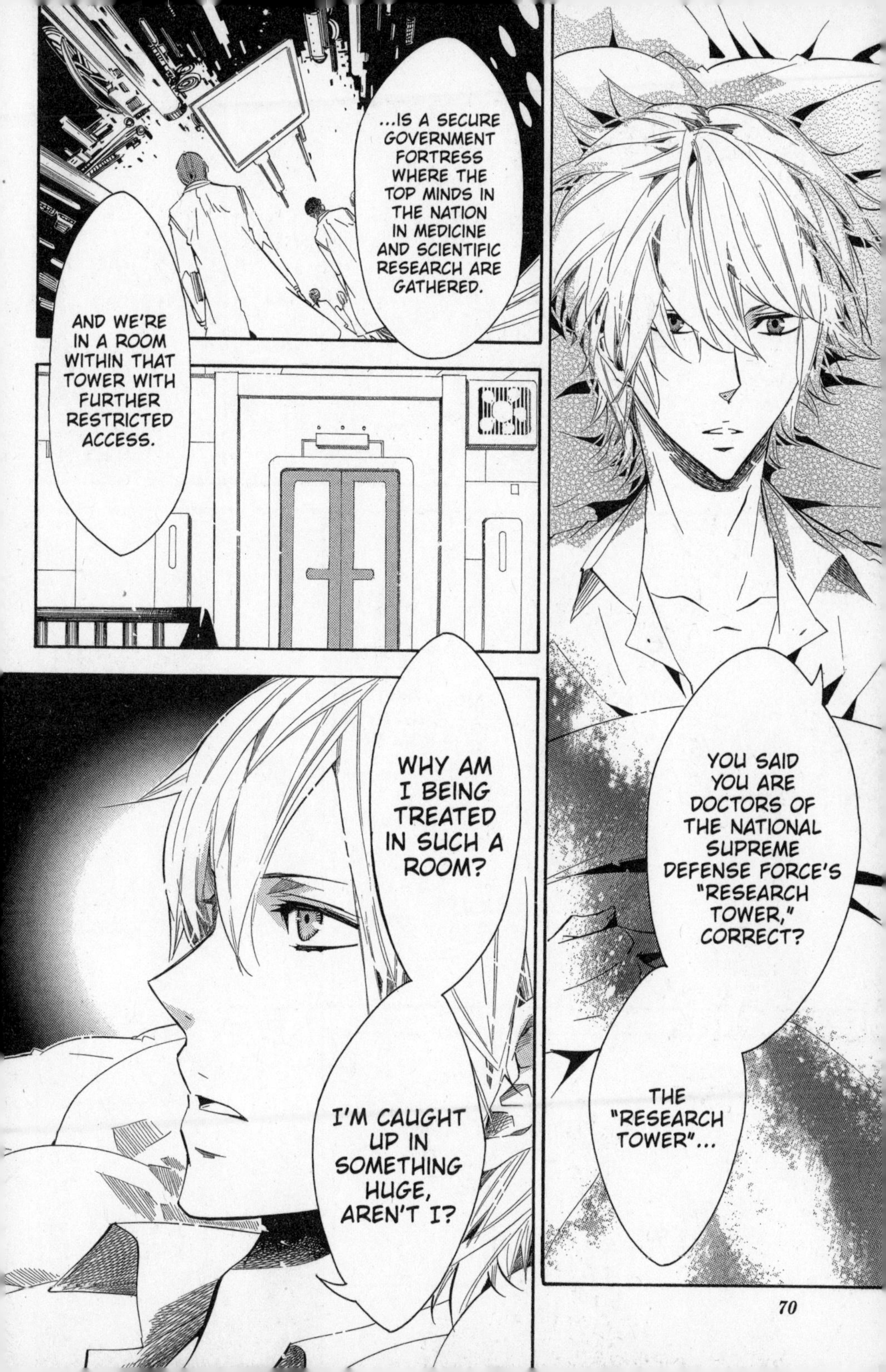
YOU SAID YOU ARE DOCTORS OF THE NATIONAL SUPREME DEFENSE FORCE'S "RESEARCH TOWER," CORRECT?
THE "RESEARCH TOWER"...
...IS A SECURE GOVERNMENT FORTRESS WHERE THE TOP MINDS IN THE NATION IN MEDICINE AND SCIENTIFIC RESEARCH ARE GATHERED.
AND WE'RE IN A ROOM WITHIN THAT TOWER WITH FURTHER RESTRICTED ACCESS.
WHY AM I BEING TREATED IN SUCH A ROOM?
I'M CAUGHT UP IN SOMETHING HUGE, AREN'T I?

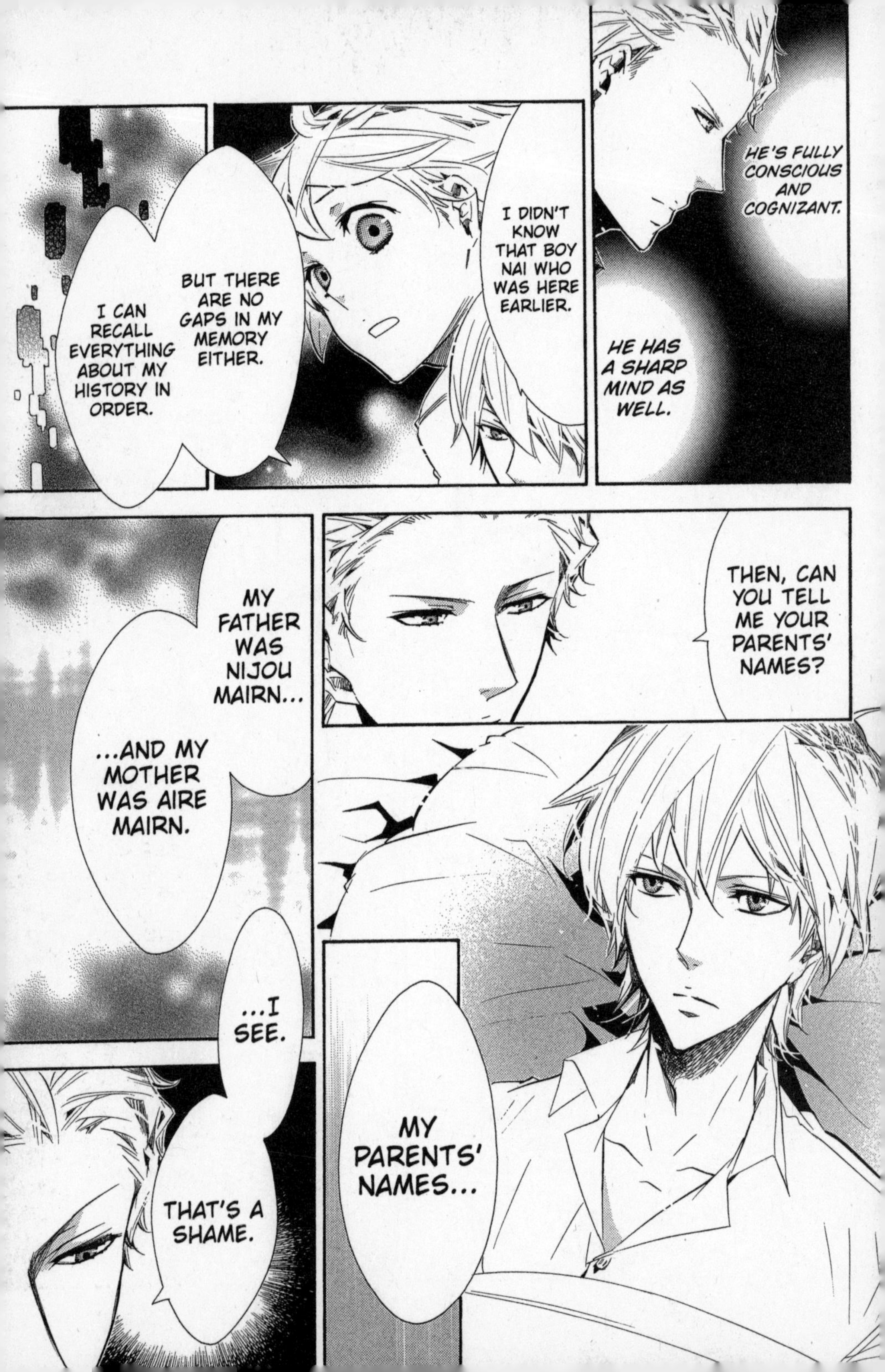
HE'S FULLY CONSCIOUS AND COGNIZANT.
HE HAS A SHARP MIND AS WELL.
I DIDN'T KNOW THAT BOY NAI WHO WAS HERE EARLIER.
BUT THERE ARE NO GAPS IN MY MEMORY EITHER.
I CAN RECALL EVERYTHING ABOUT MY HISTORY IN ORDER.
THEN, CAN YOU TELL ME YOUR PARENTS' NAMES?
MY PARENTS' NAMES...
MY FATHER WAS NIJOU MAIRN...
...AND MY MOTHER WAS AIRE MAIRN.
...I SEE.
THAT'S A SHAME.

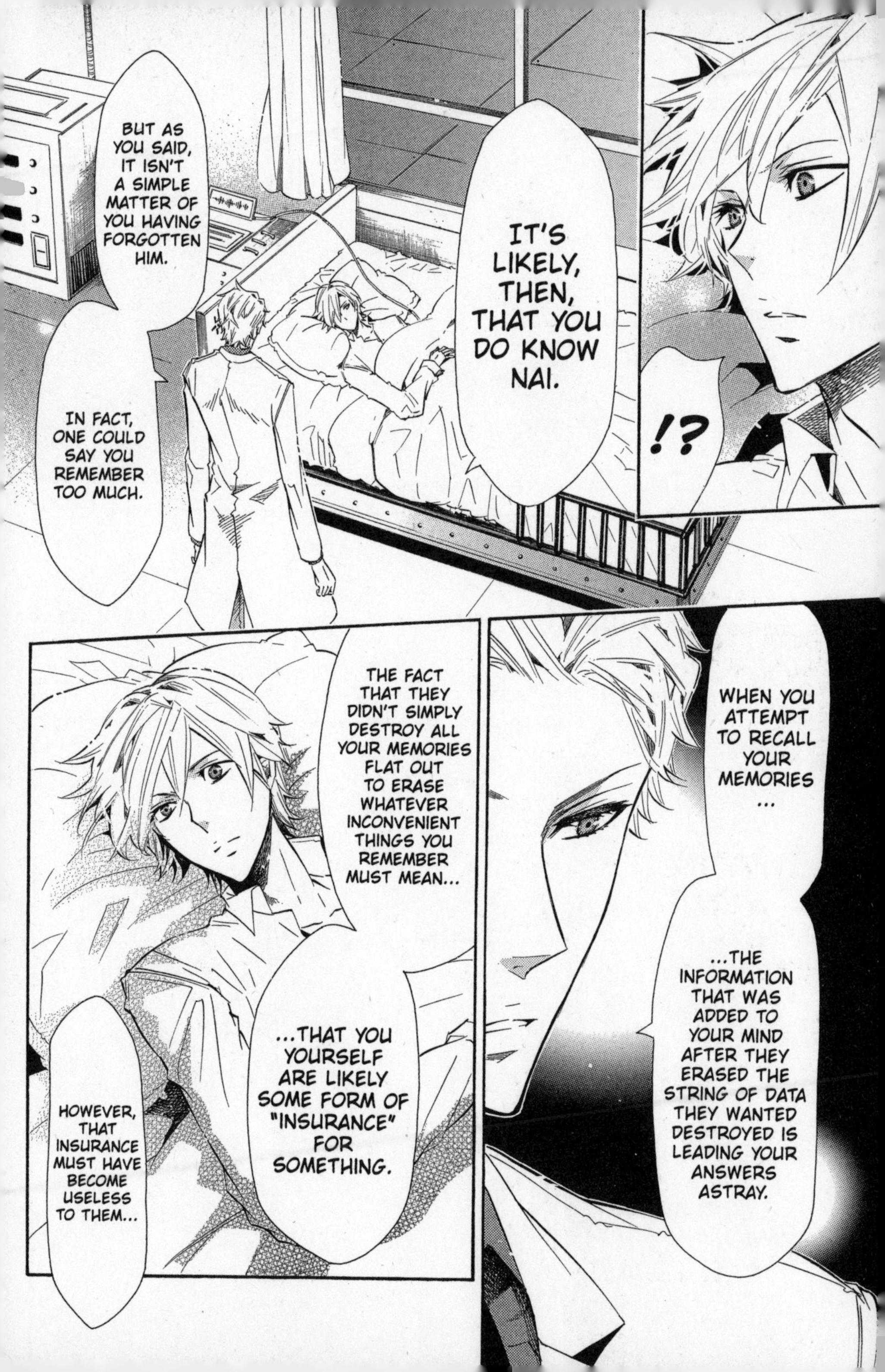
BUT AS YOU SAID, IT ISN'T A SIMPLE MATTER OF YOU HAVING FORGOTTEN HIM.
IN FACT, ONE COULD SAY YOU REMEMBER TOO MUCH.
IT'S LIKELY, THEN, THAT YOU DO KNOW NAI.
!?
WHEN YOU ATTEMPT TO RECALL YOUR MEMORIES...
...THE INFORMATION THAT WAS ADDED TO YOUR MIND AFTER THEY ERASED THE STRING OF DATA THEY WANTED DESTROYED IS LEADING YOUR ANSWERS ASTRAY.
THE FACT THAT THEY DIDN'T SIMPLY DESTROY ALL YOUR MEMORIES FLAT OUT TO ERASE WHATEVER INCONVENIENT THINGS YOU REMEMBER MUST MEAN...
...THAT YOU YOURSELF ARE LIKELY SOME FORM OF "INSURANCE" FOR SOMETHING.
HOWEVER, THAT INSURANCE MUST HAVE BECOME USELESS TO THEM...

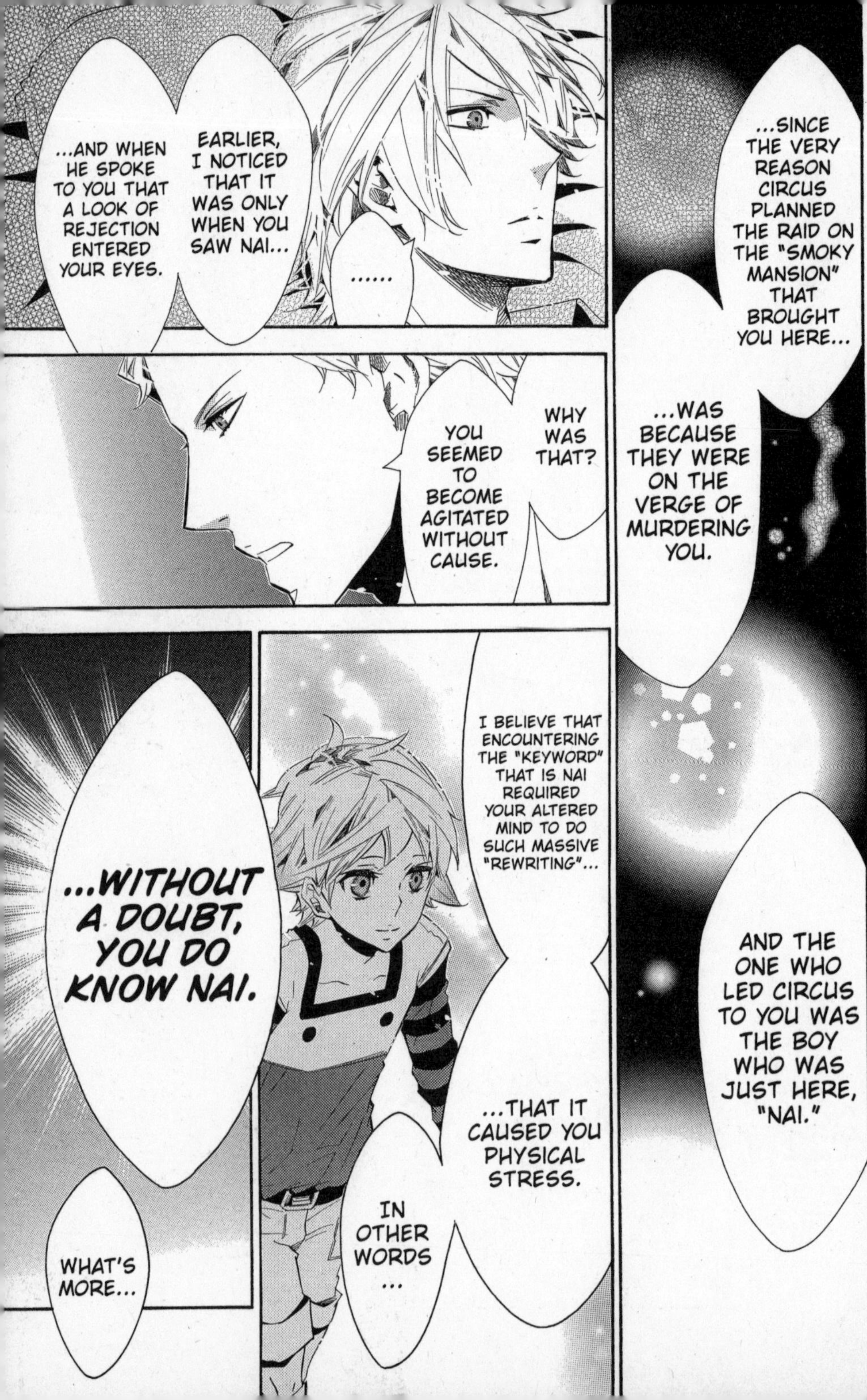
EARLIER, I NOTICED THAT IT WAS ONLY WHEN YOU SAW NAI...
...AND WHEN HE SPOKE TO YOU THAT A LOOK OF REJECTION ENTERED YOUR EYES.
......
WHY WAS THAT?
YOU SEEMED TO BECOME AGITATED WITHOUT CAUSE.
I BELIEVE THAT ENCOUNTERING THE "KEYWORD" THAT IS NAI REQUIRED YOUR ALTERED MIND TO DO SUCH MASSIVE "REWRITING"...
...THAT IT CAUSED YOU PHYSICAL STRESS.
IN OTHER WORDS...
...WITHOUT A DOUBT, YOU DO KNOW NAI.
WHAT'S MORE...
...SINCE THE VERY REASON CIRCUS PLANNED THE RAID ON THE "SMOKY MANSION" THAT BROUGHT YOU HERE...
...WAS BECAUSE THEY WERE ON THE VERGE OF MURDERING YOU.
AND THE ONE WHO LED CIRCUS TO YOU WAS THE BOY WHO WAS JUST HERE, "NAI."

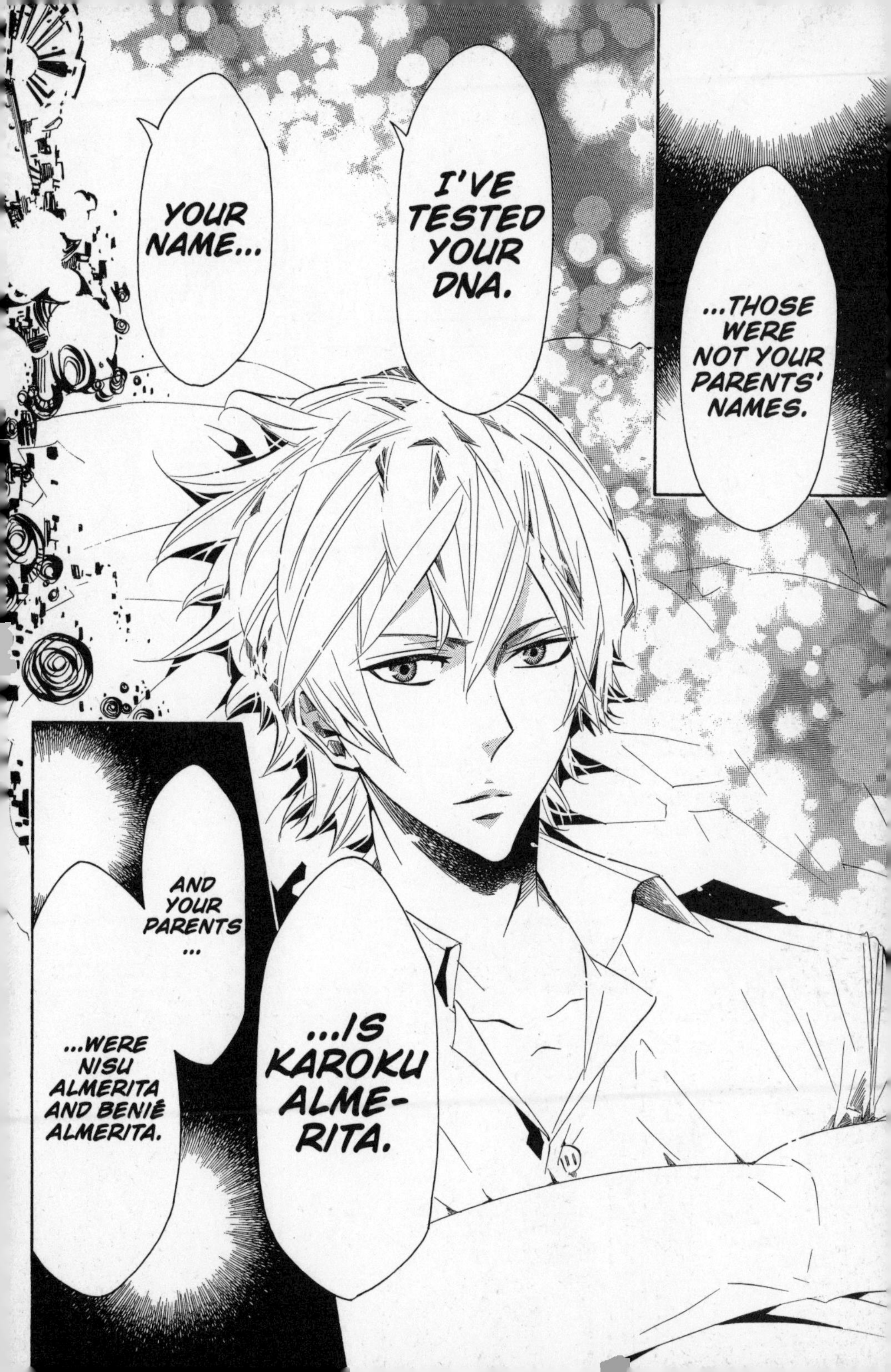
...THOSE WERE NOT YOUR PARENTS' NAMES.
I'VE TESTED YOUR DNA.
YOUR NAME...
...IS KAROKU ALME-RITA.
AND YOUR PARENTS ...
...WERE NISU ALMERITA AND BENIÉ ALMERITA.

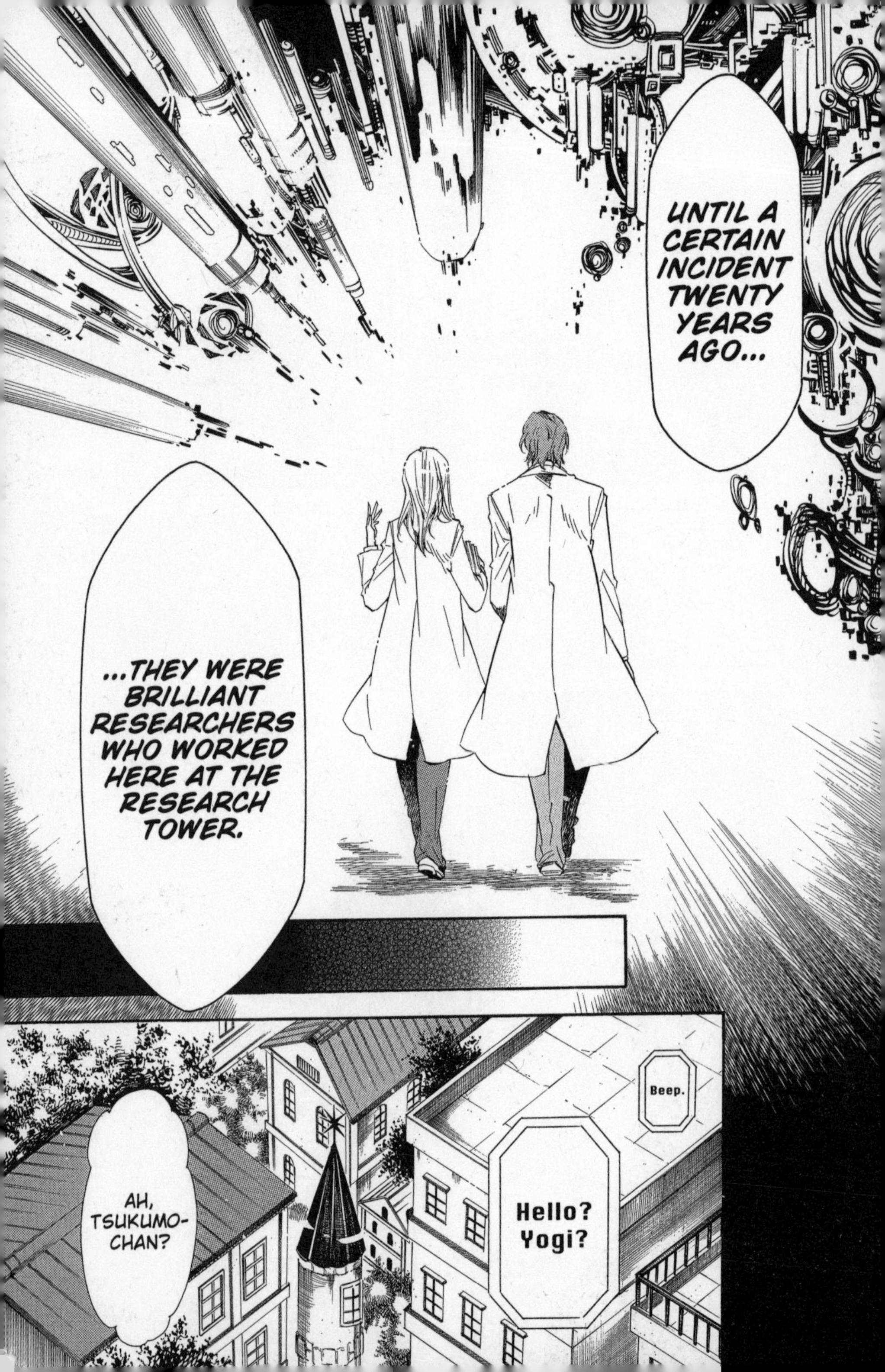
UNTIL A CERTAIN INCIDENT TWENTY YEARS AGO...
...THEY WERE BRILLIANT RESEARCHERS WHO WORKED HERE AT THE RESEARCH TOWER.
Beep.
Hello? Yogi?
AH, TSUKUMO-CHAN?

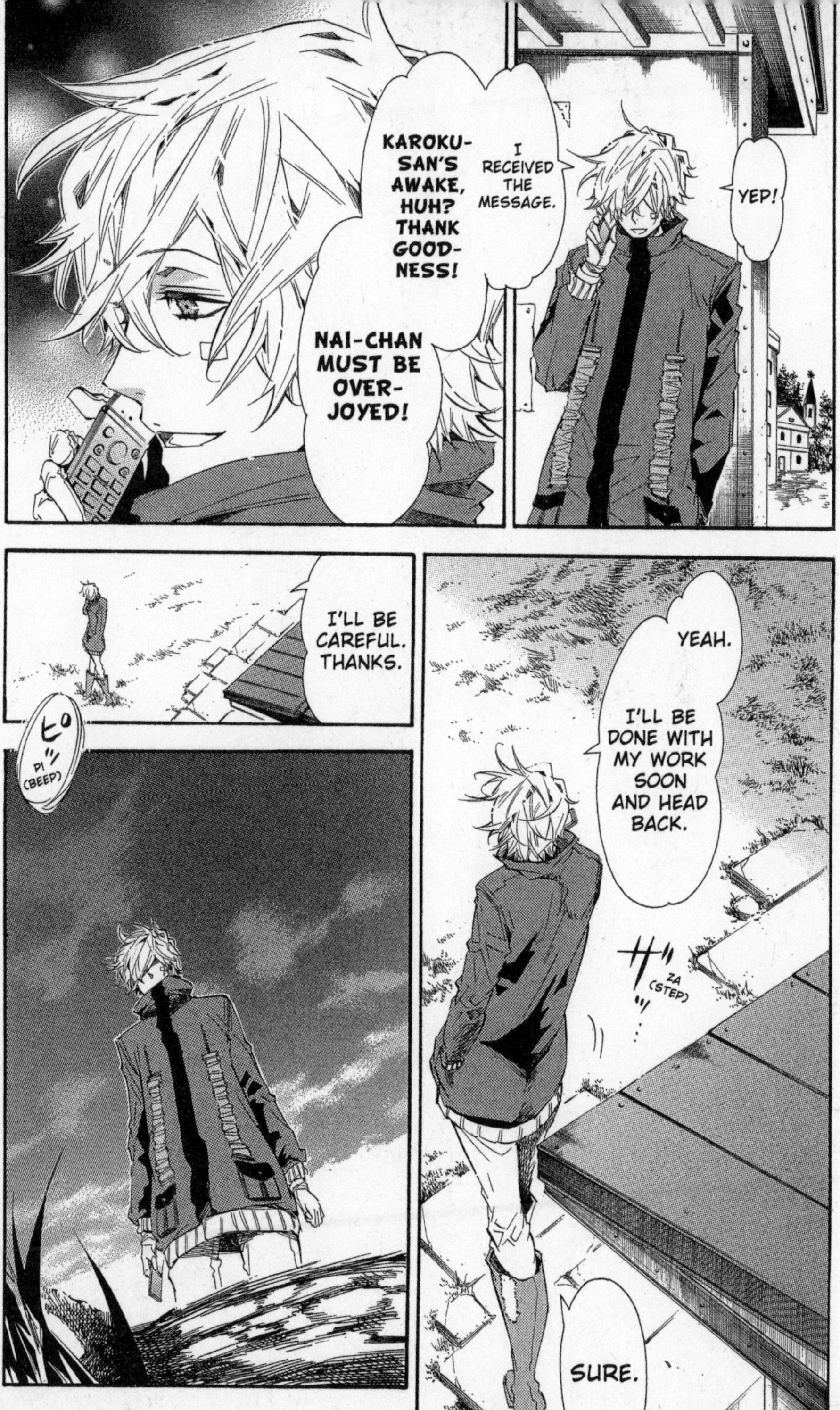
YEP!
I RECEIVED THE MESSAGE.
KAROKU-SAN'S AWAKE, HUH? THANK GOODNESS!
NAI-CHAN MUST BE OVER-JOYED!
YEAH.
I'LL BE DONE WITH MY WORK SOON AND HEAD BACK.
ザッ
ZA (STEP)
SURE.
I'LL BE CAREFUL. THANKS.
ピッ
PI (BEEP)

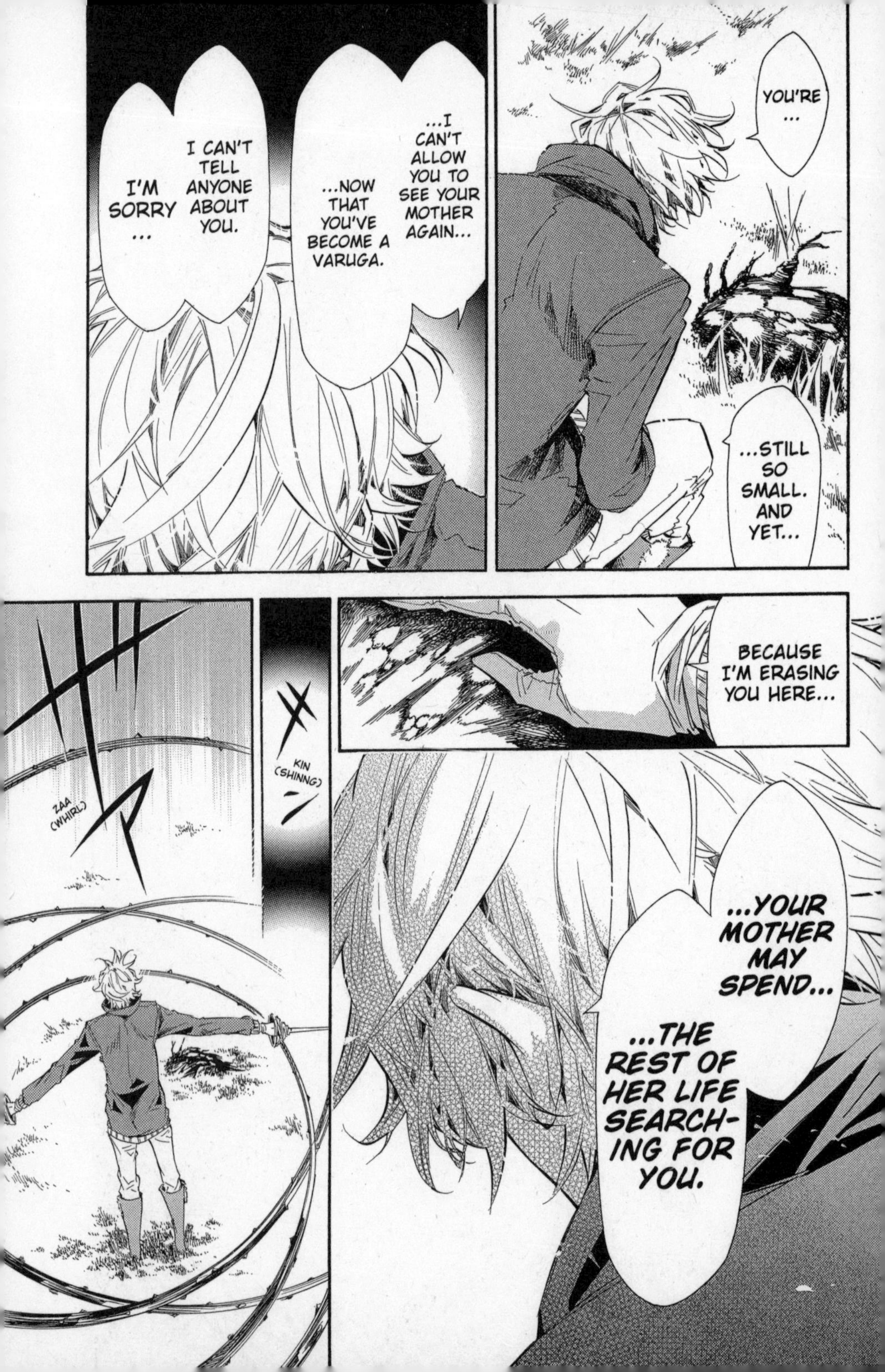
YOU'RE ...
...STILL SO SMALL. AND YET...
...I CAN'T ALLOW YOU TO SEE YOUR MOTHER AGAIN...
...NOW THAT YOU'VE BECOME A VARUGA.
I CAN'T TELL ANYONE ABOUT YOU.
I'M SORRY ...
BECAUSE I'M ERASING YOU HERE...
...YOUR MOTHER MAY SPEND...
...THE REST OF HER LIFE SEARCH-ING FOR YOU.
KIN (SHINNG)
ZAA (WHIRL)

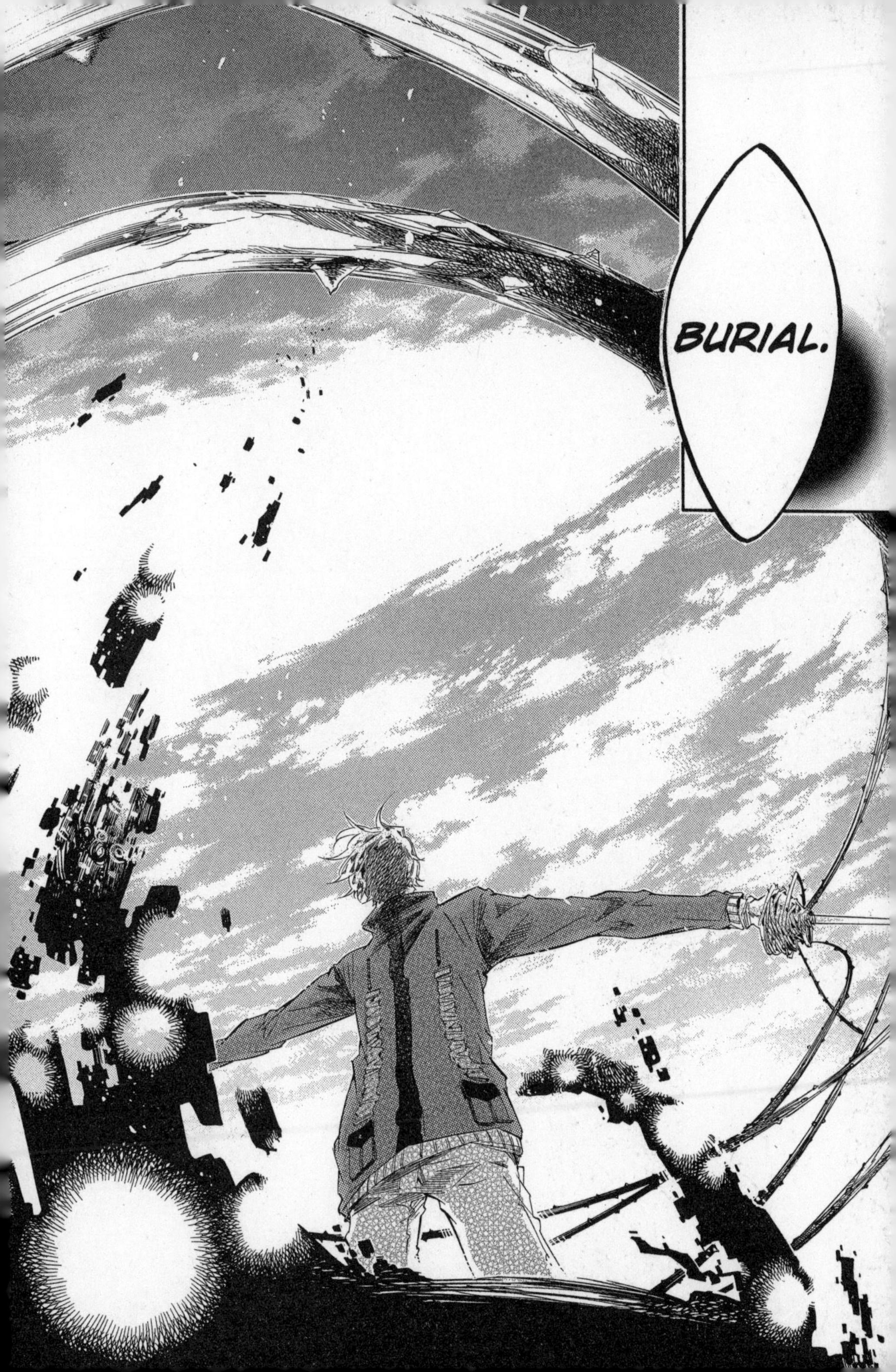
BURIAL.

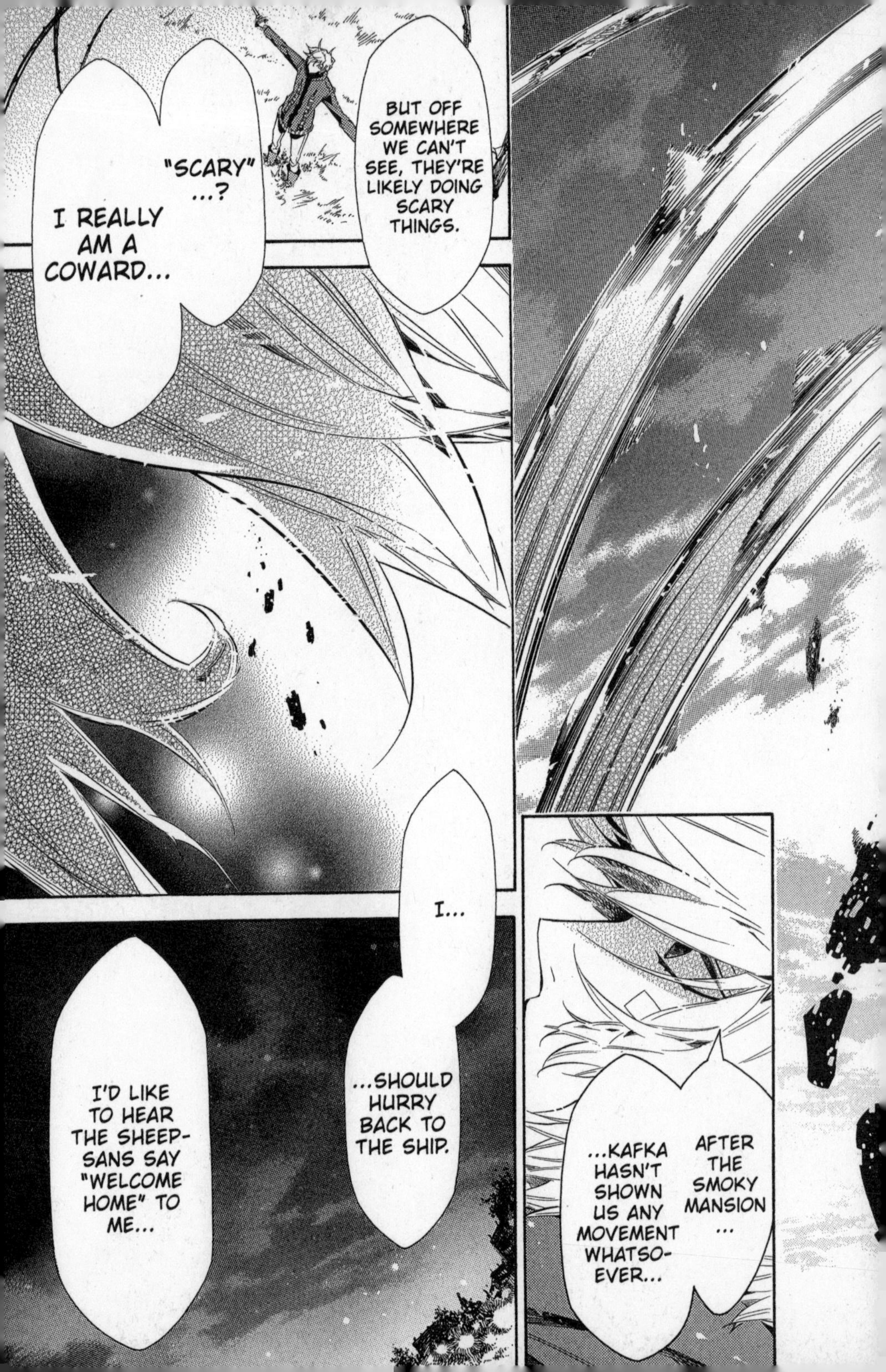
BUT OFF SOMEWHERE WE CAN'T SEE, THEY'RE LIKELY DOING SCARY THINGS.
"SCARY" ...?
I REALLY AM A COWARD...
AFTER THE SMOKY MANSION ...
...KAFKA HASN'T SHOWN US ANY MOVEMENT WHATSO-EVER...
I...
...SHOULD HURRY BACK TO THE SHIP.
I'D LIKE TO HEAR THE SHEEP-SANS SAY "WELCOME HOME" TO ME...

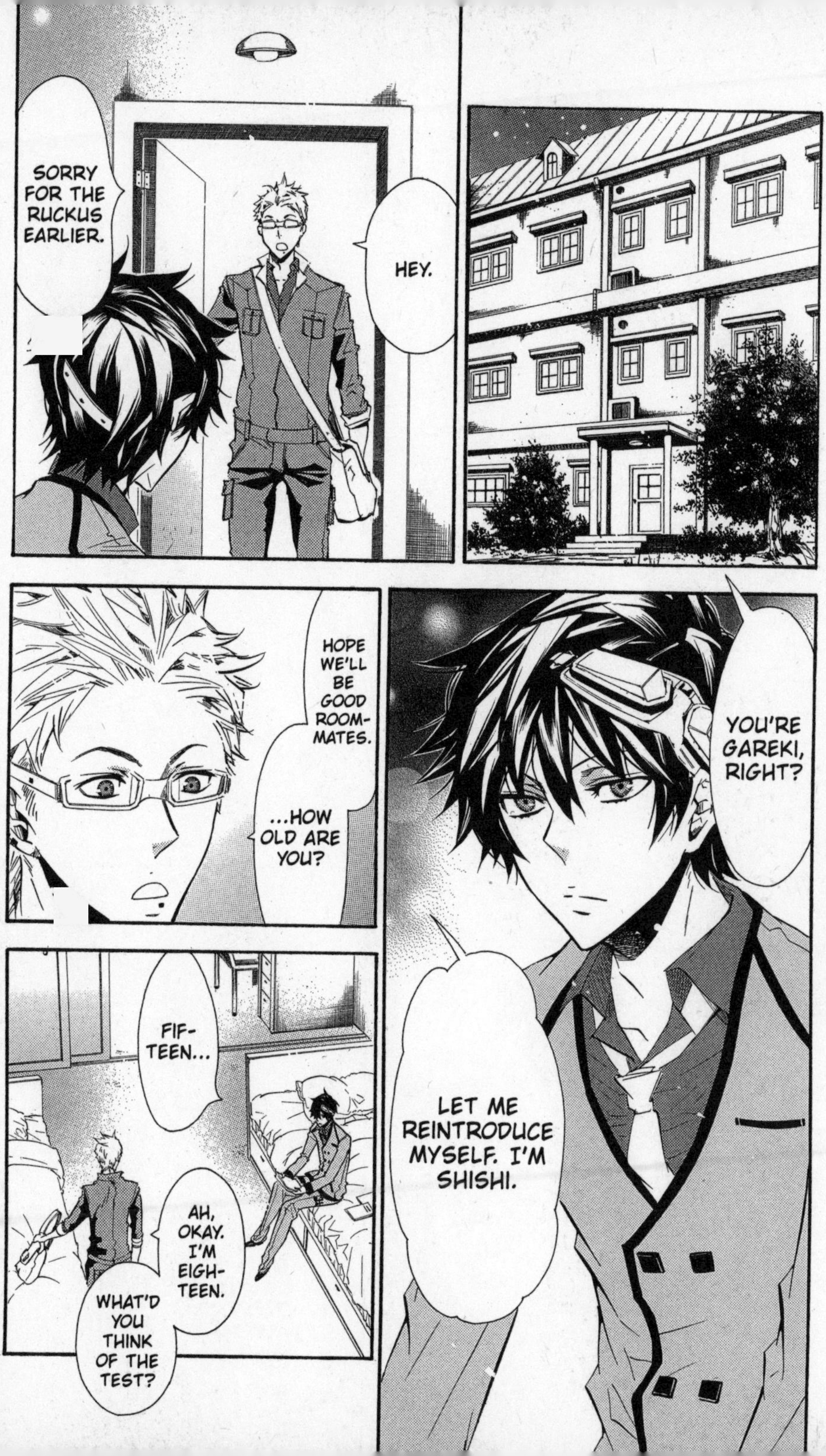
HEY.
SORRY FOR THE RUCKUS EARLIER.
YOU'RE GAREKI, RIGHT?
LET ME REINTRODUCE MYSELF. I'M SHISHI.
HOPE WE'LL BE GOOD ROOM-MATES.
...HOW OLD ARE YOU?
FIF-TEEN...
AH, OKAY. I'M EIGH-TEEN.
WHAT'D YOU THINK OF THE TEST?

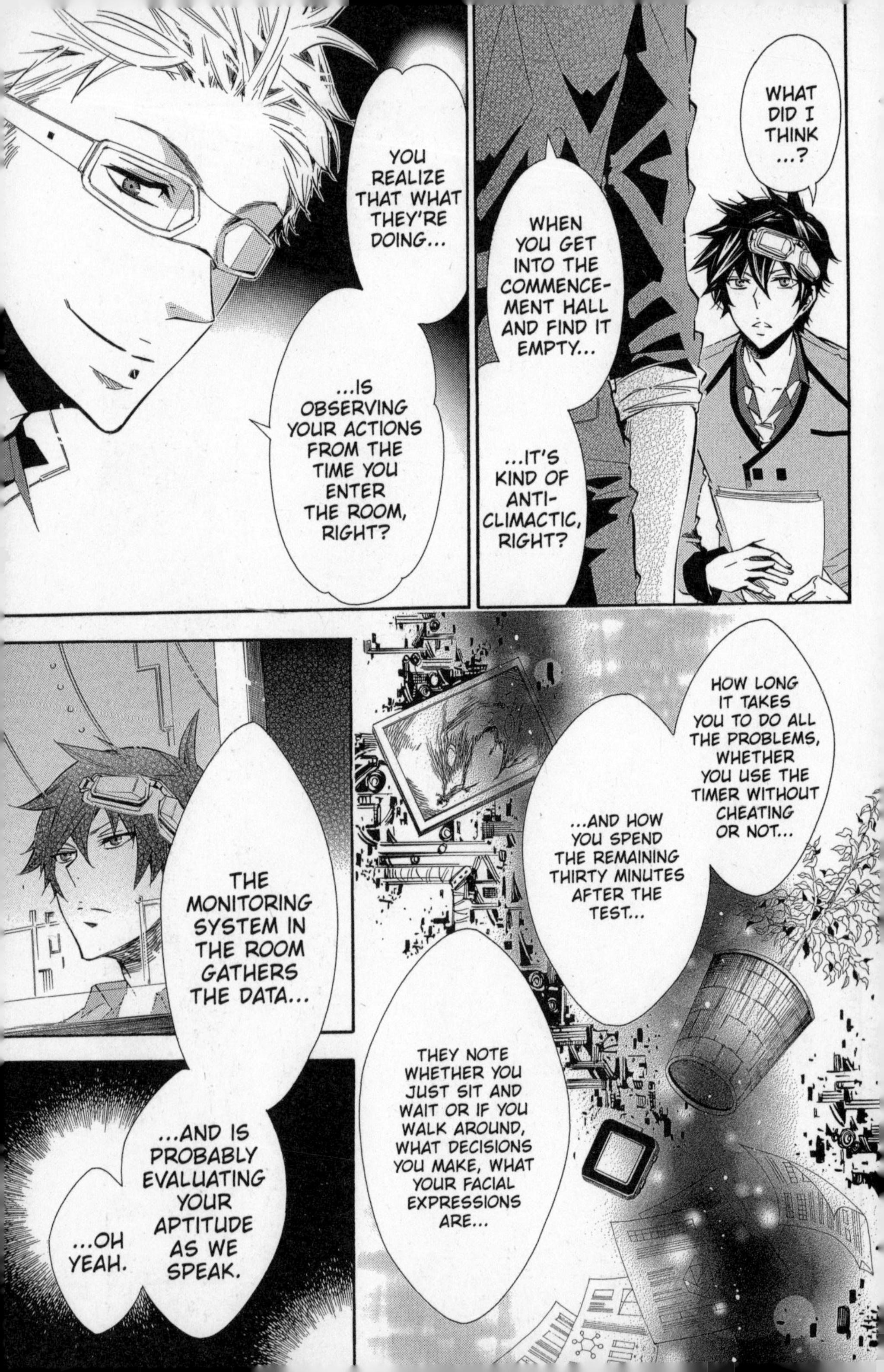
WHAT DID I THINK ...?
WHEN YOU GET INTO THE COMMENCEMENT HALL AND FIND IT EMPTY...
...IT'S KIND OF ANTI-CLIMACTIC, RIGHT?
YOU REALIZE THAT WHAT THEY'RE DOING...
...IS OBSERVING YOUR ACTIONS FROM THE TIME YOU ENTER THE ROOM, RIGHT?
HOW LONG IT TAKES YOU TO DO ALL THE PROBLEMS, WHETHER YOU USE THE TIMER WITHOUT CHEATING OR NOT...
...AND HOW YOU SPEND THE REMAINING THIRTY MINUTES AFTER THE TEST...
THEY NOTE WHETHER YOU JUST SIT AND WAIT OR IF YOU WALK AROUND, WHAT DECISIONS YOU MAKE, WHAT YOUR FACIAL EXPRESSIONS ARE...
THE MONITORING SYSTEM IN THE ROOM GATHERS THE DATA...
...AND IS PROBABLY EVALUATING YOUR APTITUDE AS WE SPEAK.
...OH YEAH.

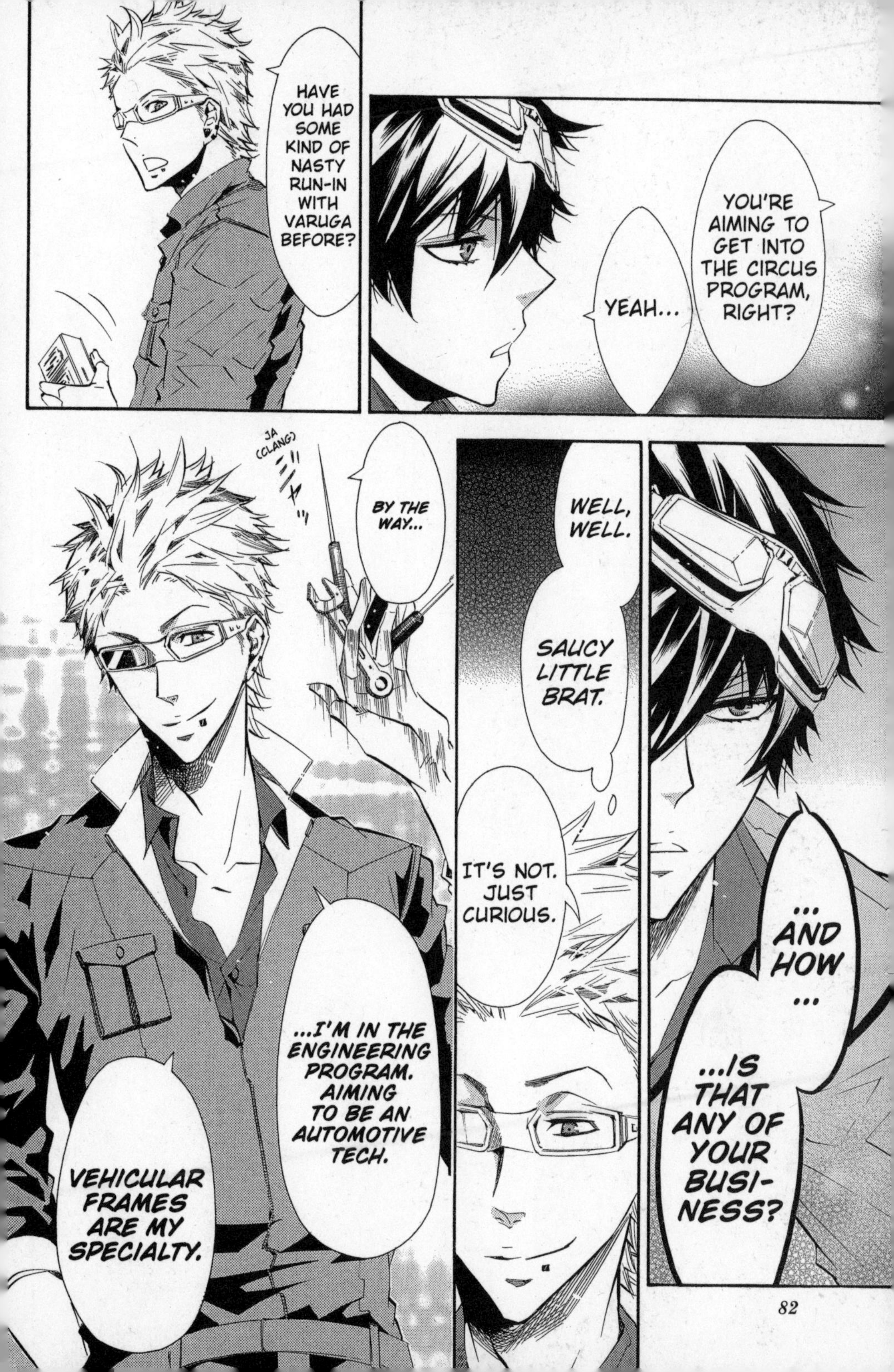
YOU'RE AIMING TO GET INTO THE CIRCUS PROGRAM, RIGHT?
YEAH...
HAVE YOU HAD SOME KIND OF NASTY RUN-IN WITH VARUGA BEFORE?
... AND HOW ...
...IS THAT ANY OF YOUR BUSI-NESS?
WELL, WELL.
SAUCY LITTLE BRAT.
IT'S NOT. JUST CURIOUS.
BY THE WAY...
JA (CLANG)
...I'M IN THE ENGINEERING PROGRAM. AIMING TO BE AN AUTOMOTIVE TECH.
VEHICULAR FRAMES ARE MY SPECIALTY.

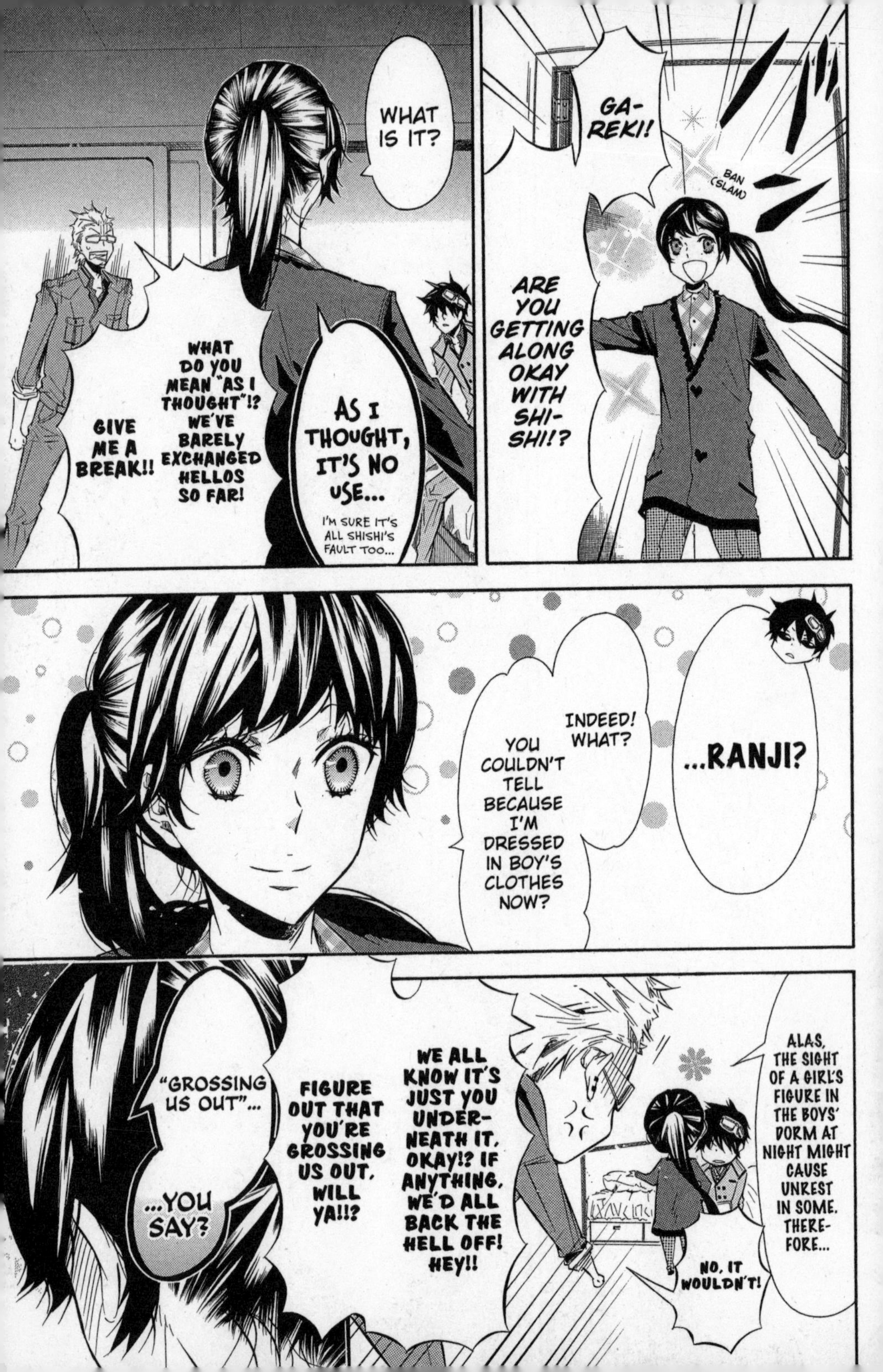
GA-REKI!
BAN (SLAM)
ARE YOU GETTING ALONG OKAY WITH SHI-SHI!?
WHAT IS IT?
AS I THOUGHT, IT'S NO USE...
I'M SURE IT'S ALL SHISHI'S FAULT TOO...
WHAT DO YOU MEAN "AS I THOUGHT"!? WE'VE BARELY EXCHANGED HELLOS SO FAR!
GIVE ME A BREAK!!
...RANJI?
INDEED! WHAT?
YOU COULDN'T TELL BECAUSE I'M DRESSED IN BOY'S CLOTHES NOW?
ALAS, THE SIGHT OF A GIRL'S FIGURE IN THE BOYS' DORM AT NIGHT MIGHT CAUSE UNREST IN SOME. THEREFORE...
NO, IT WOULDN'T!
WE ALL KNOW IT'S JUST YOU UNDER-NEATH IT, OKAY!? IF ANYTHING, WE'D ALL BACK THE HELL OFF! HEY!!
FIGURE OUT THAT YOU'RE GROSSING US OUT, WILL YA!!?
"GROSSING US OUT"...
...YOU SAY?

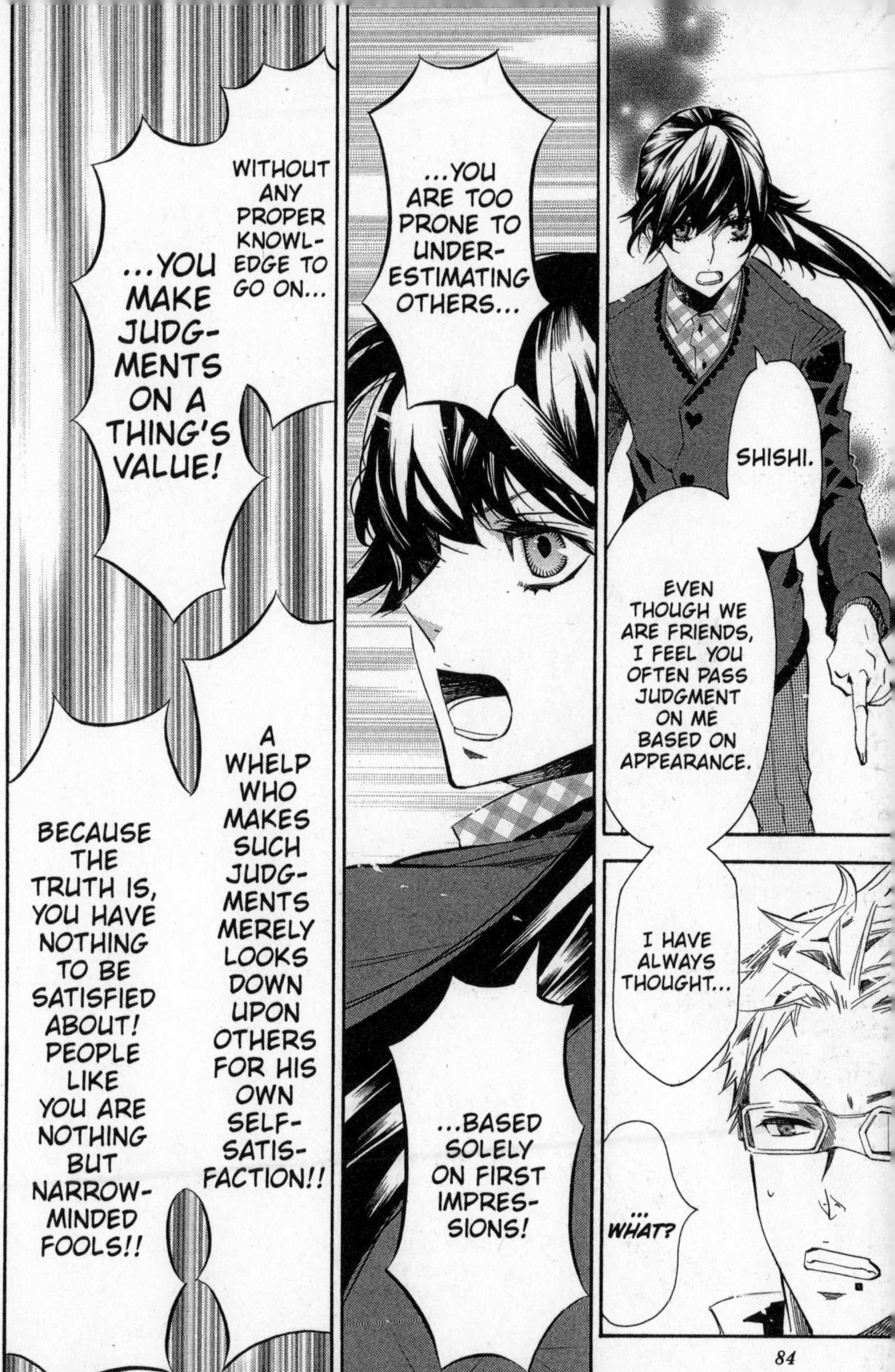
SHISHI.
EVEN THOUGH WE ARE FRIENDS, I FEEL YOU OFTEN PASS JUDGMENT ON ME BASED ON APPEARANCE.
I HAVE ALWAYS THOUGHT...
...WHAT?
...YOU ARE TOO PRONE TO UNDER-ESTIMATING OTHERS...
...BASED SOLELY ON FIRST IMPRESSIONS!
WITHOUT ANY PROPER KNOWL-EDGE TO GO ON...
...YOU MAKE JUDG-MENTS ON A THING'S VALUE!
A WHELP WHO MAKES SUCH JUDG-MENTS MERELY LOOKS DOWN UPON OTHERS FOR HIS OWN SELF-SATIS-FACTION!!
BECAUSE THE TRUTH IS, YOU HAVE NOTHING TO BE SATISFIED ABOUT! PEOPLE LIKE YOU ARE NOTHING BUT NARROW-MINDED FOOLS!!

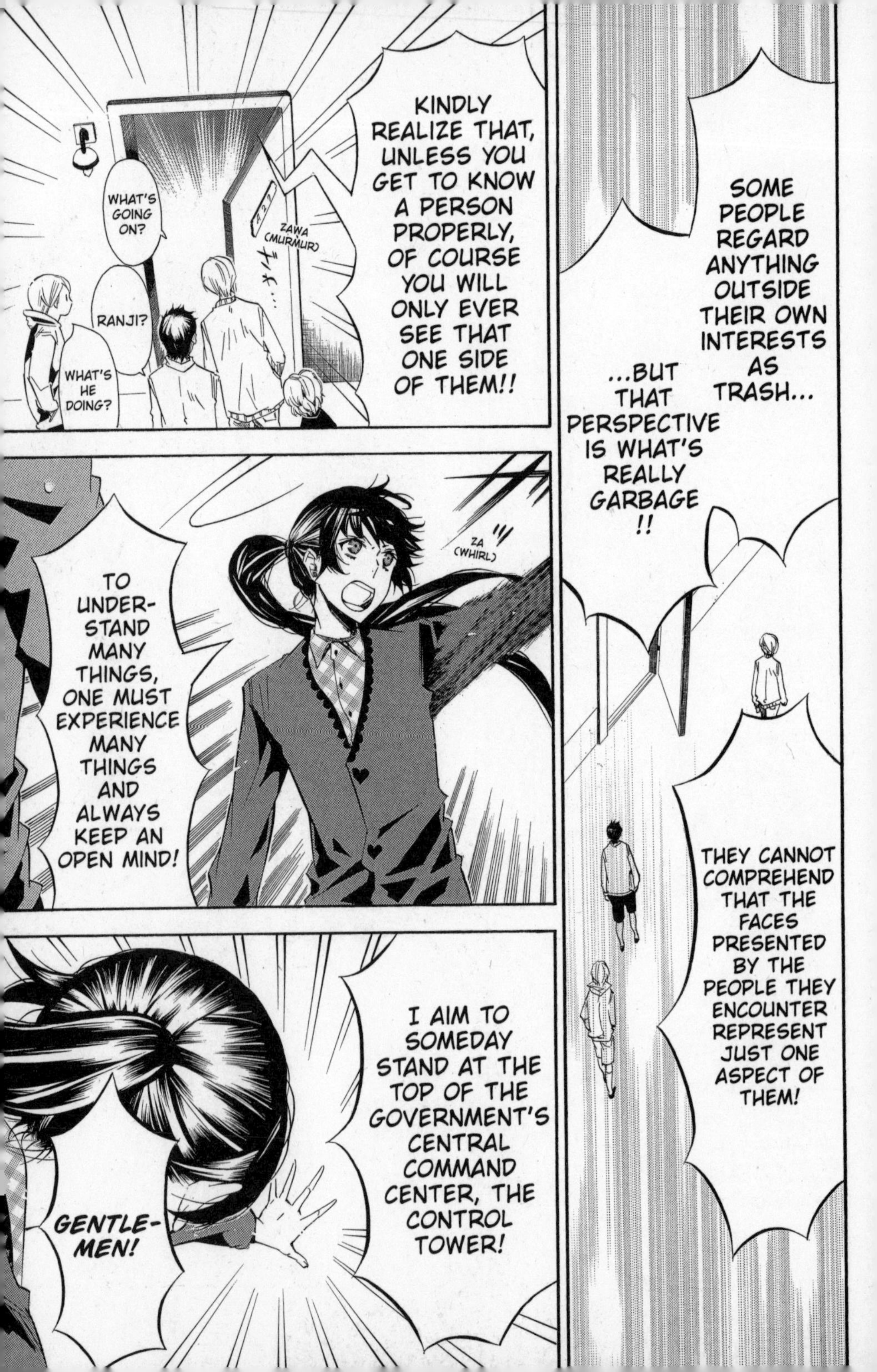
SOME PEOPLE REGARD ANYTHING OUTSIDE THEIR OWN INTERESTS AS TRASH...
...BUT THAT PERSPECTIVE IS WHAT'S REALLY GARBAGE!!
THEY CANNOT COMPREHEND THAT THE FACES PRESENTED BY THE PEOPLE THEY ENCOUNTER REPRESENT JUST ONE ASPECT OF THEM!
KINDLY REALIZE THAT, UNLESS YOU GET TO KNOW A PERSON PROPERLY, OF COURSE YOU WILL ONLY EVER SEE THAT ONE SIDE OF THEM!!
ZAWA (MURMUR)
WHAT'S GOING ON?
RANJI?
WHAT'S HE DOING?
ZA (WHIRL)
TO UNDER-STAND MANY THINGS, ONE MUST EXPERIENCE MANY THINGS AND ALWAYS KEEP AN OPEN MIND!
I AIM TO SOMEDAY STAND AT THE TOP OF THE GOVERNMENT'S CENTRAL COMMAND CENTER, THE CONTROL TOWER!
GENTLE-MEN!

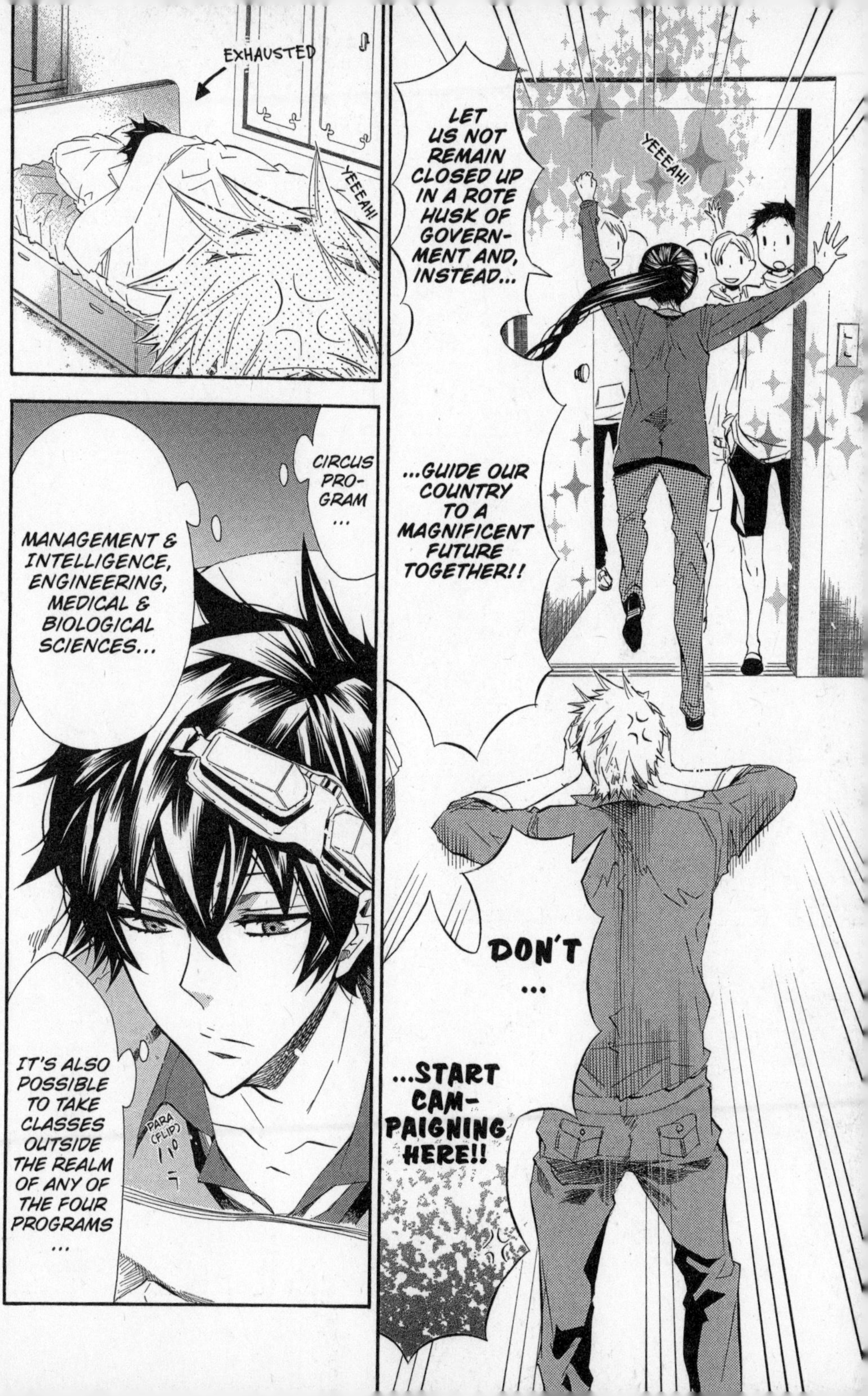
LET US NOT REMAIN CLOSED UP IN A ROTE HUSK OF GOVERNMENT AND, INSTEAD...
YEEEAH!
...GUIDE OUR COUNTRY TO A MAGNIFICENT FUTURE TOGETHER!!
DON'T ...
...START CAMPAIGNING HERE!!
EXHAUSTED
YEEEAH!
CIRCUS PROGRAM ...
MANAGEMENT & INTELLIGENCE, ENGINEERING, MEDICAL & BIOLOGICAL SCIENCES...
PARA (FLIP)
IT'S ALSO POSSIBLE TO TAKE CLASSES OUTSIDE THE REALM OF ANY OF THE FOUR PROGRAMS ...

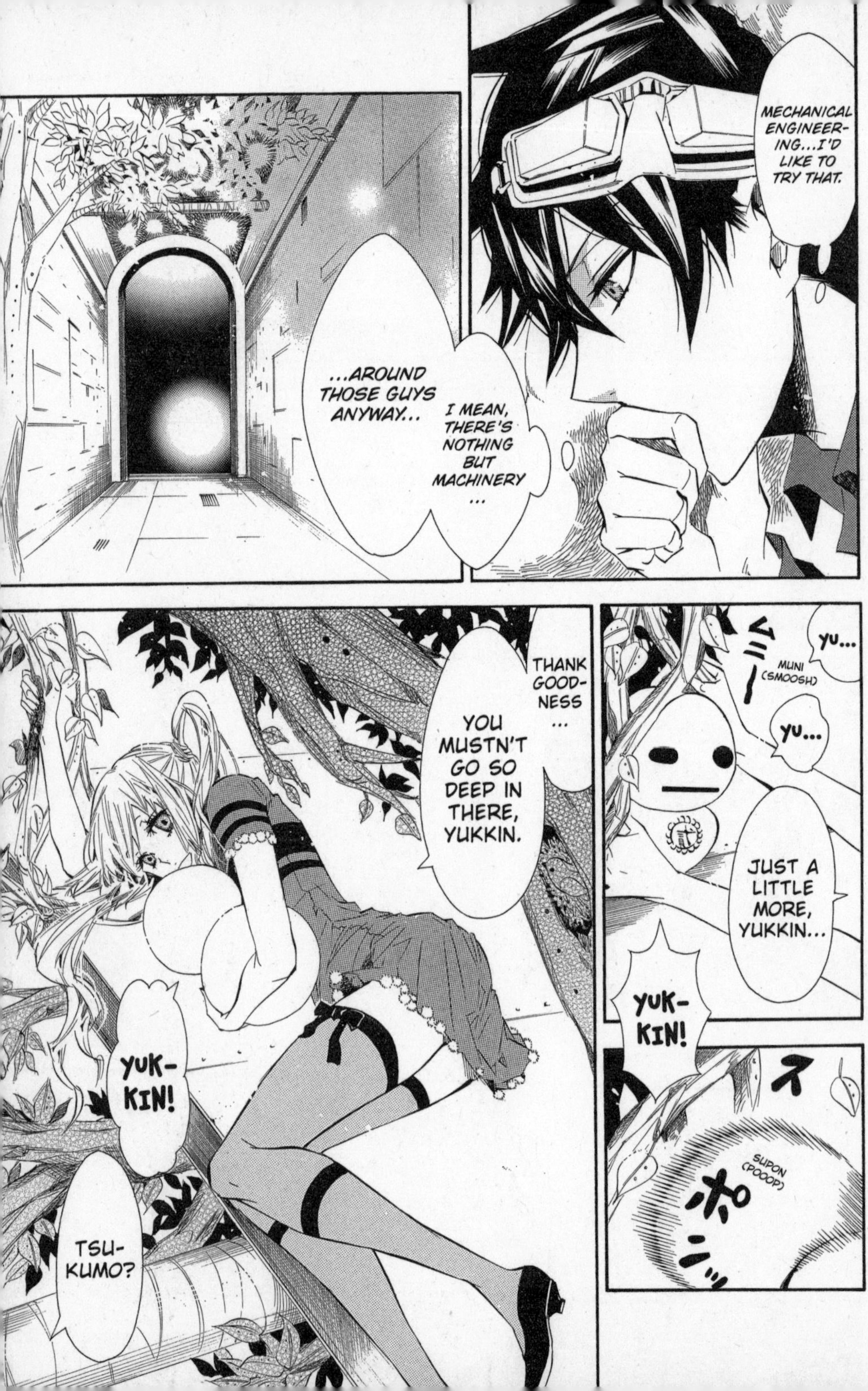
MECHANICAL ENGINEERING...I'D LIKE TO TRY THAT.
I MEAN, THERE'S NOTHING BUT MACHINERY...
...AROUND THOSE GUYS ANYWAY...
YU...
MUNI (SMOOSH)
YU...
JUST A LITTLE MORE, YUKKIN...
YUK-KIN!
SUPON (POOOP)
THANK GOODNESS...
YOU MUSTN'T GO SO DEEP IN THERE, YUKKIN.
YUK-KIN!
TSU-KUMO?

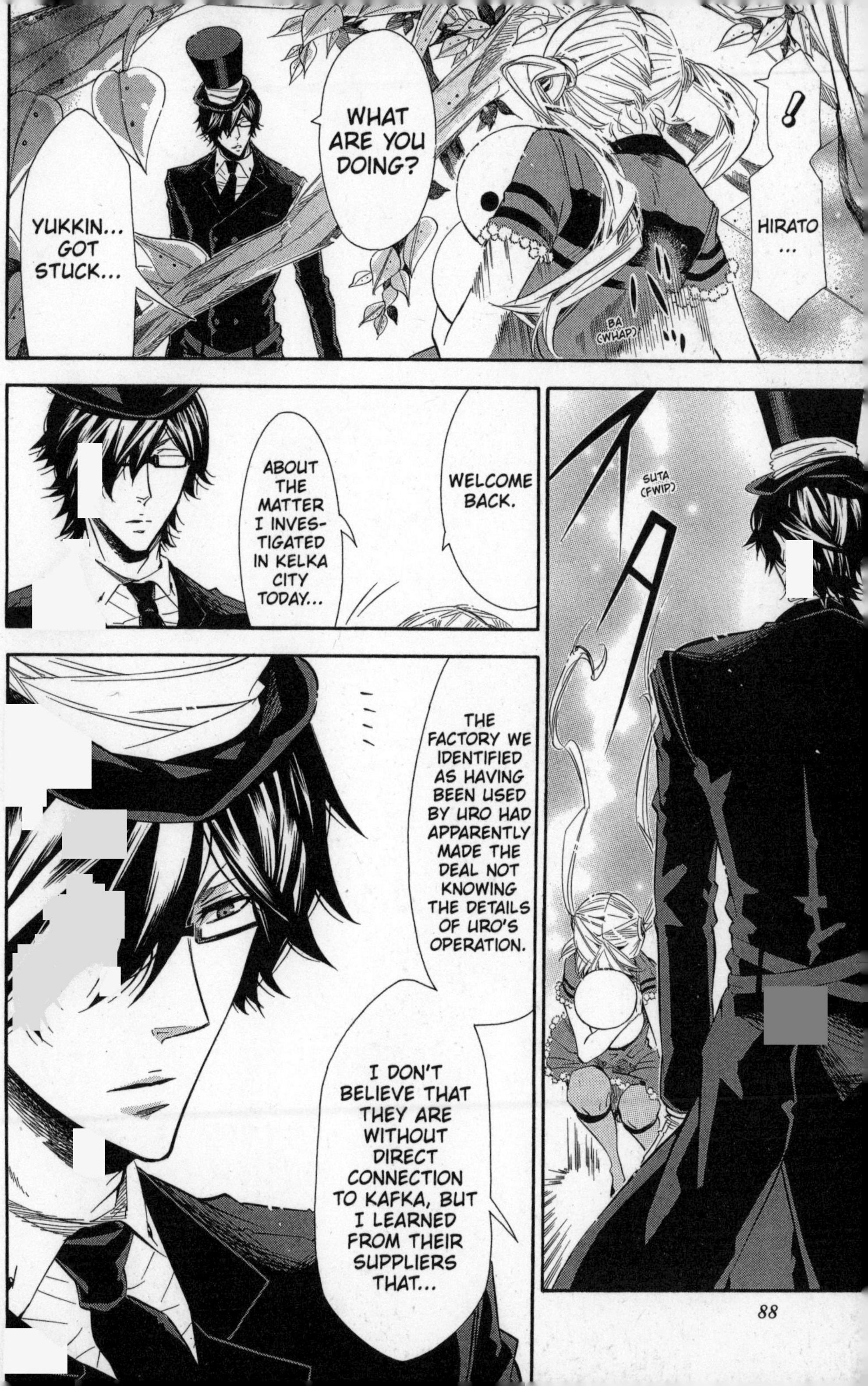
!
HIRATO ...
WHAT ARE YOU DOING?
BA (WHAP)
YUKKIN... GOT STUCK...
SUTA (FWIP)
WELCOME BACK.
ABOUT THE MATTER I INVESTIGATED IN KELKA CITY TODAY...
...
THE FACTORY WE IDENTIFIED AS HAVING BEEN USED BY URO HAD APPARENTLY MADE THE DEAL NOT KNOWING THE DETAILS OF URO'S OPERATION.
I DON'T BELIEVE THAT THEY ARE WITHOUT DIRECT CONNECTION TO KAFKA, BUT I LEARNED FROM THEIR SUPPLIERS THAT...

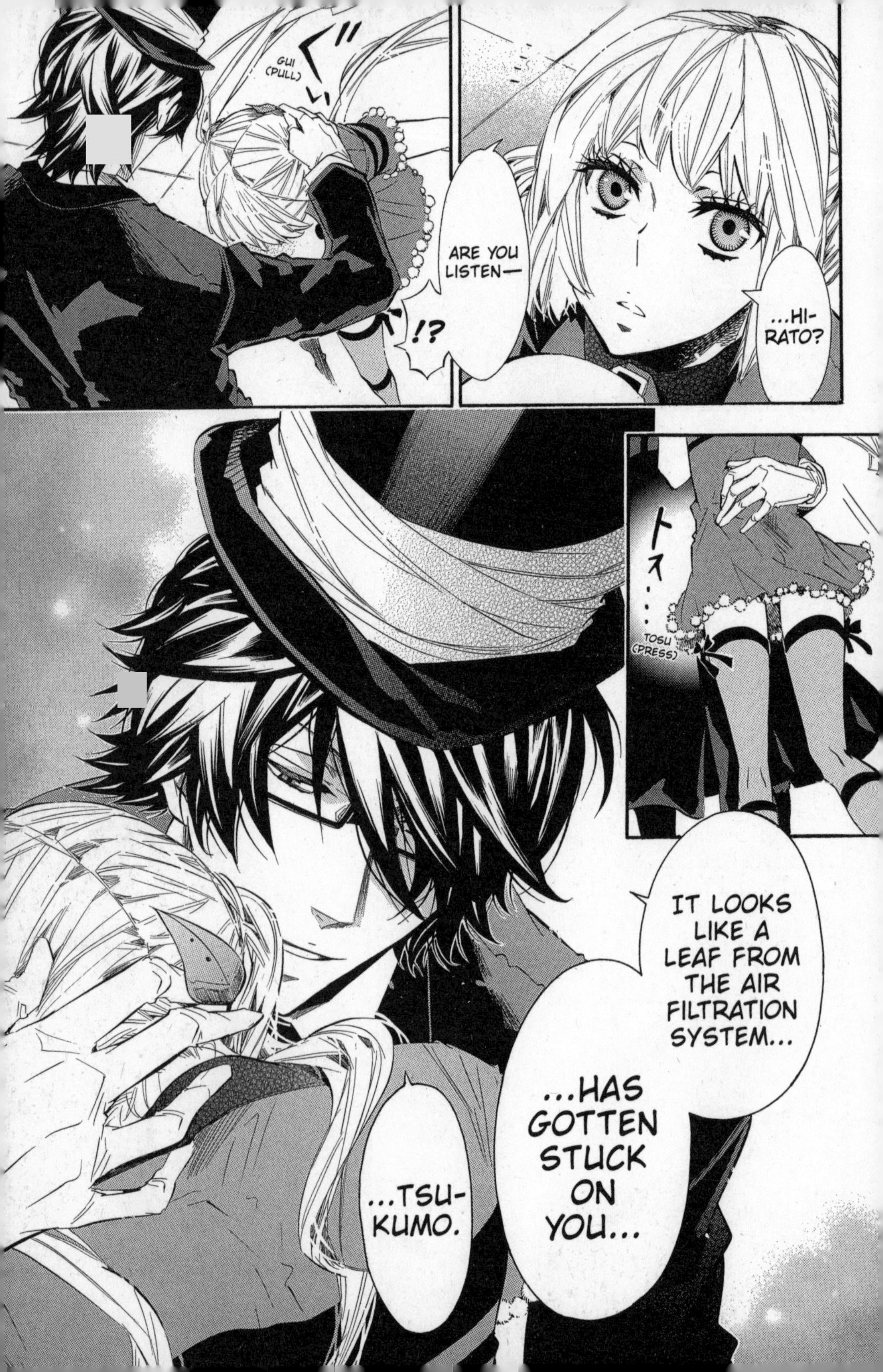
...HI-RATO?
ARE YOU LISTEN—
GUI (PULL)
!?
TOSU (PRESS)
IT LOOKS LIKE A LEAF FROM THE AIR FILTRATION SYSTEM...
...HAS GOTTEN STUCK ON YOU...
...TSU-KUMO.

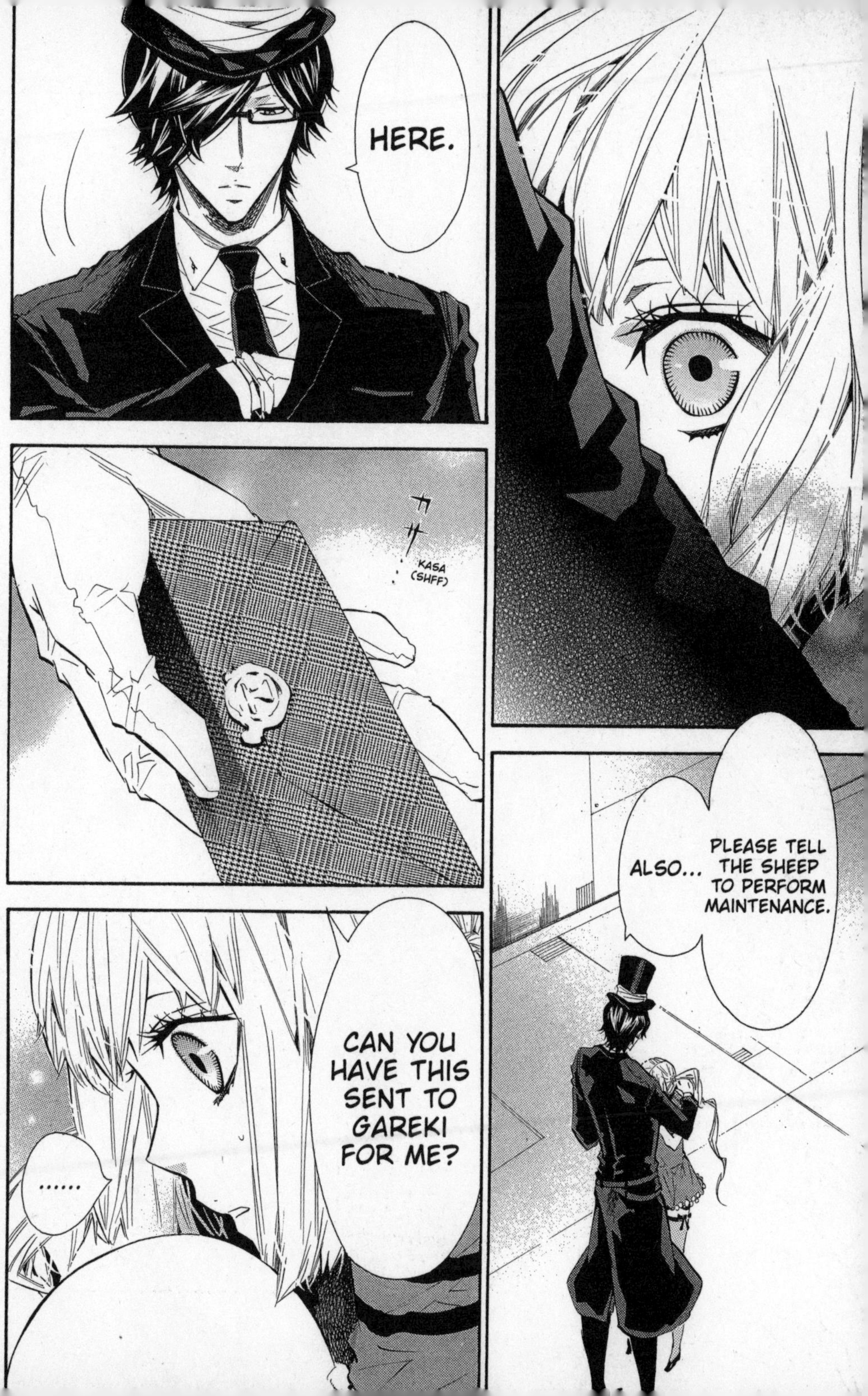
HERE.
KASA (SHFF)
CAN YOU HAVE THIS SENT TO GAREKI FOR ME?
......
ALSO... PLEASE TELL THE SHEEP TO PERFORM MAINTENANCE.

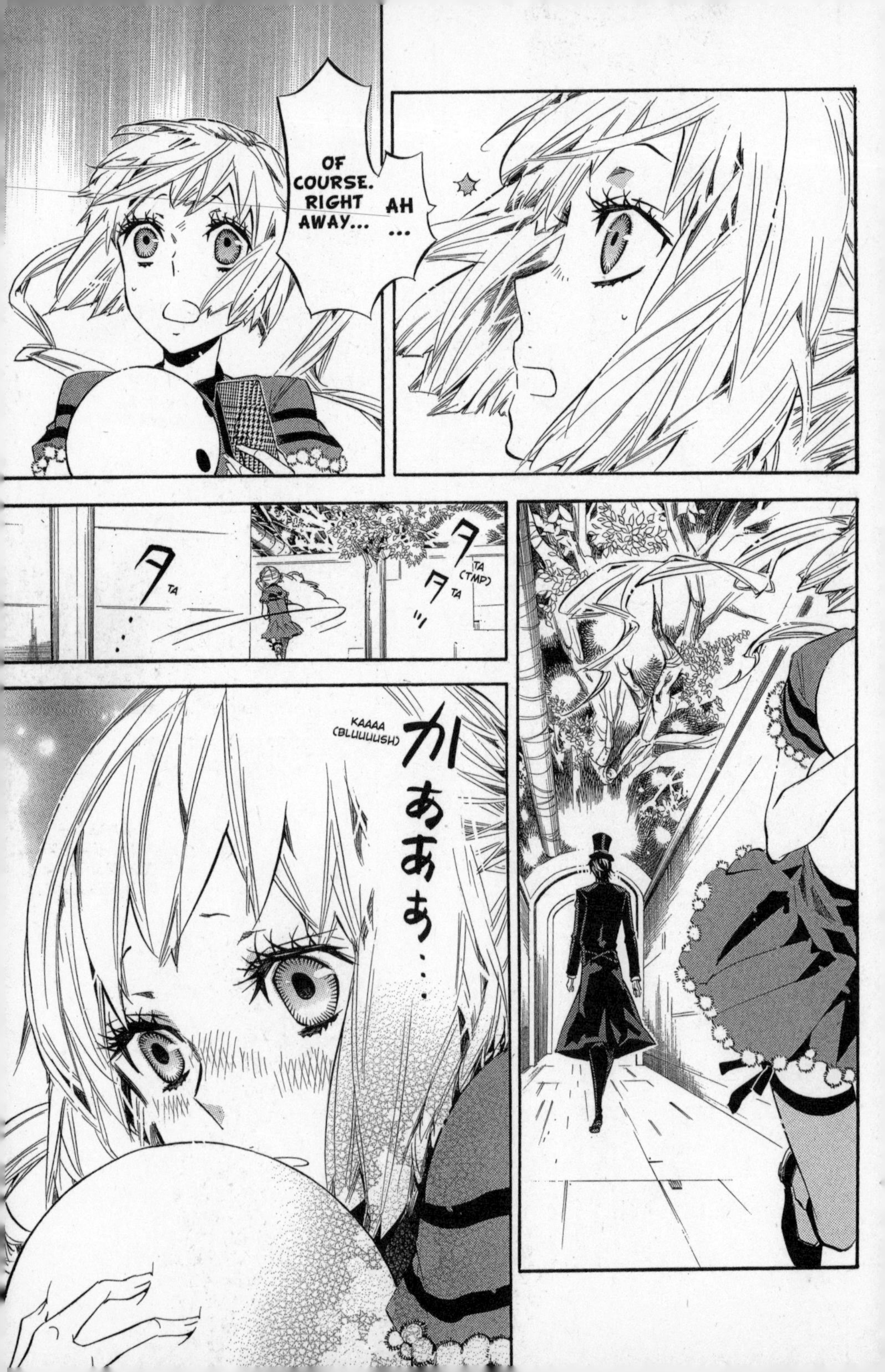
AH ...
OF COURSE. RIGHT AWAY...
タ TA (TMP)
タ TA ッ
タ TA
カあああ…
KAAAA (BLUUUUSH)

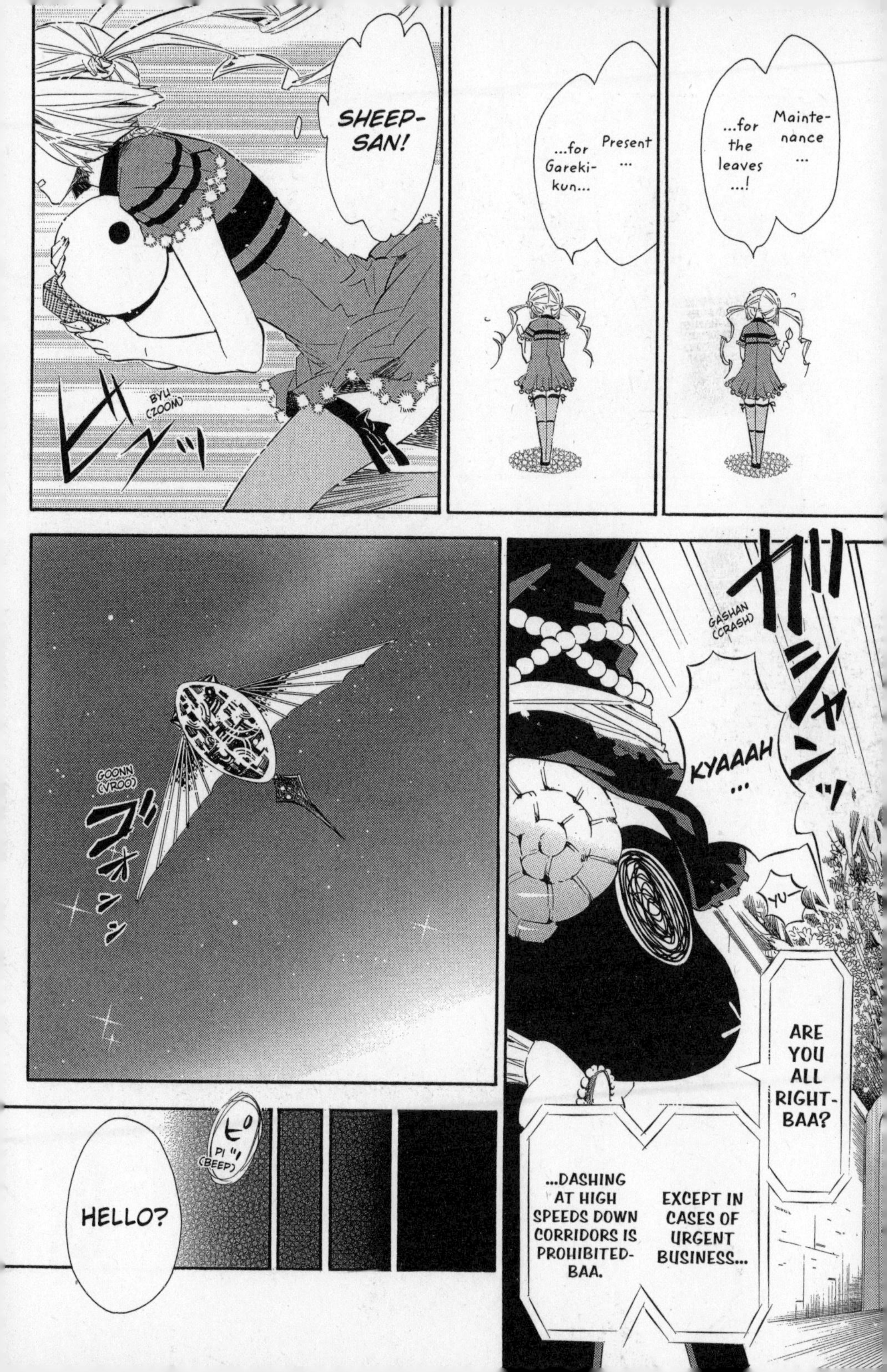

Mainte-nance... ...for the leaves...!
Present... ...for Gareki-kun...
SHEEP-SAN!
BYU (ZOOM)
GASHAN (CRASH)
KYAAAH...
YU-
ARE YOU ALL RIGHT-BAA?
EXCEPT IN CASES OF URGENT BUSINESS...
...DASHING AT HIGH SPEEDS DOWN CORRIDORS IS PROHIBITED-BAA.
GOONN (VROO)
PI (BEEP)
HELLO?

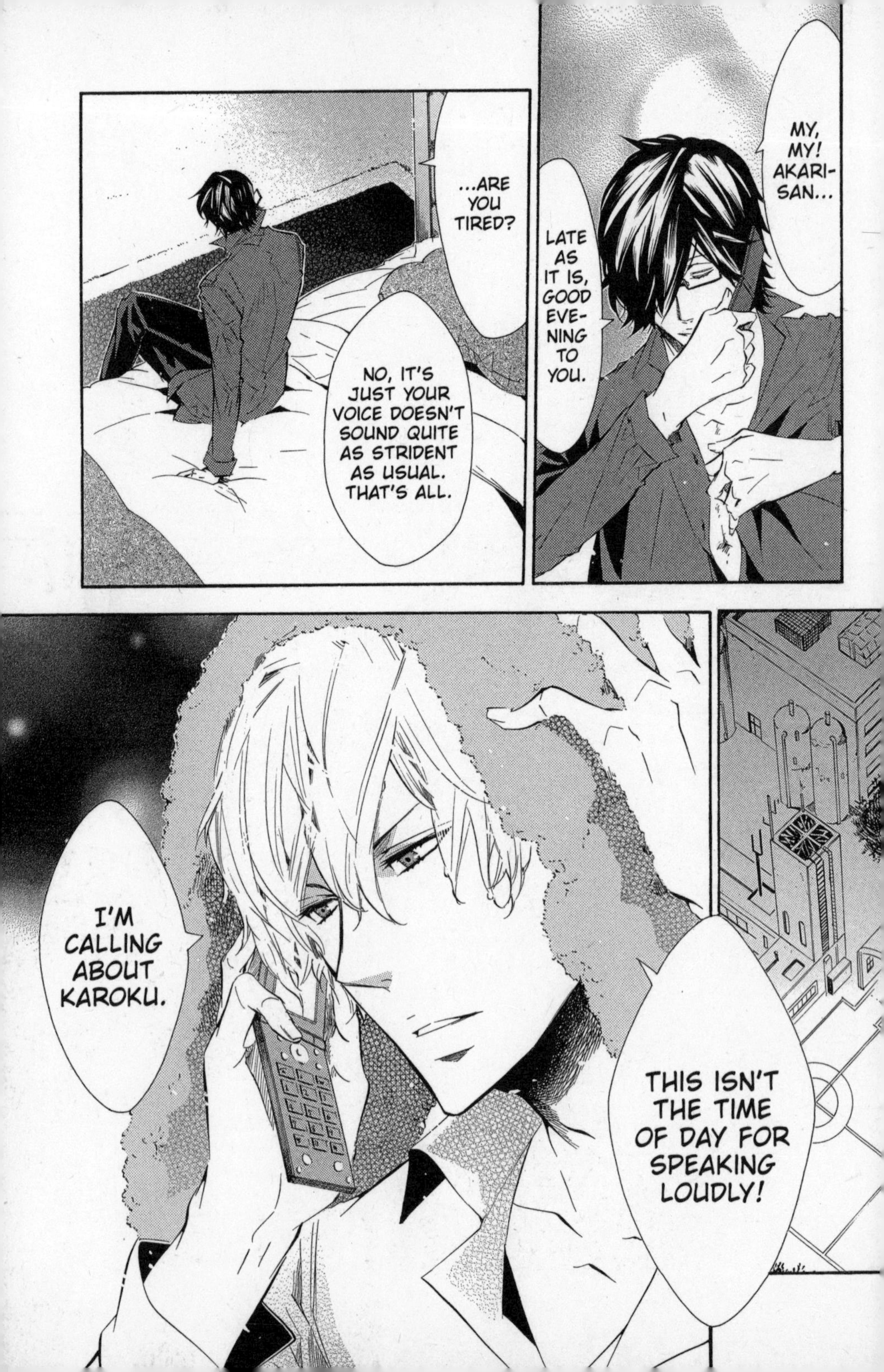
MY, MY! AKARI-SAN...
LATE AS IT IS, GOOD EVE-NING TO YOU.
...ARE YOU TIRED?
NO, IT'S JUST YOUR VOICE DOESN'T SOUND QUITE AS STRIDENT AS USUAL. THAT'S ALL.
THIS ISN'T THE TIME OF DAY FOR SPEAKING LOUDLY!
I'M CALLING ABOUT KAROKU.

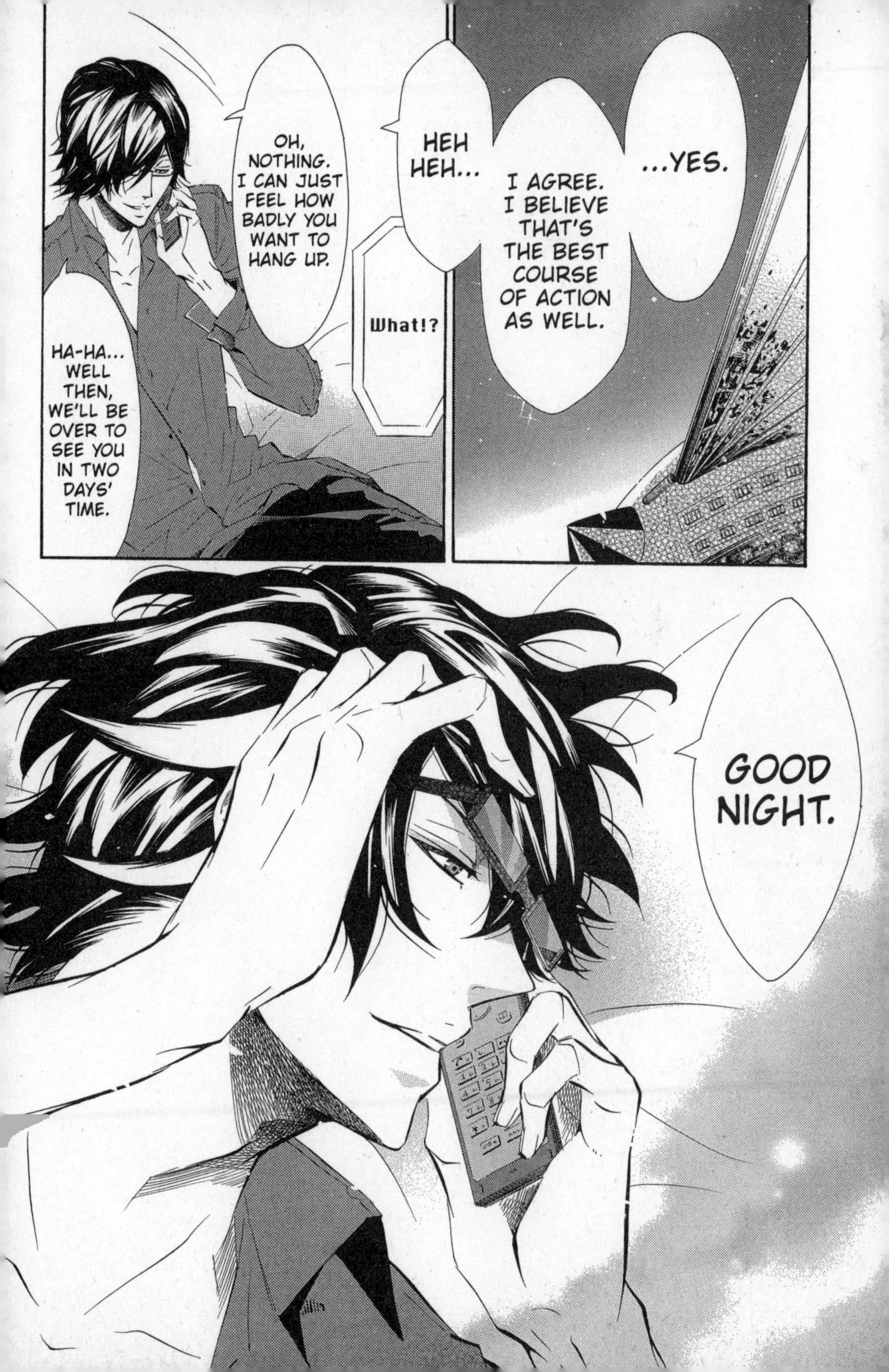
...YES.
I AGREE. I BELIEVE THAT'S THE BEST COURSE OF ACTION AS WELL.
HEH HEH...
OH, NOTHING. I CAN JUST FEEL HOW BADLY YOU WANT TO HANG UP.
What!?
HA-HA... WELL THEN, WE'LL BE OVER TO SEE YOU IN TWO DAYS' TIME.
GOOD NIGHT.

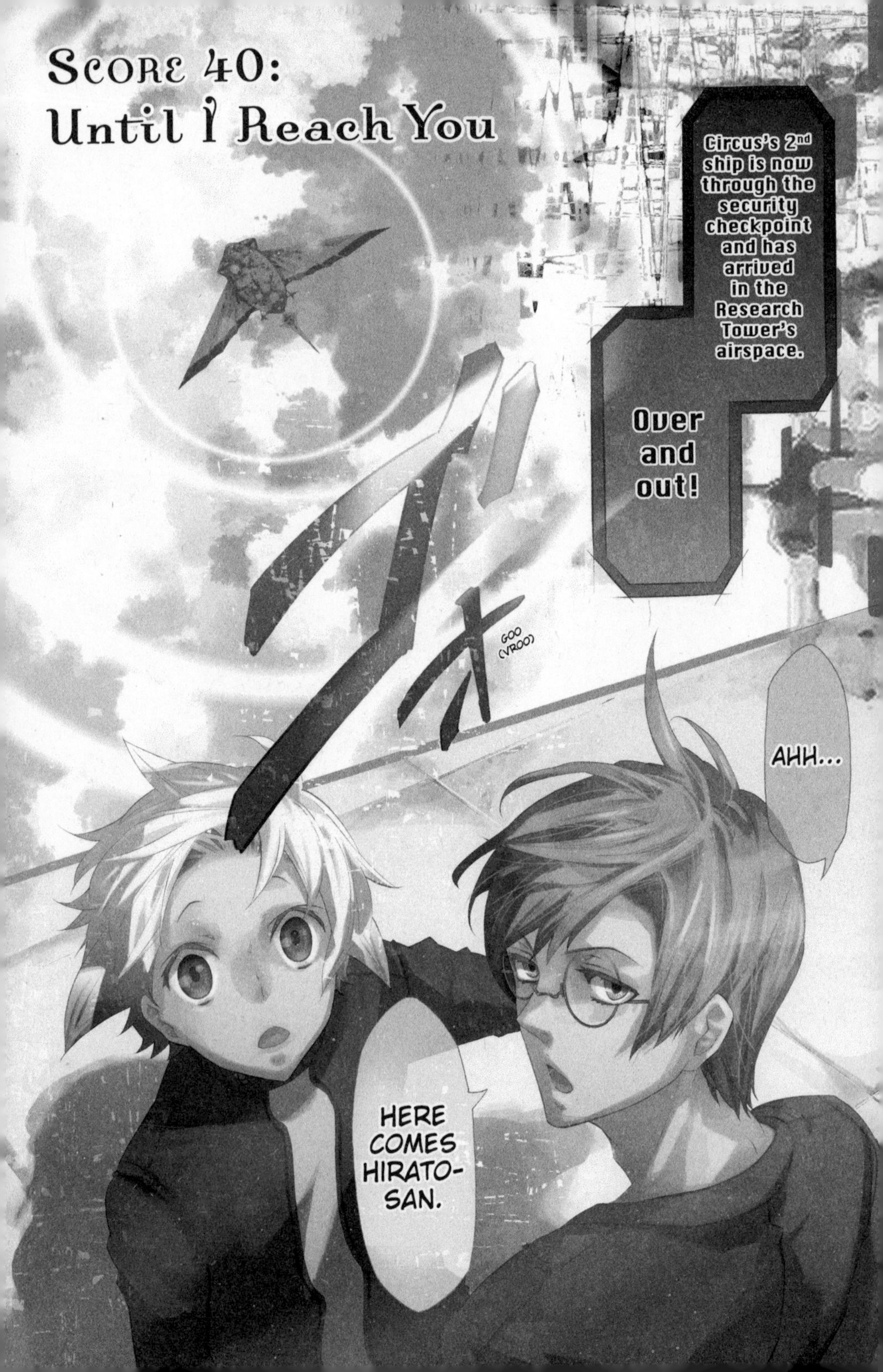
Score 40:
Until I Reach You
Circus's 2nd ship is now through the security checkpoint and has arrived in the Research Tower's airspace.
Over and out!
GOO (VROO)
AHH...
HERE COMES HIRATO-SAN.

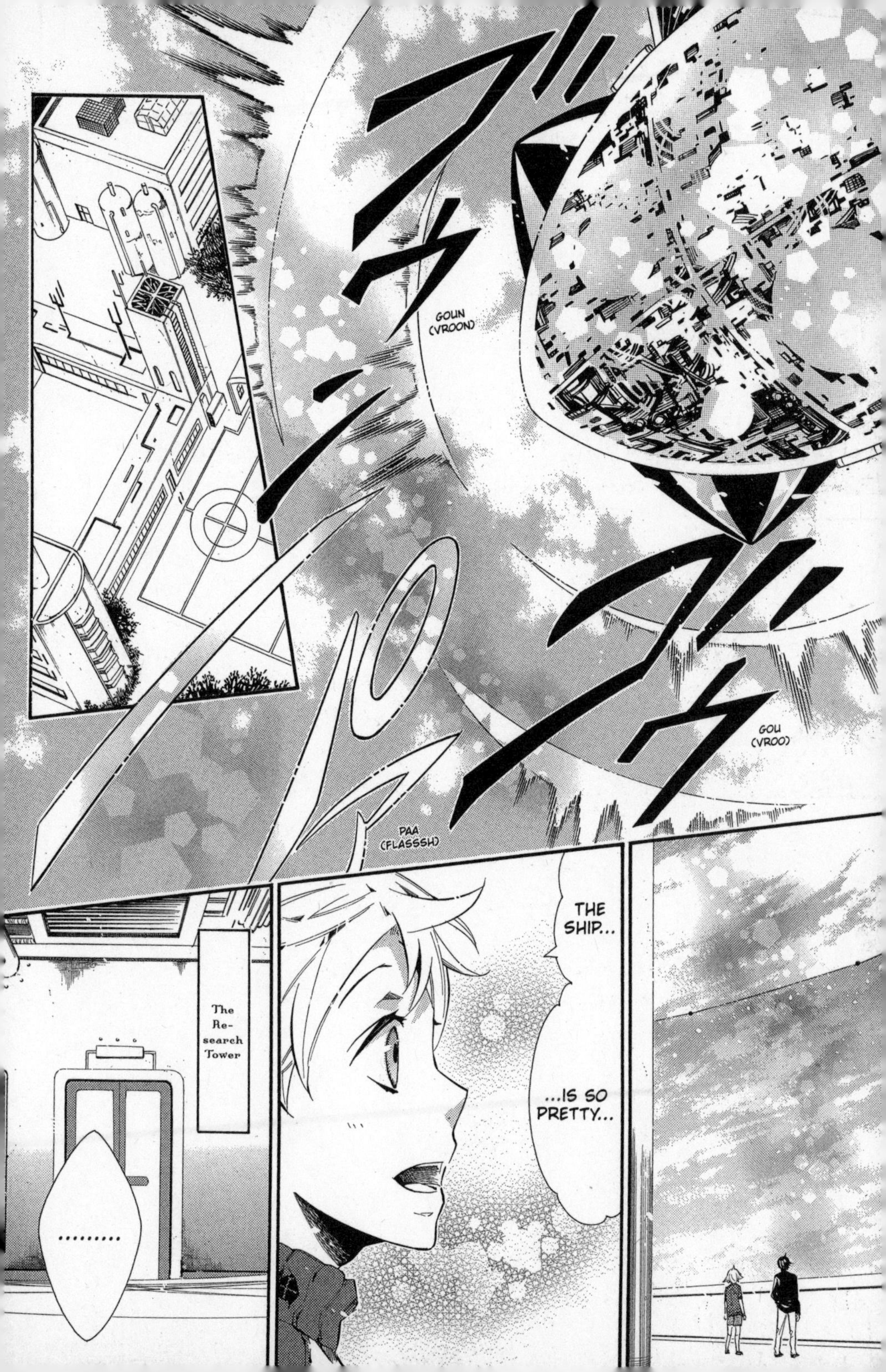
GOUN (VROON)
GOU (VROO)
PAA (FLASSSH)
THE SHIP...
...IS SO PRETTY...
The Re-search Tower
....

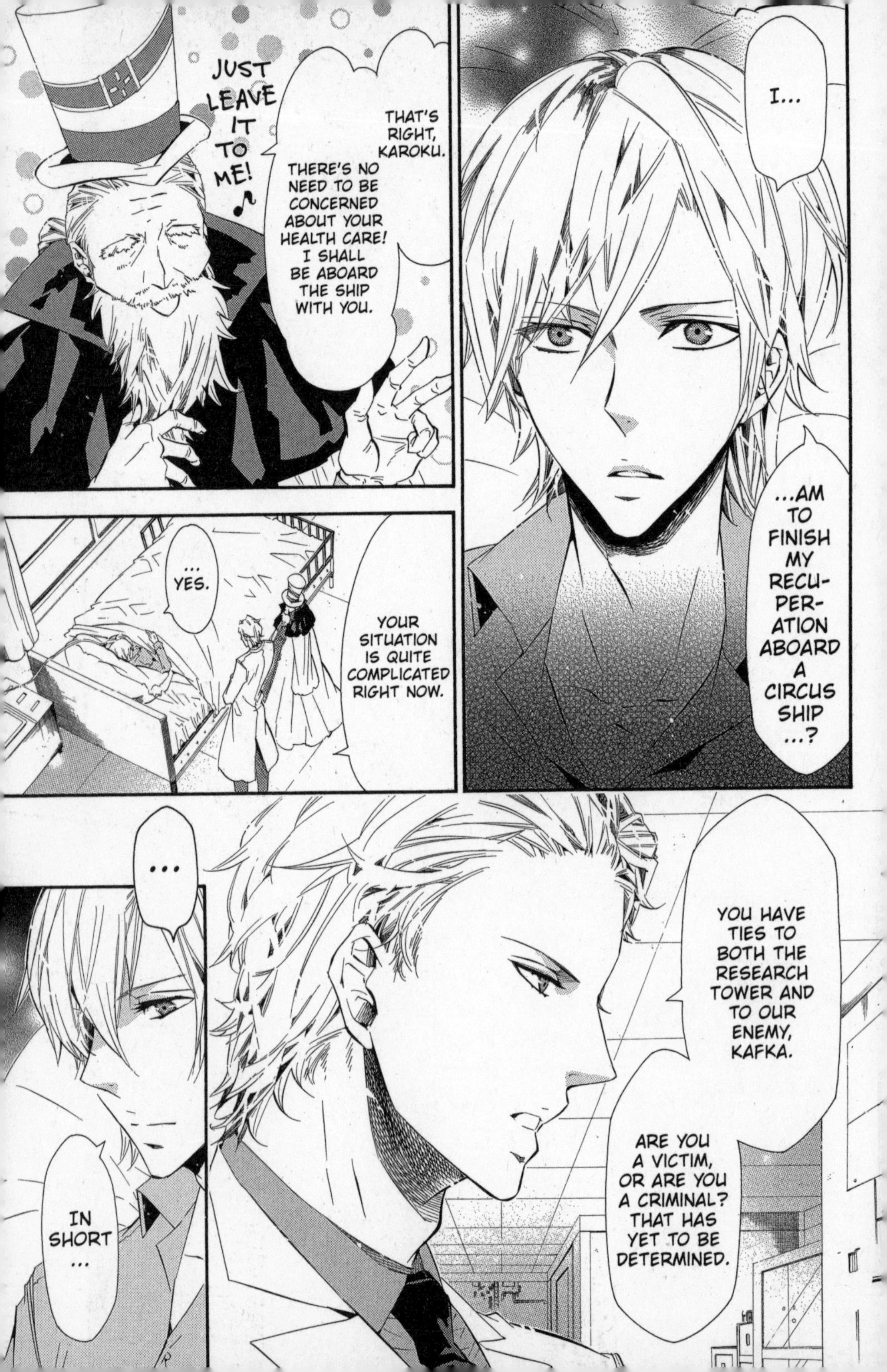
I...
...AM TO FINISH MY RECUPERATION ABOARD A CIRCUS SHIP ...?
THAT'S RIGHT, KAROKU. THERE'S NO NEED TO BE CONCERNED ABOUT YOUR HEALTH CARE! I SHALL BE ABOARD THE SHIP WITH YOU.
JUST LEAVE IT TO ME! ♪
YOUR SITUATION IS QUITE COMPLICATED RIGHT NOW.
... YES.
YOU HAVE TIES TO BOTH THE RESEARCH TOWER AND TO OUR ENEMY, KAFKA.
ARE YOU A VICTIM, OR ARE YOU A CRIMINAL? THAT HAS YET TO BE DETERMINED.
...
IN SHORT ...

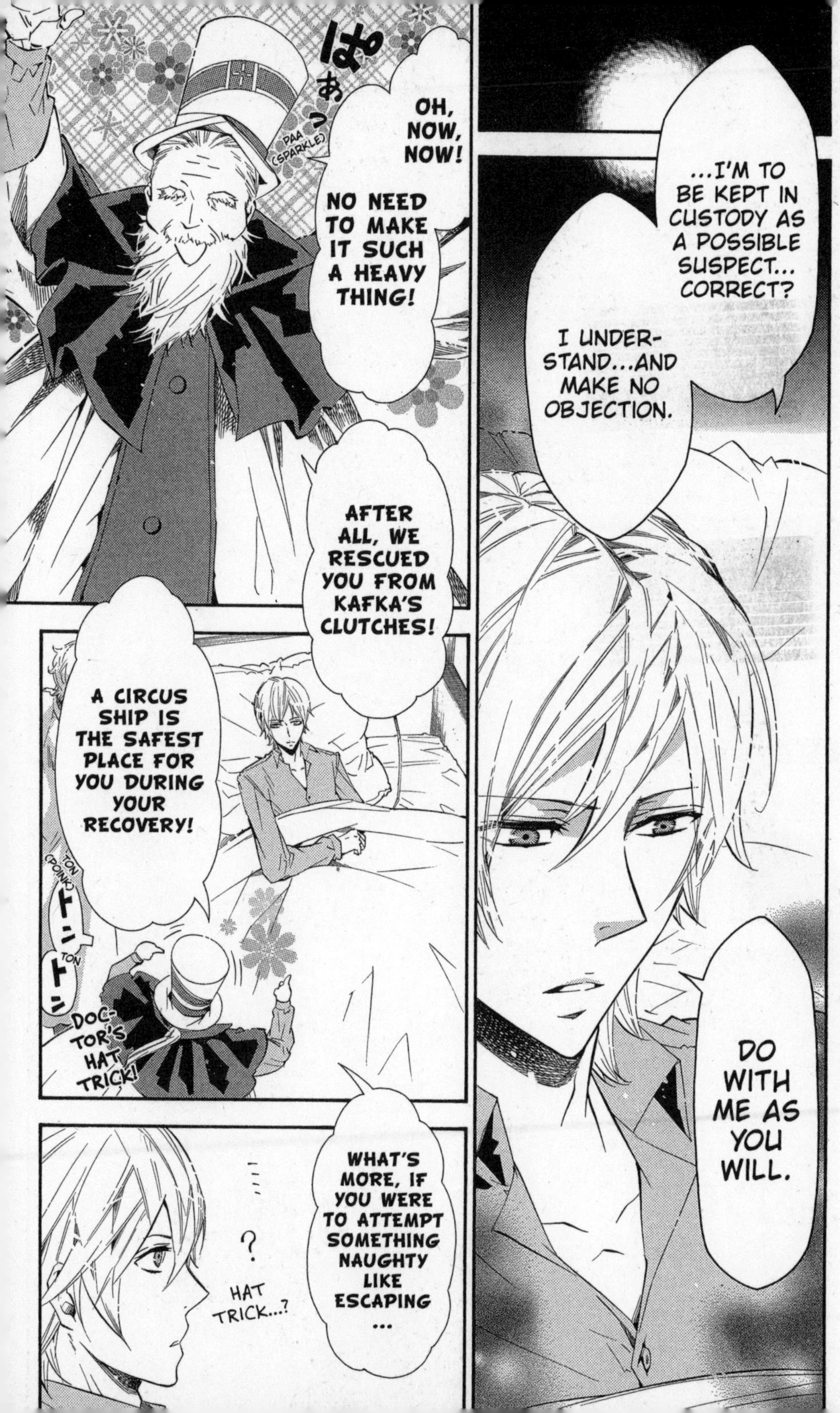
...I'M TO BE KEPT IN CUSTODY AS A POSSIBLE SUSPECT... CORRECT?
I UNDERSTAND...AND MAKE NO OBJECTION.
DO WITH ME AS YOU WILL.
ぱあっ
PAA (SPARKLE)
OH, NOW, NOW!
NO NEED TO MAKE IT SUCH A HEAVY THING!
AFTER ALL, WE RESCUED YOU FROM KAFKA'S CLUTCHES!
A CIRCUS SHIP IS THE SAFEST PLACE FOR YOU DURING YOUR RECOVERY!
トン トン
TON (POINK) TON
DOC-TOR'S HAT TRICK!
WHAT'S MORE, IF YOU WERE TO ATTEMPT SOMETHING NAUGHTY LIKE ESCAPING...
...
?
HAT TRICK...?

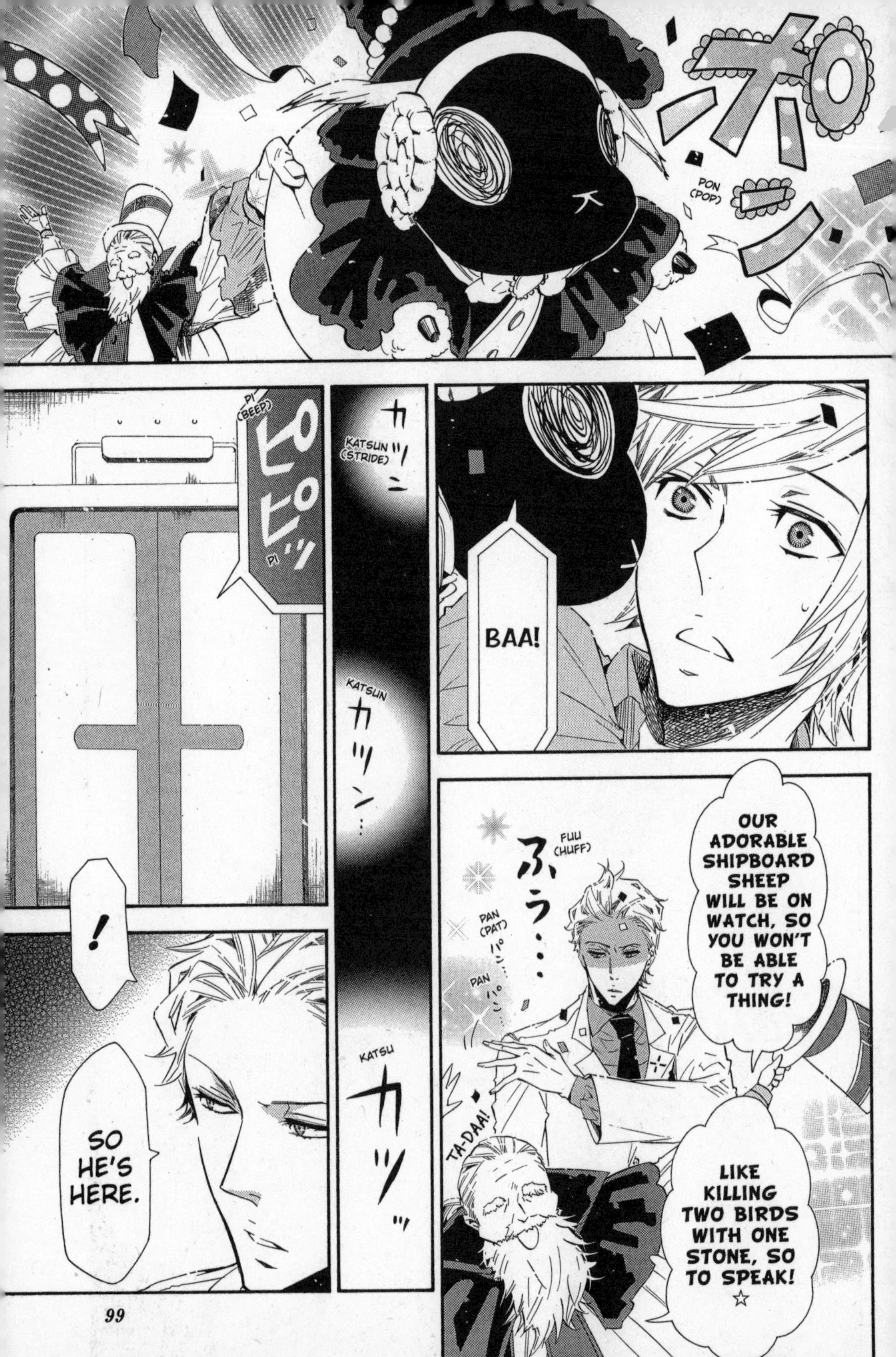
PON (POP)
BAA!
FUU (HUFF)
PAN (PAT)
PAN
OUR ADORABLE SHIPBOARD SHEEP WILL BE ON WATCH, SO YOU WON'T BE ABLE TO TRY A THING!
TA-DAA!
LIKE KILLING TWO BIRDS WITH ONE STONE, SO TO SPEAK! ☆
KATSUN (STRIDE)
KATSUN
KATSU
PI (BEEP)
PI
!
SO HE'S HERE.

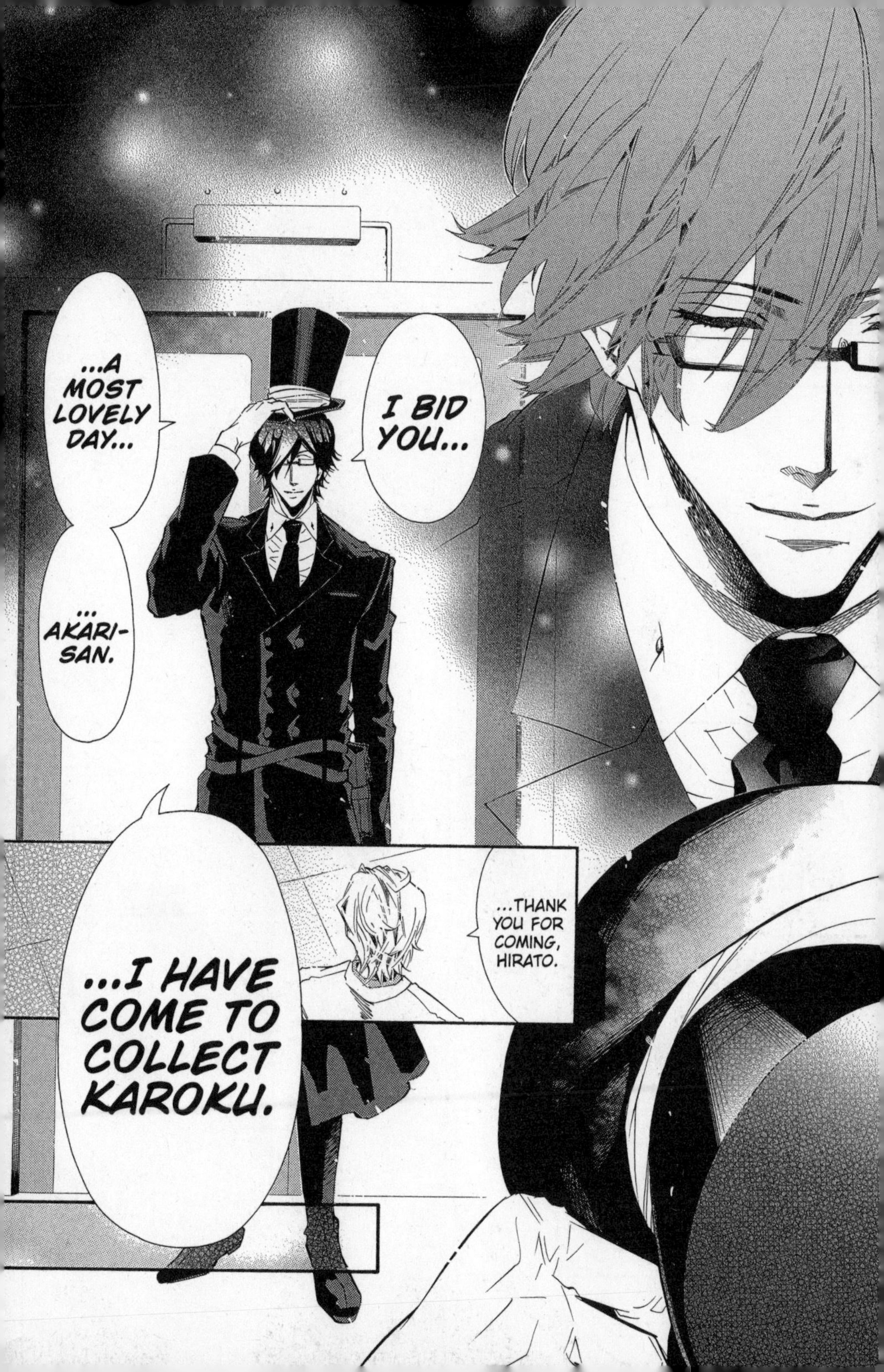
I BID YOU...
...A MOST LOVELY DAY...
...AKARI-SAN.
...I HAVE COME TO COLLECT KAROKU.
...THANK YOU FOR COMING, HIRATO.

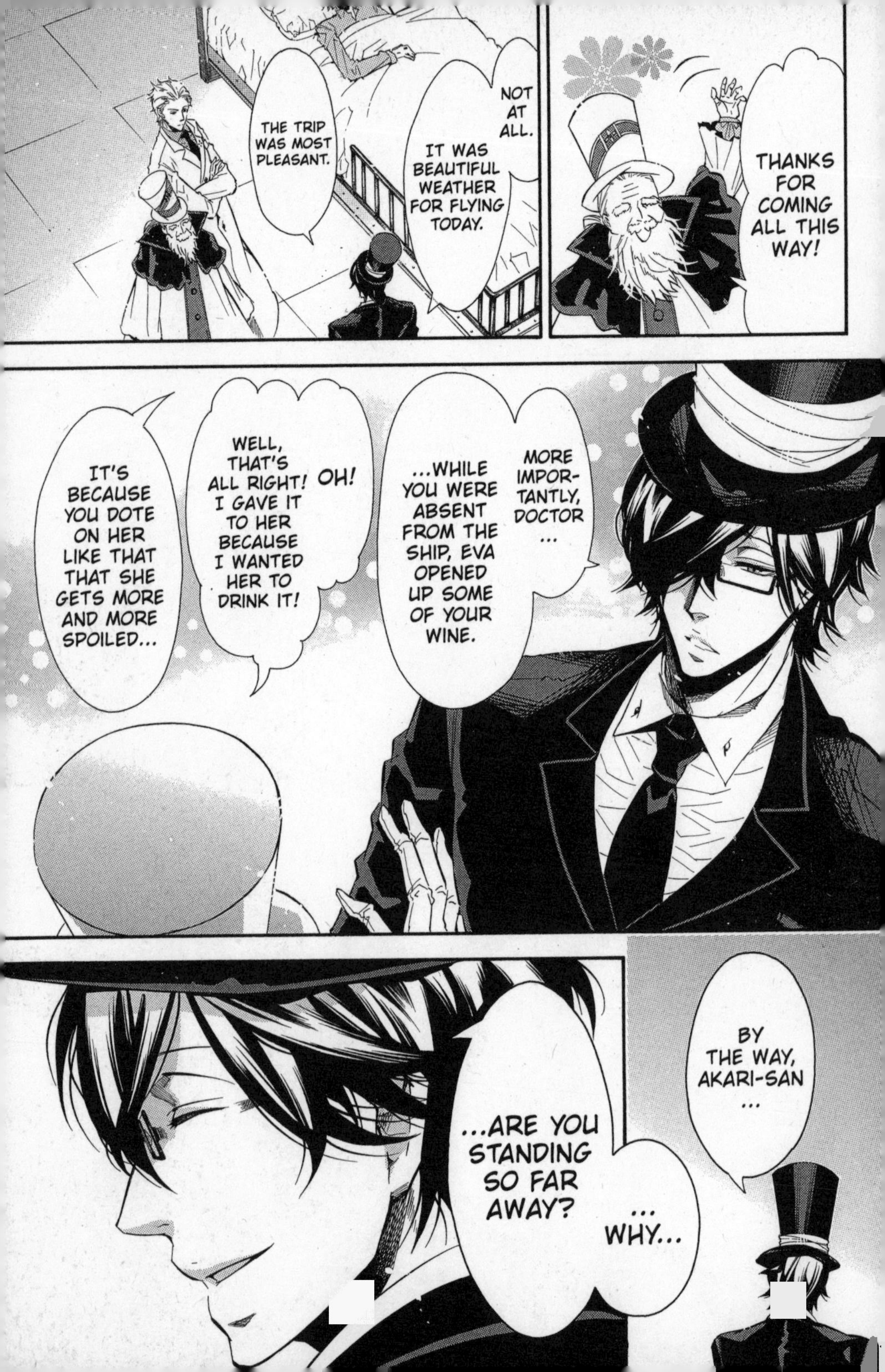
THANKS FOR COMING ALL THIS WAY!
NOT AT ALL.
IT WAS BEAUTIFUL WEATHER FOR FLYING TODAY.
THE TRIP WAS MOST PLEASANT.
MORE IMPOR-TANTLY, DOCTOR ...
...WHILE YOU WERE ABSENT FROM THE SHIP, EVA OPENED UP SOME OF YOUR WINE.
OH!
WELL, THAT'S ALL RIGHT! I GAVE IT TO HER BECAUSE I WANTED HER TO DRINK IT!
IT'S BECAUSE YOU DOTE ON HER LIKE THAT THAT SHE GETS MORE AND MORE SPOILED...
BY THE WAY, AKARI-SAN ...
... WHY...
...ARE YOU STANDING SO FAR AWAY?

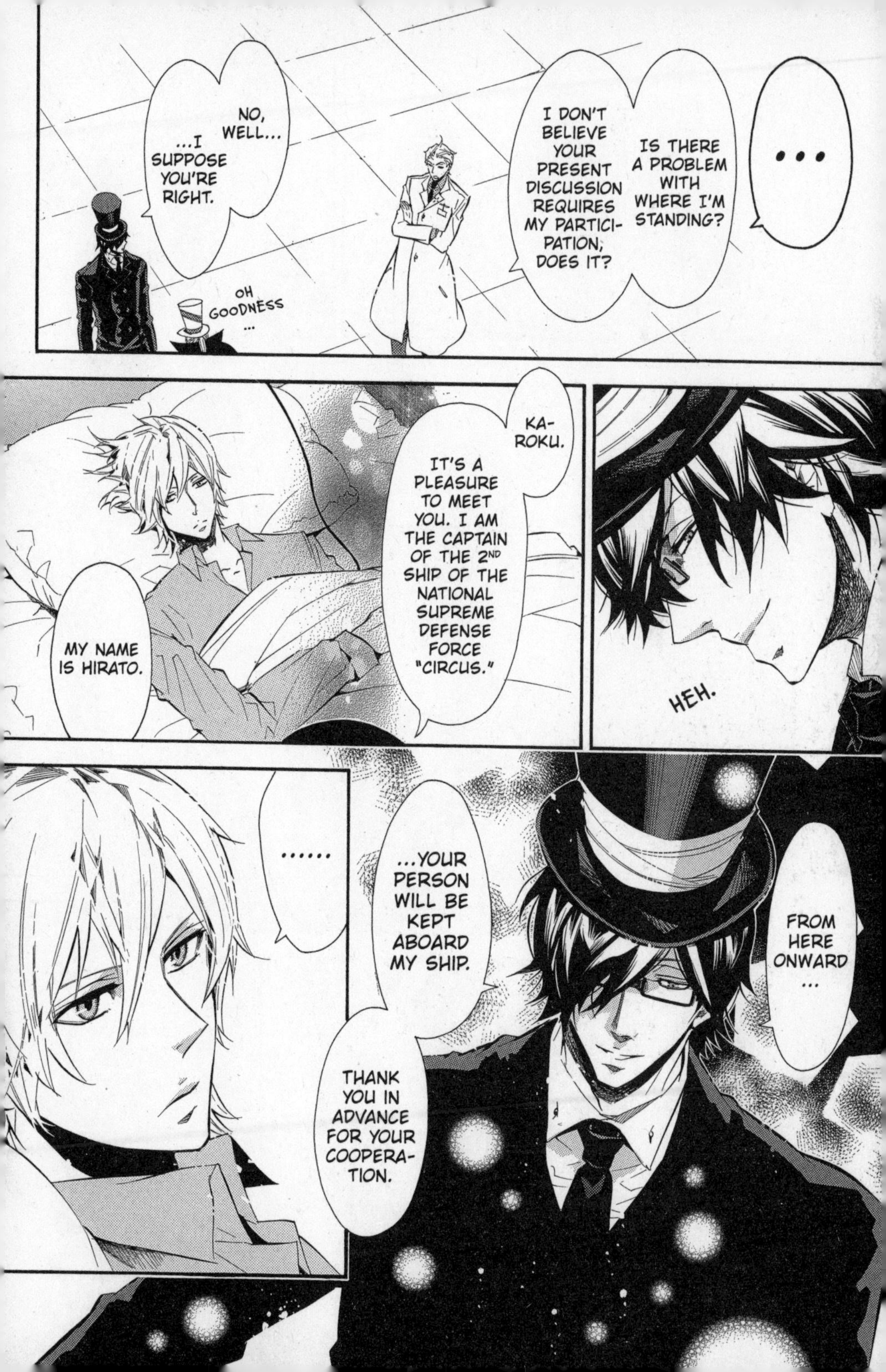
...
IS THERE A PROBLEM WITH WHERE I'M STANDING?
I DON'T BELIEVE YOUR PRESENT DISCUSSION REQUIRES MY PARTICIPATION; DOES IT?
NO, WELL... ...I SUPPOSE YOU'RE RIGHT.
OH GOODNESS ...
HEH.
KA-ROKU.
IT'S A PLEASURE TO MEET YOU. I AM THE CAPTAIN OF THE 2nd SHIP OF THE NATIONAL SUPREME DEFENSE FORCE "CIRCUS."
MY NAME IS HIRATO.
FROM HERE ONWARD ...
...YOUR PERSON WILL BE KEPT ABOARD MY SHIP.
......
THANK YOU IN ADVANCE FOR YOUR COOPERATION.

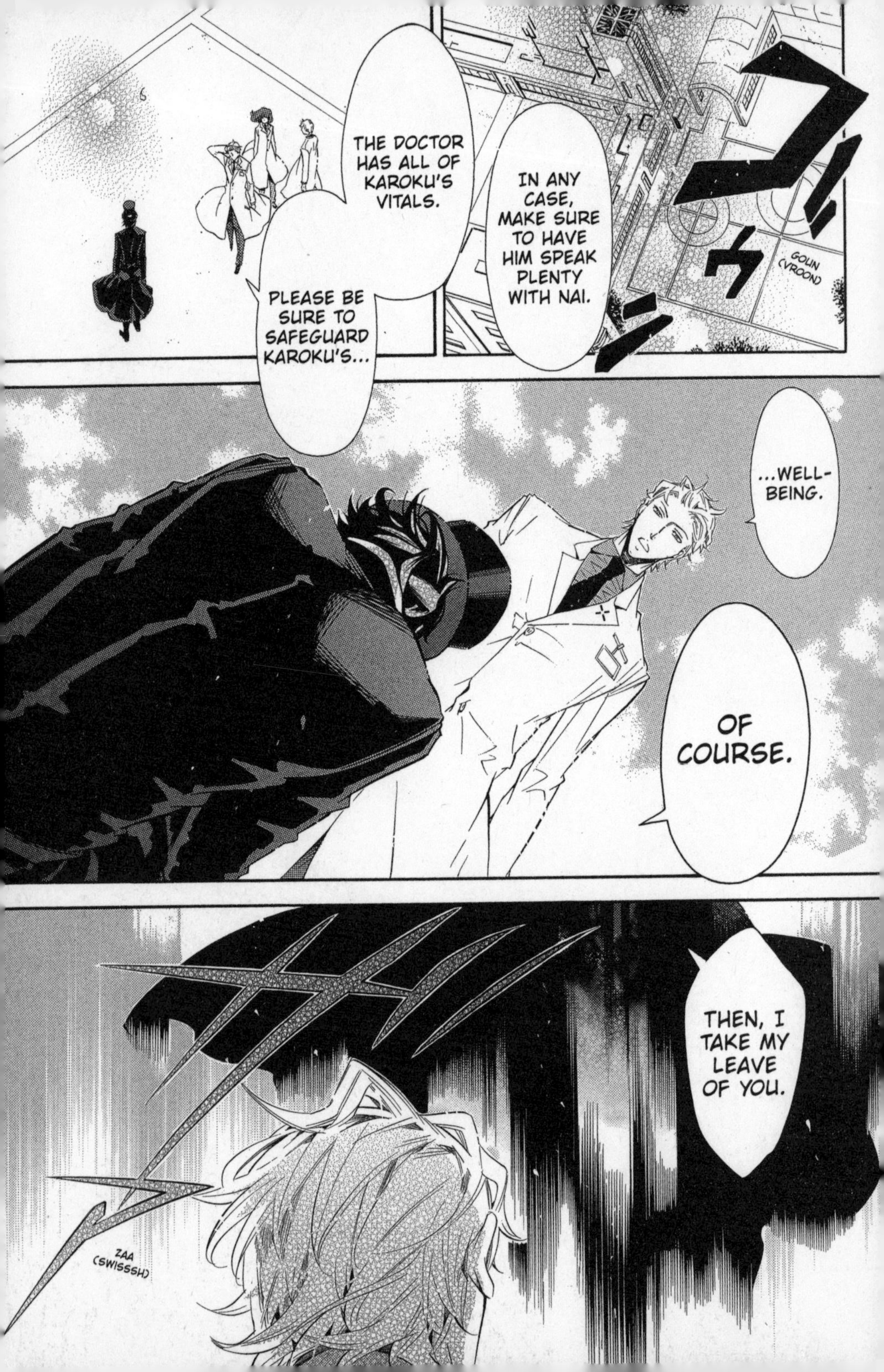
GOUN (VROON)
IN ANY CASE, MAKE SURE TO HAVE HIM SPEAK PLENTY WITH NAI.
THE DOCTOR HAS ALL OF KAROKU'S VITALS.
PLEASE BE SURE TO SAFEGUARD KAROKU'S...
...WELL-BEING.
OF COURSE.
THEN, I TAKE MY LEAVE OF YOU.
ZAA (SWISSSH)

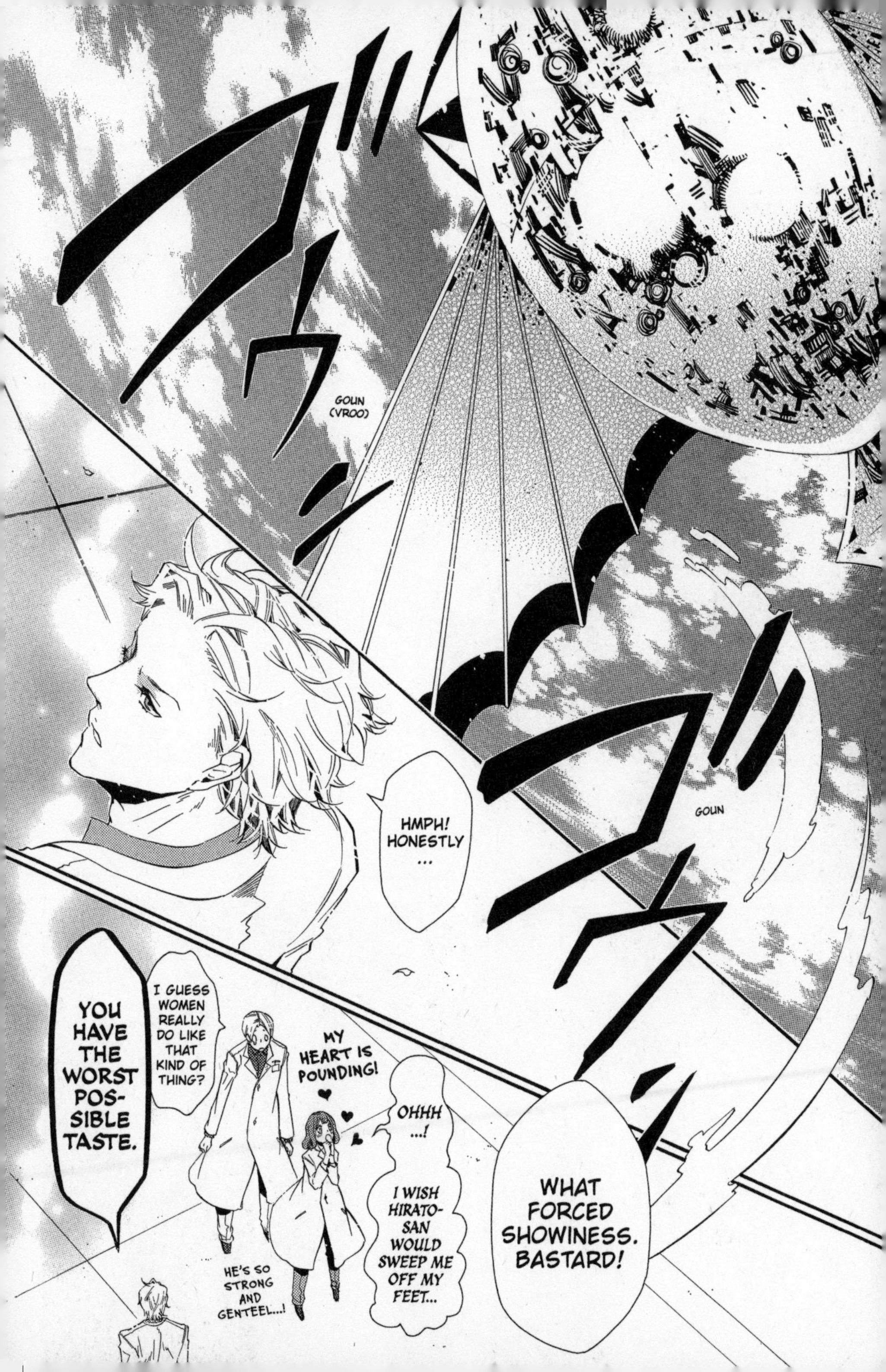
GOUN (VROO)
GOUN
HMPH! HONESTLY ...
WHAT FORCED SHOWINESS. BASTARD!
OHHH ...!
I WISH HIRATO-SAN WOULD SWEEP ME OFF MY FEET...
MY HEART IS POUNDING!
HE'S SO STRONG AND GENTEEL...!
I GUESS WOMEN REALLY DO LIKE THAT KIND OF THING?
YOU HAVE THE WORST POS-SIBLE TASTE.

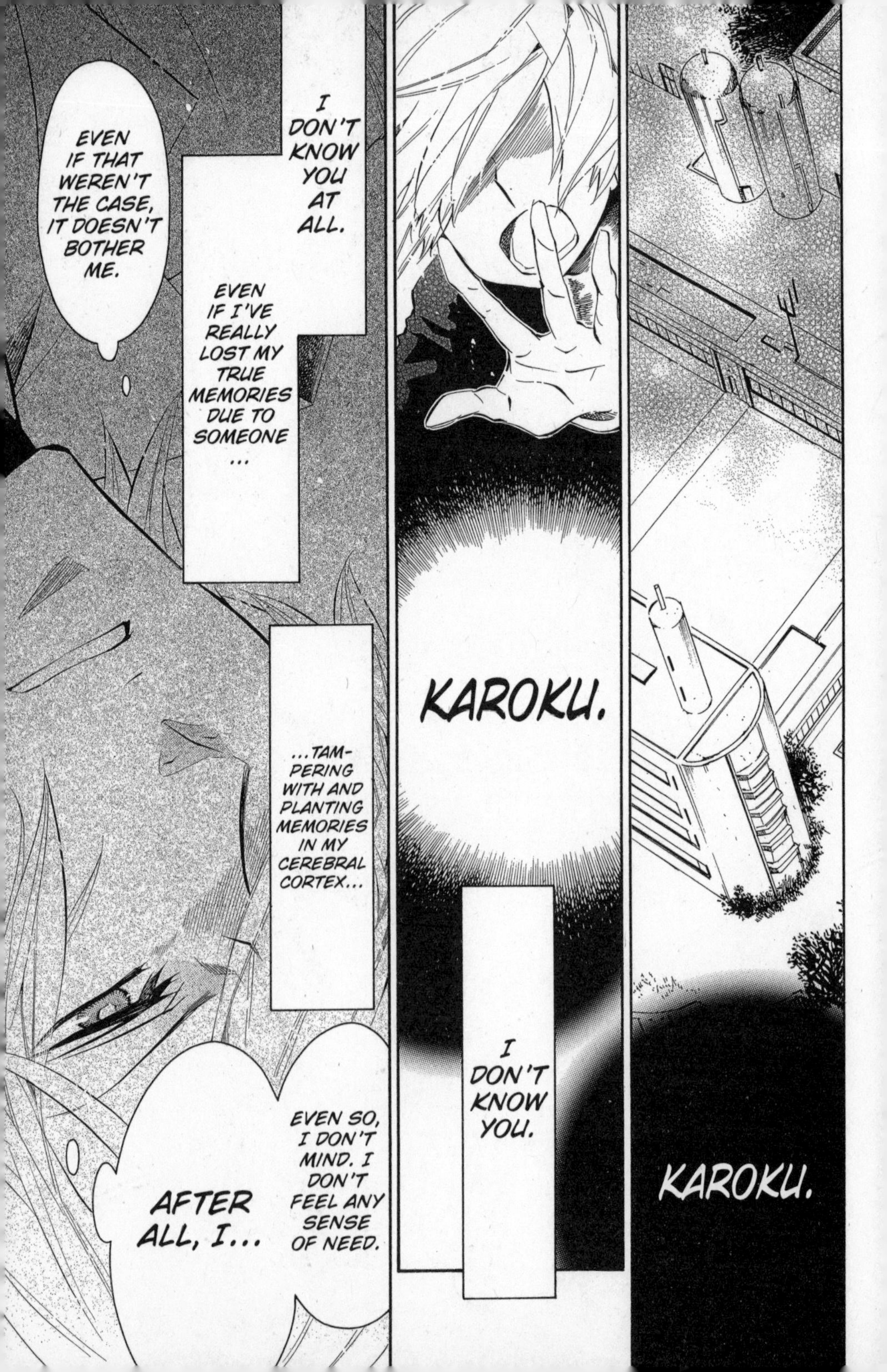
KAROKU.
KAROKU.
I DON'T KNOW YOU.
I DON'T KNOW YOU AT ALL.
EVEN IF I'VE REALLY LOST MY TRUE MEMORIES DUE TO SOMEONE ...
...TAMPERING WITH AND PLANTING MEMORIES IN MY CEREBRAL CORTEX...
EVEN IF THAT WEREN'T THE CASE, IT DOESN'T BOTHER ME.
EVEN SO, I DON'T MIND. I DON'T FEEL ANY SENSE OF NEED.
AFTER ALL, I...

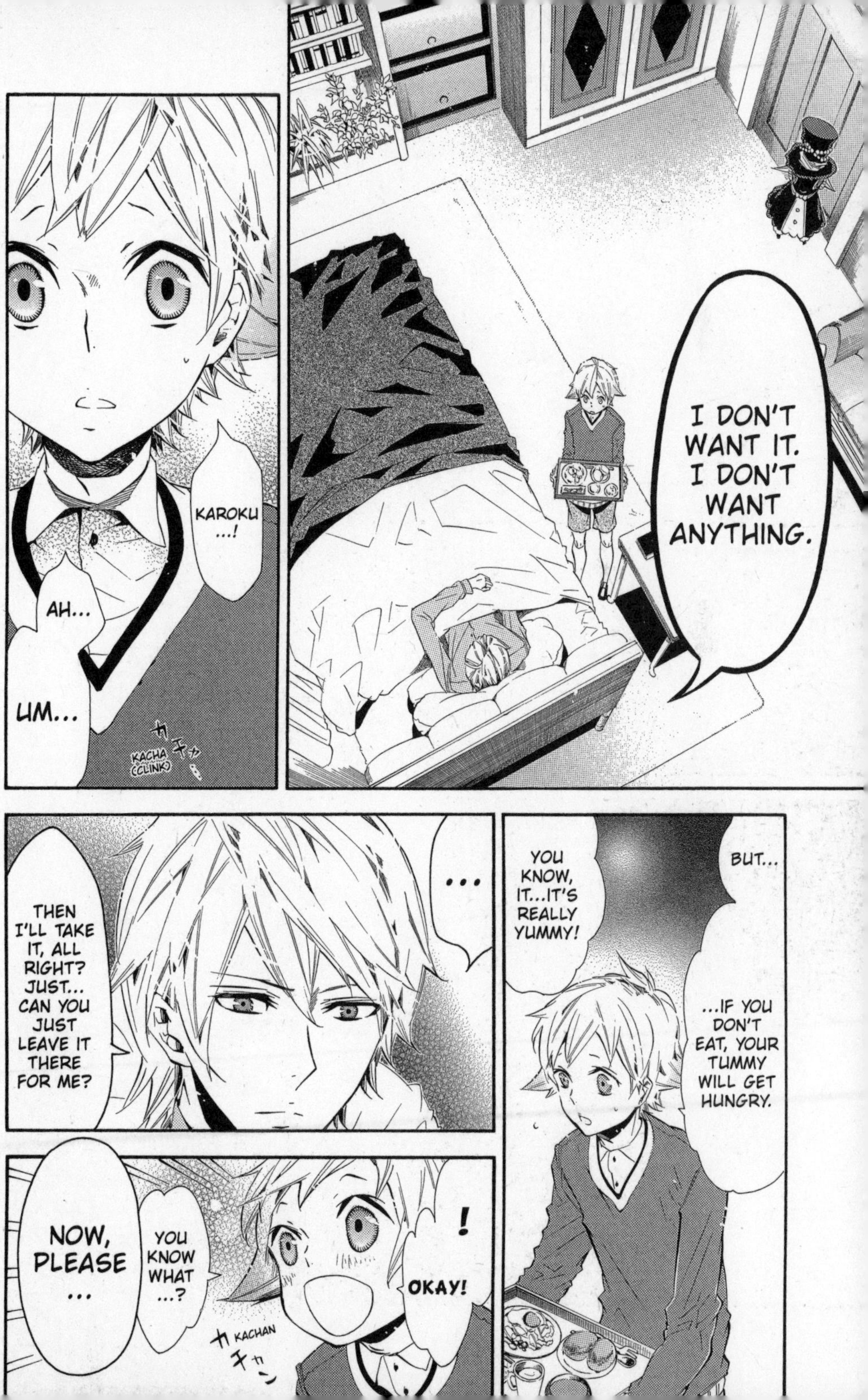
I DON'T WANT IT. I DON'T WANT ANYTHING.
KAROKU ...!
AH...
UM...
KACHA (CLINK)
BUT...
YOU KNOW, IT...IT'S REALLY YUMMY!
...IF YOU DON'T EAT, YOUR TUMMY WILL GET HUNGRY.
...
THEN I'LL TAKE IT, ALL RIGHT? JUST... CAN YOU JUST LEAVE IT THERE FOR ME?
!
OKAY!
YOU KNOW WHAT ...?
NOW, PLEASE ...
KACHAN

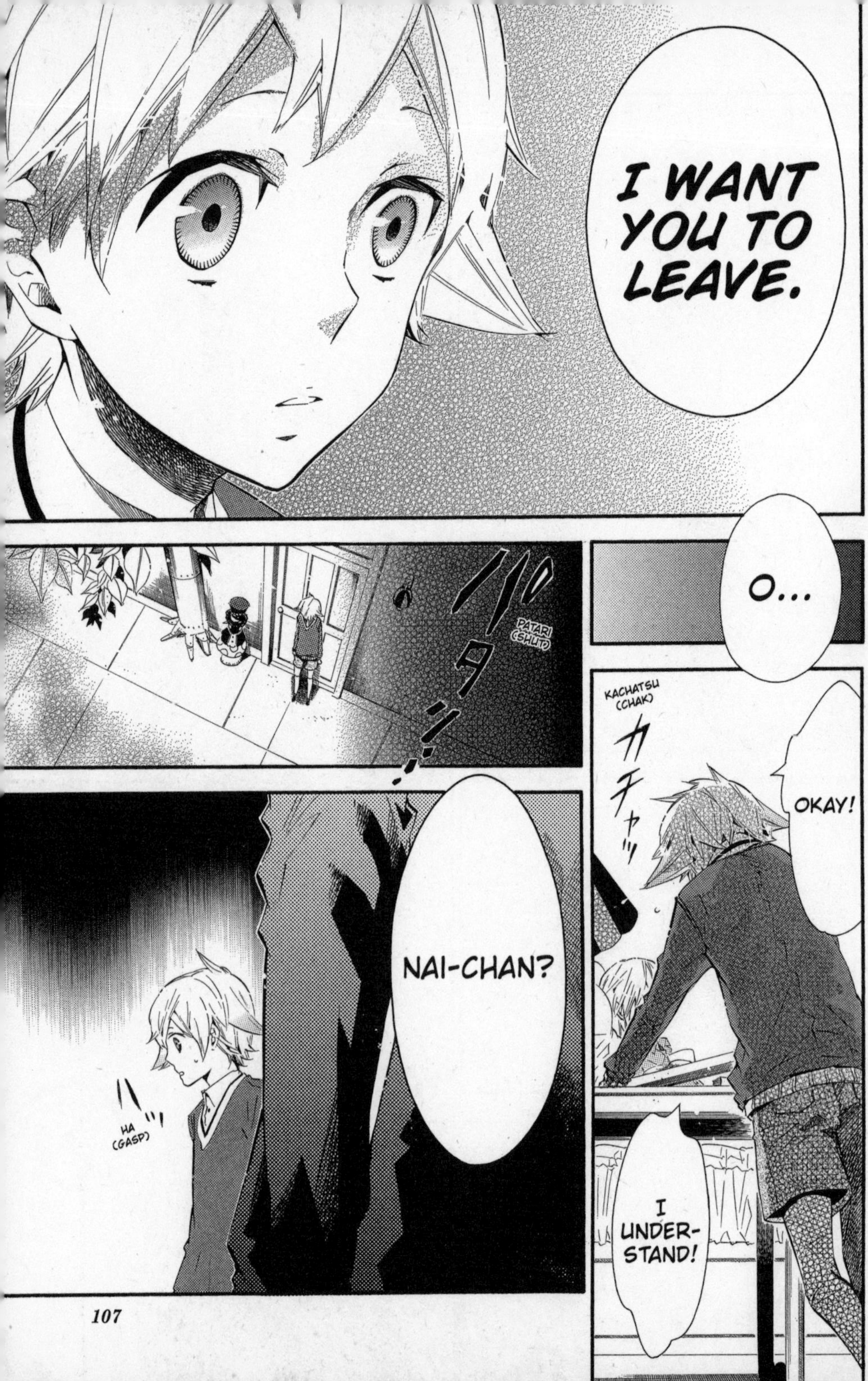
I WANT YOU TO LEAVE.
O...
KACHATSU (CHAK)
OKAY!
I UNDERSTAND!
PATARI (SHUT)
NAI-CHAN?
HA (GASP)

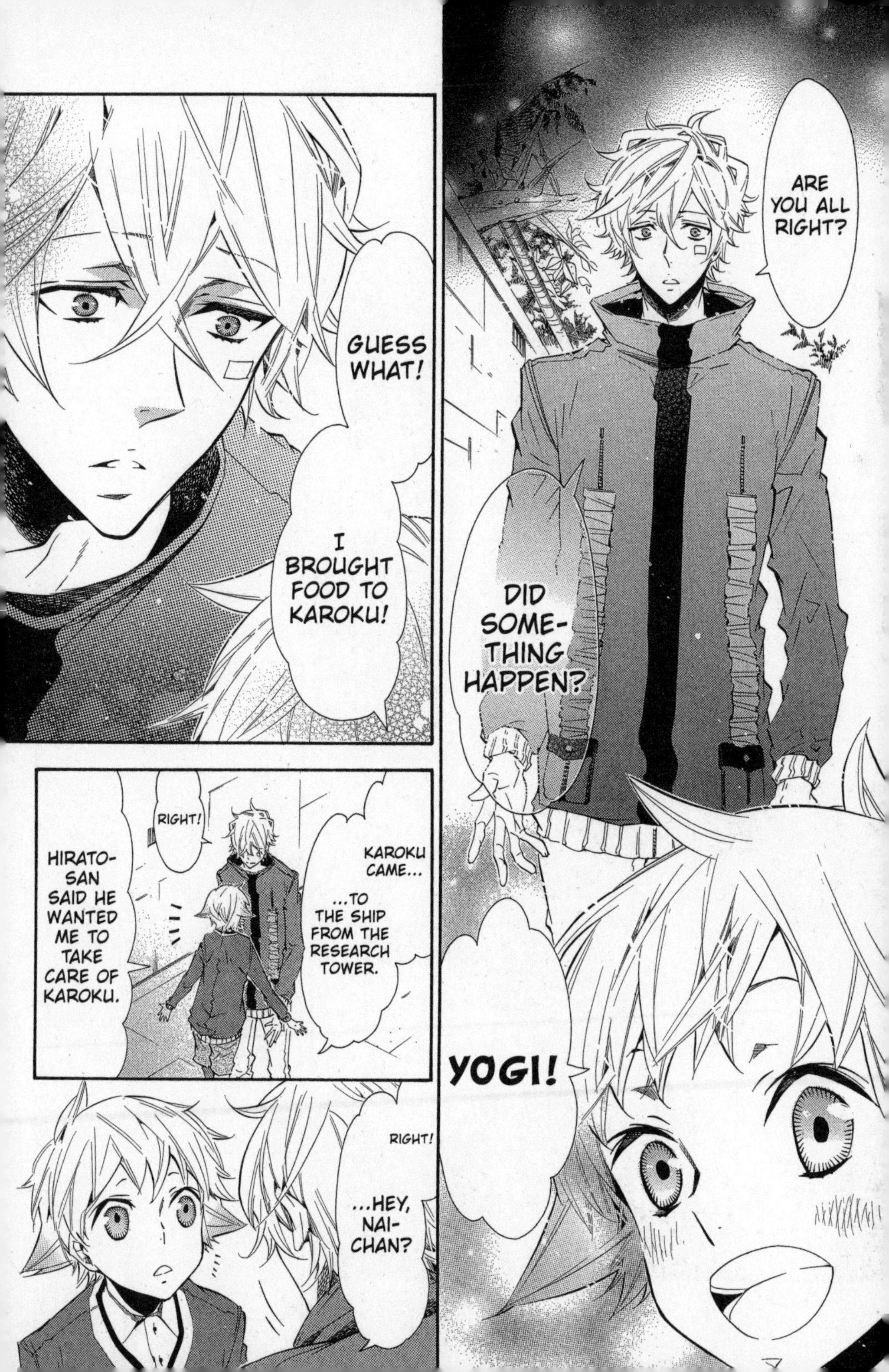
ARE YOU ALL RIGHT?
DID SOMETHING HAPPEN?
YOGI!
GUESS WHAT!
I BROUGHT FOOD TO KAROKU!
KAROKU CAME...
...TO THE SHIP FROM THE RESEARCH TOWER.
RIGHT!
HIRATO-SAN SAID HE WANTED ME TO TAKE CARE OF KAROKU.
RIGHT!
...HEY, NAI-CHAN?

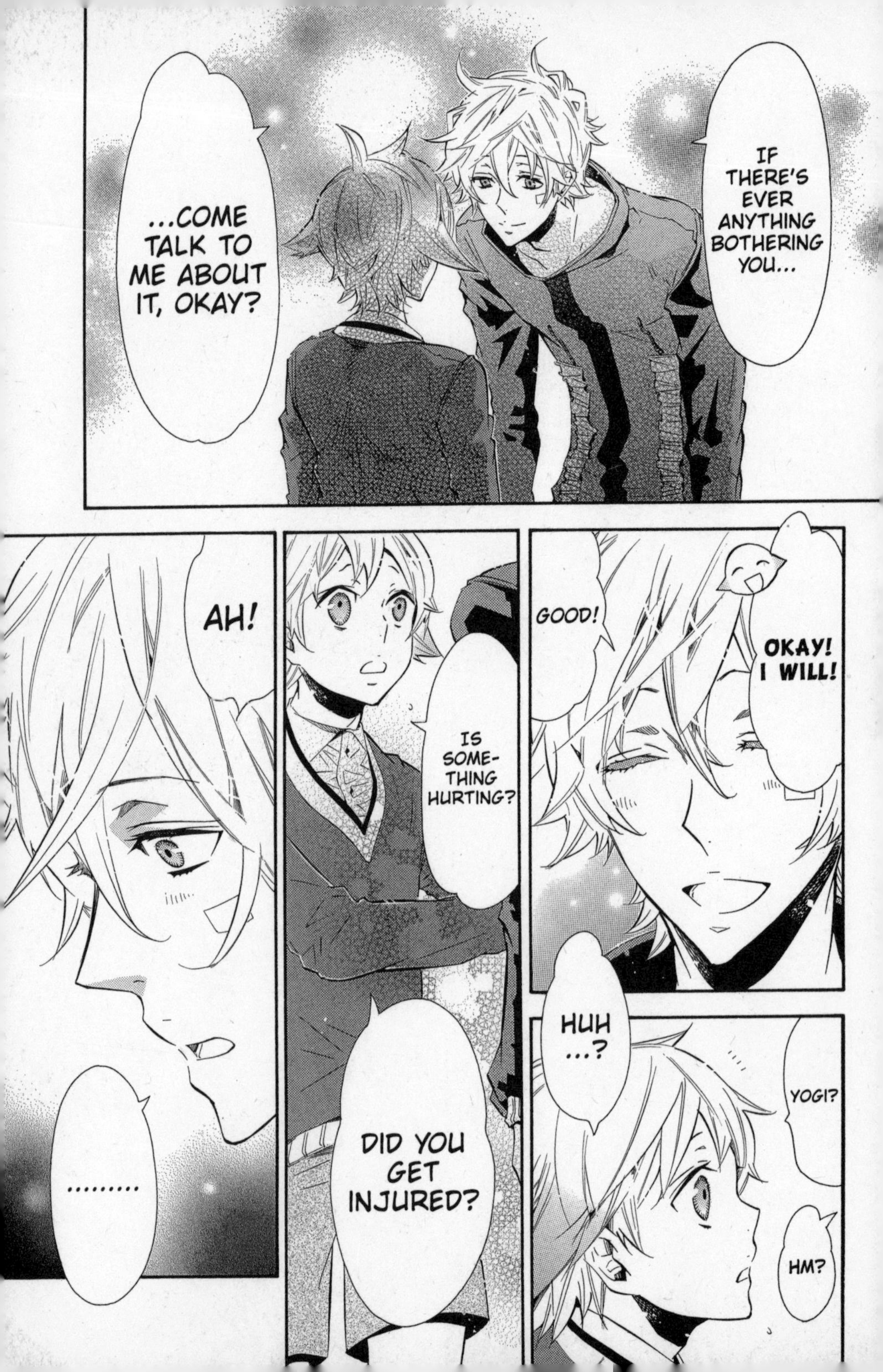
IF THERE'S EVER ANYTHING BOTHERING YOU...
...COME TALK TO ME ABOUT IT, OKAY?
OKAY! I WILL!
GOOD!
HUH ...?
YOGI?
HM?
IS SOME-THING HURTING?
DID YOU GET INJURED?
AH!
....

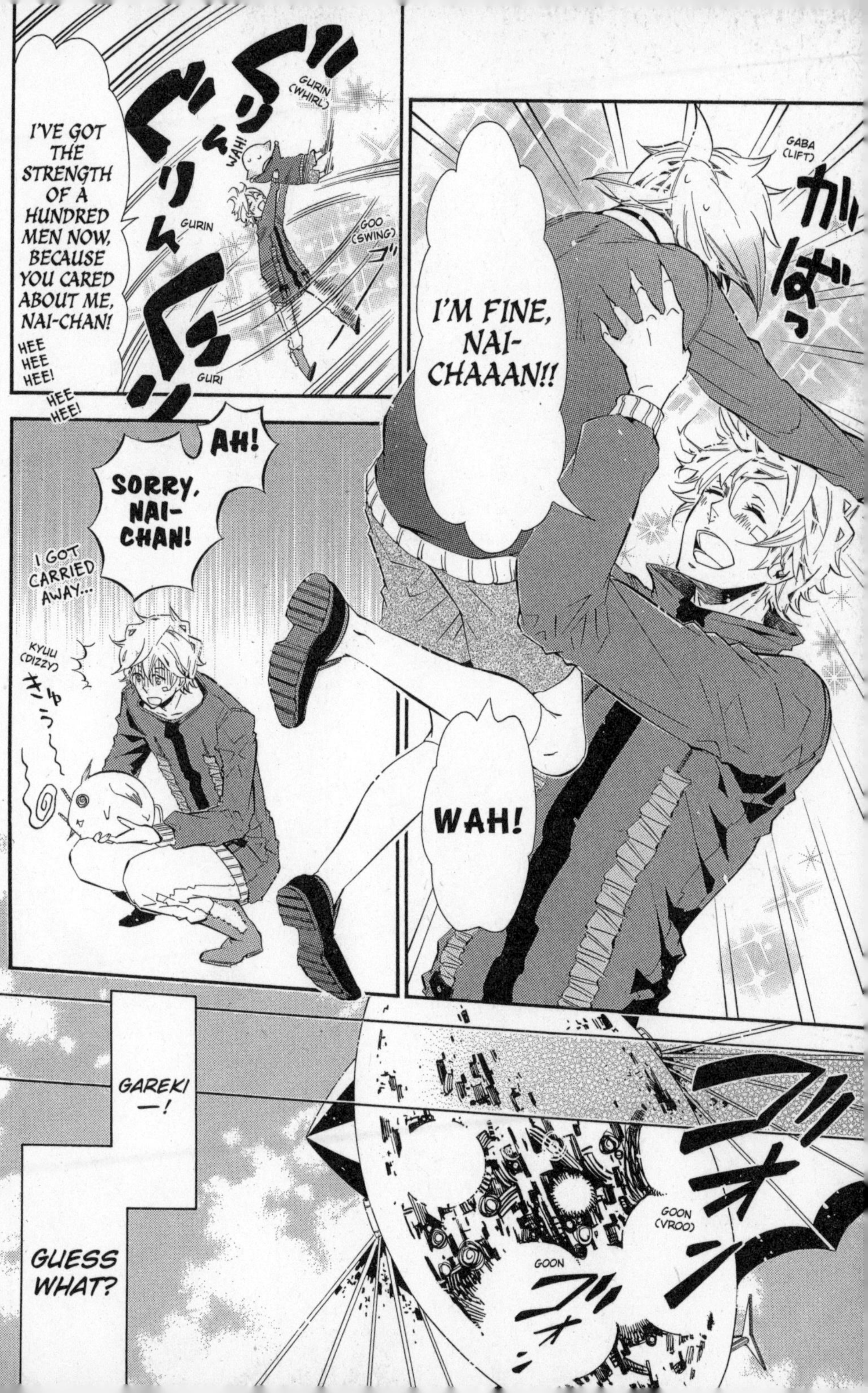
GABA (LIFT)
I'M FINE, NAI-CHAAAN!!
WAH!
GURIN (WHIRL)
WAH!
GURIN
GOO (SWING)
I'VE GOT THE STRENGTH OF A HUNDRED MEN NOW, BECAUSE YOU CARED ABOUT ME, NAI-CHAN!
HEE HEE HEE!
GURI
HEE HEE!
AH!
SORRY, NAI-CHAN!
I GOT CARRIED AWAY...
KYUU (DIZZY)
GOON (VROO)
GOON
GAREKI—!
GUESS WHAT?

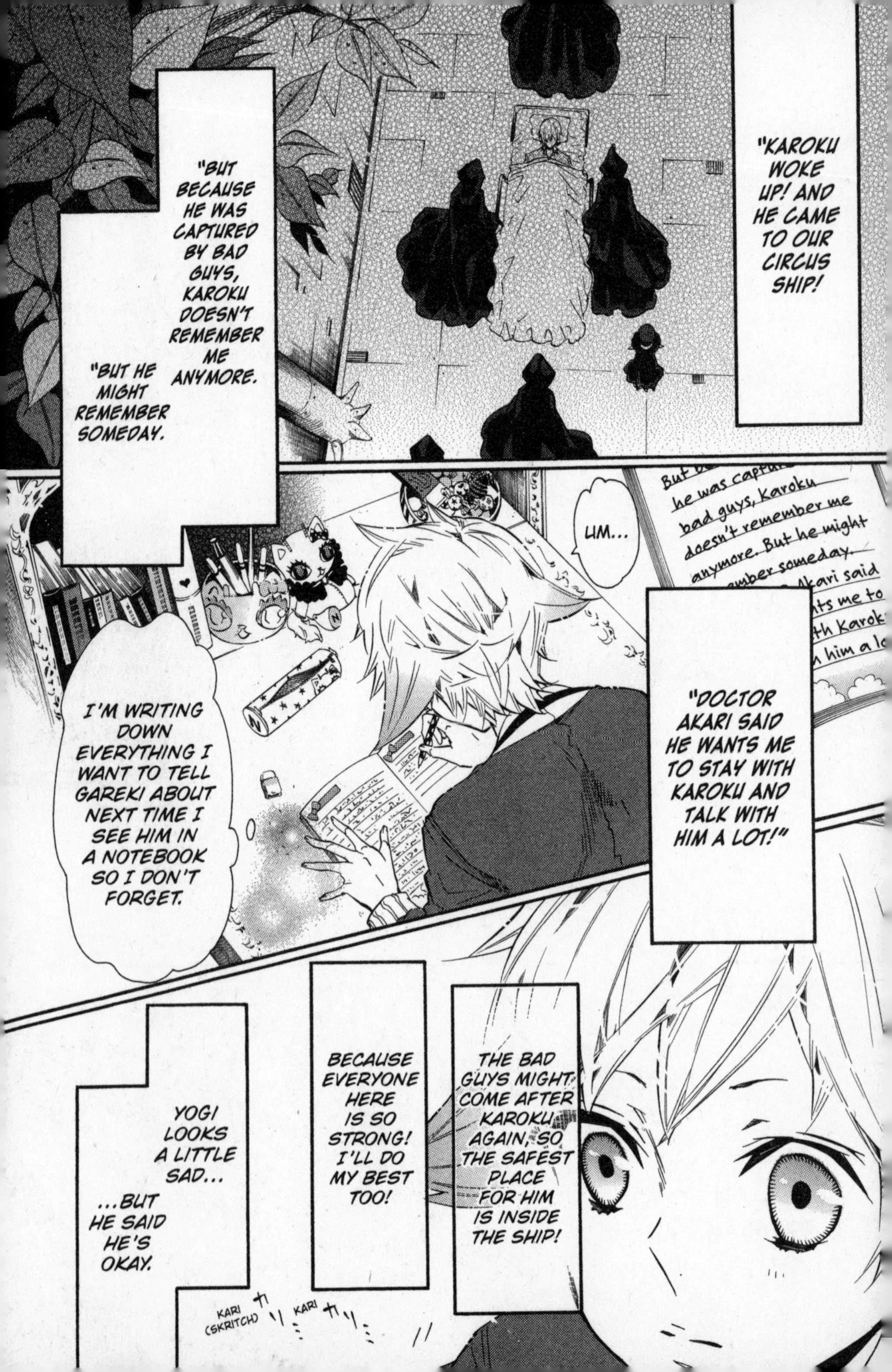
"KAROKU WOKE UP! AND HE CAME TO OUR CIRCUS SHIP!
"BUT BECAUSE HE WAS CAPTURED BY BAD GUYS, KAROKU DOESN'T REMEMBER ME ANYMORE.
"BUT HE MIGHT REMEMBER SOMEDAY.
UM...
"DOCTOR AKARI SAID HE WANTS ME TO STAY WITH KAROKU AND TALK WITH HIM A LOT!"
I'M WRITING DOWN EVERYTHING I WANT TO TELL GAREKI ABOUT NEXT TIME I SEE HIM IN A NOTEBOOK SO I DON'T FORGET.
THE BAD GUYS MIGHT COME AFTER KAROKU AGAIN, SO THE SAFEST PLACE FOR HIM IS INSIDE THE SHIP!
BECAUSE EVERYONE HERE IS SO STRONG! I'LL DO MY BEST TOO!
YOGI LOOKS A LITTLE SAD...
...BUT HE SAID HE'S OKAY.
KARI (SKRITCH)
KARI

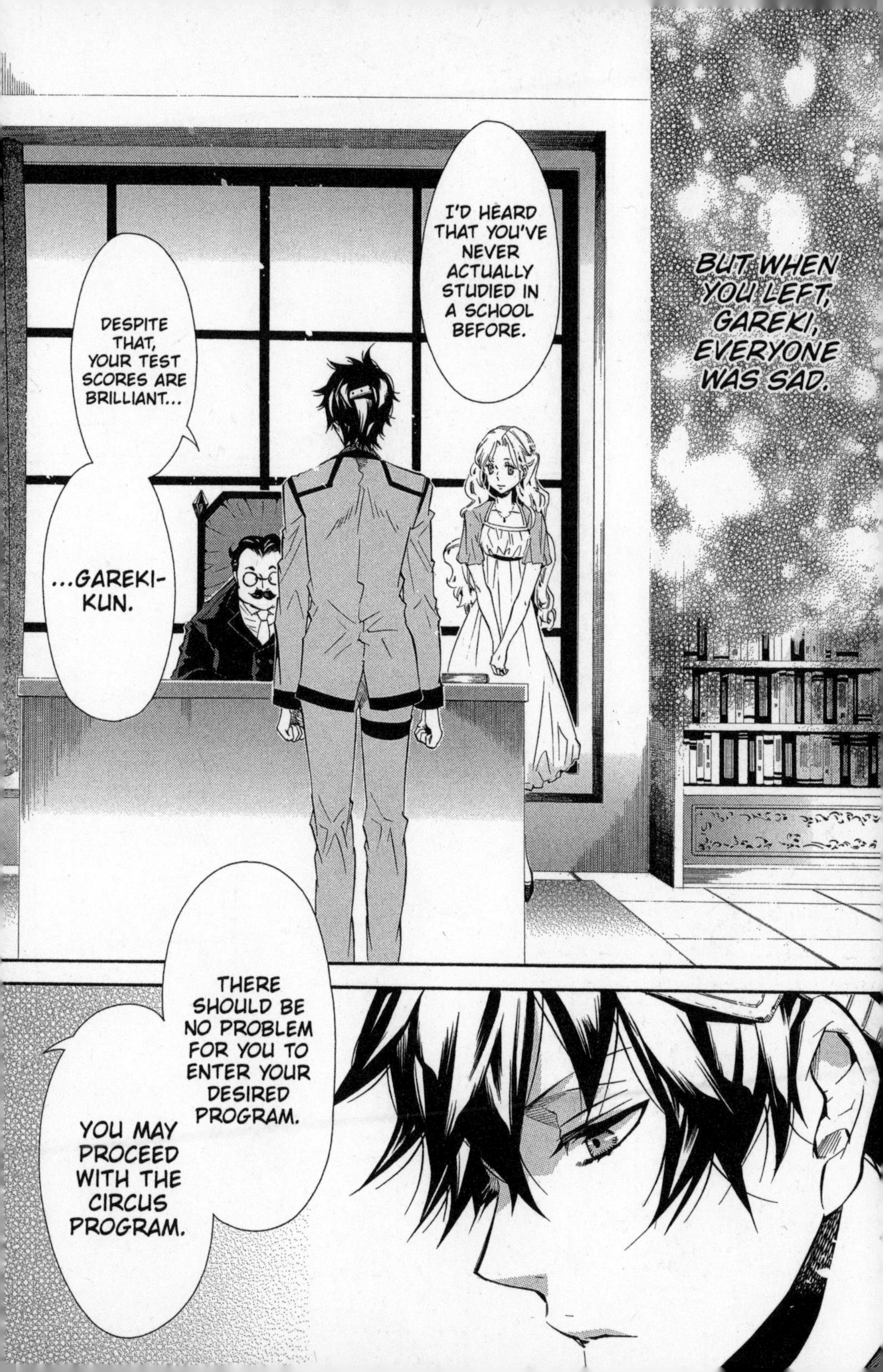
BUT WHEN YOU LEFT, GAREKI, EVERYONE WAS SAD.
I'D HEARD THAT YOU'VE NEVER ACTUALLY STUDIED IN A SCHOOL BEFORE.
DESPITE THAT, YOUR TEST SCORES ARE BRILLIANT...
...GAREKI-KUN.
THERE SHOULD BE NO PROBLEM FOR YOU TO ENTER YOUR DESIRED PROGRAM.
YOU MAY PROCEED WITH THE CIRCUS PROGRAM.

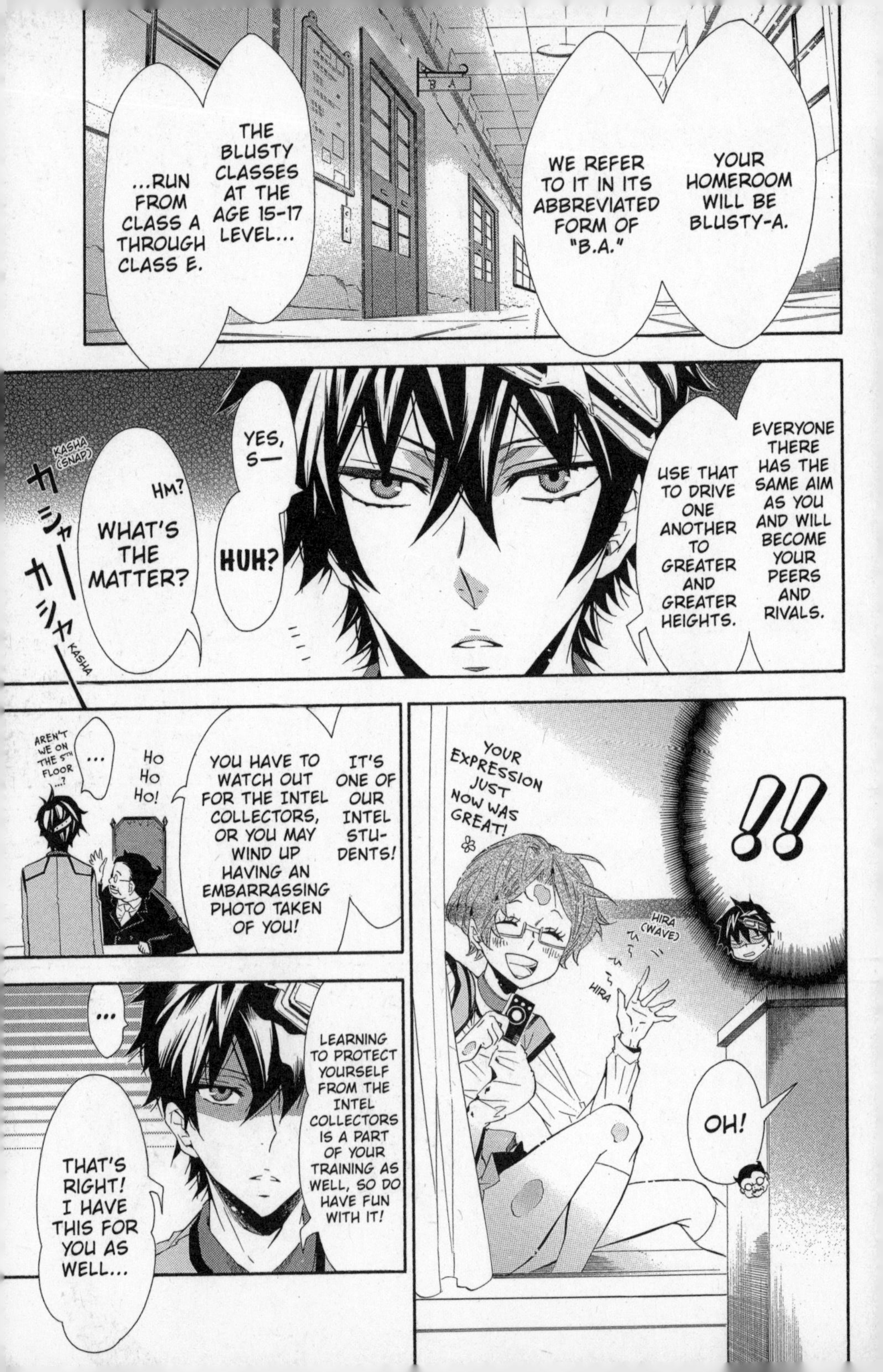
YOUR HOMEROOM WILL BE BLUSTY-A.
WE REFER TO IT IN ITS ABBREVIATED FORM OF "B.A."
THE BLUSTY CLASSES AT THE AGE 15-17 LEVEL...
...RUN FROM CLASS A THROUGH CLASS E.
EVERYONE THERE HAS THE SAME AIM AS YOU AND WILL BECOME YOUR PEERS AND RIVALS.
USE THAT TO DRIVE ONE ANOTHER TO GREATER AND GREATER HEIGHTS.
YES, S—
HUH?
カシャーカシャ
KASHA (SNAP)
KASHA
HM?
WHAT'S THE MATTER?
!!
YOUR EXPRESSION JUST NOW WAS GREAT!
HIRA (WAVE)
HIRA
OH!
IT'S ONE OF OUR INTEL STUDENTS!
YOU HAVE TO WATCH OUT FOR THE INTEL COLLECTORS, OR YOU MAY WIND UP HAVING AN EMBARRASSING PHOTO TAKEN OF YOU!
HO HO HO!
...
AREN'T WE ON THE 5TH FLOOR ...?
LEARNING TO PROTECT YOURSELF FROM THE INTEL COLLECTORS IS A PART OF YOUR TRAINING AS WELL, SO DO HAVE FUN WITH IT!
...
THAT'S RIGHT! I HAVE THIS FOR YOU AS WELL...

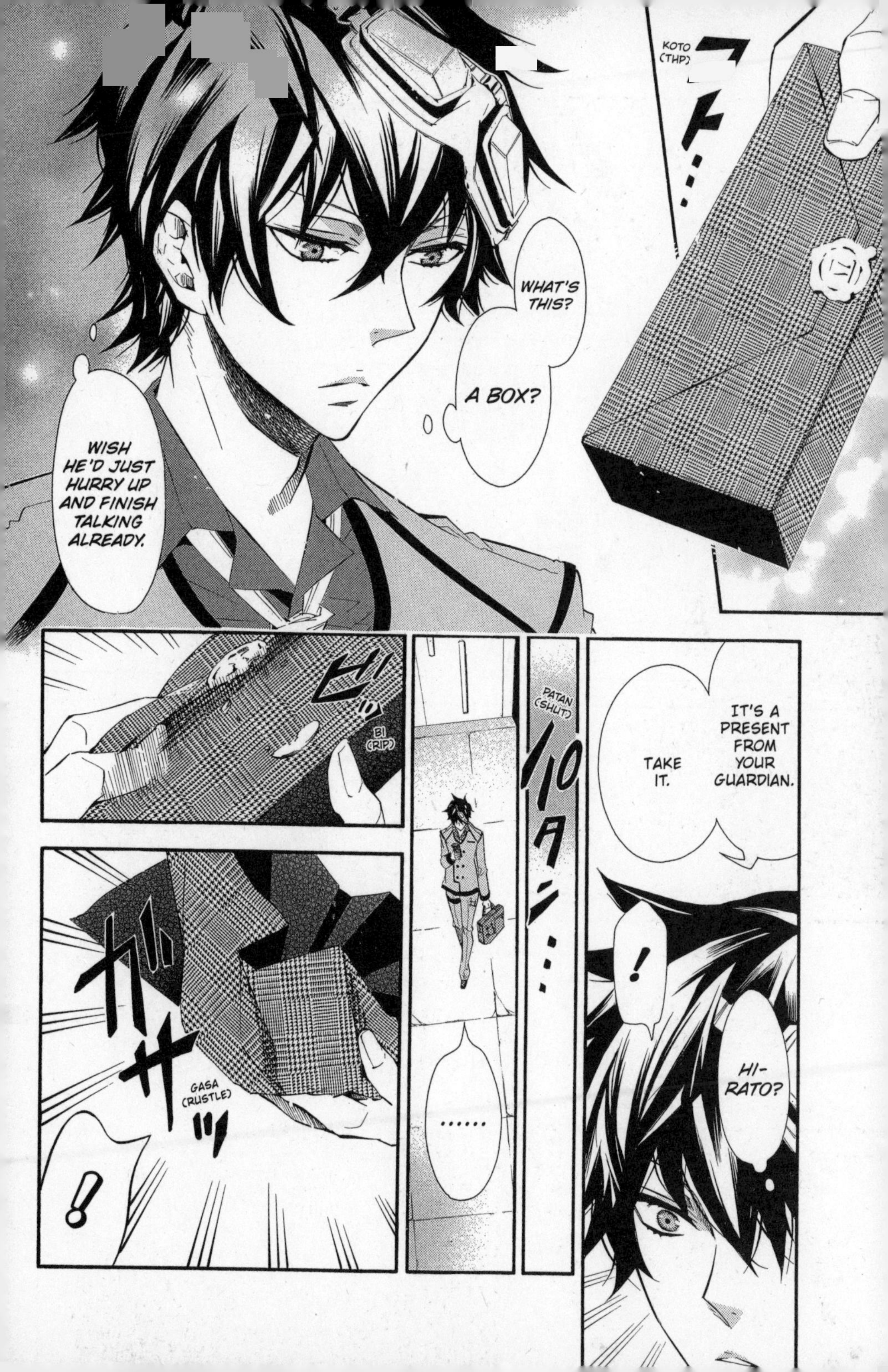
KOTO (THP)
WHAT'S THIS?
A BOX?
WISH HE'D JUST HURRY UP AND FINISH TALKING ALREADY.
IT'S A PRESENT FROM YOUR GUARDIAN.
TAKE IT.
!
HI-RATO?
PATAN (SHUT)
......
BI (RIP)
GASA (RUSTLE)
!

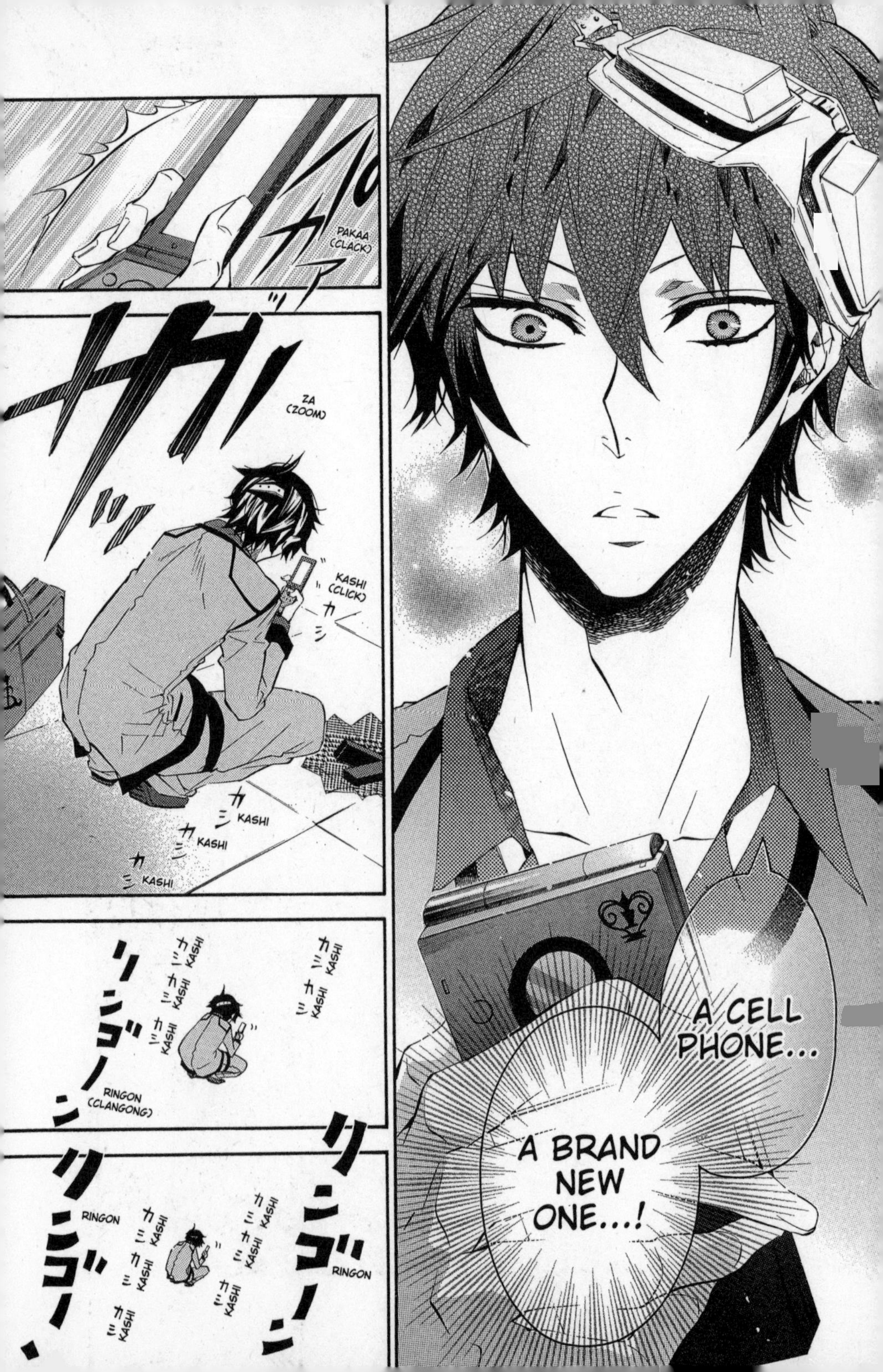
A CELL PHONE...
A BRAND NEW ONE...!
PAKAA (CLACK)
ZA (ZOOM)
KASHI (CLICK)
KASHI
KASHI
KASHI
KASHI KASHI
KASHI KASHI KASHI
RINGON (CLANGONG)
RINGON
KASHI KASHI KASHI
KASHI KASHI KASHI
RINGON

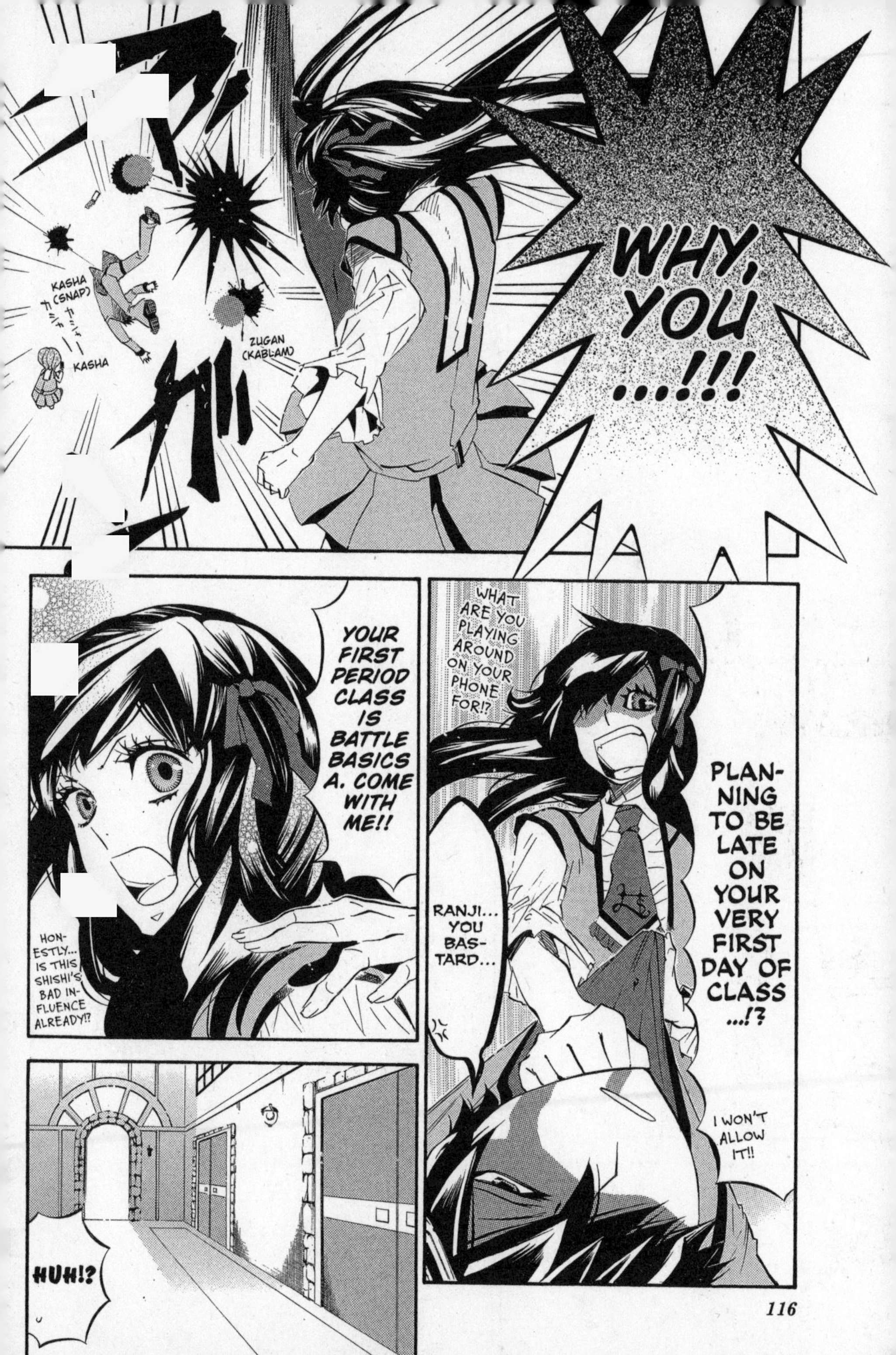
WHY, YOU ...!!!
ZUGAN (KABLAM)
KASHA (SNAP)
KASHA
WHAT ARE YOU PLAYING AROUND ON YOUR PHONE FOR!?
PLAN-NING TO BE LATE ON YOUR VERY FIRST DAY OF CLASS ...!?
RANJI... YOU BAS-TARD...
I WON'T ALLOW IT!!
YOUR FIRST PERIOD CLASS IS BATTLE BASICS A. COME WITH ME!!
HON-ESTLY... IS THIS SHISHI'S BAD IN-FLUENCE ALREADY!?
HUH!?

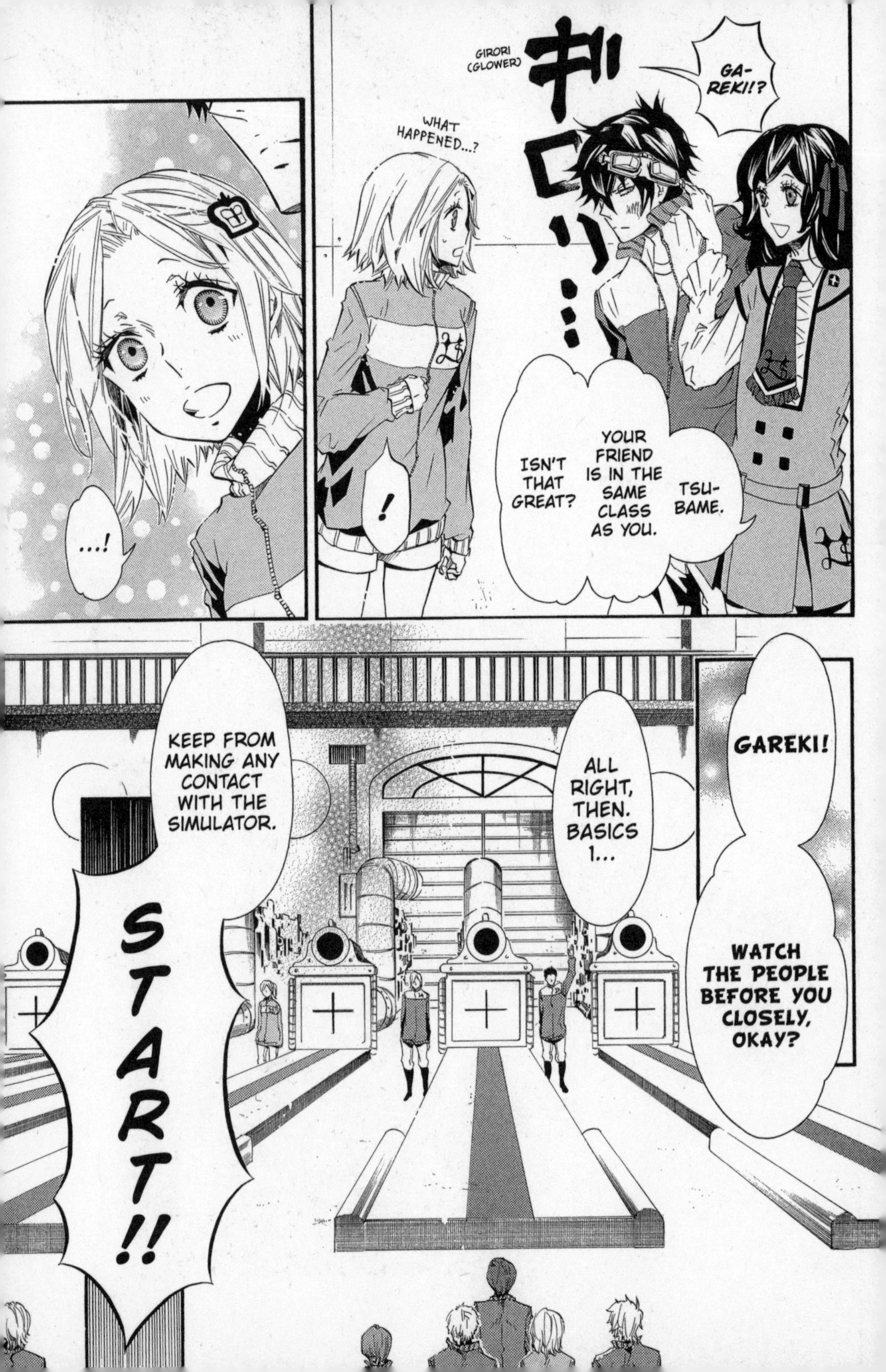
GA-REKI!?
GIRORI (GLOWER)
WHAT HAPPENED...?
TSU-BAME.
YOUR FRIEND IS IN THE SAME CLASS AS YOU.
ISN'T THAT GREAT?
!
...!
GAREKI!
WATCH THE PEOPLE BEFORE YOU CLOSELY, OKAY?
ALL RIGHT, THEN. BASICS 1...
KEEP FROM MAKING ANY CONTACT WITH THE SIMULATOR.
START!!

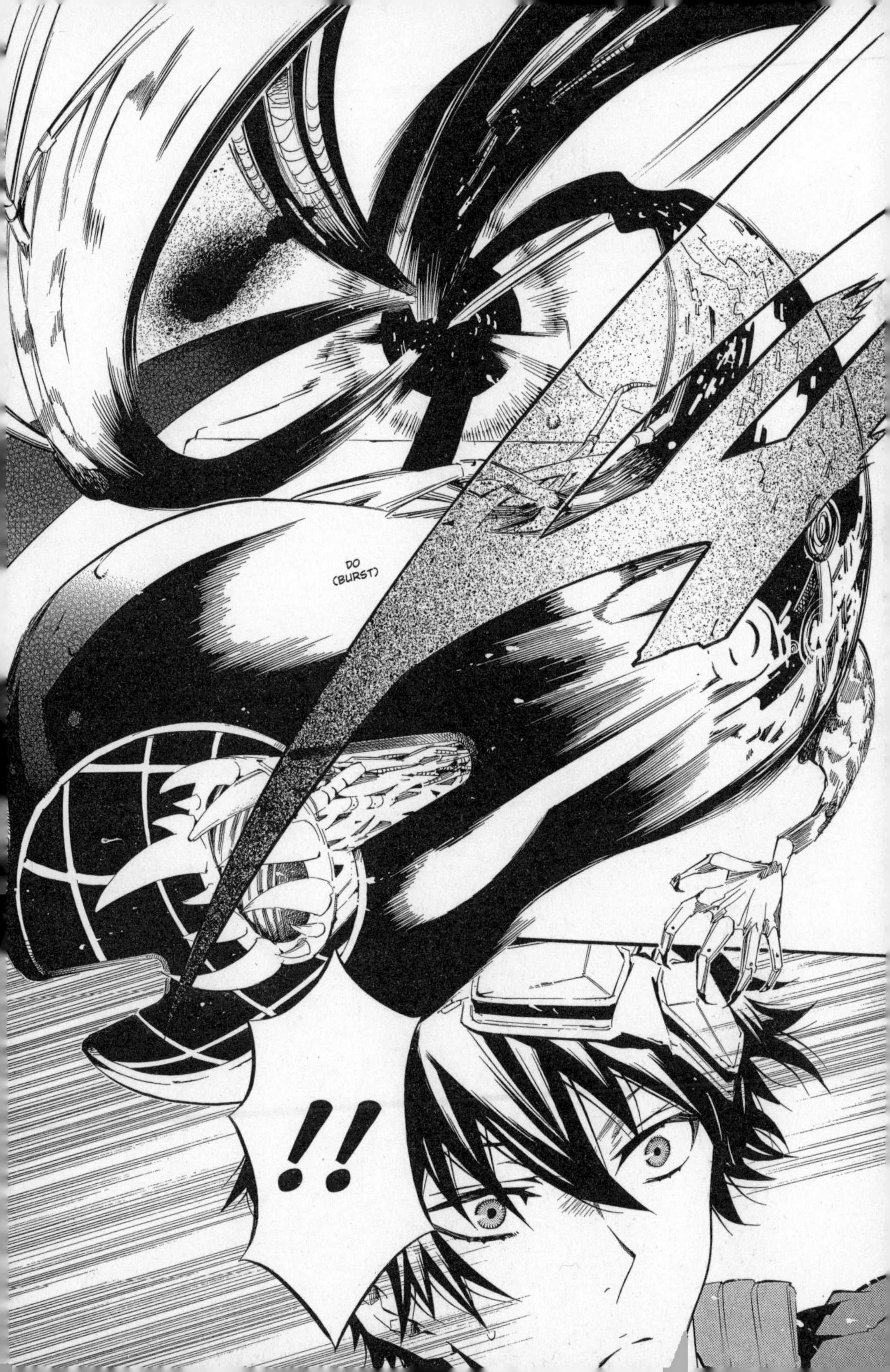
DO
(BURST)
!!

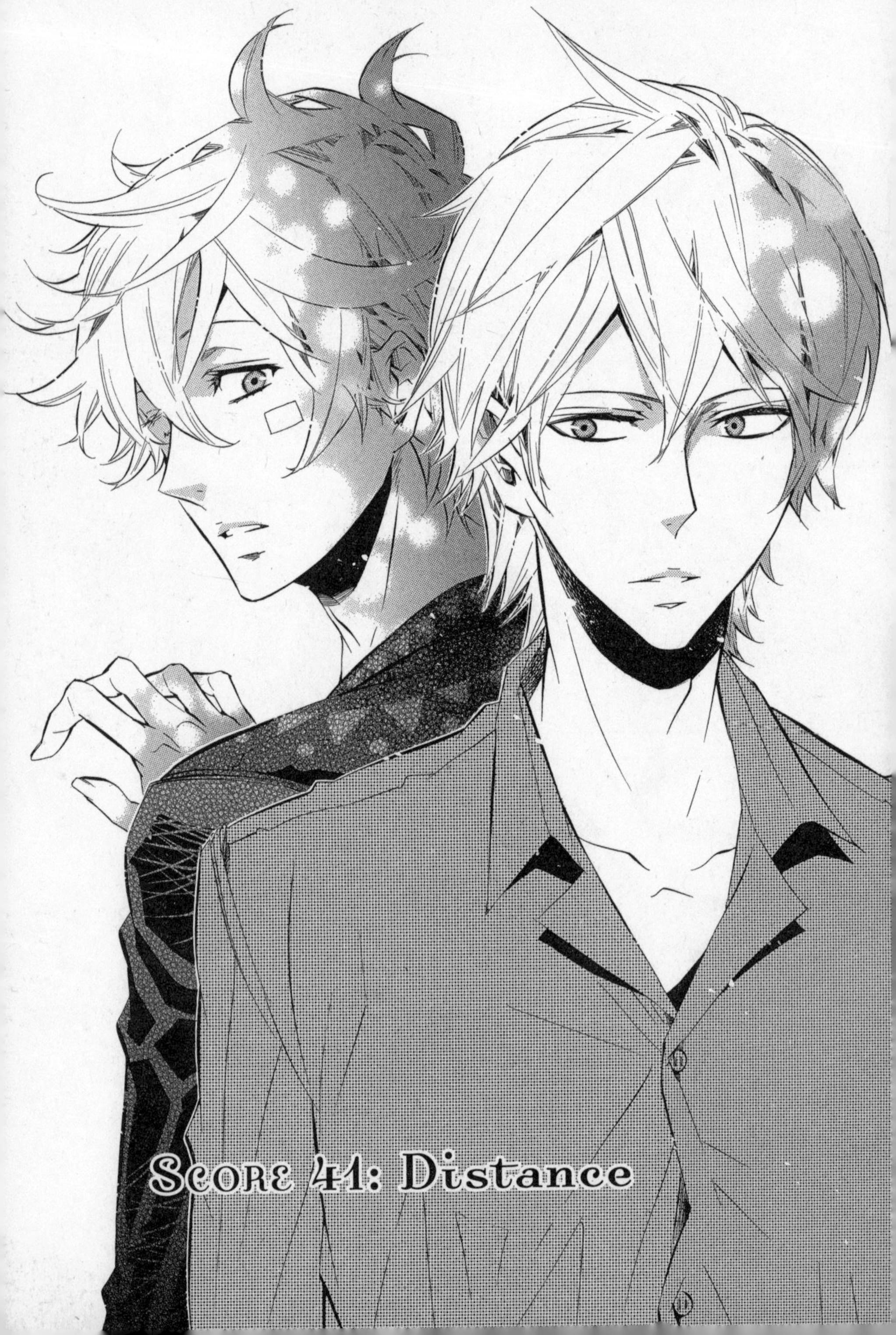
Score 41: Distance

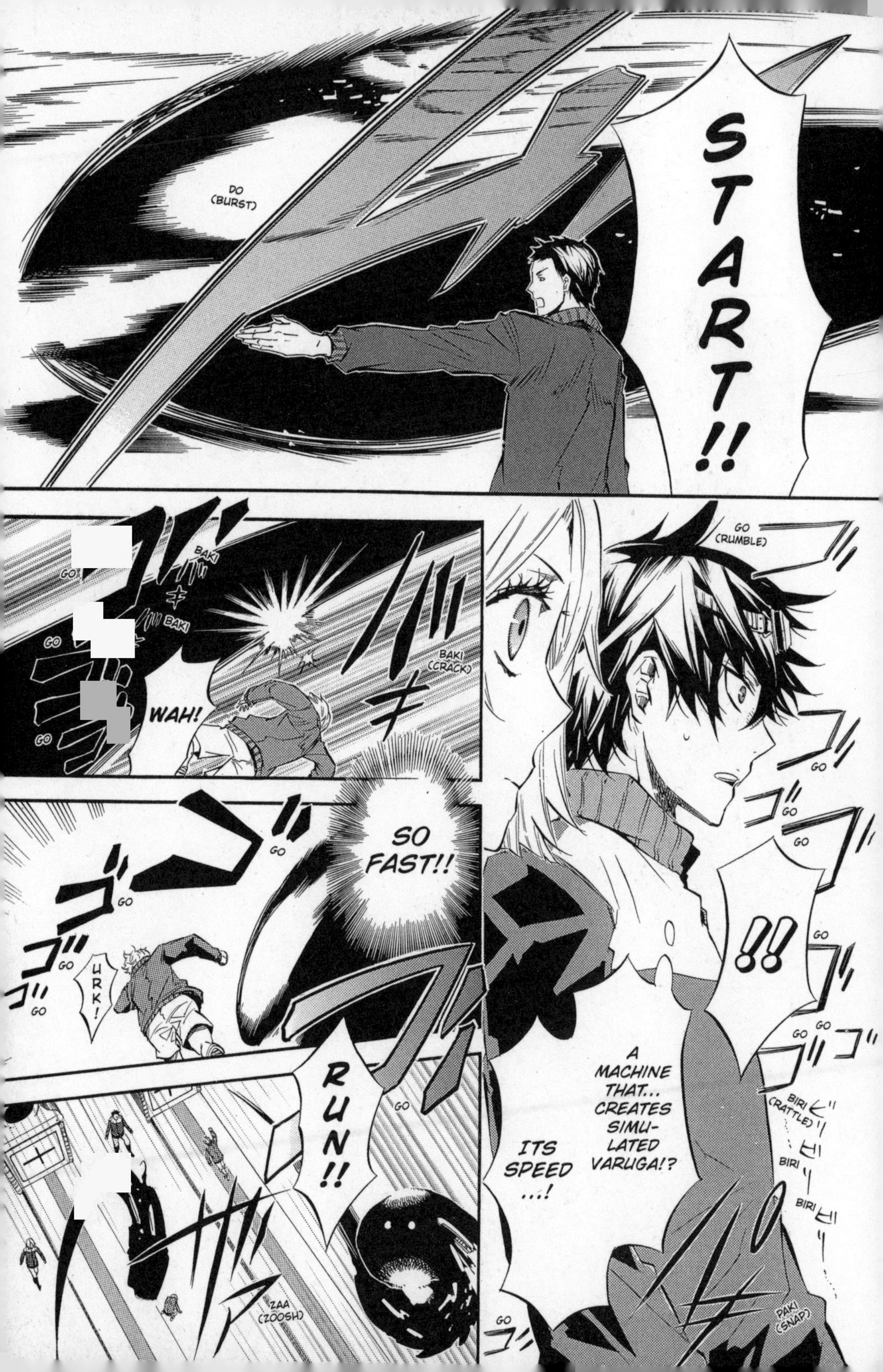
START!!
DO
(BURST)
GO
(RUMBLE)
GO
GO
GO
!!
GO
GO
GO
BIRI
(RATTLE)
BIRI
BIRI
A MACHINE THAT... CREATES SIMULATED VARUGA!?
ITS SPEED...!
PAKI
(SNAP)
GO
BAKI
GO
BAKI
GO
GO
BAKI
(CRACK)
WAH!
SO FAST!!
GO
GO
GO
GO
URK!
RUN!!
GO
ZAA
(ZOOSH)

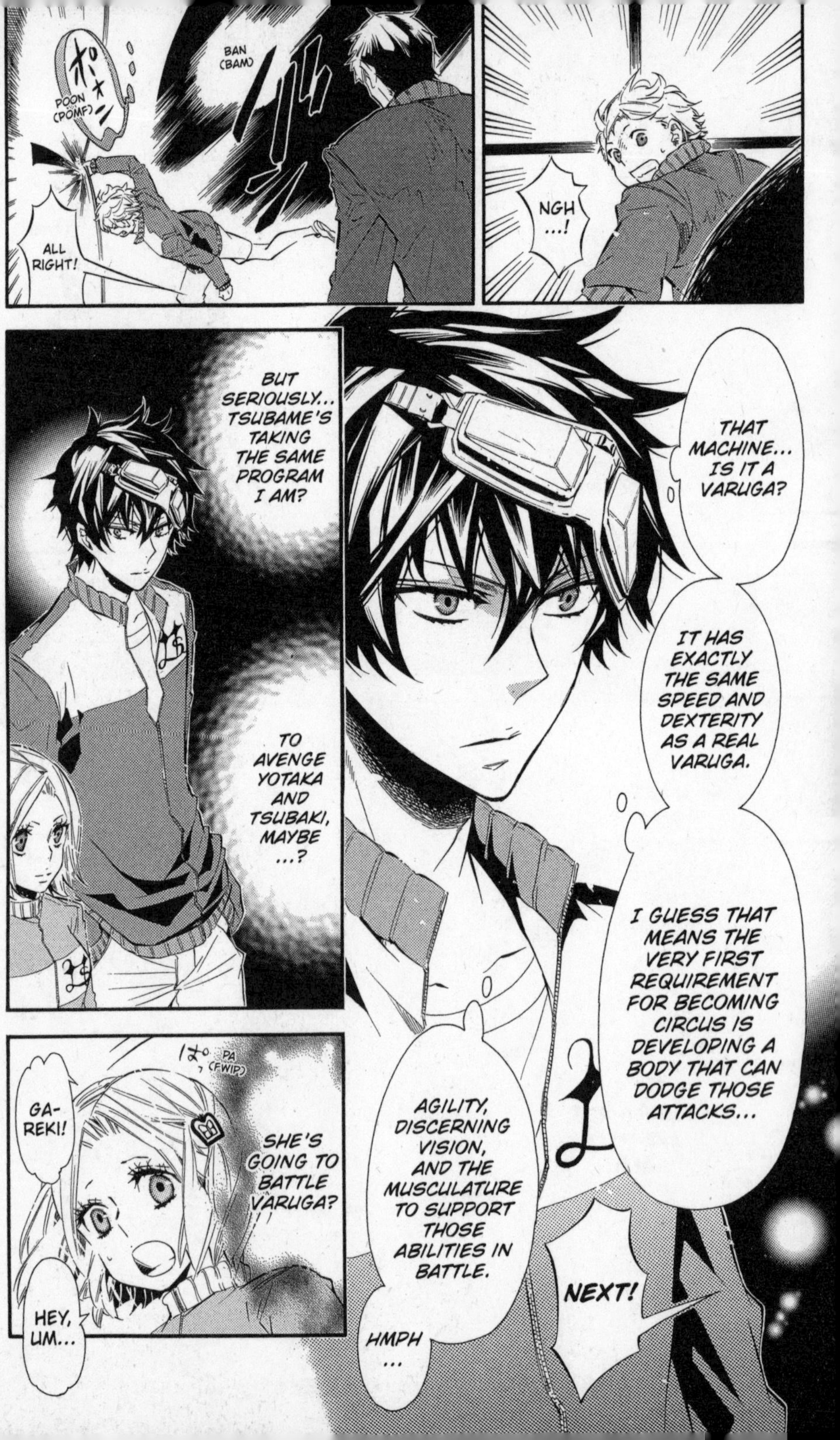
NGH ...!
BAN (BAM)
POON (POMF)
ALL RIGHT!
THAT MACHINE... IS IT A VARUGA?
IT HAS EXACTLY THE SAME SPEED AND DEXTERITY AS A REAL VARUGA.
I GUESS THAT MEANS THE VERY FIRST REQUIREMENT FOR BECOMING CIRCUS IS DEVELOPING A BODY THAT CAN DODGE THOSE ATTACKS...
AGILITY, DISCERNING VISION, AND THE MUSCULATURE TO SUPPORT THOSE ABILITIES IN BATTLE.
NEXT!
HMPH ...
BUT SERIOUSLY... TSUBAME'S TAKING THE SAME PROGRAM I AM?
TO AVENGE YOTAKA AND TSUBAKI, MAYBE ...?
PA (FWIP)
GA-REKI!
SHE'S GOING TO BATTLE VARUGA?
HEY, UM...

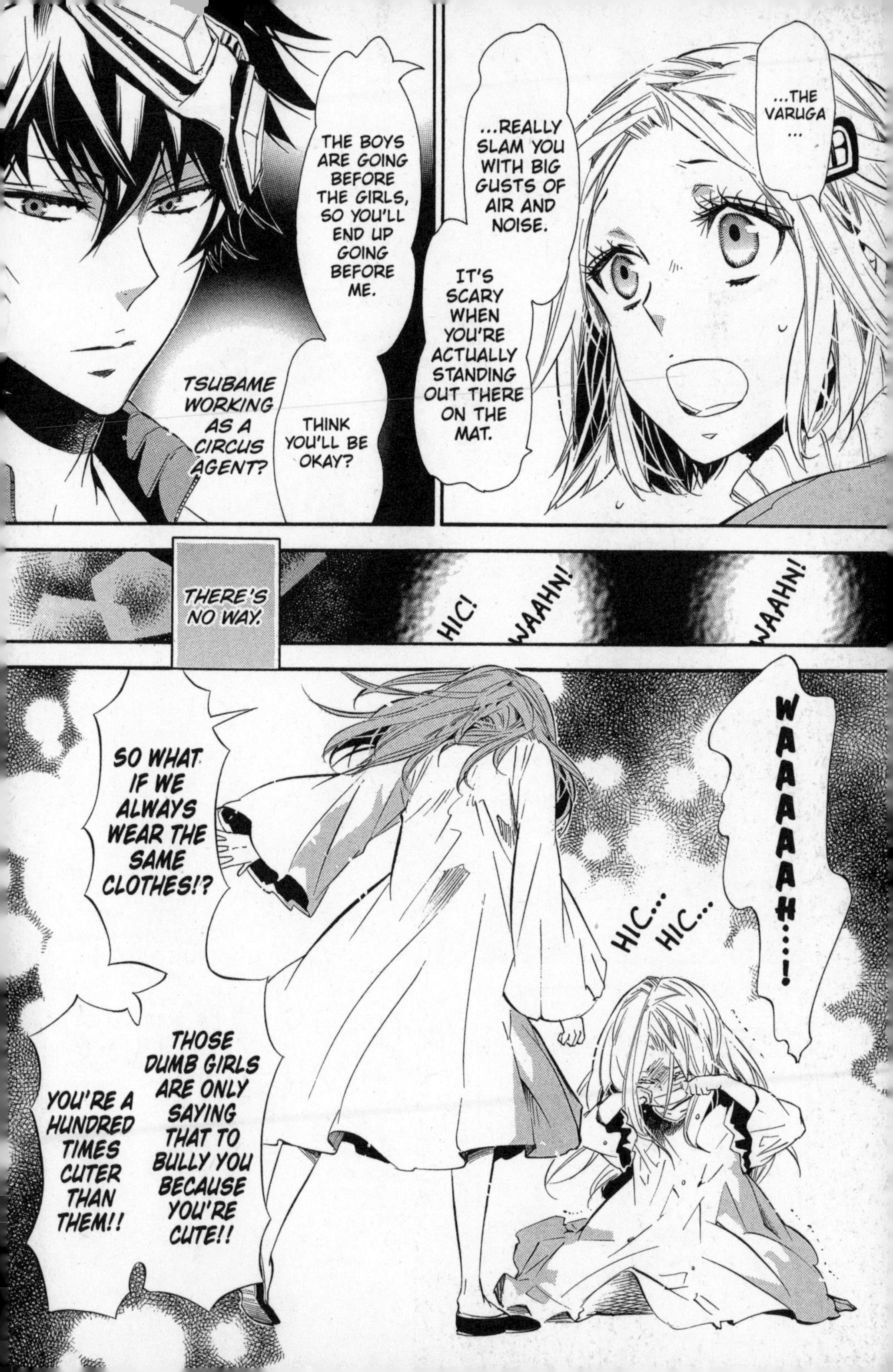
...THE VARUGA ...
...REALLY SLAM YOU WITH BIG GUSTS OF AIR AND NOISE.
IT'S SCARY WHEN YOU'RE ACTUALLY STANDING OUT THERE ON THE MAT.
THE BOYS ARE GOING BEFORE THE GIRLS, SO YOU'LL END UP GOING BEFORE ME.
THINK YOU'LL BE OKAY?
TSUBAME WORKING AS A CIRCUS AGENT?
WAAHN!
WAAHN!
HIC!
THERE'S NO WAY.
WAAAAAAH...!
HIC... HIC...
SO WHAT IF WE ALWAYS WEAR THE SAME CLOTHES!?
THOSE DUMB GIRLS ARE ONLY SAYING THAT TO BULLY YOU BECAUSE YOU'RE CUTE!!
YOU'RE A HUNDRED TIMES CUTER THAN THEM!!

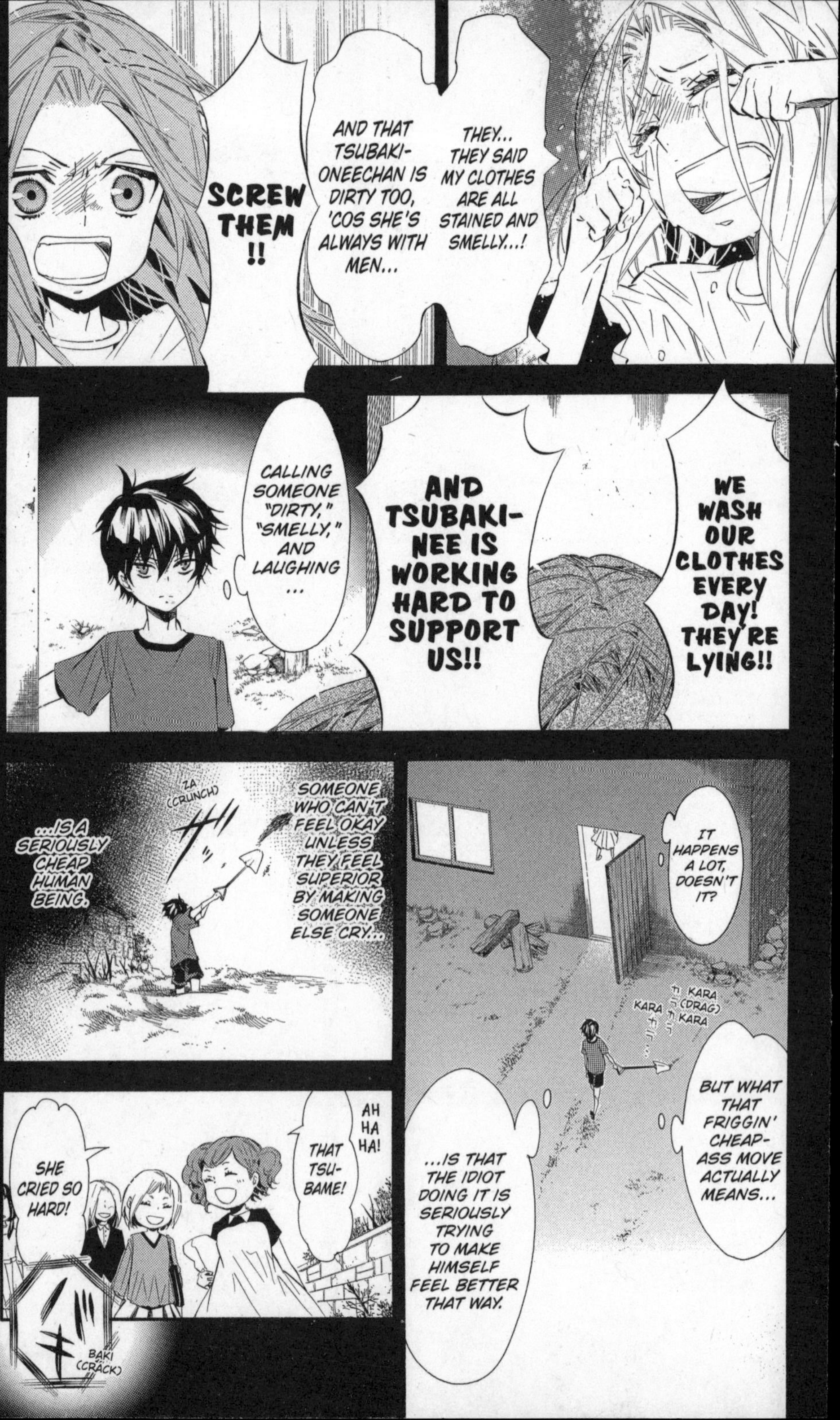
THEY... THEY SAID MY CLOTHES ARE ALL STAINED AND SMELLY...!
AND THAT TSUBAKI-ONEECHAN IS DIRTY TOO, 'COS SHE'S ALWAYS WITH MEN...
SCREW THEM!!
WE WASH OUR CLOTHES EVERY DAY! THEY'RE LYING!!
AND TSUBAKI-NEE IS WORKING HARD TO SUPPORT US!!
CALLING SOMEONE "DIRTY," "SMELLY," AND LAUGHING...
IT HAPPENS A LOT, DOESN'T IT?
KARA (DRAG) KARA
KARA
BUT WHAT THAT FRIGGIN' CHEAP-ASS MOVE ACTUALLY MEANS...
...IS THAT THE IDIOT DOING IT IS SERIOUSLY TRYING TO MAKE HIMSELF FEEL BETTER THAT WAY.
SOMEONE WHO CAN'T FEEL OKAY UNLESS THEY FEEL SUPERIOR BY MAKING SOMEONE ELSE CRY...
ZA (CRUNCH)
...IS A SERIOUSLY CHEAP HUMAN BEING.
AH HA HA! THAT TSU-BAME!
SHE CRIED SO HARD!
BAKI (CRACK)

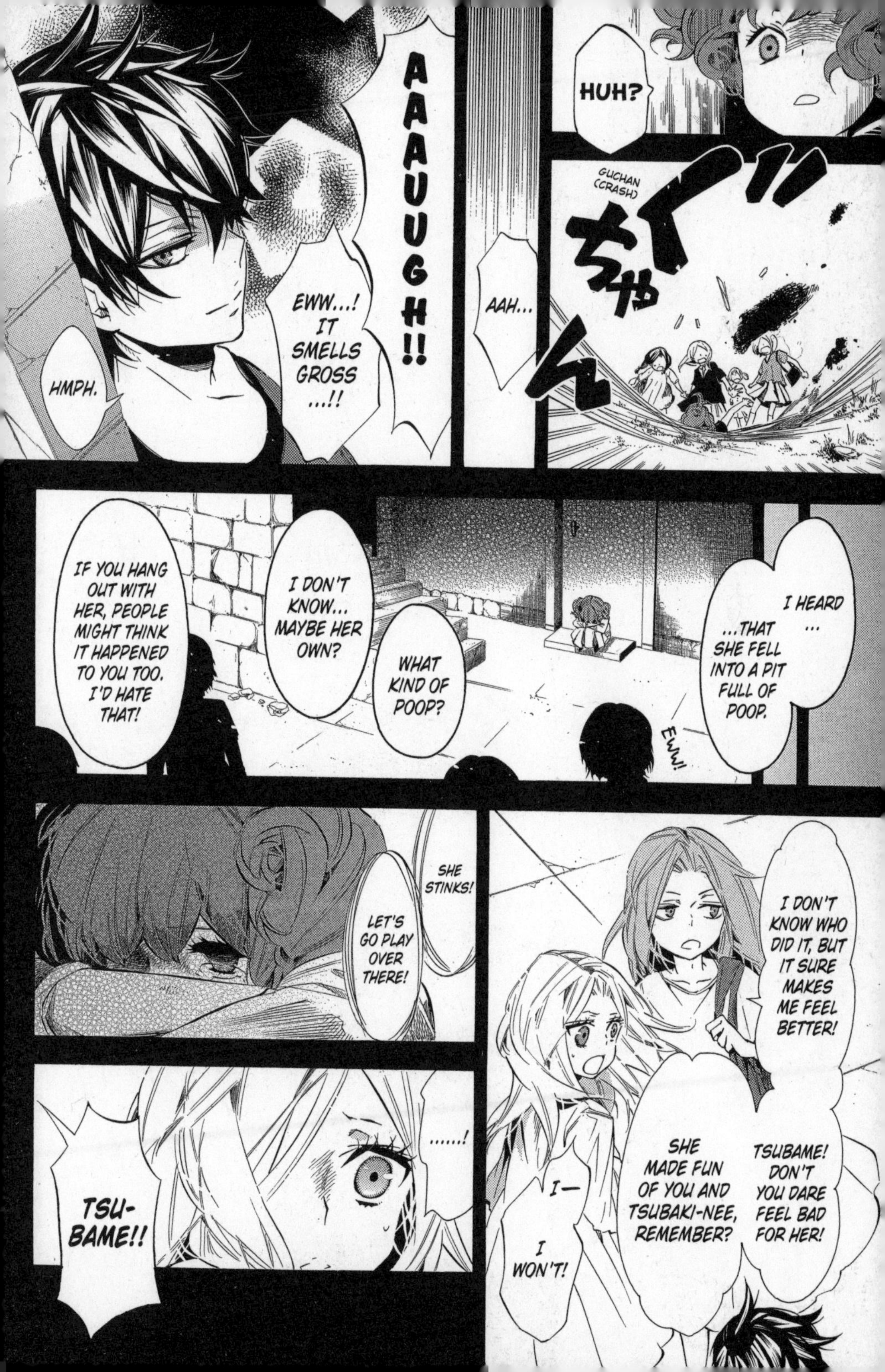
HUH?
GUCHAN (CRASH)
ぐちゃん
AAH...
AAAUUGH!!
EWW...! IT SMELLS GROSS ...!!
HMPH.
I HEARD ...
...THAT SHE FELL INTO A PIT FULL OF POOP.
EWW!
WHAT KIND OF POOP?
I DON'T KNOW... MAYBE HER OWN?
IF YOU HANG OUT WITH HER, PEOPLE MIGHT THINK IT HAPPENED TO YOU TOO. I'D HATE THAT!
I DON'T KNOW WHO DID IT, BUT IT SURE MAKES ME FEEL BETTER!
TSUBAME! DON'T YOU DARE FEEL BAD FOR HER!
SHE MADE FUN OF YOU AND TSUBAKI-NEE, REMEMBER?
I—
I WON'T!
SHE STINKS!
LET'S GO PLAY OVER THERE!
......!
TSU-BAME!!

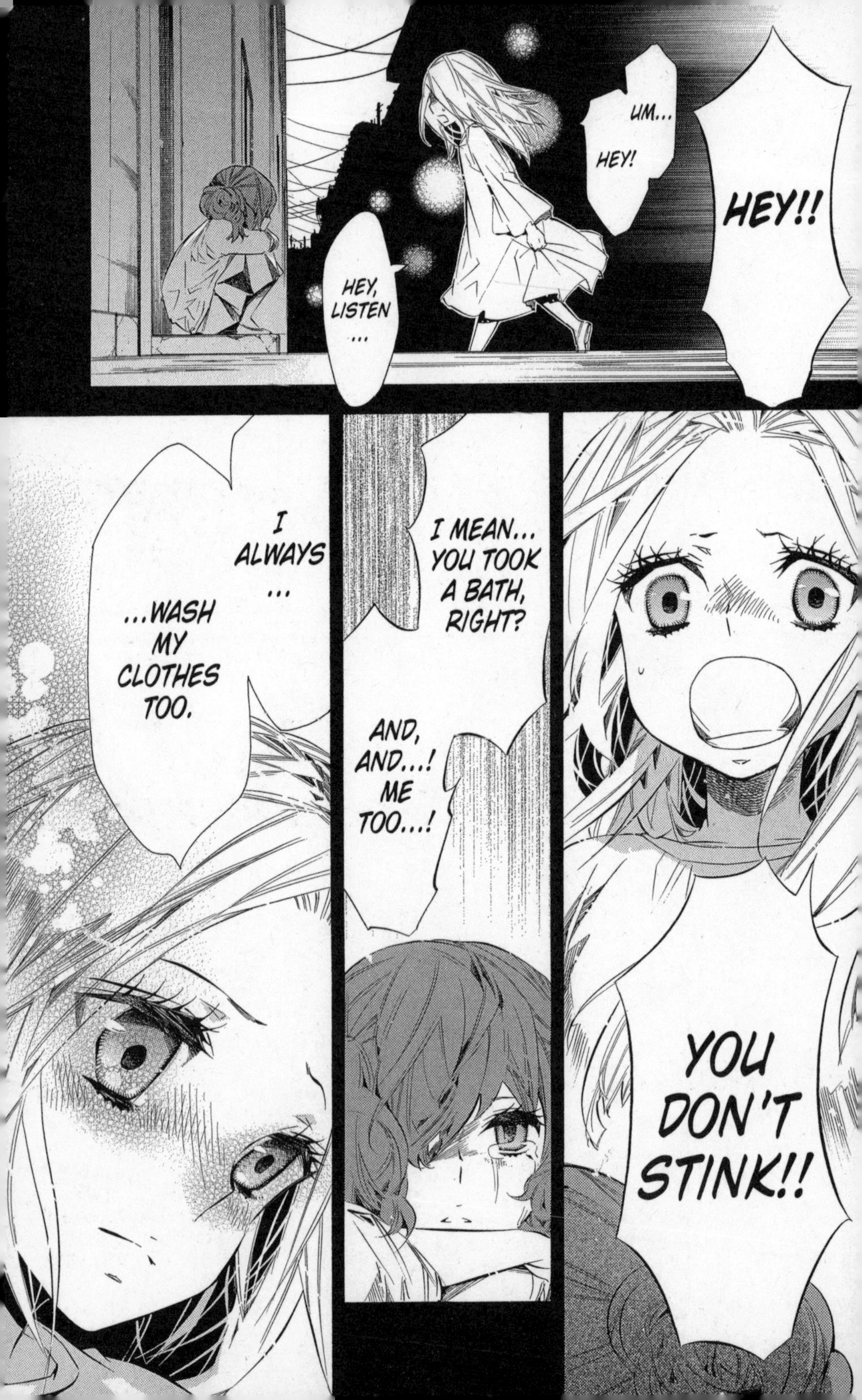
HEY!!
UM... HEY!
HEY, LISTEN ...
YOU DON'T STINK!!
I MEAN... YOU TOOK A BATH, RIGHT?
AND, AND...! ME TOO...!
I ALWAYS ...
...WASH MY CLOTHES TOO.

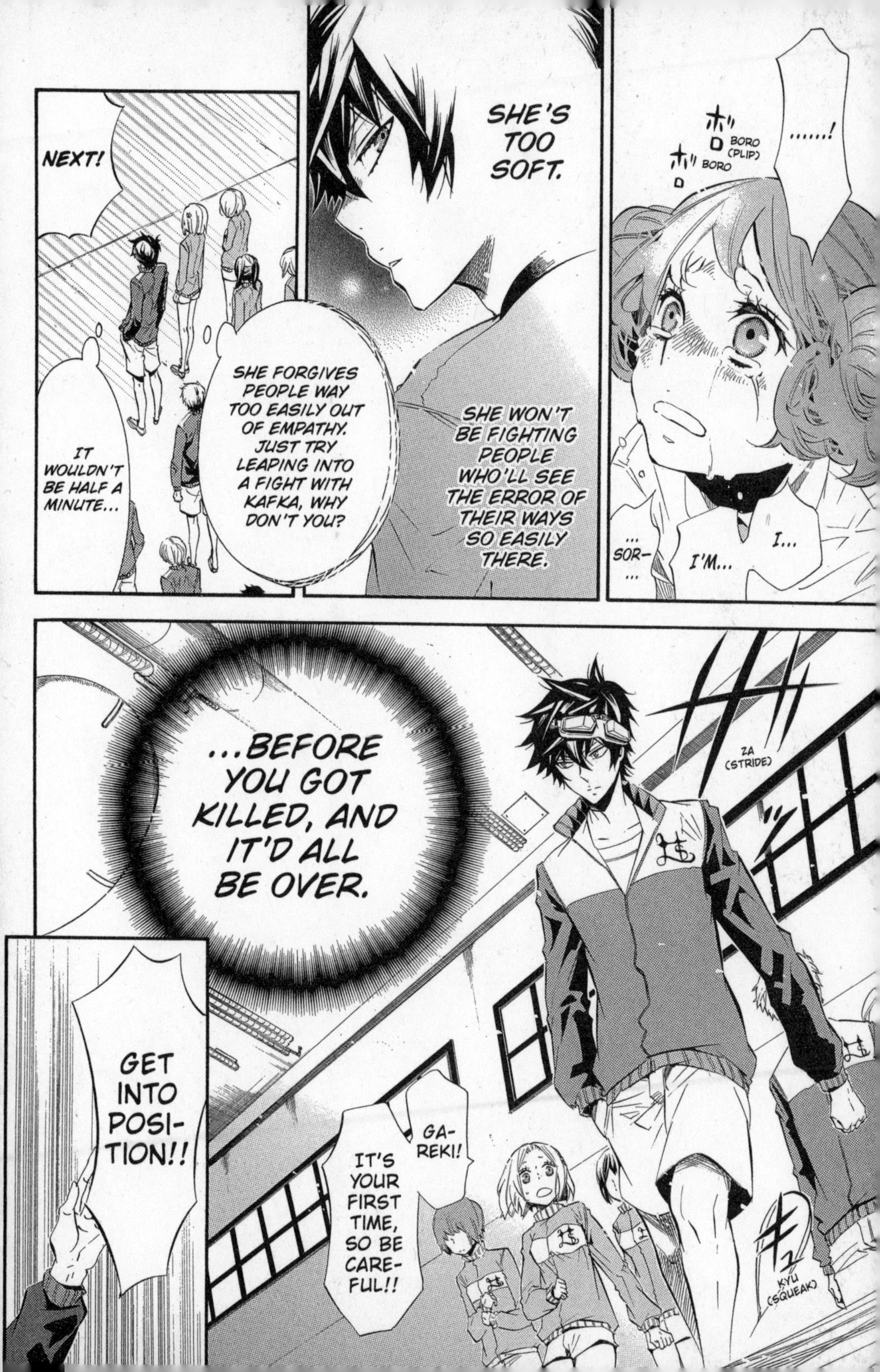
......!
ボロ BORO (PLIP)
ボロ BORO
I...
I'M...
...SOR-...
SHE'S TOO SOFT.
SHE WON'T BE FIGHTING PEOPLE WHO'LL SEE THE ERROR OF THEIR WAYS SO EASILY THERE.
SHE FORGIVES PEOPLE WAY TOO EASILY OUT OF EMPATHY. JUST TRY LEAPING INTO A FIGHT WITH KAFKA, WHY DON'T YOU?
NEXT!
IT WOULDN'T BE HALF A MINUTE...
ZA (STRIDE)
...BEFORE YOU GOT KILLED, AND IT'D ALL BE OVER.
KYU (SQUEAK)
GA-REKI!
IT'S YOUR FIRST TIME, SO BE CARE-FUL!!
GET INTO POSI-TION!!

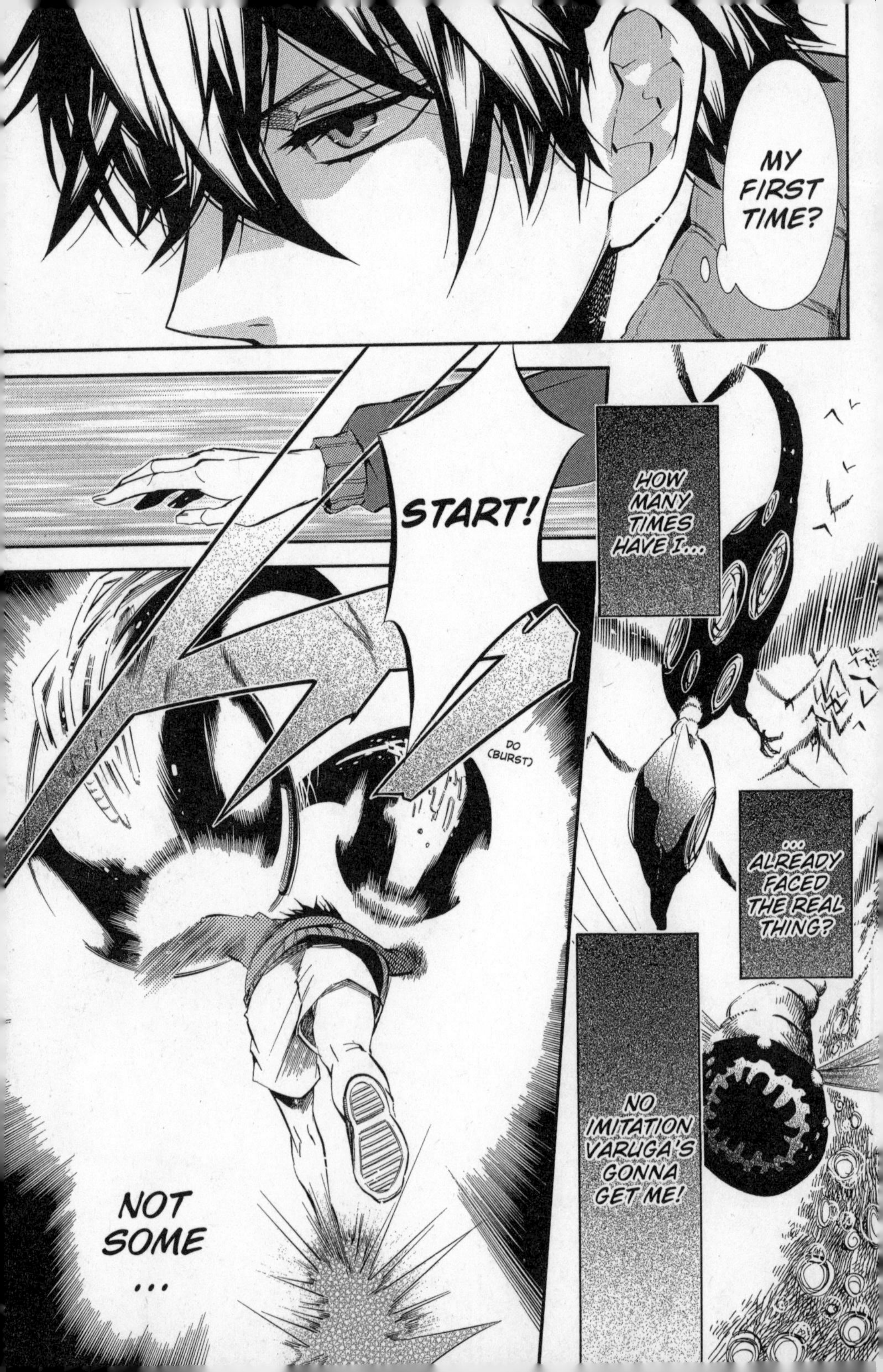
MY FIRST TIME?
START!
HOW MANY TIMES HAVE I...
...ALREADY FACED THE REAL THING?
DO (BURST)
NOT SOME ...
NO IMITATION VARUGA'S GONNA GET ME!

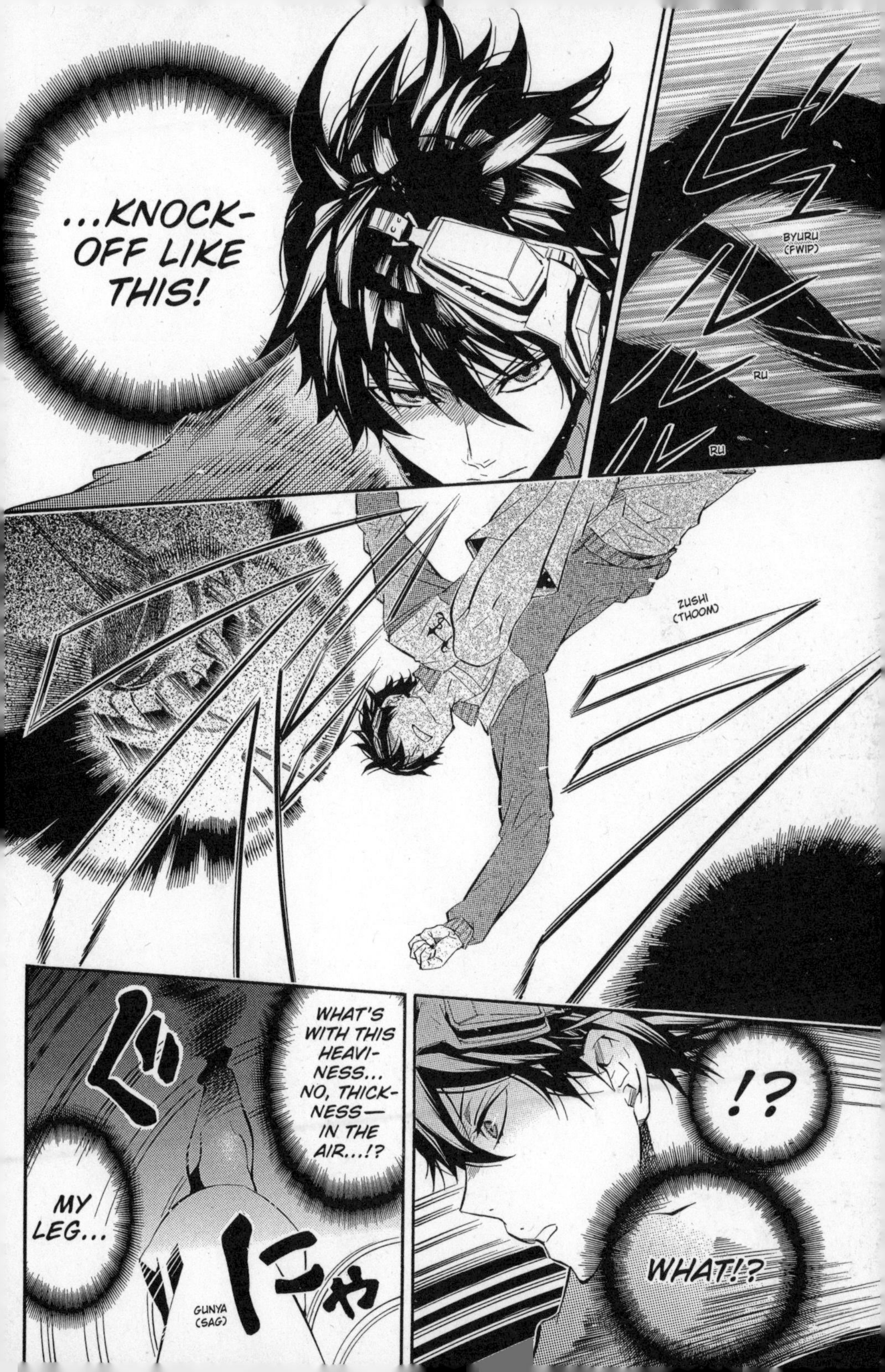
BYURU (FWIP)
RU
RU
...KNOCK-OFF LIKE THIS!
ZUSHI (THOOM)
!?
WHAT!?
WHAT'S WITH THIS HEAVINESS... NO, THICKNESS—IN THE AIR...!?
MY LEG...
ぐにゃ
GUNYA (SAG)

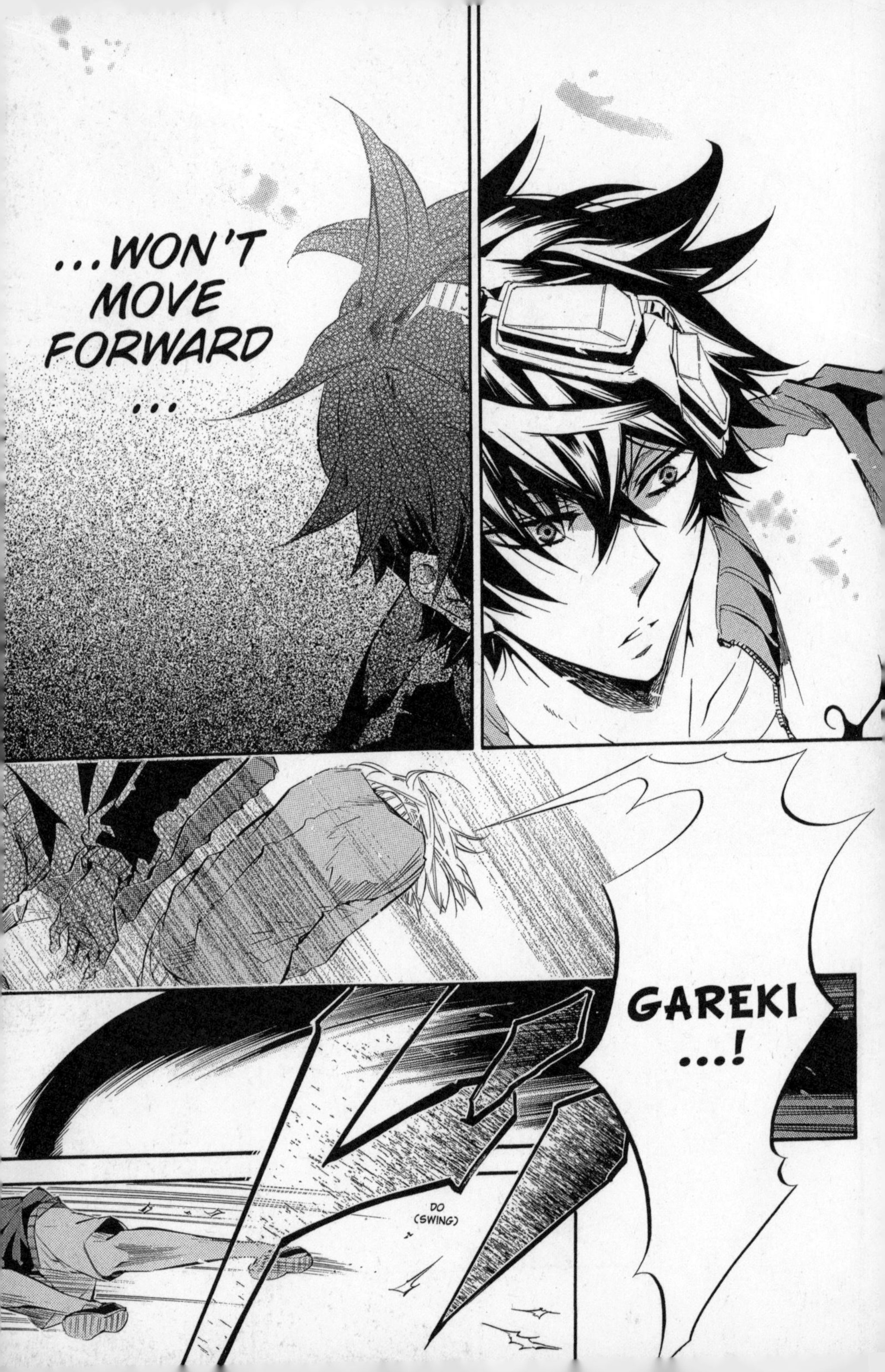
...WON'T MOVE FORWARD ...
GAREKI ...!
DO (SWING)

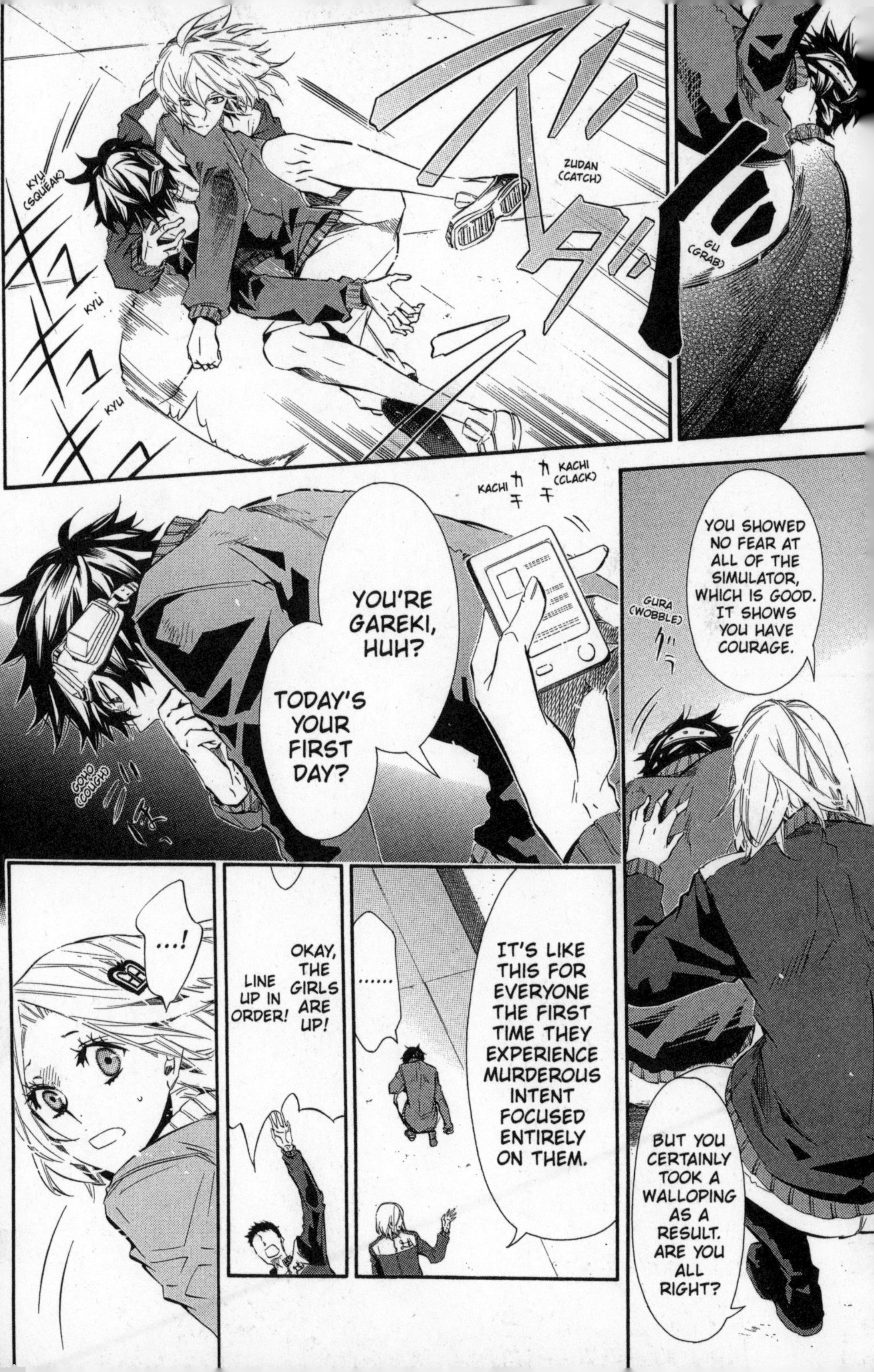
GU (GRAB)
ZUDAN (CATCH)
KYU (SQUEAK)
KYU
KYU
GURA (WOBBLE)
YOU SHOWED NO FEAR AT ALL OF THE SIMULATOR, WHICH IS GOOD. IT SHOWS YOU HAVE COURAGE.
BUT YOU CERTAINLY TOOK A WALLOPING AS A RESULT. ARE YOU ALL RIGHT?
KACHI (CLACK)
KACHI
YOU'RE GAREKI, HUH?
TODAY'S YOUR FIRST DAY?
GOHO (COUGH)
IT'S LIKE THIS FOR EVERYONE THE FIRST TIME THEY EXPERIENCE MURDEROUS INTENT FOCUSED ENTIRELY ON THEM.
......
OKAY, THE GIRLS ARE UP!
LINE UP IN ORDER!
...!

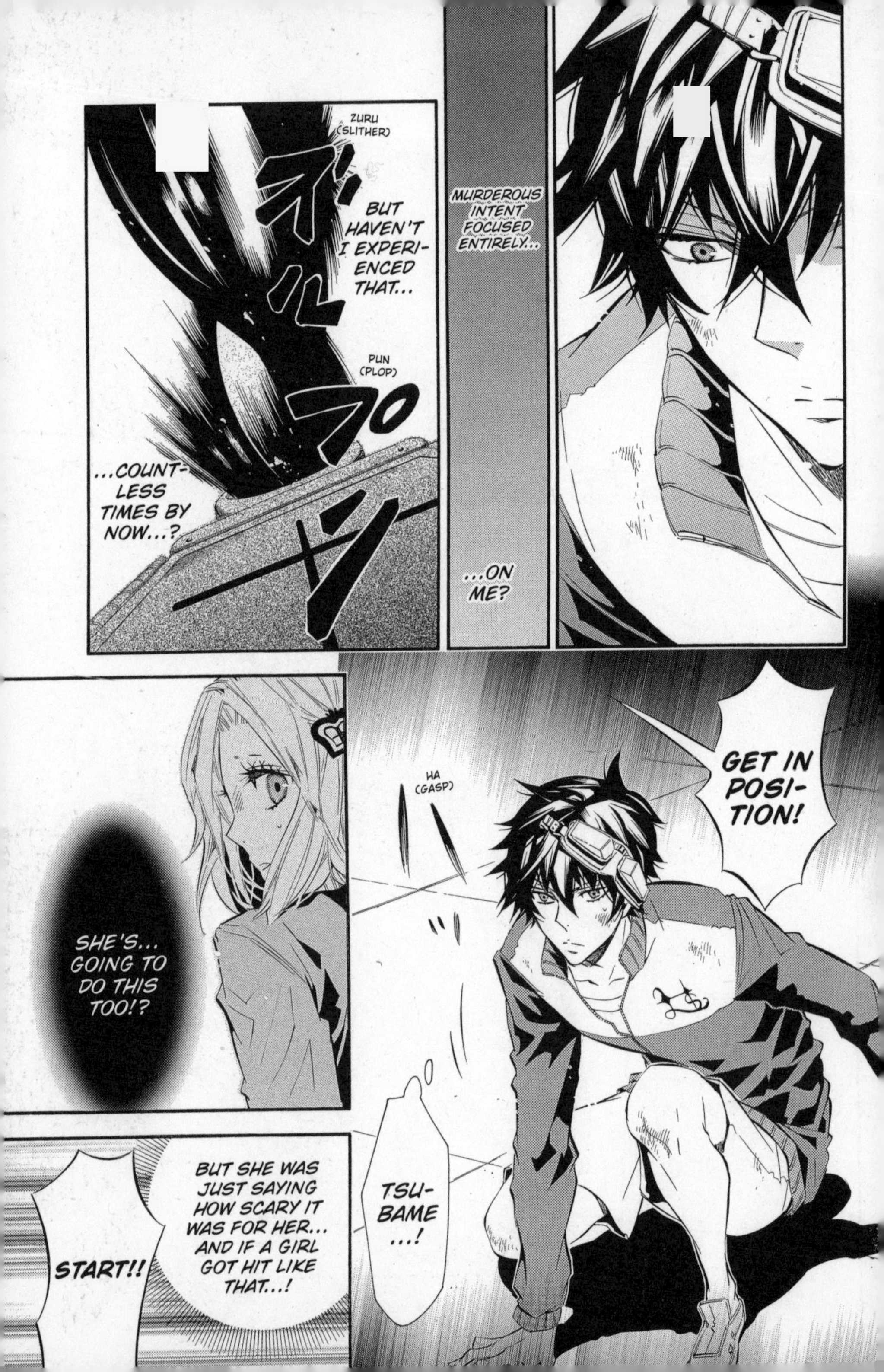
MURDEROUS INTENT FOCUSED ENTIRELY...
...ON ME?
ZURU (SLITHER)
BUT HAVEN'T I EXPERIENCED THAT...
PUN (PLOP)
...COUNTLESS TIMES BY NOW...?
GET IN POSITION!
HA (GASP)
TSUBAME...!
SHE'S... GOING TO DO THIS TOO!?
BUT SHE WAS JUST SAYING HOW SCARY IT WAS FOR HER... AND IF A GIRL GOT HIT LIKE THAT...!
START!!

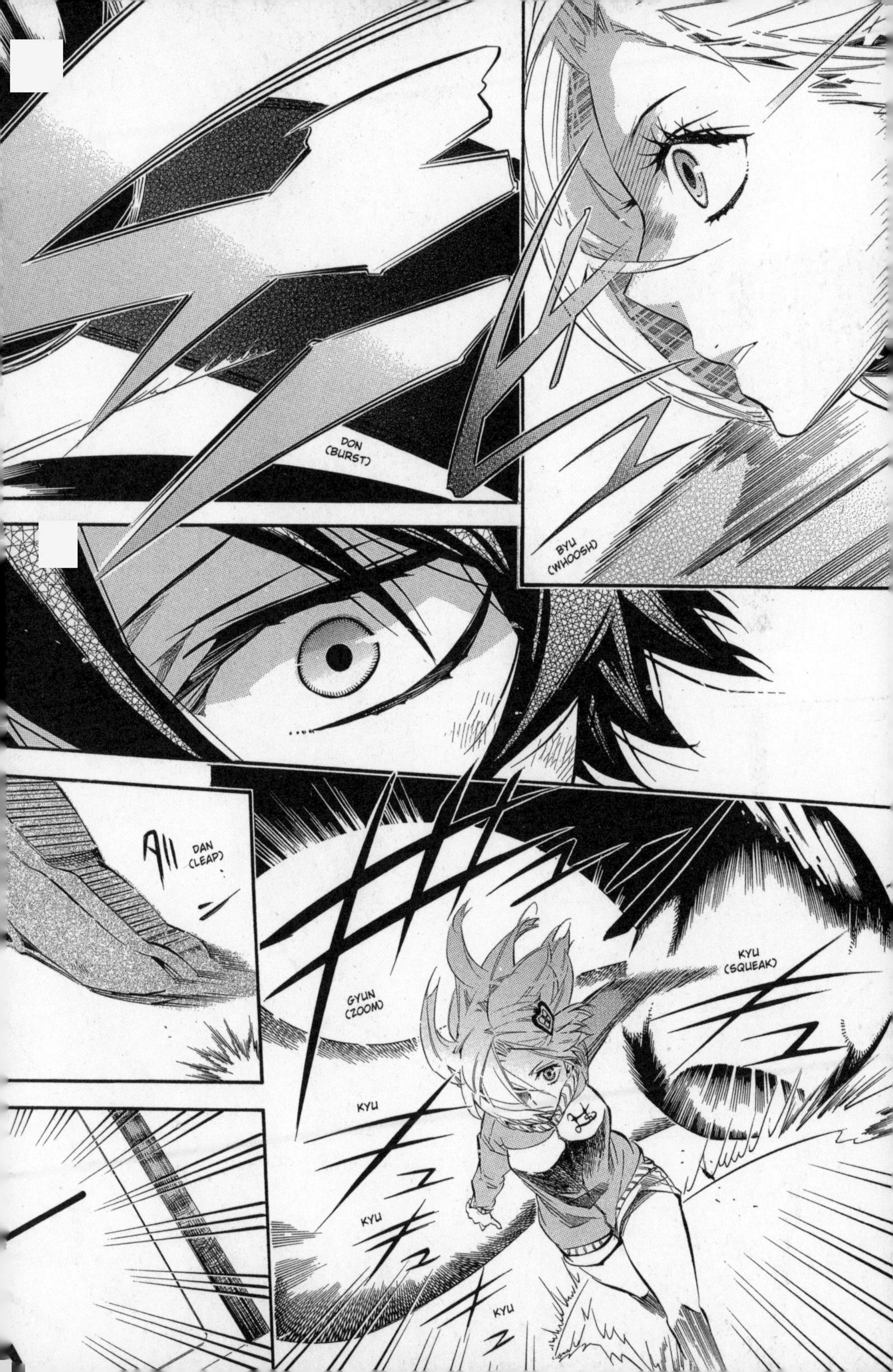
BYU
(WHOOSH)
DON
(BURST)
KYU
(SQUEAK)
GYUN
(ZOOM)
KYU
KYU
KYU
DAN
(LEAP)

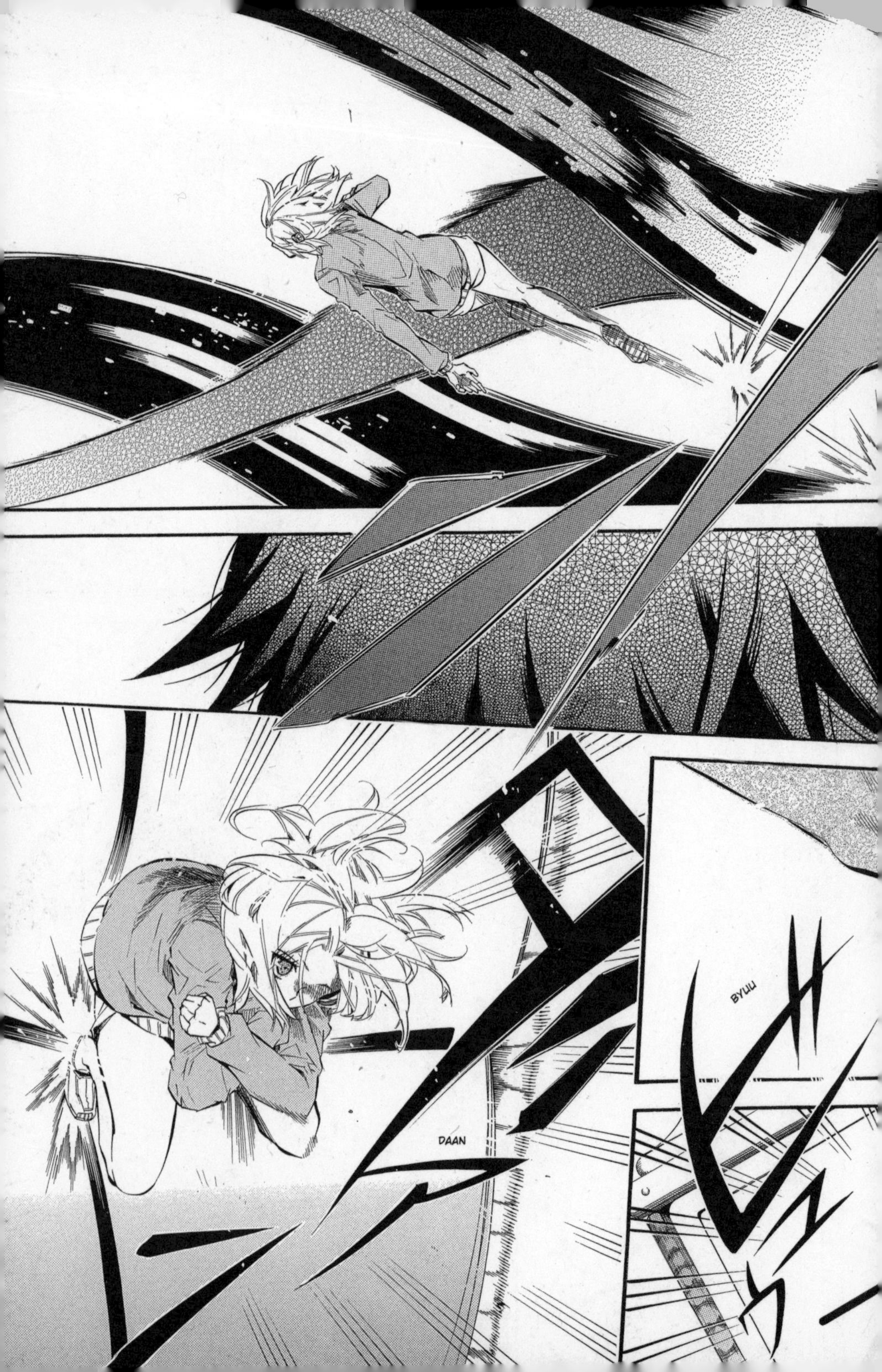
BYUU
DAAN

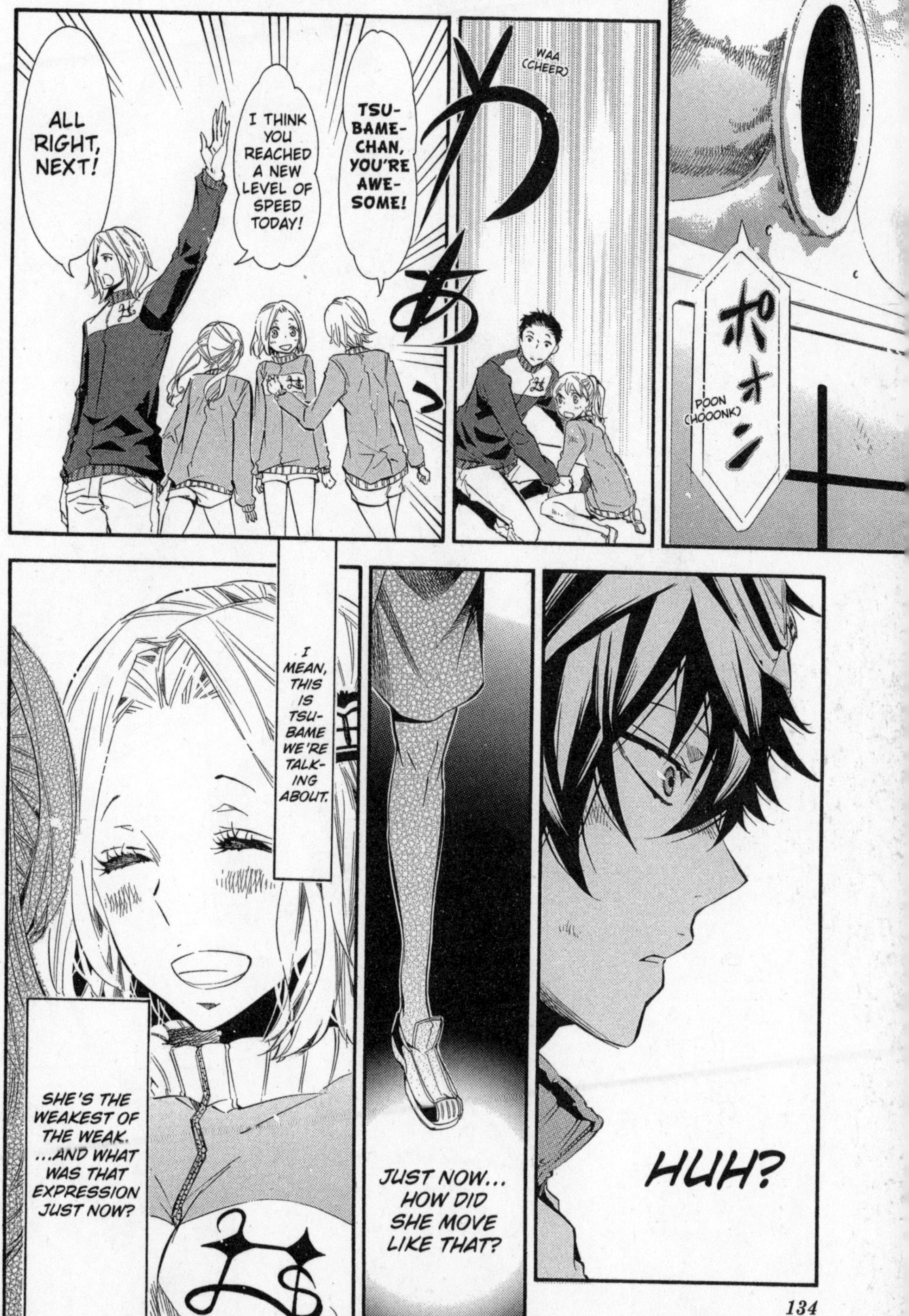
POON (HOOONK)
WAA (CHEER)
TSU-BAME-CHAN, YOU'RE AWE-SOME!
I THINK YOU REACHED A NEW LEVEL OF SPEED TODAY!
ALL RIGHT, NEXT!
HUH?
I MEAN, THIS IS TSU-BAME WE'RE TALK-ING ABOUT.
JUST NOW... HOW DID SHE MOVE LIKE THAT?
SHE'S THE WEAKEST OF THE WEAK. ...AND WHAT WAS THAT EXPRESSION JUST NOW?

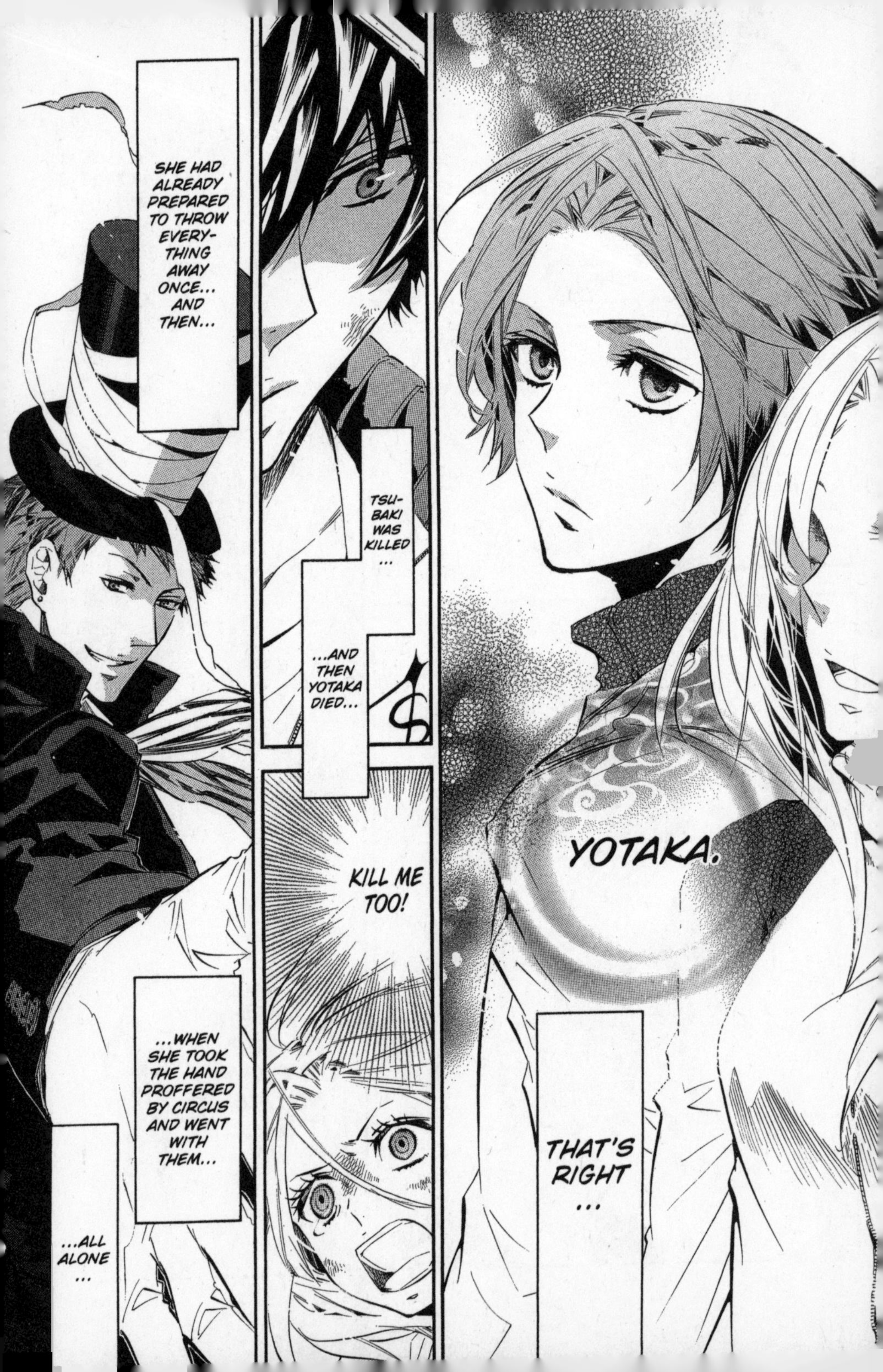
YOTAKA.
THAT'S RIGHT ...
TSU-BAKI WAS KILLED ...
...AND THEN YOTAKA DIED...
KILL ME TOO!
SHE HAD ALREADY PREPARED TO THROW EVERY-THING AWAY ONCE... AND THEN...
...WHEN SHE TOOK THE HAND PROFFERED BY CIRCUS AND WENT WITH THEM...
...ALL ALONE ...

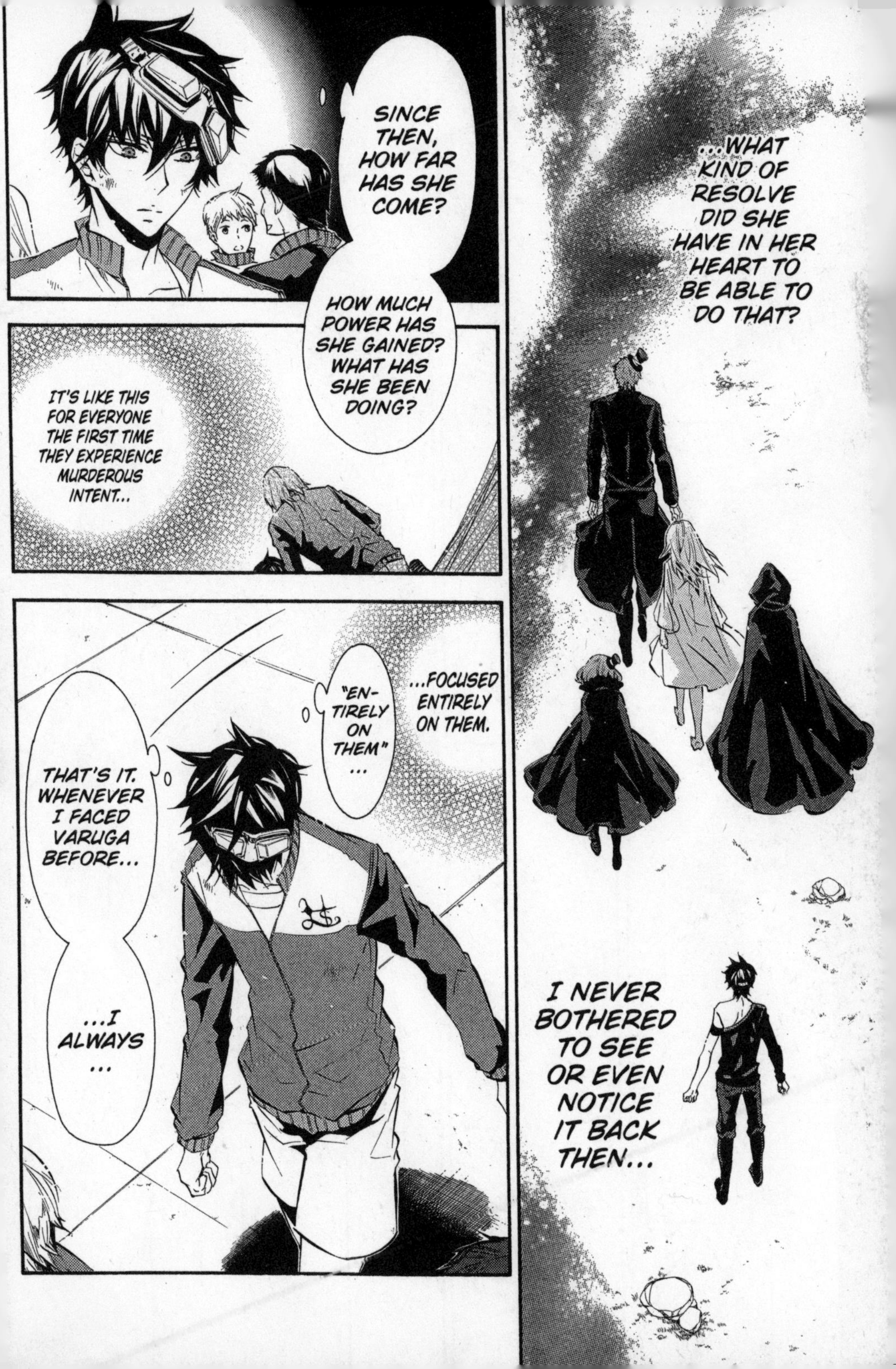
...WHAT KIND OF RESOLVE DID SHE HAVE IN HER HEART TO BE ABLE TO DO THAT?
I NEVER BOTHERED TO SEE OR EVEN NOTICE IT BACK THEN...
SINCE THEN, HOW FAR HAS SHE COME?
HOW MUCH POWER HAS SHE GAINED? WHAT HAS SHE BEEN DOING?
IT'S LIKE THIS FOR EVERYONE THE FIRST TIME THEY EXPERIENCE MURDEROUS INTENT...
...FOCUSED ENTIRELY ON THEM.
"EN-TIRELY ON THEM" ...
THAT'S IT. WHENEVER I FACED VARUGA BEFORE...
...I ALWAYS ...

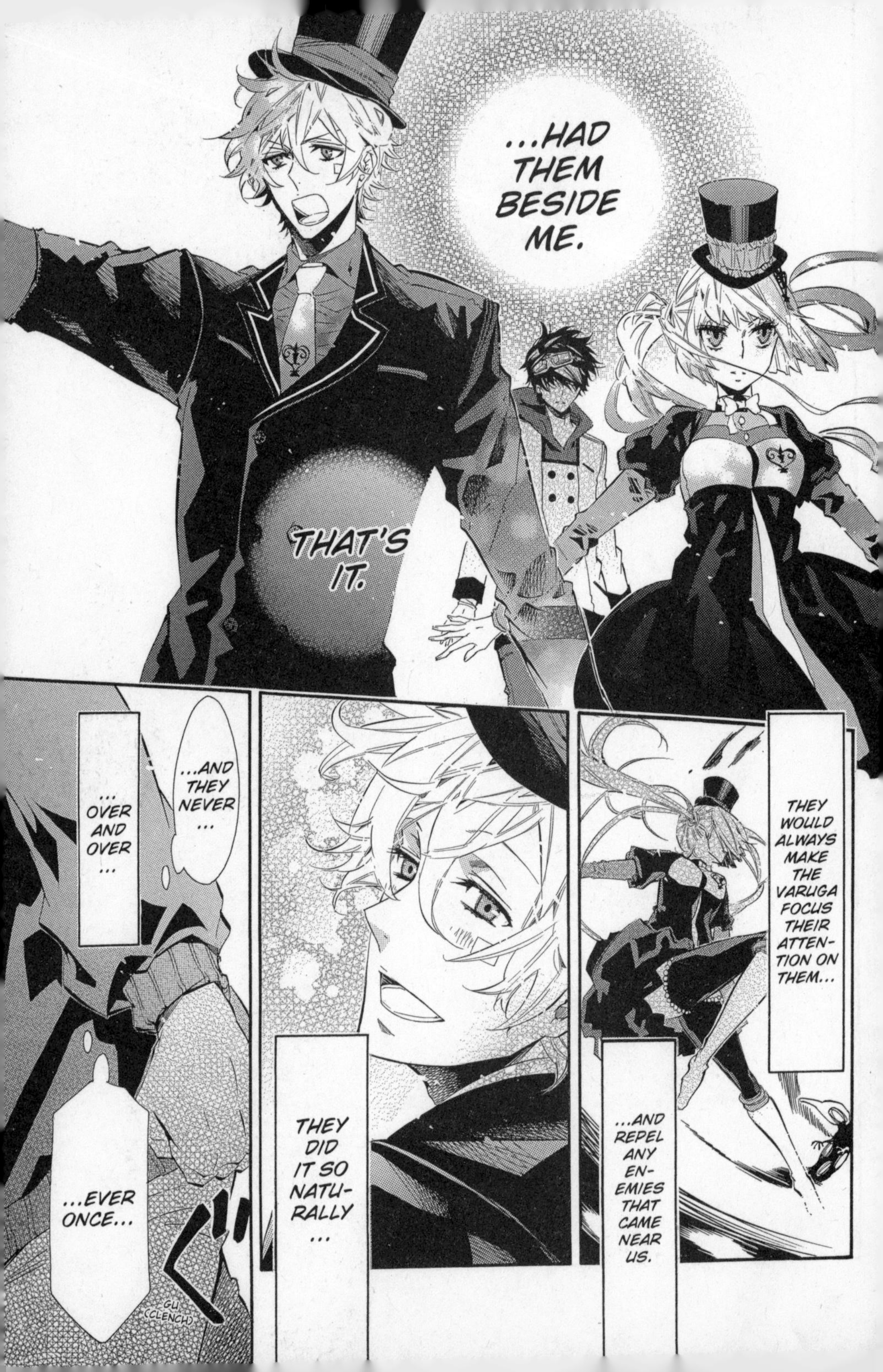
...HAD THEM BESIDE ME.
THAT'S IT.
THEY WOULD ALWAYS MAKE THE VARUGA FOCUS THEIR ATTENTION ON THEM...
...AND REPEL ANY ENEMIES THAT CAME NEAR US.
THEY DID IT SO NATURALLY...
...AND THEY NEVER...
...OVER AND OVER...
...EVER ONCE...
GU (CLENCH)

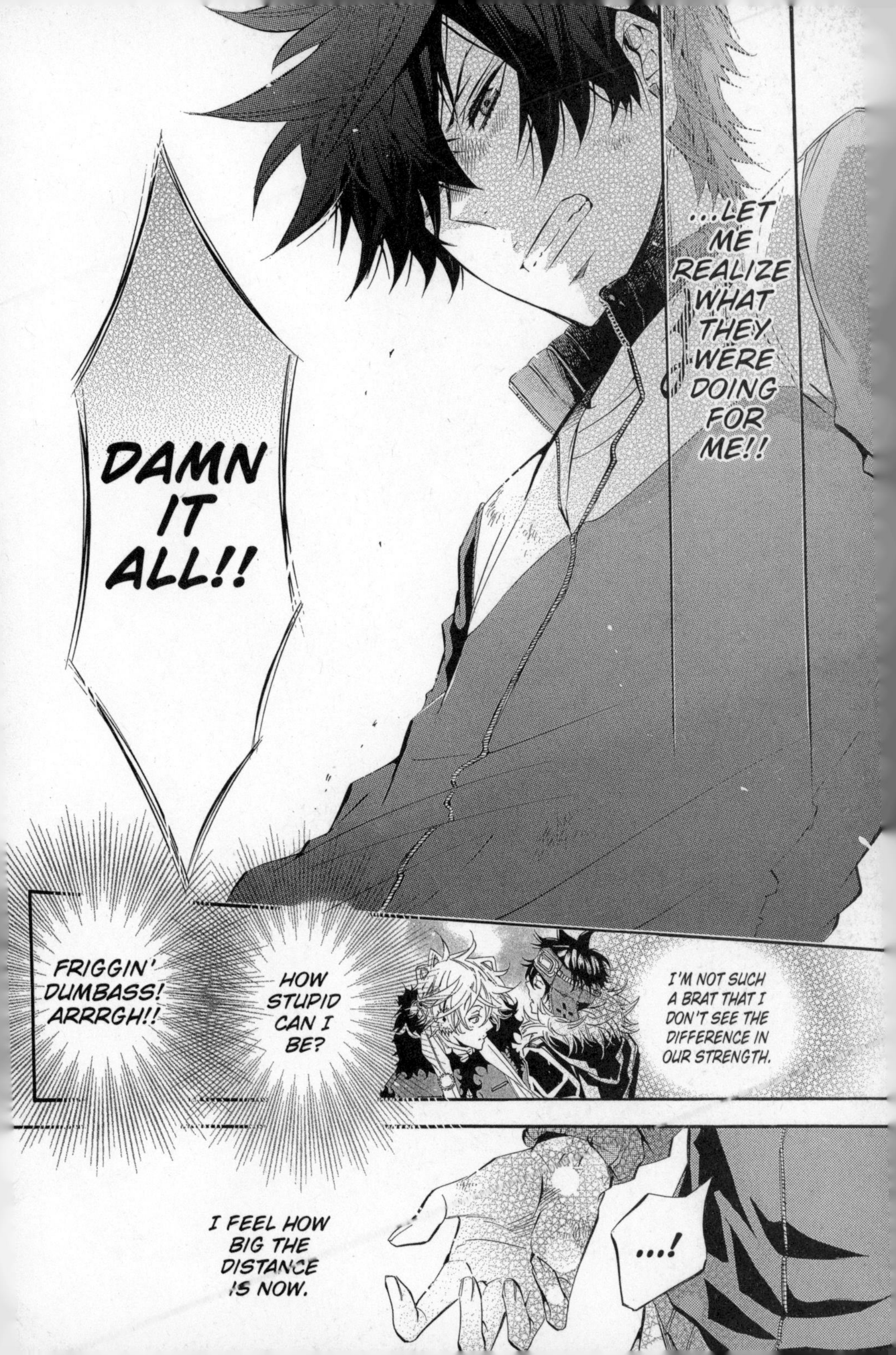
...LET ME REALIZE WHAT THEY WERE DOING FOR ME!!
DAMN IT ALL!!
I'M NOT SUCH A BRAT THAT I DON'T SEE THE DIFFERENCE IN OUR STRENGTH.
HOW STUPID CAN I BE?
FRIGGIN' DUMBASS! ARRRGH!!
...!
I FEEL HOW BIG THE DISTANCE IS NOW.

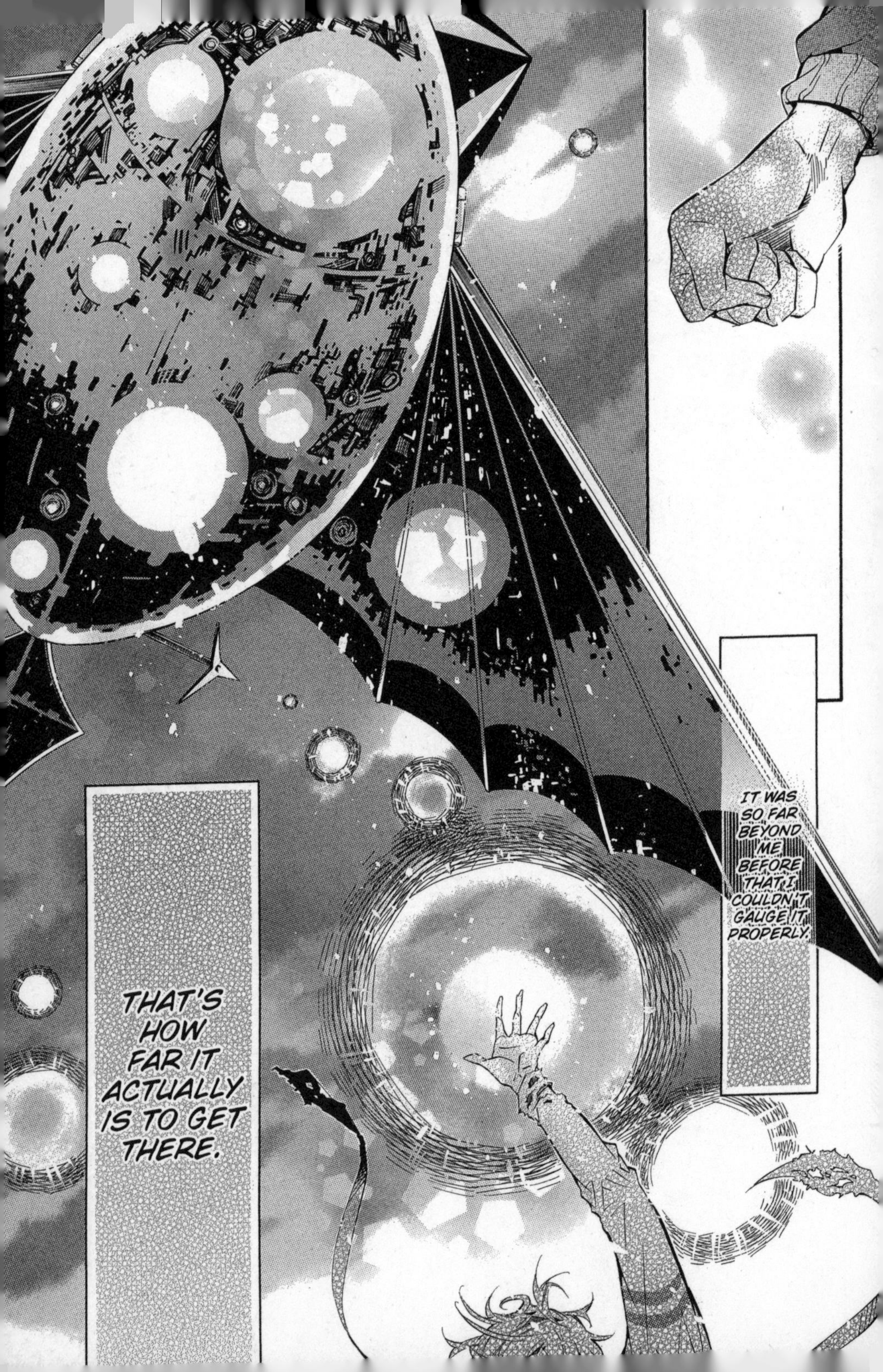
IT WAS SO FAR BEYOND ME BEFORE THAT I COULDN'T GAUGE IT PROPERLY.
THAT'S HOW FAR IT ACTUALLY IS TO GET THERE.

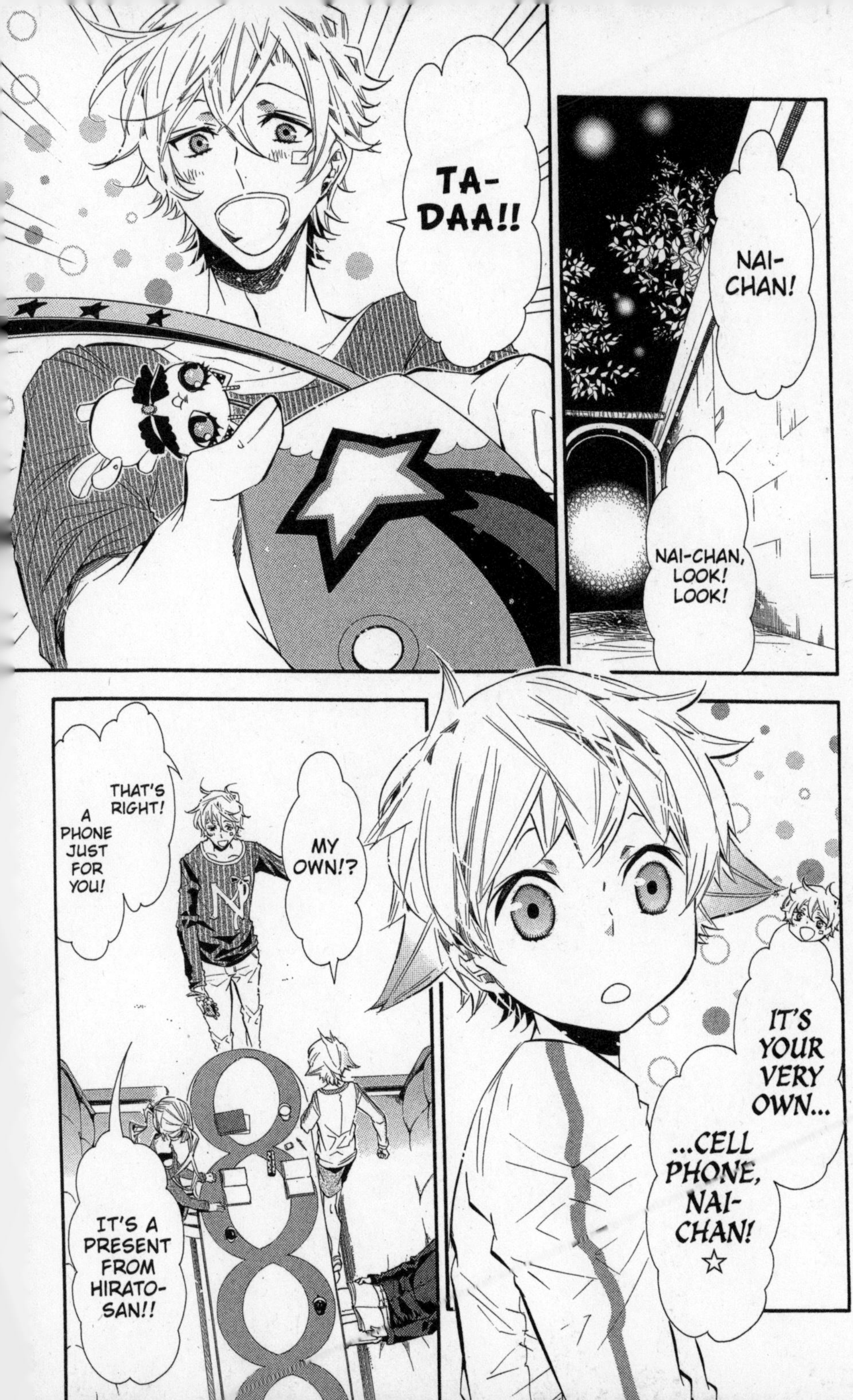
NAI-CHAN!
NAI-CHAN, LOOK! LOOK!
TA-DAA!!
IT'S YOUR VERY OWN...
...CELL PHONE, NAI-CHAN! ☆
MY OWN!?
THAT'S RIGHT! A PHONE JUST FOR YOU!
IT'S A PRESENT FROM HIRATO-SAN!!

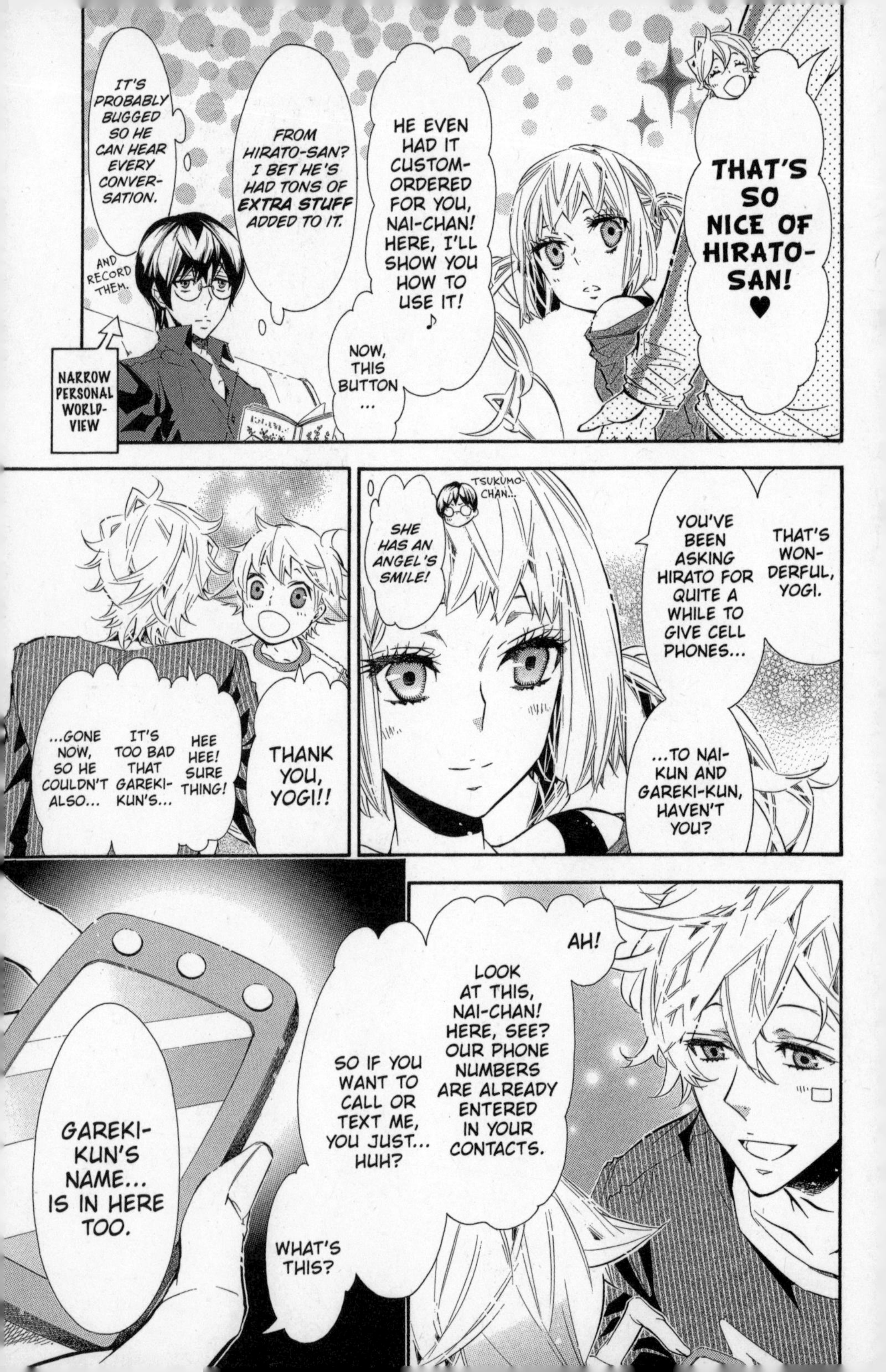
THAT'S SO NICE OF HIRATO-SAN! ♥
HE EVEN HAD IT CUSTOM-ORDERED FOR YOU, NAI-CHAN! HERE, I'LL SHOW YOU HOW TO USE IT! ♪
NOW, THIS BUTTON...
FROM HIRATO-SAN? I BET HE'S HAD TONS OF EXTRA STUFF ADDED TO IT.
IT'S PROBABLY BUGGED SO HE CAN HEAR EVERY CONVERSATION.
AND RECORD THEM.
NARROW PERSONAL WORLD-VIEW
THAT'S WONDERFUL, YOGI.
YOU'VE BEEN ASKING HIRATO FOR QUITE A WHILE TO GIVE CELL PHONES...
...TO NAI-KUN AND GAREKI-KUN, HAVEN'T YOU?
TSUKUMO-CHAN...
SHE HAS AN ANGEL'S SMILE!
THANK YOU, YOGI!!
HEE HEE! SURE THING!
IT'S TOO BAD THAT GAREKI-KUN'S...
...GONE NOW, SO HE COULDN'T ALSO...
AH!
LOOK AT THIS, NAI-CHAN! HERE, SEE? OUR PHONE NUMBERS ARE ALREADY ENTERED IN YOUR CONTACTS.
SO IF YOU WANT TO CALL OR TEXT ME, YOU JUST... HUH?
WHAT'S THIS?
GAREKI-KUN'S NAME... IS IN HERE TOO.

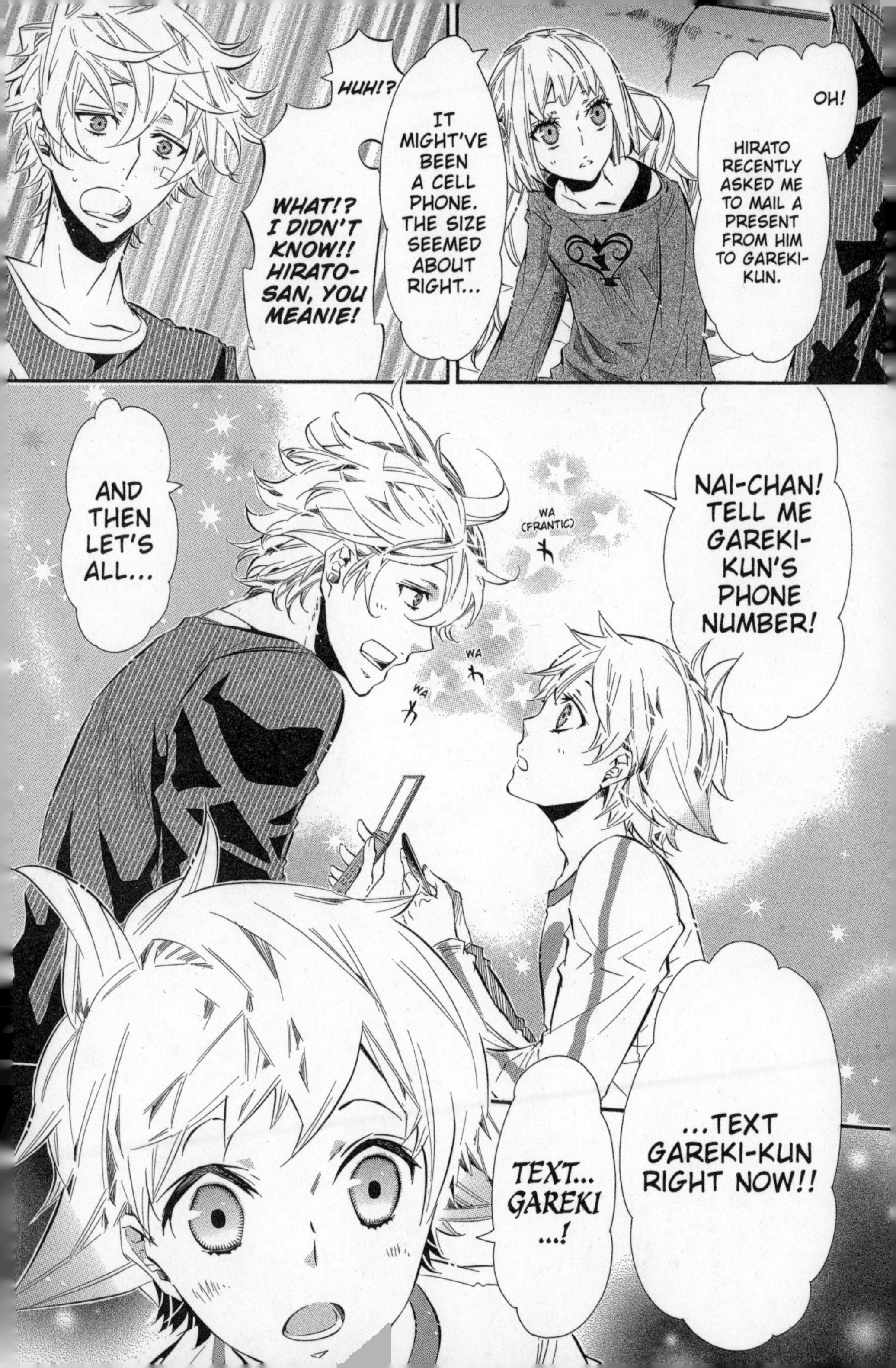
OH!
HIRATO RECENTLY ASKED ME TO MAIL A PRESENT FROM HIM TO GAREKI-KUN.
IT MIGHT'VE BEEN A CELL PHONE. THE SIZE SEEMED ABOUT RIGHT...
HUH!?
WHAT!? I DIDN'T KNOW!! HIRATO-SAN, YOU MEANIE!
NAI-CHAN! TELL ME GAREKI-KUN'S PHONE NUMBER!
WA (FRANTIC)
WA
WA
AND THEN LET'S ALL...
...TEXT GAREKI-KUN RIGHT NOW!!
TEXT... GAREKI ...!

KARNEVAL

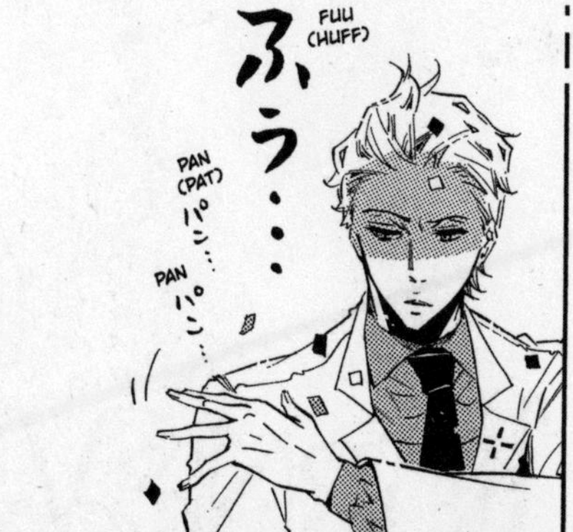

FUU (HUFF)
ふう・・・
PAN (PAT)
パン…
PAN
パン…

KARNEVAL

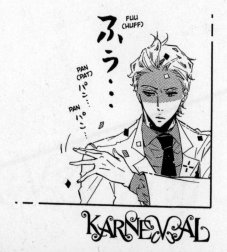

Score 42: Beneath the Starry Sky

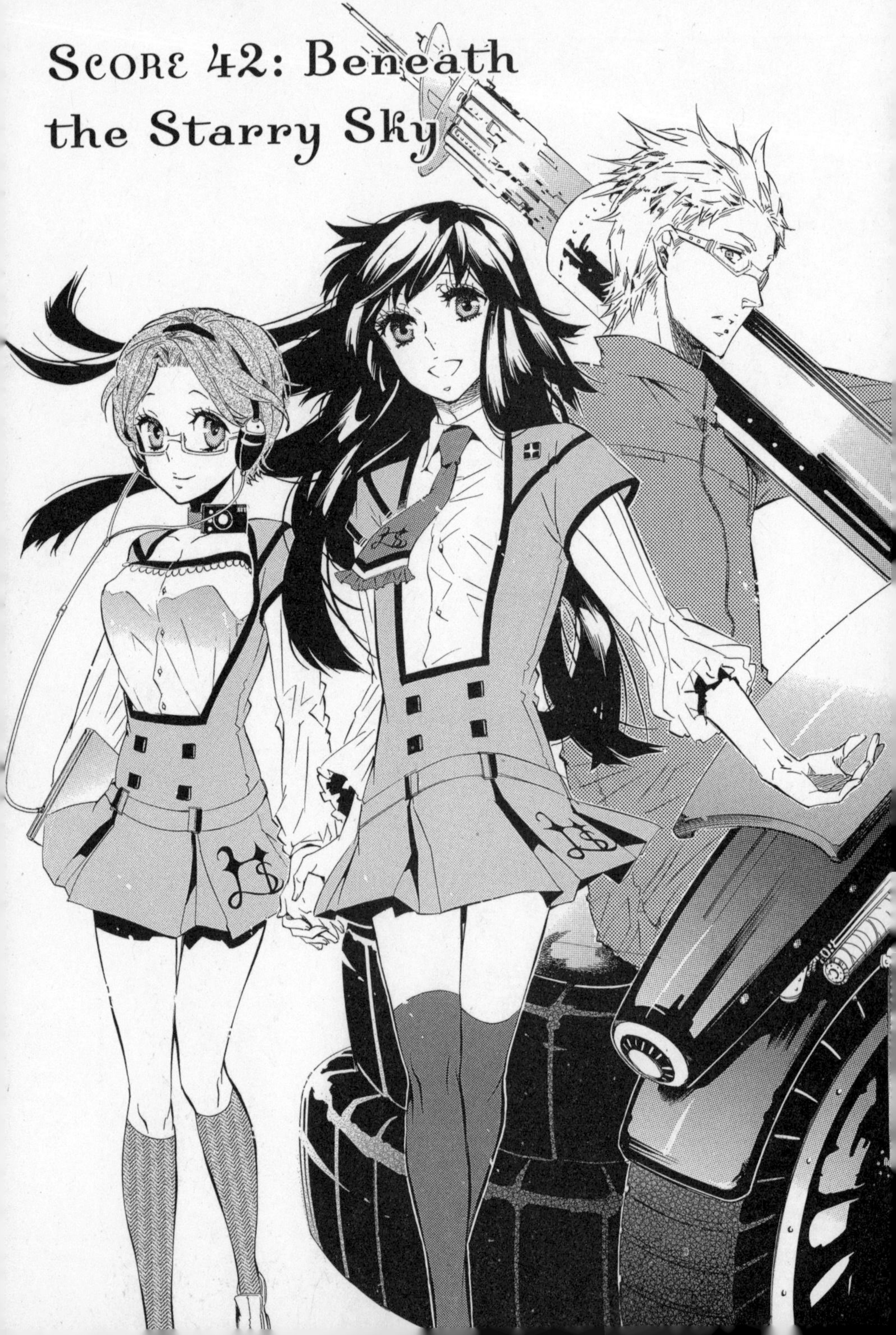

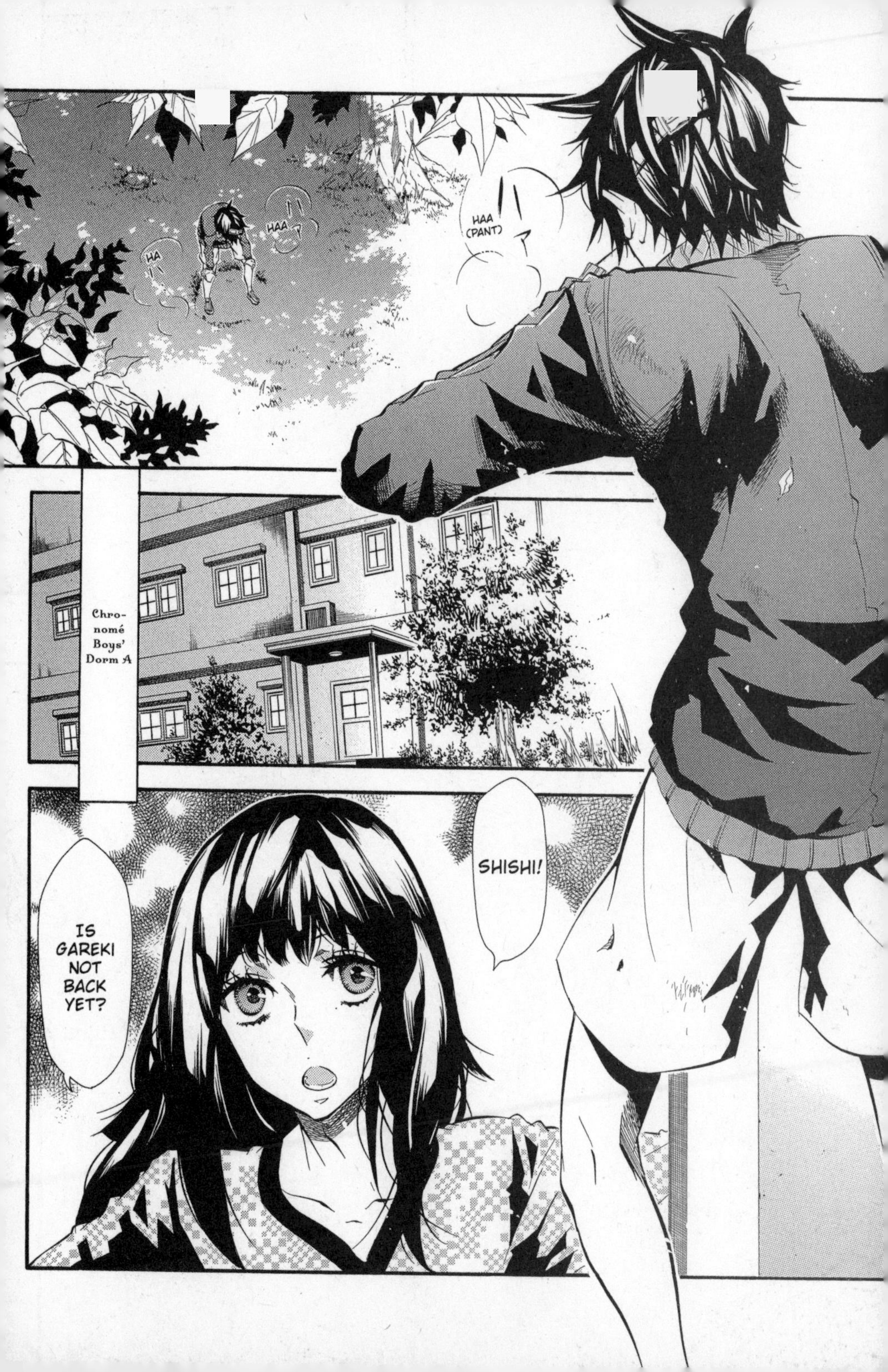
HAA (PANT)
HAA
HA
Chro-nomé Boys' Dorm A
SHISHI!
IS GAREKI NOT BACK YET?

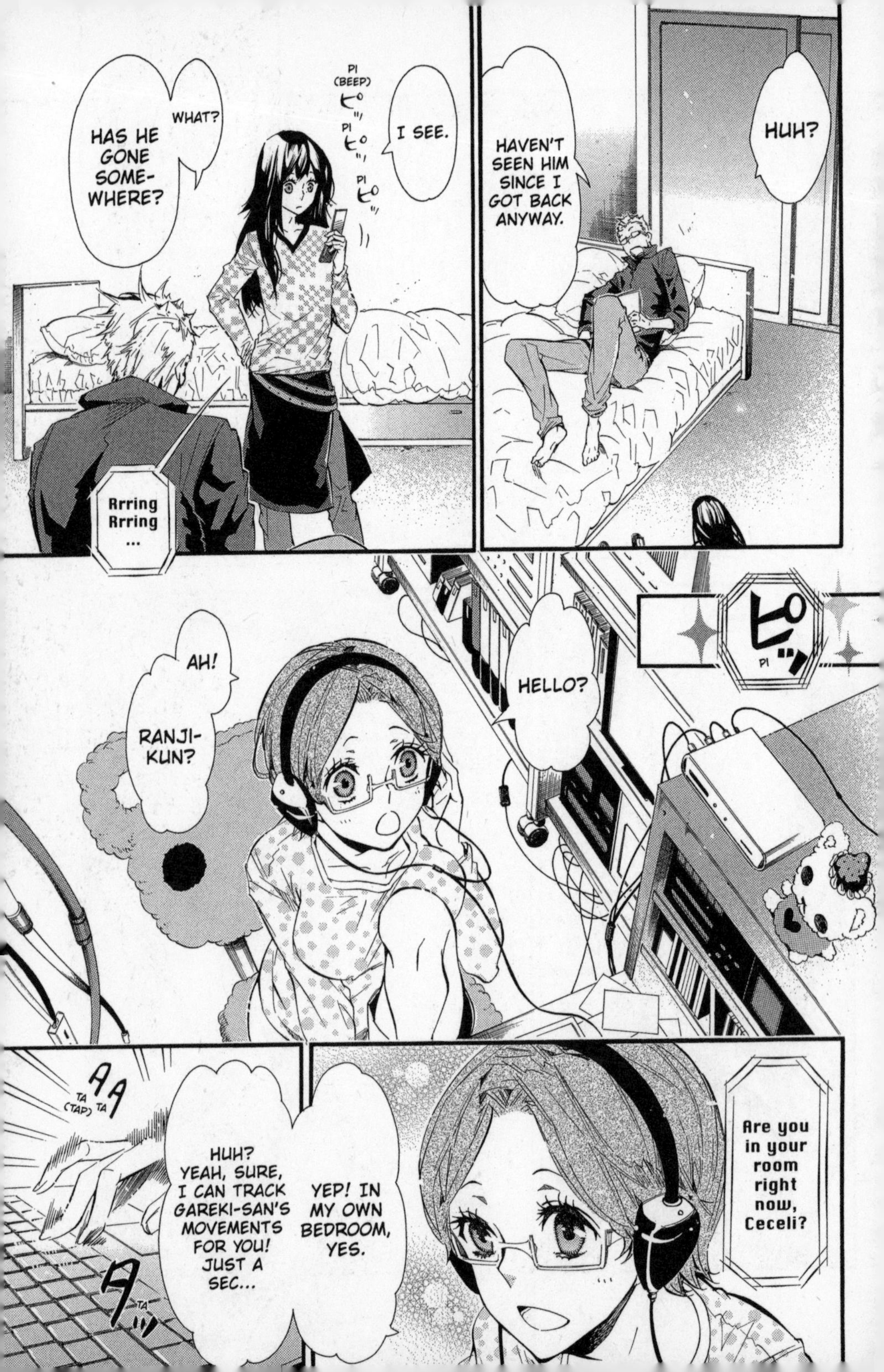
HUH?
HAVEN'T SEEN HIM SINCE I GOT BACK ANYWAY.
I SEE.
PI (BEEP)
PI
PI
WHAT?
HAS HE GONE SOME-WHERE?
Rrring Rrring ...
PI
HELLO?
AH!
RANJI-KUN?
Are you in your room right now, Ceceli?
YEP! IN MY OWN BEDROOM, YES.
HUH? YEAH, SURE, I CAN TRACK GAREKI-SAN'S MOVEMENTS FOR YOU! JUST A SEC...
TA (TAP) TA
TA

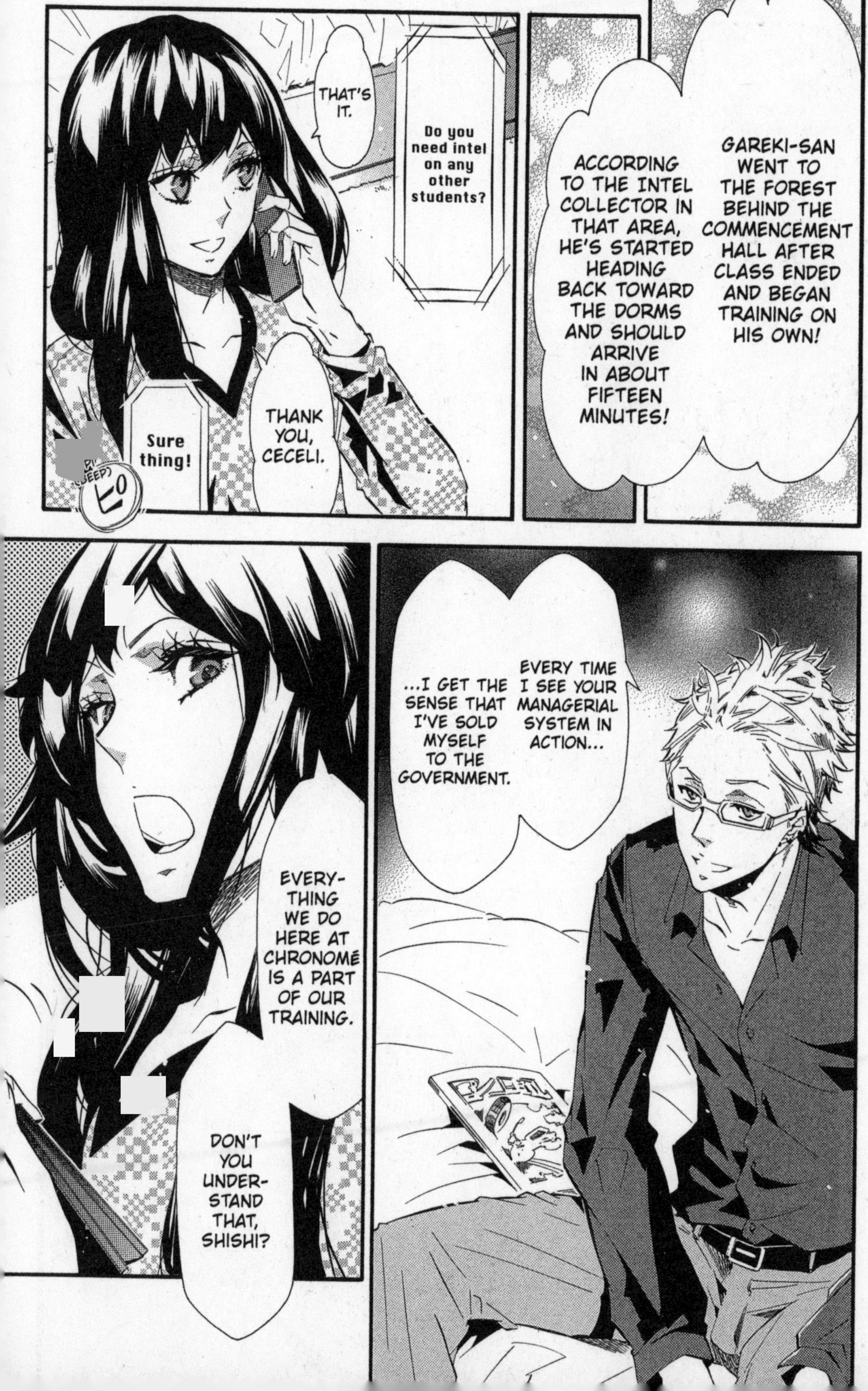

GAREKI-SAN WENT TO THE FOREST BEHIND THE COMMENCEMENT HALL AFTER CLASS ENDED AND BEGAN TRAINING ON HIS OWN!
ACCORDING TO THE INTEL COLLECTOR IN THAT AREA, HE'S STARTED HEADING BACK TOWARD THE DORMS AND SHOULD ARRIVE IN ABOUT FIFTEEN MINUTES!
Do you need intel on any other students?
THAT'S IT.
THANK YOU, CECELI.
Sure thing!
(BEEP)
ピ
EVERY TIME I SEE YOUR MANAGERIAL SYSTEM IN ACTION...
...I GET THE SENSE THAT I'VE SOLD MYSELF TO THE GOVERNMENT.
EVERYTHING WE DO HERE AT CHRONOMÉ IS A PART OF OUR TRAINING.
DON'T YOU UNDERSTAND THAT, SHISHI?

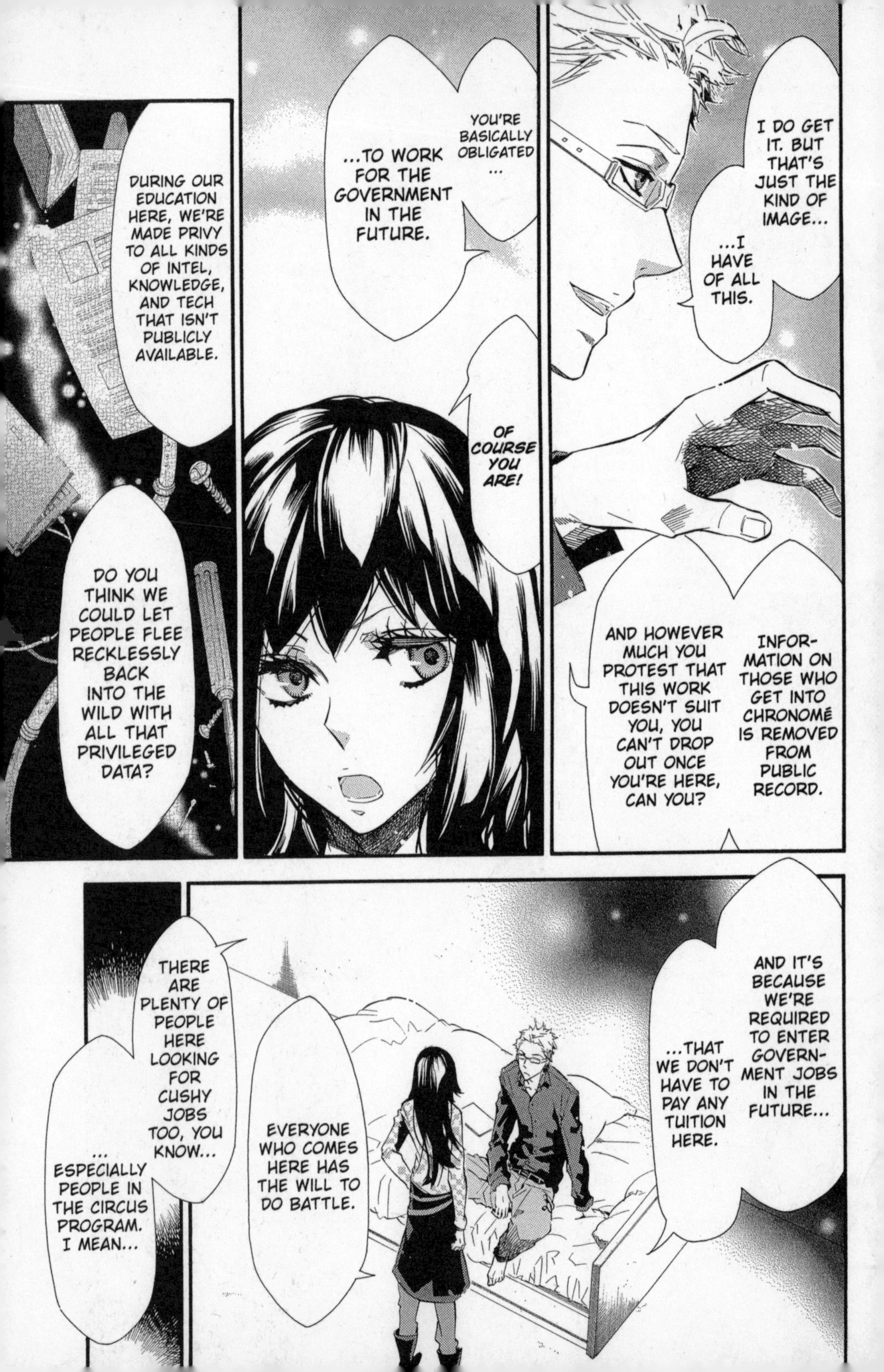
I DO GET IT. BUT THAT'S JUST THE KIND OF IMAGE...
...I HAVE OF ALL THIS.
INFORMATION ON THOSE WHO GET INTO CHRONOMÉ IS REMOVED FROM PUBLIC RECORD.
AND HOWEVER MUCH YOU PROTEST THAT THIS WORK DOESN'T SUIT YOU, YOU CAN'T DROP OUT ONCE YOU'RE HERE, CAN YOU?
YOU'RE BASICALLY OBLIGATED...
...TO WORK FOR THE GOVERNMENT IN THE FUTURE.
OF COURSE YOU ARE!
DURING OUR EDUCATION HERE, WE'RE MADE PRIVY TO ALL KINDS OF INTEL, KNOWLEDGE, AND TECH THAT ISN'T PUBLICLY AVAILABLE.
DO YOU THINK WE COULD LET PEOPLE FLEE RECKLESSLY BACK INTO THE WILD WITH ALL THAT PRIVILEGED DATA?
AND IT'S BECAUSE WE'RE REQUIRED TO ENTER GOVERNMENT JOBS IN THE FUTURE...
...THAT WE DON'T HAVE TO PAY ANY TUITION HERE.
EVERYONE WHO COMES HERE HAS THE WILL TO DO BATTLE.
THERE ARE PLENTY OF PEOPLE HERE LOOKING FOR CUSHY JOBS TOO, YOU KNOW...
...ESPECIALLY PEOPLE IN THE CIRCUS PROGRAM. I MEAN...

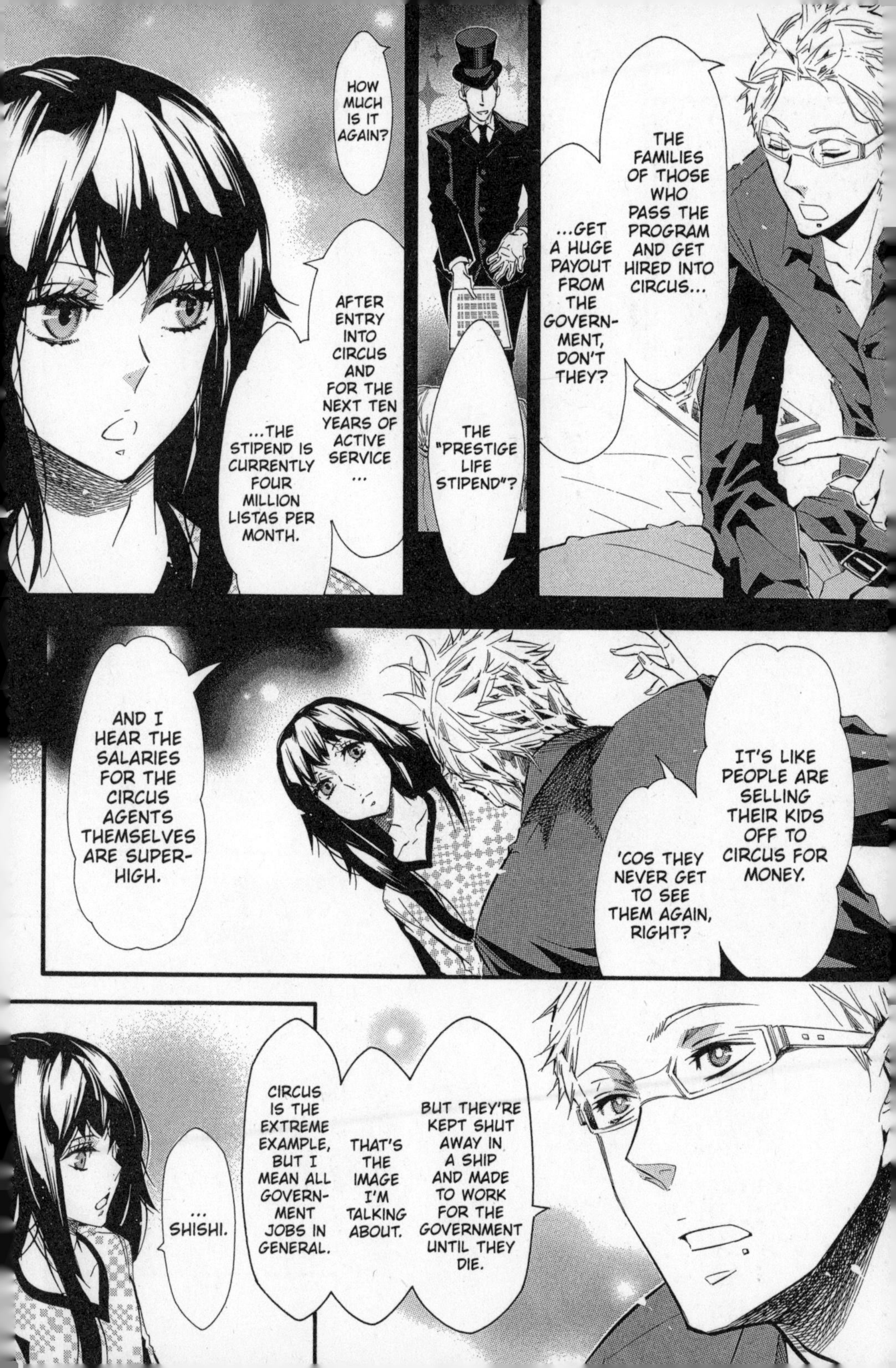
THE FAMILIES OF THOSE WHO PASS THE PROGRAM AND GET HIRED INTO CIRCUS...
...GET A HUGE PAYOUT FROM THE GOVERNMENT, DON'T THEY?
HOW MUCH IS IT AGAIN?
THE "PRESTIGE LIFE STIPEND"?
AFTER ENTRY INTO CIRCUS AND FOR THE NEXT TEN YEARS OF ACTIVE SERVICE...
...THE STIPEND IS CURRENTLY FOUR MILLION LISTAS PER MONTH.
IT'S LIKE PEOPLE ARE SELLING THEIR KIDS OFF TO CIRCUS FOR MONEY.
'COS THEY NEVER GET TO SEE THEM AGAIN, RIGHT?
AND I HEAR THE SALARIES FOR THE CIRCUS AGENTS THEMSELVES ARE SUPER-HIGH.
BUT THEY'RE KEPT SHUT AWAY IN A SHIP AND MADE TO WORK FOR THE GOVERNMENT UNTIL THEY DIE.
THAT'S THE IMAGE I'M TALKING ABOUT.
CIRCUS IS THE EXTREME EXAMPLE, BUT I MEAN ALL GOVERNMENT JOBS IN GENERAL.
...SHISHI.

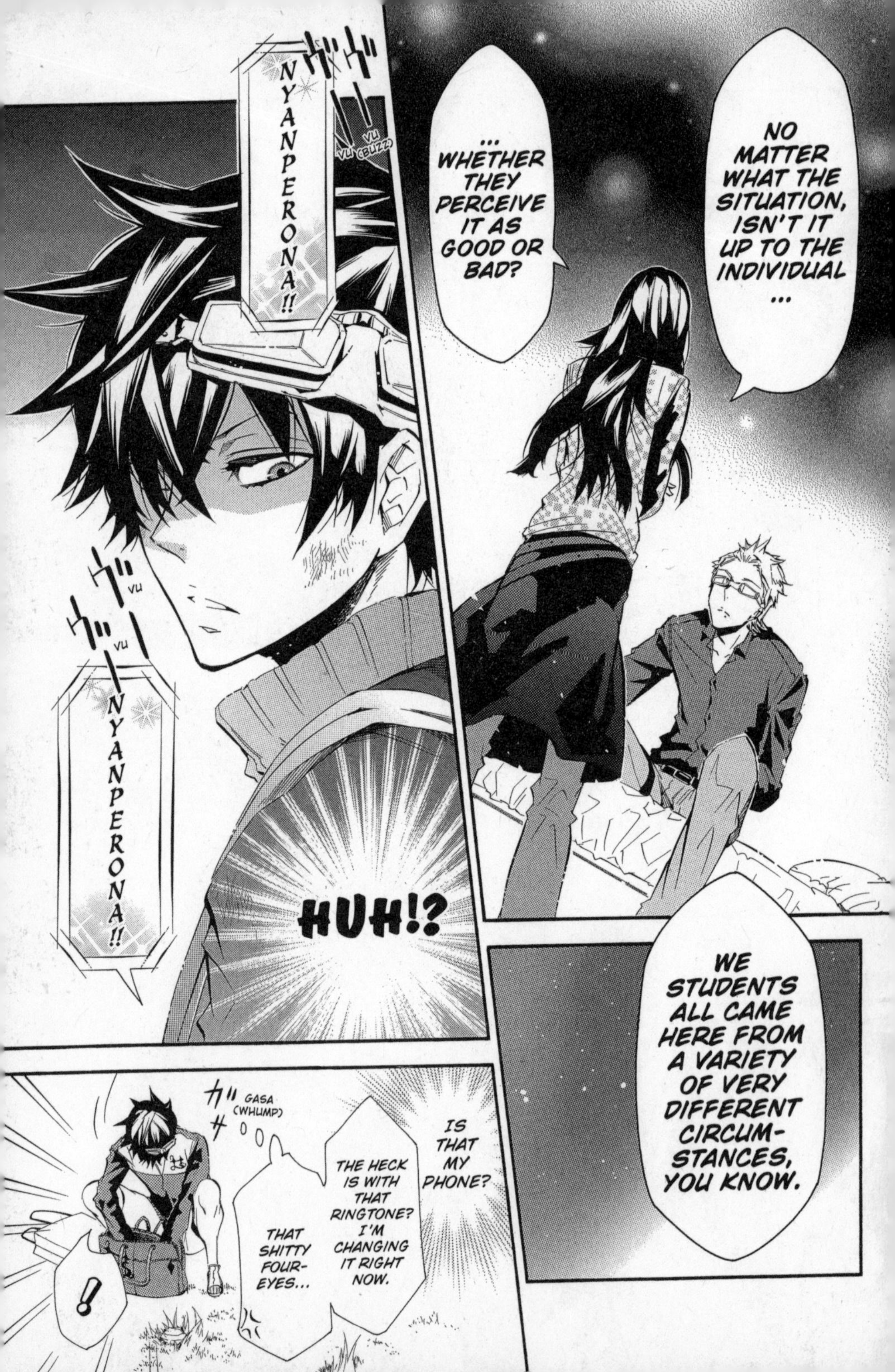
NO MATTER WHAT THE SITUATION, ISN'T IT UP TO THE INDIVIDUAL...
...WHETHER THEY PERCEIVE IT AS GOOD OR BAD?
WE STUDENTS ALL CAME HERE FROM A VARIETY OF VERY DIFFERENT CIRCUM-STANCES, YOU KNOW.
VU VU (BUZZ)
NYANPERONA!!
VU
VU
NYANPERONA!!
HUH!?
IS THAT MY PHONE?
THE HECK IS WITH THAT RINGTONE? I'M CHANGING IT RIGHT NOW.
THAT SHITTY FOUR-EYES...
GASA (WHUMP)
!

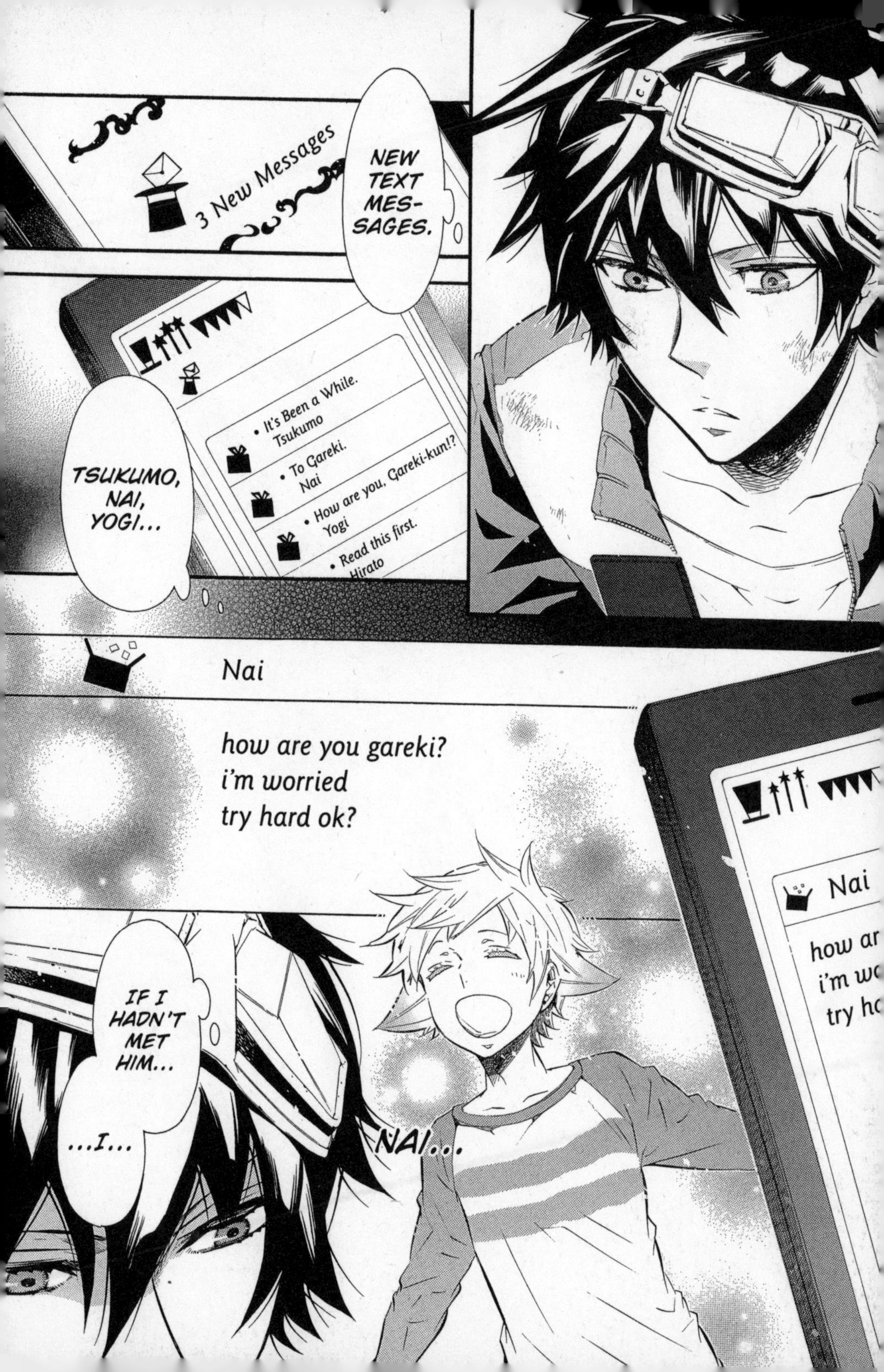
3 New Messages
NEW TEXT MESSAGES.
• It's Been a While. Tsukumo
• To Gareki. Nai
• How are you, Gareki-kun!? Yogi
• Read this first. Hirato
TSUKUMO, NAI, YOGI...
Nai
how are you gareki?
i'm worried
try hard ok?
IF I HADN'T MET HIM...
...I...
NAI...

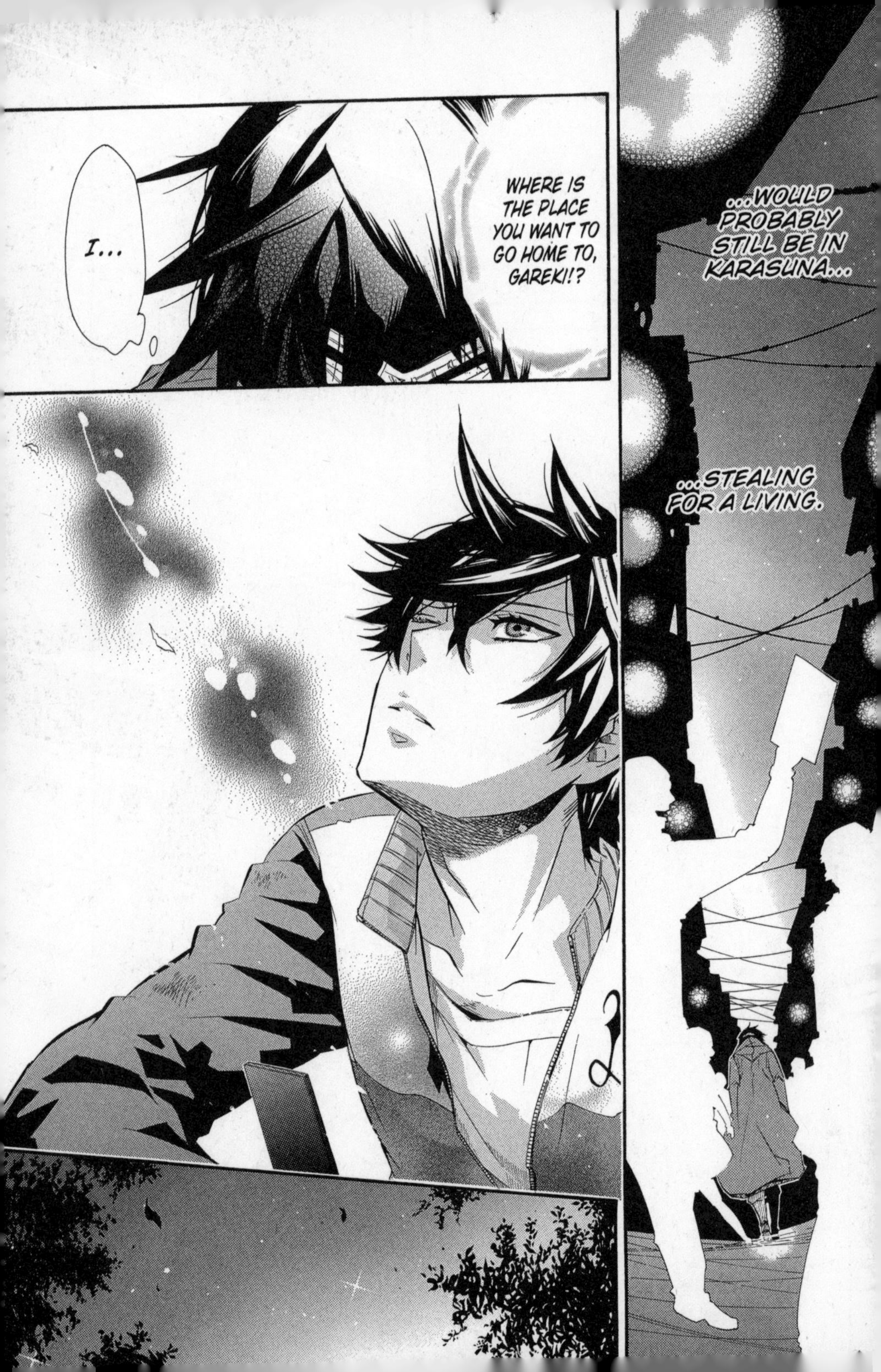
WHERE IS THE PLACE YOU WANT TO GO HOME TO, GAREKI!?
I...
...WOULD PROBABLY STILL BE IN KARASUNA...
...STEALING FOR A LIVING.

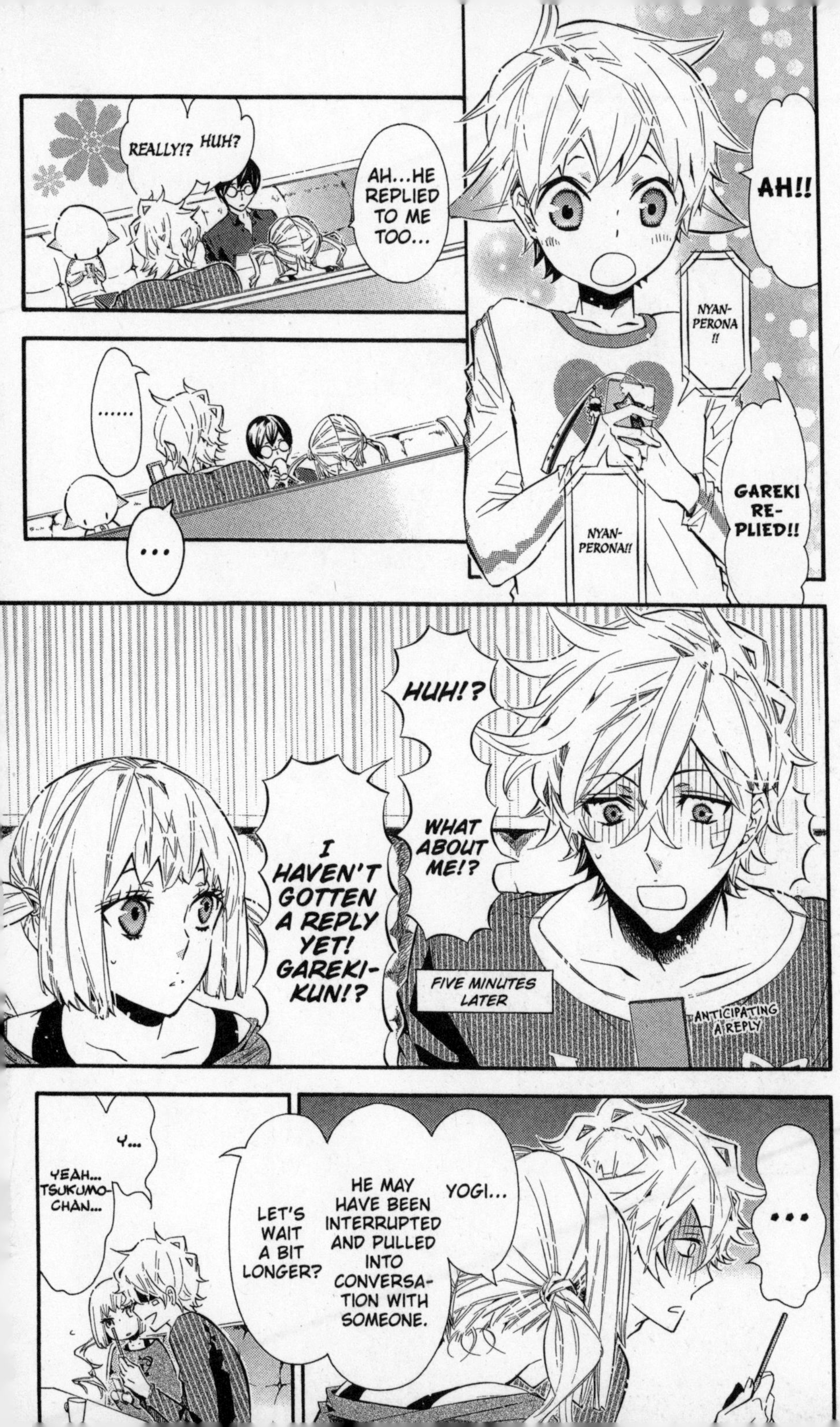
AH!!
NYAN-PERONA!!
GAREKI RE-PLIED!!
NYAN-PERONA!!
AH...HE REPLIED TO ME TOO...
HUH?
REALLY!?
......
...
HUH!?
WHAT ABOUT ME!?
I HAVEN'T GOTTEN A REPLY YET! GAREKI-KUN!?
ANTICIPATING A REPLY
FIVE MINUTES LATER
...
YOGI...
HE MAY HAVE BEEN INTERRUPTED AND PULLED INTO CONVERSA-TION WITH SOMEONE.
LET'S WAIT A BIT LONGER?
Y...
YEAH... TSUKUMO-CHAN...

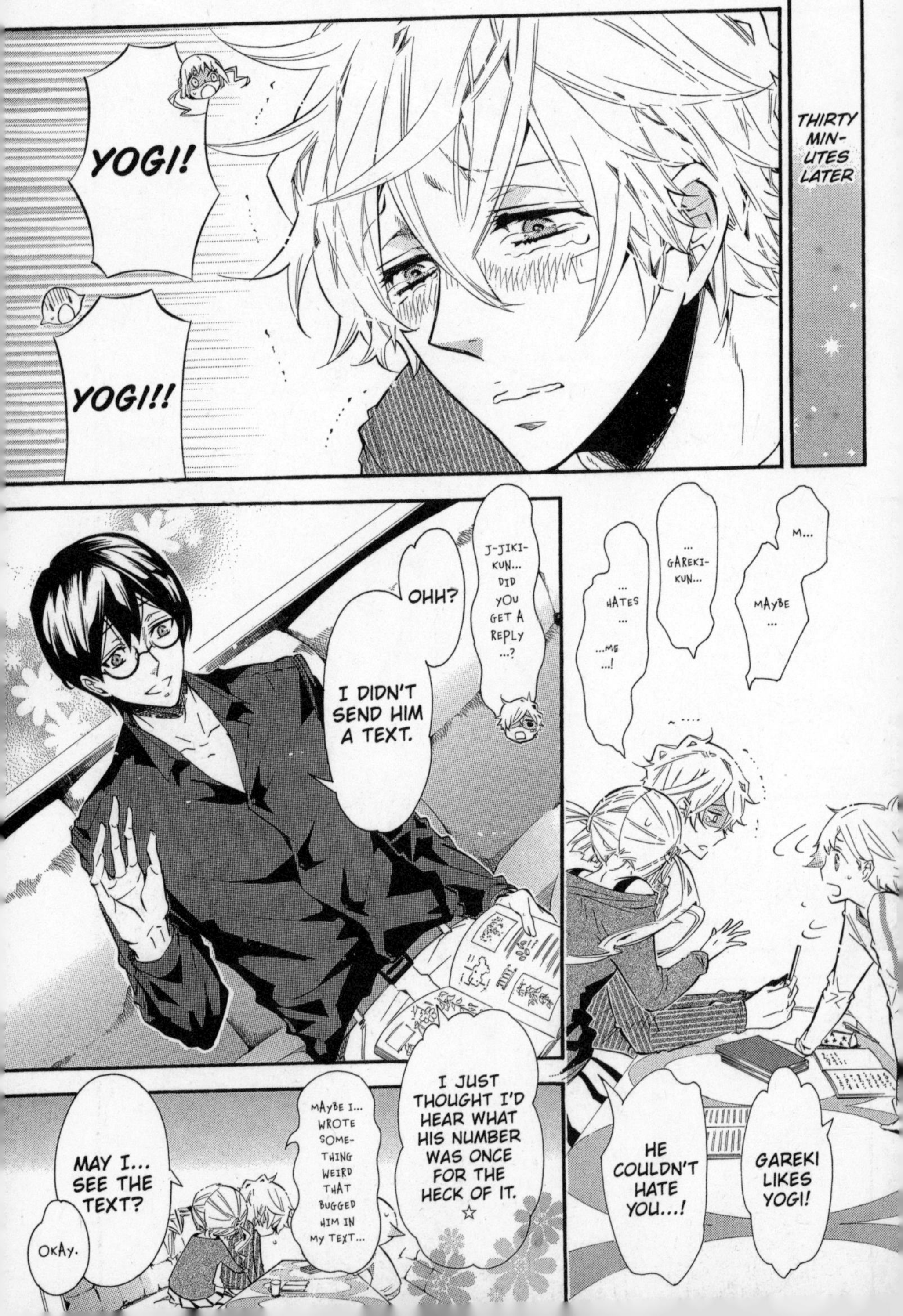
THIRTY MIN-UTES LATER
YOGI!
YOGI!!
M... MAYBE ...
... GAREKI-KUN...
... HATES ... ...ME ...!
~....
J-JIKI-KUN... DID YOU GET A REPLY ...?
OHH?
I DIDN'T SEND HIM A TEXT.
GAREKI LIKES YOGI!
HE COULDN'T HATE YOU...!
I JUST THOUGHT I'D HEAR WHAT HIS NUMBER WAS ONCE FOR THE HECK OF IT. ☆
MAYBE I... WROTE SOMETHING WEIRD THAT BUGGED HIM IN MY TEXT...
MAY I... SEE THE TEXT?
OKAY.

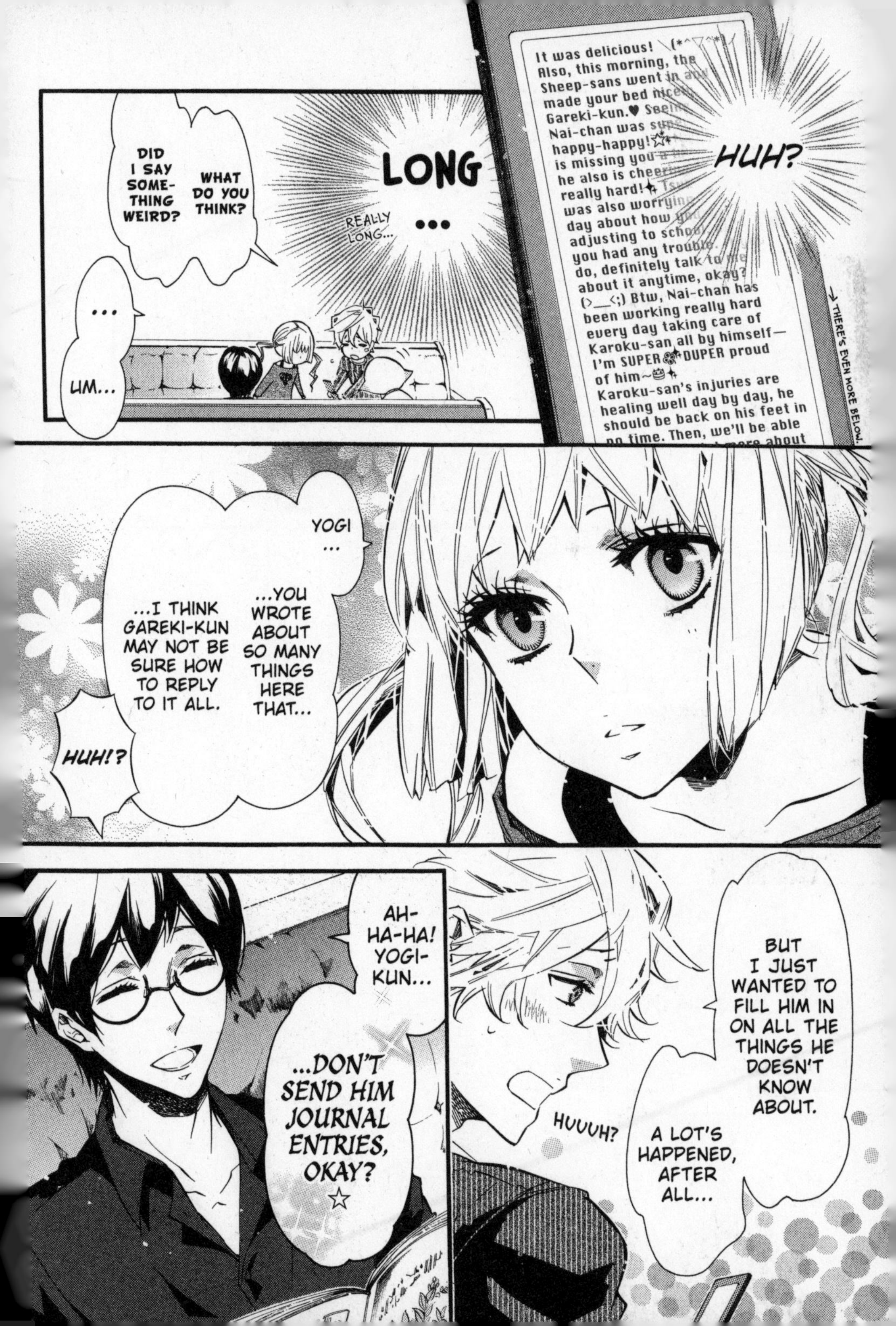
It was delicious! ＼(*^▽^*)ノ
Also, this morning, the
Sheep-sans went in and
made your bed nicely,
Gareki-kun.♥ Seeing
Nai-chan was super
happy-happy!☆
is missing you a
he also is cheering
really hard!✦ Tsu
was also worrying
day about how you
adjusting to school
you had any trouble.
do, definitely talk to me
about it anytime, okay?
(>_<;) Btw, Nai-chan has
been working really hard
every day taking care of
Karoku-san all by himself—
I'm SUPER DUPER proud
of him~
Karoku-san's injuries are
healing well day by day, he
should be back on his feet in
no time. Then, we'll be able
THERE'S EVEN MORE BELOW.
HUH?
LONG ...
REALLY LONG...
WHAT DO YOU THINK?
DID I SAY SOME-THING WEIRD?
...
UM...
YOGI ...
...YOU WROTE ABOUT SO MANY THINGS HERE THAT...
...I THINK GAREKI-KUN MAY NOT BE SURE HOW TO REPLY TO IT ALL.
HUH!?
BUT I JUST WANTED TO FILL HIM IN ON ALL THE THINGS HE DOESN'T KNOW ABOUT.
A LOT'S HAPPENED, AFTER ALL...
HUUUH?
AH-HA-HA! YOGI-KUN...
...DON'T SEND HIM JOURNAL ENTRIES, OKAY? ☆

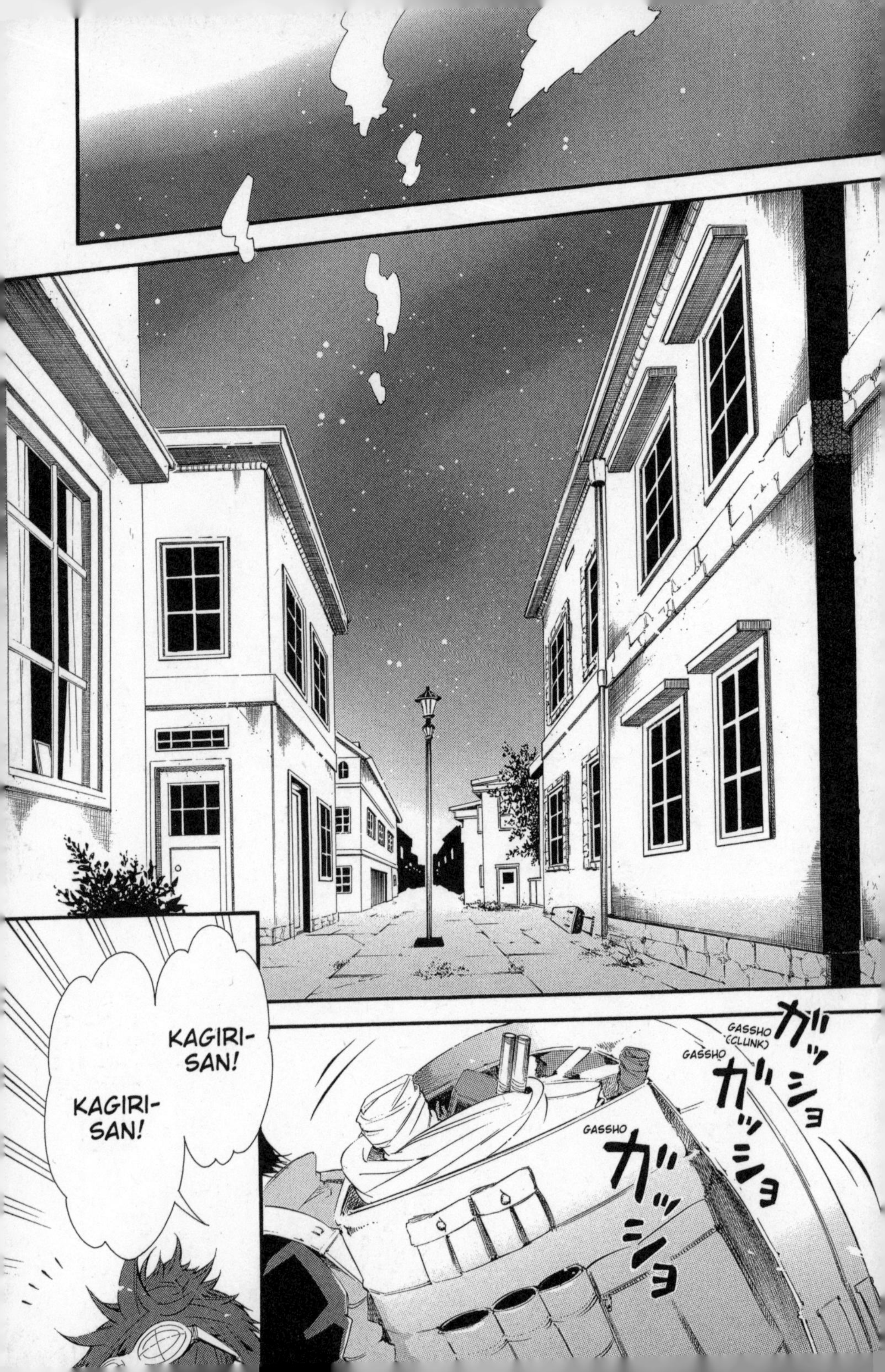
ガッショ
GASSHO (CLUNK)
ガッショ
GASSHO
ガッショ
GASSHO
KAGIRI-SAN!
KAGIRI-SAN!

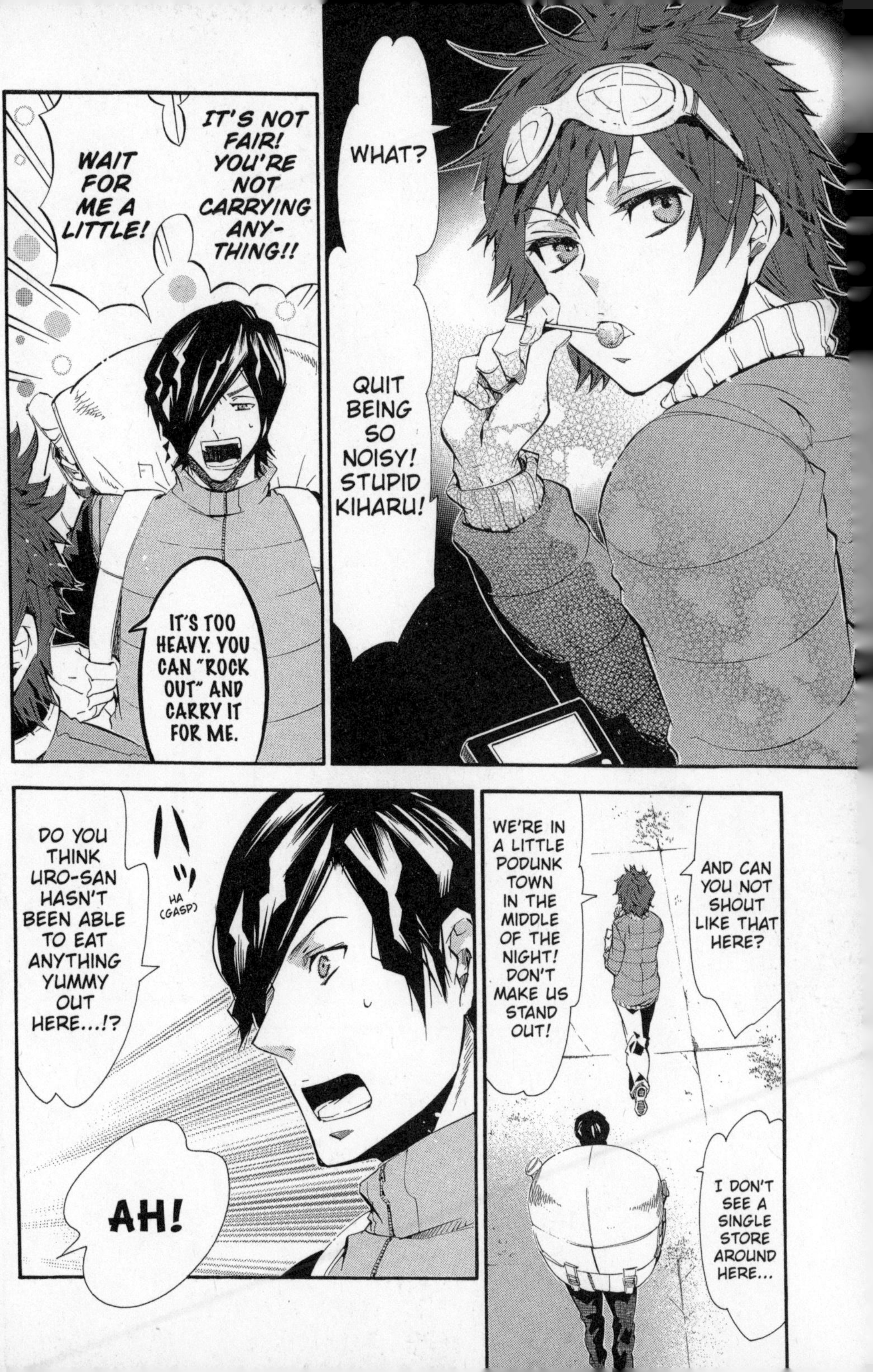
WAIT FOR ME A LITTLE!
IT'S NOT FAIR! YOU'RE NOT CARRYING ANYTHING!!
IT'S TOO HEAVY. YOU CAN "ROCK OUT" AND CARRY IT FOR ME.
WHAT?
QUIT BEING SO NOISY! STUPID KIHARU!
DO YOU THINK URO-SAN HASN'T BEEN ABLE TO EAT ANYTHING YUMMY OUT HERE...!?
HA (GASP)
AH!
WE'RE IN A LITTLE PODUNK TOWN IN THE MIDDLE OF THE NIGHT! DON'T MAKE US STAND OUT!
AND CAN YOU NOT SHOUT LIKE THAT HERE?
I DON'T SEE A SINGLE STORE AROUND HERE...

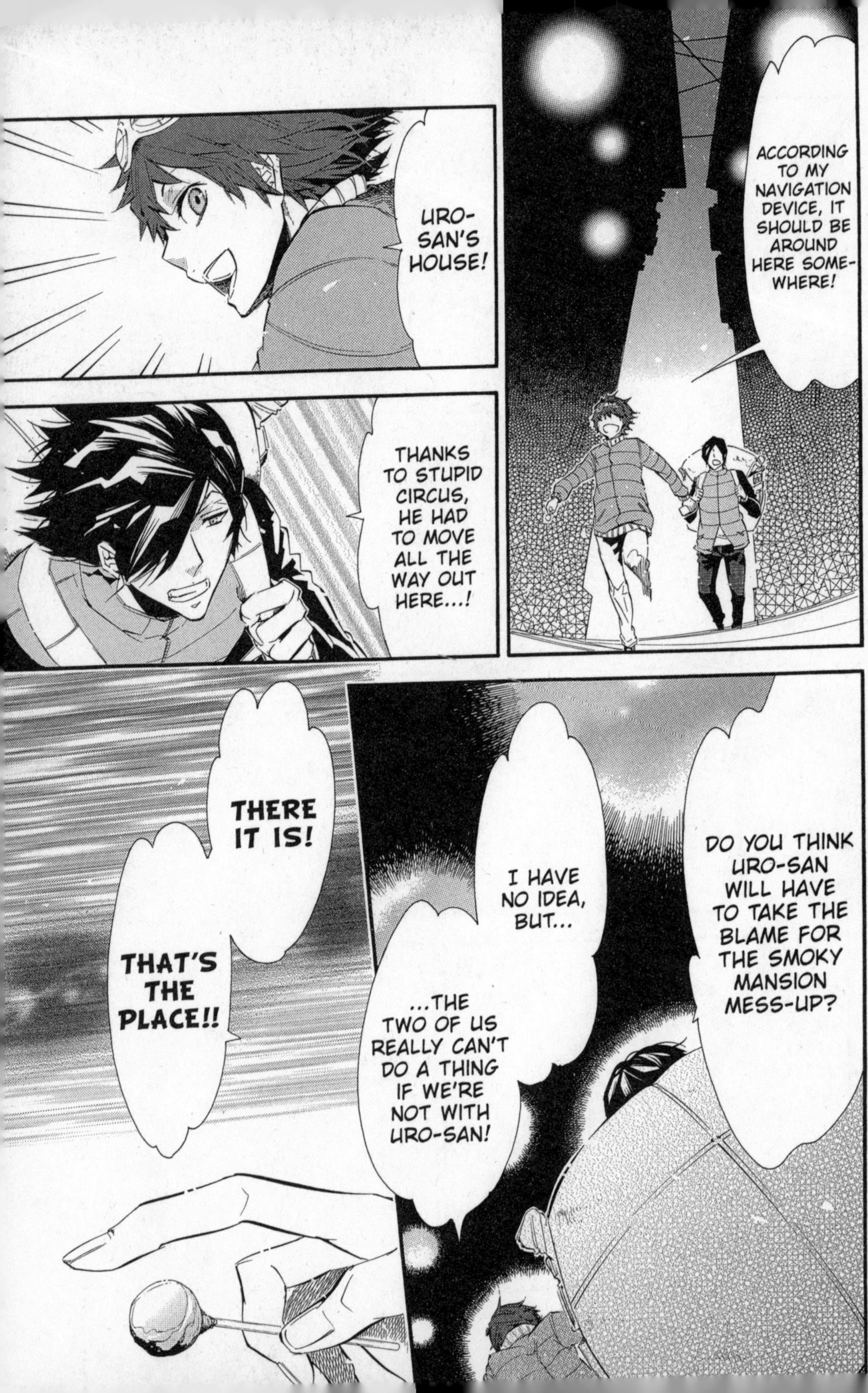
ACCORDING TO MY NAVIGATION DEVICE, IT SHOULD BE AROUND HERE SOME-WHERE!
URO-SAN'S HOUSE!
THANKS TO STUPID CIRCUS, HE HAD TO MOVE ALL THE WAY OUT HERE...!
DO YOU THINK URO-SAN WILL HAVE TO TAKE THE BLAME FOR THE SMOKY MANSION MESS-UP?
I HAVE NO IDEA, BUT...
...THE TWO OF US REALLY CAN'T DO A THING IF WE'RE NOT WITH URO-SAN!
THERE IT IS!
THAT'S THE PLACE!!

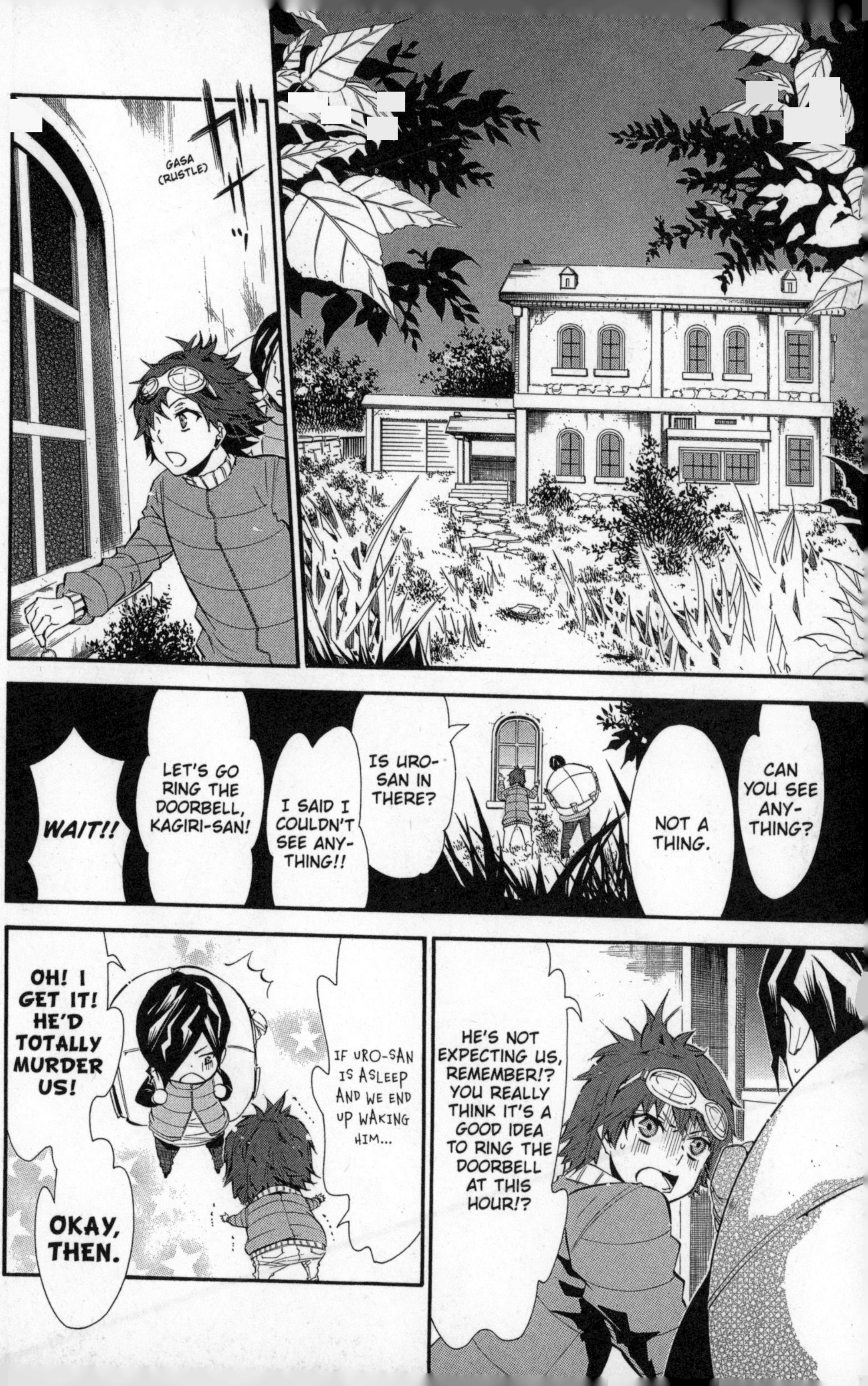
GASA (RUSTLE)
CAN YOU SEE ANYTHING?
NOT A THING.
IS URO-SAN IN THERE?
I SAID I COULDN'T SEE ANYTHING!!
LET'S GO RING THE DOORBELL, KAGIRI-SAN!
WAIT!!
HE'S NOT EXPECTING US, REMEMBER!? YOU REALLY THINK IT'S A GOOD IDEA TO RING THE DOORBELL AT THIS HOUR!?
IF URO-SAN IS ASLEEP AND WE END UP WAKING HIM...
OH! I GET IT! HE'D TOTALLY MURDER US!
OKAY, THEN.

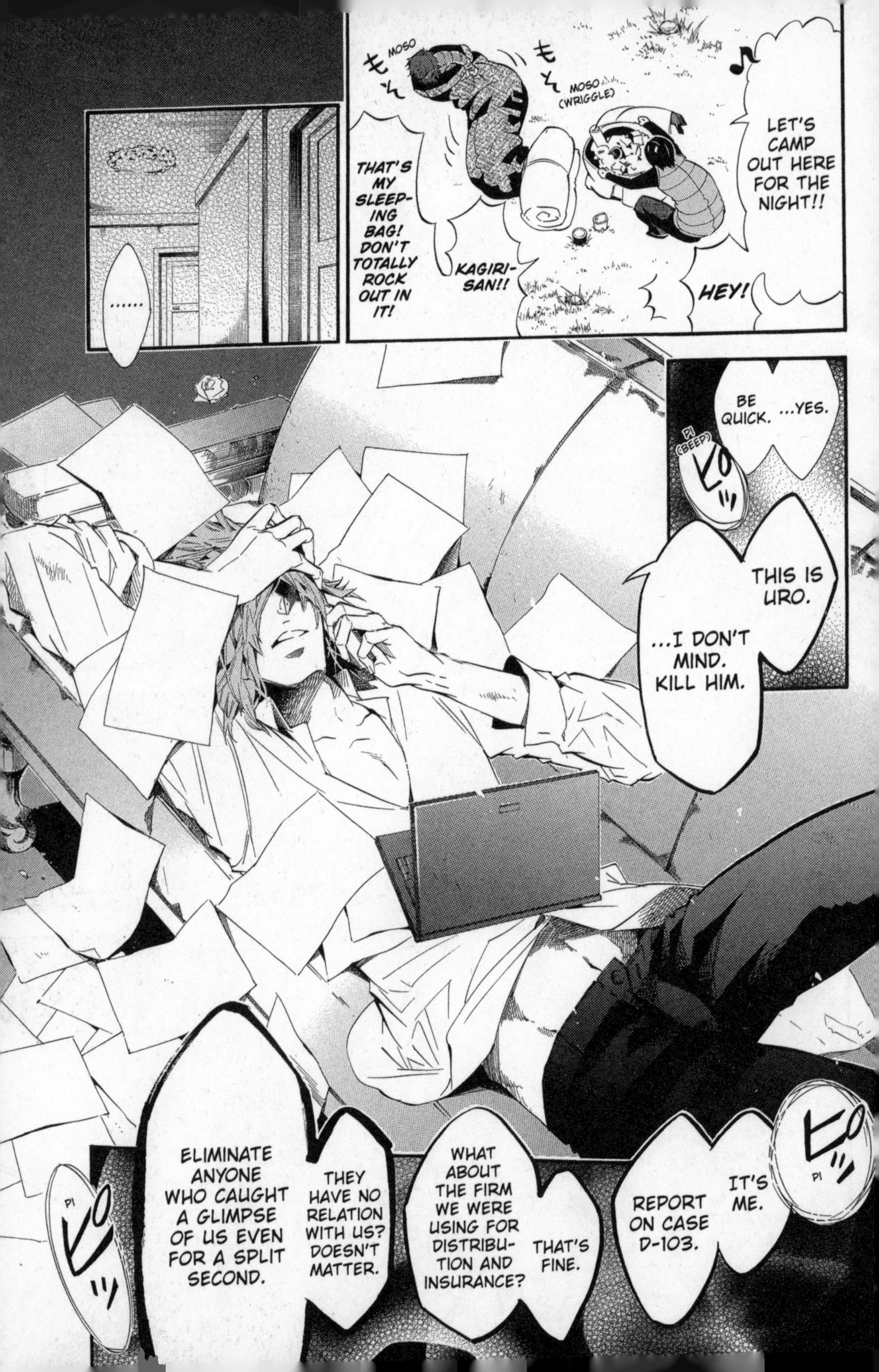
LET'S CAMP OUT HERE FOR THE NIGHT!!
HEY!
MOSO (WRIGGLE)
KAGIRI-SAN!!
THAT'S MY SLEEPING BAG! DON'T TOTALLY ROCK OUT IN IT!
MOSO
......
BE QUICK. ...YES.
PI (BEEP)
THIS IS URO.
...I DON'T MIND. KILL HIM.
PI
IT'S ME.
REPORT ON CASE D-103.
THAT'S FINE.
WHAT ABOUT THE FIRM WE WERE USING FOR DISTRIBUTION AND INSURANCE?
THEY HAVE NO RELATION WITH US? DOESN'T MATTER.
ELIMINATE ANYONE WHO CAUGHT A GLIMPSE OF US EVEN FOR A SPLIT SECOND.
PI

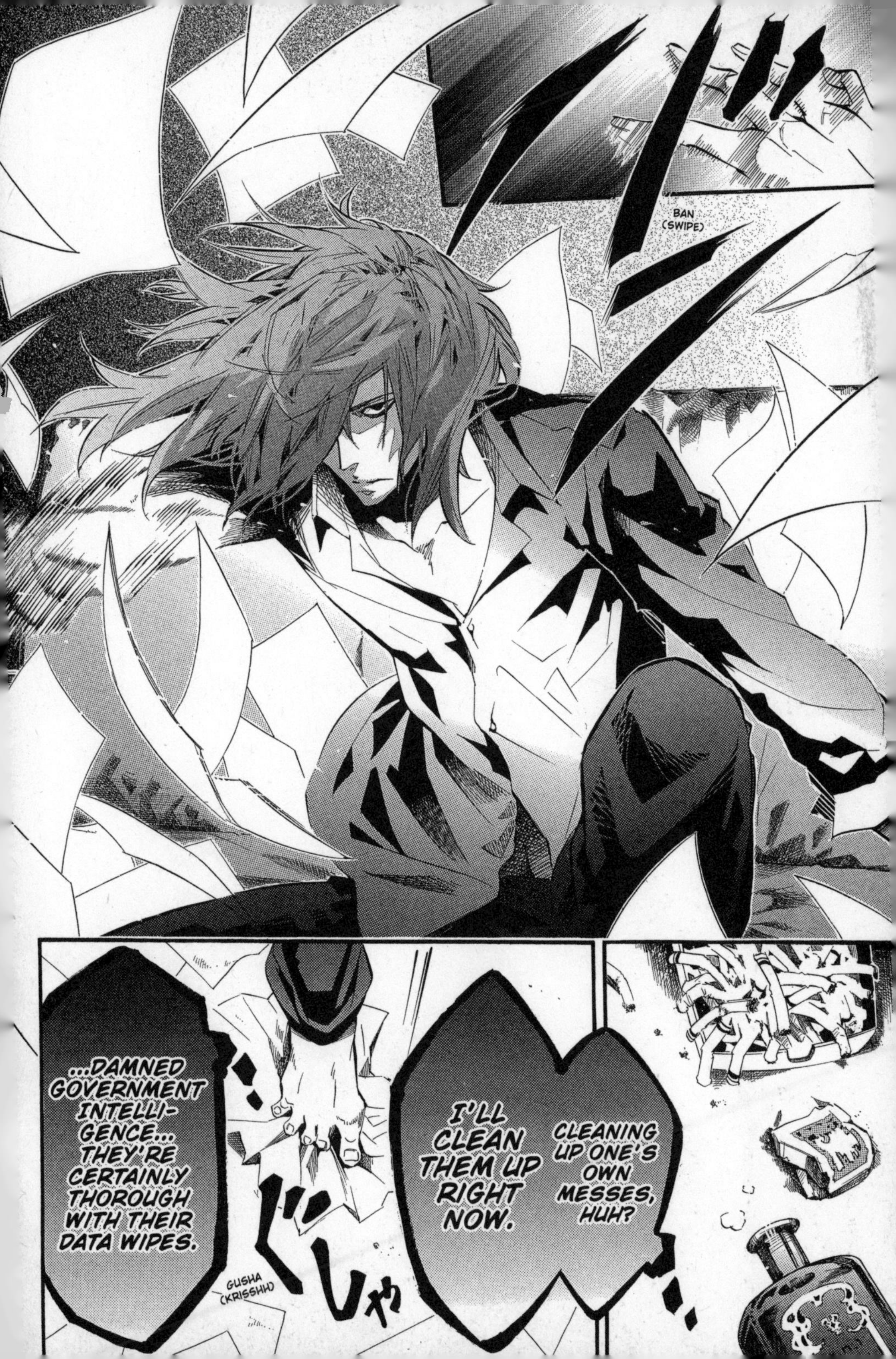
BAN (SWIPE)
CLEANING UP ONE'S OWN MESSES, HUH?
I'LL CLEAN THEM UP RIGHT NOW.
GUSHA (KRISSHH)
...DAMNED GOVERNMENT INTELLI-GENCE... THEY'RE CERTAINLY THOROUGH WITH THEIR DATA WIPES.

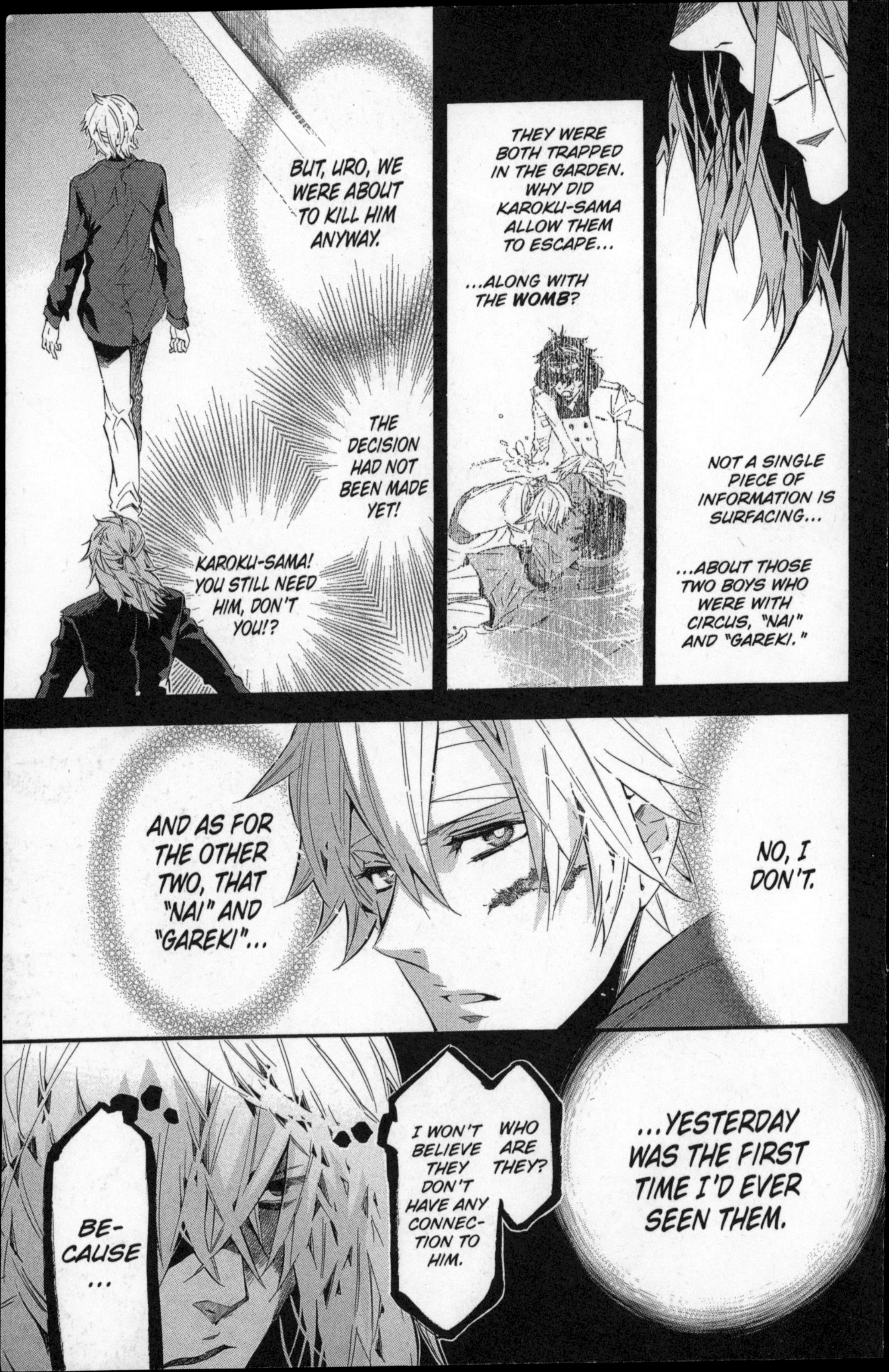
NOT A SINGLE PIECE OF INFORMATION IS SURFACING...
...ABOUT THOSE TWO BOYS WHO WERE WITH CIRCUS, "NAI" AND "GAREKI."
THEY WERE BOTH TRAPPED IN THE GARDEN. WHY DID KAROKU-SAMA ALLOW THEM TO ESCAPE...
...ALONG WITH THE **WOMB**?
BUT, URO, WE WERE ABOUT TO KILL HIM ANYWAY.
THE DECISION HAD NOT BEEN MADE YET!
KAROKU-SAMA! YOU STILL NEED HIM, DON'T YOU!?
NO, I DON'T.
AND AS FOR THE OTHER TWO, THAT "NAI" AND "GAREKI"...
...YESTERDAY WAS THE FIRST TIME I'D EVER SEEN THEM.
WHO ARE THEY?
I WON'T BELIEVE THEY DON'T HAVE ANY CONNECTION TO HIM.
BE-CAUSE ...

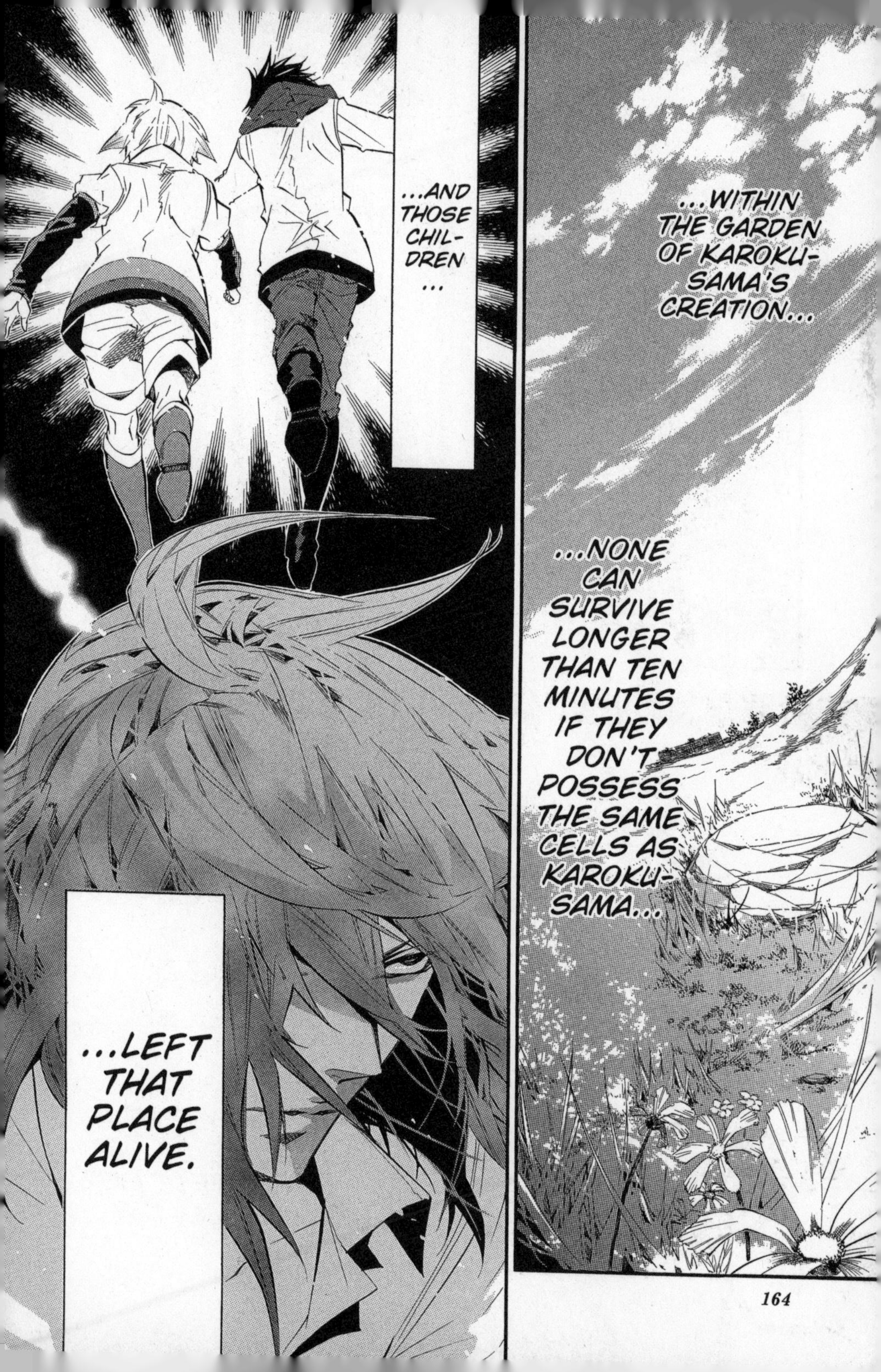
...WITHIN THE GARDEN OF KAROKU-SAMA'S CREATION...
...NONE CAN SURVIVE LONGER THAN TEN MINUTES IF THEY DON'T POSSESS THE SAME CELLS AS KAROKU-SAMA...
...AND THOSE CHIL-DREN...
...LEFT THAT PLACE ALIVE.

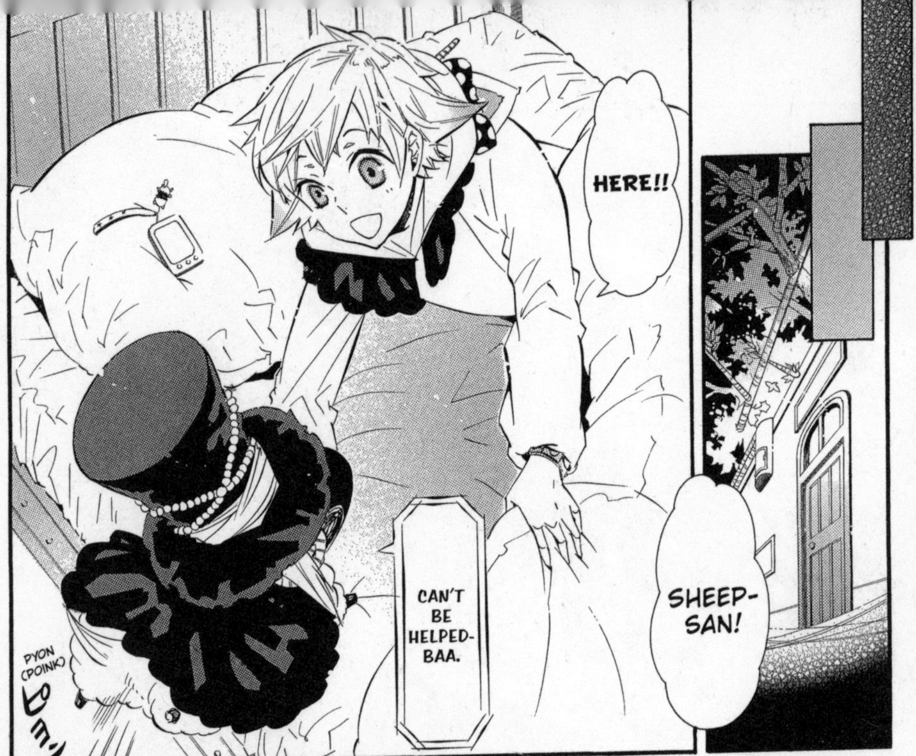
SHEEP-SAN!
HERE!!
CAN'T BE HELPED-BAA.
PYON (POINK)
ピョン

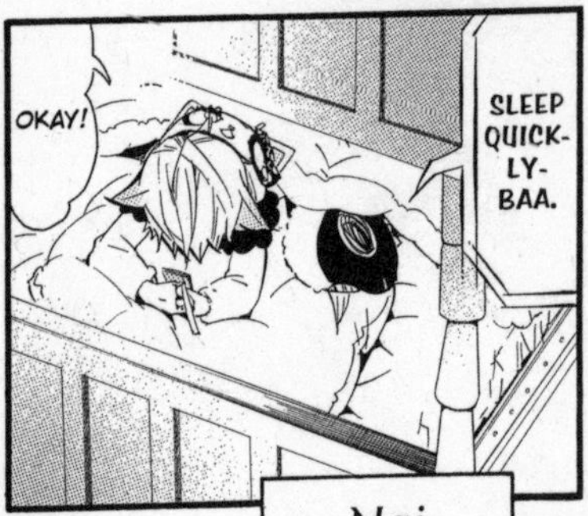
SLEEP QUICKLY-BAA.
OKAY!

Nai

You're the one who's gotta try hard. If there's anything you don't get though, you can text me and ask about it.

That said, don't just text me carelessly either. Think about it for five minutes first. If you can't figure it out by then, just stop, 'cos it'd be a huge waste of time with your brain's processing power. You can send a text and ask me then.

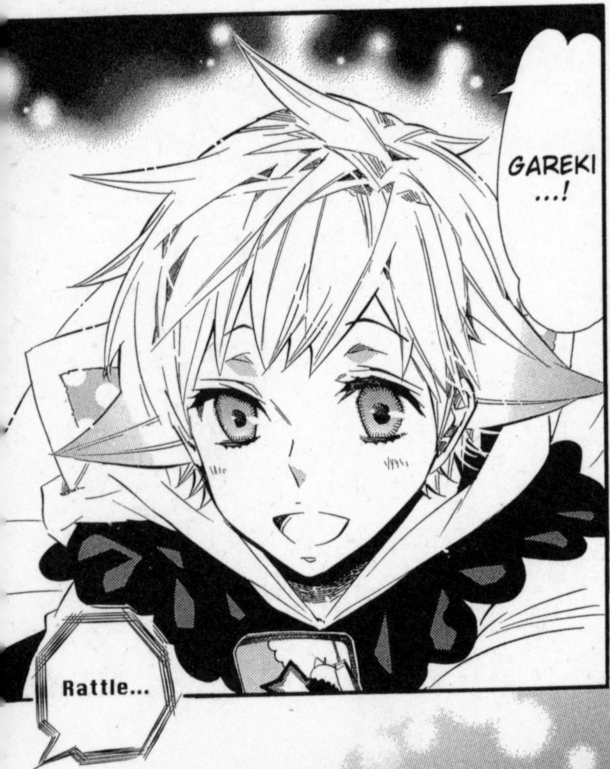
GAREKI ...!
Rattle...

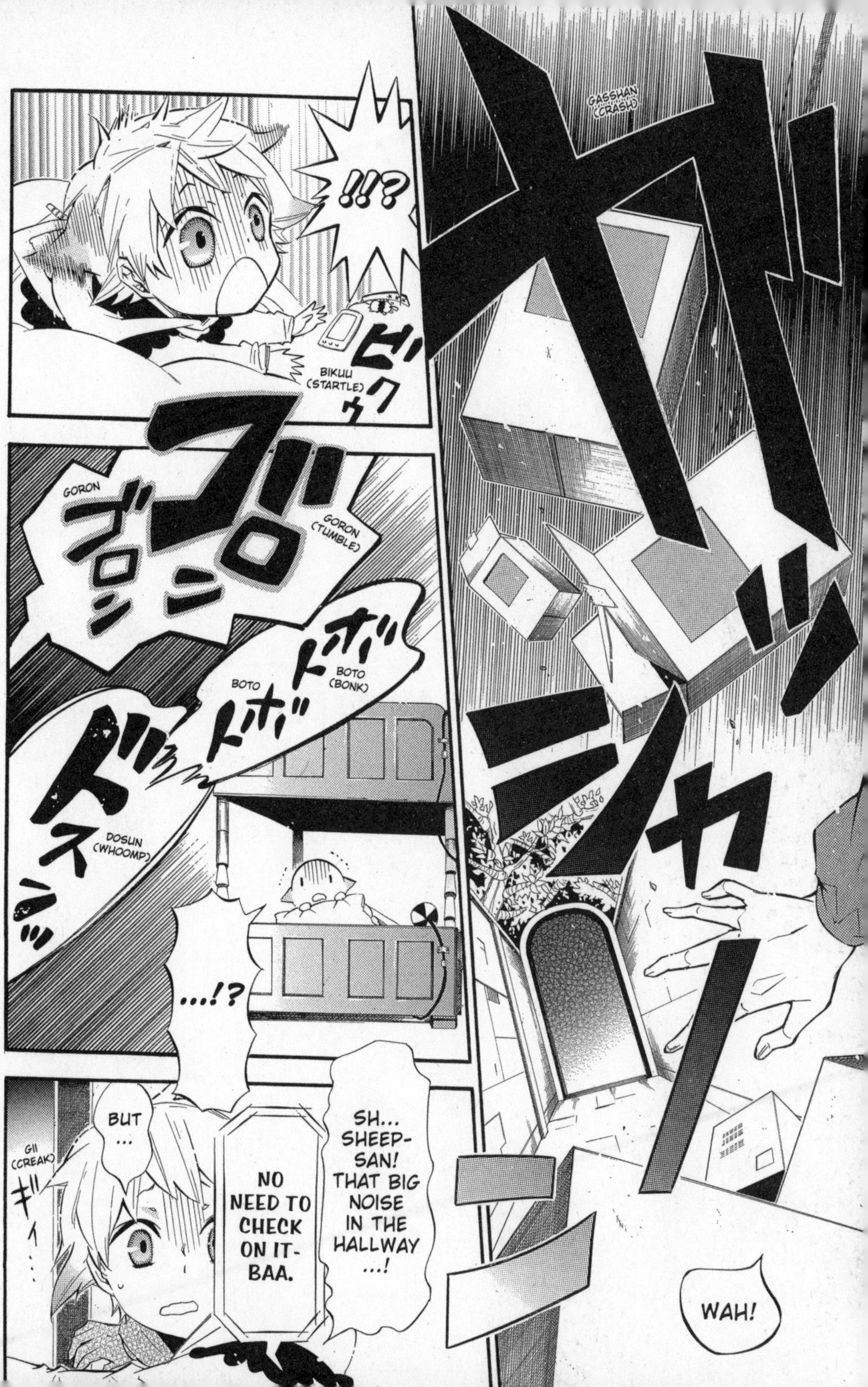
GASSHAN (CRASH)
WAH!
!!?
BIKUU (STARTLE)
GORON
GORON (TUMBLE)
BOTO
BOTO (BONK)
DOSUN (WHOOMP)
...!?
SH... SHEEP-SAN! THAT BIG NOISE IN THE HALLWAY ...!
NO NEED TO CHECK ON IT-BAA.
BUT ...
GII (CREAK)

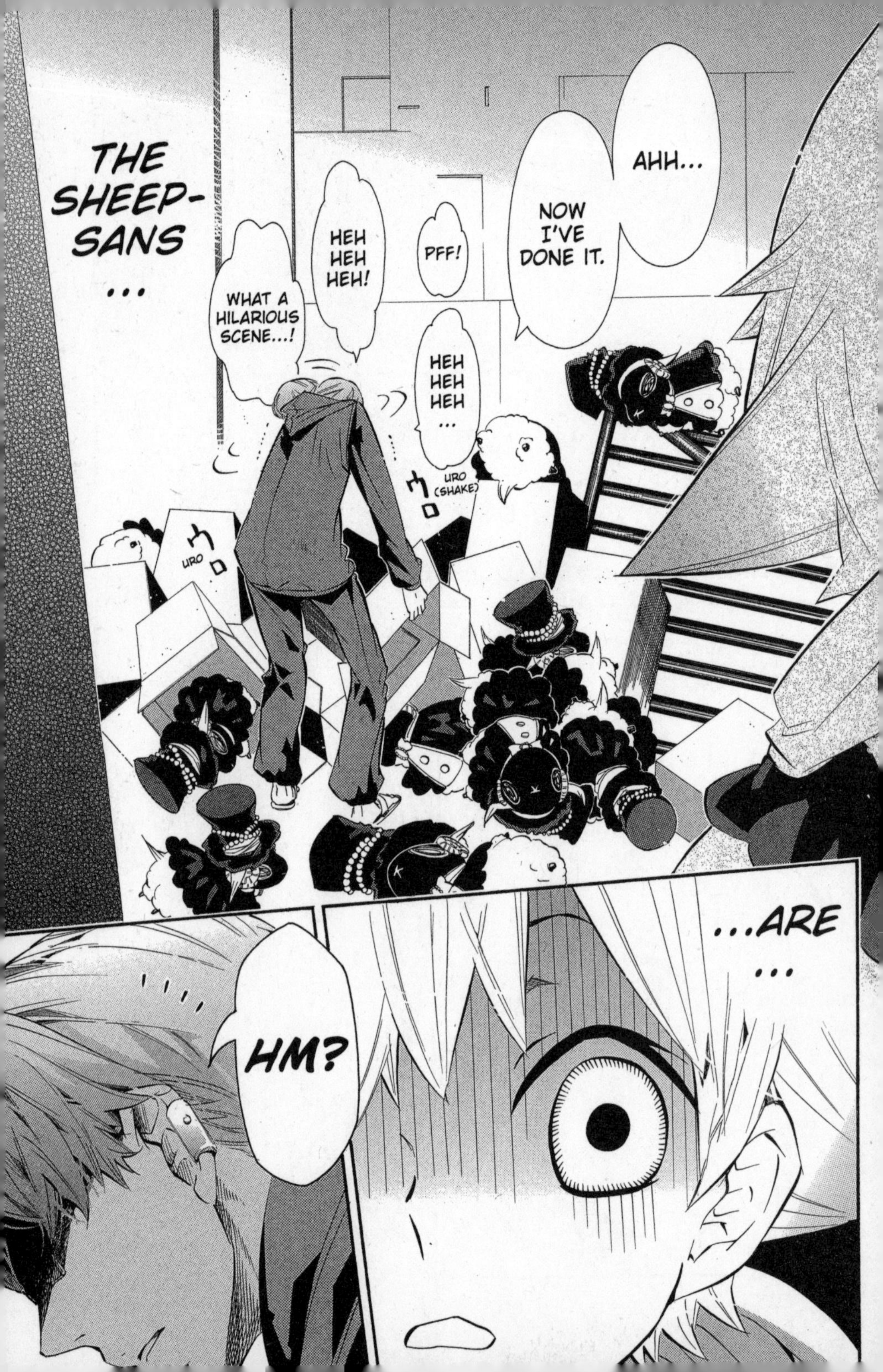

AHH...
NOW I'VE DONE IT.
PFF!
HEH HEH HEH!
HEH HEH HEH ...
WHAT A HILARIOUS SCENE...!
URO (SHAKE)
URO
THE SHEEP-SANS ...
...ARE ...
HM?
...

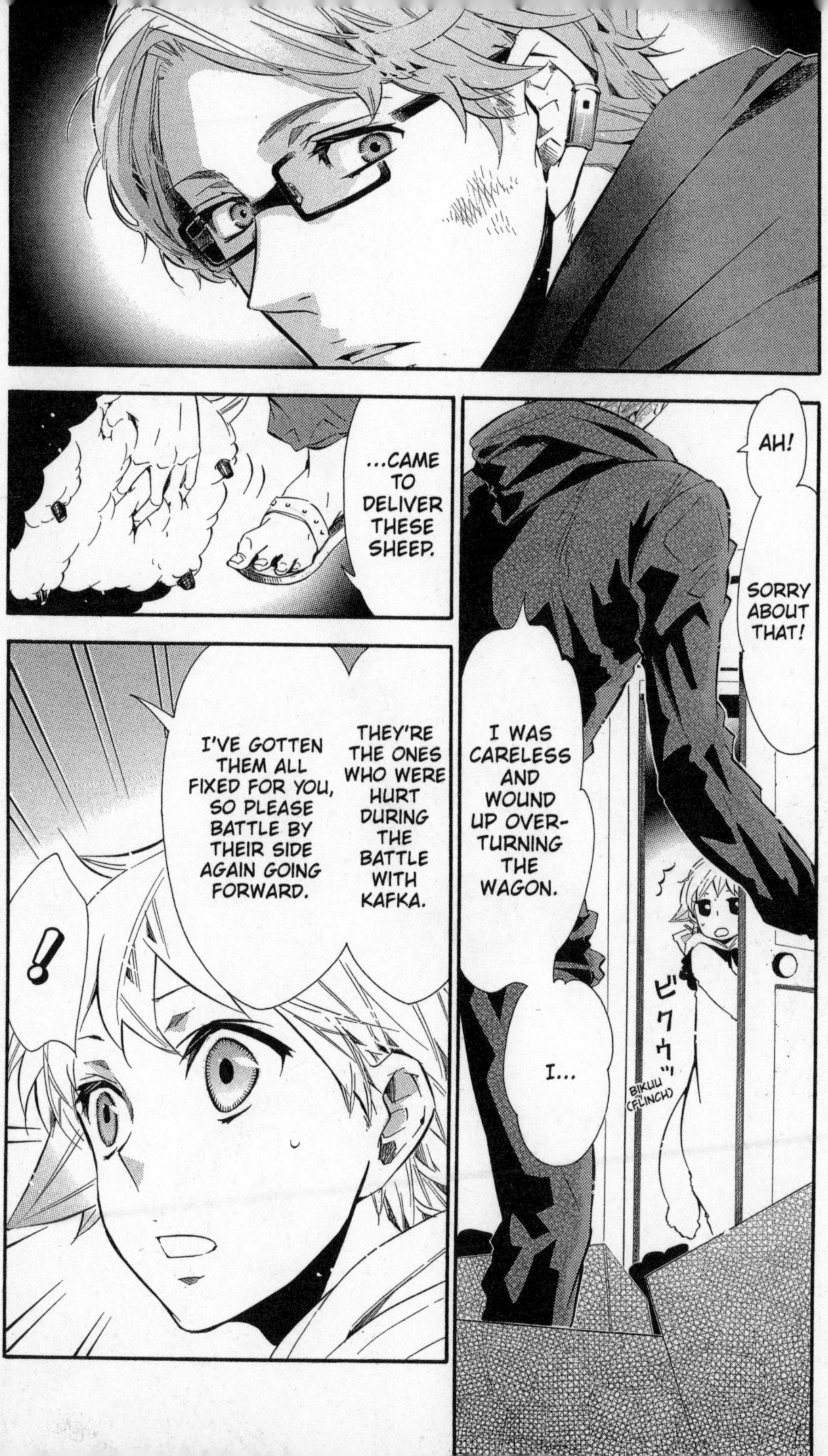
AH!
SORRY ABOUT THAT!
I WAS CARELESS AND WOUND UP OVER-TURNING THE WAGON.
ビクゥッ
BIKUU (FLINCH)
I...
...CAME TO DELIVER THESE SHEEP.
THEY'RE THE ONES WHO WERE HURT DURING THE BATTLE WITH KAFKA.
I'VE GOTTEN THEM ALL FIXED FOR YOU, SO PLEASE BATTLE BY THEIR SIDE AGAIN GOING FORWARD.
!

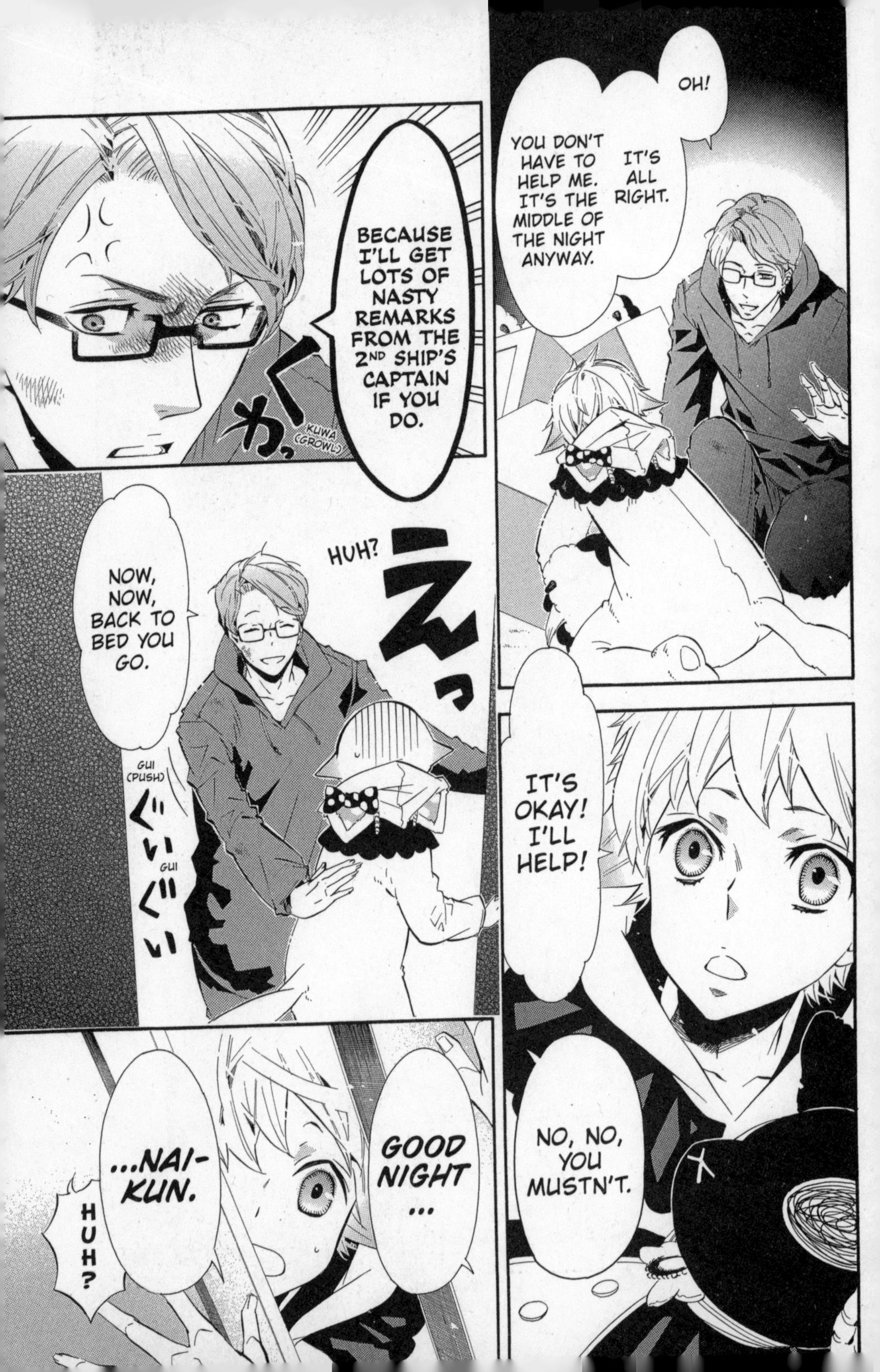
OH!
IT'S ALL RIGHT.
YOU DON'T HAVE TO HELP ME. IT'S THE MIDDLE OF THE NIGHT ANYWAY.
IT'S OKAY! I'LL HELP!
NO, NO, YOU MUSTN'T.
BECAUSE I'LL GET LOTS OF NASTY REMARKS FROM THE 2ND SHIP'S CAPTAIN IF YOU DO.
KUWA (GROWL)
HUH?
NOW, NOW, BACK TO BED YOU GO.
GUI (PUSH)
GUI
GOOD NIGHT...
...NAI-KUN.
HUH?

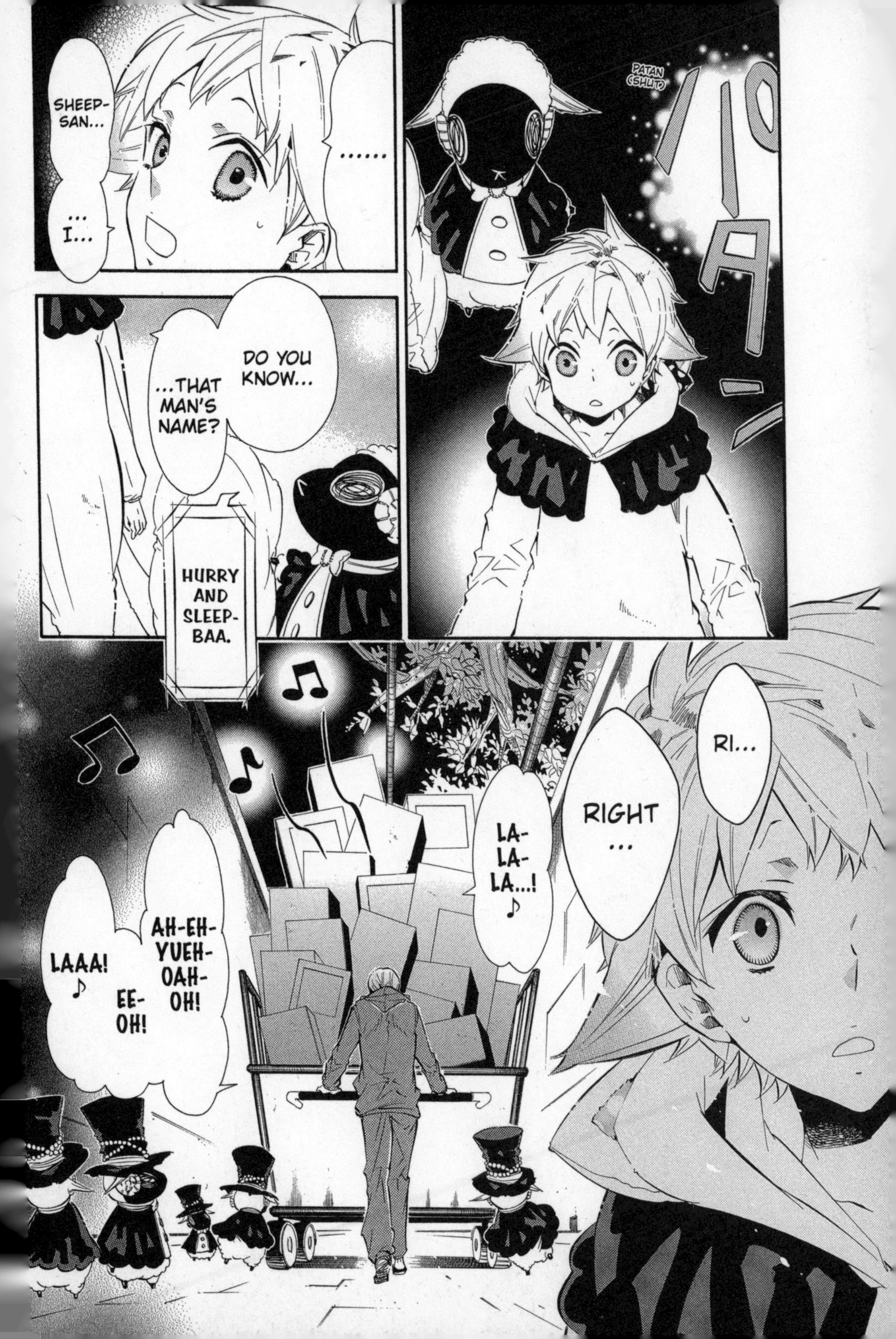
PATAN (SHUT)
SHEEP-SAN...
......
...I...
DO YOU KNOW...
...THAT MAN'S NAME?
HURRY AND SLEEP-BAA.
RI...
RIGHT ...
LA-LA-LA...! ♪
AH-EH-YUEH-OAH-OH!
EE-OH!
LAAA! ♪

KARNEVAL

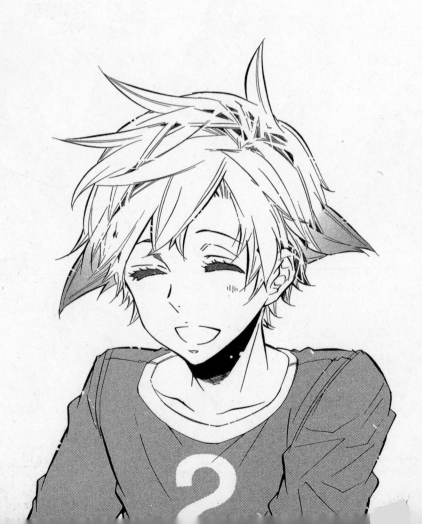

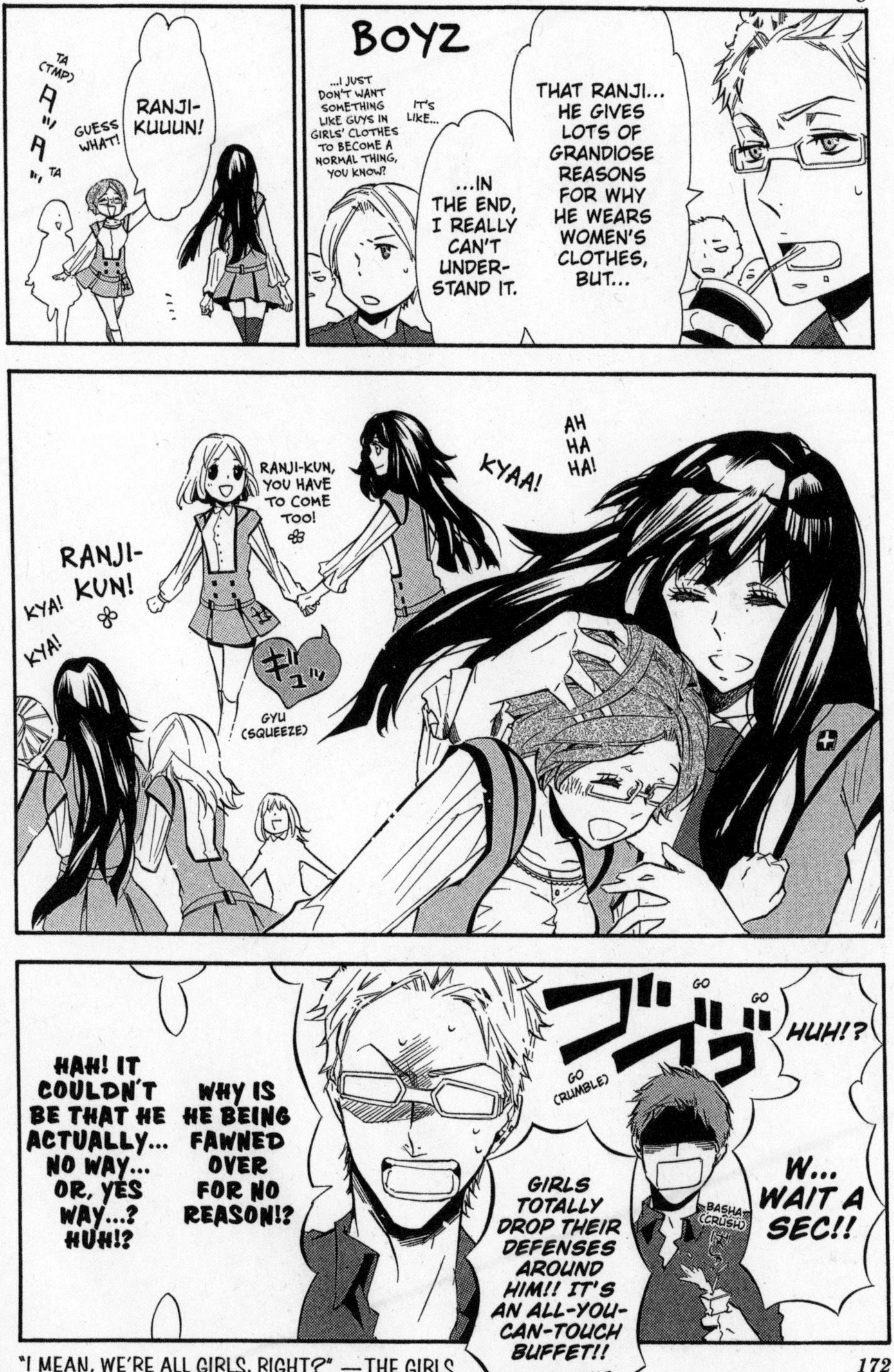
BOYZ
THAT RANJI... HE GIVES LOTS OF GRANDIOSE REASONS FOR WHY HE WEARS WOMEN'S CLOTHES, BUT...
...IN THE END, I REALLY CAN'T UNDERSTAND IT.
IT'S LIKE...
...I JUST DON'T WANT SOMETHING LIKE GUYS IN GIRLS' CLOTHES TO BECOME A NORMAL THING, YOU KNOW?
RANJI-KUUUN!
GUESS WHAT!
TA (TMP) TA
AH HA HA!
KYAA!
RANJI-KUN, YOU HAVE TO COME TOO!
RANJI-KUN!
KYA! KYA!
GYU (SQUEEZE)
HUH!?
GO GO GO (RUMBLE)
W... WAIT A SEC!!
GIRLS TOTALLY DROP THEIR DEFENSES AROUND HIM!! IT'S AN ALL-YOU-CAN-TOUCH BUFFET!! OF THE FEMALE BODY...
BASHA (CRUSH)
WHY IS HE BEING FAWNED OVER FOR NO REASON!?
HAH! IT COULDN'T BE THAT HE ACTUALLY... NO WAY... OR, YES WAY...? HUH!?

"I MEAN, WE'RE ALL GIRLS, RIGHT?" —THE GIRLS

The Circus Ship Resident Guardian

Bonus Comic 2 - Who Cleans the Floors Till They Sparkle—"Mokkyu"

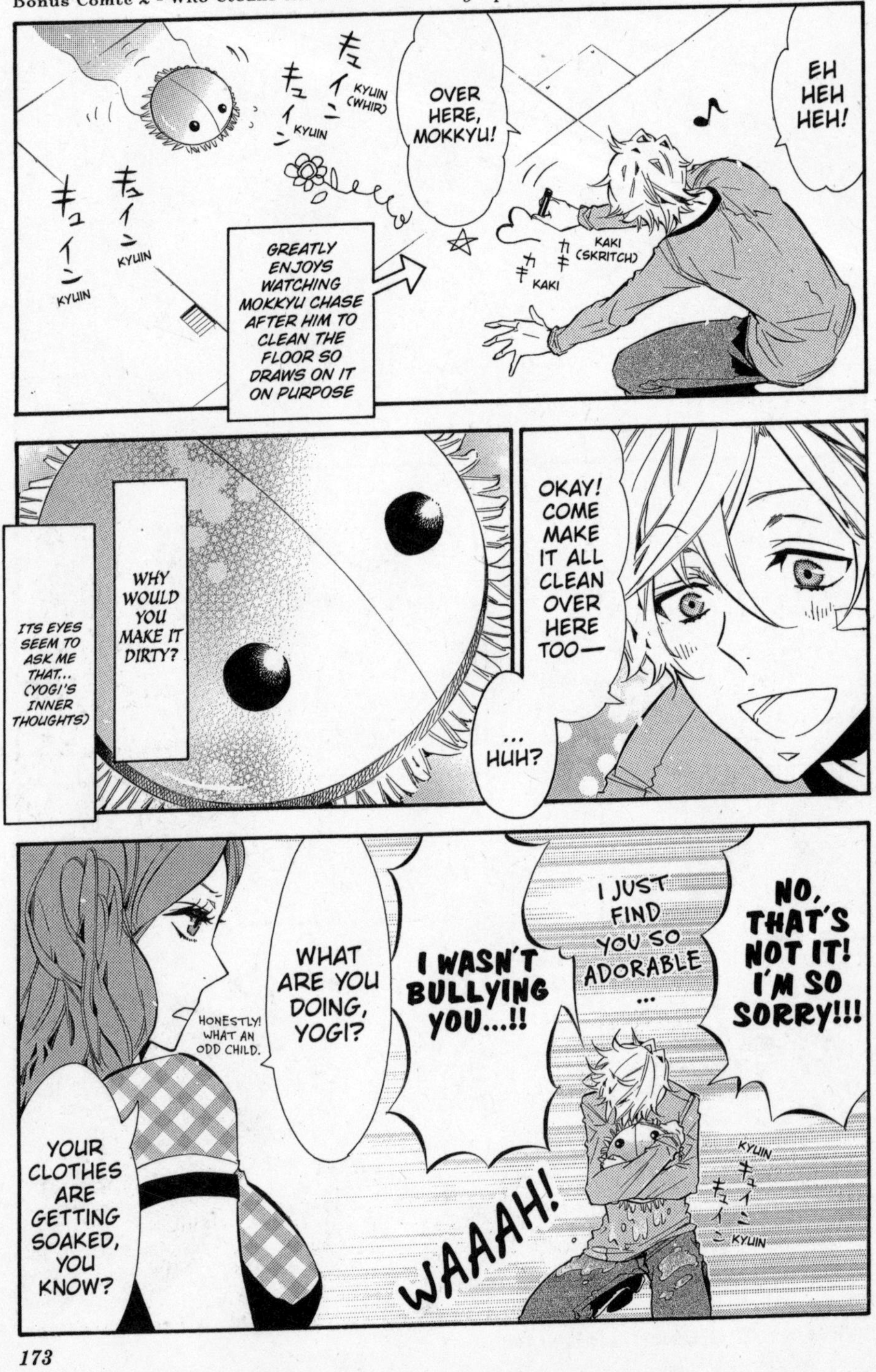
EH HEH HEH!
KAKI (SKRITCH)
KAKI
OVER HERE, MOKKYU!
GREATLY ENJOYS WATCHING MOKKYU CHASE AFTER HIM TO CLEAN THE FLOOR SO DRAWS ON IT ON PURPOSE
KYUIN (WHIR)
KYUIN
KYUIN
KYUIN
OKAY! COME MAKE IT ALL CLEAN OVER HERE TOO—
... HUH?
WHY WOULD YOU MAKE IT DIRTY?
ITS EYES SEEM TO ASK ME THAT... (YOGI'S INNER THOUGHTS)
NO, THAT'S NOT IT! I'M SO SORRY!!!
I JUST FIND YOU SO ADORABLE ...
I WASN'T BULLYING YOU...!!
KYUIN
KYUIN
WAAAH!
WHAT ARE YOU DOING, YOGI?
HONESTLY! WHAT AN ODD CHILD.
YOUR CLOTHES ARE GETTING SOAKED, YOU KNOW?

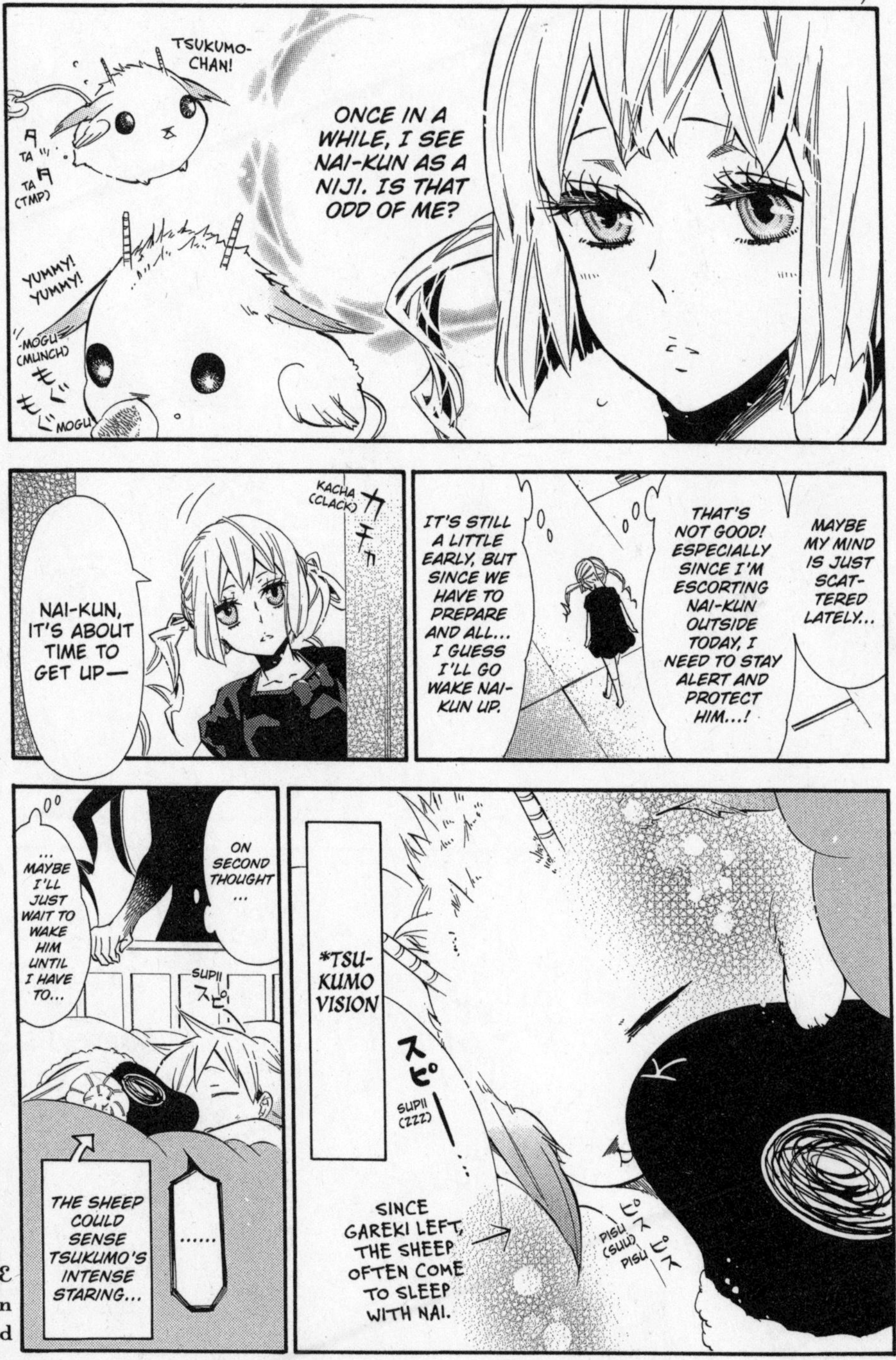
ONCE IN A WHILE, I SEE NAI-KUN AS A NIJI. IS THAT ODD OF ME?
TSUKUMO-CHAN!
タ TA タ TA (TMP)
YUMMY! YUMMY!
もぐ MOGU (MUNCH) もぐ MOGU
MAYBE MY MIND IS JUST SCAT-TERED LATELY...
THAT'S NOT GOOD! ESPECIALLY SINCE I'M ESCORTING NAI-KUN OUTSIDE TODAY, I NEED TO STAY ALERT AND PROTECT HIM...!
IT'S STILL A LITTLE EARLY, BUT SINCE WE HAVE TO PREPARE AND ALL... I GUESS I'LL GO WAKE NAI-KUN UP.
カチャ KACHA (CLACK)
NAI-KUN, IT'S ABOUT TIME TO GET UP—
*TSU-KUMO VISION
スピー SUPII (ZZZ)
ピス PISU (SUU) ピス PISU
SINCE GAREKI LEFT, THE SHEEP OFTEN COME TO SLEEP WITH NAI.
ON SECOND THOUGHT...
...MAYBE I'LL JUST WAIT TO WAKE HIM UNTIL I HAVE TO...
スピ SUPII
THE SHEEP COULD SENSE TSUKUMO'S INTENSE STARING...
......

End

COME RIDE OUR SHIP WITH ME, AND LET'S SOAR ONWARD TO-GETHER. —TSU-KUMO

THE KIND OF PET TSUKUMO WANTS TO OWN: A NIJI.

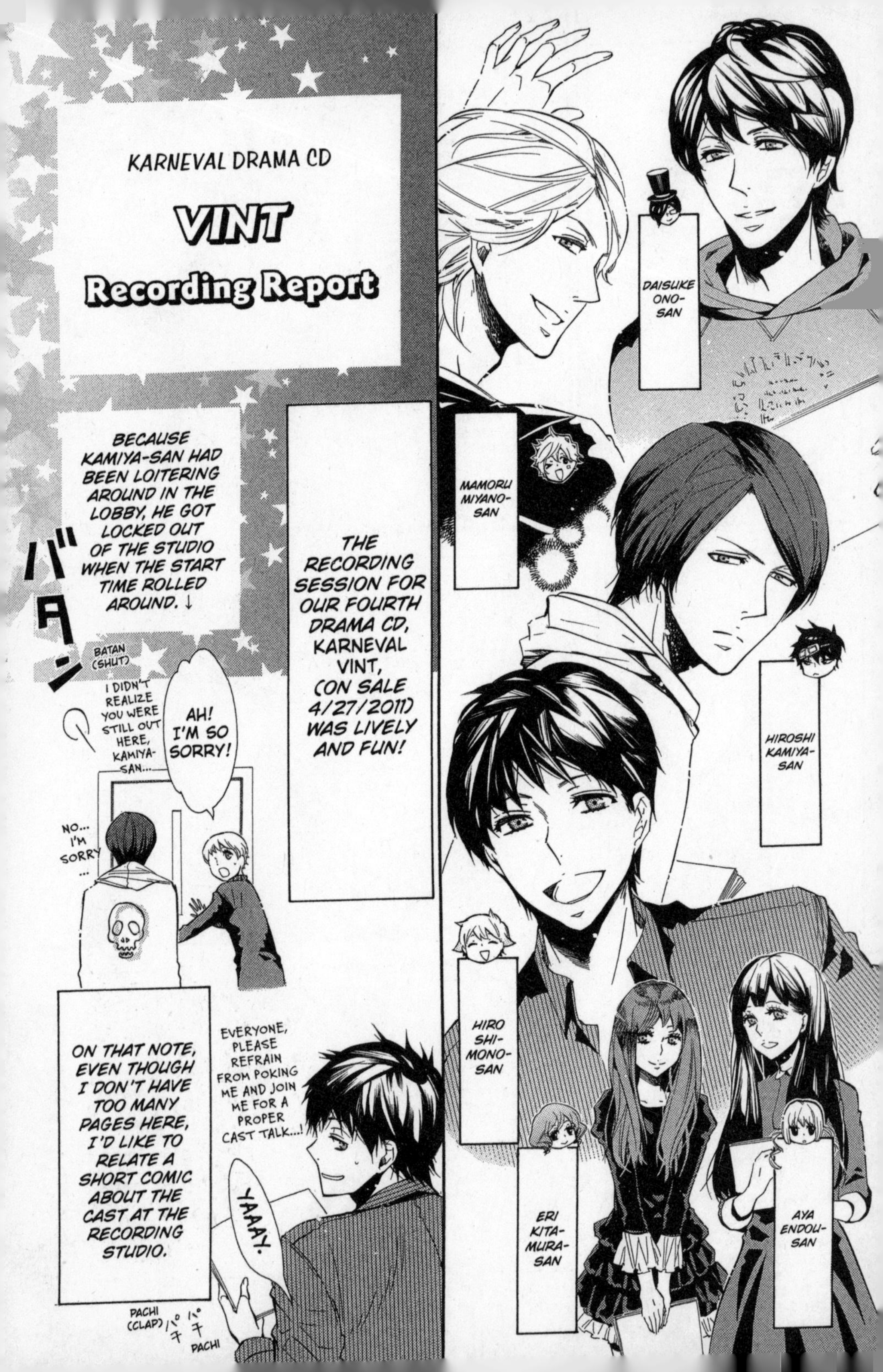
DAISUKE ONO-SAN
MAMORU MIYANO-SAN
HIROSHI KAMIYA-SAN
HIRO SHIMONO-SAN
AYA ENDOU-SAN
ERI KITAMURA-SAN
KARNEVAL DRAMA CD
VINT
Recording Report
THE RECORDING SESSION FOR OUR FOURTH DRAMA CD, KARNEVAL VINT, (ON SALE 4/27/2011) WAS LIVELY AND FUN!
BECAUSE KAMIYA-SAN HAD BEEN LOITERING AROUND IN THE LOBBY, HE GOT LOCKED OUT OF THE STUDIO WHEN THE START TIME ROLLED AROUND. ↓
バタン
BATAN (SHUT)
AH! I'M SO SORRY!
I DIDN'T REALIZE YOU WERE STILL OUT HERE, KAMIYA-SAN...
NO... I'M SORRY...
EVERYONE, PLEASE REFRAIN FROM POKING ME AND JOIN ME FOR A PROPER CAST TALK...!
YAAAY.
パチ パチ
PACHI (CLAP) PACHI
ON THAT NOTE, EVEN THOUGH I DON'T HAVE TOO MANY PAGES HERE, I'D LIKE TO RELATE A SHORT COMIC ABOUT THE CAST AT THE RECORDING STUDIO.

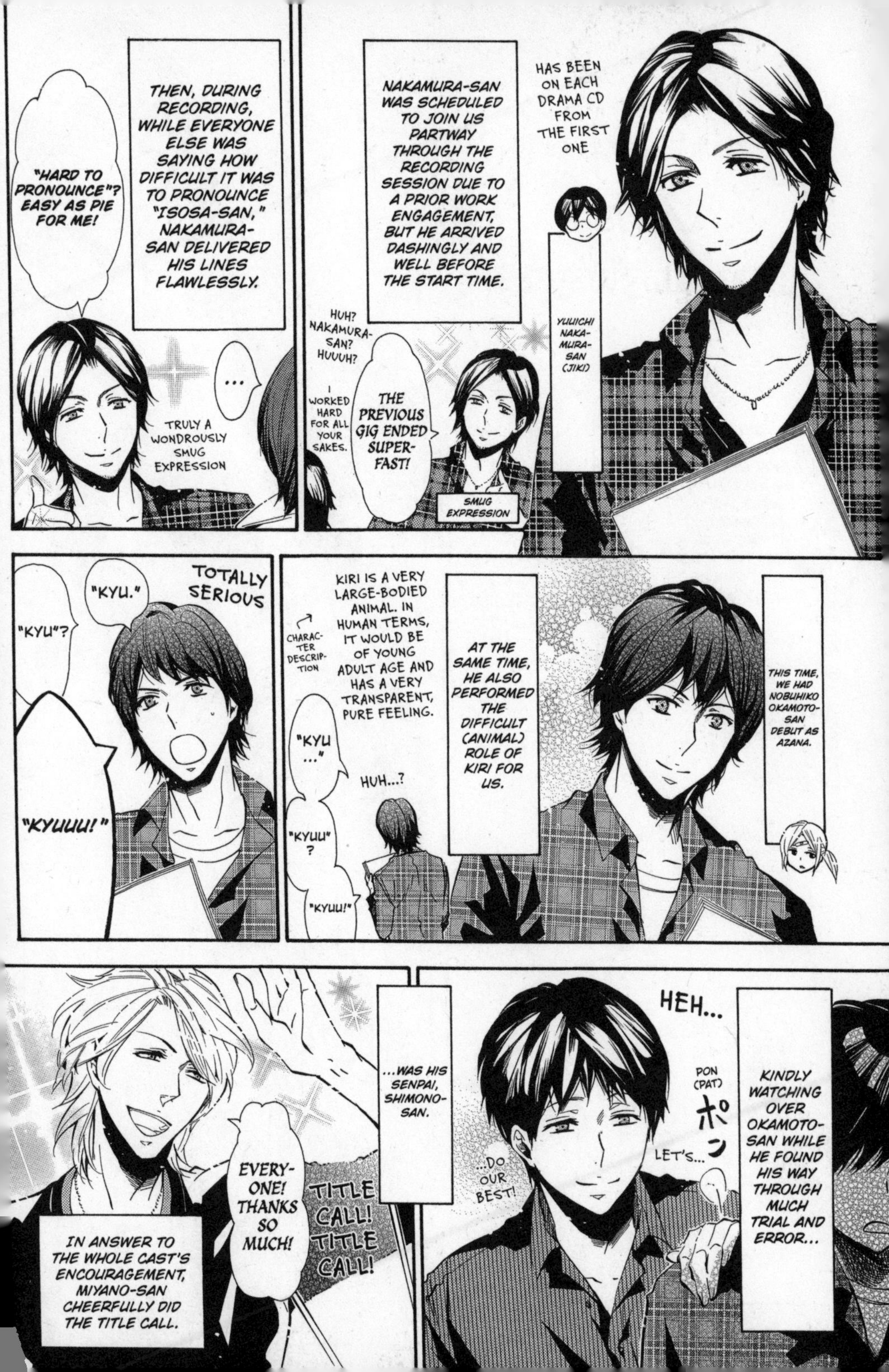
HAS BEEN ON EACH DRAMA CD FROM THE FIRST ONE
YUUICHI NAKAMURA-SAN (JIKI)
NAKAMURA-SAN WAS SCHEDULED TO JOIN US PARTWAY THROUGH THE RECORDING SESSION DUE TO A PRIOR WORK ENGAGEMENT, BUT HE ARRIVED DASHINGLY AND WELL BEFORE THE START TIME.
HUH? NAKAMURA-SAN? HUUUH?
THE PREVIOUS GIG ENDED SUPER-FAST!
I WORKED HARD FOR ALL YOUR SAKES.
SMUG EXPRESSION
THEN, DURING RECORDING, WHILE EVERYONE ELSE WAS SAYING HOW DIFFICULT IT WAS TO PRONOUNCE "ISOSA-SAN," NAKAMURA-SAN DELIVERED HIS LINES FLAWLESSLY.
"HARD TO PRONOUNCE"? EASY AS PIE FOR ME!
...
TRULY A WONDROUSLY SMUG EXPRESSION
THIS TIME, WE HAD NOBUHIKO OKAMOTO-SAN DEBUT AS AZANA.
AT THE SAME TIME, HE ALSO PERFORMED THE DIFFICULT (ANIMAL) ROLE OF KIRI FOR US.
KIRI IS A VERY LARGE-BODIED ANIMAL. IN HUMAN TERMS, IT WOULD BE OF YOUNG ADULT AGE AND HAS A VERY TRANSPARENT, PURE FEELING.
CHARACTER DESCRIPTION
HUH...?
"KYU..."
"KYUU"?
"KYUU!"
TOTALLY SERIOUS
"KYU."
"KYU"?
"KYUUU!"
KINDLY WATCHING OVER OKAMOTO-SAN WHILE HE FOUND HIS WAY THROUGH MUCH TRIAL AND ERROR...
HEH...
PON (PAT)
ポン
LET'S...
...DO OUR BEST!
...WAS HIS SENPAI, SHIMONO-SAN.
TITLE CALL! TITLE CALL!
EVERY-ONE! THANKS SO MUCH!
IN ANSWER TO THE WHOLE CAST'S ENCOURAGEMENT, MIYANO-SAN CHEERFULLY DID THE TITLE CALL.

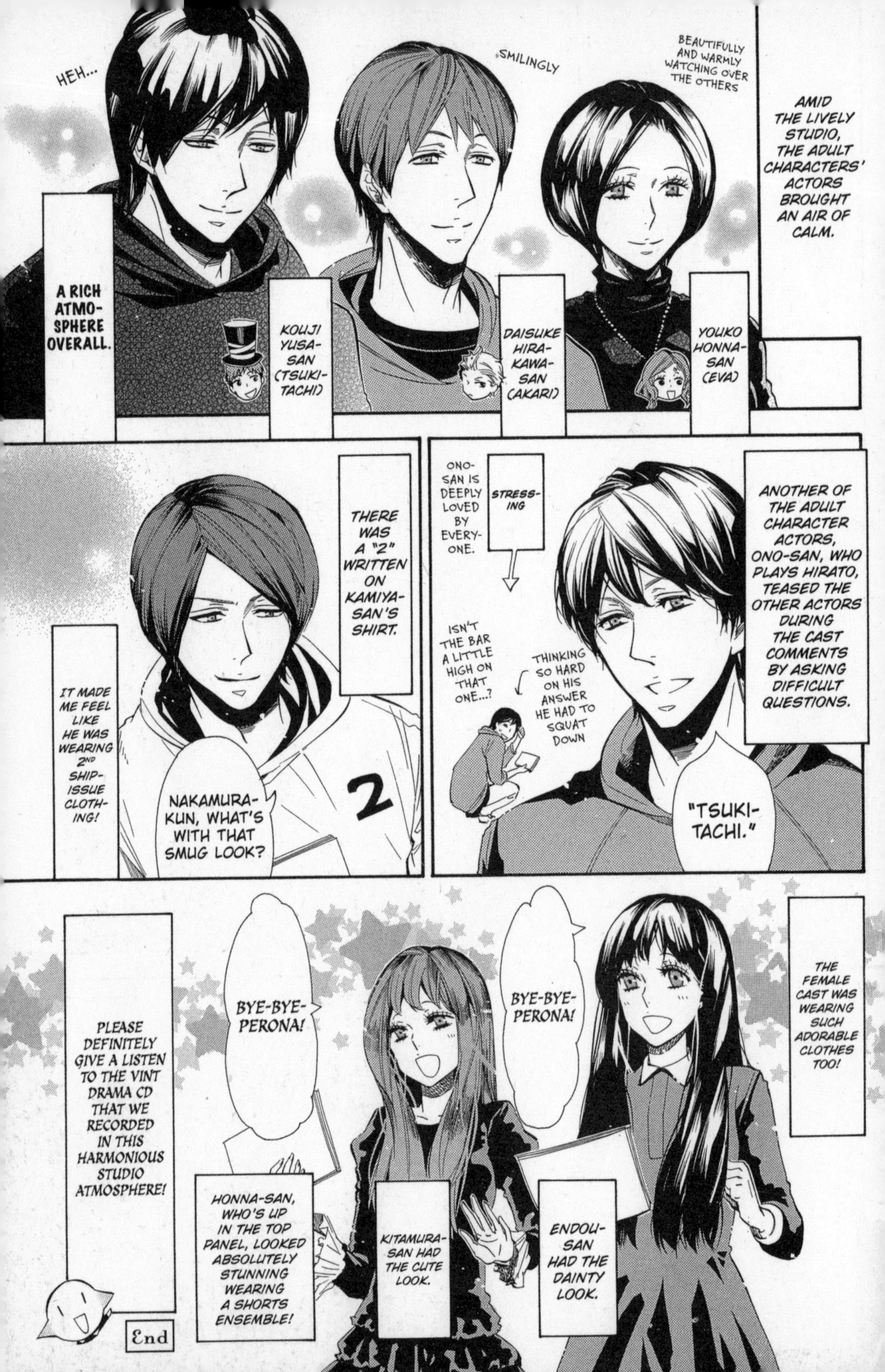
AMID THE LIVELY STUDIO, THE ADULT CHARACTERS' ACTORS BROUGHT AN AIR OF CALM.
BEAUTIFULLY AND WARMLY WATCHING OVER THE OTHERS
YOUKO HONNA-SAN (EVA)
SMILINGLY
DAISUKE HIRA-KAWA-SAN (AKARI)
HEH...
KOUJI YUSA-SAN (TSUKI-TACHI)
A RICH ATMO-SPHERE OVERALL.
ANOTHER OF THE ADULT CHARACTER ACTORS, ONO-SAN, WHO PLAYS HIRATO, TEASED THE OTHER ACTORS DURING THE CAST COMMENTS BY ASKING DIFFICULT QUESTIONS.
"TSUKI-TACHI."
STRESS-ING
ONO-SAN IS DEEPLY LOVED BY EVERY-ONE.
THINKING SO HARD ON HIS ANSWER HE HAD TO SQUAT DOWN
ISN'T THE BAR A LITTLE HIGH ON THAT ONE...?
THERE WAS A "2" WRITTEN ON KAMIYA-SAN'S SHIRT.
2
NAKAMURA-KUN, WHAT'S WITH THAT SMUG LOOK?
IT MADE ME FEEL LIKE HE WAS WEARING 2ND SHIP-ISSUE CLOTH-ING!
THE FEMALE CAST WAS WEARING SUCH ADORABLE CLOTHES TOO!
BYE-BYE-PERONA!
ENDOU-SAN HAD THE DAINTY LOOK.
BYE-BYE-PERONA!
KITAMURA-SAN HAD THE CUTE LOOK.
HONNA-SAN, WHO'S UP IN THE TOP PANEL, LOOKED ABSOLUTELY STUNNING WEARING A SHORTS ENSEMBLE!
PLEASE DEFINITELY GIVE A LISTEN TO THE VINT DRAMA CD THAT WE RECORDED IN THIS HARMONIOUS STUDIO ATMOSPHERE!
End

KASHI (CLICK)
カシ
KASHI
カシ
KASHI
カシ
KASHI
カシ
KASHI
カシ

KARNEVAL

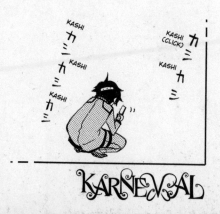

HELLO, THIS IS MIKANAGI. THANK YOU FOR ALWAYS READING KARNEVAL. I'M REALLY HAPPY THAT LATELY MOVIC HAS BEEN RELEASING QUITE A FEW NEW PIECES OF MERCHANDISE FOR KARNEVAL TOO. THERE'S A NYANPERONA PHONE STRAP, AS WELL AS A BADGE OF THE 2ND SHIP COAT OF ARMS FEATURED ON YOGI'S SHIRT ON THE FRONT COVER OF VOLUME 2, AND OTHER THINGS LIKE TRADING CARDS AND SO ON, WHICH THEY HAVE DESIGNED VERY CUTELY. THE NYANPE PHONE STRAP THEY MADE MATCHES THE ONE YOGI GAVE TO NAI, SO I WAS ACTUALLY THINKING ABOUT GETTING ONE FOR MYSELF.

AS I WAS WORKING ON THESE BONUS PAGES FOR THIS VOLUME, WE HAD THE TOHOKU EARTHQUAKE. I PRAY FROM MY HEART THAT ALL THOSE AFFECTED BY THE QUAKE WILL BE ABLE TO RETURN TO A PEACEFUL, SAFE DAILY LIFE AS QUICKLY AS POSSIBLE.
IF THERE ARE VICTIMS OF THE TOHOKU EARTHQUAKE AMONG MY READERS AS WELL, I PRAY THAT WHEN THINGS SETTLE DOWN AND YOU CAN READ THIS VOLUME, IT WILL PROVIDE YOU WITH EVEN A MOMENT'S RESPITE OF FUN. AS THIS IS WHAT I'M PROBABLY BEST ABLE TO DO TO HELP, I WILL CONTINUE DOING MY BEST DRAWING THIS MANGA.

TOUYA MIKANAGI

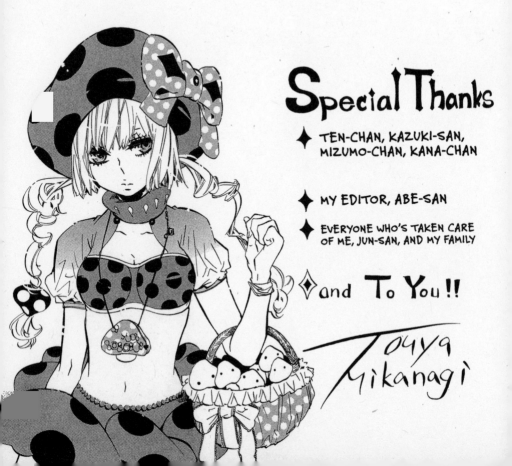

Special Thanks

- ◆ TEN-CHAN, KAZUKI-SAN, MIZUMO-CHAN, KANA-CHAN

- ◆ MY EDITOR, ABE-SAN

- ◆ EVERYONE WHO'S TAKEN CARE OF ME, JUN-SAN, AND MY FAMILY

◆ and To You!!

Touya Mikanagi

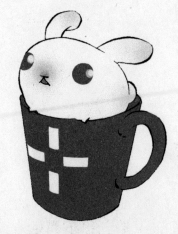

Score 43: Rejection

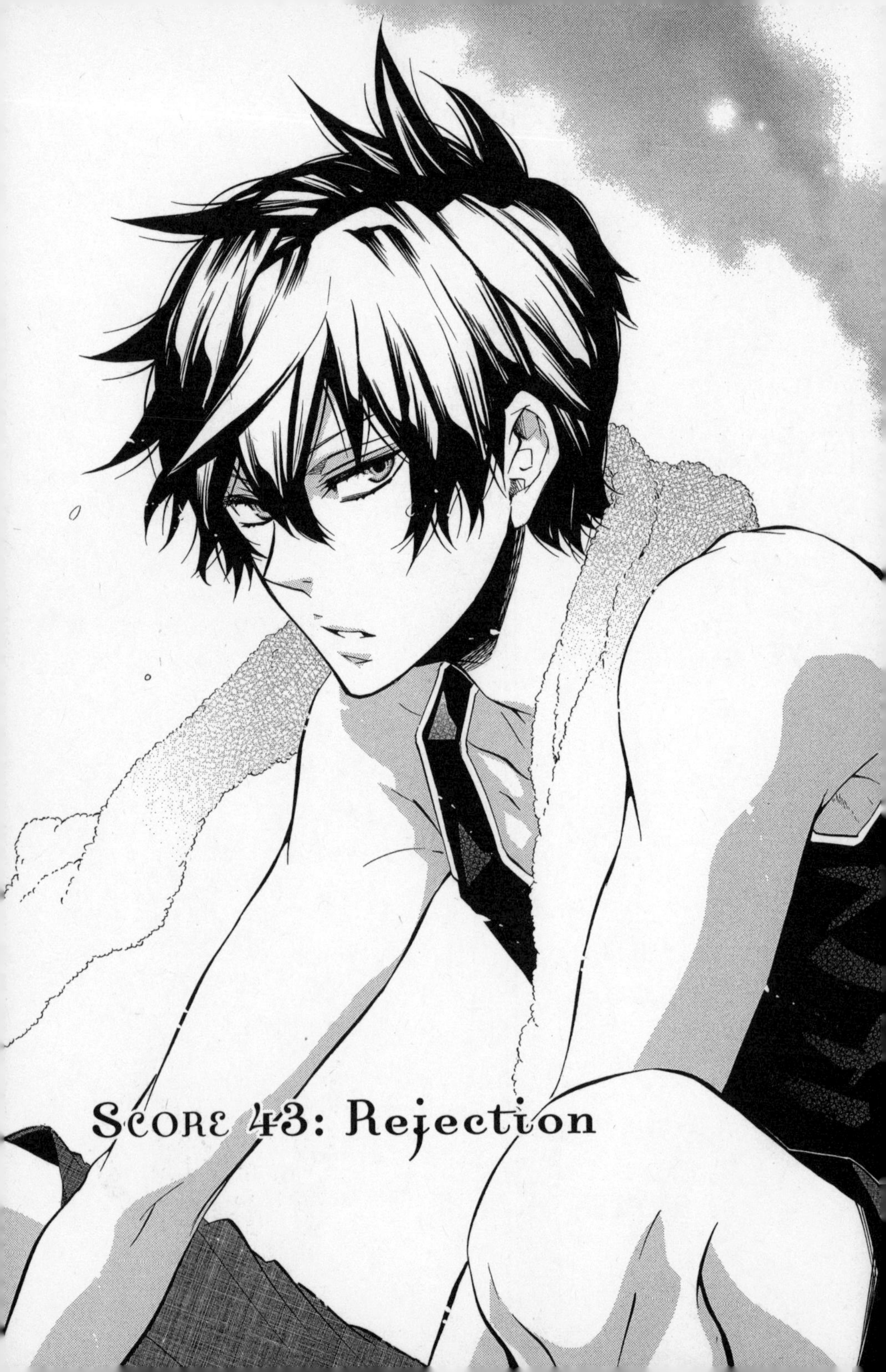

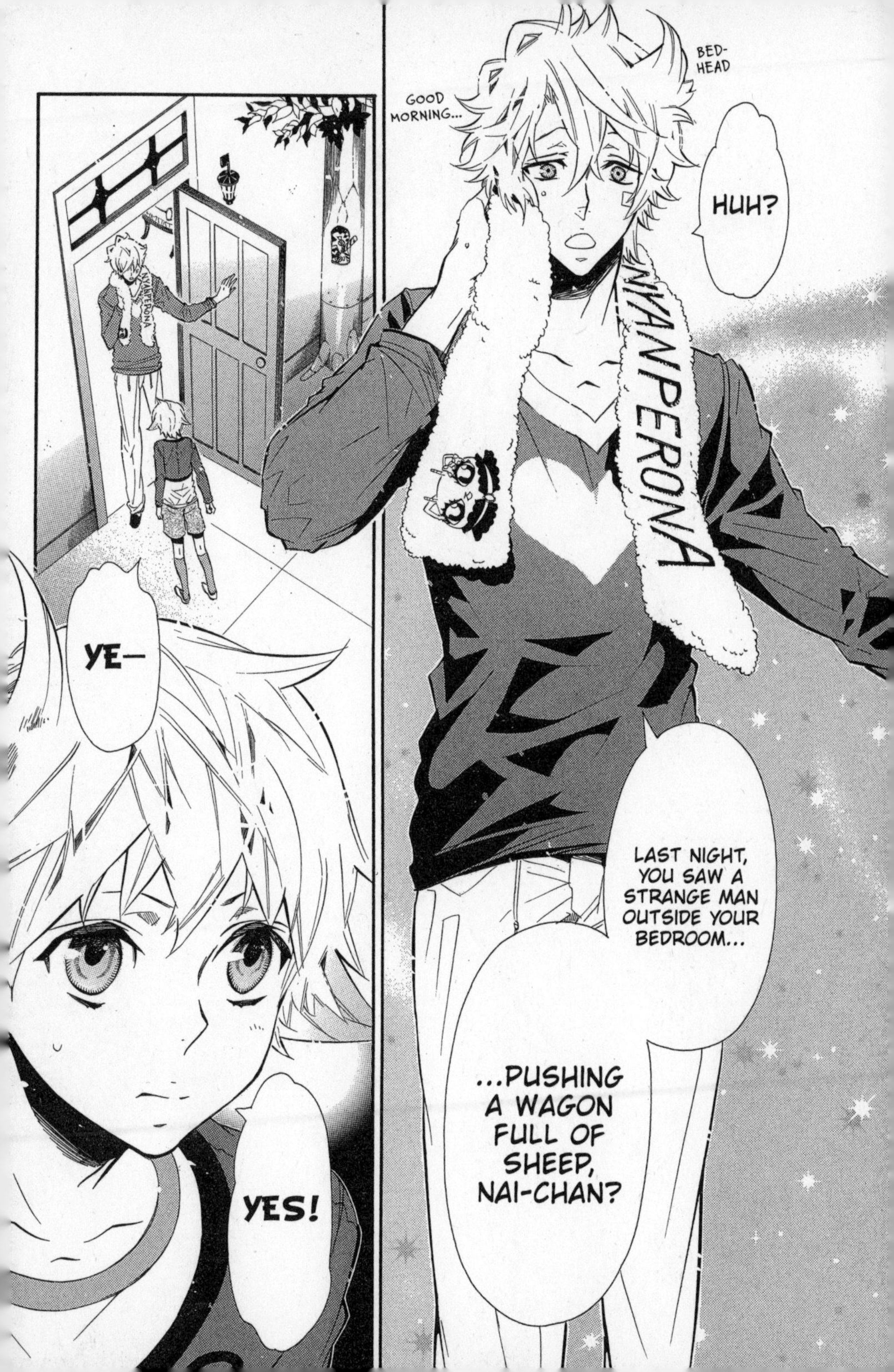
BED-HEAD
GOOD MORNING...
HUH?
NYANPERONA
LAST NIGHT, YOU SAW A STRANGE MAN OUTSIDE YOUR BEDROOM...
...PUSHING A WAGON FULL OF SHEEP, NAI-CHAN?
NYANPERONA
YE—
YES!

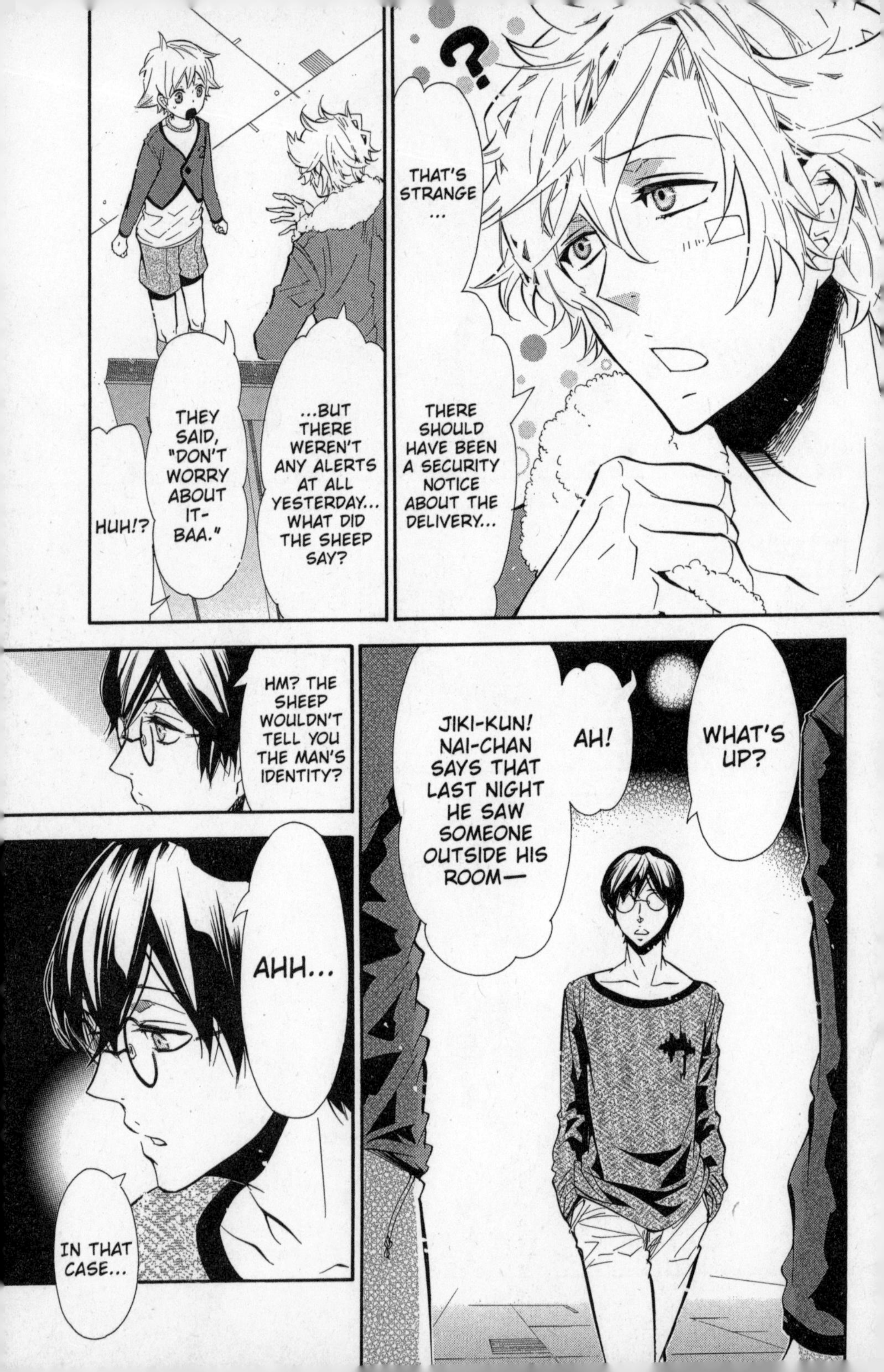
?
THAT'S STRANGE...
THERE SHOULD HAVE BEEN A SECURITY NOTICE ABOUT THE DELIVERY...
...BUT THERE WEREN'T ANY ALERTS AT ALL YESTERDAY... WHAT DID THE SHEEP SAY?
THEY SAID, "DON'T WORRY ABOUT IT-BAA."
HUH!?
WHAT'S UP?
AH!
JIKI-KUN! NAI-CHAN SAYS THAT LAST NIGHT HE SAW SOMEONE OUTSIDE HIS ROOM—
HM? THE SHEEP WOULDN'T TELL YOU THE MAN'S IDENTITY?
AHH...
IN THAT CASE...

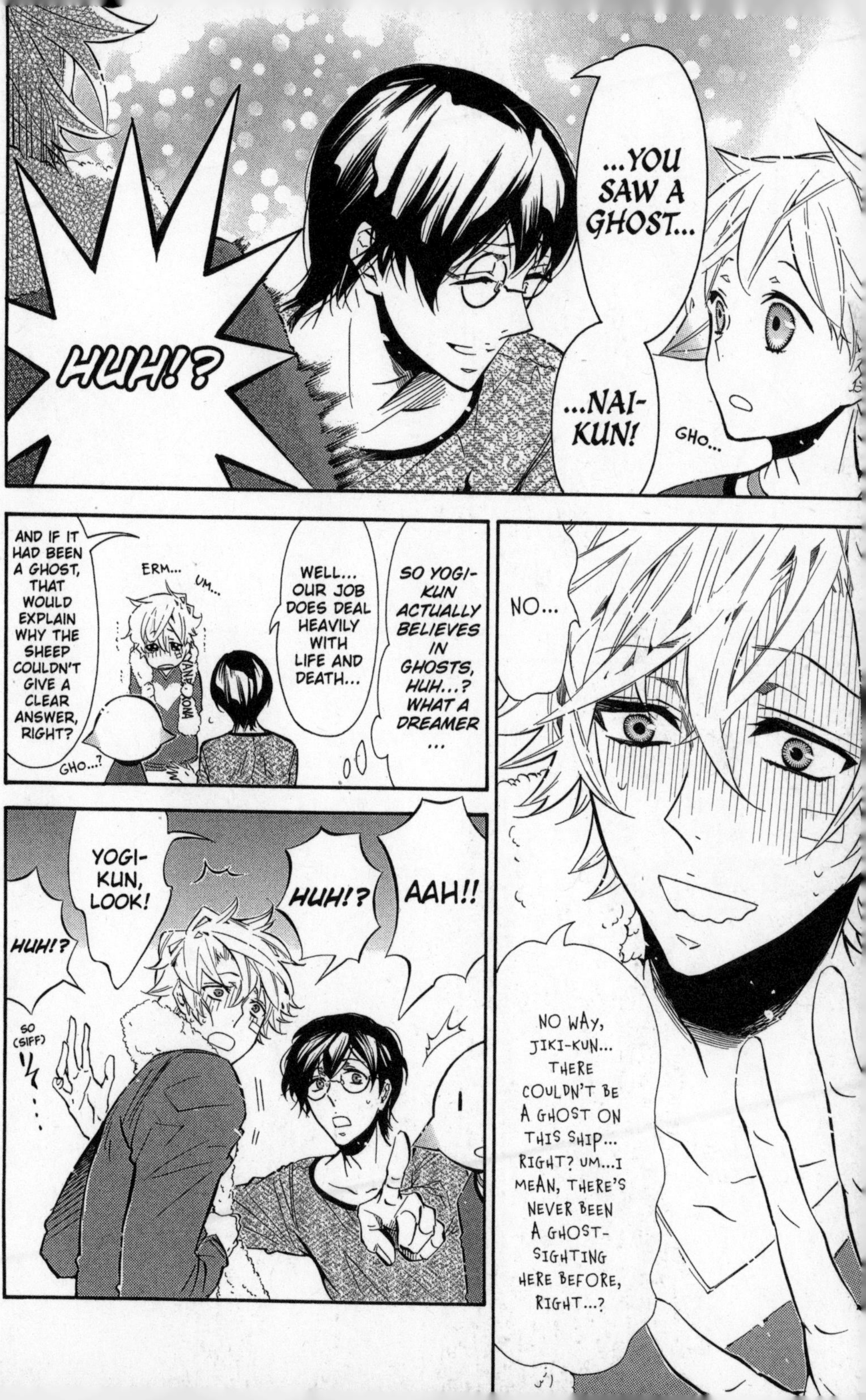
...YOU SAW A GHOST...
GHO...
...NAI-KUN!
HUH!?
NO...
NO WAY, JIKI-KUN... THERE COULDN'T BE A GHOST ON THIS SHIP... RIGHT? UM...I MEAN, THERE'S NEVER BEEN A GHOST-SIGHTING HERE BEFORE, RIGHT...?
SO YOGI-KUN ACTUALLY BELIEVES IN GHOSTS, HUH...? WHAT A DREAMER...
WELL... OUR JOB DOES DEAL HEAVILY WITH LIFE AND DEATH...
UM...
ERM...
AND IF IT HAD BEEN A GHOST, THAT WOULD EXPLAIN WHY THE SHEEP COULDN'T GIVE A CLEAR ANSWER, RIGHT?
GHO...?
AAH!!
HUH!?
YOGI-KUN, LOOK!
HUH!?
SO (SIFF)

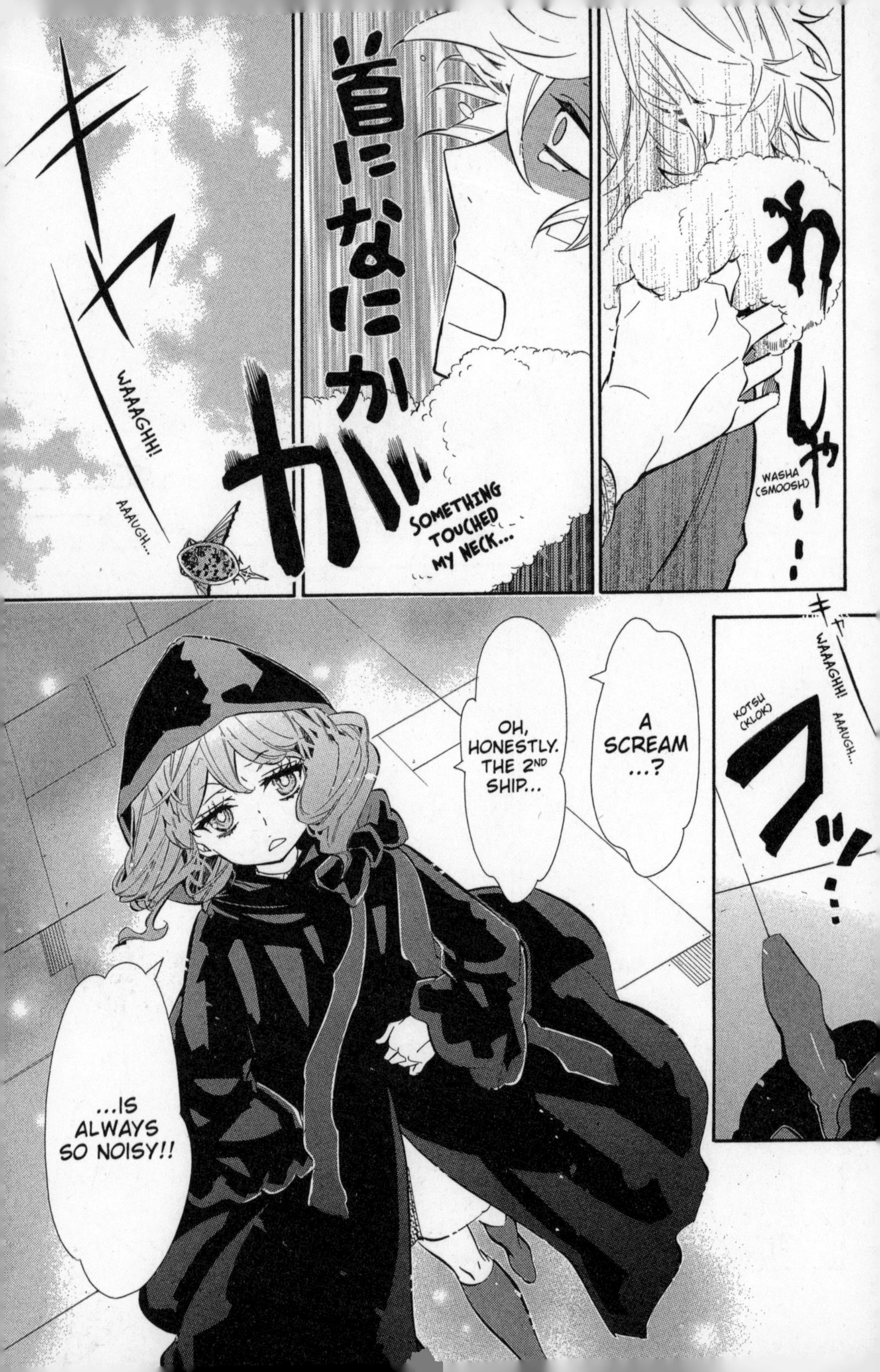
わしゃ…
WASHA (SMOOSH)
首になにか
ガッ
SOMETHING TOUCHED MY NECK...
キャ
WAAAGHH!
AAAUGH...
キャ
WAAAGHH!
AAAUGH...
KOTSU (KLOK)
コッ…
A SCREAM ...?
OH, HONESTLY. THE 2ND SHIP...
...IS ALWAYS SO NOISY!!

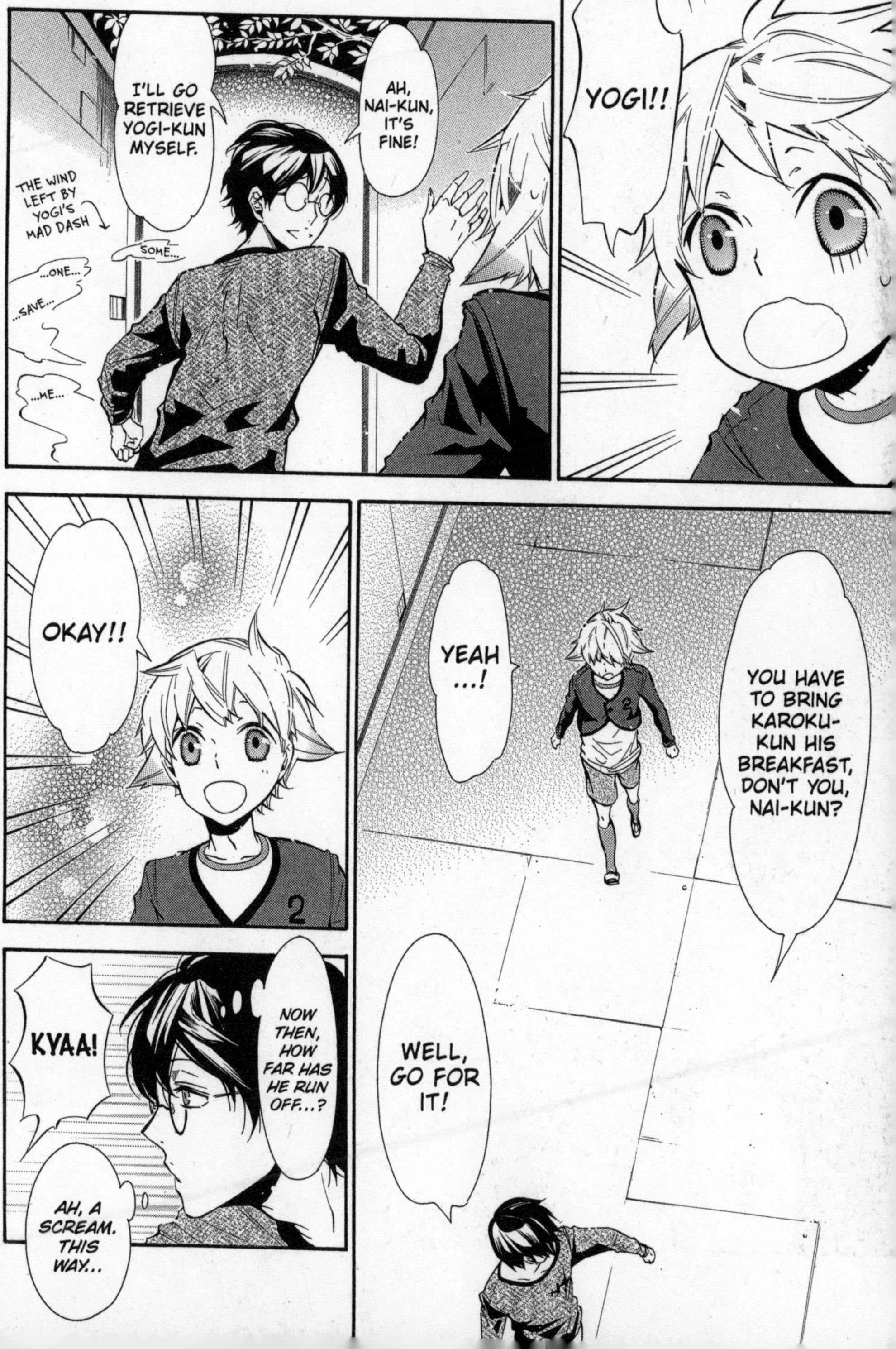
YOGI!!
AH, NAI-KUN, IT'S FINE!
I'LL GO RETRIEVE YOGI-KUN MYSELF.
THE WIND LEFT BY YOGI'S MAD DASH
SOME...
...ONE...
...SAVE...
...ME...
YOU HAVE TO BRING KAROKU-KUN HIS BREAKFAST, DON'T YOU, NAI-KUN?
YEAH ...!
WELL, GO FOR IT!
OKAY!!
NOW THEN, HOW FAR HAS HE RUN OFF...?
KYAA!
AH, A SCREAM. THIS WAY...

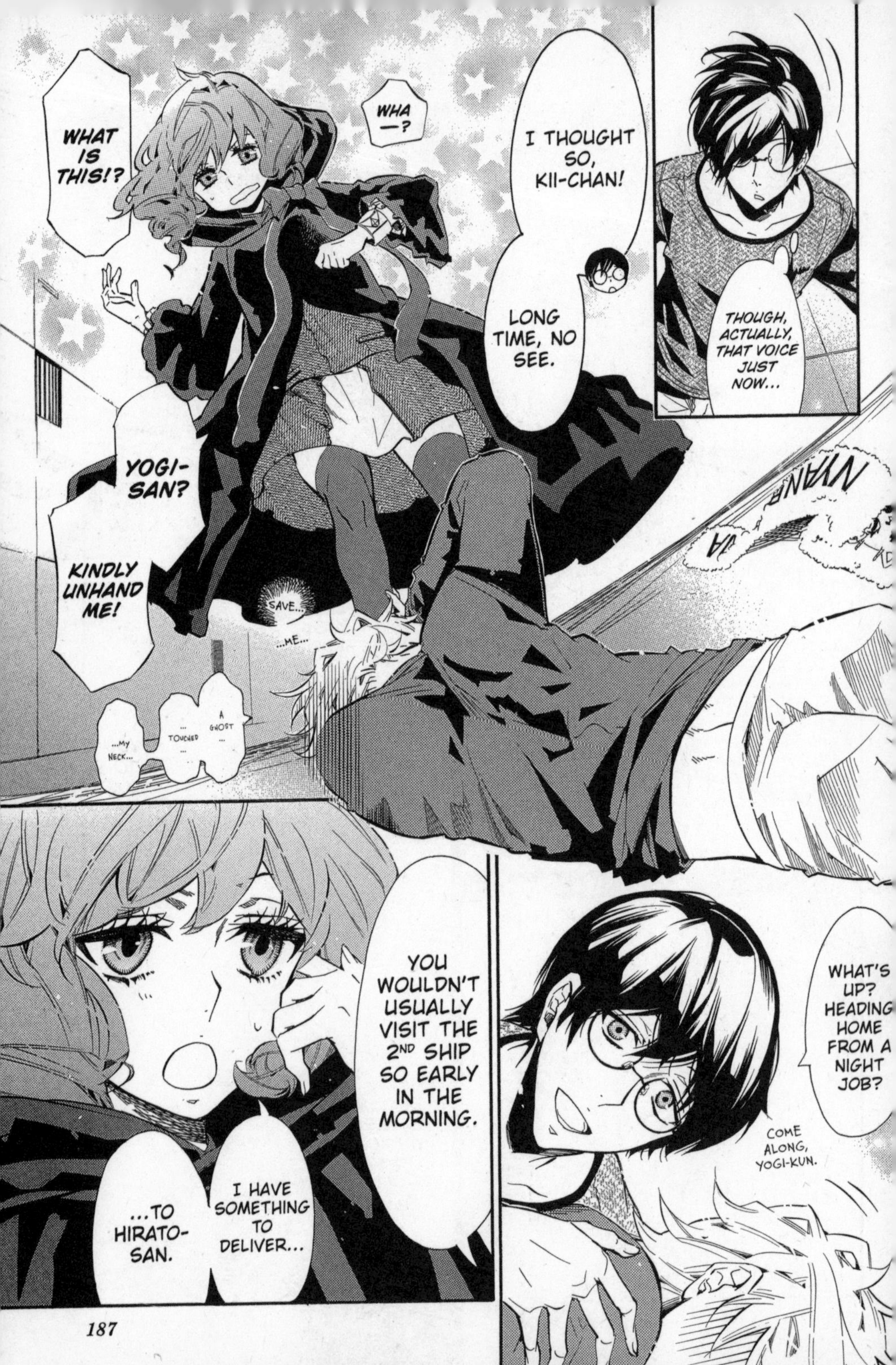
THOUGH, ACTUALLY, THAT VOICE JUST NOW...
I THOUGHT SO, KII-CHAN!
LONG TIME, NO SEE.
WHA—?
WHAT IS THIS!?
YOGI-SAN?
KINDLY UNHAND ME!
SAVE...
...ME...
A GHOST ...
... TOUCHED ...
...MY NECK...
WHAT'S UP? HEADING HOME FROM A NIGHT JOB?
COME ALONG, YOGI-KUN.
YOU WOULDN'T USUALLY VISIT THE 2ND SHIP SO EARLY IN THE MORNING.
I HAVE SOMETHING TO DELIVER...
...TO HIRATO-SAN.

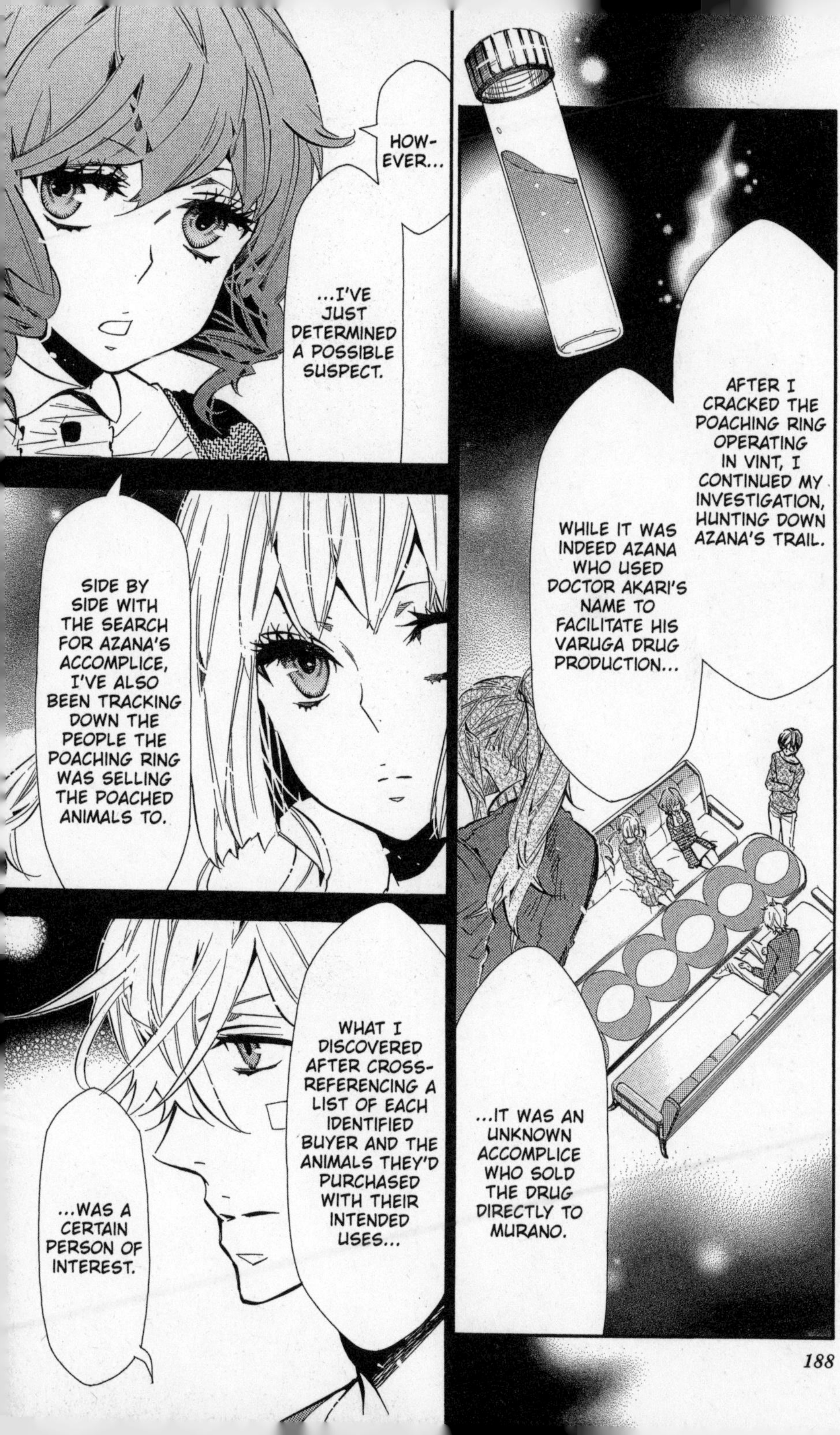
AFTER I CRACKED THE POACHING RING OPERATING IN VINT, I CONTINUED MY INVESTIGATION, HUNTING DOWN AZANA'S TRAIL.
WHILE IT WAS INDEED AZANA WHO USED DOCTOR AKARI'S NAME TO FACILITATE HIS VARUGA DRUG PRODUCTION...
...IT WAS AN UNKNOWN ACCOMPLICE WHO SOLD THE DRUG DIRECTLY TO MURANO.
HOW-EVER...
...I'VE JUST DETERMINED A POSSIBLE SUSPECT.
SIDE BY SIDE WITH THE SEARCH FOR AZANA'S ACCOMPLICE, I'VE ALSO BEEN TRACKING DOWN THE PEOPLE THE POACHING RING WAS SELLING THE POACHED ANIMALS TO.
WHAT I DISCOVERED AFTER CROSS-REFERENCING A LIST OF EACH IDENTIFIED BUYER AND THE ANIMALS THEY'D PURCHASED WITH THEIR INTENDED USES...
...WAS A CERTAIN PERSON OF INTEREST.

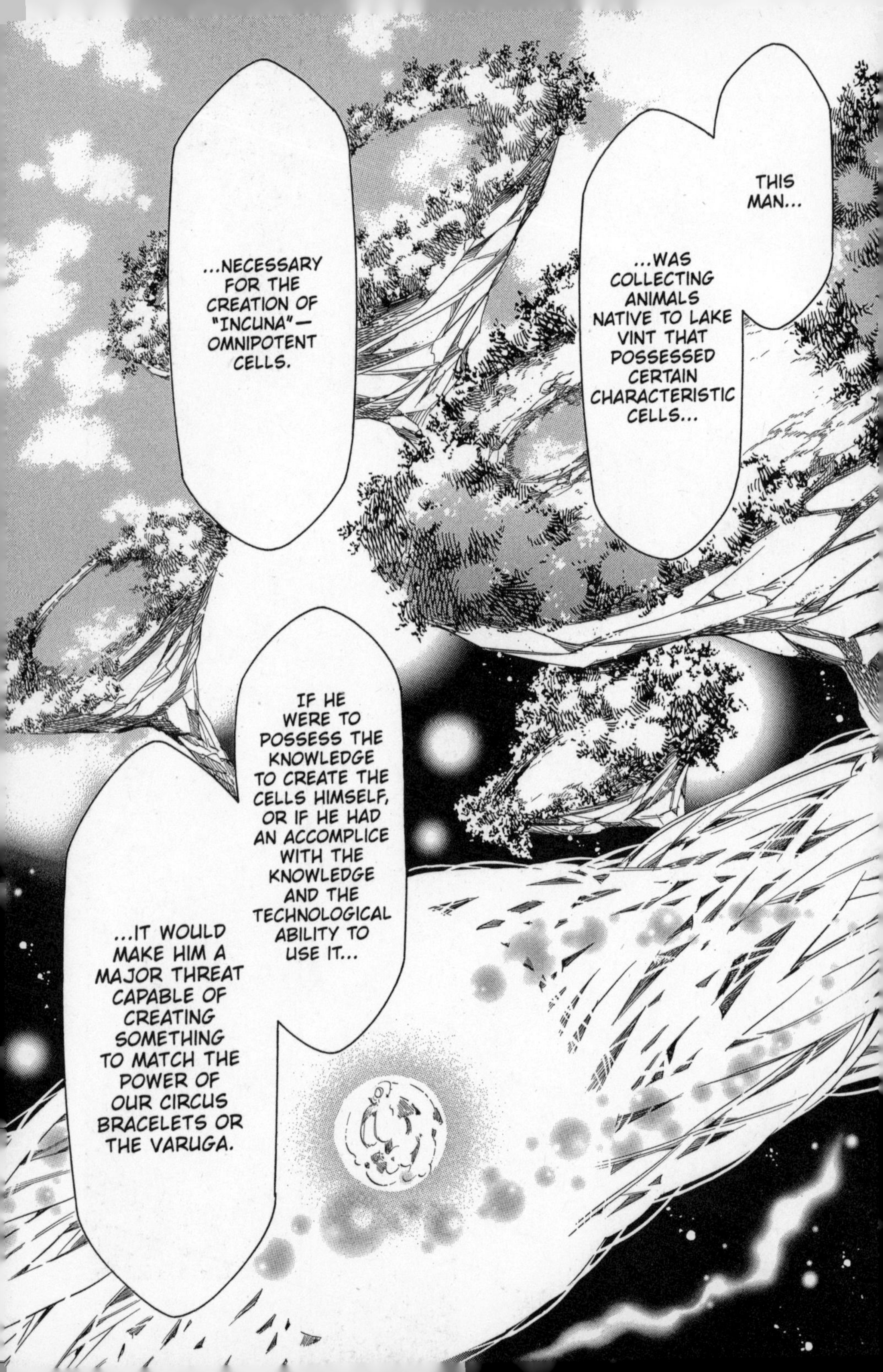
THIS MAN...
...WAS COLLECTING ANIMALS NATIVE TO LAKE VINT THAT POSSESSED CERTAIN CHARACTERISTIC CELLS...
...NECESSARY FOR THE CREATION OF "INCUNA"—OMNIPOTENT CELLS.
IF HE WERE TO POSSESS THE KNOWLEDGE TO CREATE THE CELLS HIMSELF, OR IF HE HAD AN ACCOMPLICE WITH THE KNOWLEDGE AND THE TECHNOLOGICAL ABILITY TO USE IT...
...IT WOULD MAKE HIM A MAJOR THREAT CAPABLE OF CREATING SOMETHING TO MATCH THE POWER OF OUR CIRCUS BRACELETS OR THE VARUGA.

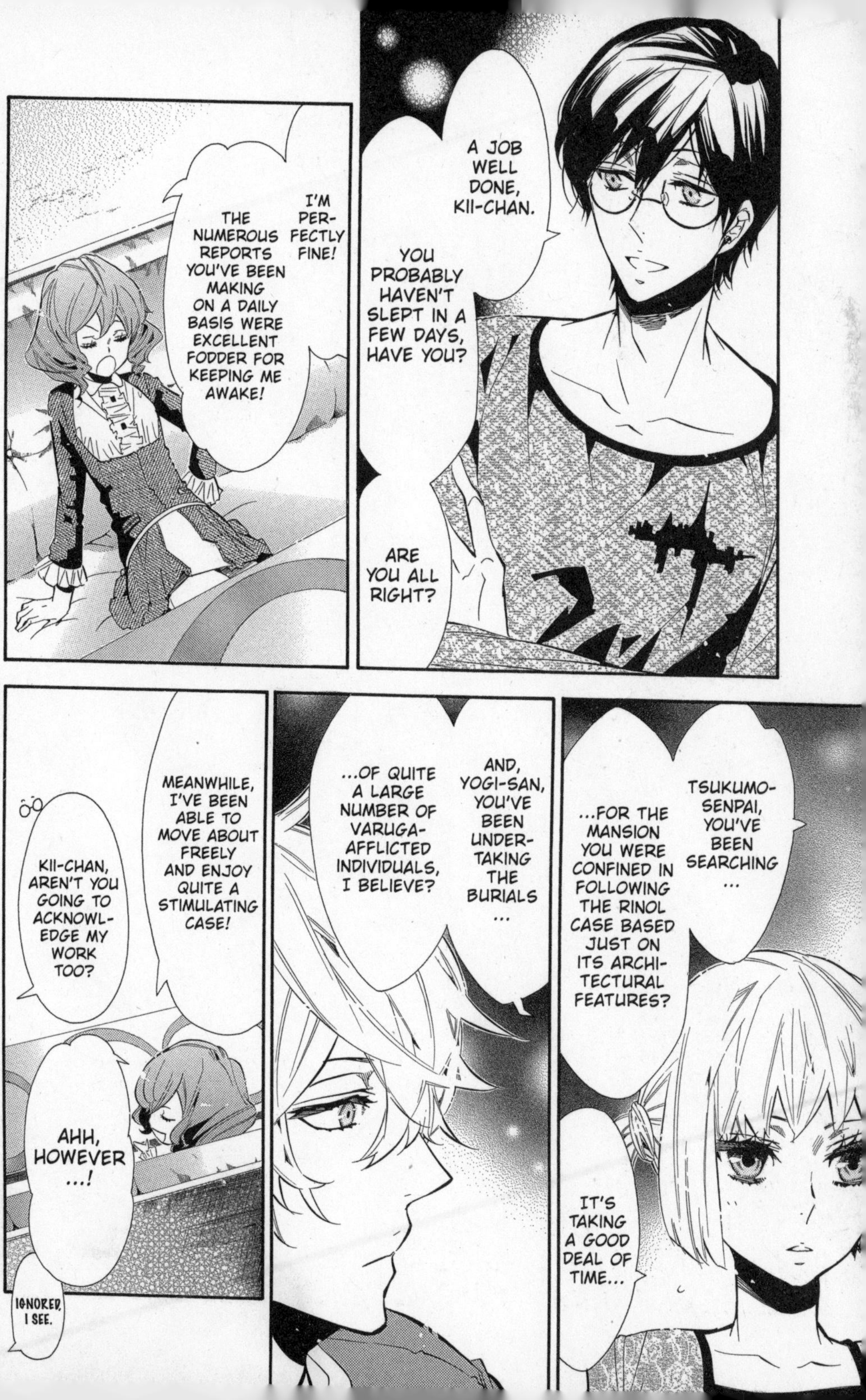
A JOB WELL DONE, KII-CHAN.
YOU PROBABLY HAVEN'T SLEPT IN A FEW DAYS, HAVE YOU?
ARE YOU ALL RIGHT?
I'M PER-FECTLY FINE!
THE NUMEROUS REPORTS YOU'VE BEEN MAKING ON A DAILY BASIS WERE EXCELLENT FODDER FOR KEEPING ME AWAKE!
TSUKUMO-SENPAI, YOU'VE BEEN SEARCHING...
...FOR THE MANSION YOU WERE CONFINED IN FOLLOWING THE RINOL CASE BASED JUST ON ITS ARCHI-TECTURAL FEATURES?
IT'S TAKING A GOOD DEAL OF TIME...
AND, YOGI-SAN, YOU'VE BEEN UNDER-TAKING THE BURIALS...
...OF QUITE A LARGE NUMBER OF VARUGA-AFFLICTED INDIVIDUALS, I BELIEVE?
MEANWHILE, I'VE BEEN ABLE TO MOVE ABOUT FREELY AND ENJOY QUITE A STIMULATING CASE!
KII-CHAN, AREN'T YOU GOING TO ACKNOWL-EDGE MY WORK TOO?
AHH, HOWEVER...!
IGNORED, I SEE.

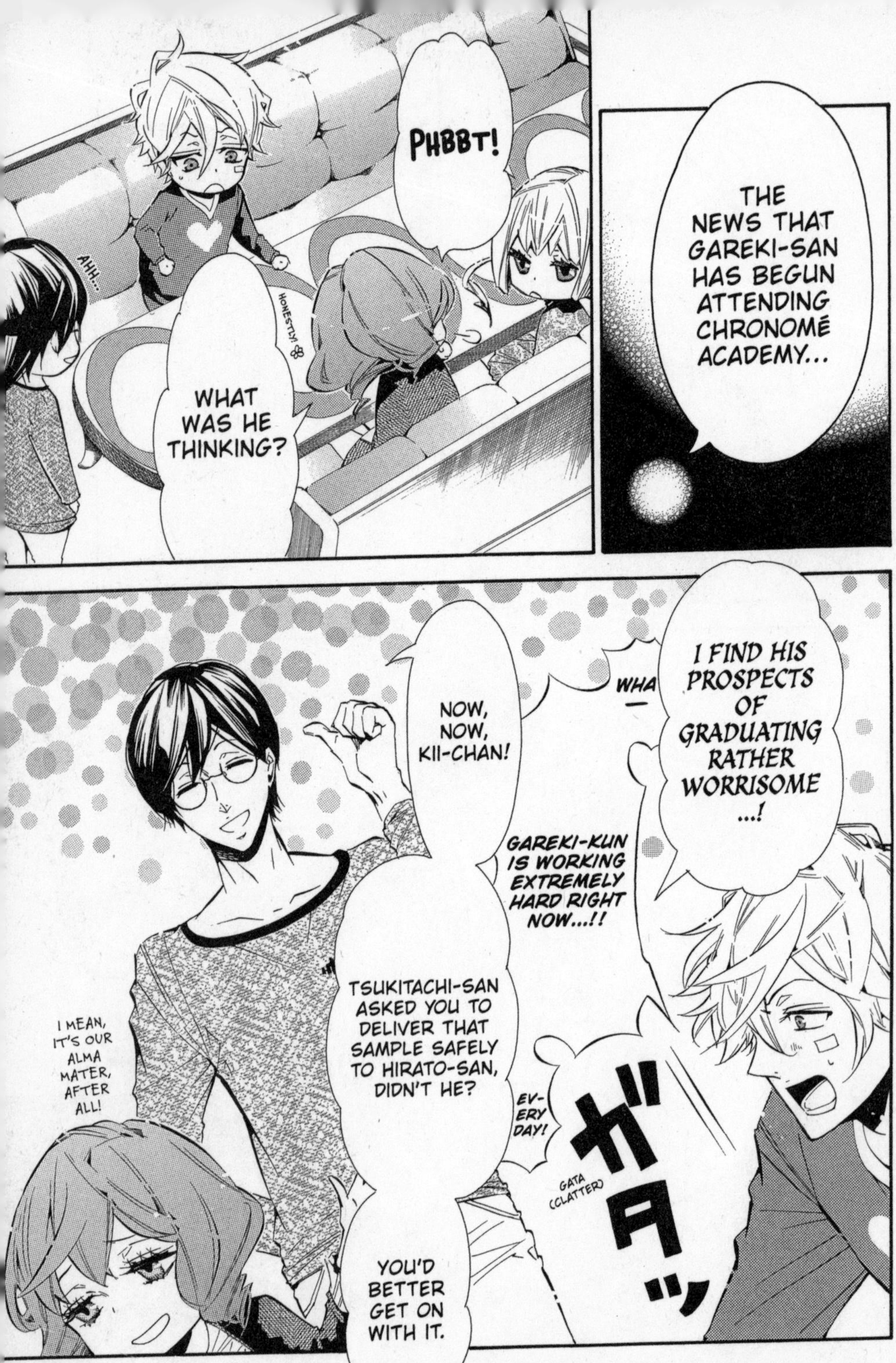
THE NEWS THAT GAREKI-SAN HAS BEGUN ATTENDING CHRONOMÉ ACADEMY...
PHBBT!
HONESTLY!
WHAT WAS HE THINKING?
AHH...
I FIND HIS PROSPECTS OF GRADUATING RATHER WORRISOME ...!
WHA—
NOW, NOW, KII-CHAN!
GAREKI-KUN IS WORKING EXTREMELY HARD RIGHT NOW...!!
EV-ERY DAY!
GATA (CLATTER)
TSUKITACHI-SAN ASKED YOU TO DELIVER THAT SAMPLE SAFELY TO HIRATO-SAN, DIDN'T HE?
I MEAN, IT'S OUR ALMA MATER, AFTER ALL!
YOU'D BETTER GET ON WITH IT.

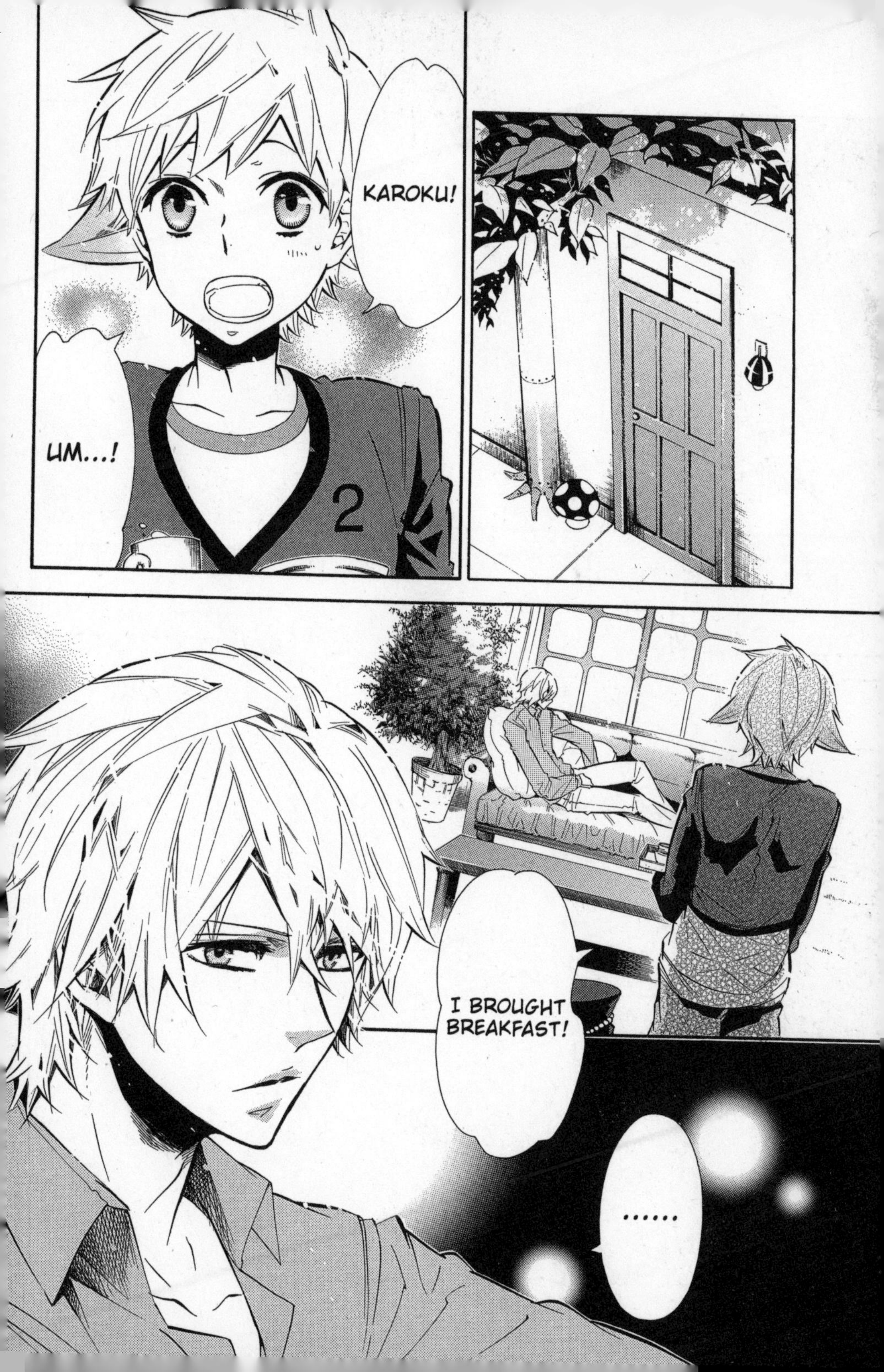
KAROKU!
UM...!
I BROUGHT BREAKFAST!
......

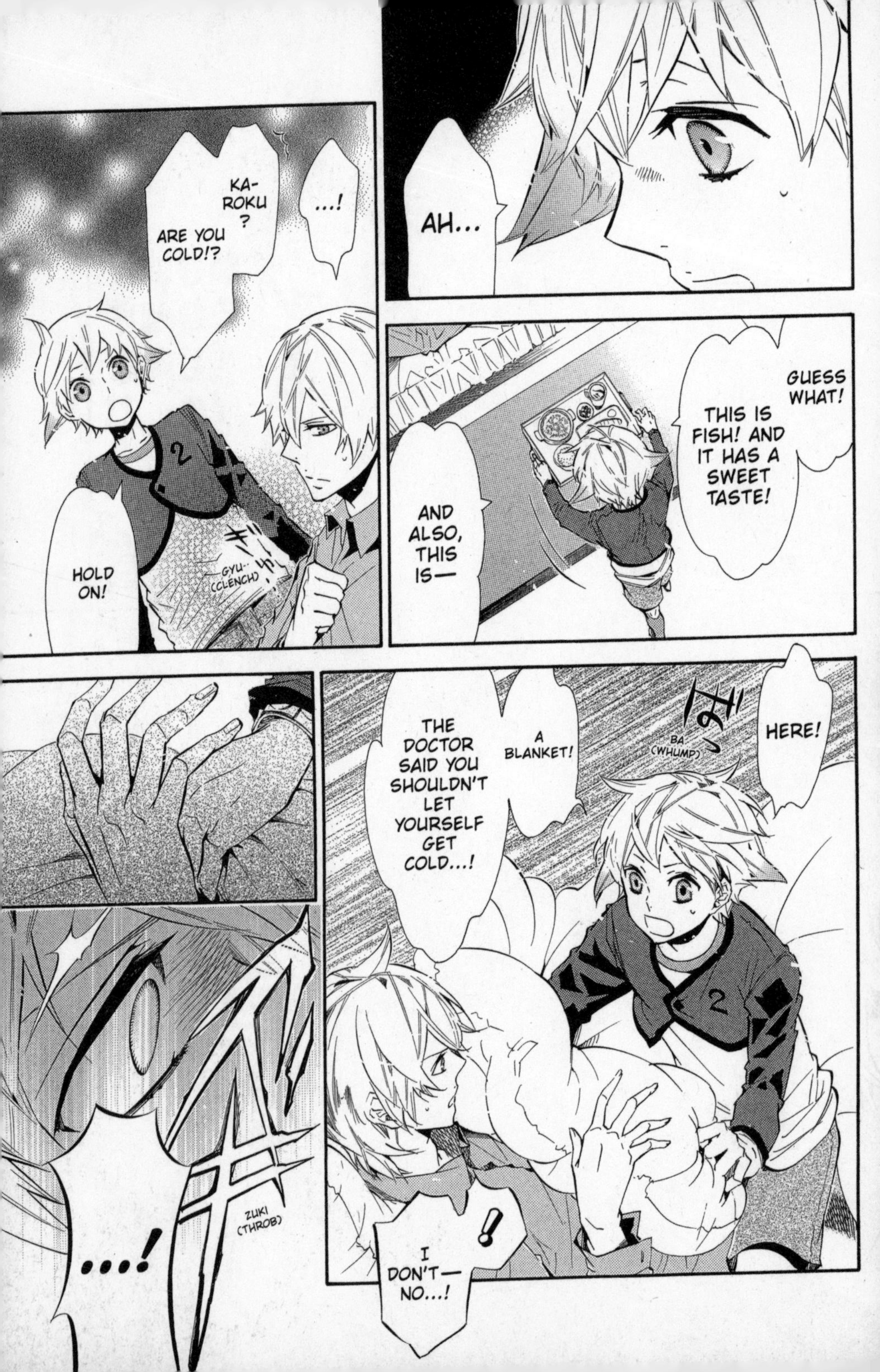
AH...
GUESS WHAT!
THIS IS FISH! AND IT HAS A SWEET TASTE!
AND ALSO, THIS IS—
...!
KA-ROKU? ARE YOU COLD!?
GYU (CLENCH)
HOLD ON!
HERE!
BA (WHUMP)
A BLANKET!
THE DOCTOR SAID YOU SHOULDN'T LET YOURSELF GET COLD...!
!
I DON'T— NO...!
ZUKI (THROB)
...!

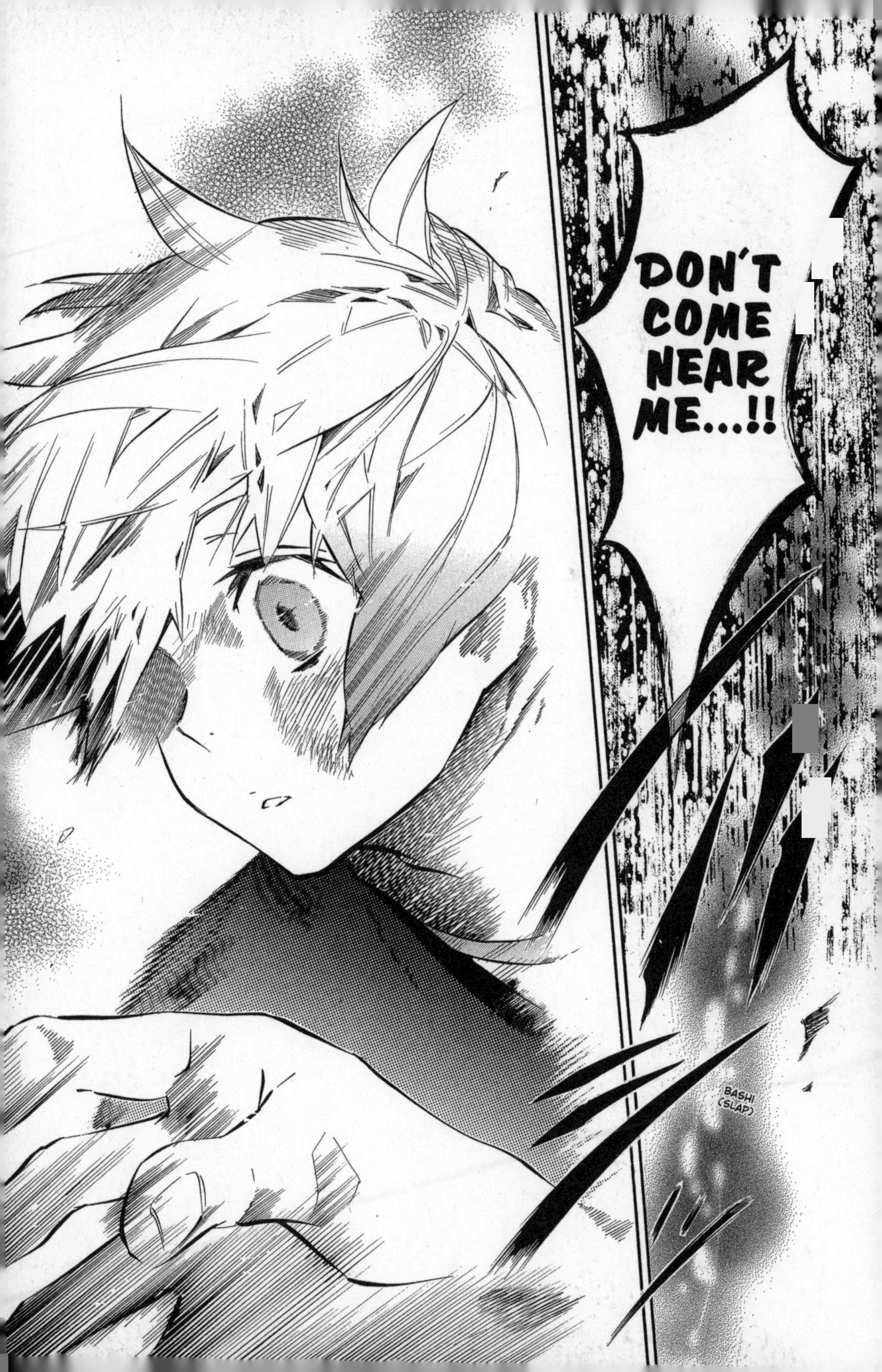
DON'T COME NEAR ME...!!
BASHI (SLAP)

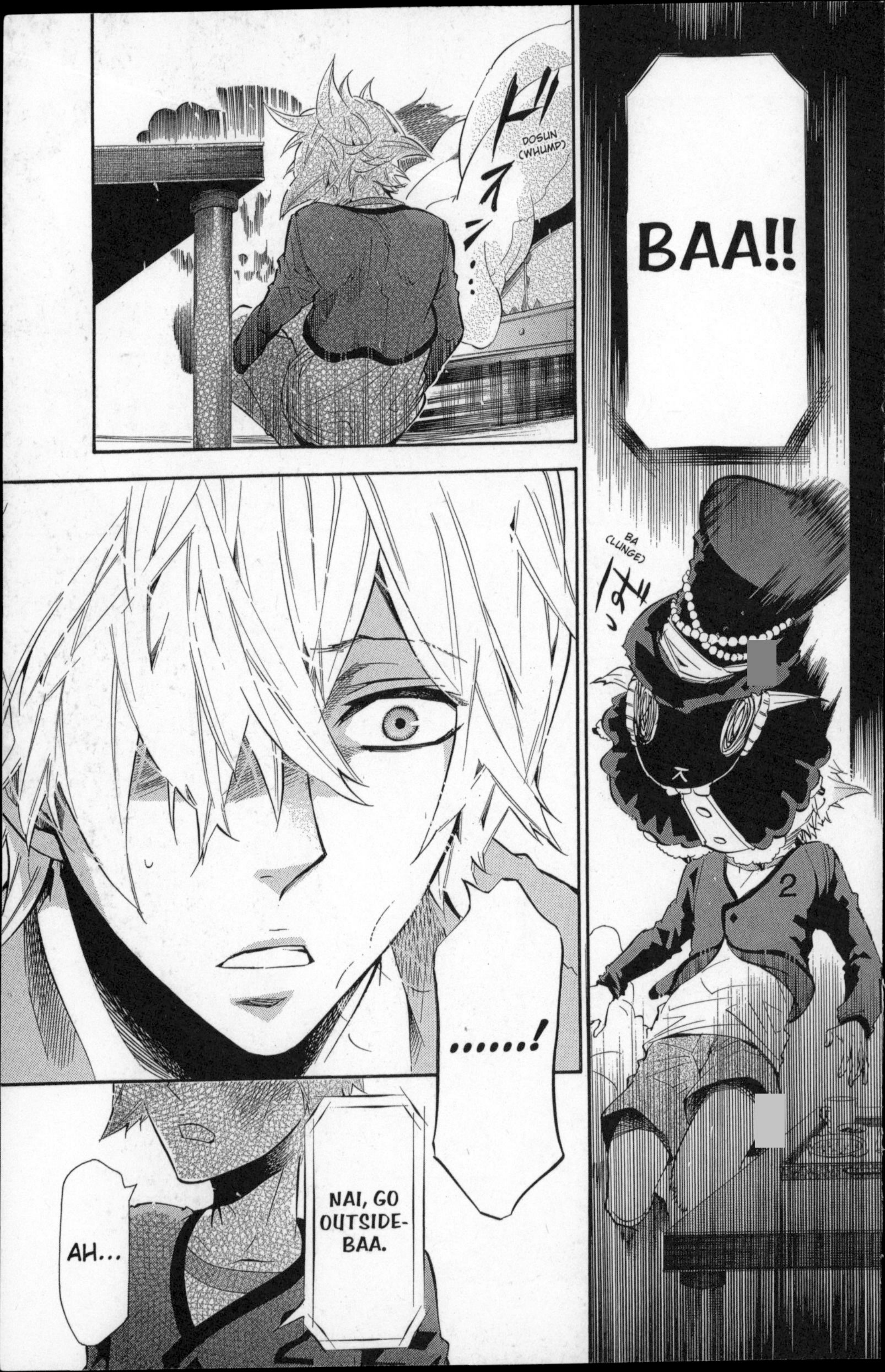
BAA!!
BA (LUNGE)
DOSUN (WHUMP)
......!
NAI, GO OUTSIDE-BAA.
AH...

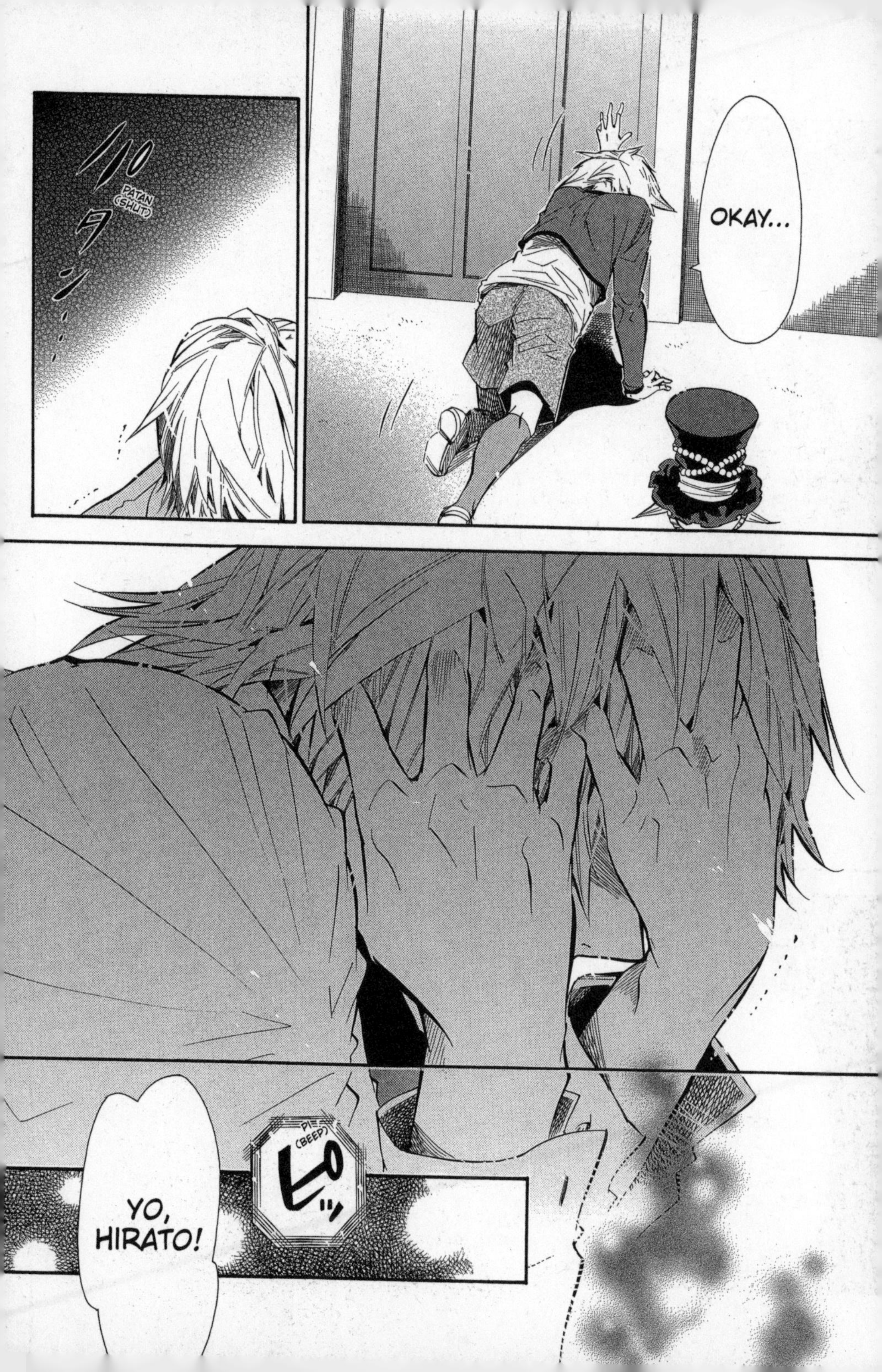
OKAY...
パタン…
PATAN (SHUT)
ピッ
PI (BEEP)
YO, HIRATO!

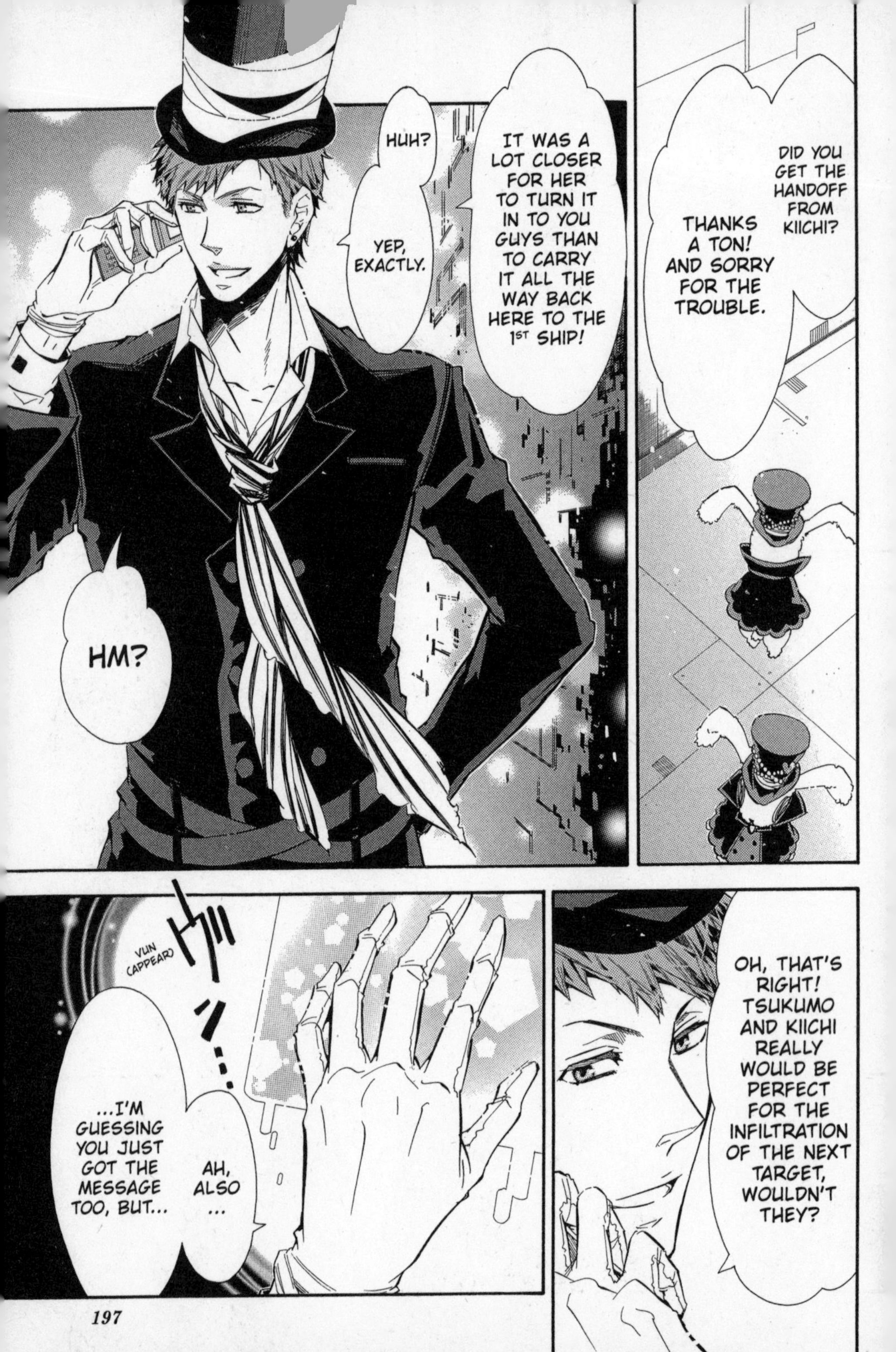
DID YOU GET THE HANDOFF FROM KIICHI?
THANKS A TON! AND SORRY FOR THE TROUBLE.
IT WAS A LOT CLOSER FOR HER TO TURN IT IN TO YOU GUYS THAN TO CARRY IT ALL THE WAY BACK HERE TO THE 1ST SHIP!
HUH?
YEP, EXACTLY.
HM?
OH, THAT'S RIGHT! TSUKUMO AND KIICHI REALLY WOULD BE PERFECT FOR THE INFILTRATION OF THE NEXT TARGET, WOULDN'T THEY?
VUN (APPEAR)
AH, ALSO ...
...I'M GUESSING YOU JUST GOT THE MESSAGE TOO, BUT...

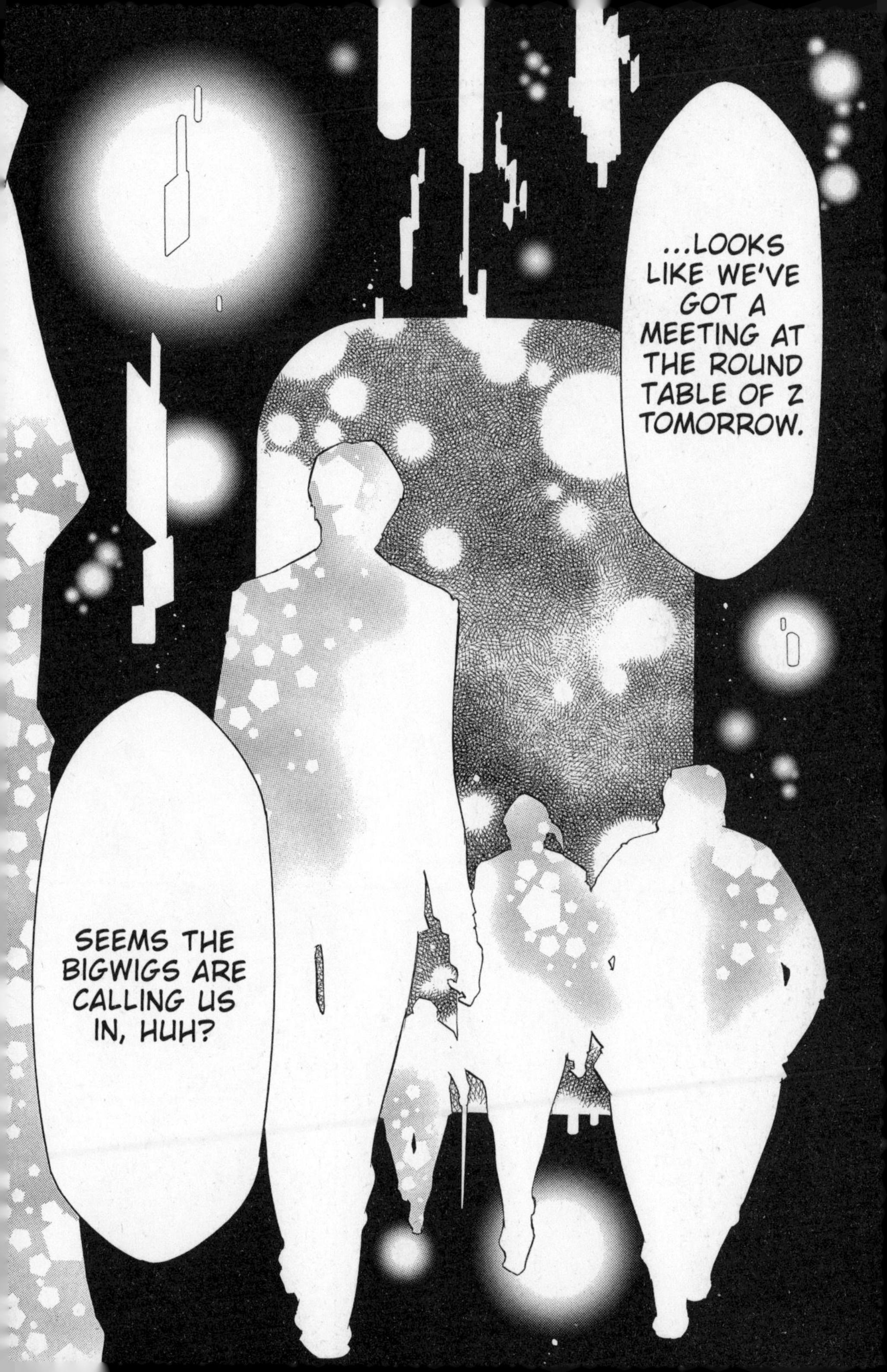
...LOOKS LIKE WE'VE GOT A MEETING AT THE ROUND TABLE OF Z TOMORROW.
SEEMS THE BIGWIGS ARE CALLING US IN, HUH?

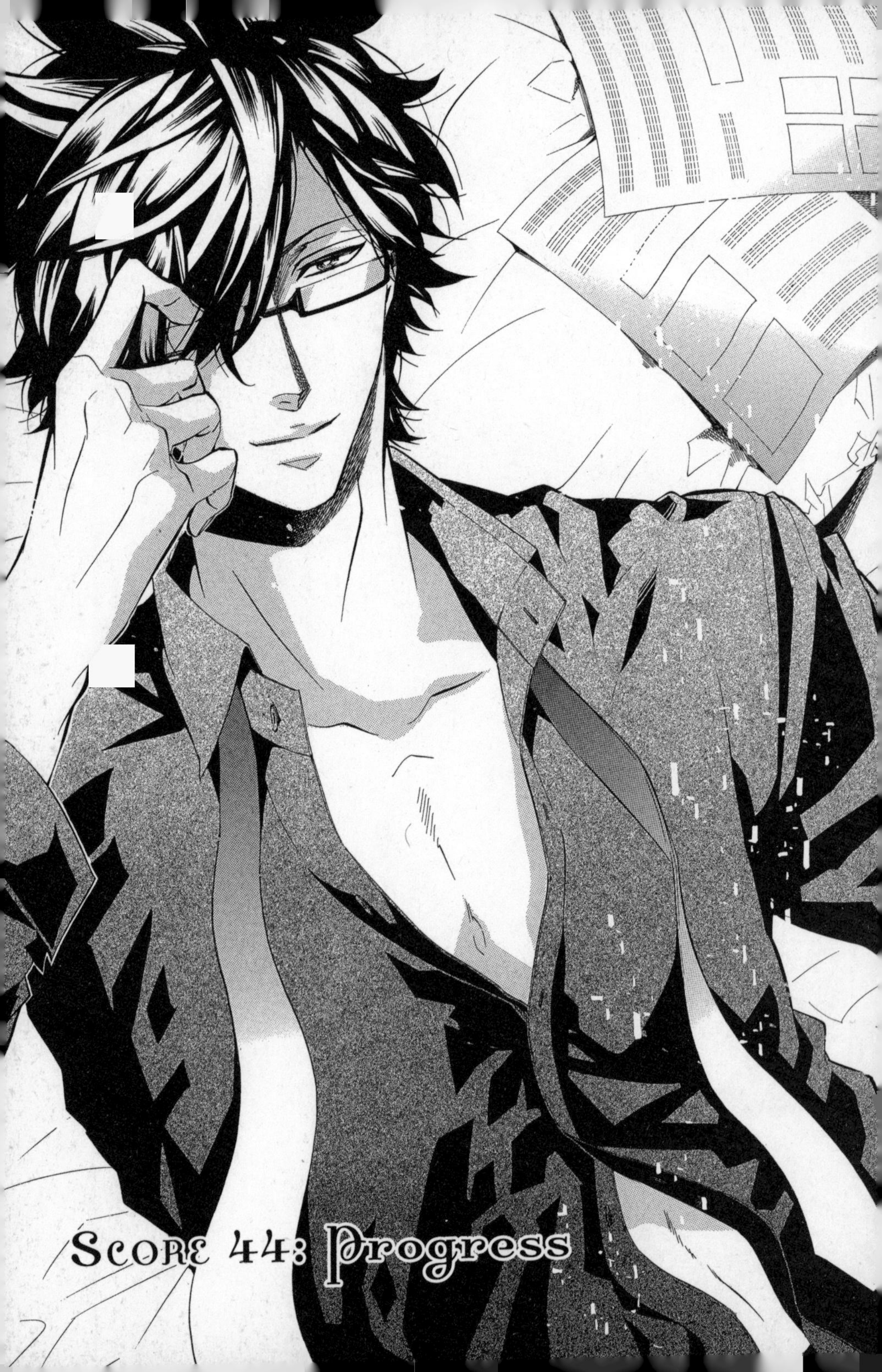
Score 44: Progress

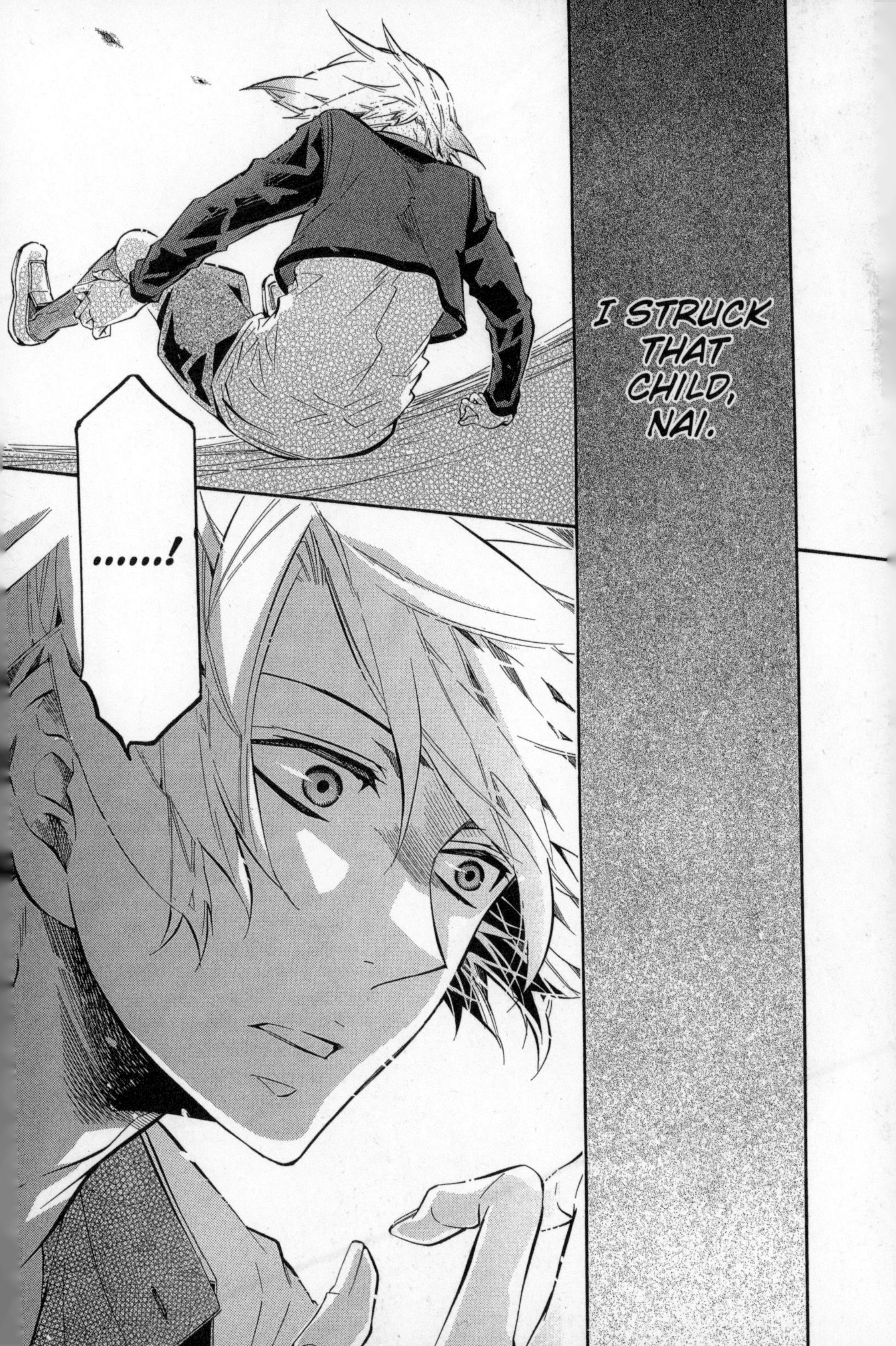
I STRUCK THAT CHILD, NAI.
......!

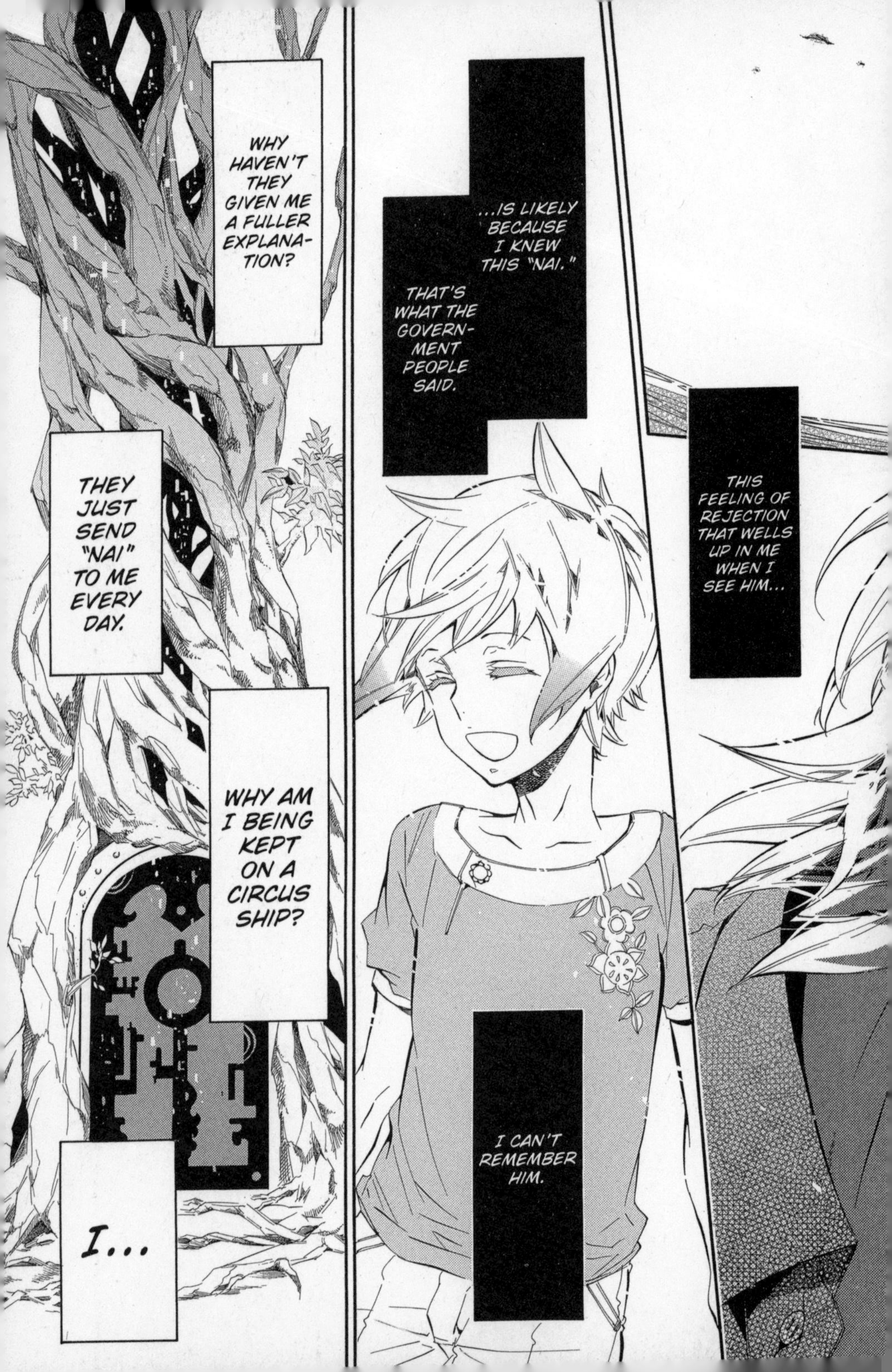
THIS FEELING OF REJECTION THAT WELLS UP IN ME WHEN I SEE HIM...
...IS LIKELY BECAUSE I KNEW THIS "NAI."
THAT'S WHAT THE GOVERNMENT PEOPLE SAID.
I CAN'T REMEMBER HIM.
WHY HAVEN'T THEY GIVEN ME A FULLER EXPLANATION?
THEY JUST SEND "NAI" TO ME EVERY DAY.
WHY AM I BEING KEPT ON A CIRCUS SHIP?
I...

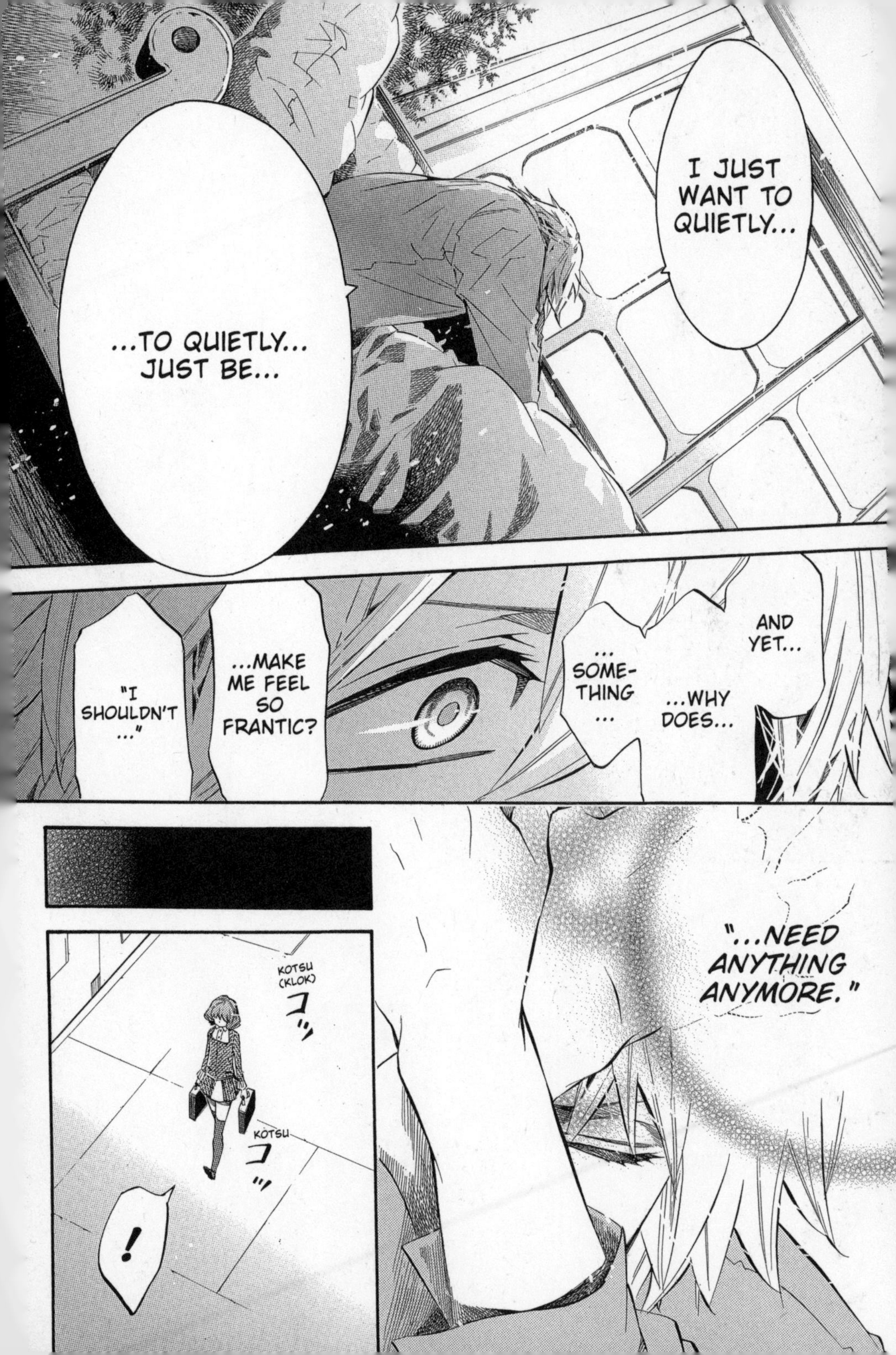
I JUST WANT TO QUIETLY...
...TO QUIETLY... JUST BE...
AND YET...
...WHY DOES...
... SOME-THING ...
...MAKE ME FEEL SO FRANTIC?
"I SHOULDN'T ..."
"...NEED ANYTHING ANYMORE."
KOTSU (KLOK)
KOTSU
!

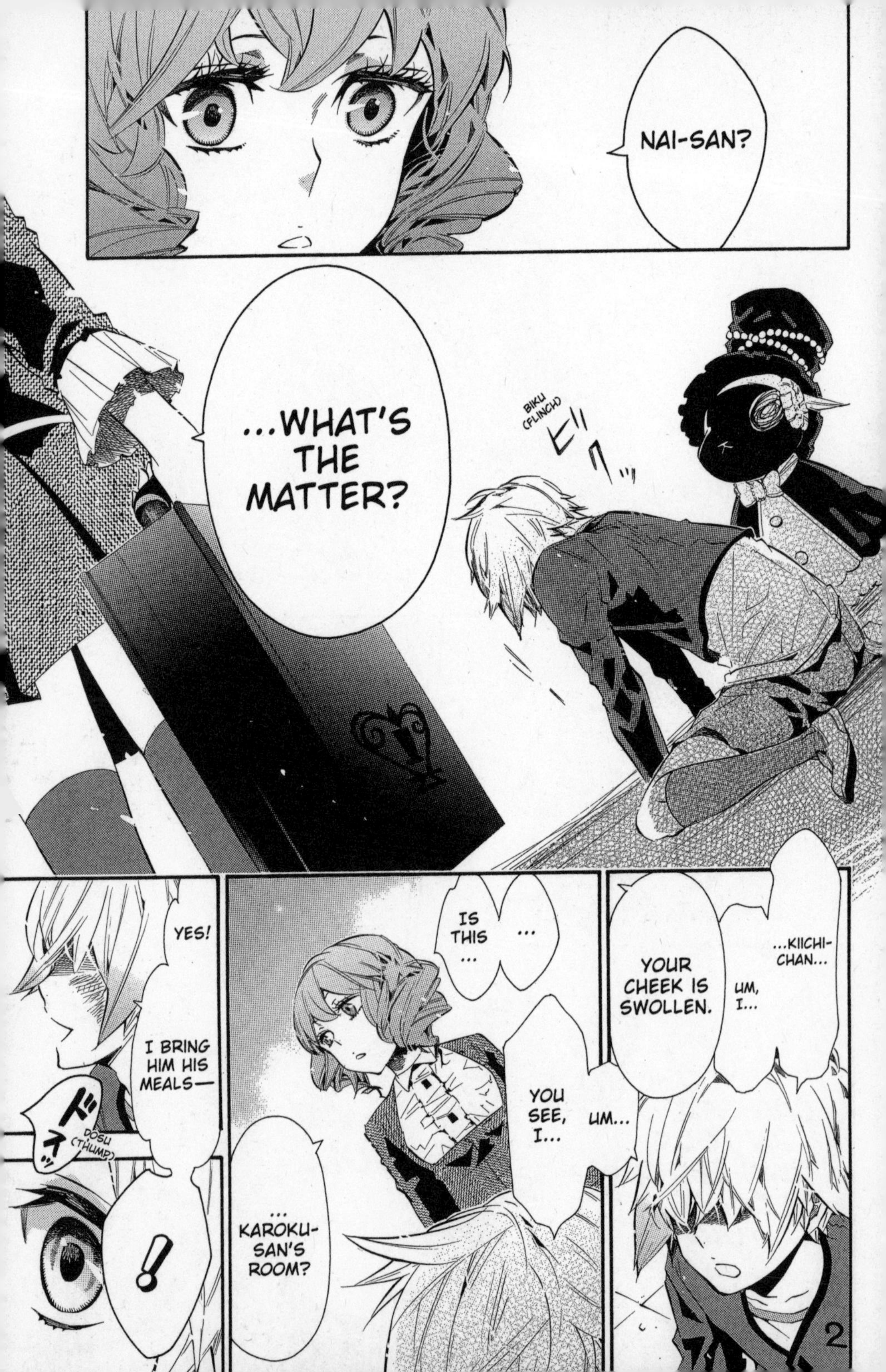
NAI-SAN?
BIKU (FLINCH)
...WHAT'S THE MATTER?
...KIICHI-CHAN...
UM, I...
YOUR CHEEK IS SWOLLEN.
UM...
YOU SEE, I...
...
IS THIS ...
... KAROKU-SAN'S ROOM?
YES!
I BRING HIM HIS MEALS—
DOSU (THUMP)
!

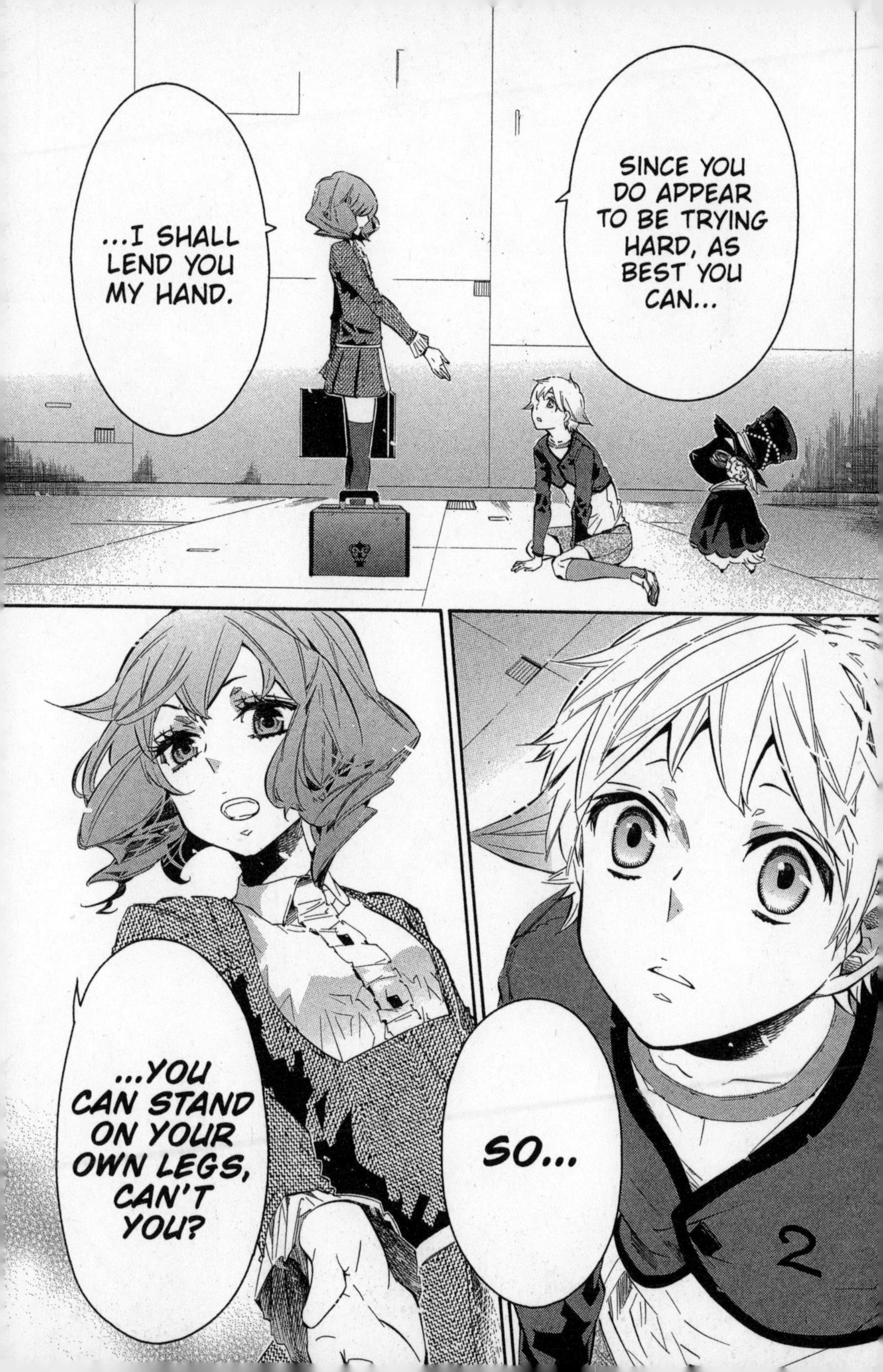
SINCE YOU DO APPEAR TO BE TRYING HARD, AS BEST YOU CAN...
...I SHALL LEND YOU MY HAND.
SO...
...YOU CAN STAND ON YOUR OWN LEGS, CAN'T YOU?

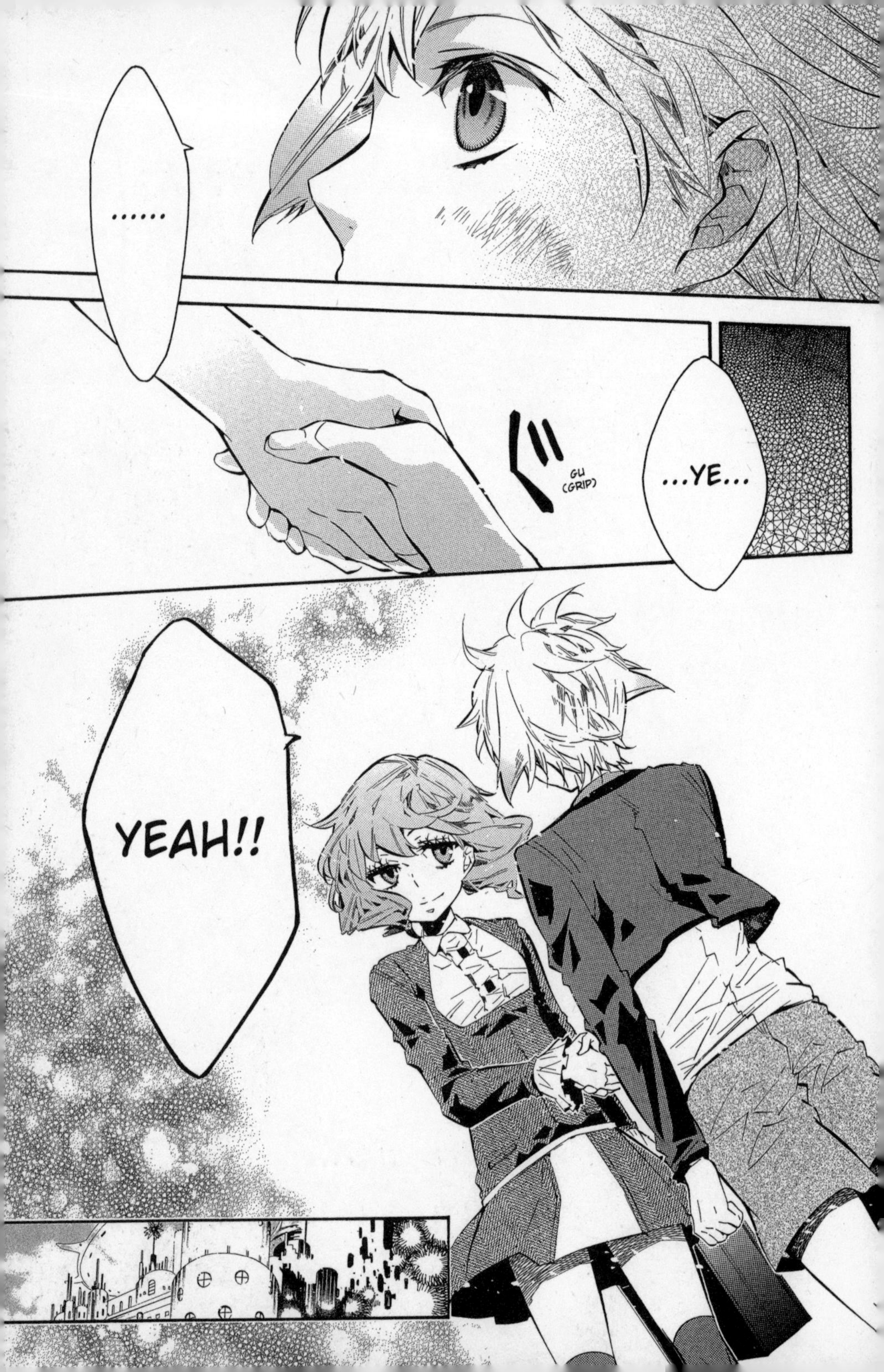
......
...YE...
GU (GRIP)
YEAH!!

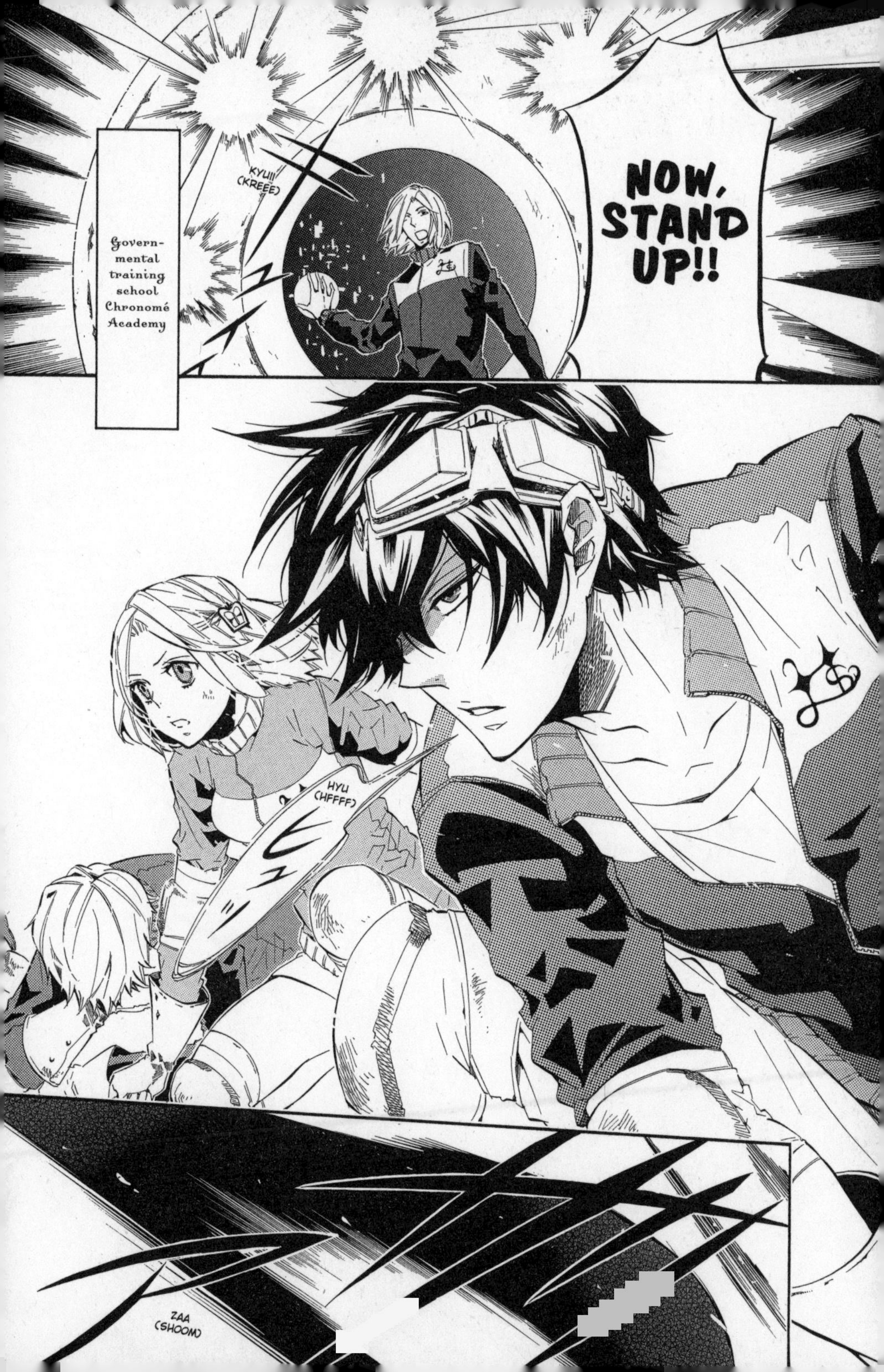
NOW, STAND UP!!
KYUII (KREEE)
Govern-mental training school Chronomé Academy
HYU (HFFFF)
ZAA (SHOOM)

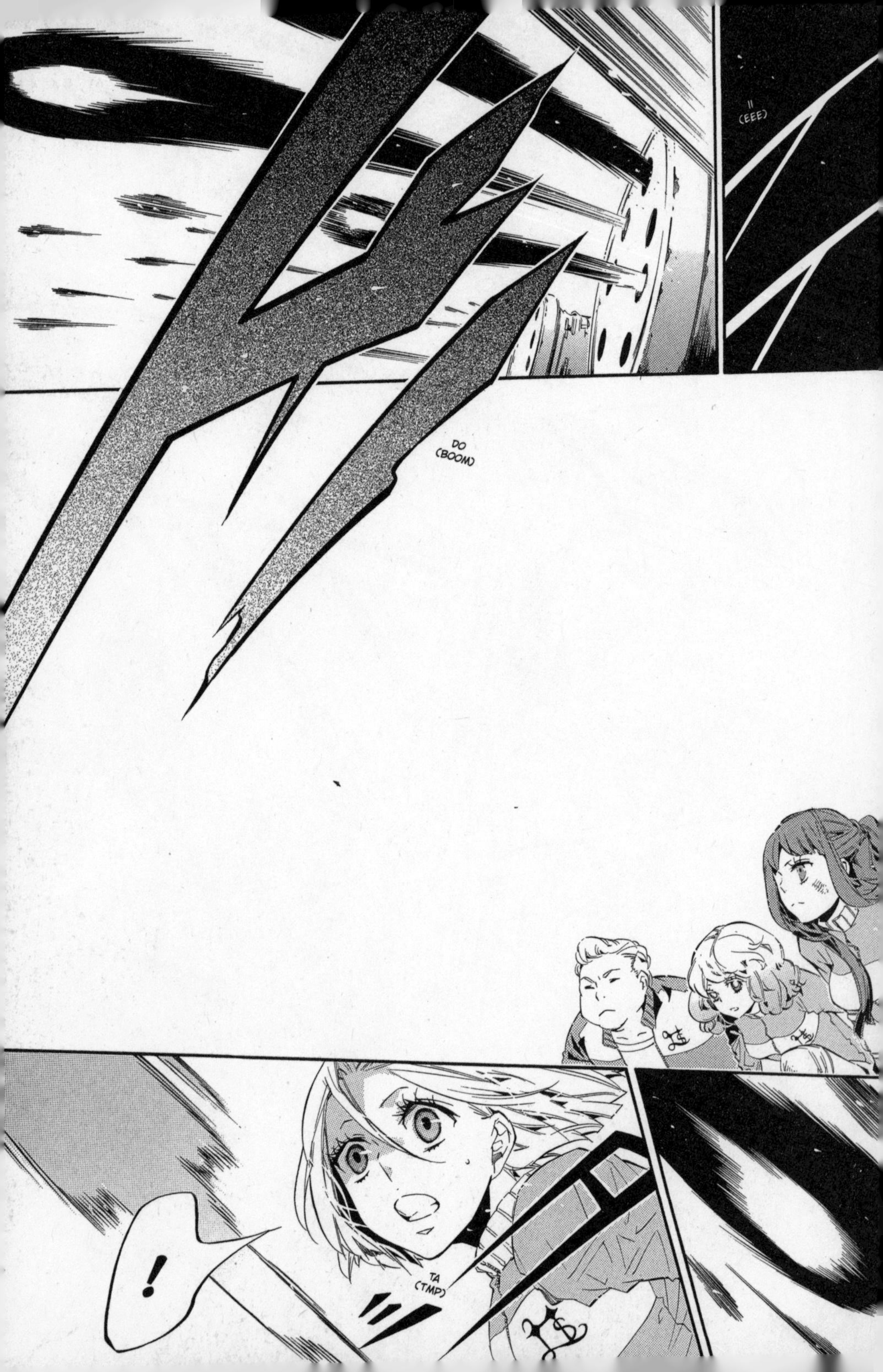
II
(EEE)
DO
(BOOM)
TA
(TMP)
!

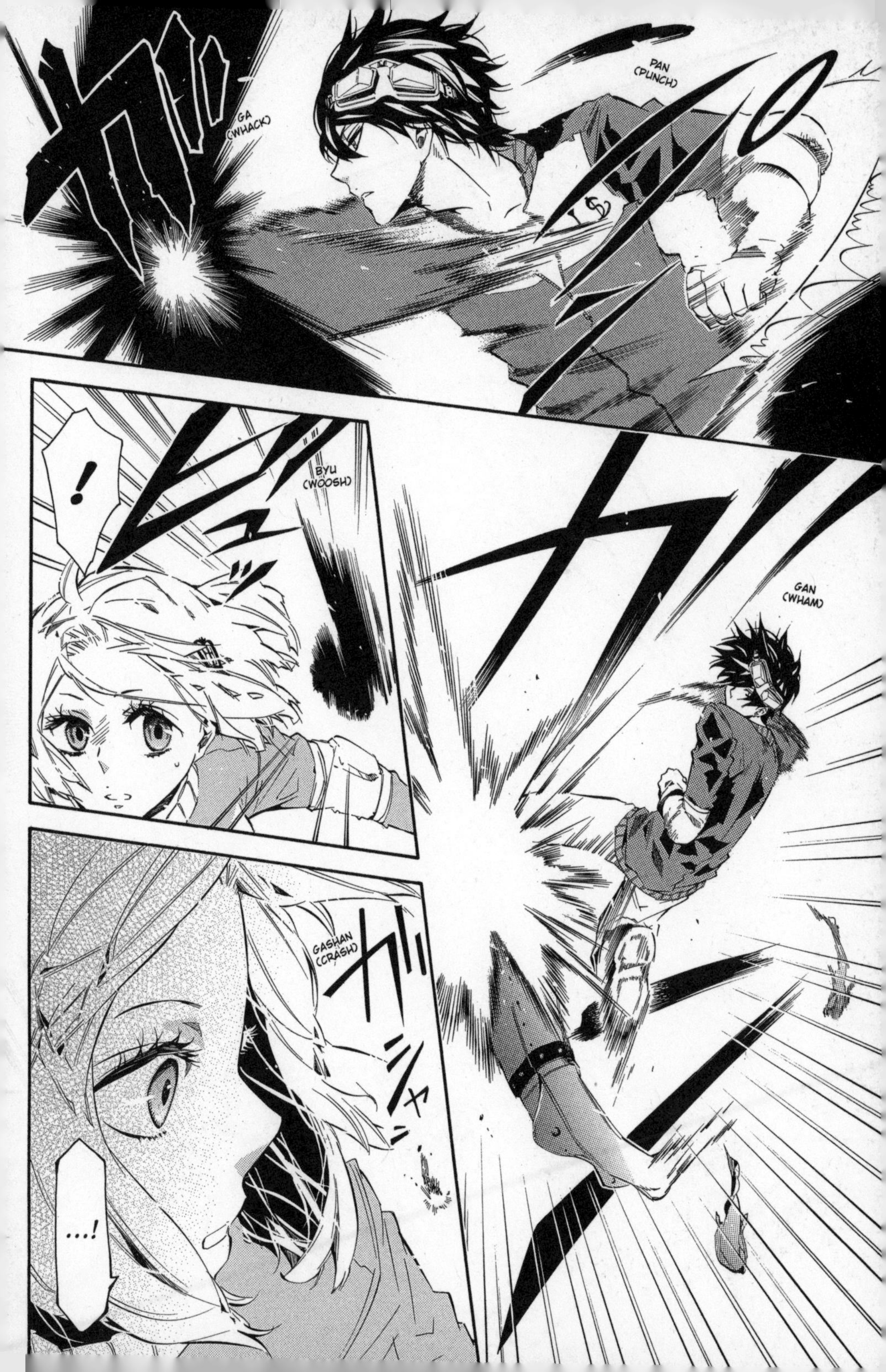

PAN (PUNCH)
GA (WHACK)
GAN (WHAM)
BYU (WOOSH)
!
GASHAN (CRASH)
...!

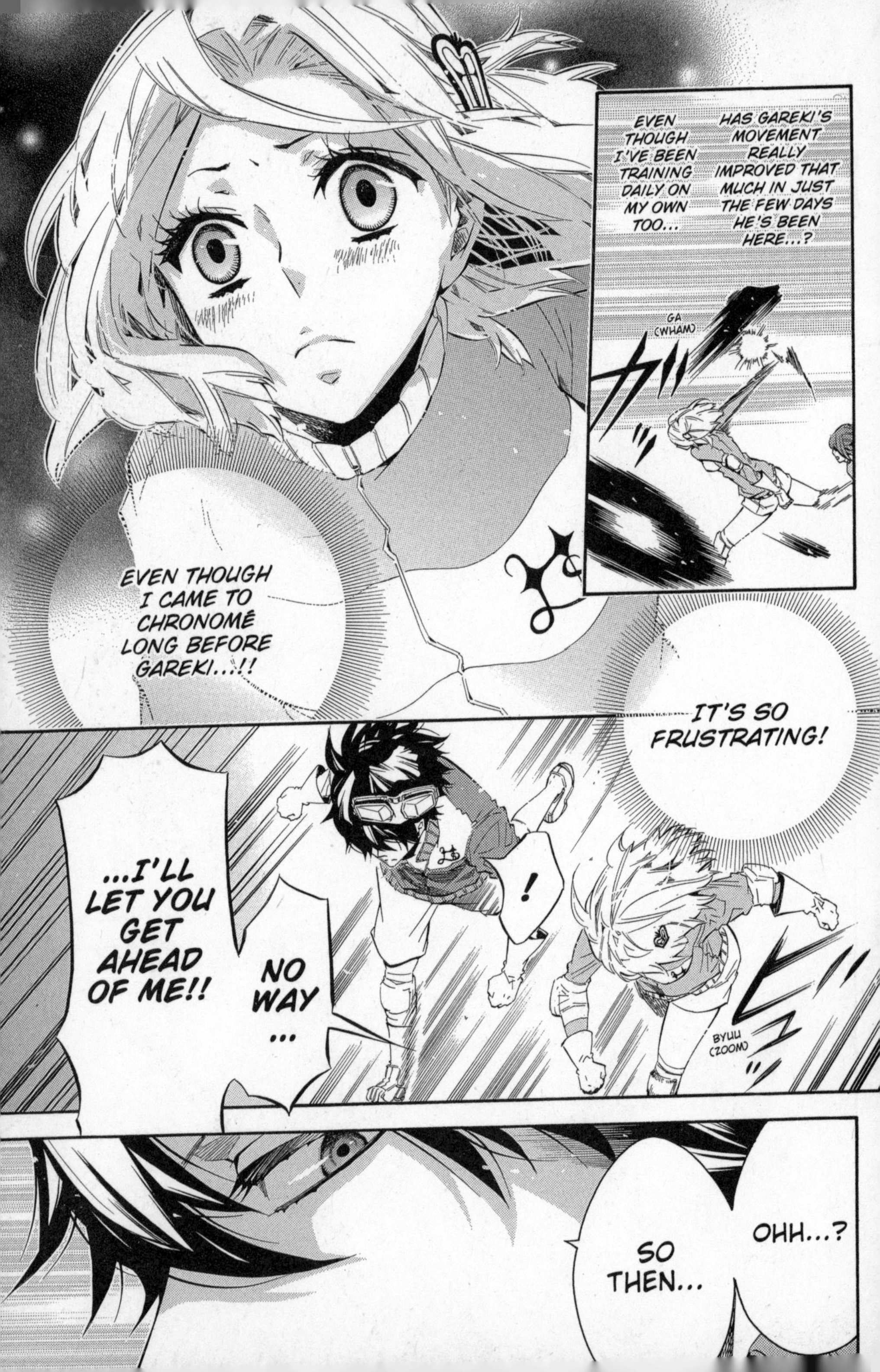

HAS GAREKI'S MOVEMENT REALLY IMPROVED THAT MUCH IN JUST THE FEW DAYS HE'S BEEN HERE...?
EVEN THOUGH I'VE BEEN TRAINING DAILY ON MY OWN TOO...
GA (WHAM)
EVEN THOUGH I CAME TO CHRONOMÉ LONG BEFORE GAREKI...!!
--IT'S SO FRUSTRATING!
BYUU (ZOOM)
!
NO WAY...
...I'LL LET YOU GET AHEAD OF ME!!
OHH...?
SO THEN...

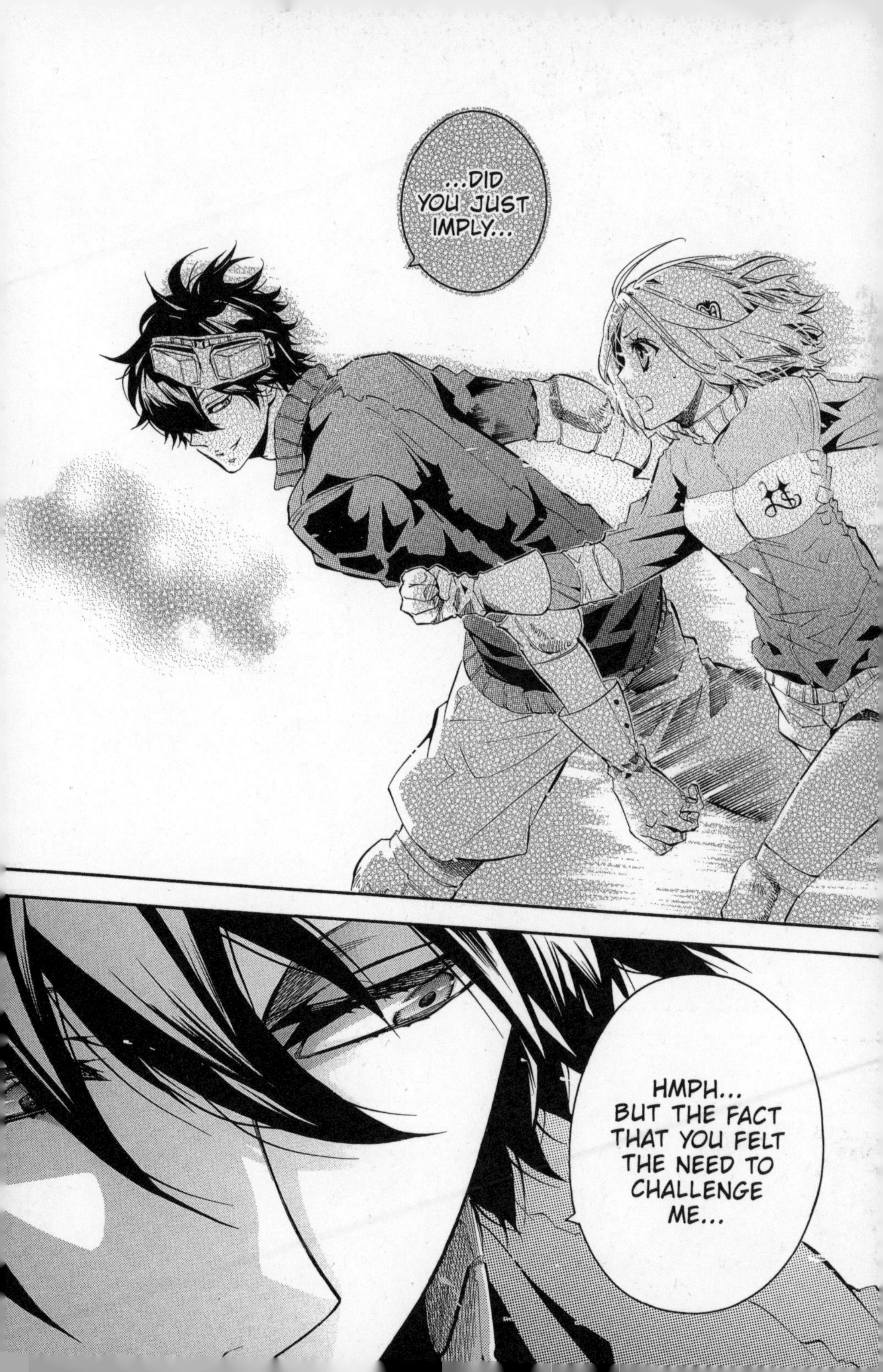
...DID YOU JUST IMPLY...
HMPH... BUT THE FACT THAT YOU FELT THE NEED TO CHALLENGE ME...

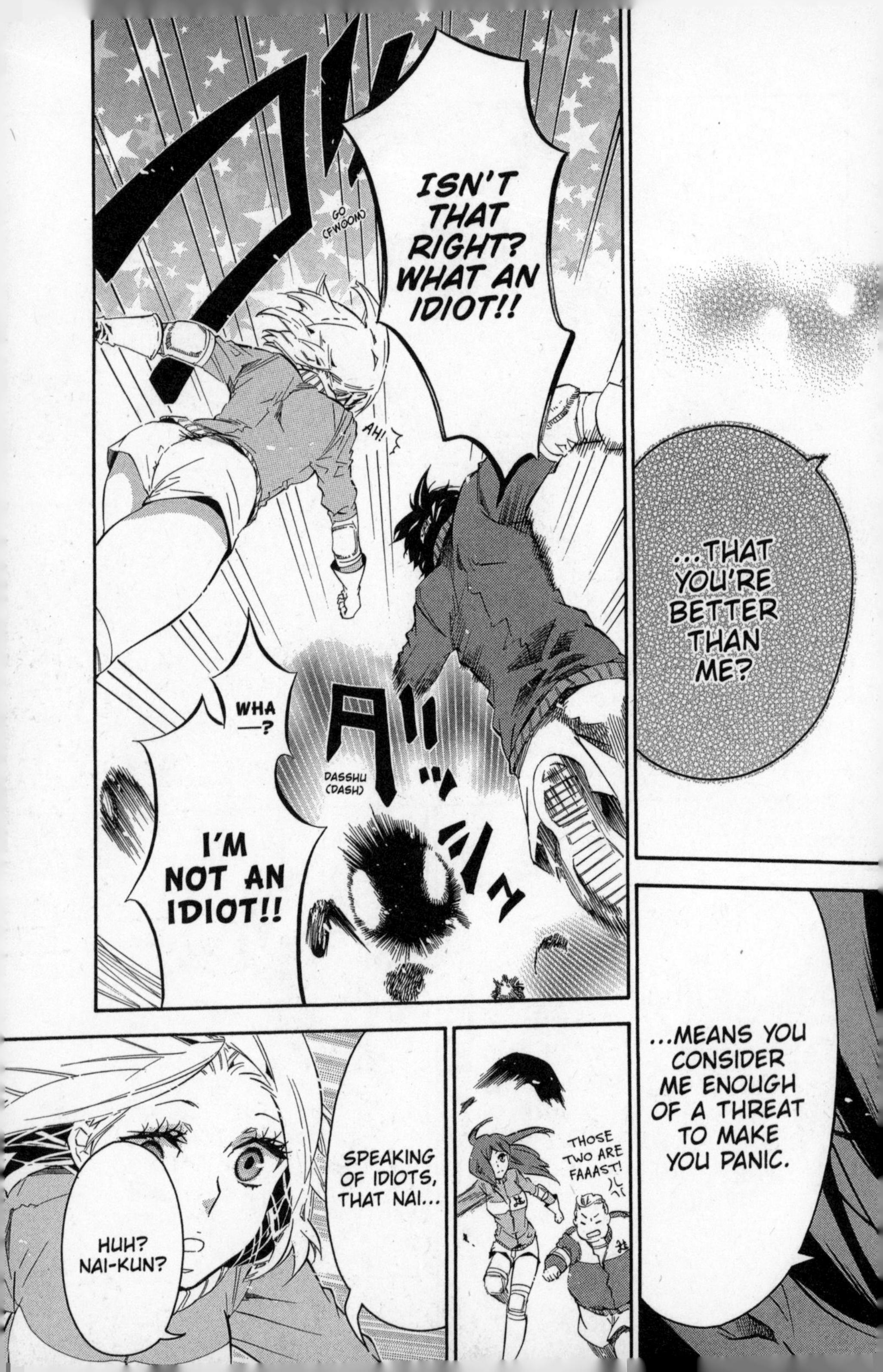

...THAT YOU'RE BETTER THAN ME?
...MEANS YOU CONSIDER ME ENOUGH OF A THREAT TO MAKE YOU PANIC.
ISN'T THAT RIGHT? WHAT AN IDIOT!!
GO (FWOOM)
AH!
WHA—?
DASSHU (DASH)
I'M NOT AN IDIOT!!
THOSE TWO ARE FAAAST!
SPEAKING OF IDIOTS, THAT NAI...
HUH? NAI-KUN?

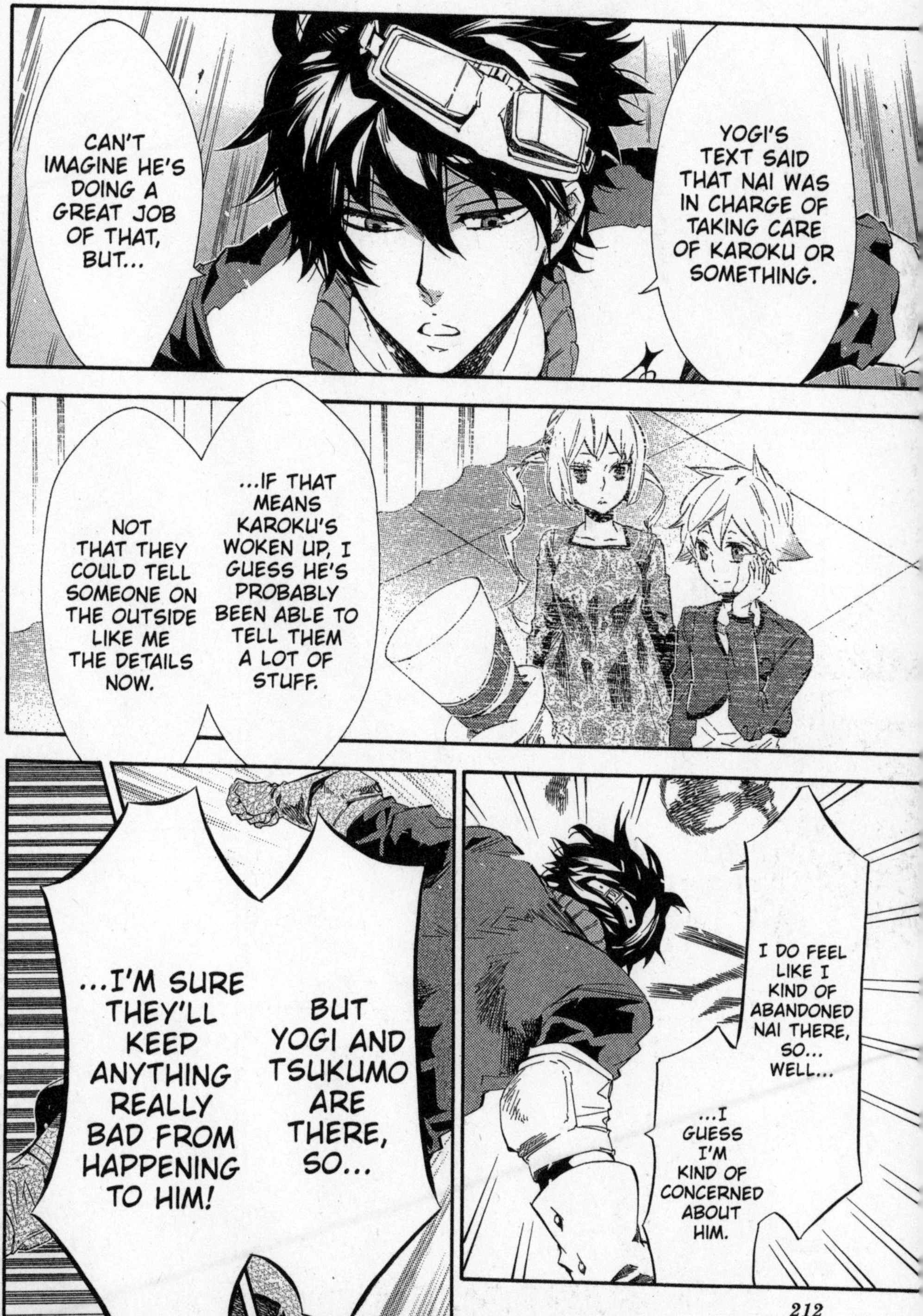
YOGI'S TEXT SAID THAT NAI WAS IN CHARGE OF TAKING CARE OF KAROKU OR SOMETHING.
CAN'T IMAGINE HE'S DOING A GREAT JOB OF THAT, BUT...
...IF THAT MEANS KAROKU'S WOKEN UP, I GUESS HE'S PROBABLY BEEN ABLE TO TELL THEM A LOT OF STUFF.
NOT THAT THEY COULD TELL SOMEONE ON THE OUTSIDE LIKE ME THE DETAILS NOW.
I DO FEEL LIKE I KIND OF ABANDONED NAI THERE, SO... WELL...
...I GUESS I'M KIND OF CONCERNED ABOUT HIM.
BUT YOGI AND TSUKUMO ARE THERE, SO...
...I'M SURE THEY'LL KEEP ANYTHING REALLY BAD FROM HAPPENING TO HIM!

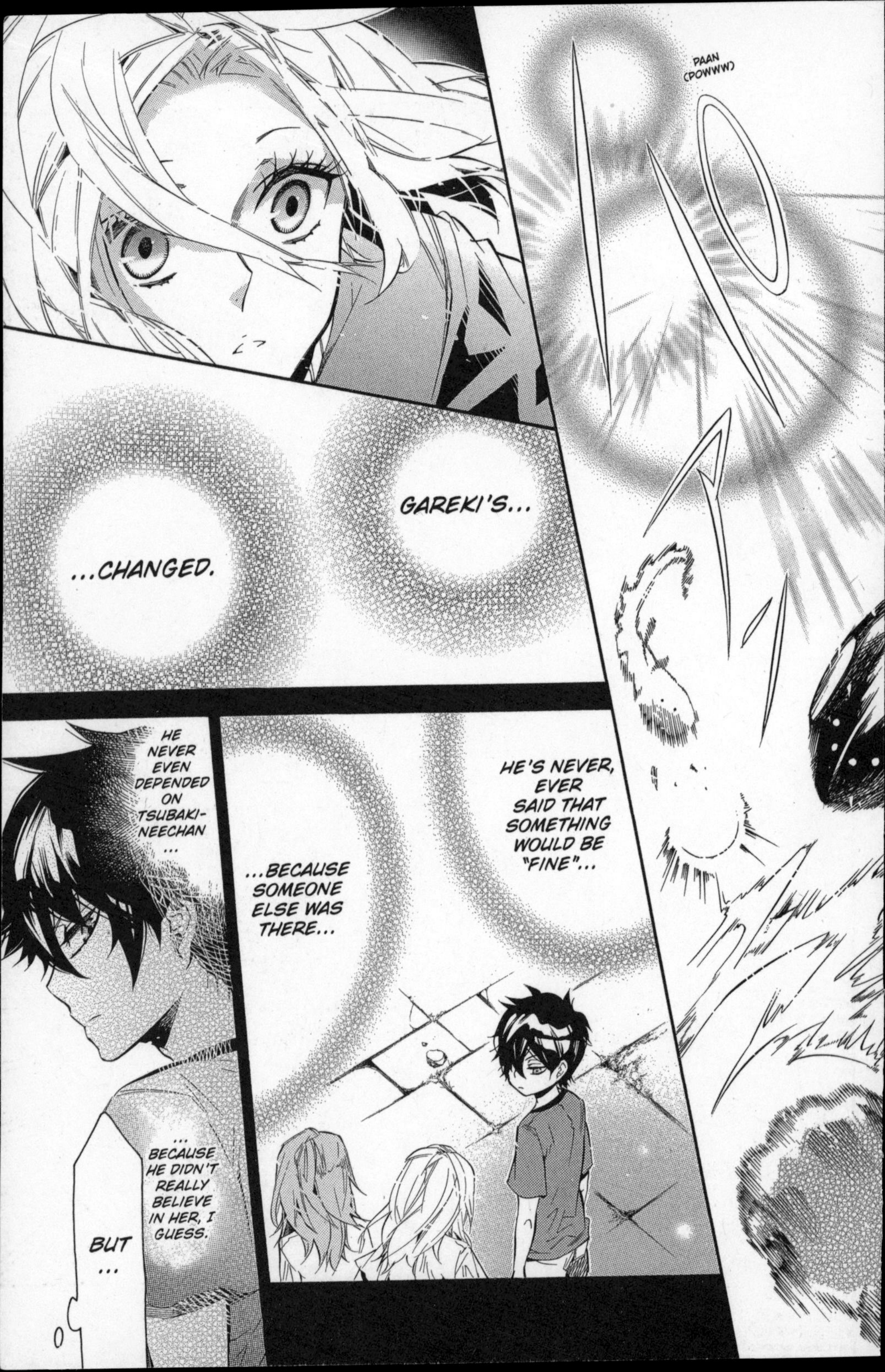
PAAN (POWWW)
GAREKI'S...
...CHANGED.
HE'S NEVER, EVER SAID THAT SOMETHING WOULD BE "FINE"...
...BECAUSE SOMEONE ELSE WAS THERE...
HE NEVER EVEN DEPENDED ON TSUBAKI-NEECHAN...
...BECAUSE HE DIDN'T REALLY BELIEVE IN HER, I GUESS.
BUT...

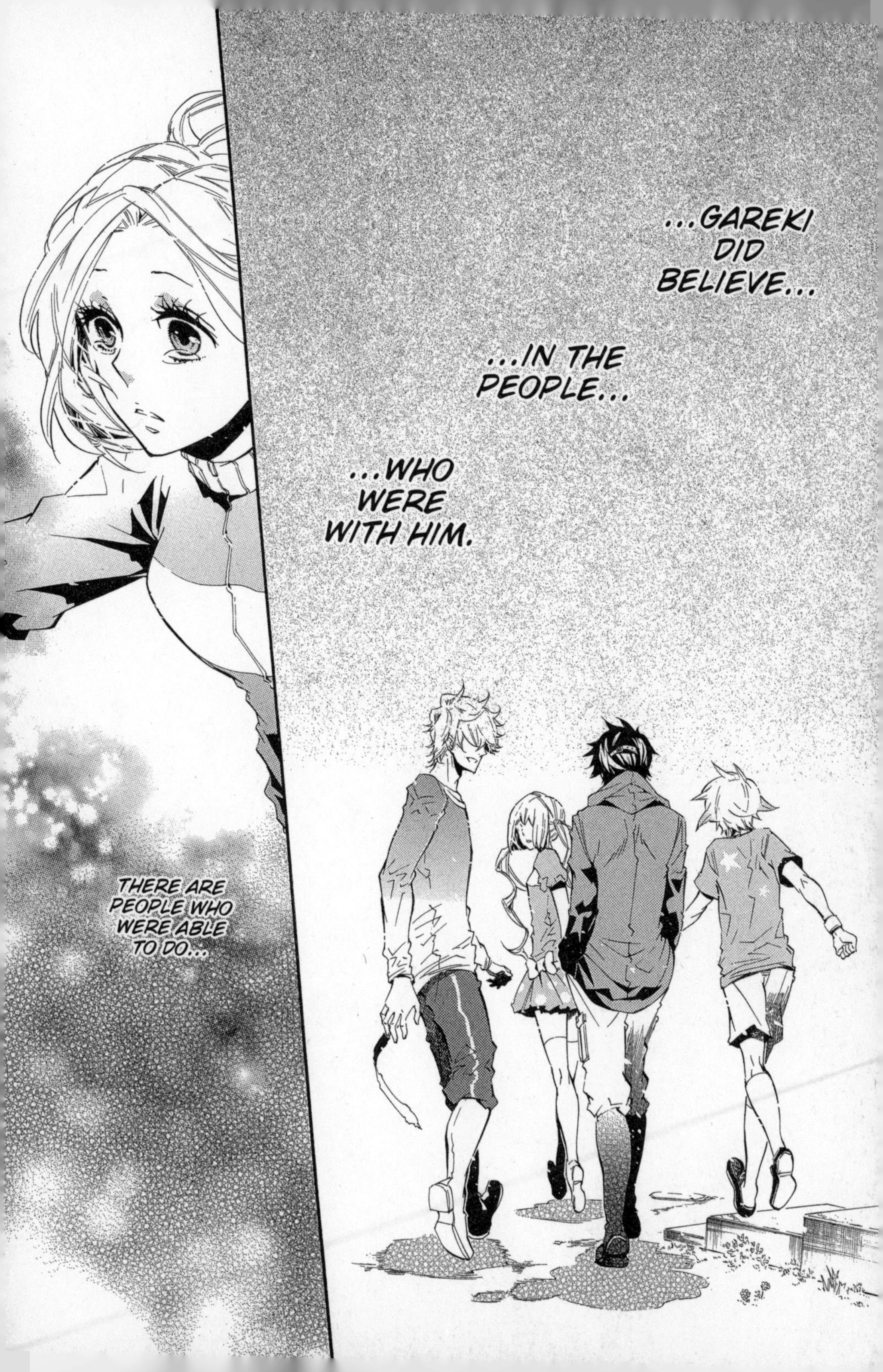
...GAREKI DID BELIEVE...
...IN THE PEOPLE...
...WHO WERE WITH HIM.
THERE ARE PEOPLE WHO WERE ABLE TO DO...

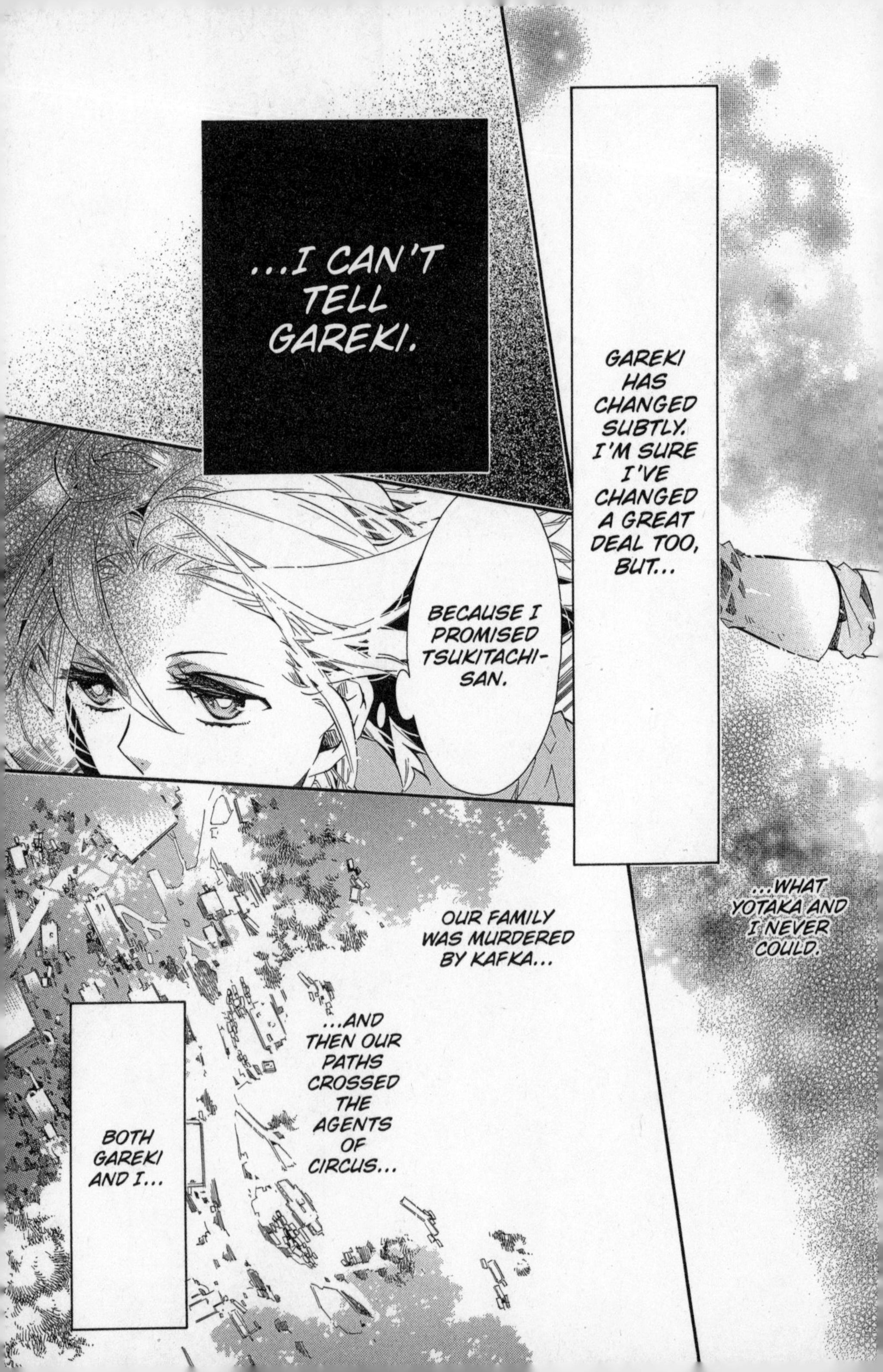
GAREKI HAS CHANGED SUBTLY. I'M SURE I'VE CHANGED A GREAT DEAL TOO, BUT...
...I CAN'T TELL GAREKI.
BECAUSE I PROMISED TSUKITACHI-SAN.
BOTH GAREKI AND I...
OUR FAMILY WAS MURDERED BY KAFKA...
...AND THEN OUR PATHS CROSSED THE AGENTS OF CIRCUS...
...WHAT YOTAKA AND I NEVER COULD.

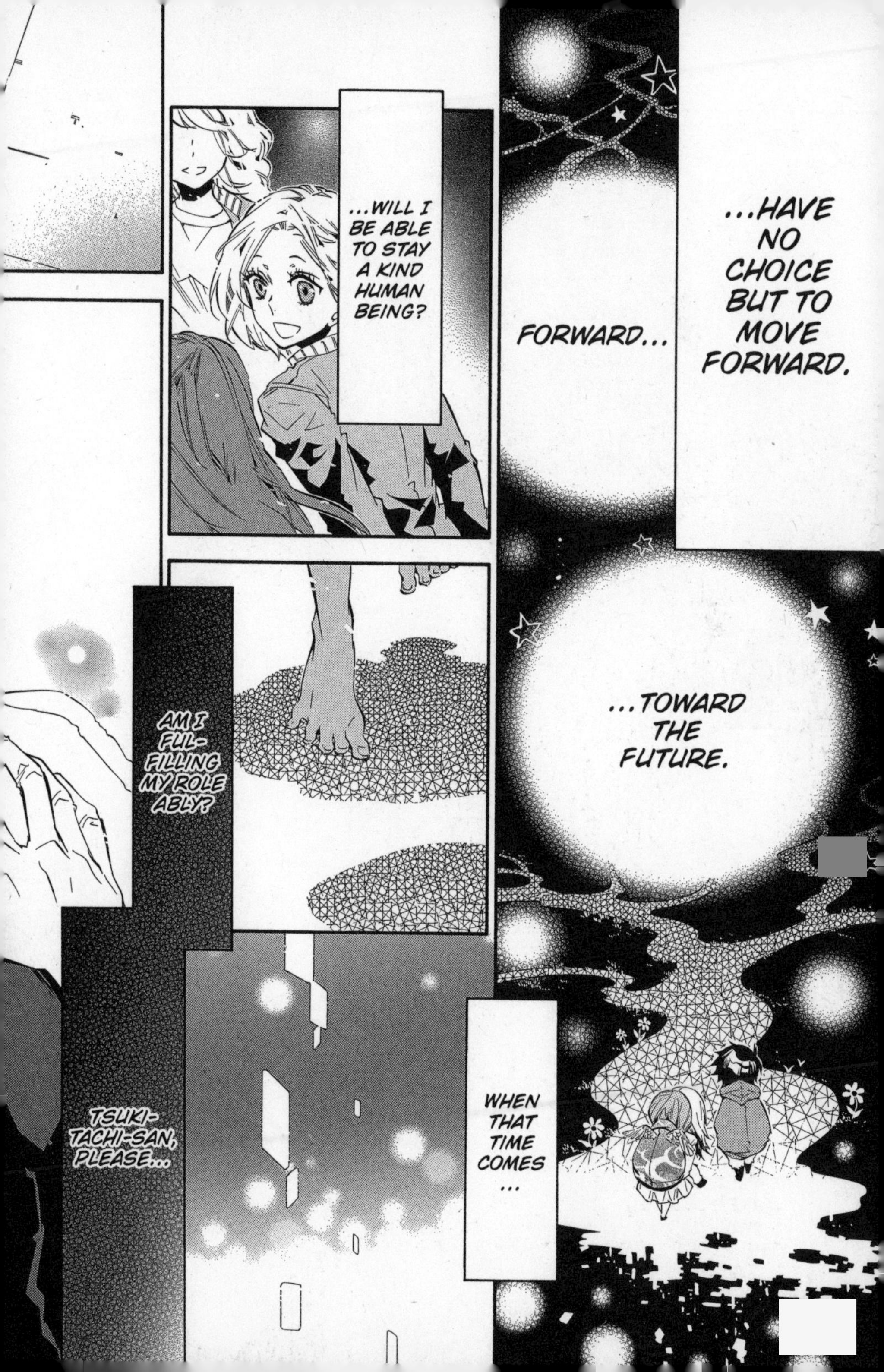
...HAVE NO CHOICE BUT TO MOVE FORWARD.
FORWARD...
...TOWARD THE FUTURE.
WHEN THAT TIME COMES ...
...WILL I BE ABLE TO STAY A KIND HUMAN BEING?
AM I FUL-FILLING MY ROLE ABLY?
TSUKI-TACHI-SAN, PLEASE...

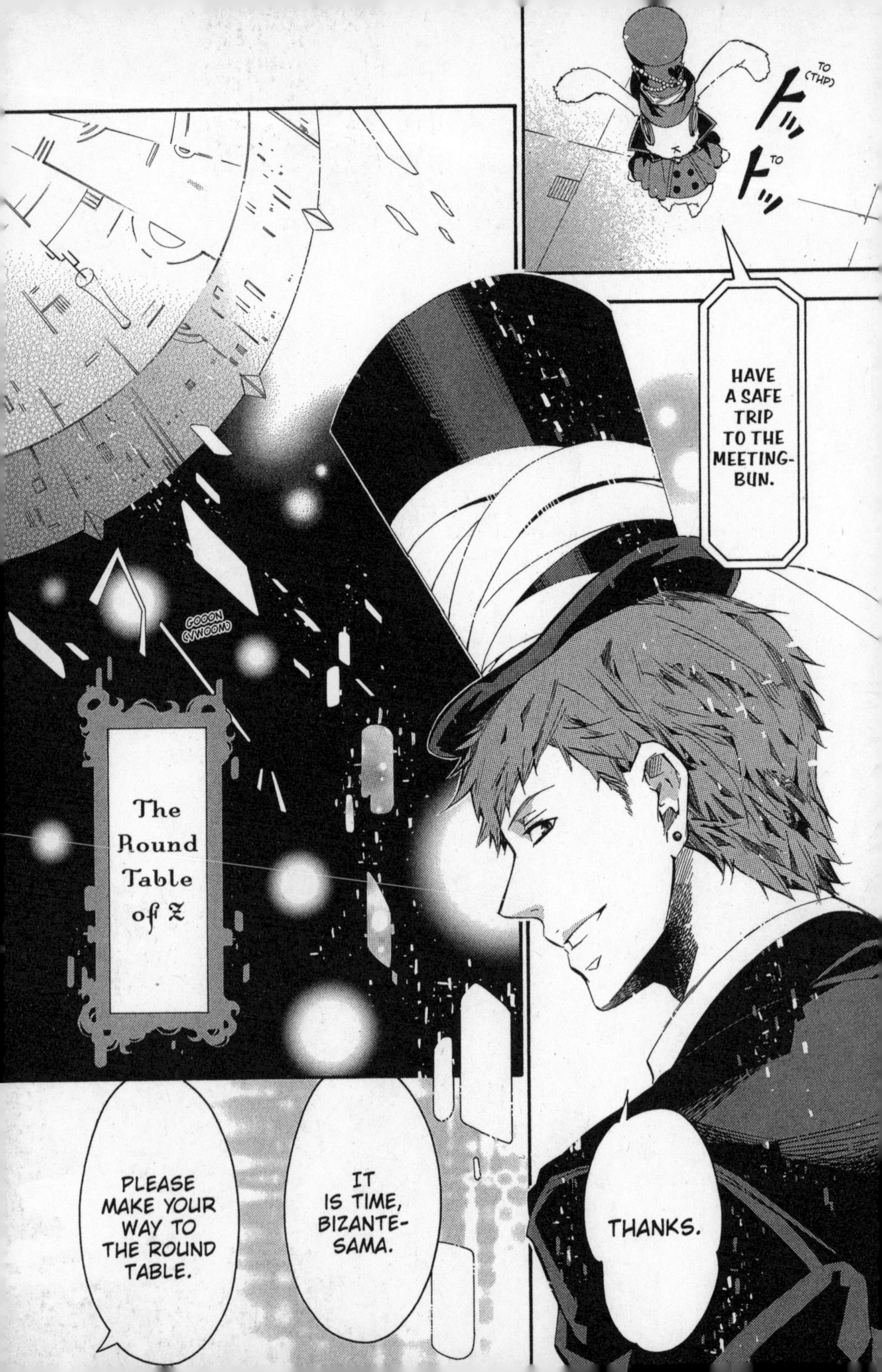
トッ TO (THP)
トッ TO
HAVE A SAFE TRIP TO THE MEETING-BUN.
GOOON (VWOOM)
The Round Table of Z
THANKS.
IT IS TIME, BIZANTE-SAMA.
PLEASE MAKE YOUR WAY TO THE ROUND TABLE.

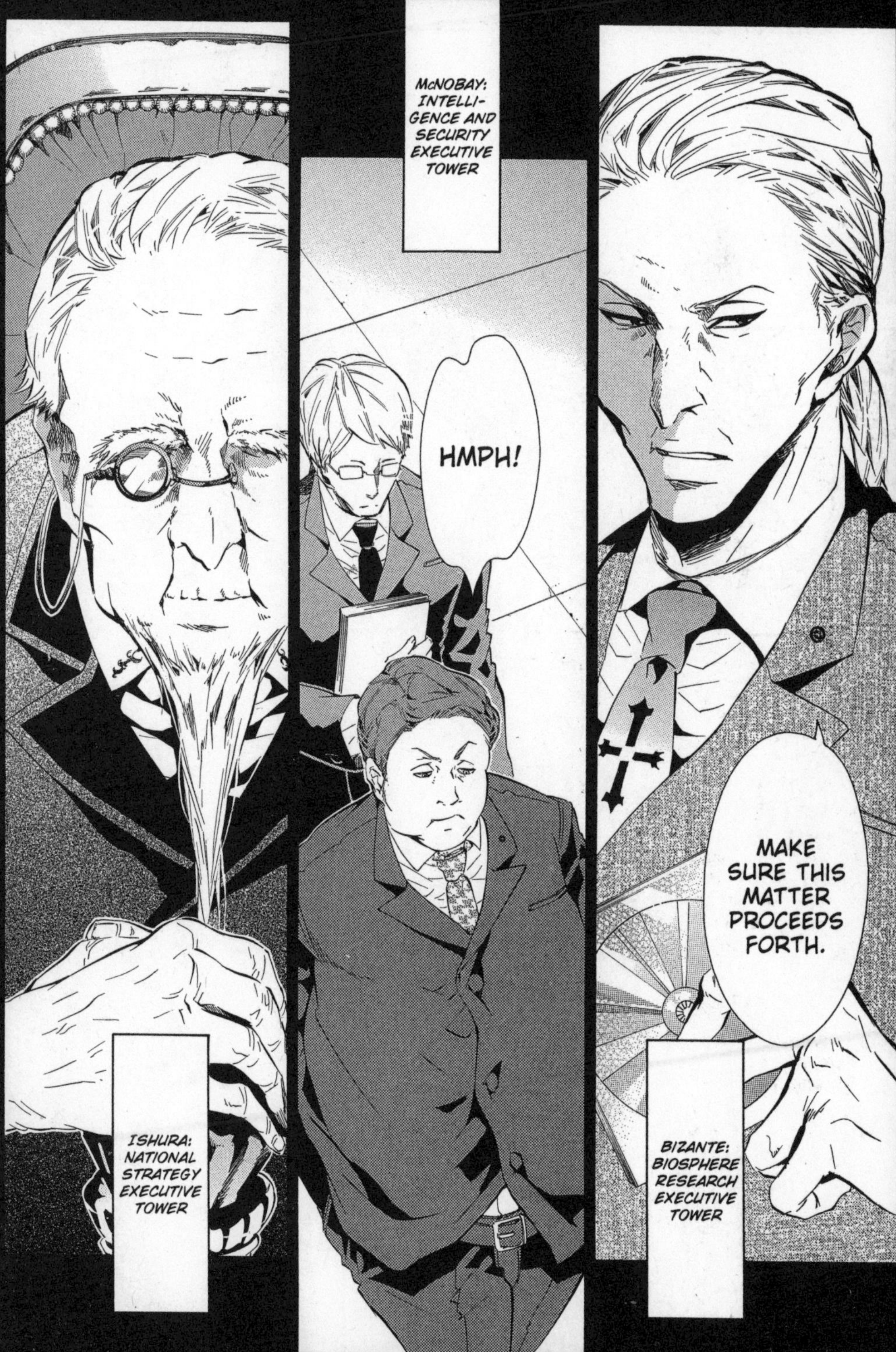
MAKE SURE THIS MATTER PROCEEDS FORTH.
BIZANTE: BIOSPHERE RESEARCH EXECUTIVE TOWER
McNOBAY: INTELLIGENCE AND SECURITY EXECUTIVE TOWER
HMPH!
ISHURA: NATIONAL STRATEGY EXECUTIVE TOWER

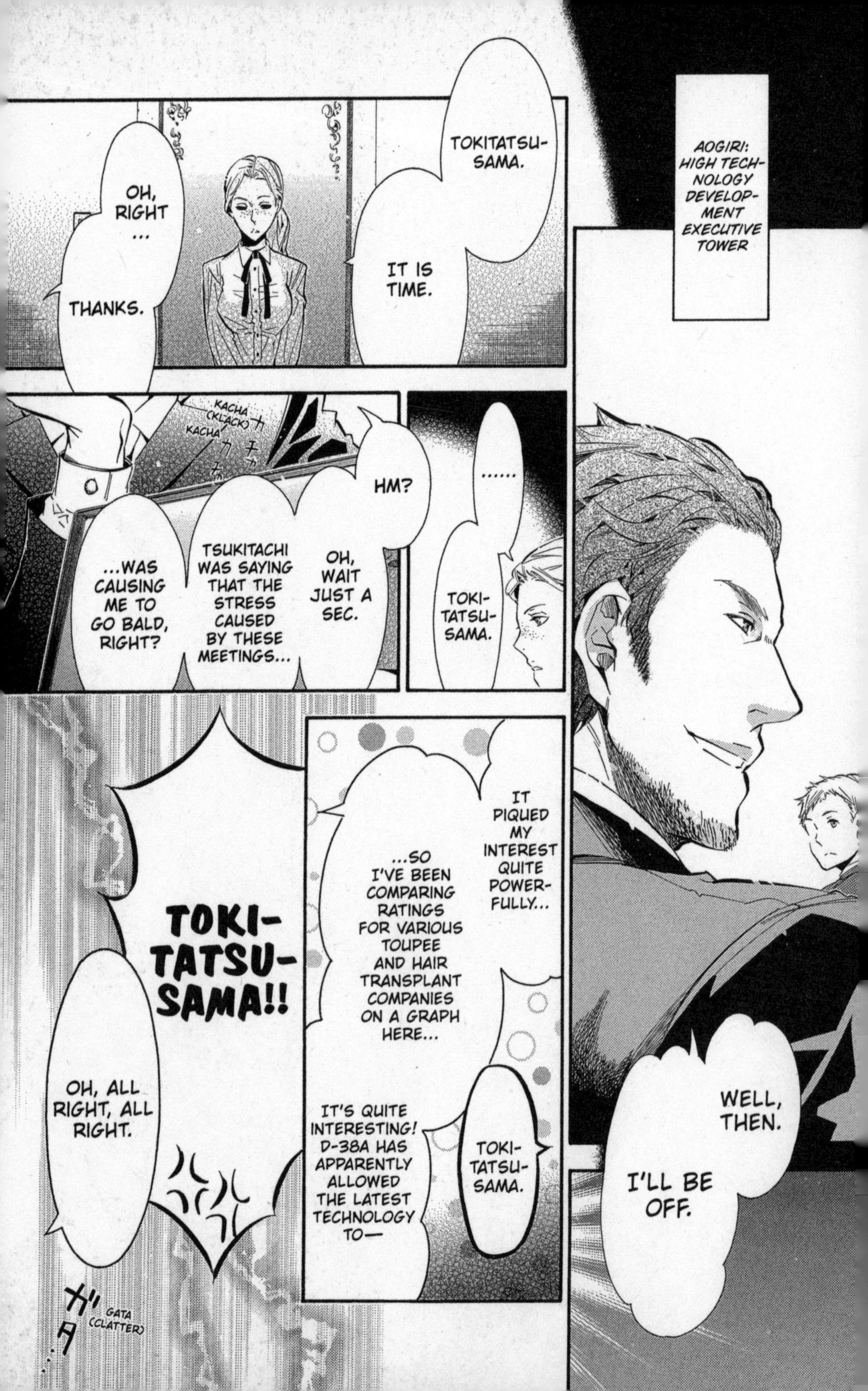
AOGIRI: HIGH TECHNOLOGY DEVELOPMENT EXECUTIVE TOWER
WELL, THEN.
I'LL BE OFF.
TOKITATSU-SAMA.
IT IS TIME.
OH, RIGHT ...
THANKS.
......
TOKITATSU-SAMA.
HM?
KACHA (KLACK) KACHA
OH, WAIT JUST A SEC.
TSUKITACHI WAS SAYING THAT THE STRESS CAUSED BY THESE MEETINGS...
...WAS CAUSING ME TO GO BALD, RIGHT?
IT PIQUED MY INTEREST QUITE POWERFULLY...
...SO I'VE BEEN COMPARING RATINGS FOR VARIOUS TOUPEE AND HAIR TRANSPLANT COMPANIES ON A GRAPH HERE...
TOKITATSU-SAMA.
IT'S QUITE INTERESTING! D-38A HAS APPARENTLY ALLOWED THE LATEST TECHNOLOGY TO—
TOKITATSU-SAMA!!
OH, ALL RIGHT, ALL RIGHT.
GATA (CLATTER)

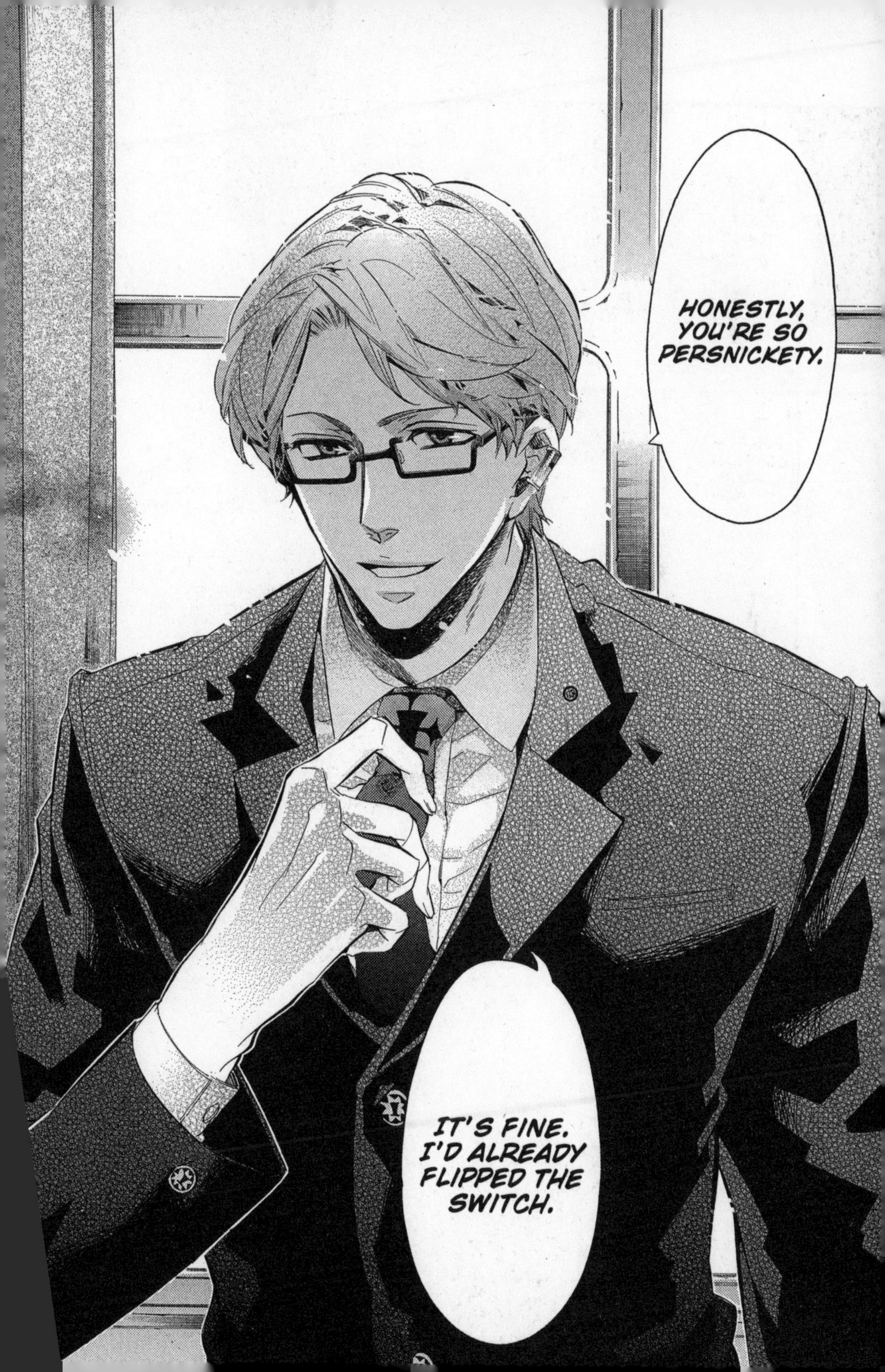
HONESTLY, YOU'RE SO PERSNICKETY.
IT'S FINE. I'D ALREADY FLIPPED THE SWITCH.

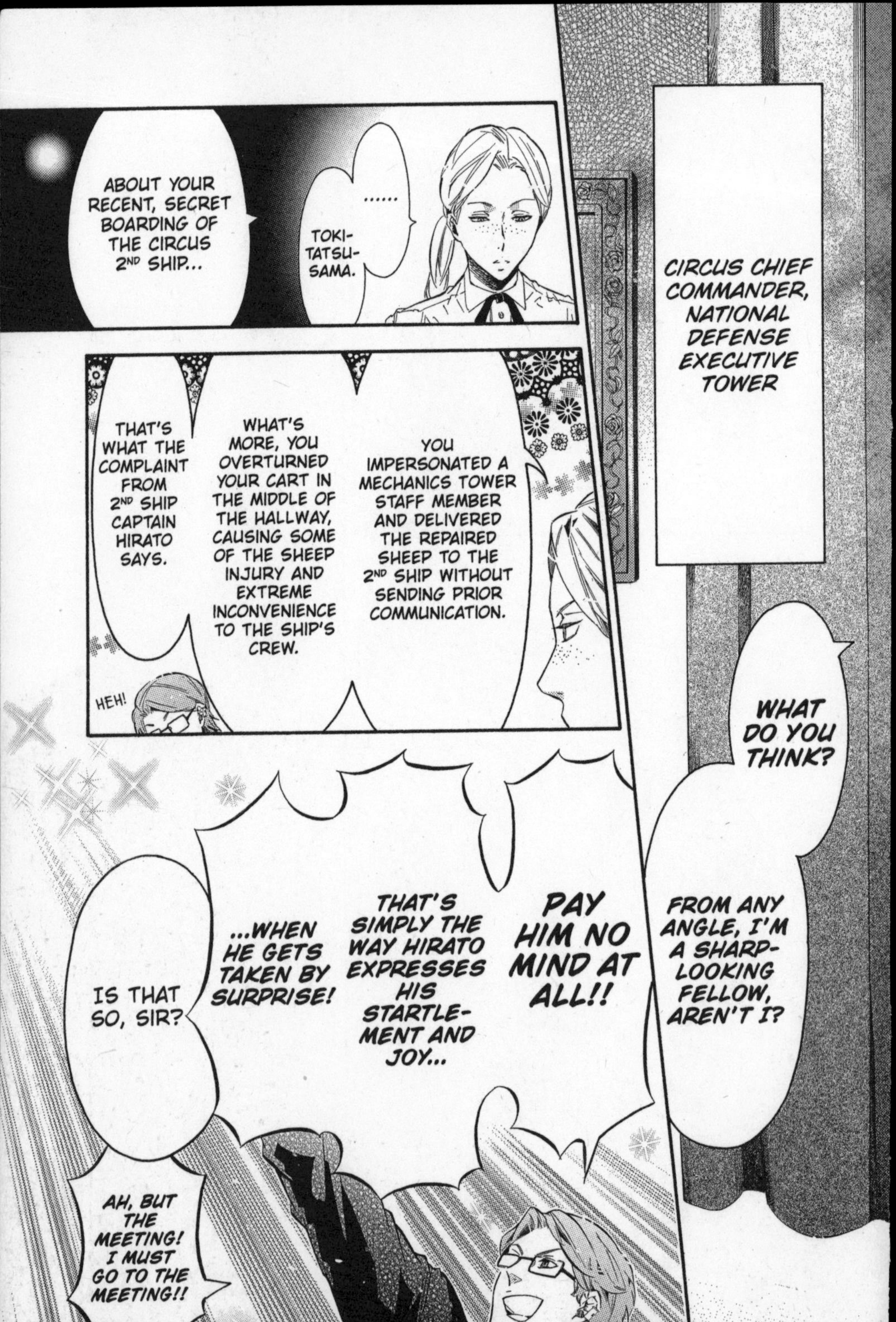

CIRCUS CHIEF COMMANDER, NATIONAL DEFENSE EXECUTIVE TOWER
......
TOKI-TATSU-SAMA.
ABOUT YOUR RECENT, SECRET BOARDING OF THE CIRCUS 2ND SHIP...
YOU IMPERSONATED A MECHANICS TOWER STAFF MEMBER AND DELIVERED THE REPAIRED SHEEP TO THE 2ND SHIP WITHOUT SENDING PRIOR COMMUNICATION.
WHAT'S MORE, YOU OVERTURNED YOUR CART IN THE MIDDLE OF THE HALLWAY, CAUSING SOME OF THE SHEEP INJURY AND EXTREME INCONVENIENCE TO THE SHIP'S CREW.
THAT'S WHAT THE COMPLAINT FROM 2ND SHIP CAPTAIN HIRATO SAYS.
HEH!
WHAT DO YOU THINK?
FROM ANY ANGLE, I'M A SHARP-LOOKING FELLOW, AREN'T I?
PAY HIM NO MIND AT ALL!!
THAT'S SIMPLY THE WAY HIRATO EXPRESSES HIS STARTLEMENT AND JOY...
...WHEN HE GETS TAKEN BY SURPRISE!
IS THAT SO, SIR?
AH, BUT THE MEETING! I MUST GO TO THE MEETING!!

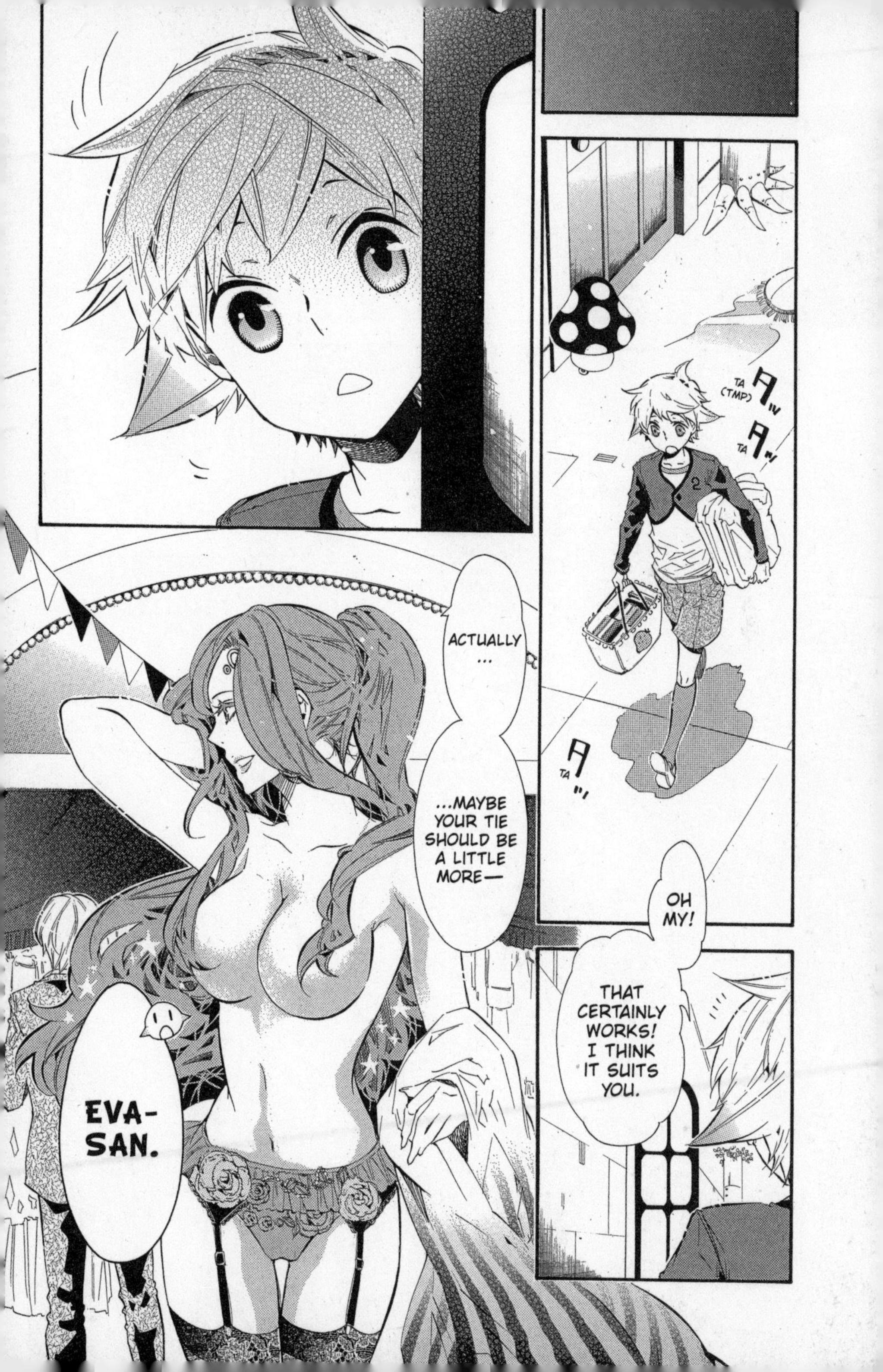
TA (TMP)
TA
TA
OH MY!
THAT CERTAINLY WORKS! I THINK IT SUITS YOU.
ACTUALLY...
...MAYBE YOUR TIE SHOULD BE A LITTLE MORE—
EVA-SAN.

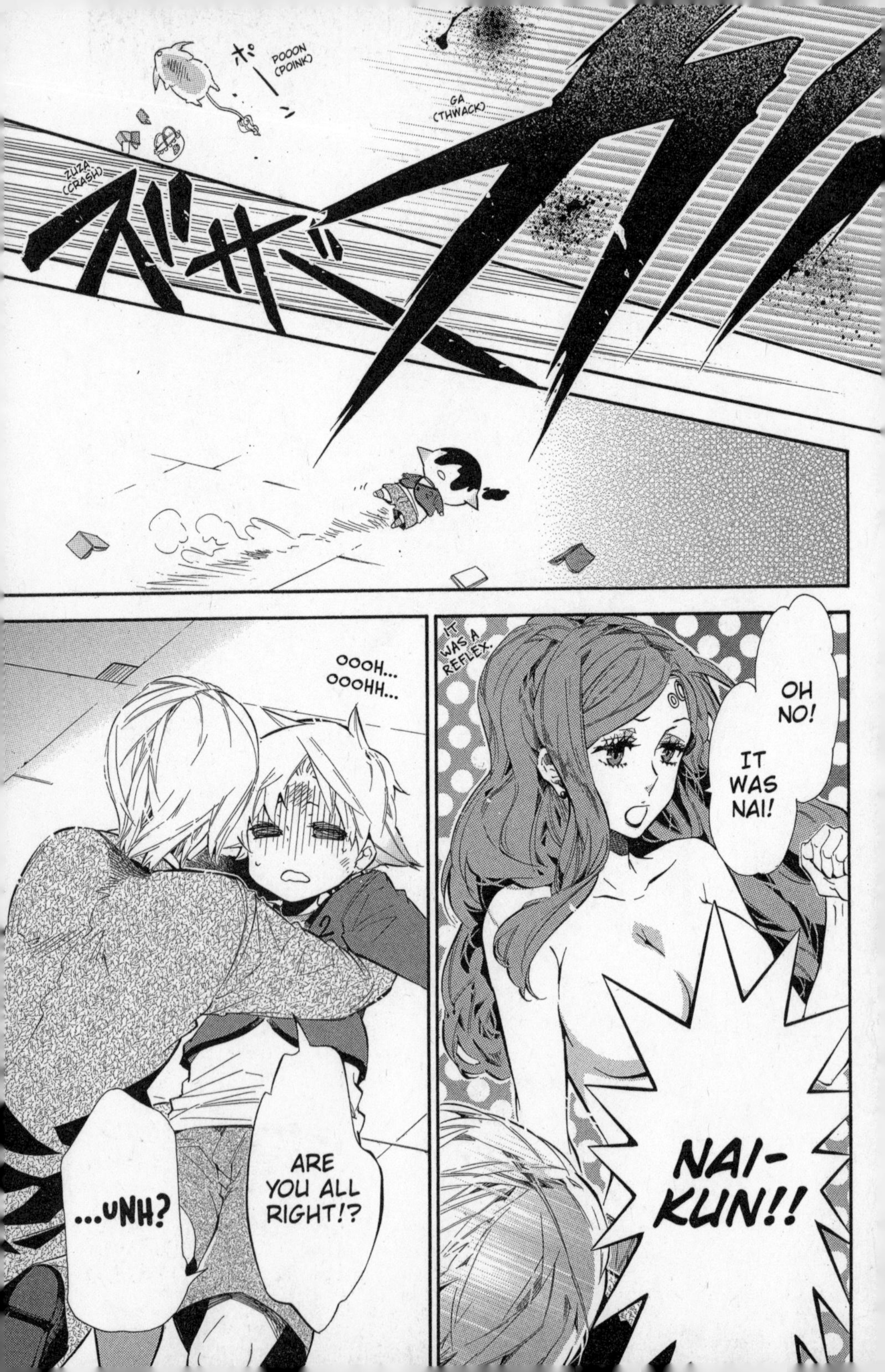
GA (THWACK)
POOON (POINK)
ZUZA (CRASH)
OH NO!
IT WAS NAI!
IT WAS A REFLEX.
NAI-KUN!!
OOOH... OOOHH...
ARE YOU ALL RIGHT!?
...UNH?

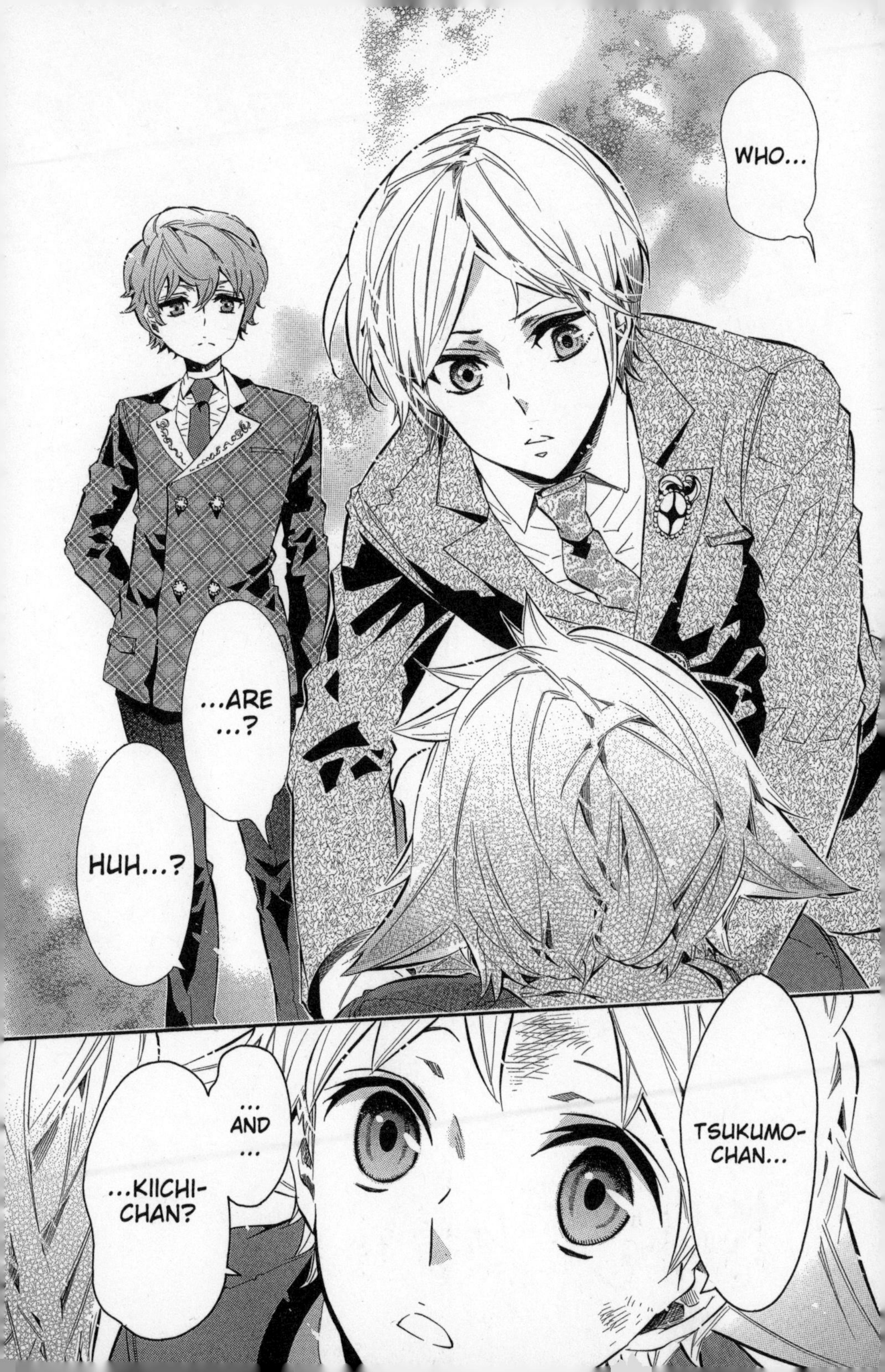
WHO...
...ARE ...?
HUH...?
TSUKUMO-CHAN...
...AND...
...KIICHI-CHAN?

KARNEVAL

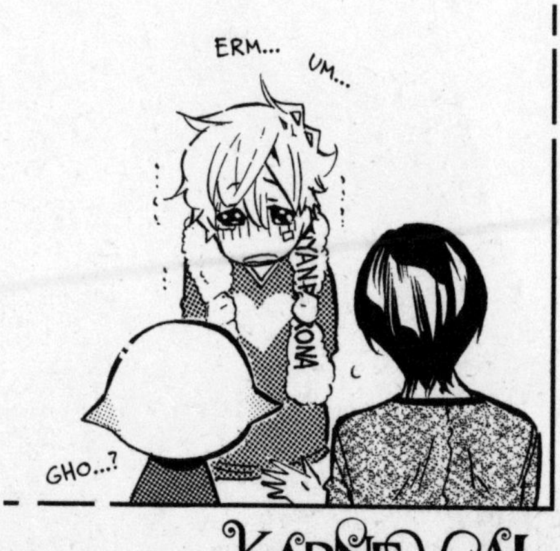
ERM...
UM...
GHO...?

KARNEVAL

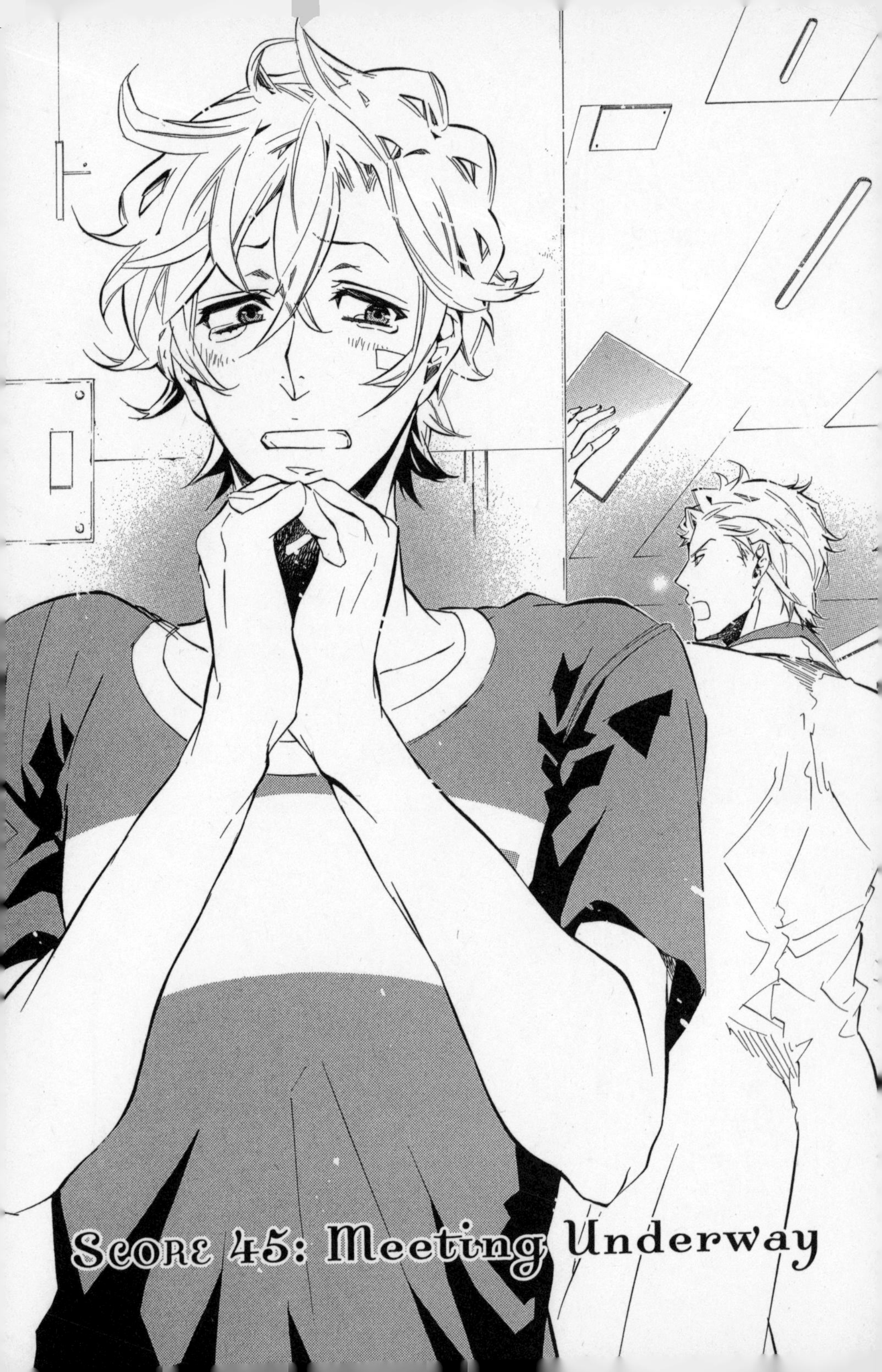
Score 45: Meeting Underway

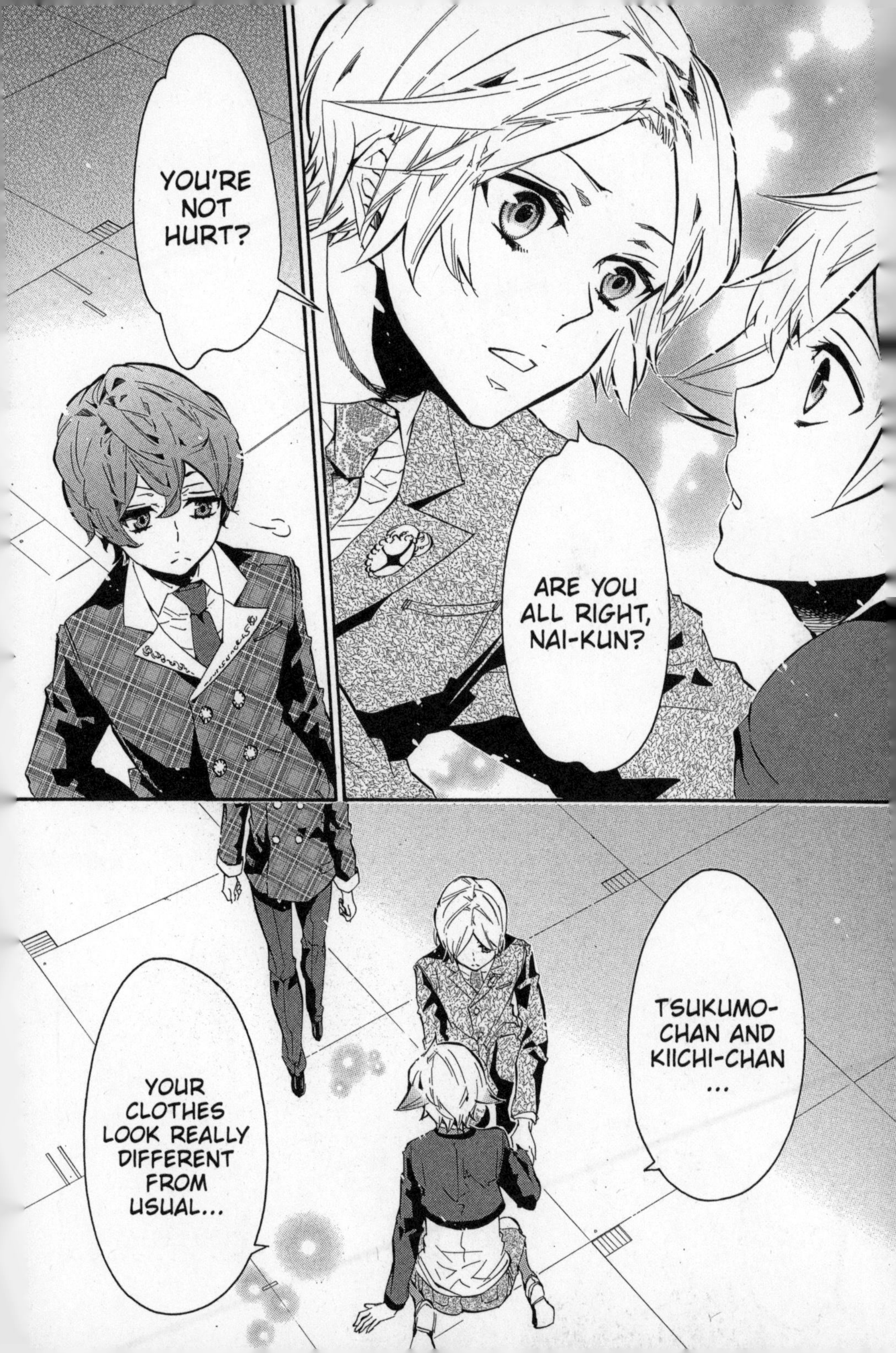
ARE YOU ALL RIGHT, NAI-KUN?
YOU'RE NOT HURT?
TSUKUMO-CHAN AND KIICHI-CHAN ...
YOUR CLOTHES LOOK REALLY DIFFERENT FROM USUAL...

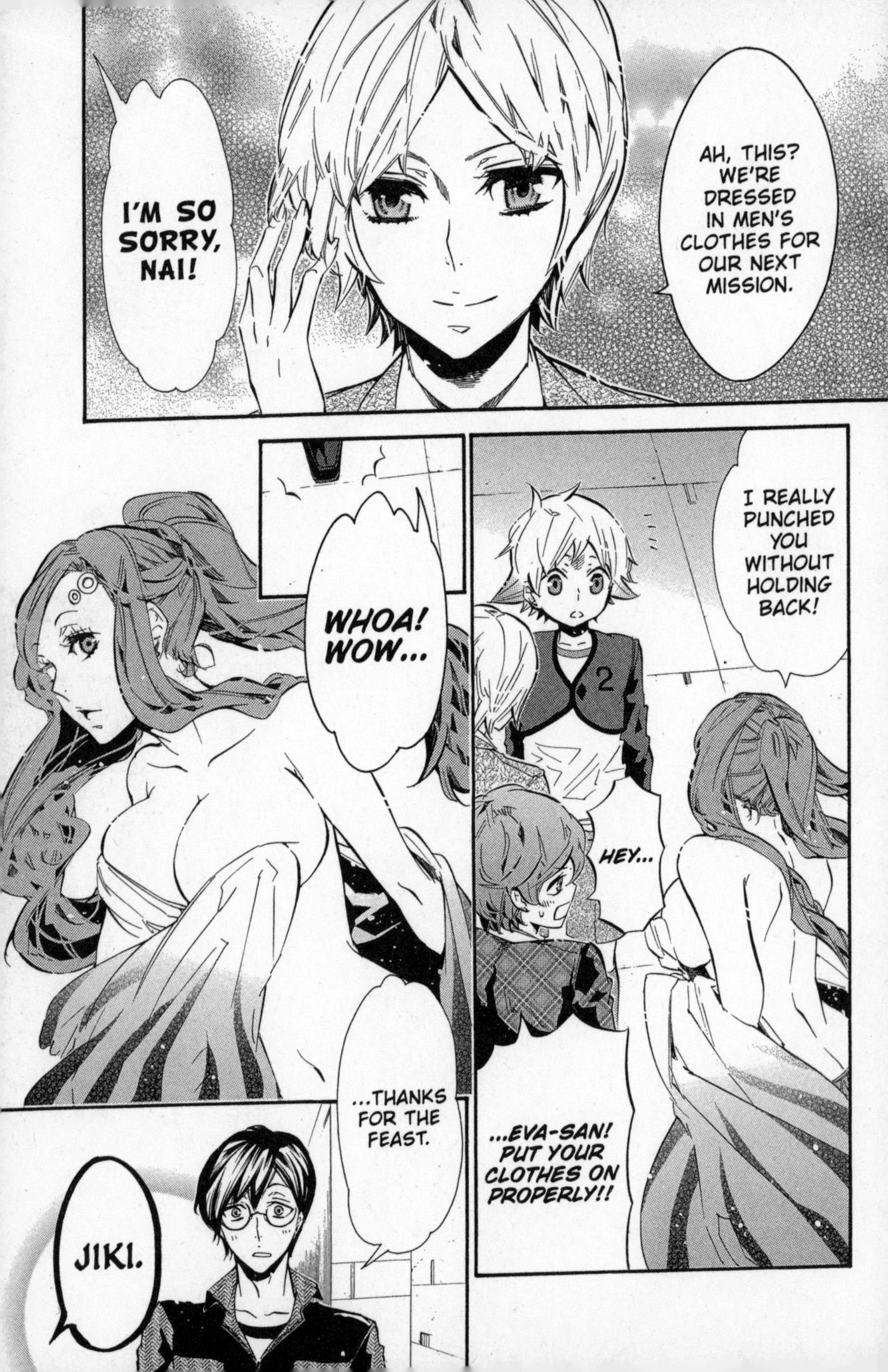
AH, THIS? WE'RE DRESSED IN MEN'S CLOTHES FOR OUR NEXT MISSION.
I'M SO SORRY, NAI!
I REALLY PUNCHED YOU WITHOUT HOLDING BACK!
HEY...
...EVA-SAN! PUT YOUR CLOTHES ON PROPERLY!!
WHOA! WOW...
...THANKS FOR THE FEAST.
JIKI.

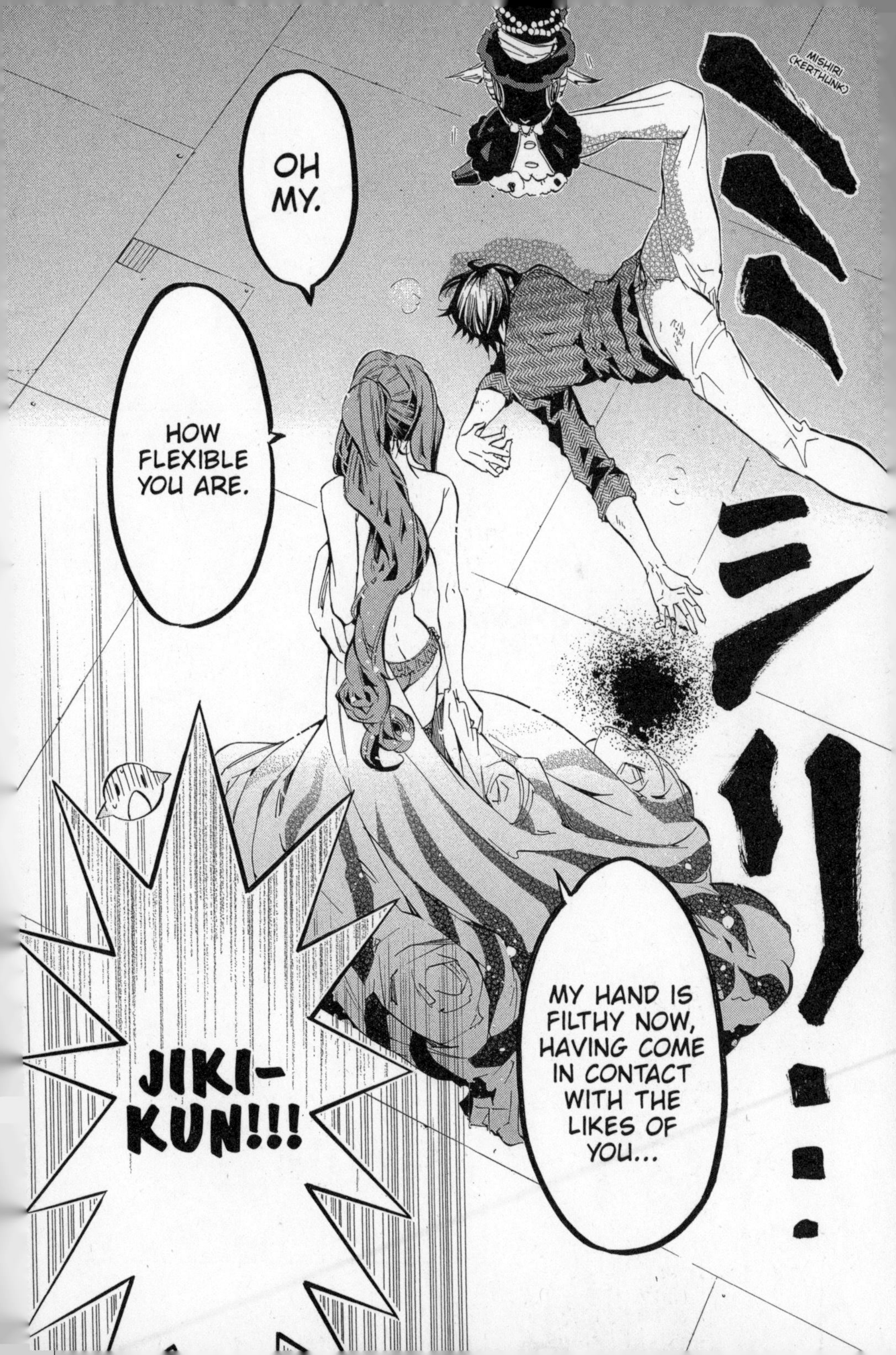
MISHIRI (KERTHUNK)
OH MY.
HOW FLEXIBLE YOU ARE.
MY HAND IS FILTHY NOW, HAVING COME IN CONTACT WITH THE LIKES OF YOU...
JIKI-KUN!!!

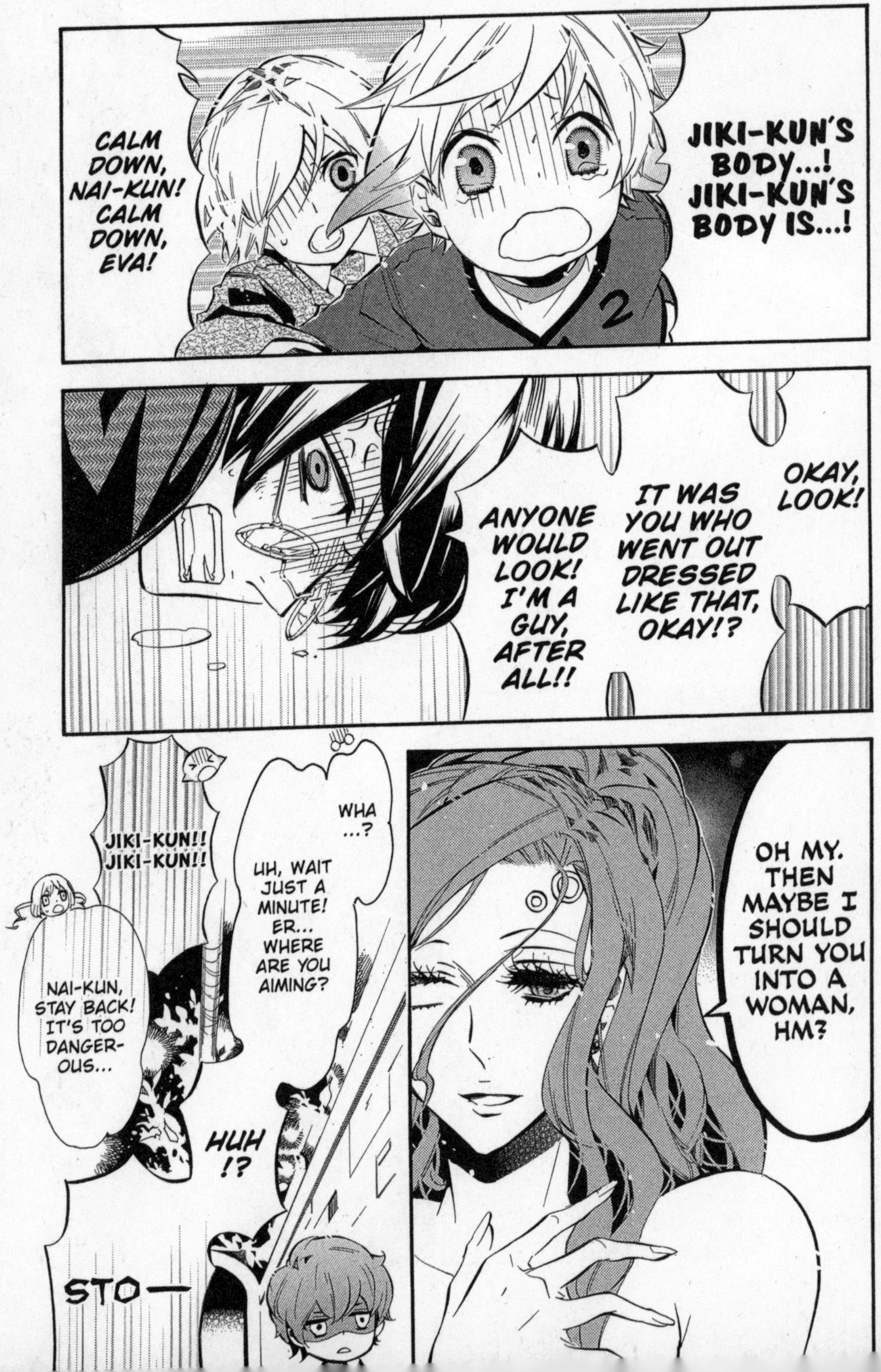
JIKI-KUN'S BODY...! JIKI-KUN'S BODY IS...!
CALM DOWN, NAI-KUN! CALM DOWN, EVA!
OKAY, LOOK!
IT WAS YOU WHO WENT OUT DRESSED LIKE THAT, OKAY!?
ANYONE WOULD LOOK! I'M A GUY, AFTER ALL!!
OH MY. THEN MAYBE I SHOULD TURN YOU INTO A WOMAN, HM?
WHA...?
UH, WAIT JUST A MINUTE! ER... WHERE ARE YOU AIMING?
HUH!?
JIKI-KUN!! JIKI-KUN!!
NAI-KUN, STAY BACK! IT'S TOO DANGER-OUS...
STO—

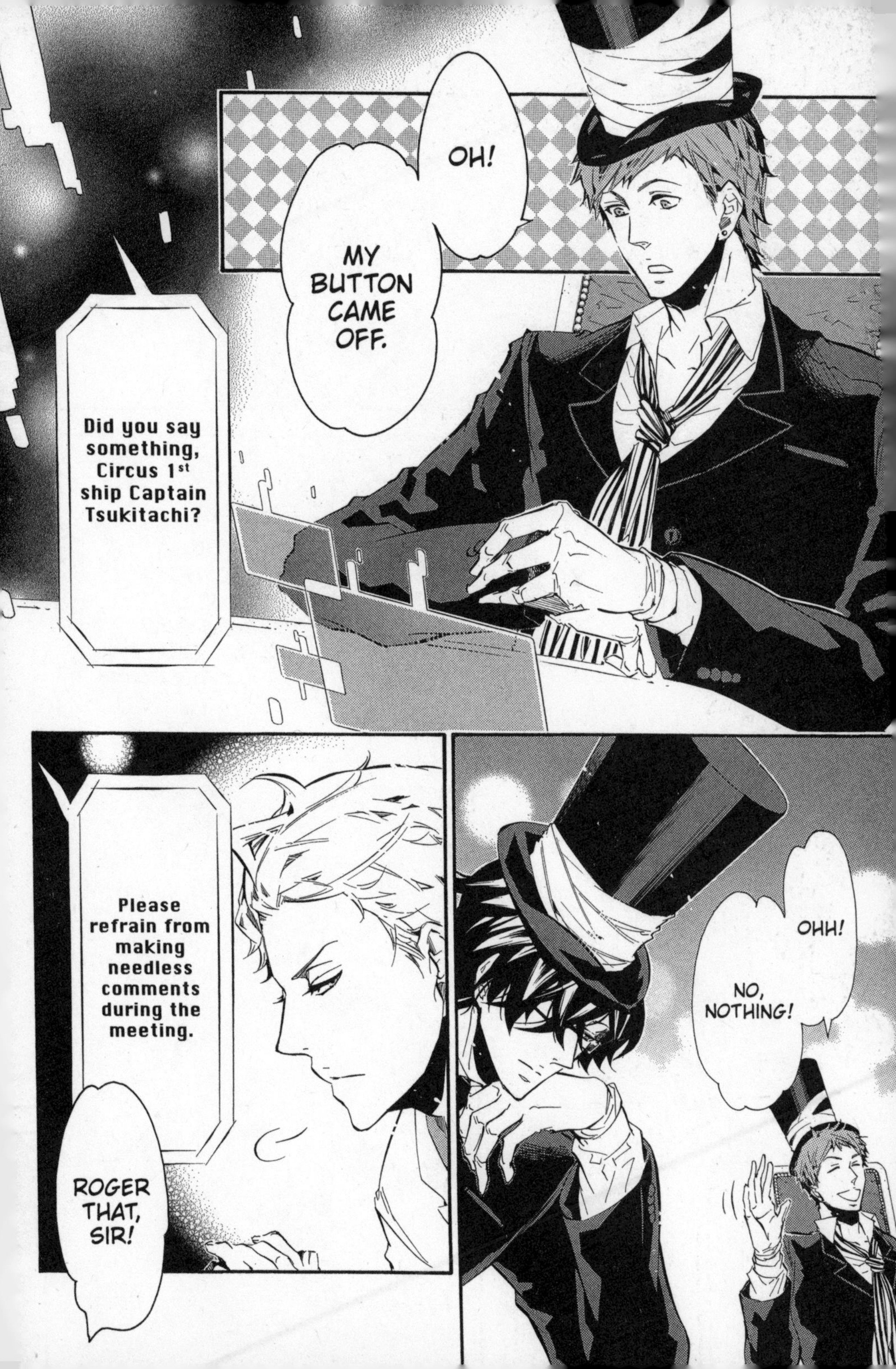
OH!
MY BUTTON CAME OFF.
Did you say something, Circus 1st ship Captain Tsukitachi?
OHH!
NO, NOTHING!
Please refrain from making needless comments during the meeting.
ROGER THAT, SIR!

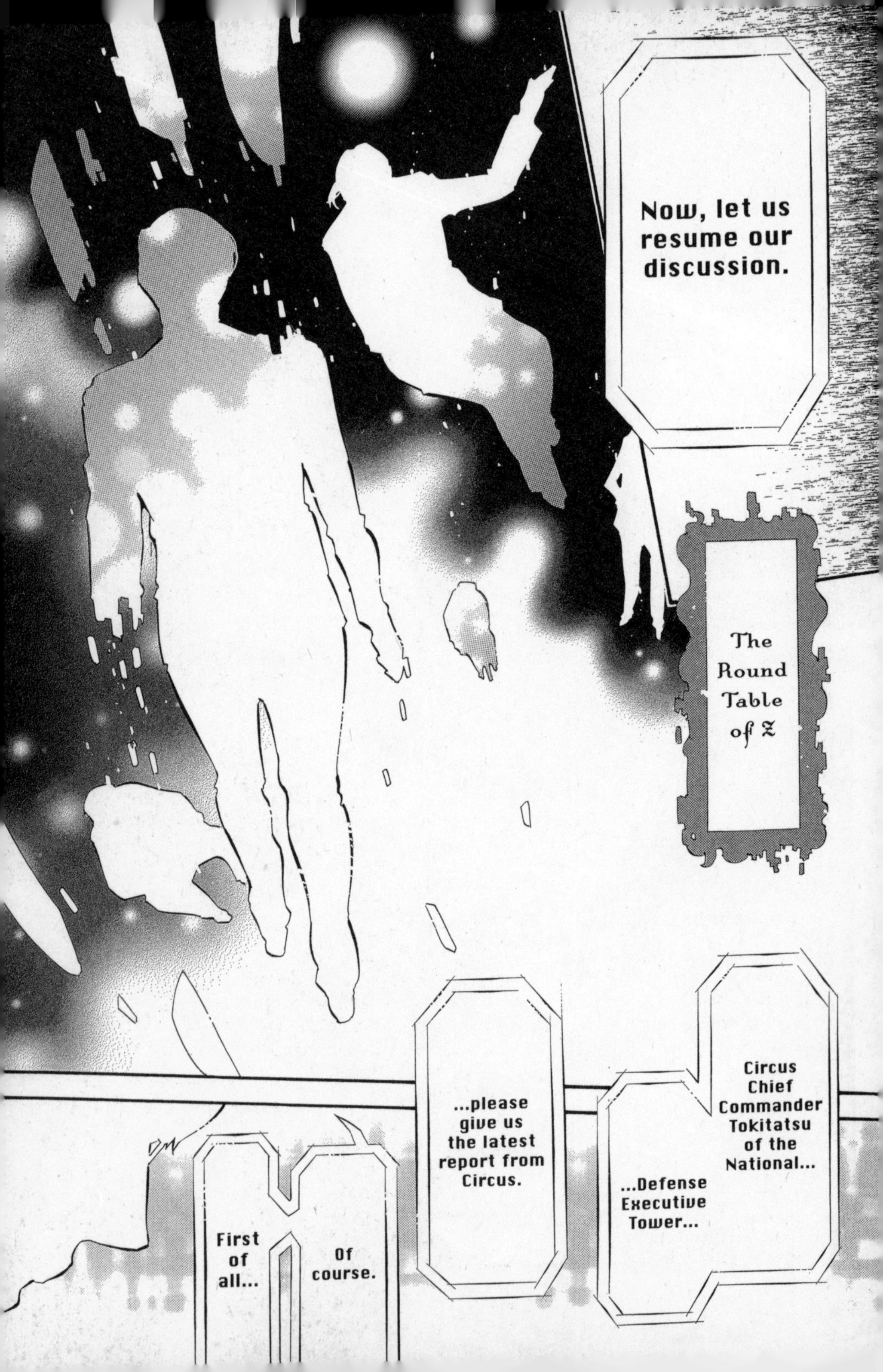
Now, let us resume our discussion.
The Round Table of Z
Circus Chief Commander Tokitatsu of the National...
...Defense Executive Tower...
...please give us the latest report from Circus.
Of course.
First of all...

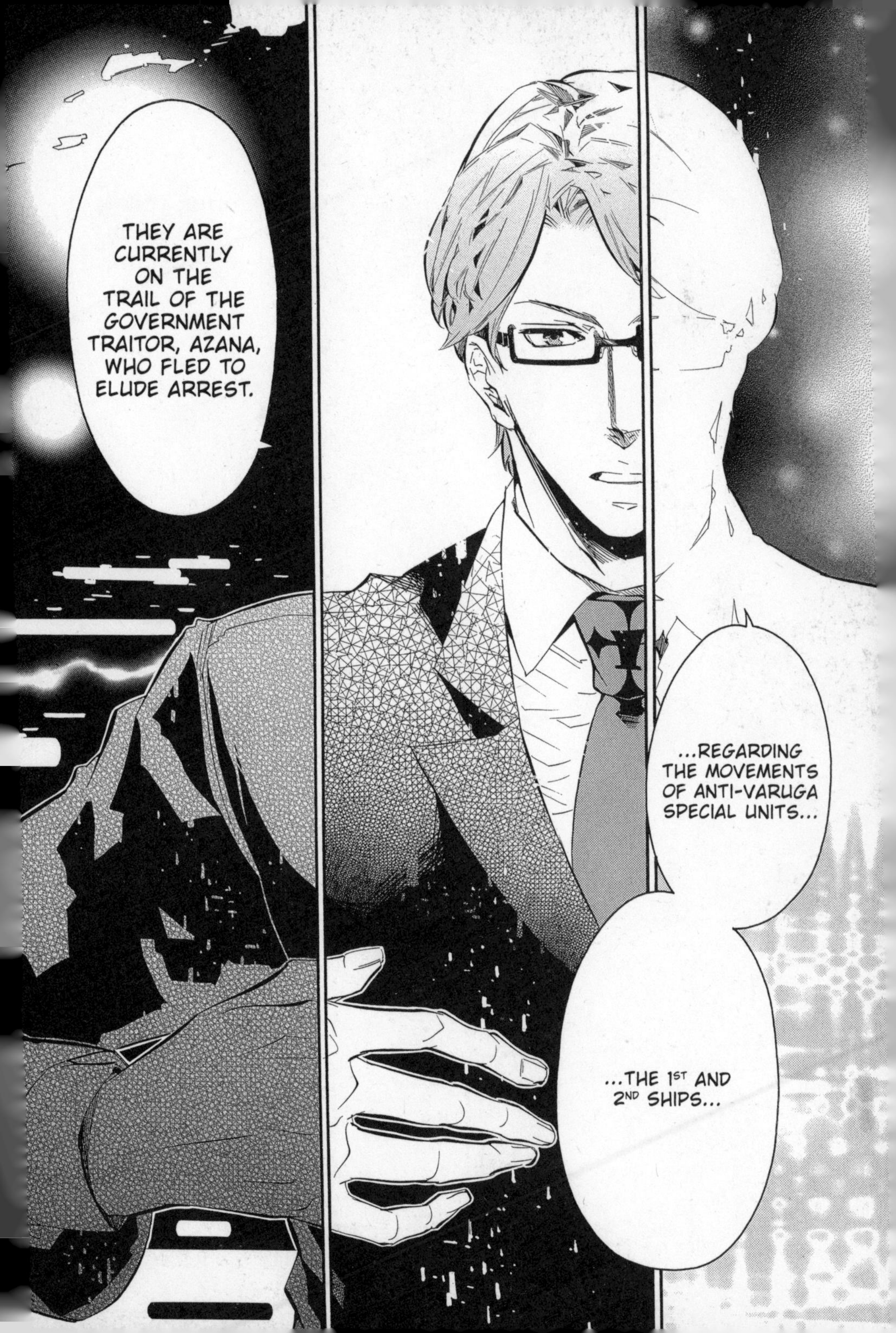
...REGARDING THE MOVEMENTS OF ANTI-VARUGA SPECIAL UNITS...
...THE 1ST AND 2ND SHIPS...
THEY ARE CURRENTLY ON THE TRAIL OF THE GOVERNMENT TRAITOR, AZANA, WHO FLED TO ELUDE ARREST.

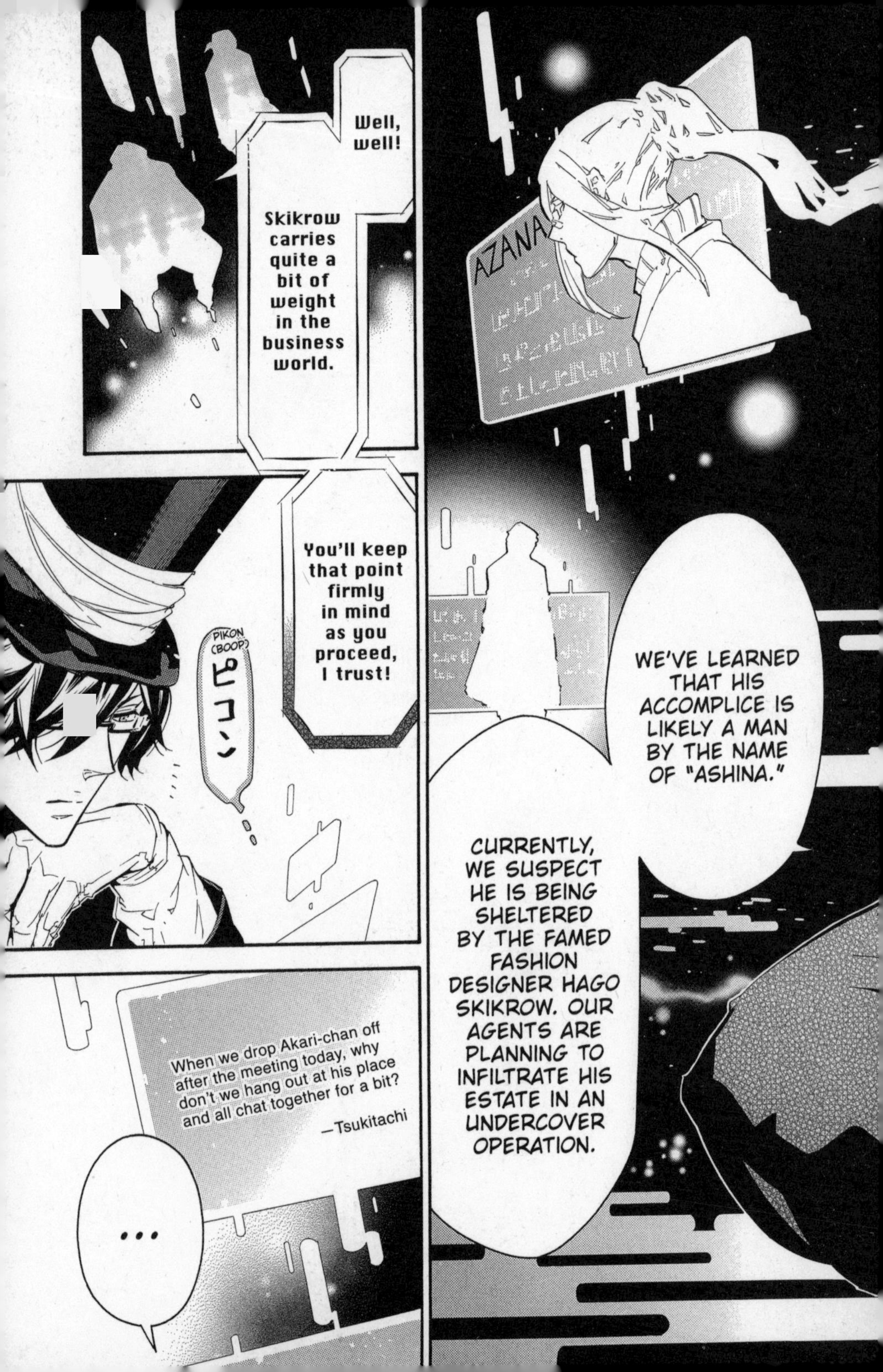
AZANA
WE'VE LEARNED THAT HIS ACCOMPLICE IS LIKELY A MAN BY THE NAME OF "ASHINA."
CURRENTLY, WE SUSPECT HE IS BEING SHELTERED BY THE FAMED FASHION DESIGNER HAGO SKIKROW. OUR AGENTS ARE PLANNING TO INFILTRATE HIS ESTATE IN AN UNDERCOVER OPERATION.
Well, well!
Skikrow carries quite a bit of weight in the business world.
You'll keep that point firmly in mind as you proceed, I trust!
PIKON (BOOP)
ピコン
When we drop Akari-chan off after the meeting today, why don't we hang out at his place and all chat together for a bit?
—Tsukitachi
...

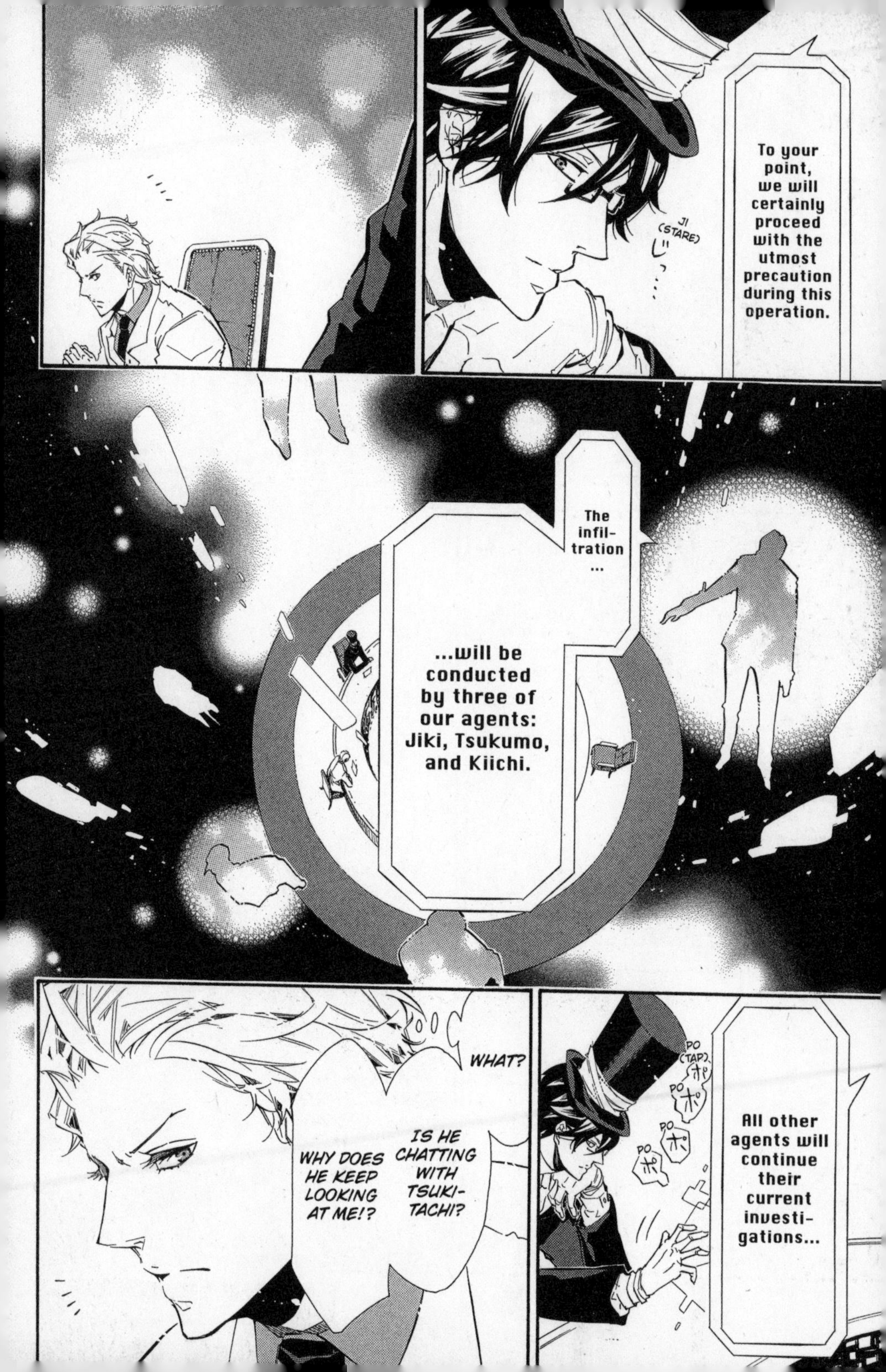
To your point, we will certainly proceed with the utmost precaution during this operation.
JI (STARE)
The infil-tration...
...will be conducted by three of our agents: Jiki, Tsukumo, and Kiichi.
All other agents will continue their current investi-gations...
PO (TAP) PO PO PO
WHAT?
IS HE CHATTING WITH TSUKI-TACHI?
WHY DOES HE KEEP LOOKING AT ME!?

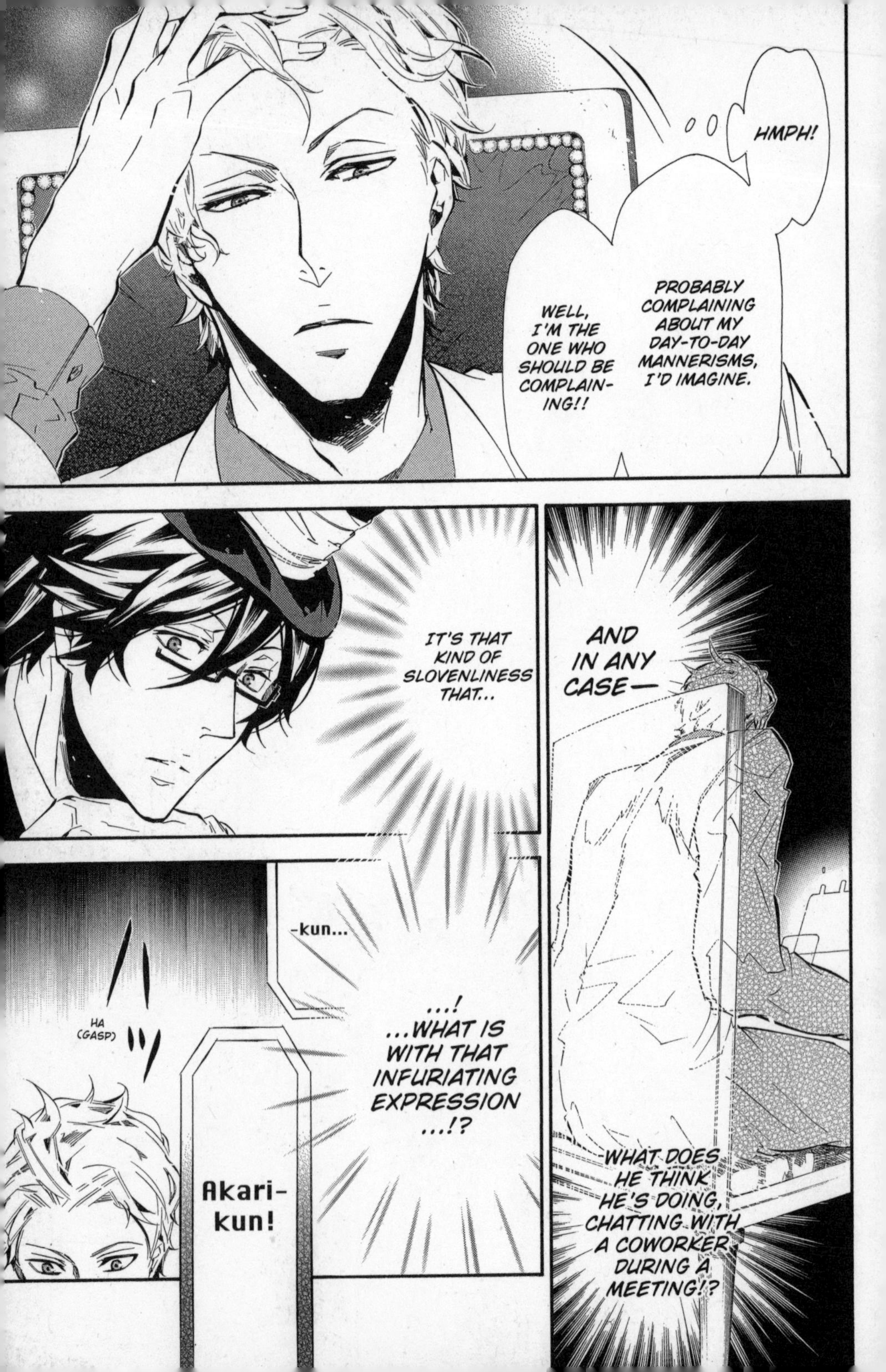
HMPH!
PROBABLY COMPLAINING ABOUT MY DAY-TO-DAY MANNERISMS, I'D IMAGINE.
WELL, I'M THE ONE WHO SHOULD BE COMPLAIN-ING!!
AND IN ANY CASE—
—WHAT DOES HE THINK HE'S DOING, CHATTING WITH A COWORKER DURING A MEETING!?
IT'S THAT KIND OF SLOVENLINESS THAT...
-kun...
...!
...WHAT IS WITH THAT INFURIATING EXPRESSION ...!?
Akari-kun!
HA (GASP)

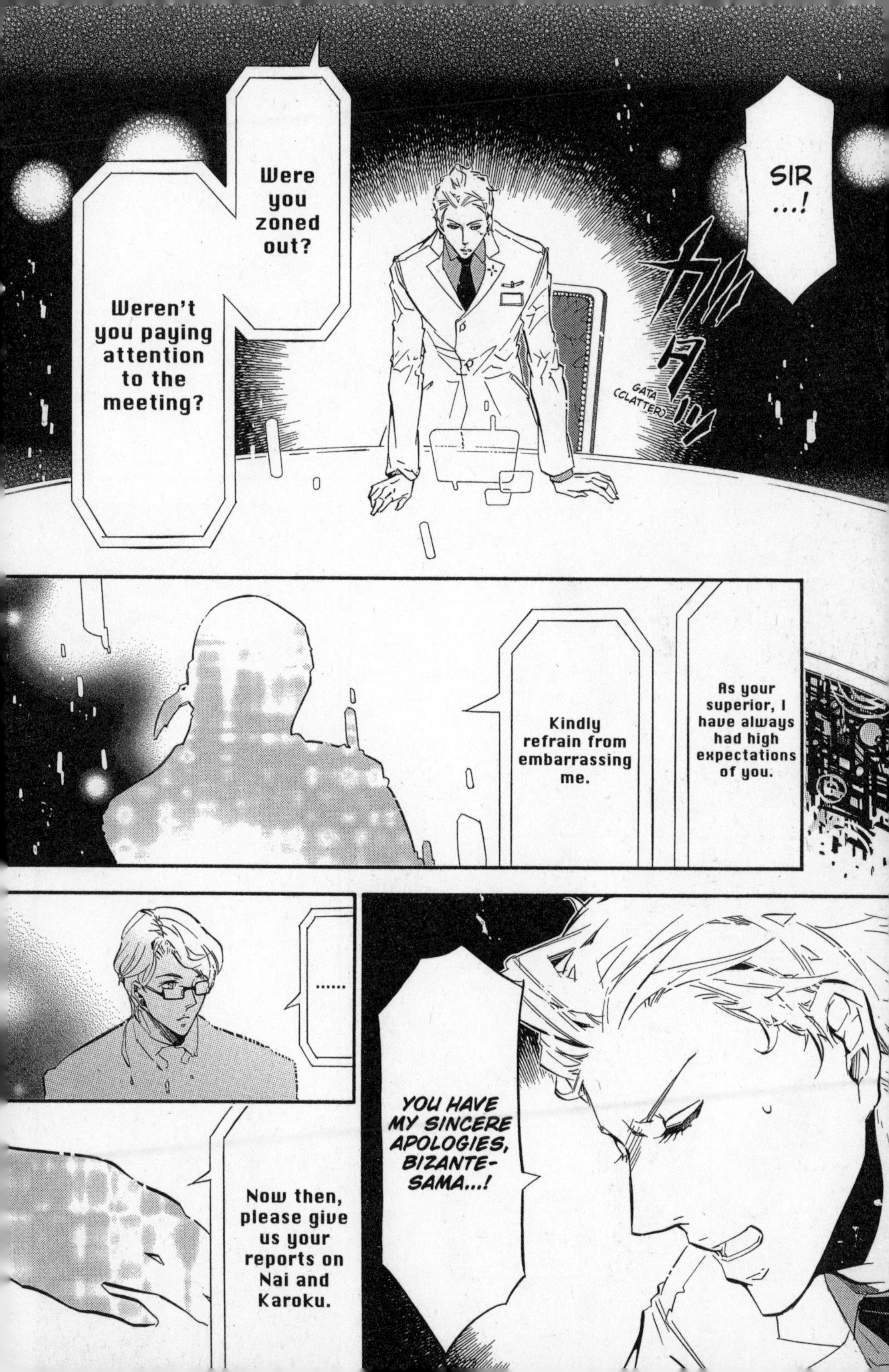
SIR ...!
GATA (CLATTER)
Were you zoned out?
Weren't you paying attention to the meeting?
As your superior, I have always had high expectations of you.
Kindly refrain from embarrassing me.
YOU HAVE MY SINCERE APOLOGIES, BIZANTE-SAMA...!
......
Now then, please give us your reports on Nai and Karoku.

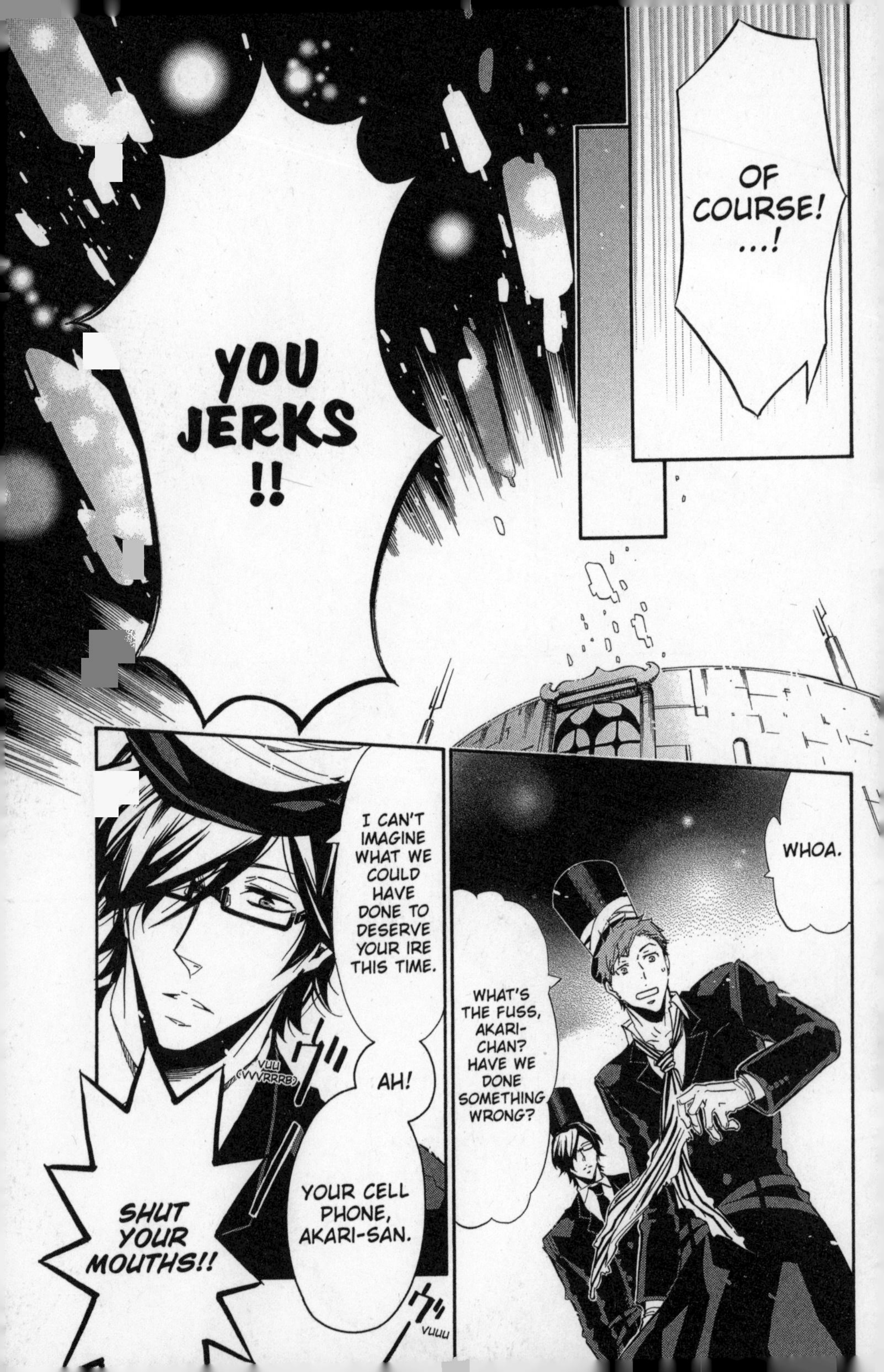
OF COURSE! ...!
YOU JERKS!!
WHOA.
WHAT'S THE FUSS, AKARI-CHAN? HAVE WE DONE SOMETHING WRONG?
I CAN'T IMAGINE WHAT WE COULD HAVE DONE TO DESERVE YOUR IRE THIS TIME.
VUU (VVVRRRB)
AH!
YOUR CELL PHONE, AKARI-SAN.
VUUU
SHUT YOUR MOUTHS!!

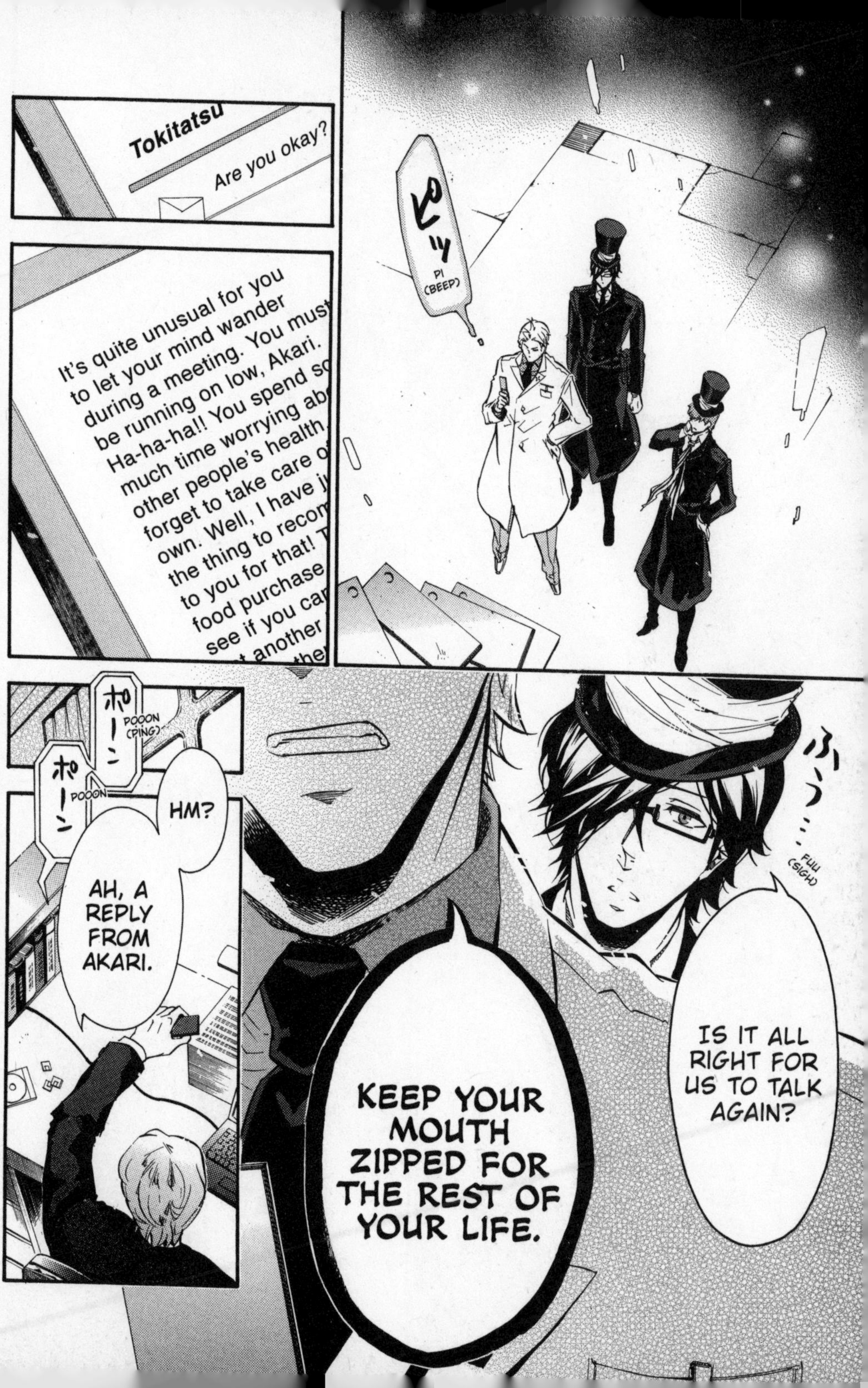
ピッ
PI (BEEP)
Tokitatsu
Are you okay?
It's quite unusual for you to let your mind wander during a meeting. You must be running on low, Akari. Ha-ha-ha!! You spend so much time worrying ab other people's health, forget to take care o own. Well, I have j the thing to recom to you for that! T to you for that! T food purchase see if you ca another
ふう…
FUU (SIGH)
IS IT ALL RIGHT FOR US TO TALK AGAIN?
KEEP YOUR MOUTH ZIPPED FOR THE REST OF YOUR LIFE.
ポーン
POOON (PING)
ポーン
POOON
HM?
AH, A REPLY FROM AKARI.

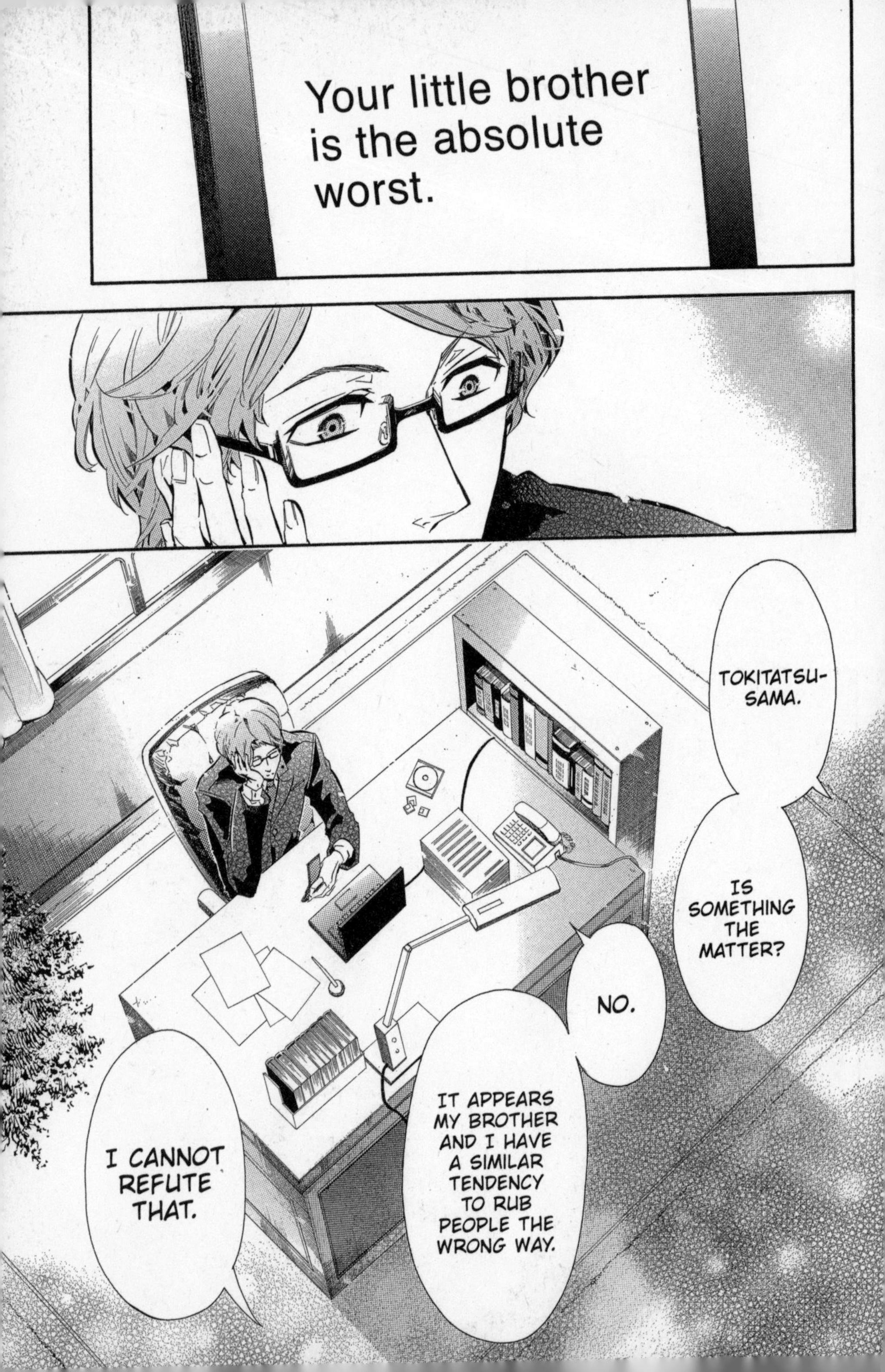
Your little brother is the absolute worst.
TOKITATSU-SAMA.
IS SOMETHING THE MATTER?
NO.
IT APPEARS MY BROTHER AND I HAVE A SIMILAR TENDENCY TO RUB PEOPLE THE WRONG WAY.
I CANNOT REFUTE THAT.

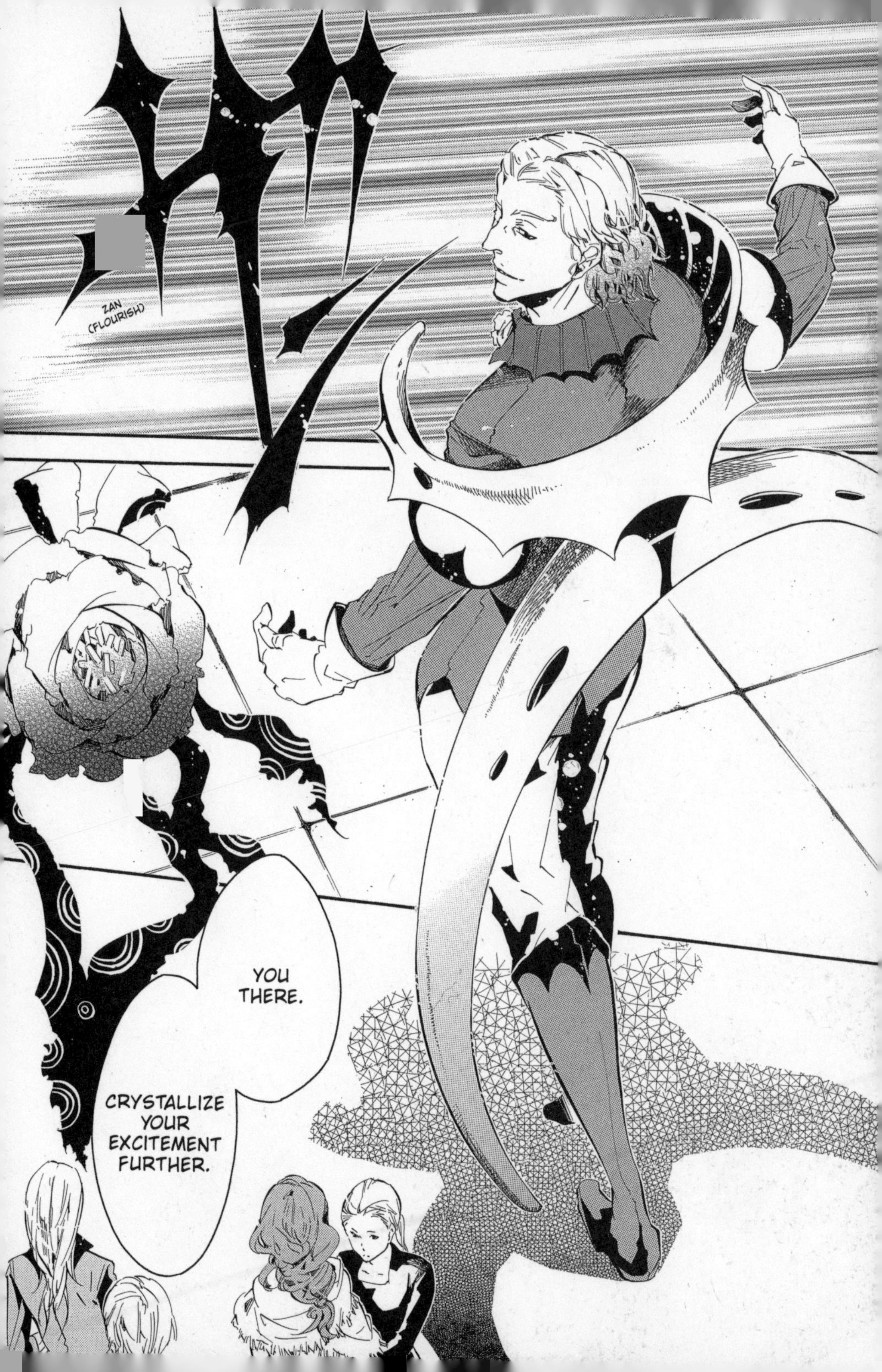
ZAN (FLOURISH)
YOU THERE.
CRYSTALLIZE YOUR EXCITEMENT FURTHER.

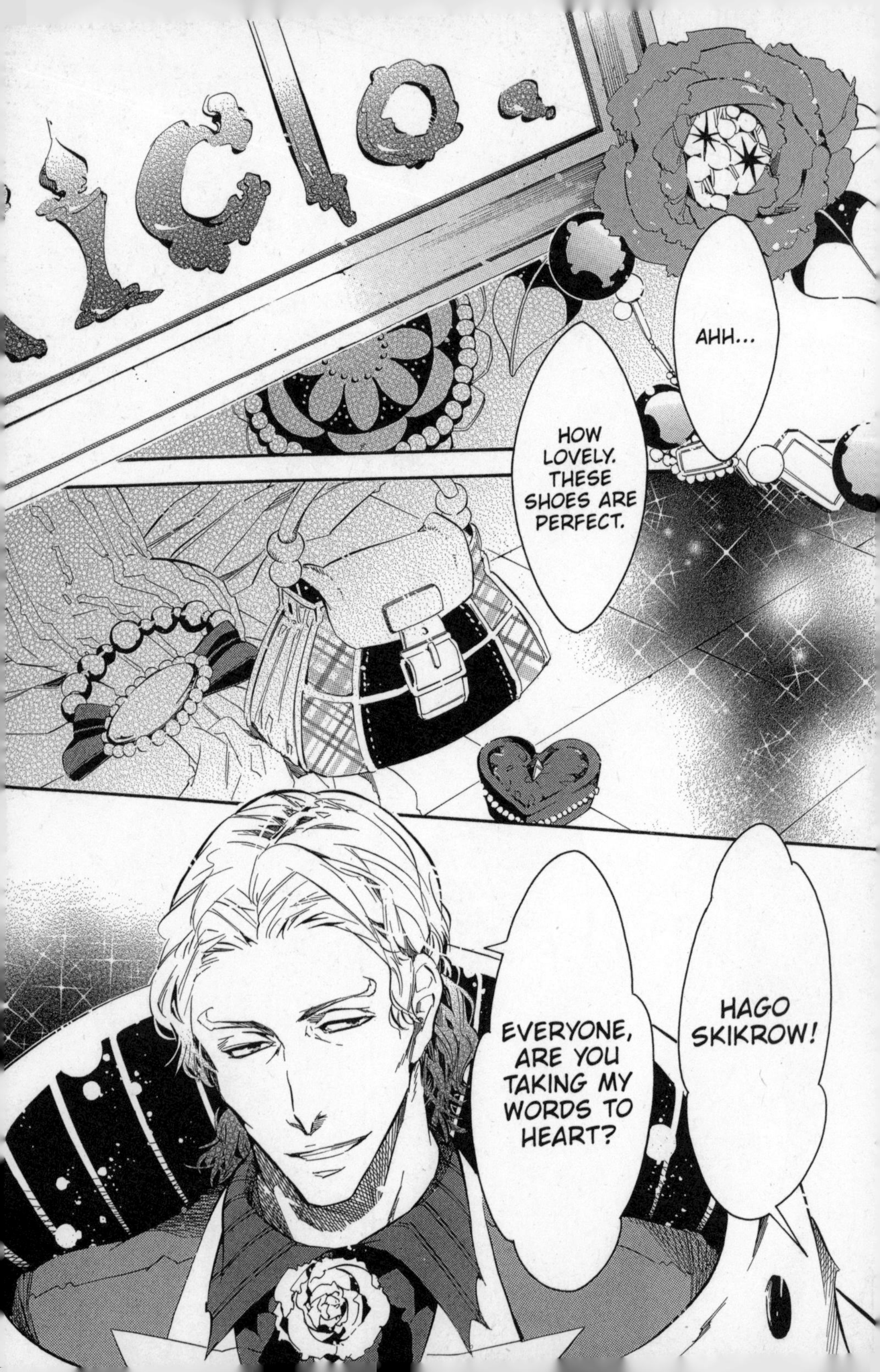
AHH...
HOW LOVELY. THESE SHOES ARE PERFECT.
HAGO SKIKROW!
EVERYONE, ARE YOU TAKING MY WORDS TO HEART?

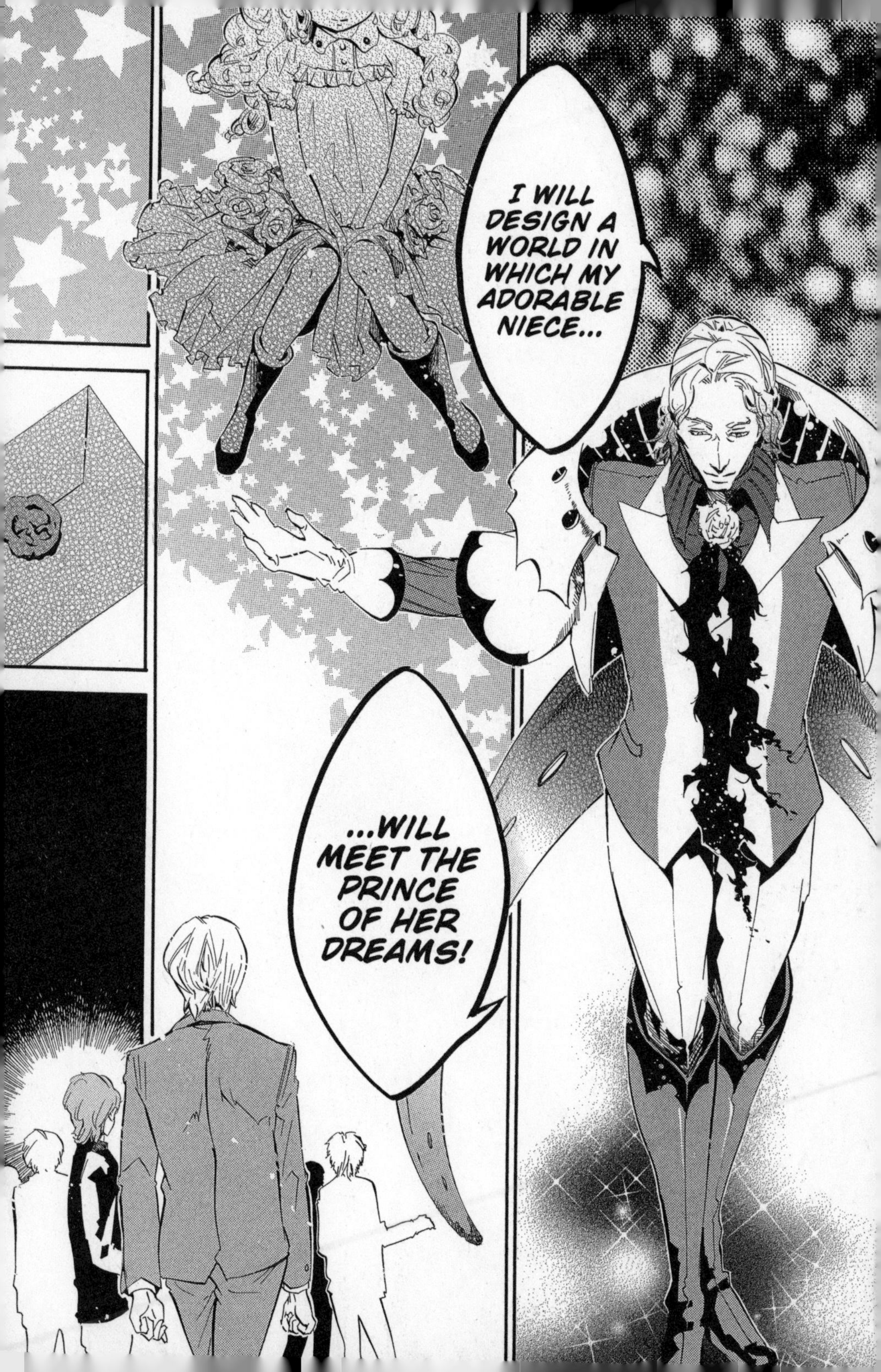
I WILL DESIGN A WORLD IN WHICH MY ADORABLE NIECE...
...WILL MEET THE PRINCE OF HER DREAMS!

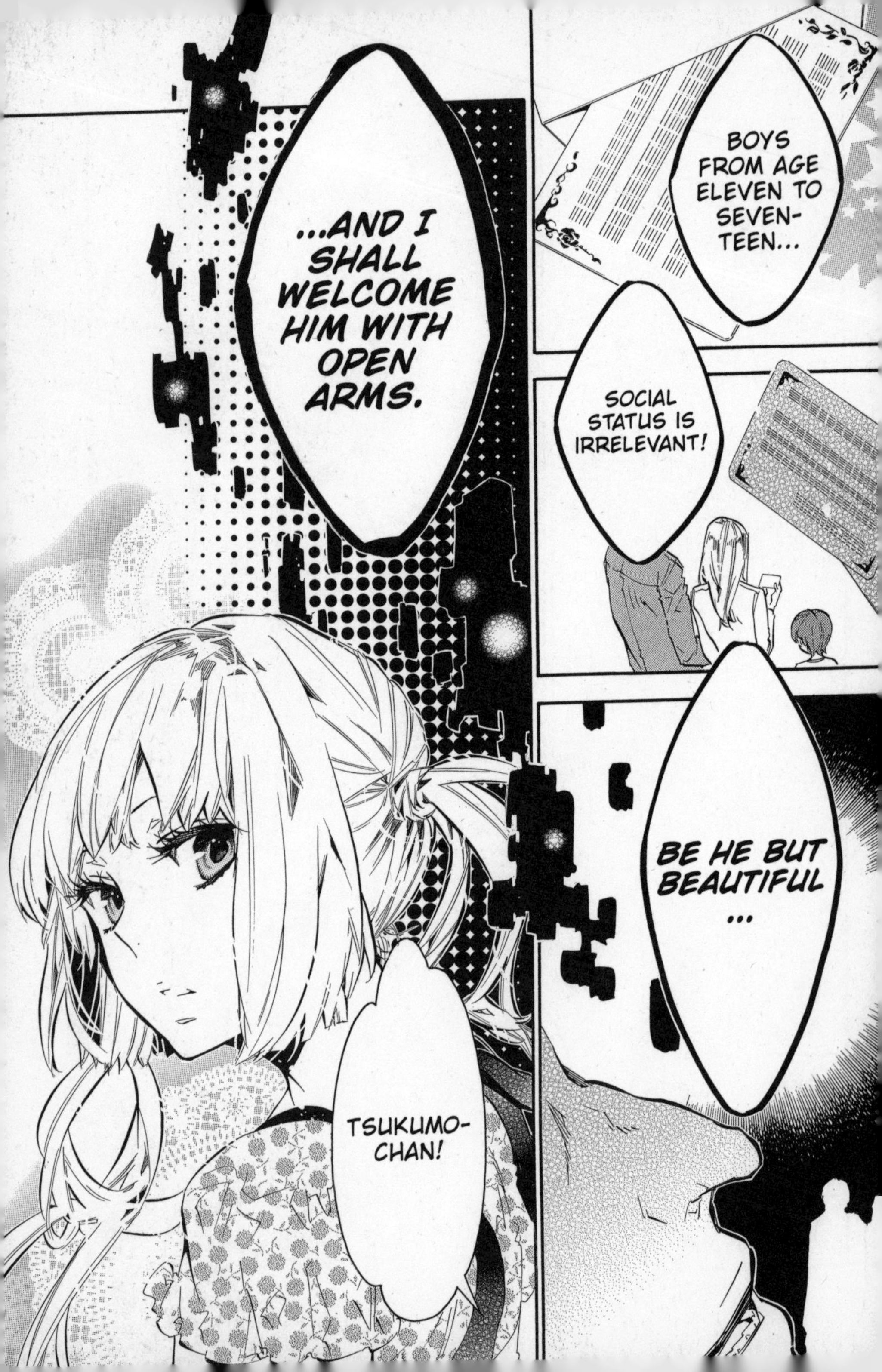
BOYS FROM AGE ELEVEN TO SEVENTEEN...
SOCIAL STATUS IS IRRELEVANT!
BE HE BUT BEAUTIFUL...
...AND I SHALL WELCOME HIM WITH OPEN ARMS.
TSUKUMO-CHAN!

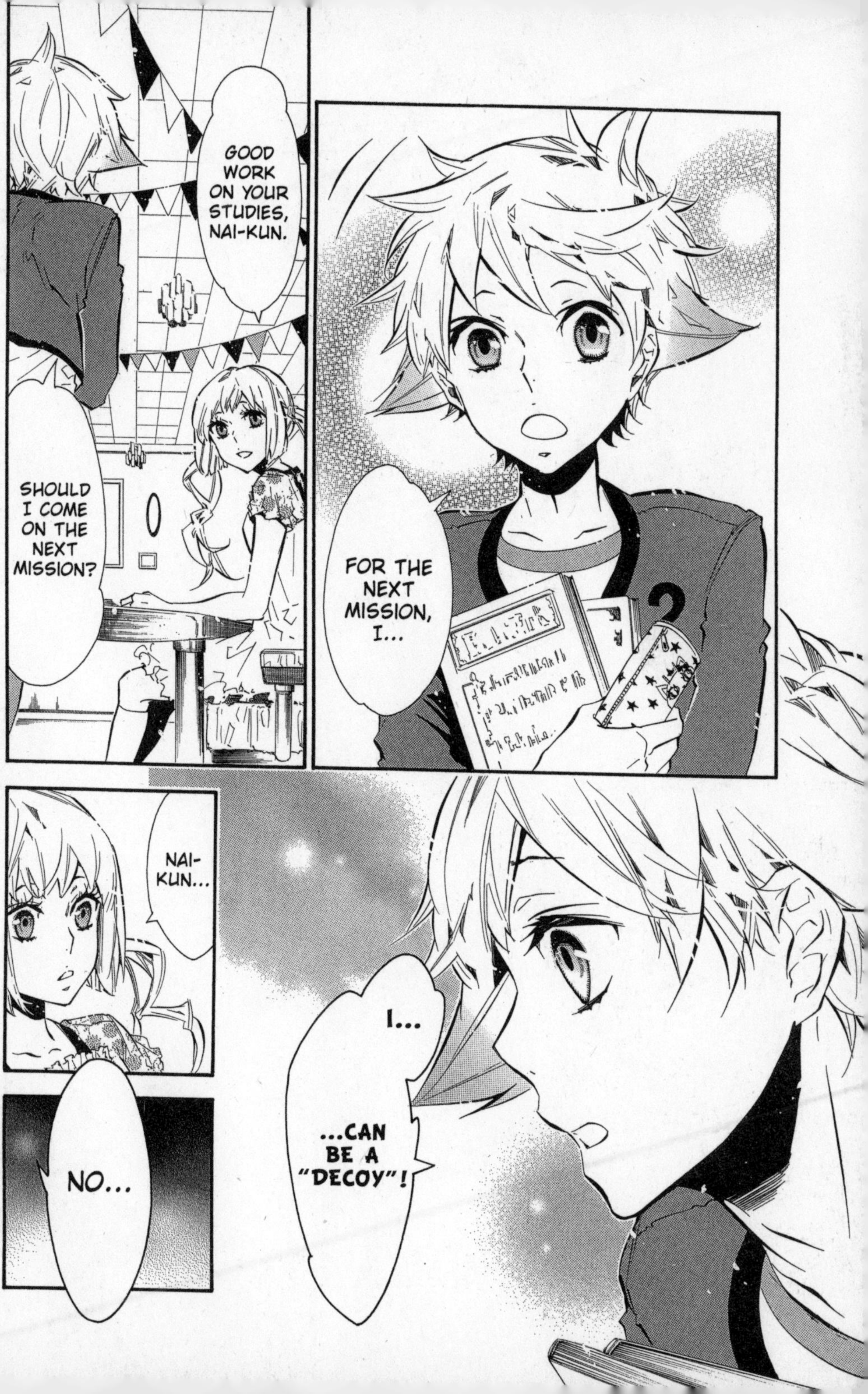
FOR THE NEXT MISSION, I...
GOOD WORK ON YOUR STUDIES, NAI-KUN.
SHOULD I COME ON THE NEXT MISSION?
I...
...CAN BE A "DECOY"!
NAI-KUN...
NO...

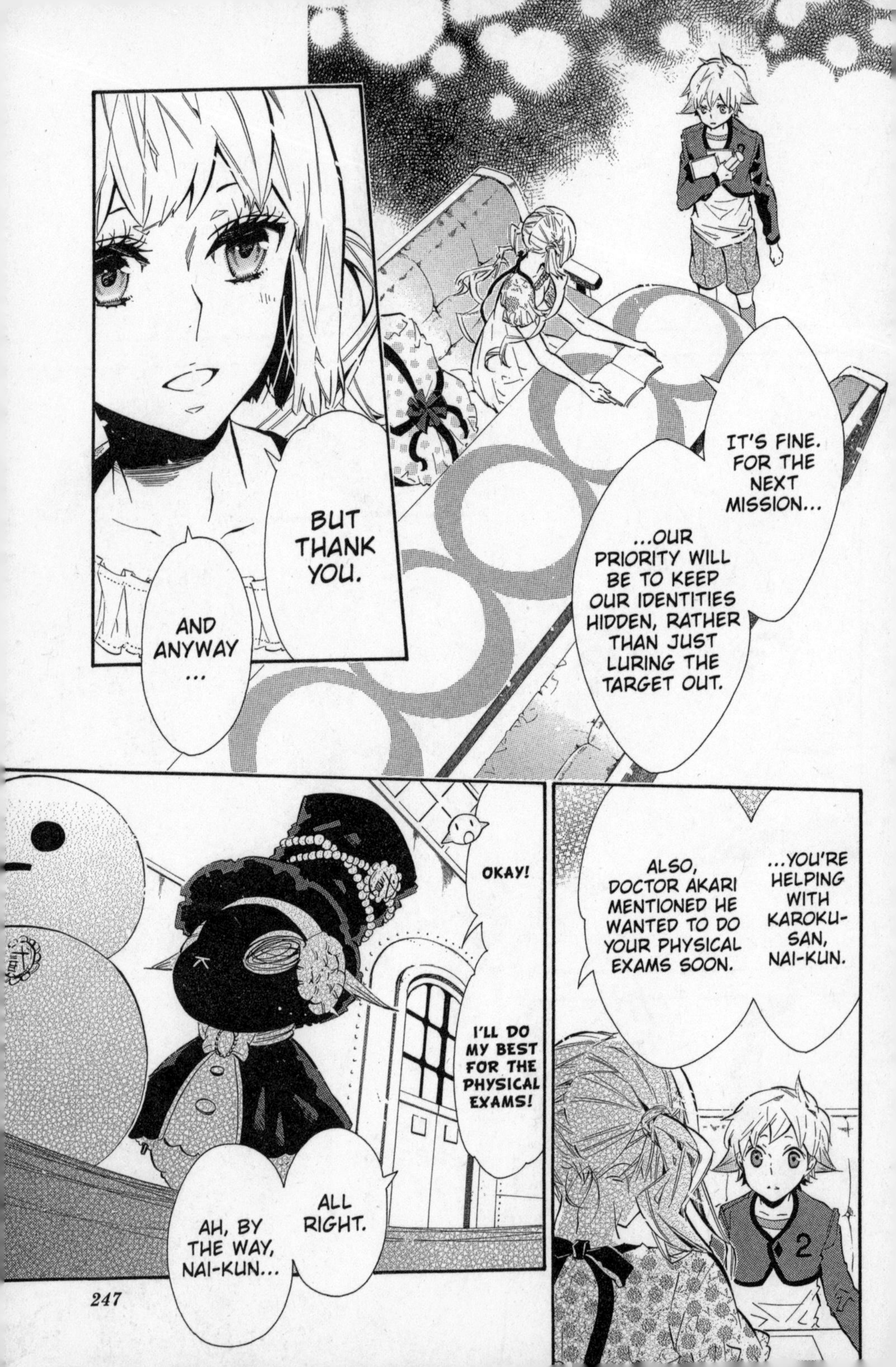
IT'S FINE. FOR THE NEXT MISSION...
...OUR PRIORITY WILL BE TO KEEP OUR IDENTITIES HIDDEN, RATHER THAN JUST LURING THE TARGET OUT.
BUT THANK YOU.
AND ANYWAY...
...YOU'RE HELPING WITH KAROKU-SAN, NAI-KUN.
ALSO, DOCTOR AKARI MENTIONED HE WANTED TO DO YOUR PHYSICAL EXAMS SOON.
OKAY!
I'LL DO MY BEST FOR THE PHYSICAL EXAMS!
ALL RIGHT.
AH, BY THE WAY, NAI-KUN...

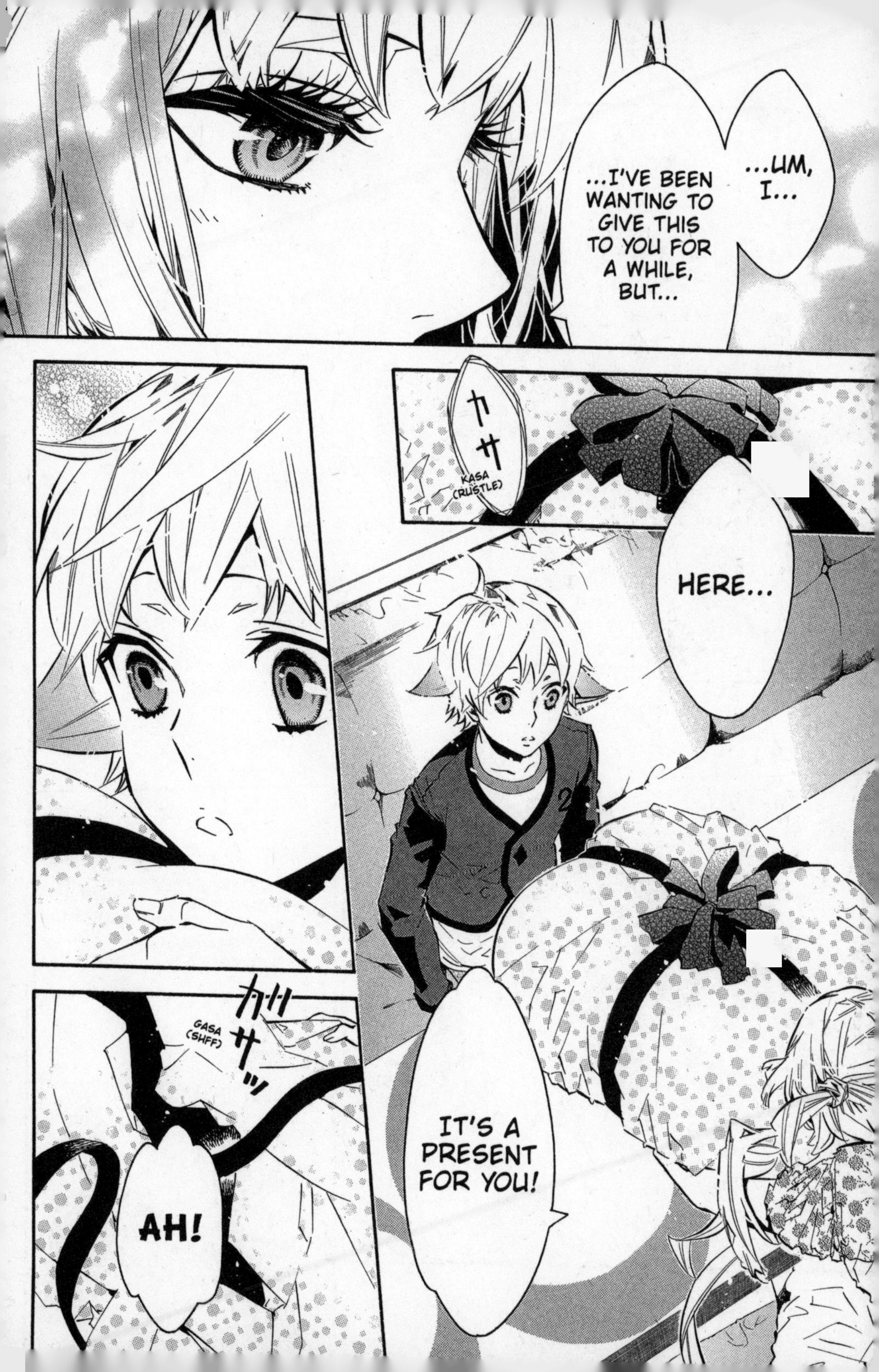
...UM, I...
...I'VE BEEN WANTING TO GIVE THIS TO YOU FOR A WHILE, BUT...
カサ
KASA (RUSTLE)
HERE...
IT'S A PRESENT FOR YOU!
ガサッ
GASA (SHFF)
AH!

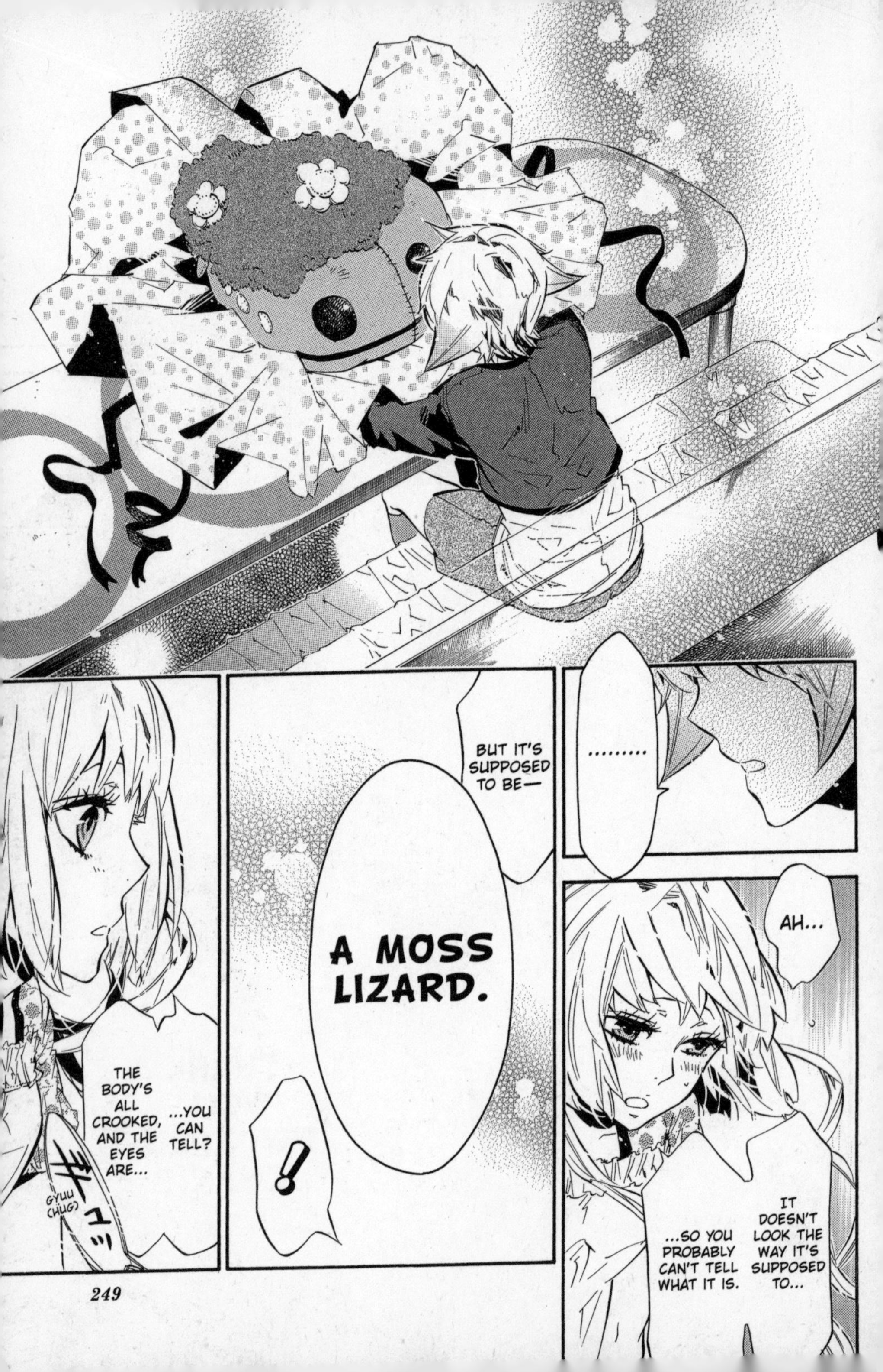
....
AH...
IT DOESN'T LOOK THE WAY IT'S SUPPOSED TO...
...SO YOU PROBABLY CAN'T TELL WHAT IT IS.
BUT IT'S SUPPOSED TO BE—
A MOSS LIZARD.
!
...YOU CAN TELL?
THE BODY'S ALL CROOKED, AND THE EYES ARE...
ギュッ
GYUU (HUG)

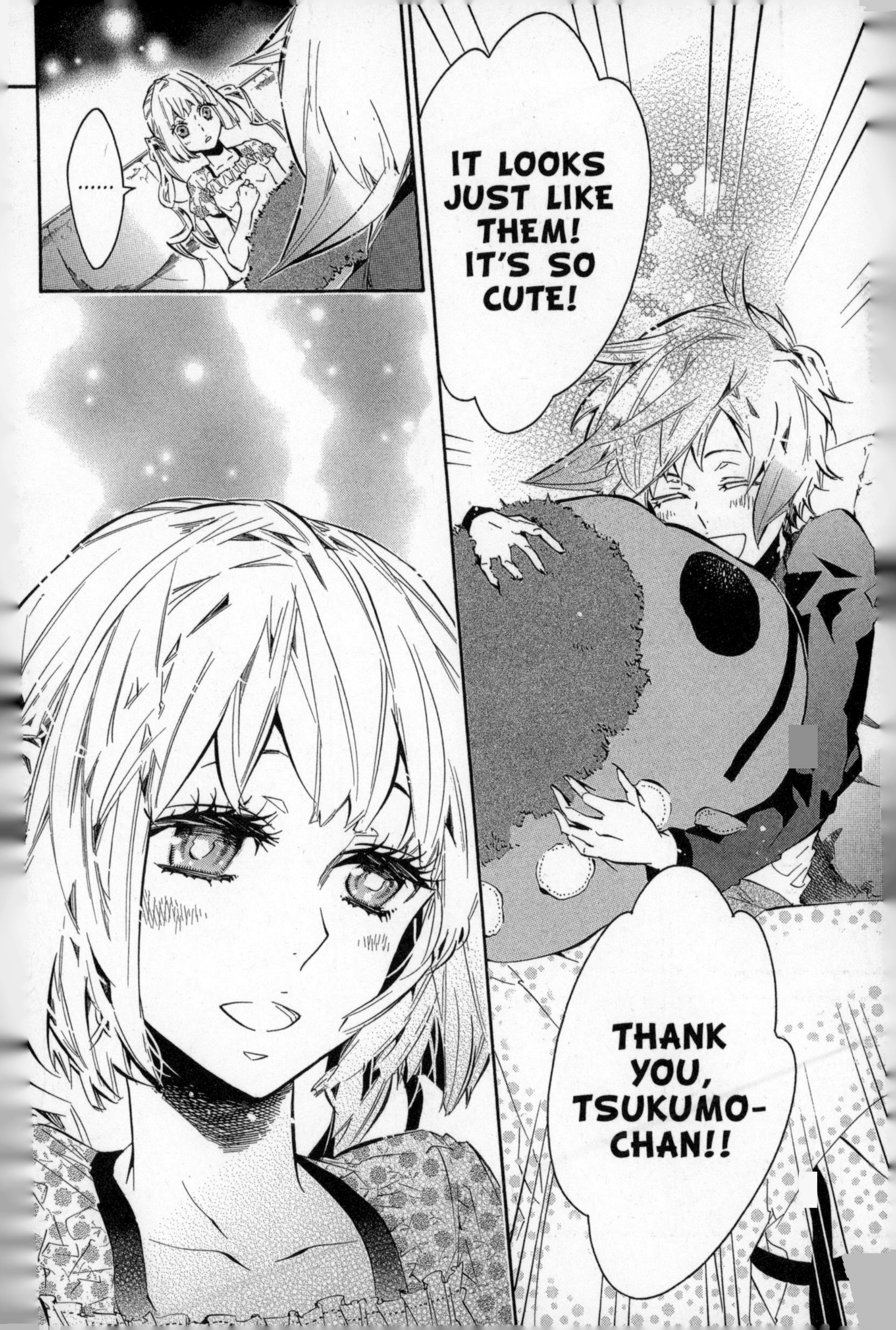
IT LOOKS JUST LIKE THEM! IT'S SO CUTE!
THANK YOU, TSUKUMO-CHAN!!
......

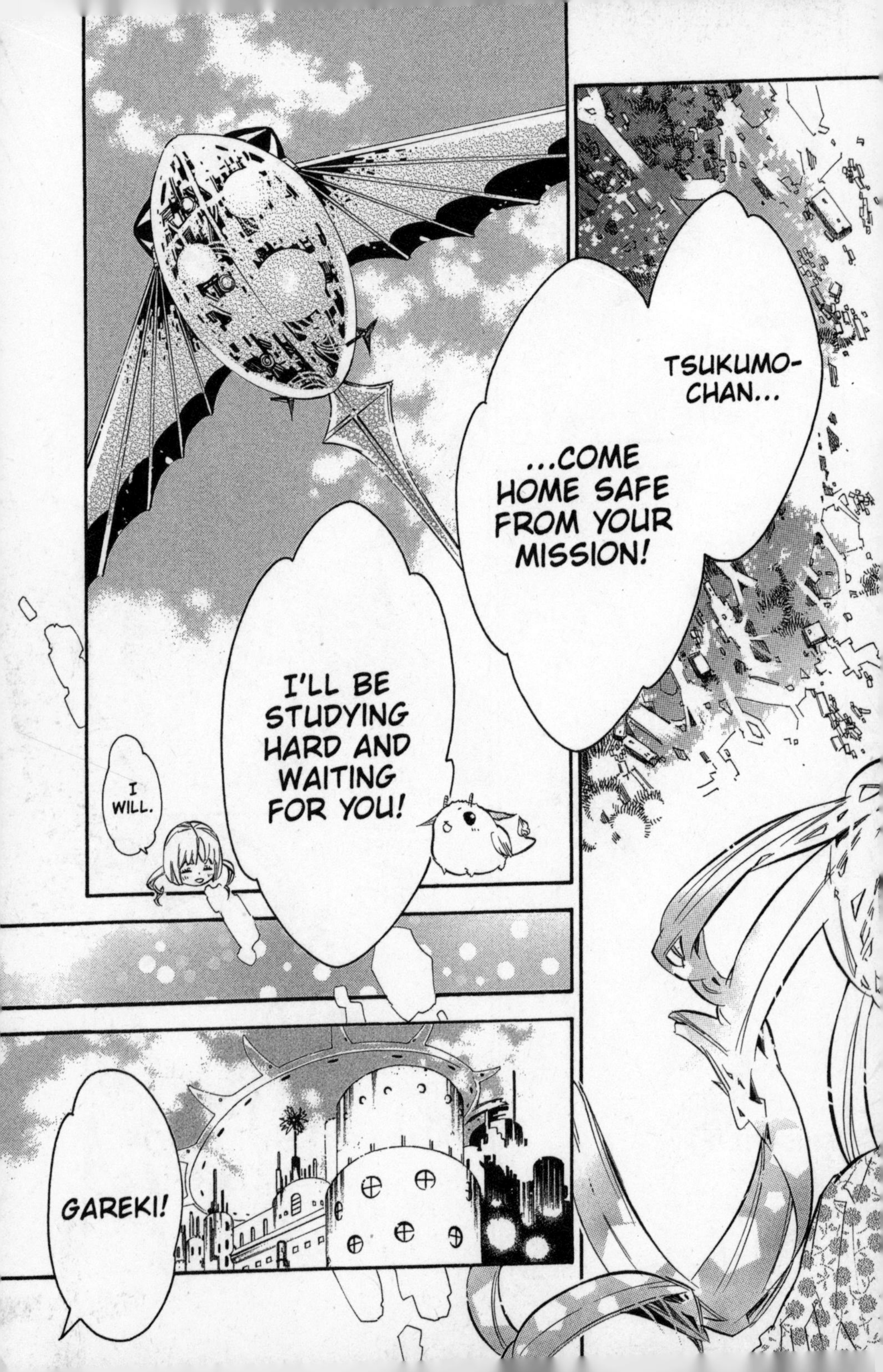
TSUKUMO-CHAN...
...COME HOME SAFE FROM YOUR MISSION!
I'LL BE STUDYING HARD AND WAITING FOR YOU!
I WILL.
GAREKI!

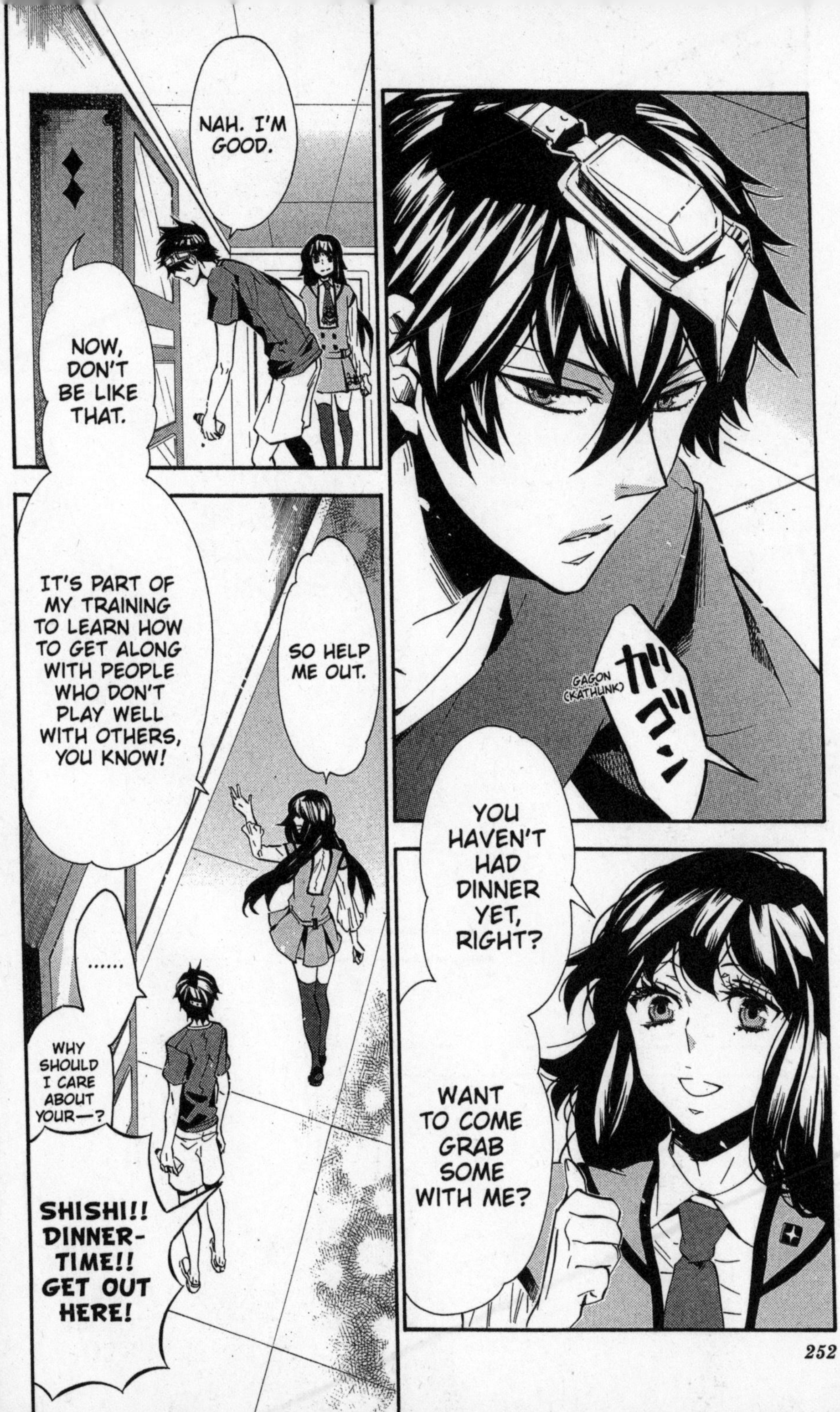
GAGON (KATHUNK)
YOU HAVEN'T HAD DINNER YET, RIGHT?
WANT TO COME GRAB SOME WITH ME?
NAH. I'M GOOD.
NOW, DON'T BE LIKE THAT.
IT'S PART OF MY TRAINING TO LEARN HOW TO GET ALONG WITH PEOPLE WHO DON'T PLAY WELL WITH OTHERS, YOU KNOW!
SO HELP ME OUT.
......
WHY SHOULD I CARE ABOUT YOUR—?
SHISHI!! DINNER-TIME!! GET OUT HERE!

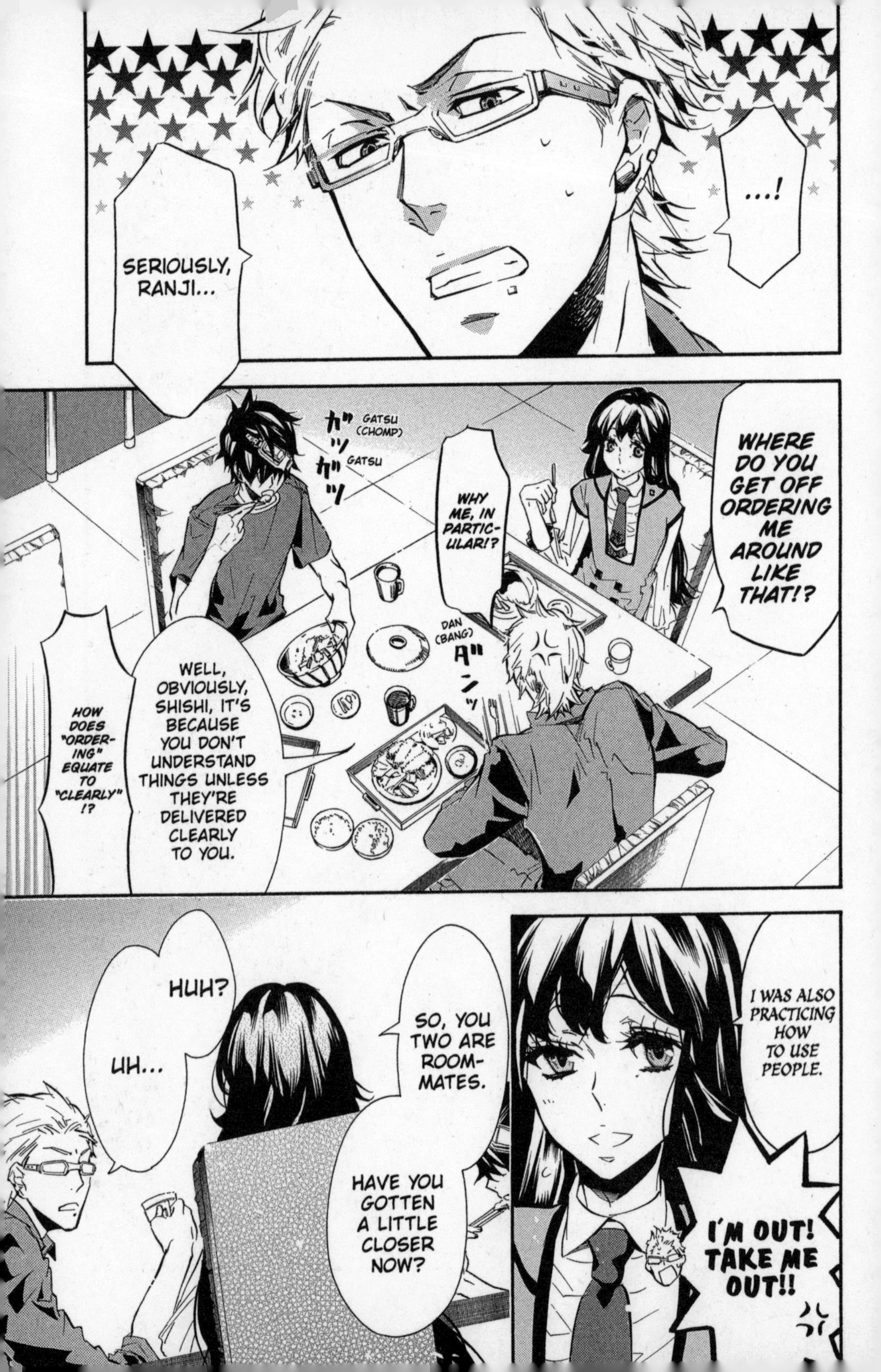
...!
SERIOUSLY, RANJI...
WHERE DO YOU GET OFF ORDERING ME AROUND LIKE THAT!?
WHY ME, IN PARTICULAR!?
ガッ GATSU (CHOMP)
ガツ GATSU
ダンッ DAN (BANG)
WELL, OBVIOUSLY, SHISHI, IT'S BECAUSE YOU DON'T UNDERSTAND THINGS UNLESS THEY'RE DELIVERED CLEARLY TO YOU.
HOW DOES "ORDERING" EQUATE TO "CLEARLY" !?
I WAS ALSO PRACTICING HOW TO USE PEOPLE.
I'M OUT! TAKE ME OUT!!
SO, YOU TWO ARE ROOM-MATES.
HAVE YOU GOTTEN A LITTLE CLOSER NOW?
HUH?
UH...

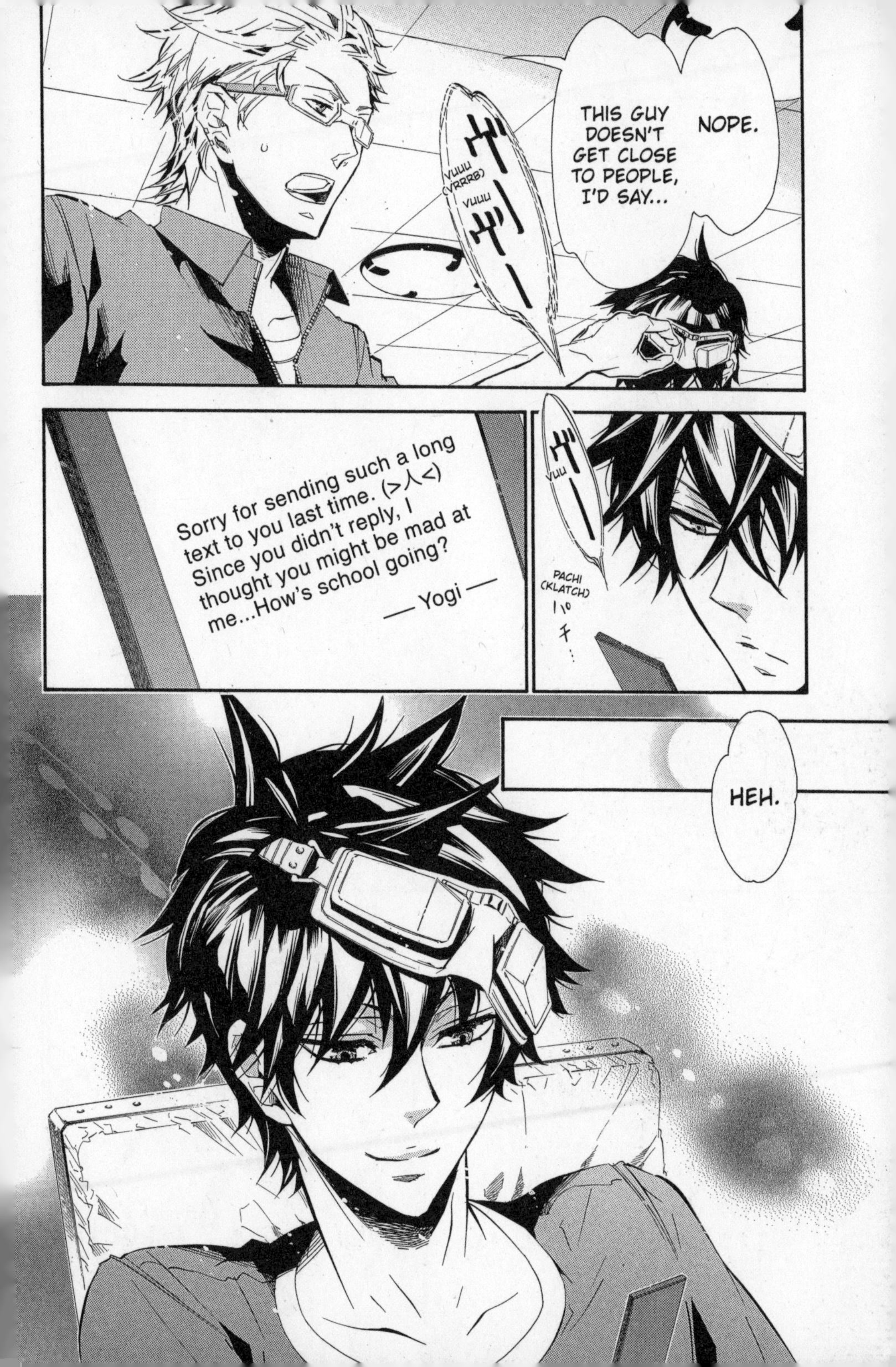
NOPE.
THIS GUY DOESN'T GET CLOSE TO PEOPLE, I'D SAY...
ヴーヴーー
VUUU (VRRRB) VUUU
ヴー
VUUU
PACHI (KLATCH)
パチ…
Sorry for sending such a long text to you last time. (>人<) Since you didn't reply, I thought you might be mad at me...How's school going?
—Yogi—
HEH.

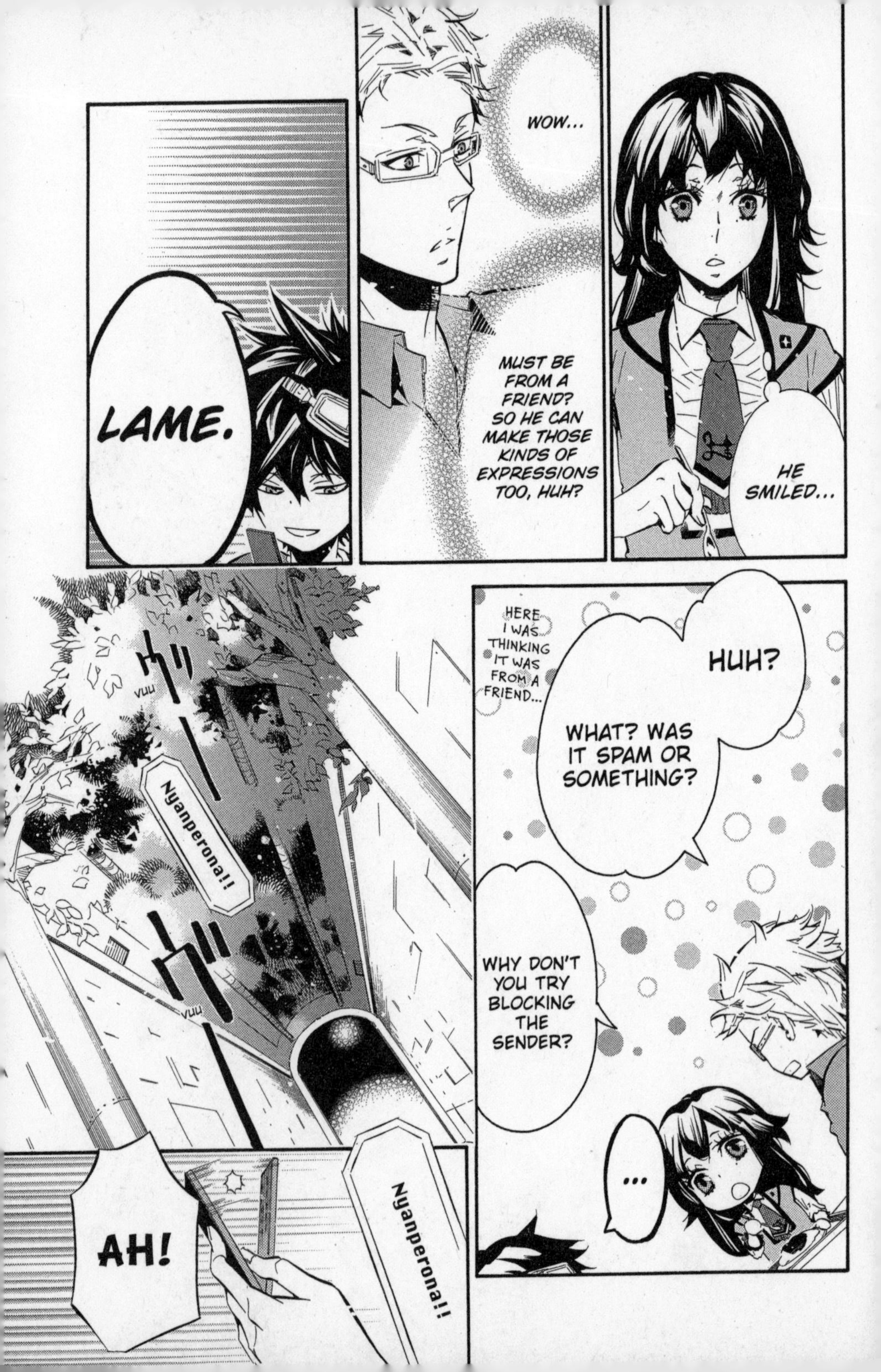
HE SMILED...
WOW...
MUST BE FROM A FRIEND? SO HE CAN MAKE THOSE KINDS OF EXPRESSIONS TOO, HUH?
LAME.
HUH?
HERE I WAS THINKING IT WAS FROM A FRIEND...
WHAT? WAS IT SPAM OR SOMETHING?
WHY DON'T YOU TRY BLOCKING THE SENDER?
...
VUU
Nyanperona!!
VUU
Nyanperona!!
AH!

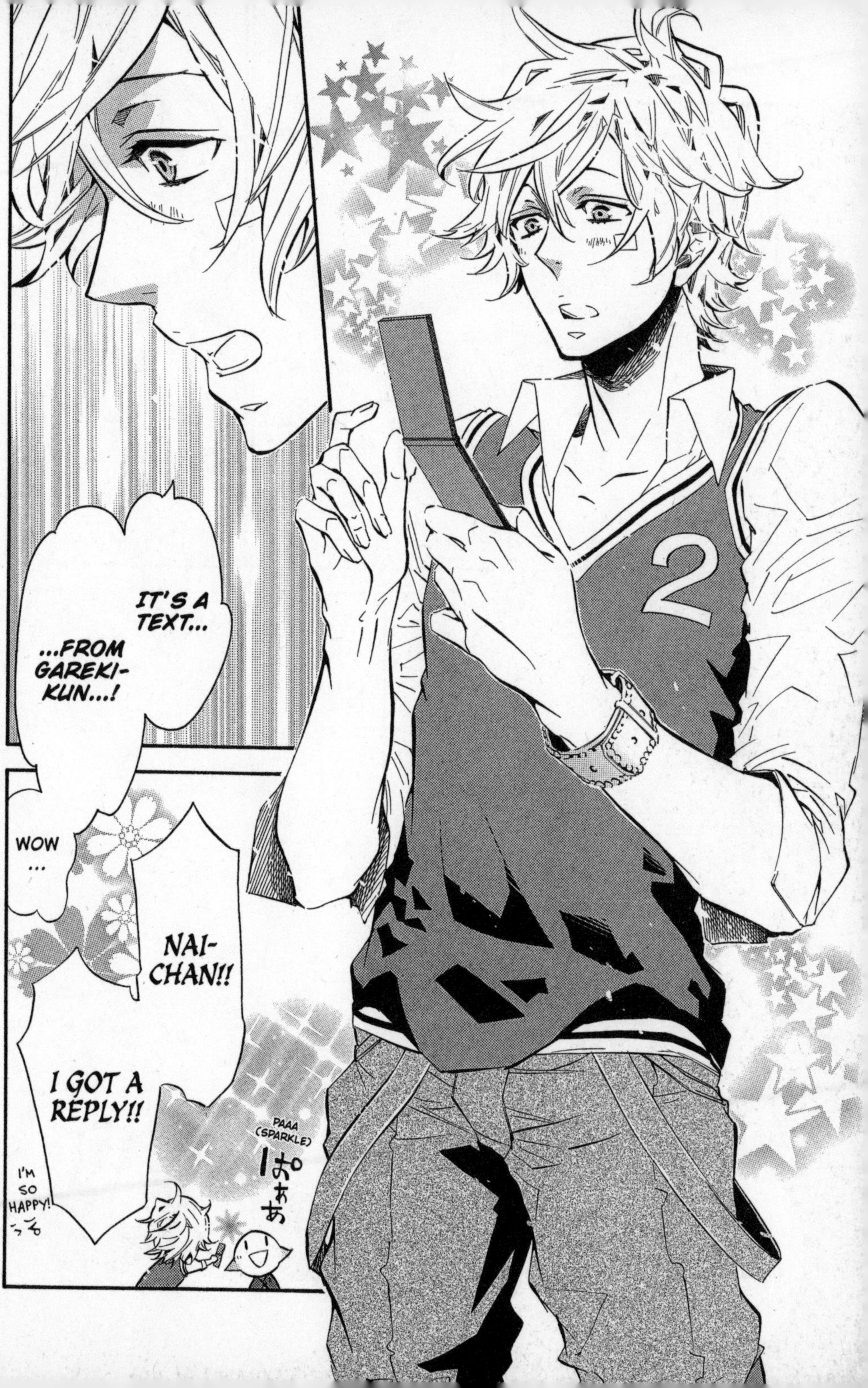
IT'S A TEXT...
...FROM GAREKI-KUN...!
WOW...
NAI-CHAN!!
I GOT A REPLY!!
PAAA (SPARKLE)
I'M SO HAPPY!

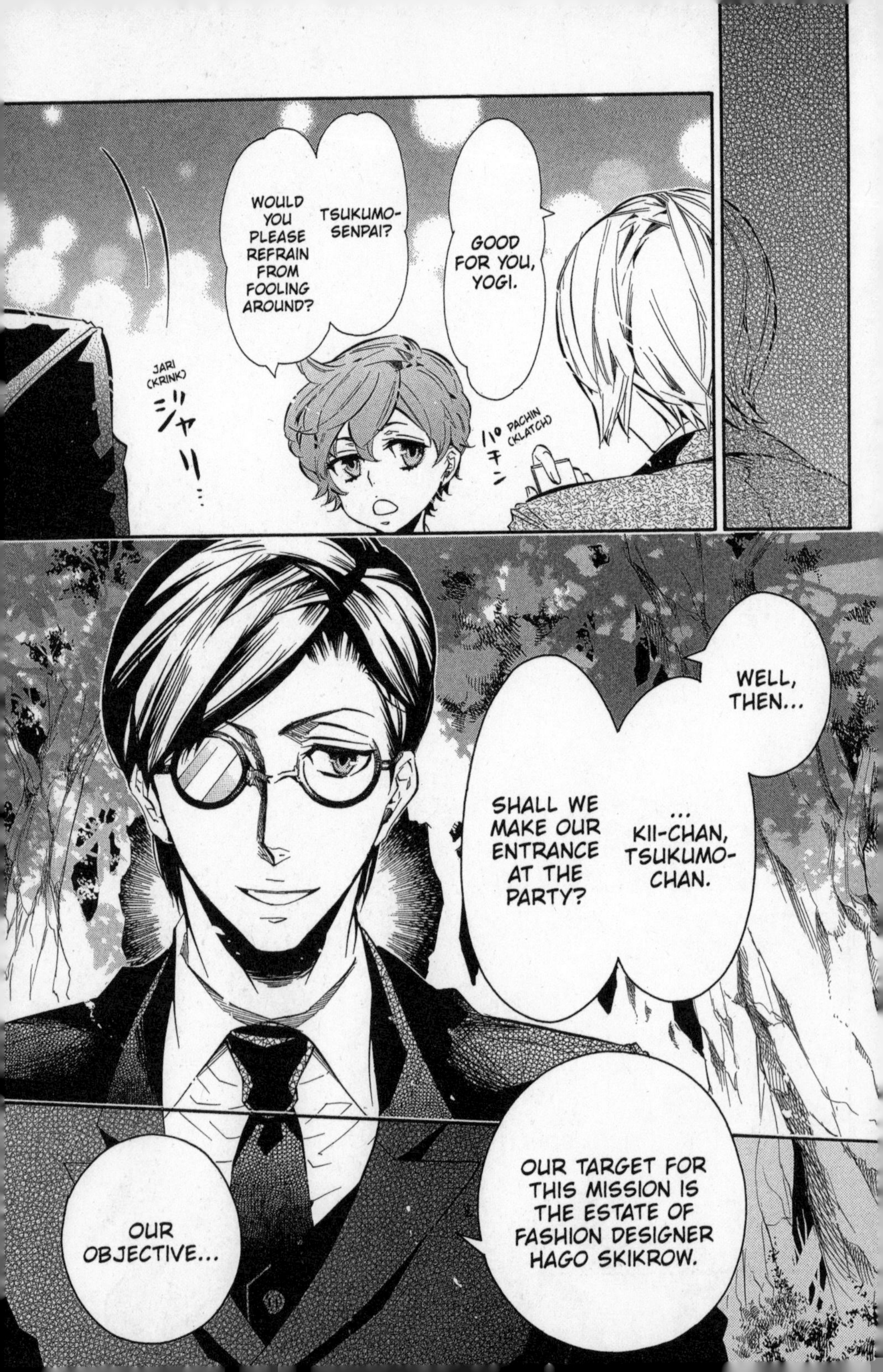
GOOD FOR YOU, YOGI.
パチン
PACHIN (KLATCH)
TSUKUMO-SENPAI? WOULD YOU PLEASE REFRAIN FROM FOOLING AROUND?
ジャリ…
JARI (KRINK)
WELL, THEN...
...KII-CHAN, TSUKUMO-CHAN.
SHALL WE MAKE OUR ENTRANCE AT THE PARTY?
OUR TARGET FOR THIS MISSION IS THE ESTATE OF FASHION DESIGNER HAGO SKIKROW.
OUR OBJECTIVE...

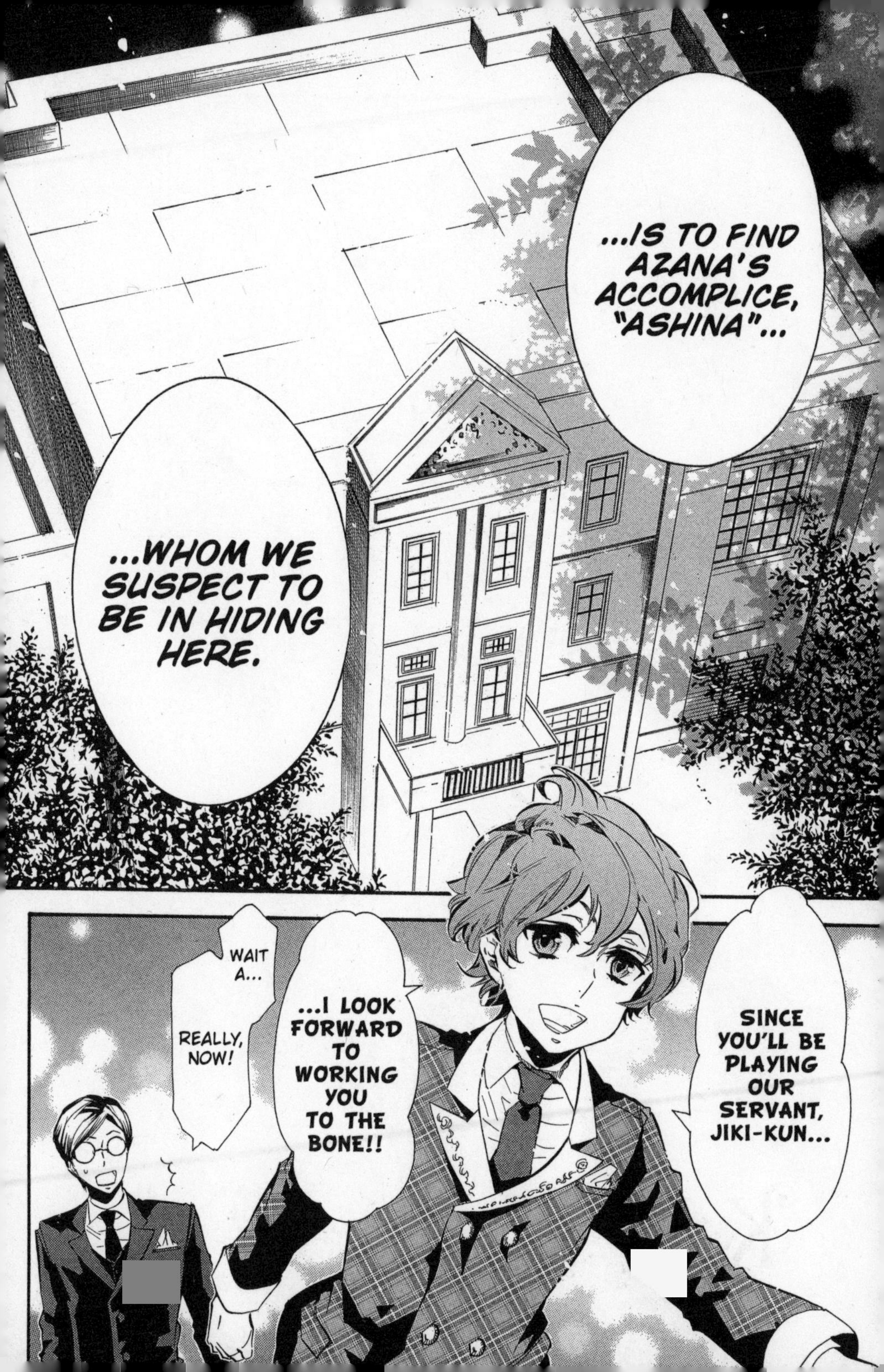
...IS TO FIND AZANA'S ACCOMPLICE, "ASHINA"...
...WHOM WE SUSPECT TO BE IN HIDING HERE.
SINCE YOU'LL BE PLAYING OUR SERVANT, JIKI-KUN...
...I LOOK FORWARD TO WORKING YOU TO THE BONE!!
WAIT A...
REALLY, NOW!

KARNEVAL

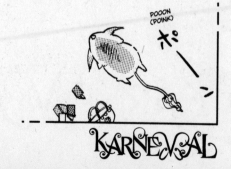

POOON
(POINK)

ポーン

KARNEVAL

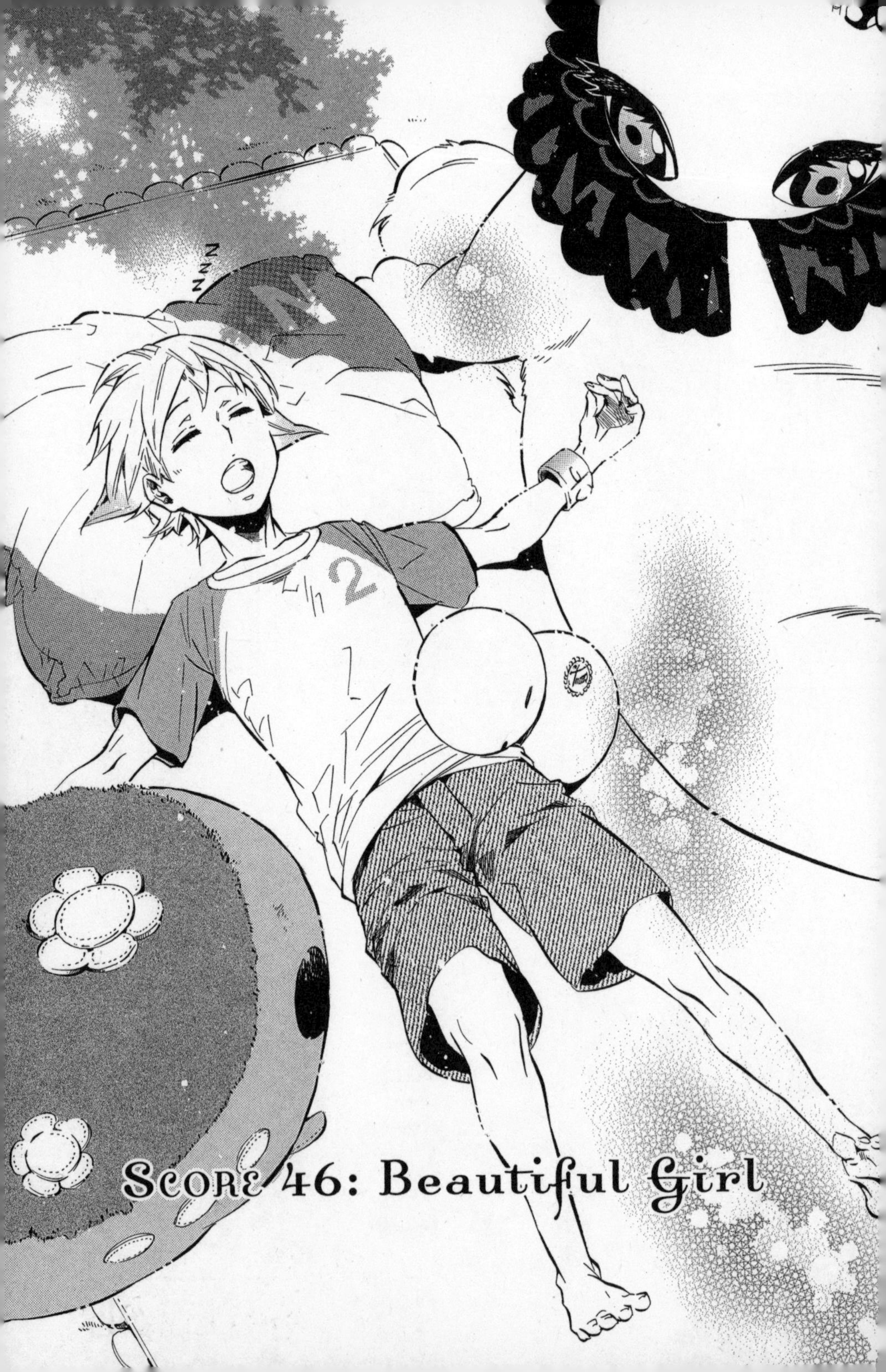
Score 46: Beautiful Girl

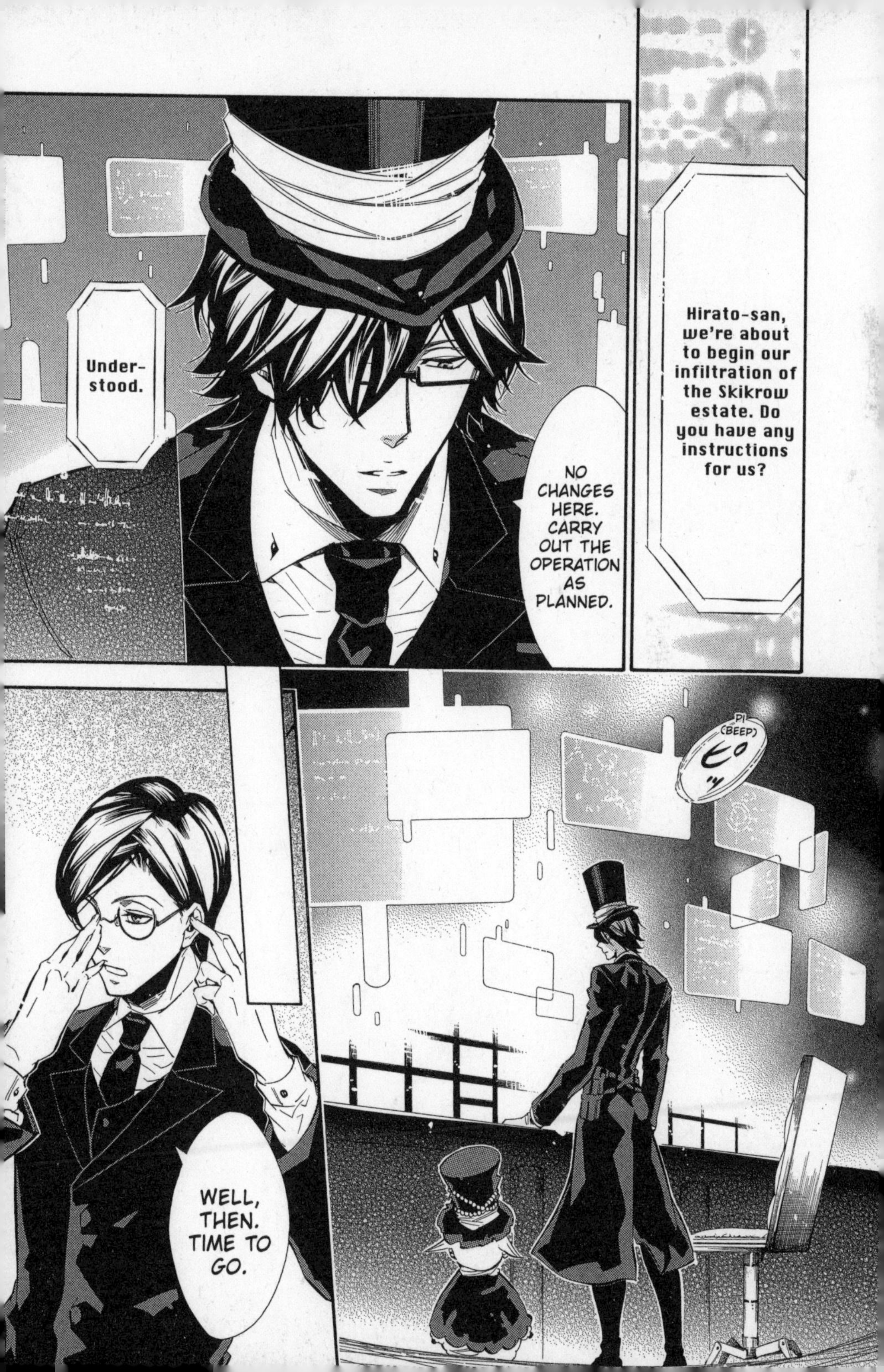
Hirato-san, we're about to begin our infiltration of the Skikrow estate. Do you have any instructions for us?
NO CHANGES HERE. CARRY OUT THE OPERATION AS PLANNED.
Under-stood.
PI (BEEP)
WELL, THEN. TIME TO GO.

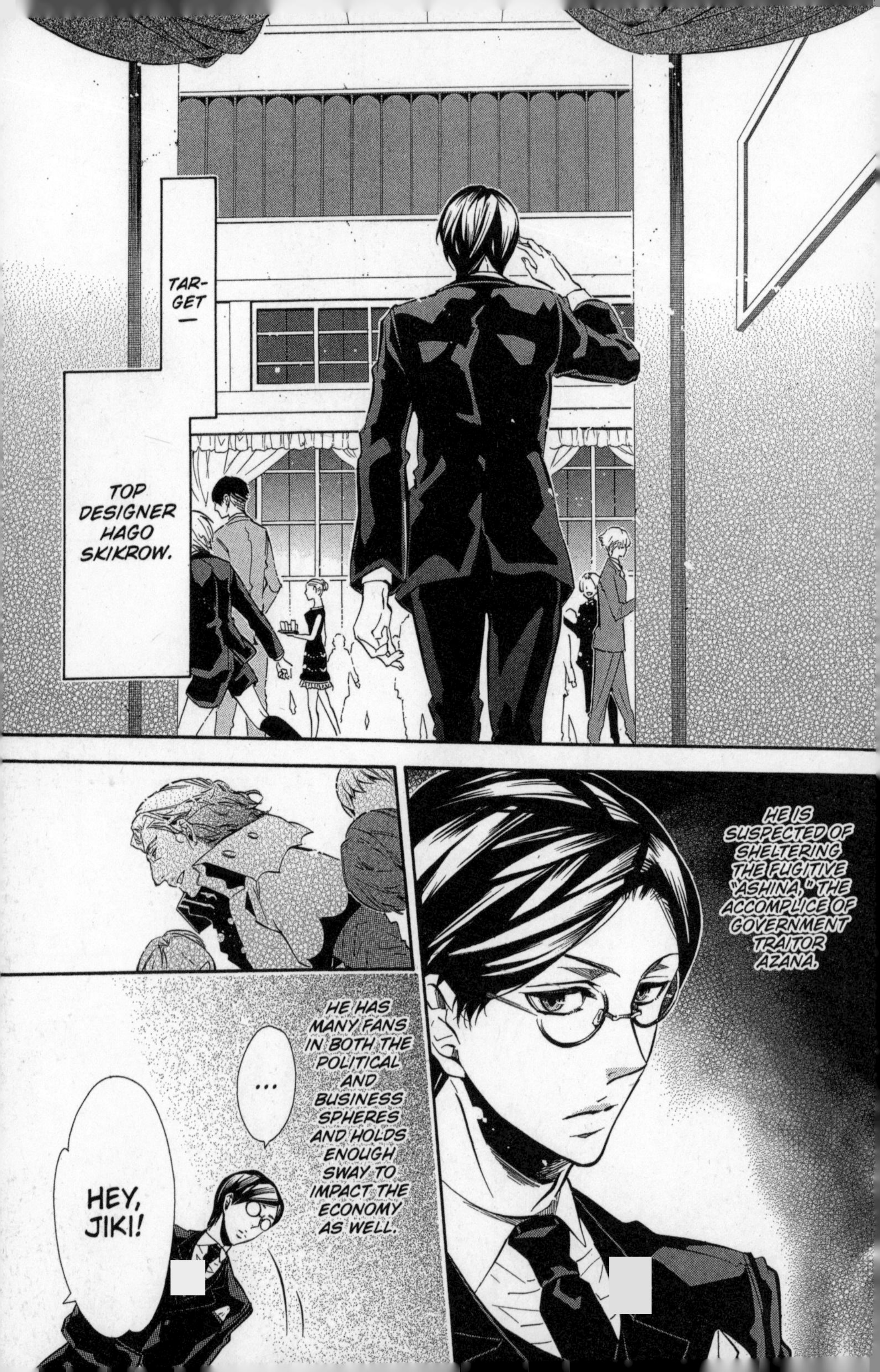
TAR-GET —
TOP DESIGNER HAGO SKIKROW.
HE IS SUSPECTED OF SHELTERING THE FUGITIVE "ASHINA," THE ACCOMPLICE OF GOVERNMENT TRAITOR AZANA.
HE HAS MANY FANS IN BOTH THE POLITICAL AND BUSINESS SPHERES AND HOLDS ENOUGH SWAY TO IMPACT THE ECONOMY AS WELL.
...
HEY, JIKI!

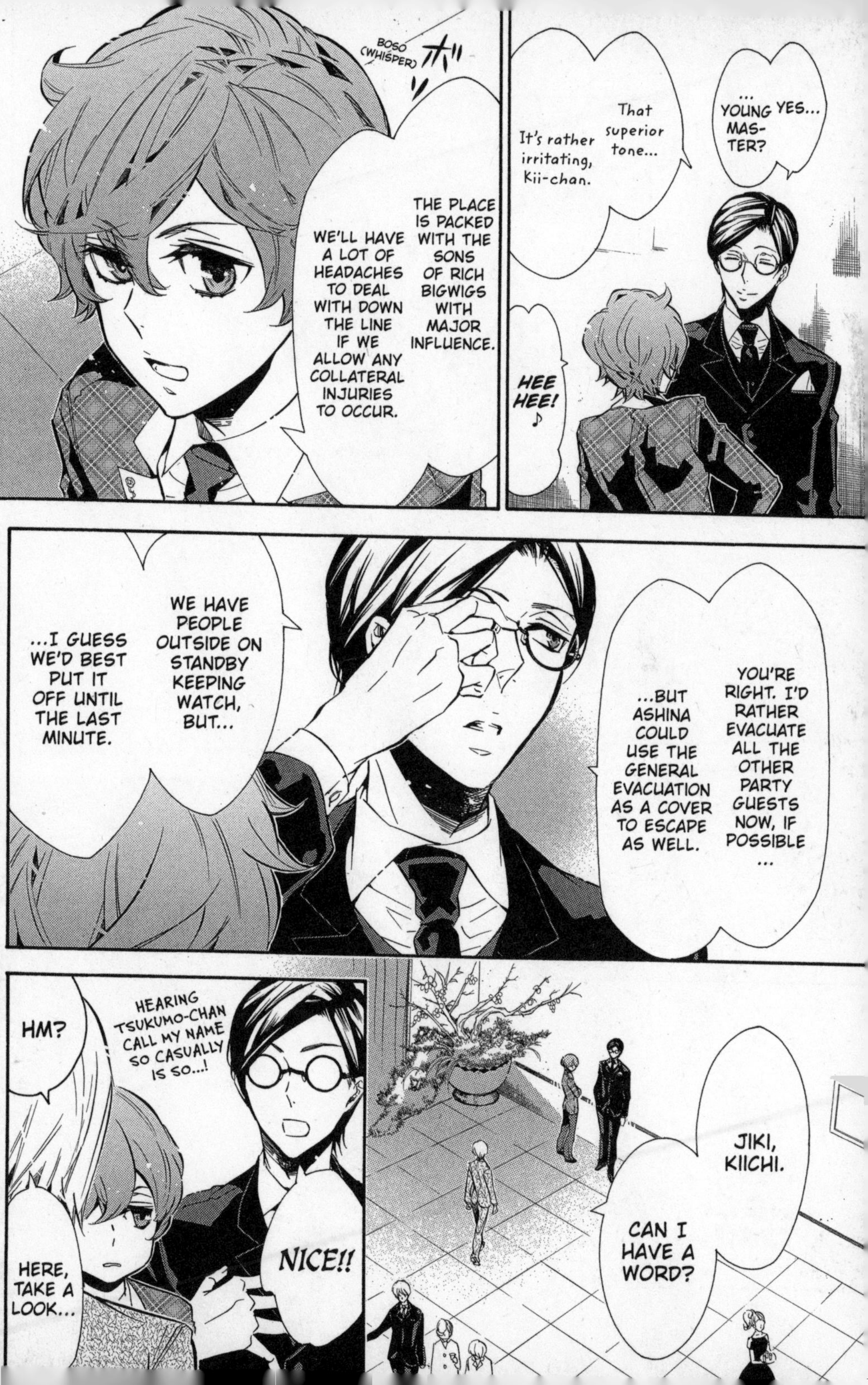
...YES... YOUNG MASTER?
That superior tone...
It's rather irritating, Kii-chan.
HEE HEE! ♪
BOSO (WHISPER)
THE PLACE IS PACKED WITH THE SONS OF RICH BIGWIGS WITH MAJOR INFLUENCE.
WE'LL HAVE A LOT OF HEADACHES TO DEAL WITH DOWN THE LINE IF WE ALLOW ANY COLLATERAL INJURIES TO OCCUR.
YOU'RE RIGHT. I'D RATHER EVACUATE ALL THE OTHER PARTY GUESTS NOW, IF POSSIBLE...
...BUT ASHINA COULD USE THE GENERAL EVACUATION AS A COVER TO ESCAPE AS WELL.
WE HAVE PEOPLE OUTSIDE ON STANDBY KEEPING WATCH, BUT...
...I GUESS WE'D BEST PUT IT OFF UNTIL THE LAST MINUTE.
JIKI, KIICHI.
CAN I HAVE A WORD?
HEARING TSUKUMO-CHAN CALL MY NAME SO CASUALLY IS SO...!
HM?
NICE!!
HERE, TAKE A LOOK...

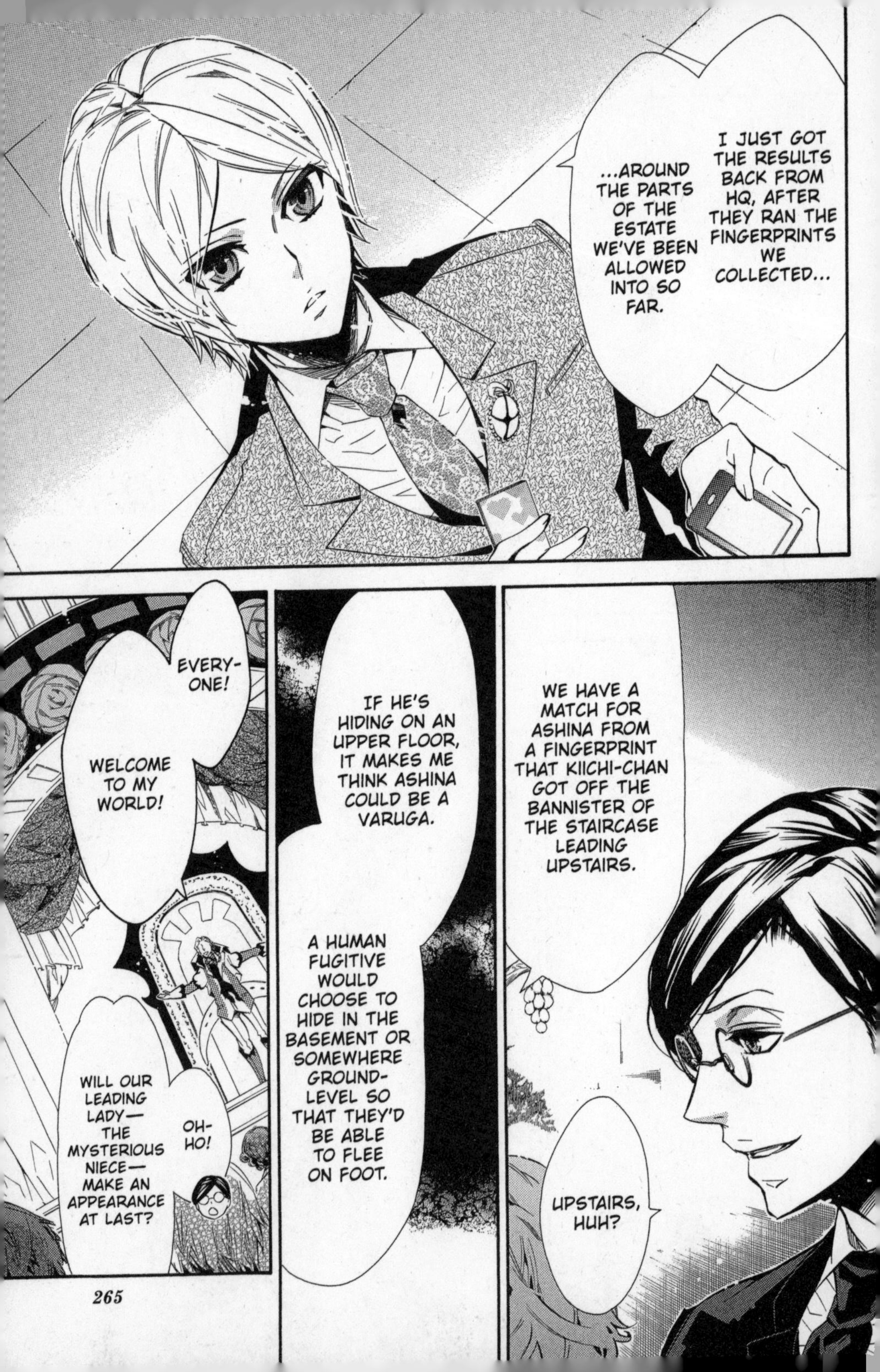
I JUST GOT THE RESULTS BACK FROM HQ, AFTER THEY RAN THE FINGERPRINTS WE COLLECTED...
...AROUND THE PARTS OF THE ESTATE WE'VE BEEN ALLOWED INTO SO FAR.
WE HAVE A MATCH FOR ASHINA FROM A FINGERPRINT THAT KIICHI-CHAN GOT OFF THE BANNISTER OF THE STAIRCASE LEADING UPSTAIRS.
UPSTAIRS, HUH?
IF HE'S HIDING ON AN UPPER FLOOR, IT MAKES ME THINK ASHINA COULD BE A VARUGA.
A HUMAN FUGITIVE WOULD CHOOSE TO HIDE IN THE BASEMENT OR SOMEWHERE GROUND-LEVEL SO THAT THEY'D BE ABLE TO FLEE ON FOOT.
EVERY-ONE!
WELCOME TO MY WORLD!
OH-HO!
WILL OUR LEADING LADY—THE MYSTERIOUS NIECE—MAKE AN APPEARANCE AT LAST?

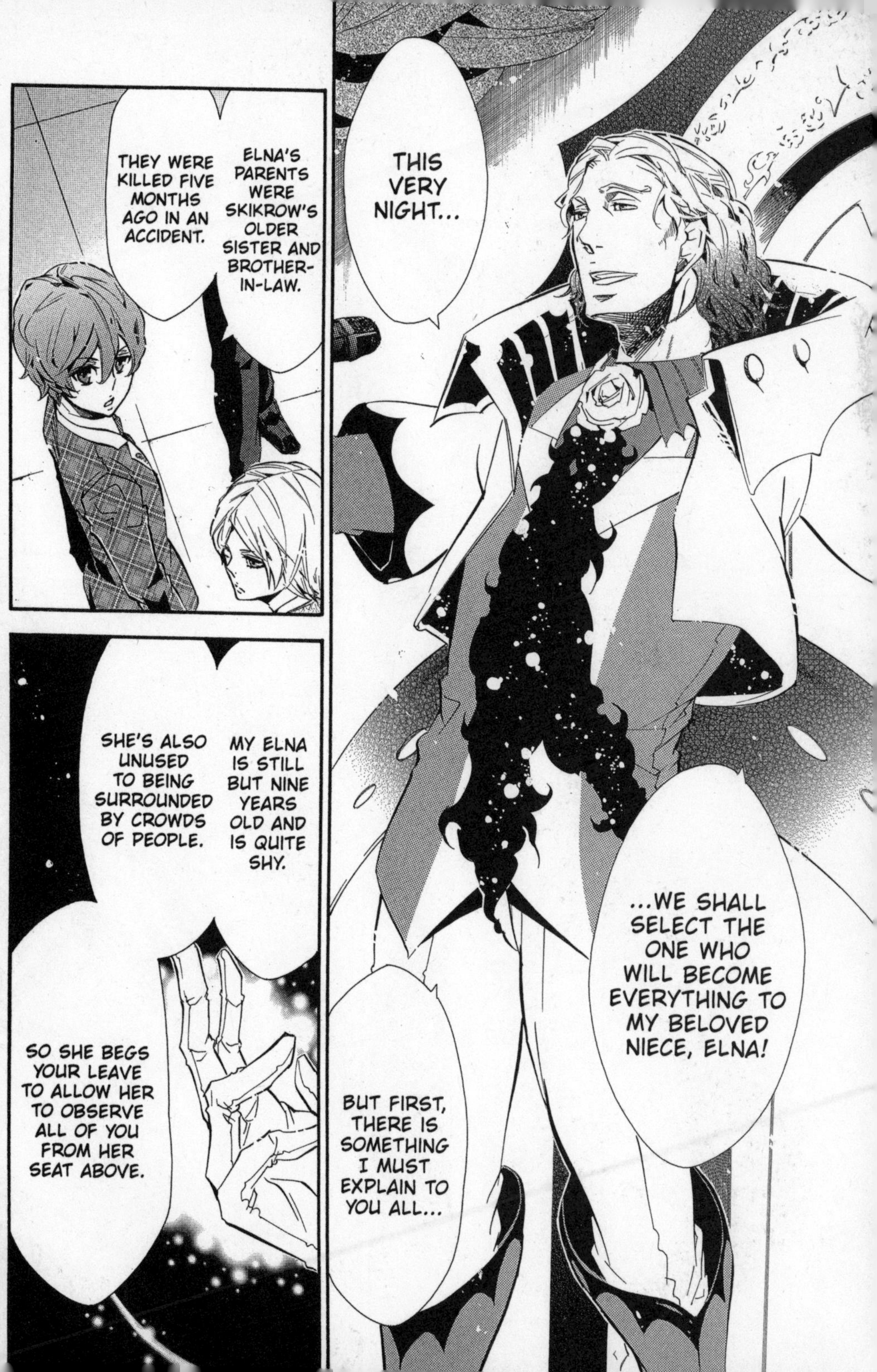
THIS VERY NIGHT...
...WE SHALL SELECT THE ONE WHO WILL BECOME EVERYTHING TO MY BELOVED NIECE, ELNA!
BUT FIRST, THERE IS SOMETHING I MUST EXPLAIN TO YOU ALL...
ELNA'S PARENTS WERE SKIKROW'S OLDER SISTER AND BROTHER-IN-LAW.
THEY WERE KILLED FIVE MONTHS AGO IN AN ACCIDENT.
MY ELNA IS STILL BUT NINE YEARS OLD AND IS QUITE SHY.
SHE'S ALSO UNUSED TO BEING SURROUNDED BY CROWDS OF PEOPLE.
SO SHE BEGS YOUR LEAVE TO ALLOW HER TO OBSERVE ALL OF YOU FROM HER SEAT ABOVE.

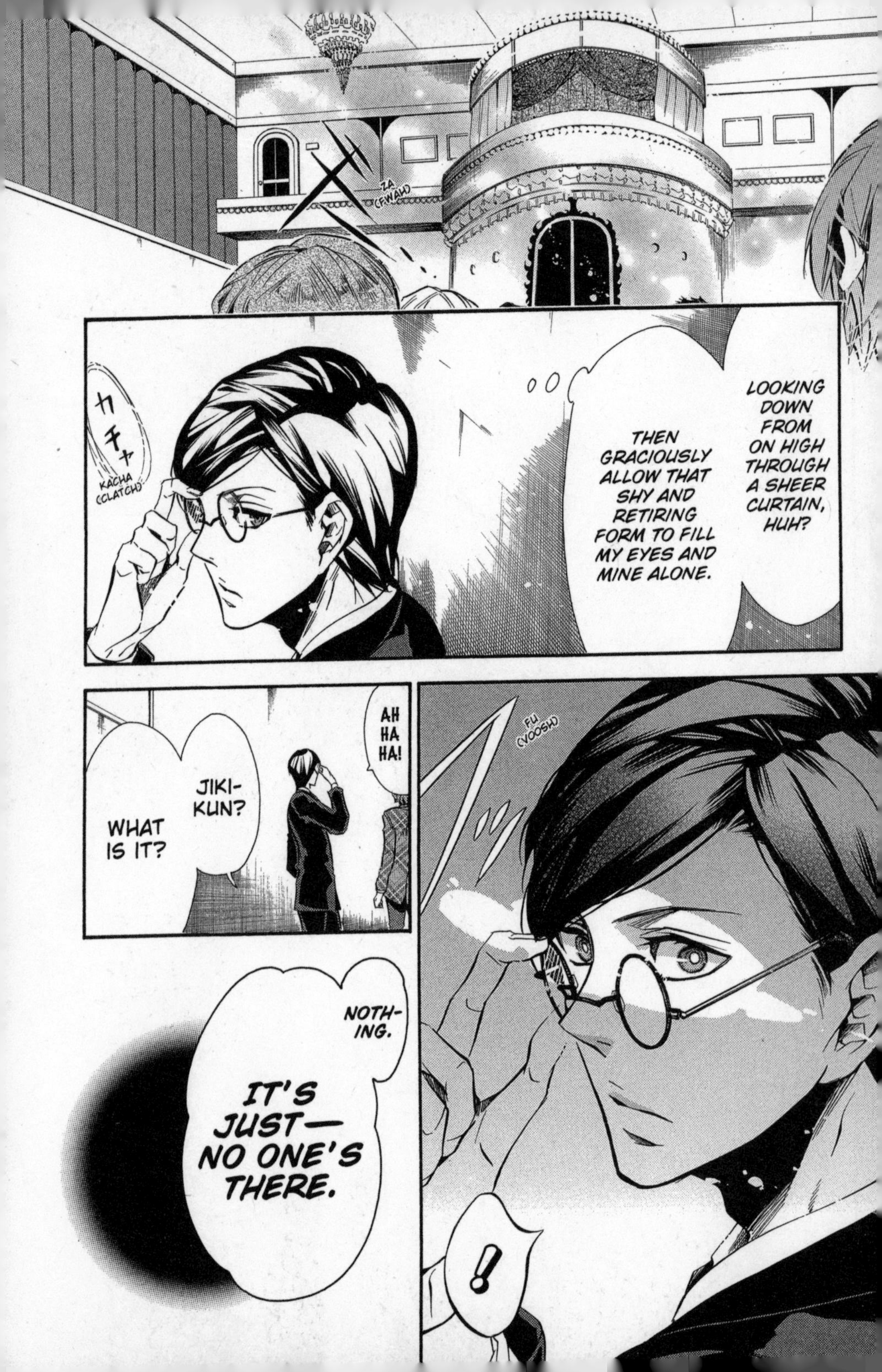
ZA (FWAH)
LOOKING DOWN FROM ON HIGH THROUGH A SHEER CURTAIN, HUH?
THEN GRACIOUSLY ALLOW THAT SHY AND RETIRING FORM TO FILL MY EYES AND MINE ALONE.
カチャ
KACHA (CLATCH)
FU (VOOSH)
!
AH HA HA!
JIKI-KUN?
WHAT IS IT?
NOTH-ING.
IT'S JUST— NO ONE'S THERE.

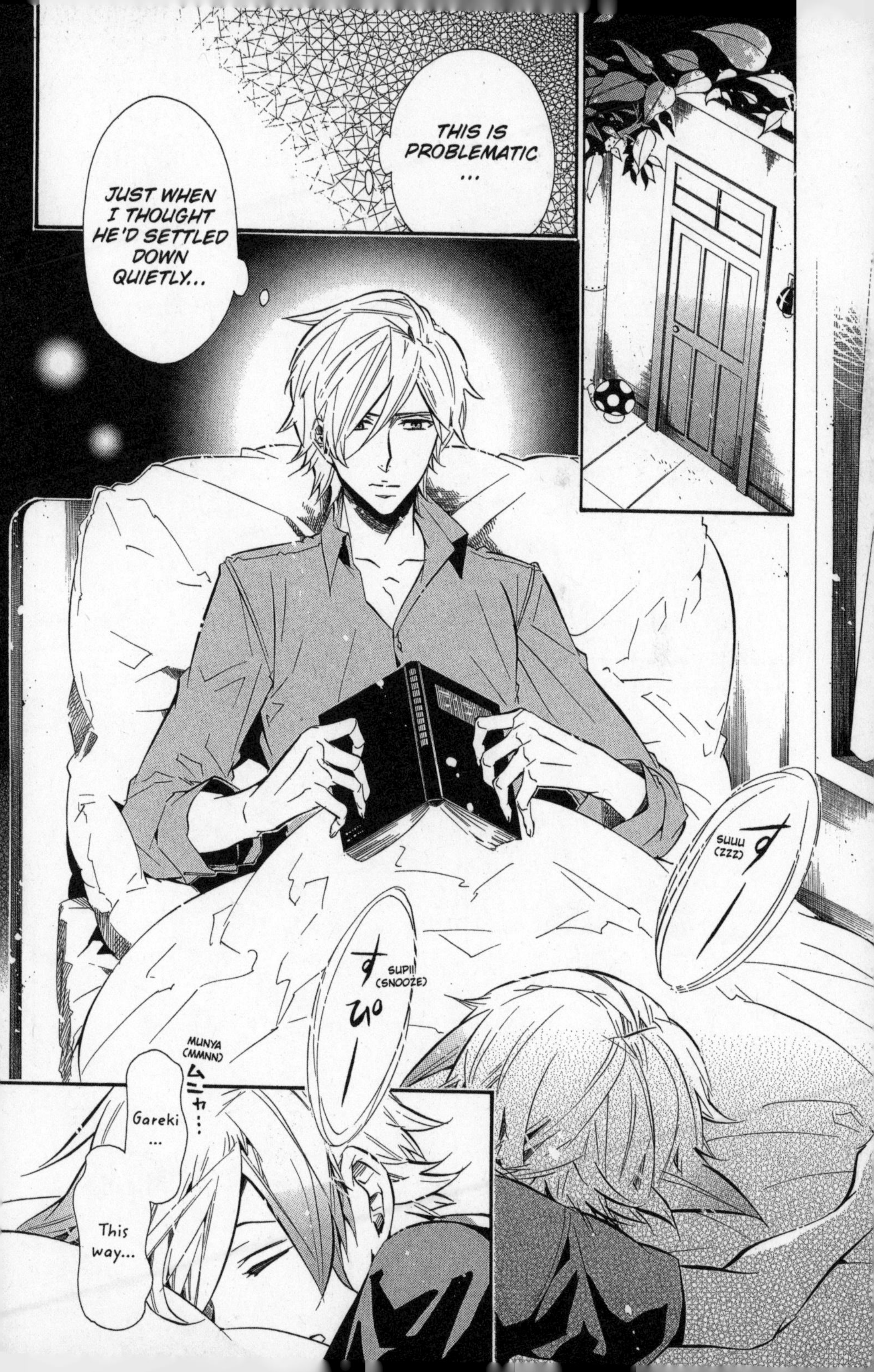
THIS IS PROBLEMATIC ...
JUST WHEN I THOUGHT HE'D SETTLED DOWN QUIETLY...
す
SUUU (ZZZ)
す ぴー
SUPII (SNOOZE)
ムニャ…
MUNYA (MMNN)
Gareki ...
This way...

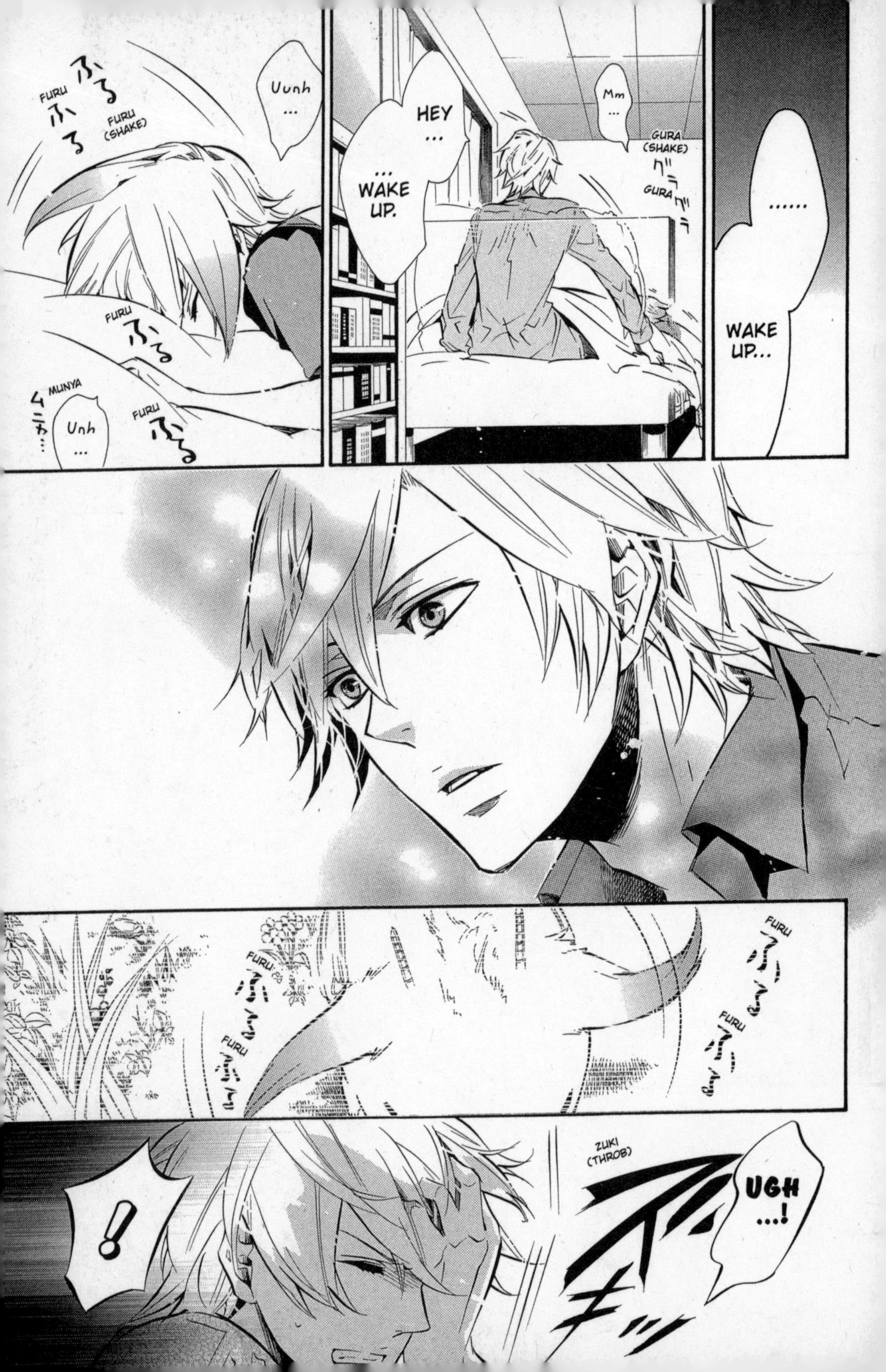
......
WAKE UP...
Mm ...
GURA (SHAKE)
グラ
GURA
グラ
HEY ...
... WAKE UP.
Uunh ...
ふる
FURU
ふる
FURU (SHAKE)
FURU
ふる
FURU
ふる
MUNYA
ムニャ...
Unh ...
FURU
FURU
FURU
ZUKI (THROB)
ズキッ
UGH ...!
!

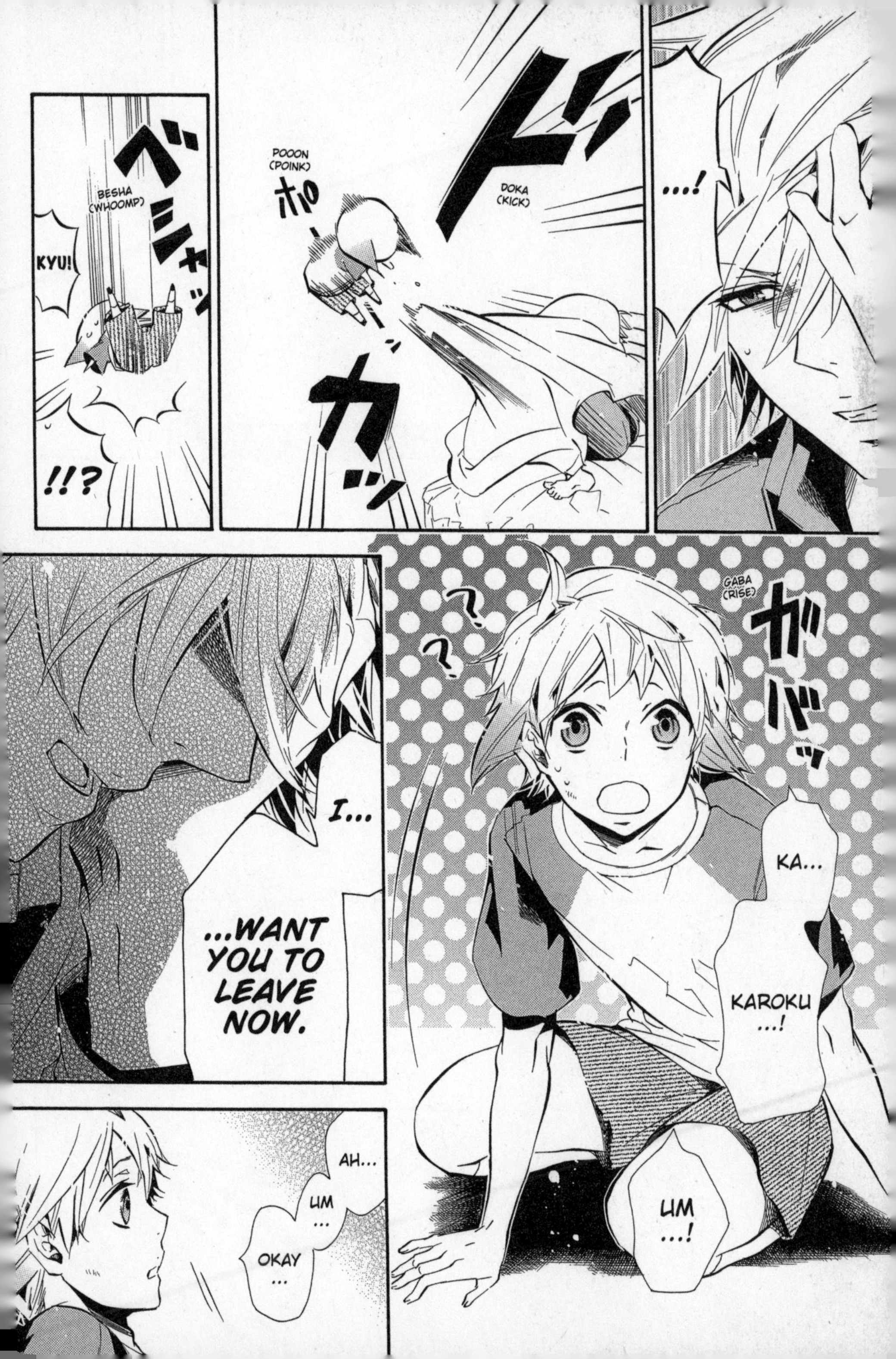
...!
DOKA (KICK)
POOON (POINK)
BESHA (WHOOMP)
KYU!
!!?
GABA (RISE)
KA...
KAROKU ...!
UM ...!
I...
...WANT YOU TO LEAVE NOW.
AH...
UM ...
OKAY ...

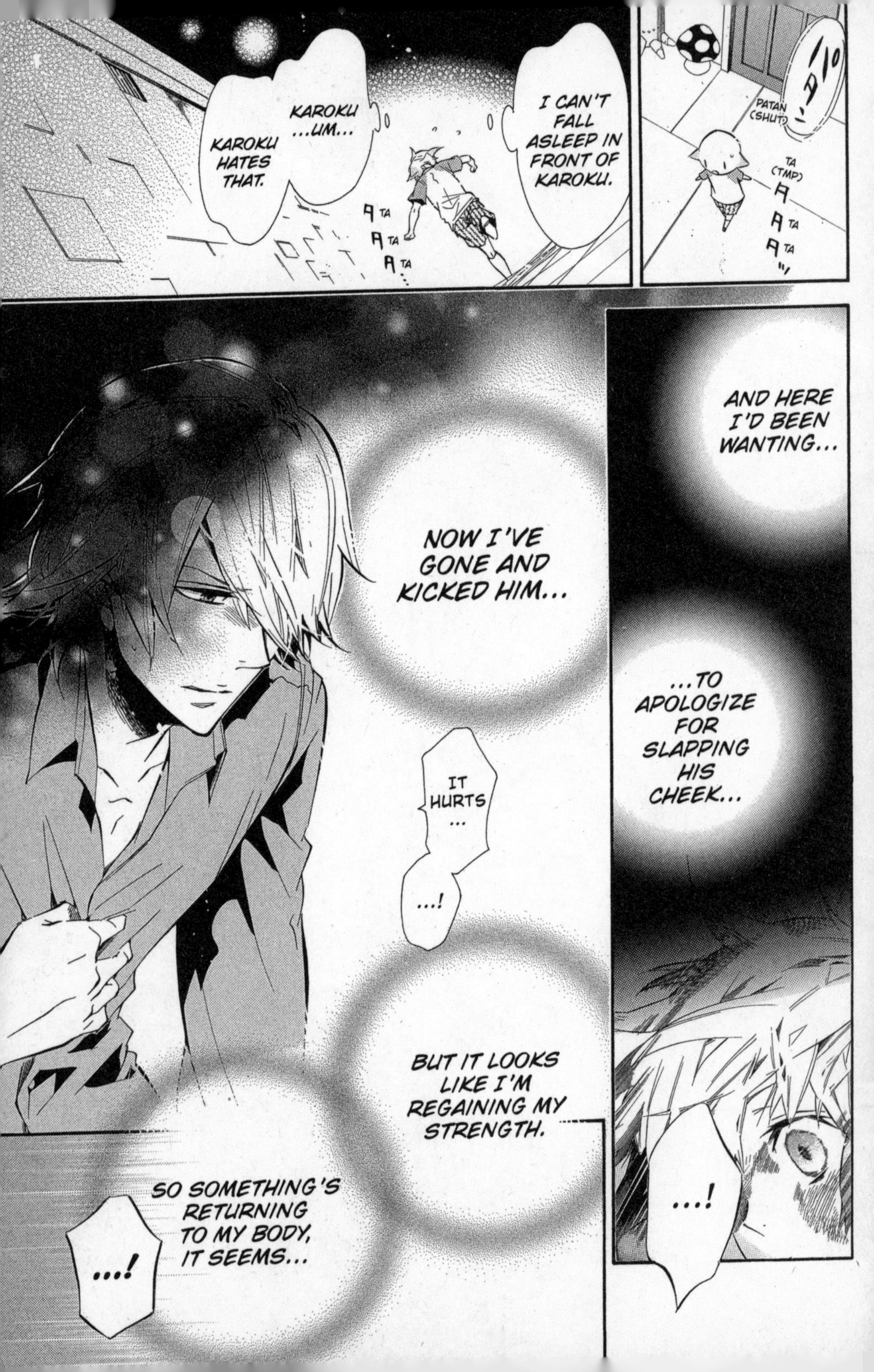
PATAN (SHUT)
TA (TMP)
TA
TA
TA
I CAN'T FALL ASLEEP IN FRONT OF KAROKU.
KAROKU ...UM...
KAROKU HATES THAT.
TA
TA
TA
AND HERE I'D BEEN WANTING...
...TO APOLOGIZE FOR SLAPPING HIS CHEEK...
...!
NOW I'VE GONE AND KICKED HIM...
IT HURTS...
...!
BUT IT LOOKS LIKE I'M REGAINING MY STRENGTH.
SO SOMETHING'S RETURNING TO MY BODY, IT SEEMS...
...!

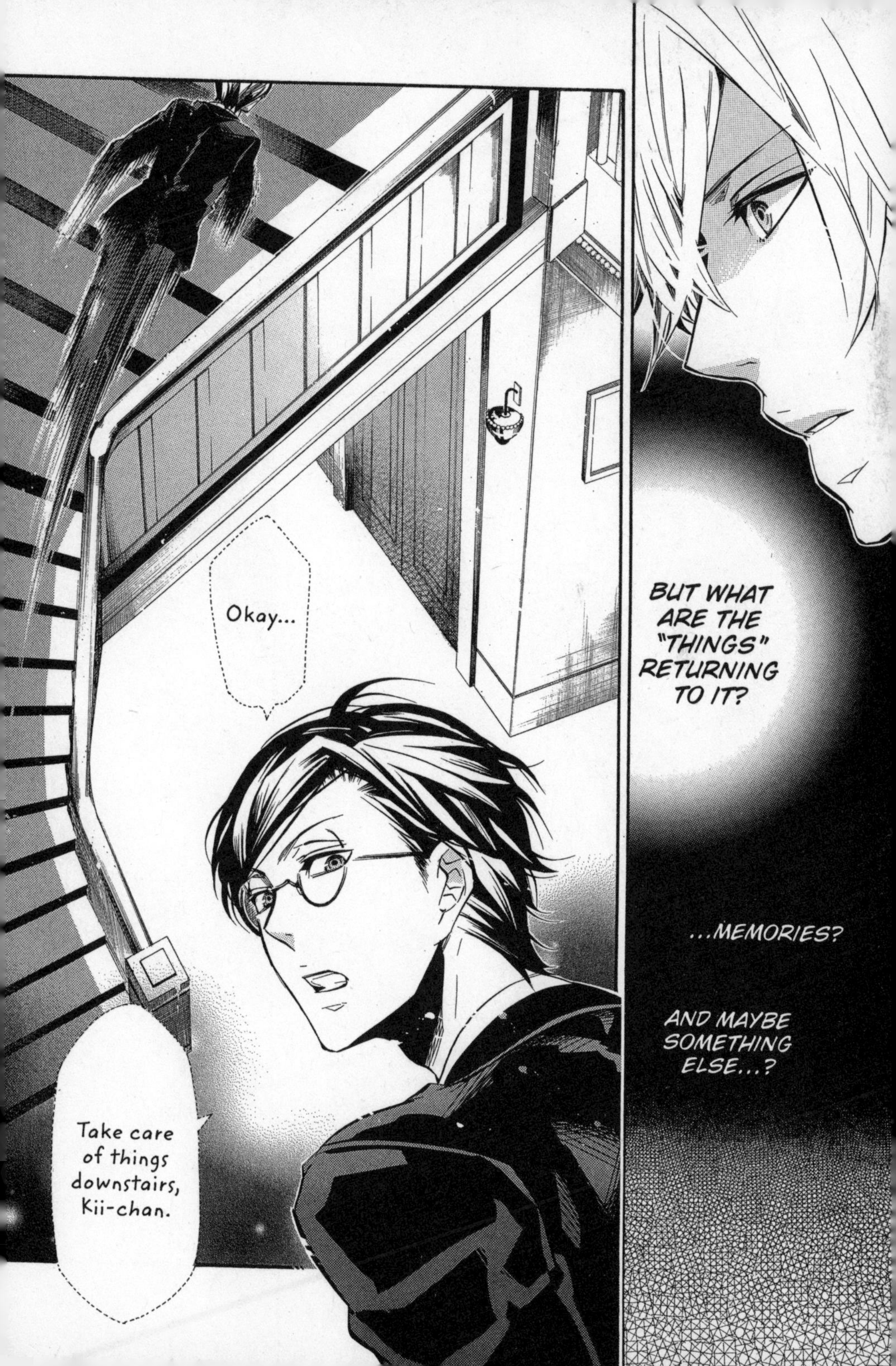
BUT WHAT ARE THE "THINGS" RETURNING TO IT?
...MEMORIES?
AND MAYBE SOMETHING ELSE...?
Okay...
Take care of things downstairs, Kii-chan.

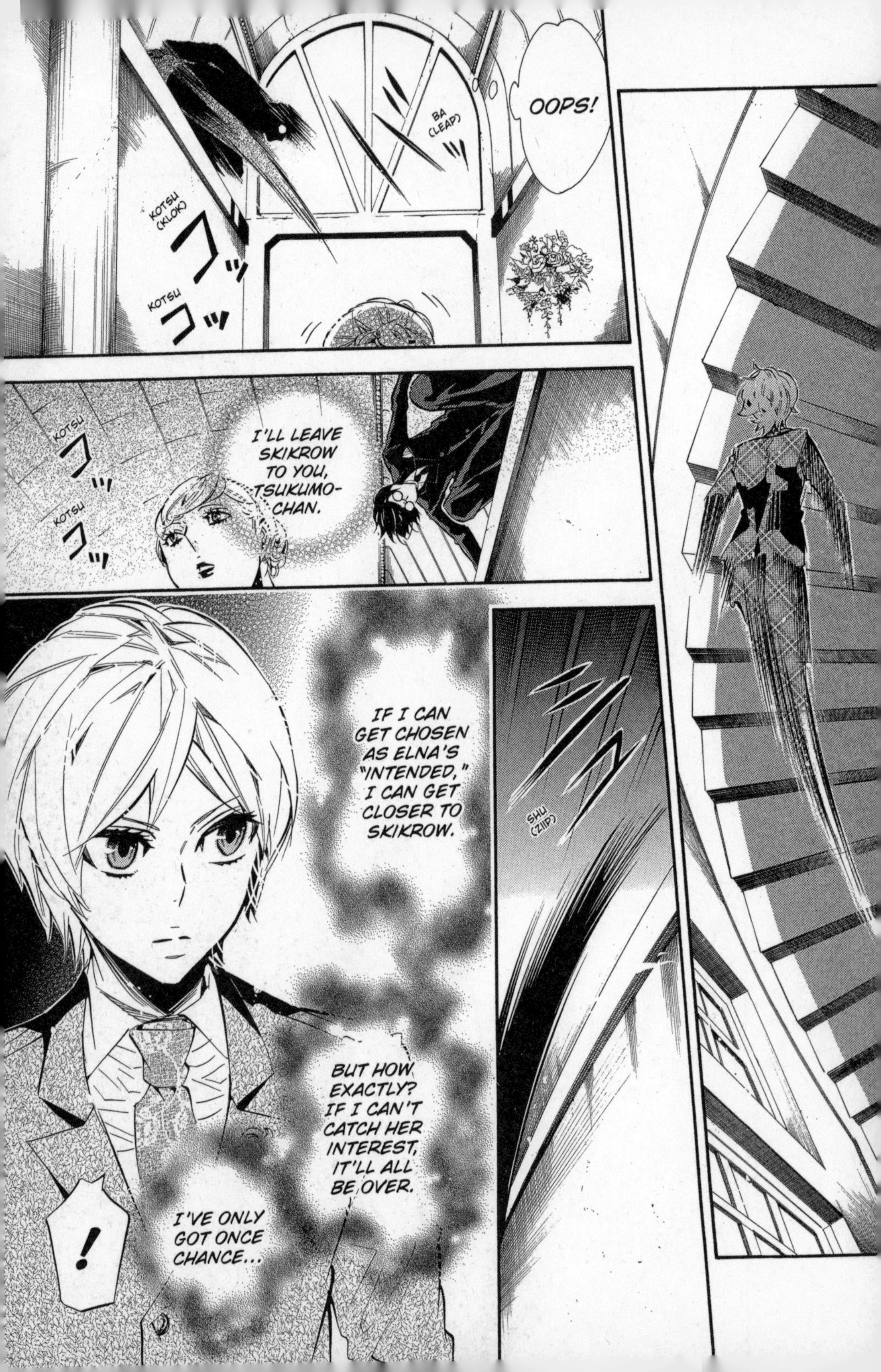
OOPS!
BA (LEAP)
KOTSU (KLOK)
KOTSU
I'LL LEAVE SKIKROW TO YOU, TSUKUMO-CHAN.
KOTSU
KOTSU
SHU (ZIIP)
IF I CAN GET CHOSEN AS ELNA'S "INTENDED," I CAN GET CLOSER TO SKIKROW.
BUT HOW EXACTLY? IF I CAN'T CATCH HER INTEREST, IT'LL ALL BE OVER.
I'VE ONLY GOT ONCE CHANCE...
!

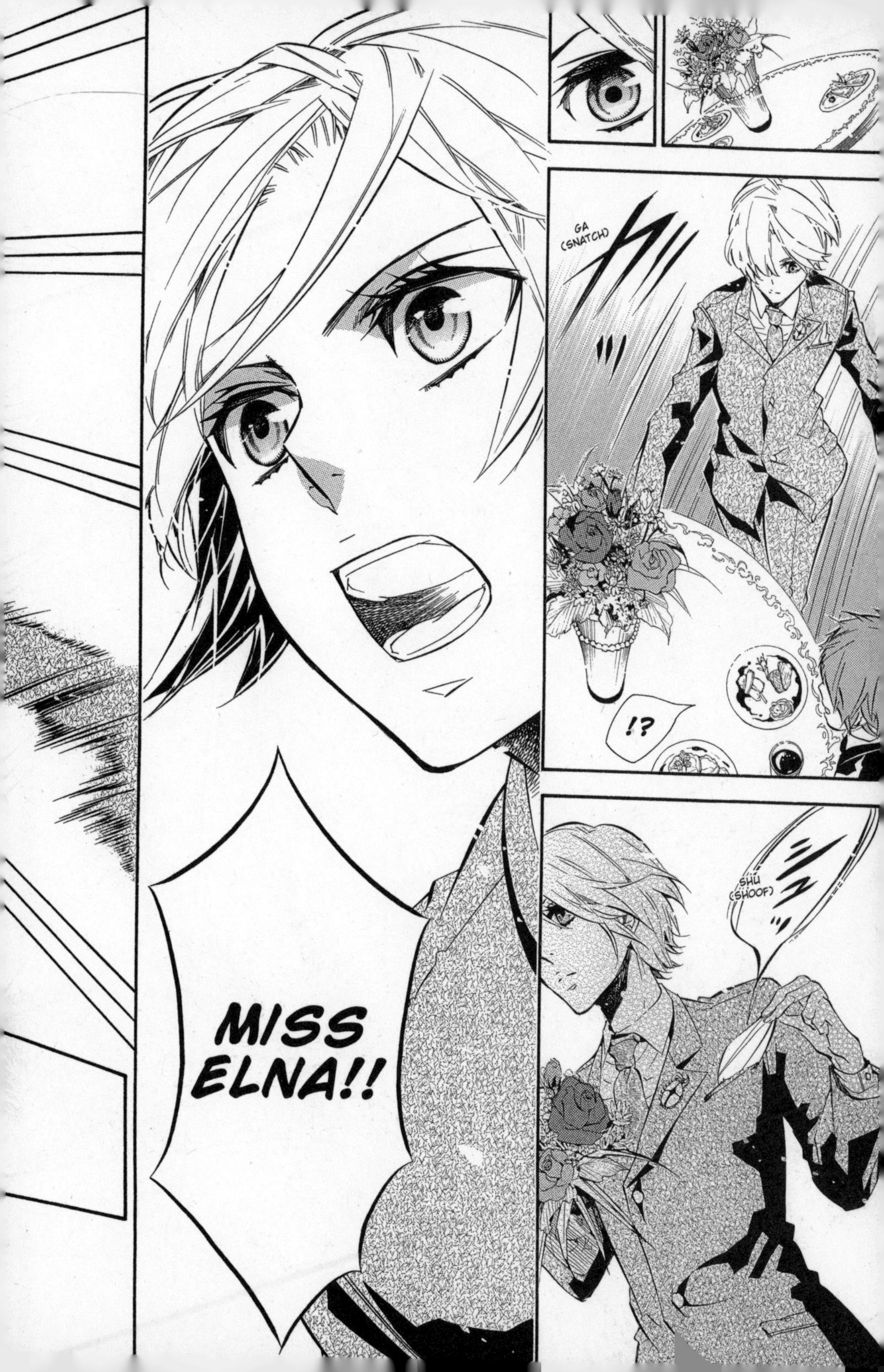
GA
(SNATCH)
!?
SHU
(SHOOF)
MISS
ELNA!!

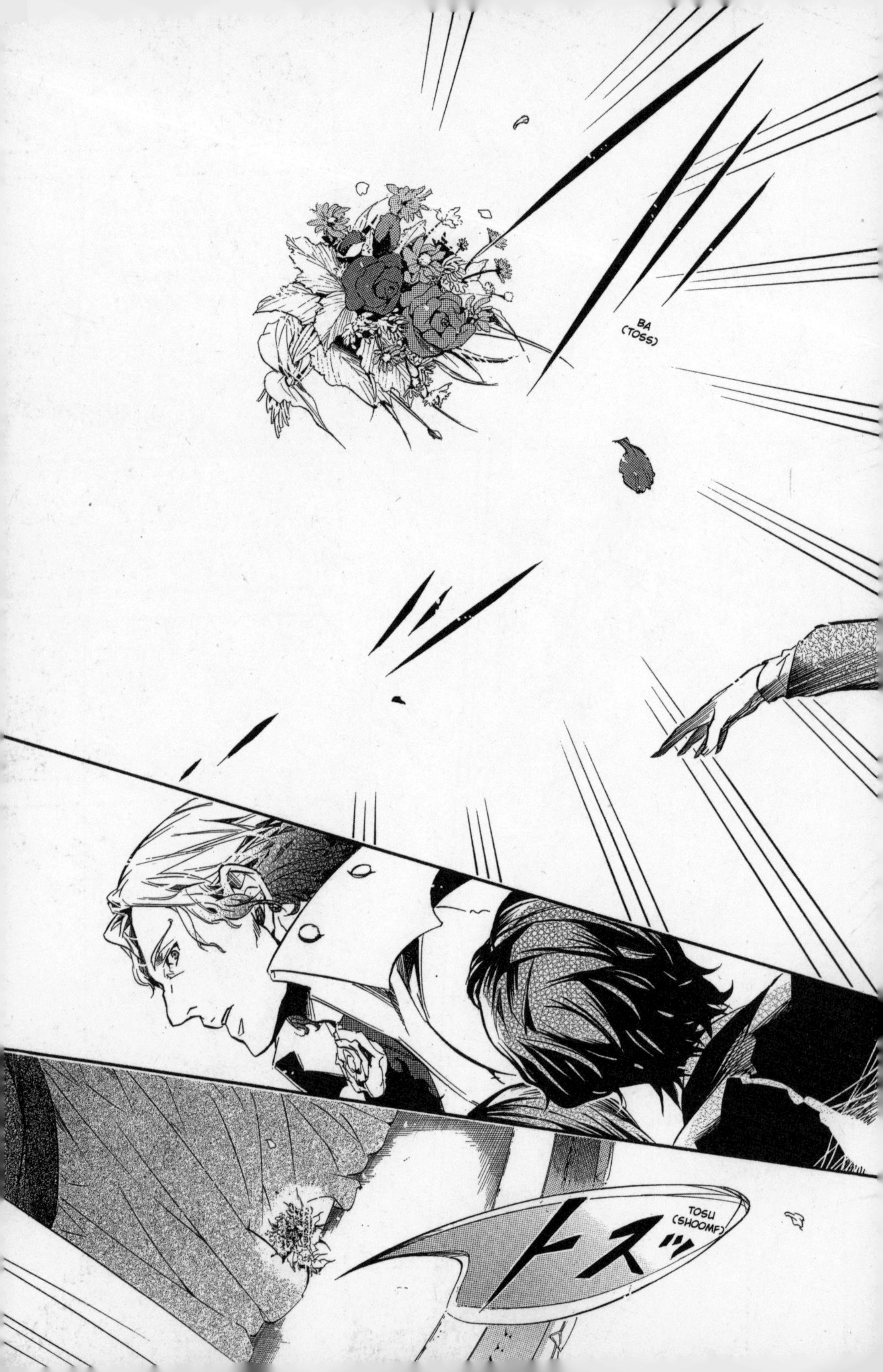
BA
(TOSS)
トスッ
TOSU
(SHOOMF)

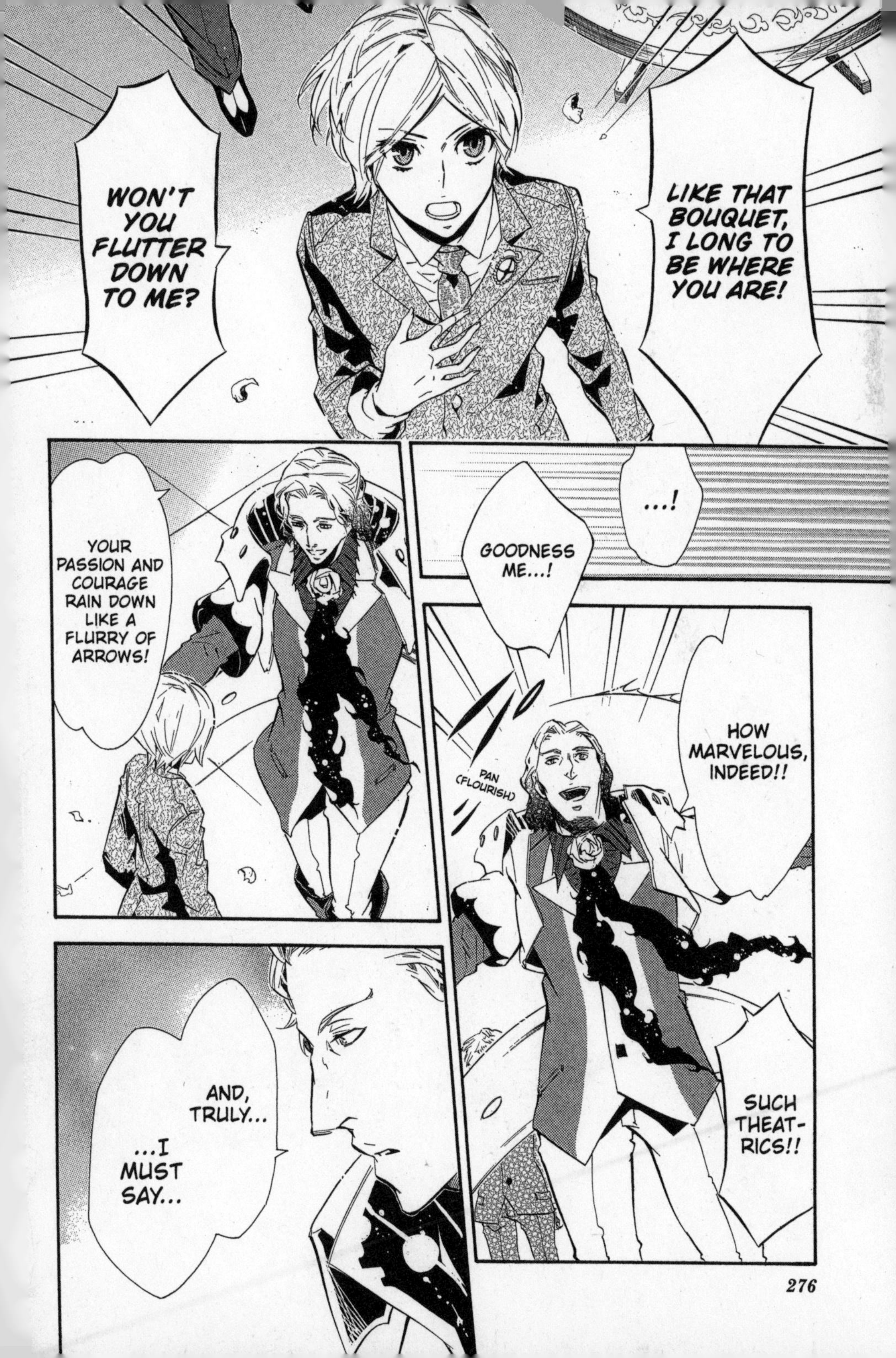
LIKE THAT BOUQUET, I LONG TO BE WHERE YOU ARE!
WON'T YOU FLUTTER DOWN TO ME?
...!
GOODNESS ME...!
YOUR PASSION AND COURAGE RAIN DOWN LIKE A FLURRY OF ARROWS!
PAN (FLOURISH)
HOW MARVELOUS, INDEED!!
SUCH THEAT-RICS!!
AND, TRULY...
...I MUST SAY...

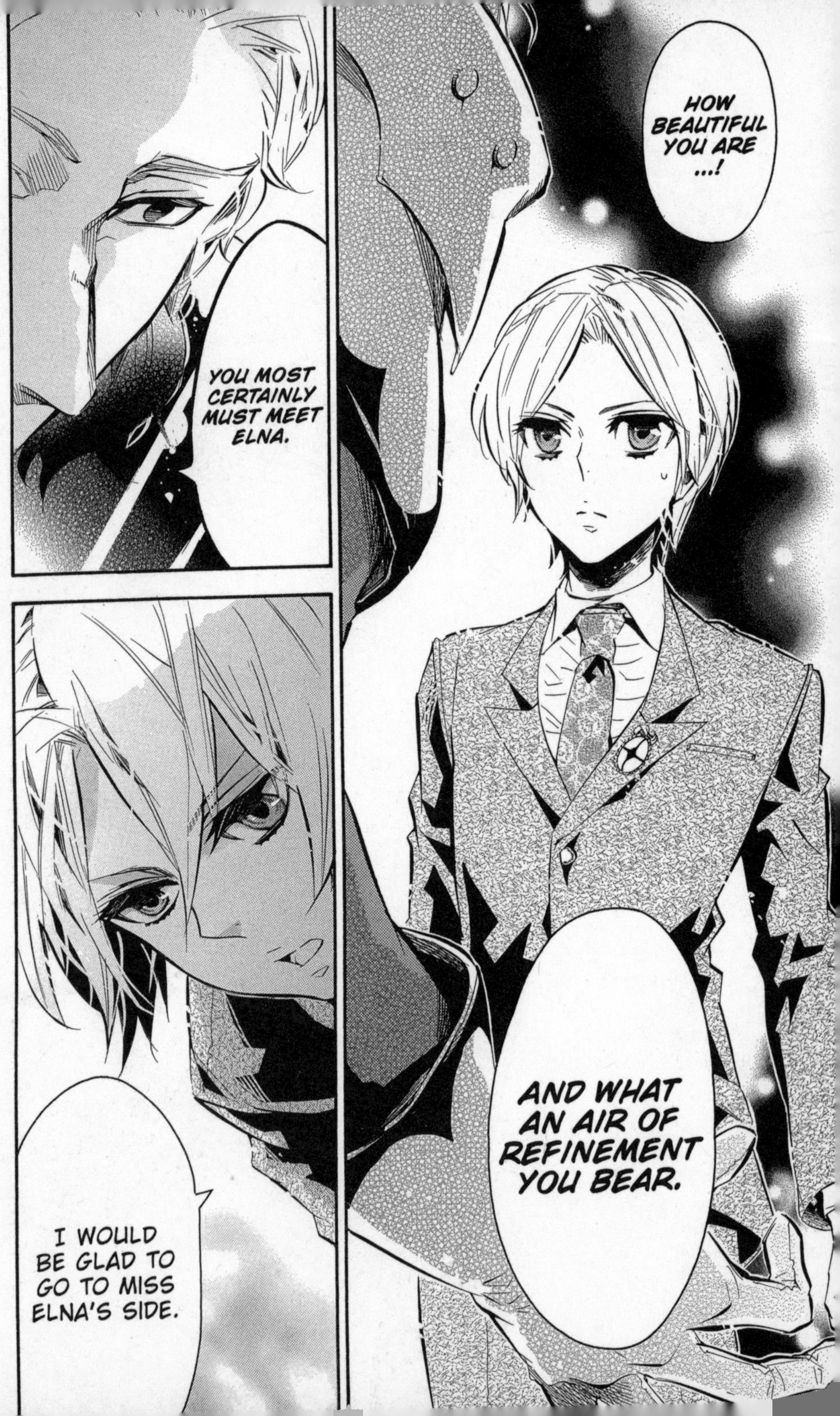
HOW BEAUTIFUL YOU ARE ...!
AND WHAT AN AIR OF REFINEMENT YOU BEAR.
YOU MOST CERTAINLY MUST MEET ELNA.
I WOULD BE GLAD TO GO TO MISS ELNA'S SIDE.

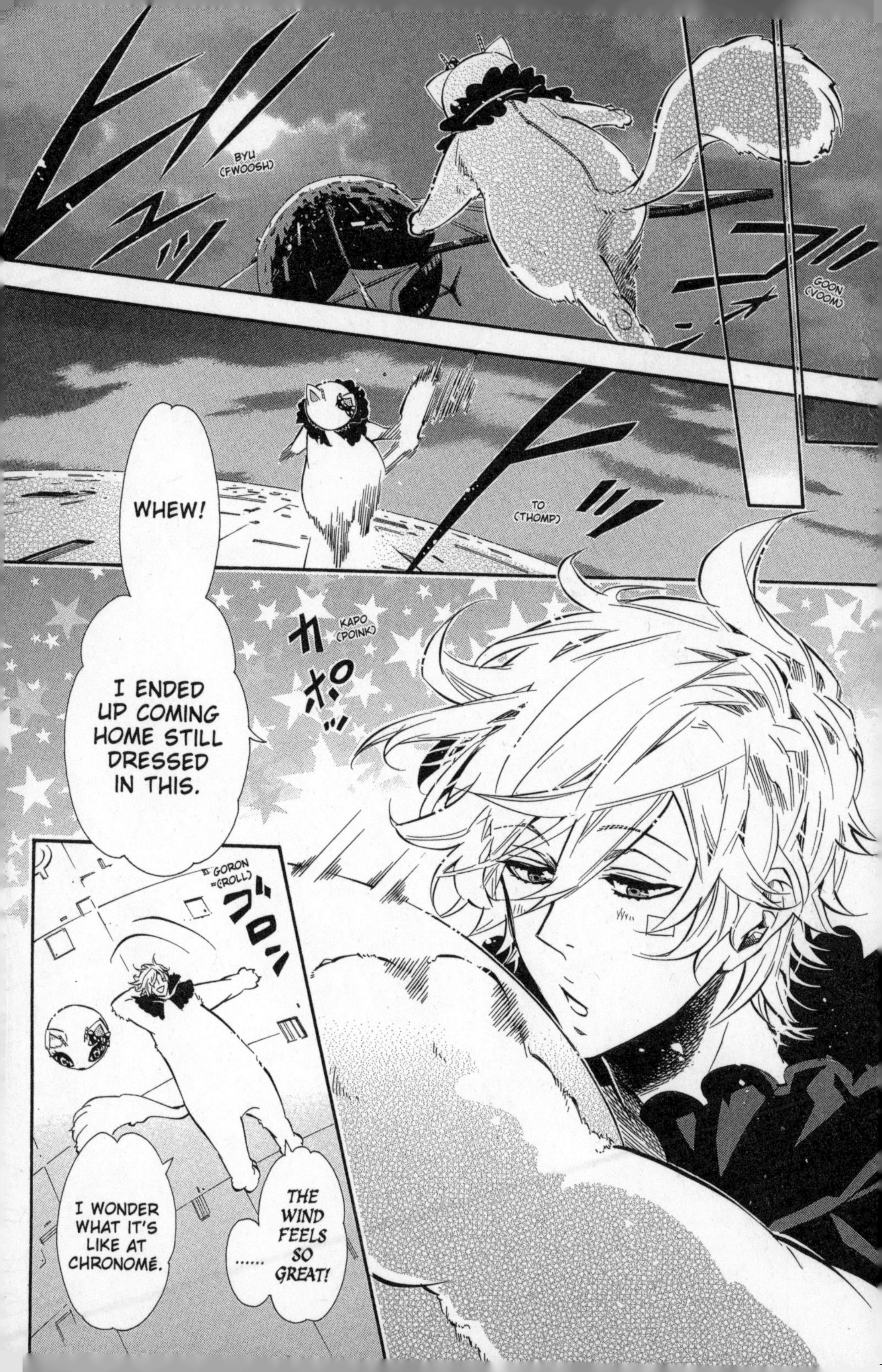
GOON (VOOM)
BYU (FWOOSH)
TO (THOMP)
WHEW!
KAPO (POINK)
I ENDED UP COMING HOME STILL DRESSED IN THIS.
GORON (ROLL)
THE WIND FEELS SO GREAT!
......
I WONDER WHAT IT'S LIKE AT CHRONOMÉ.

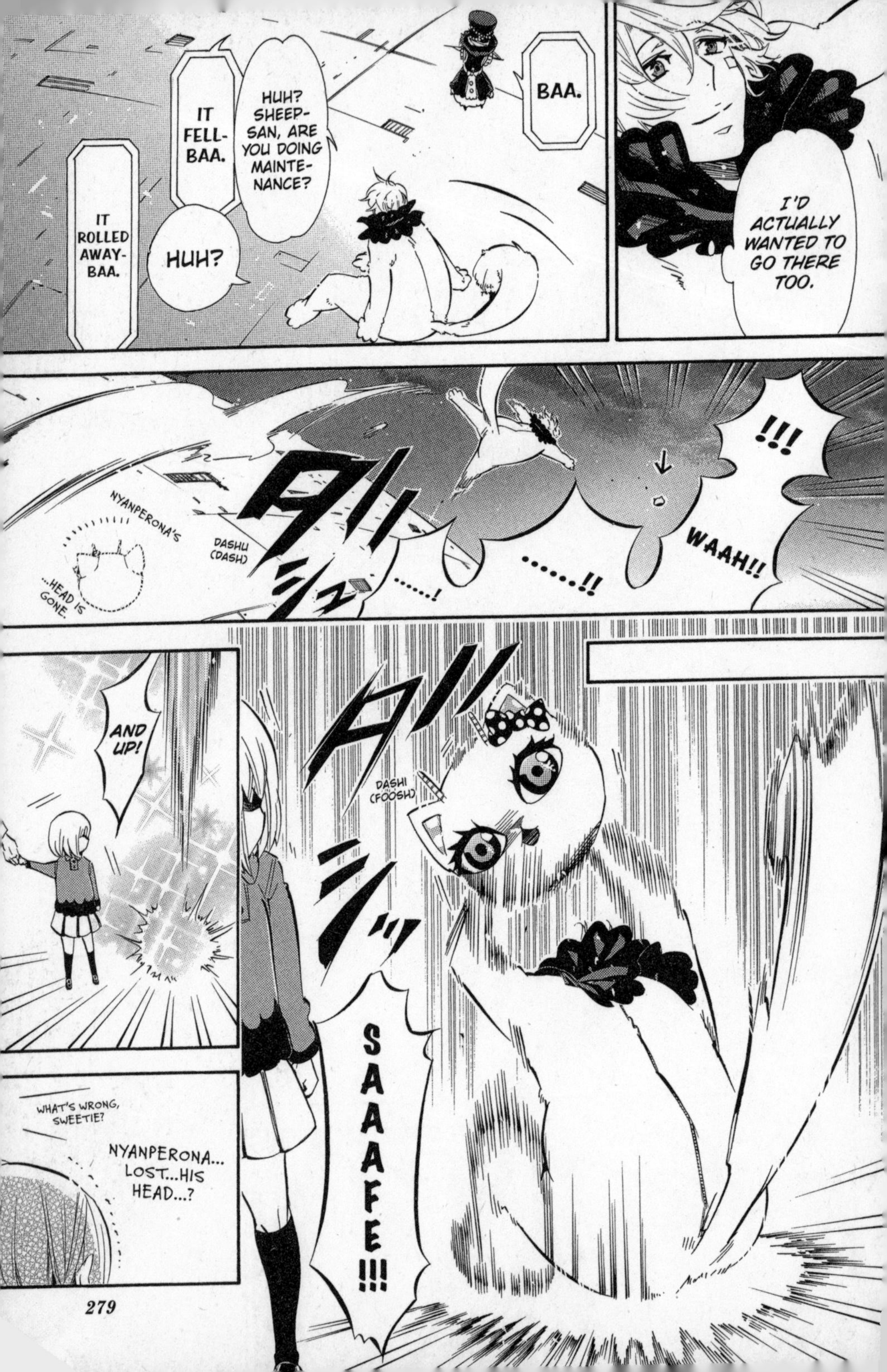

I'D ACTUALLY WANTED TO GO THERE TOO.
BAA.
HUH? SHEEP-SAN, ARE YOU DOING MAINTENANCE?
IT FELL-BAA.
HUH?
IT ROLLED AWAY-BAA.
!!!
WAAH!!
......!!
......!
DASHU (DASH)
NYANPERONA'S ...HEAD IS GONE.
DASHI (FOOSH)
SAAAFE!!!
AND UP!
WHAT'S WRONG, SWEETIE?
NYANPERONA... LOST...HIS HEAD...?

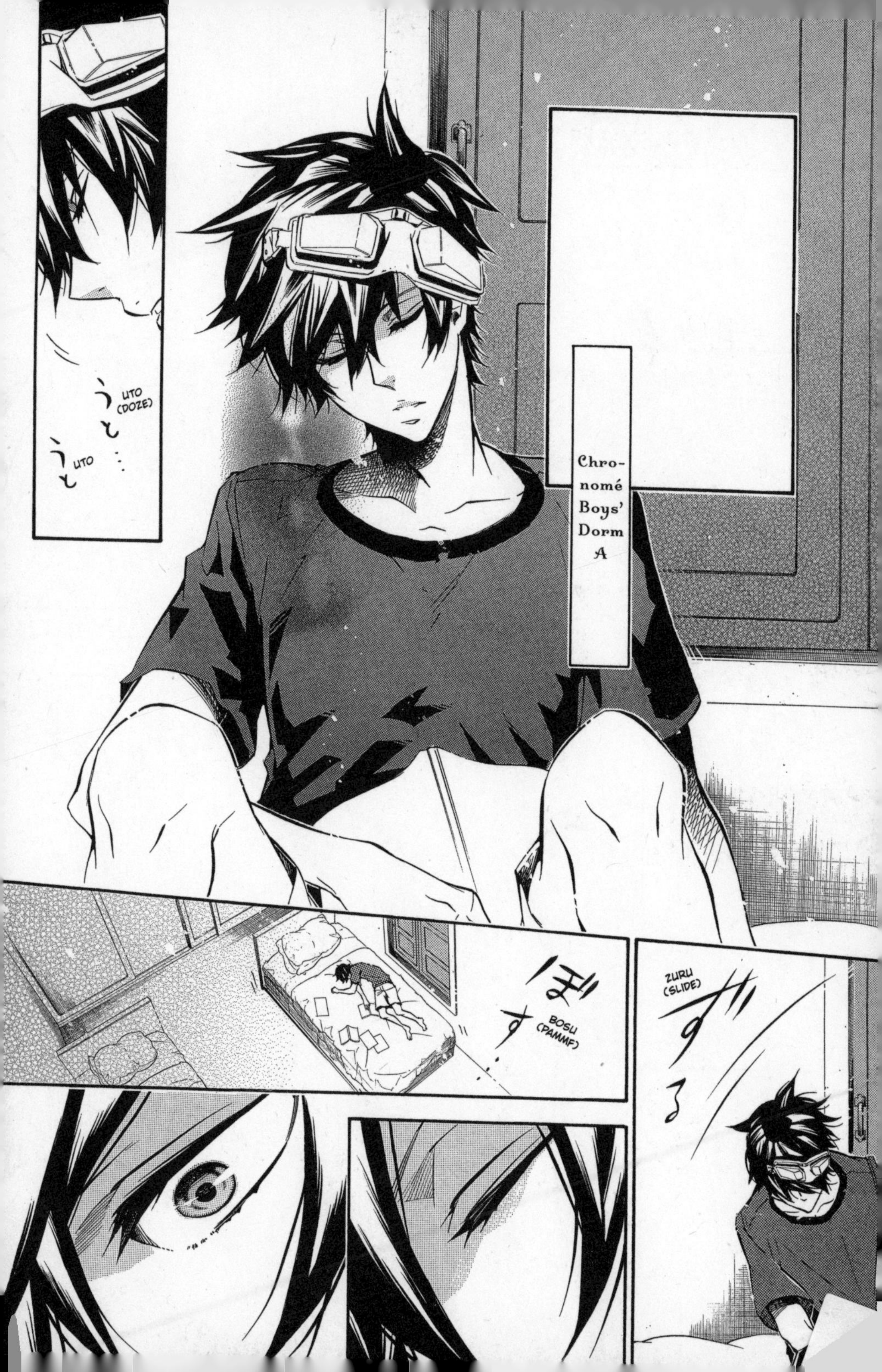
Chro-
nomé
Boys'
Dorm
A
うと UTO (DOZE)
うと UTO
ずる ZURU (SLIDE)
ぼす BOSU (PAMMF)

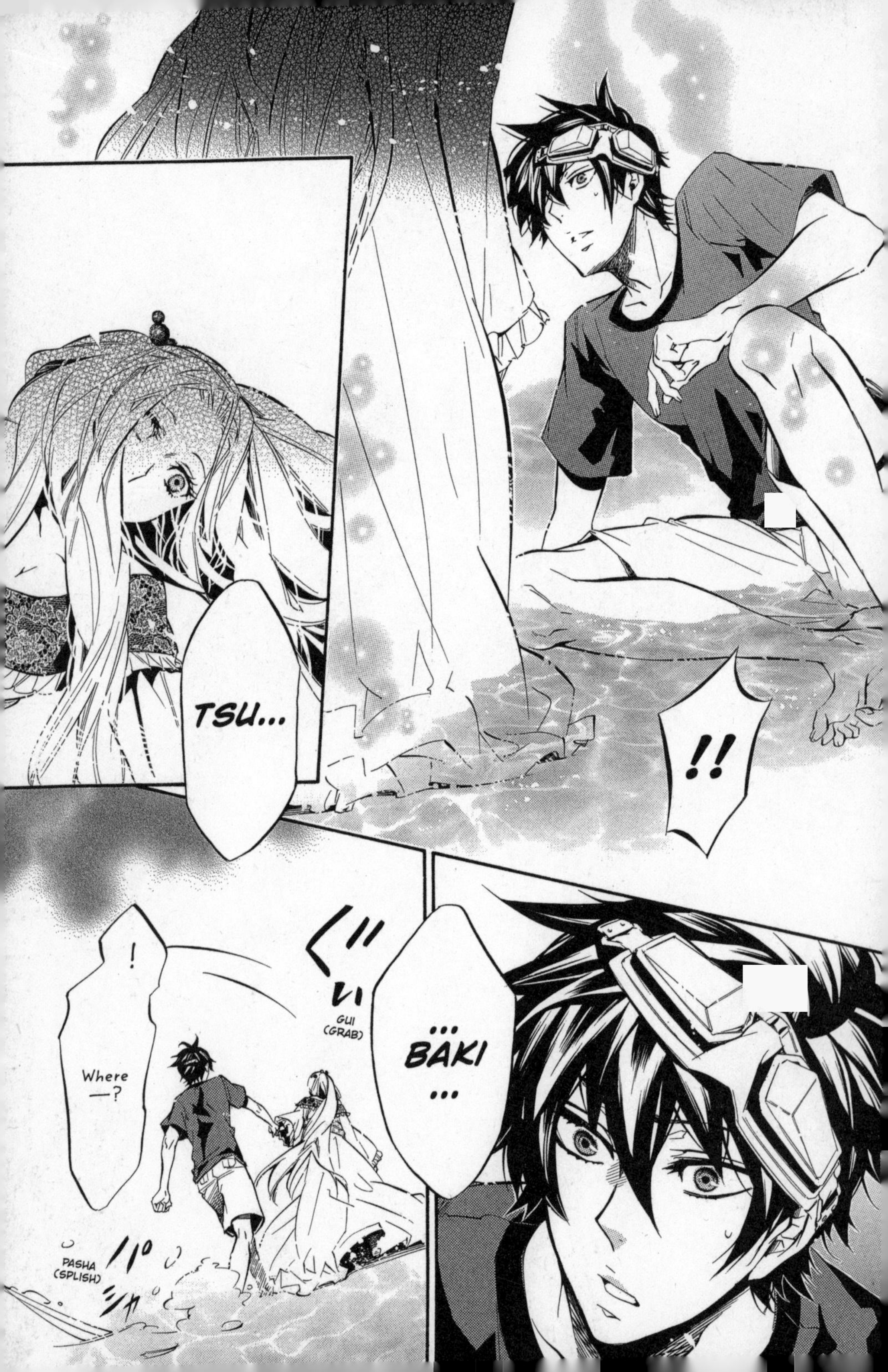
!!
TSU...
...BÄKI...
ぐい
GUI (GRAB)
!
Where—?
パシャ
PASHA (SPLISH)

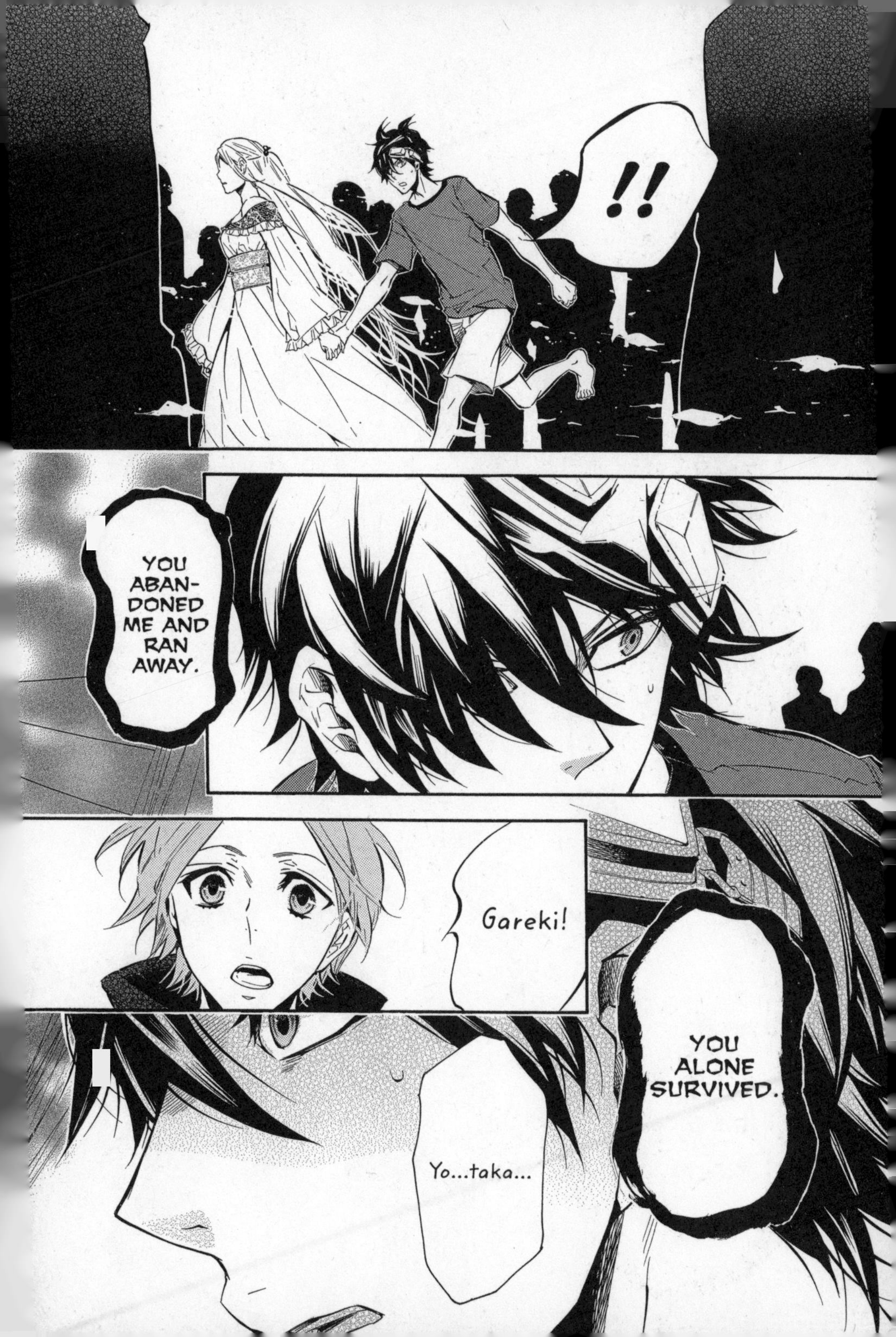
!!
YOU ABAN-DONED ME AND RAN AWAY.
Gareki!
YOU ALONE SURVIVED.
Yo...taka...

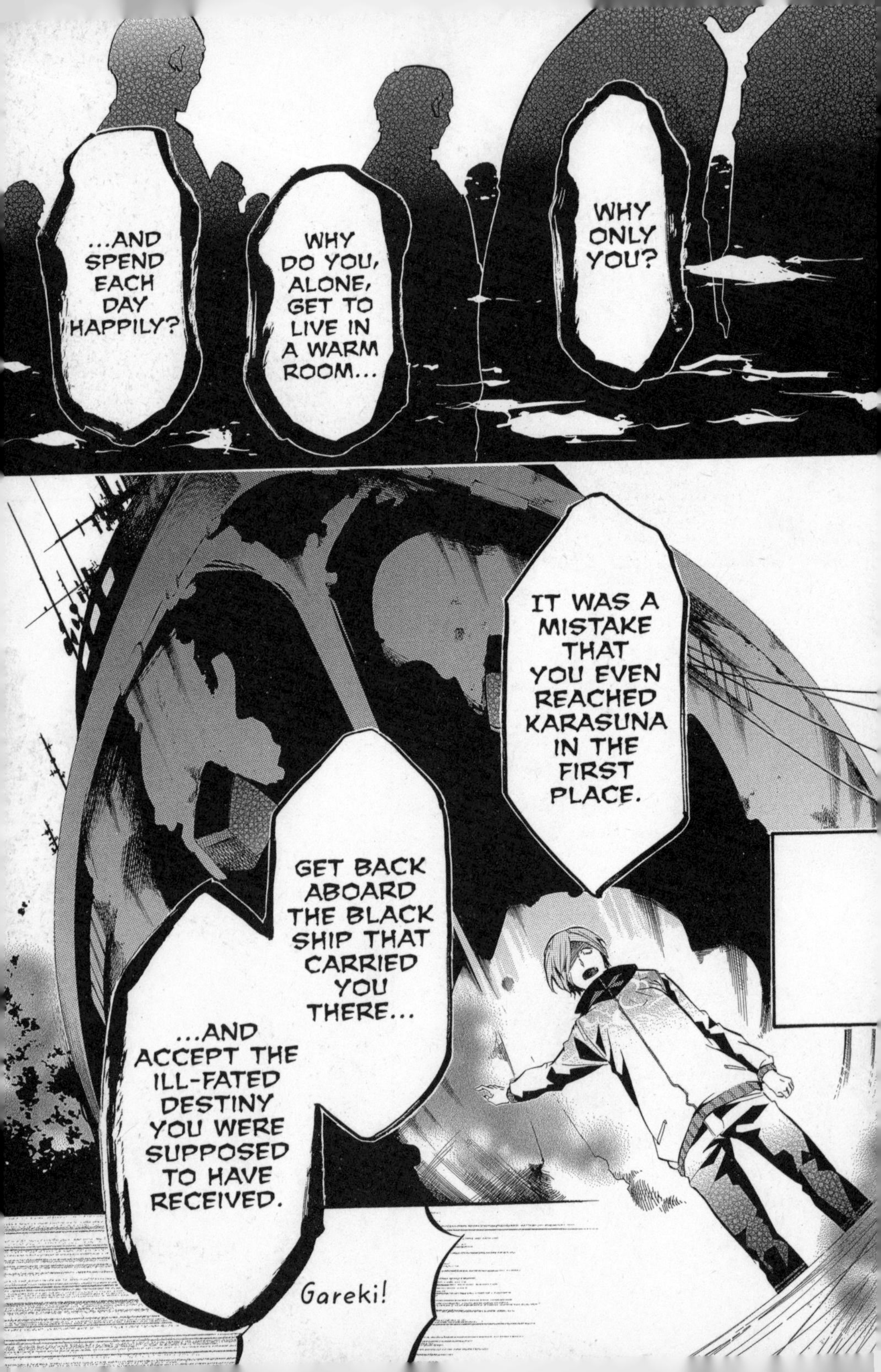
WHY ONLY YOU?
WHY DO YOU, ALONE, GET TO LIVE IN A WARM ROOM...
...AND SPEND EACH DAY HAPPILY?
IT WAS A MISTAKE THAT YOU EVEN REACHED KARASUNA IN THE FIRST PLACE.
GET BACK ABOARD THE BLACK SHIP THAT CARRIED YOU THERE...
...AND ACCEPT THE ILL-FATED DESTINY YOU WERE SUPPOSED TO HAVE RECEIVED.
Gareki!

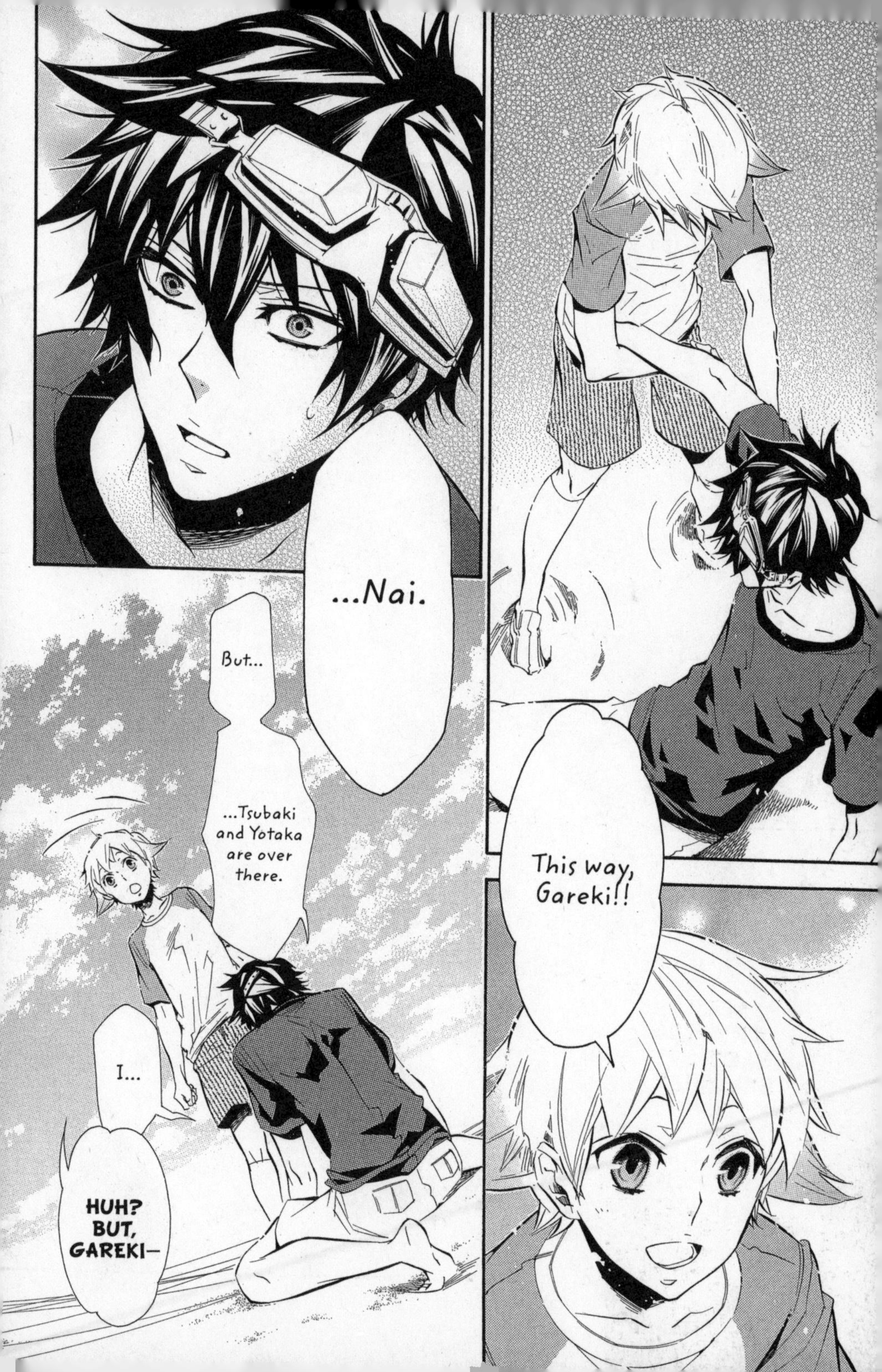
This way, Gareki!!
...Nai.
But...
...Tsubaki and Yotaka are over there.
I...
HUH? BUT, GAREKI—

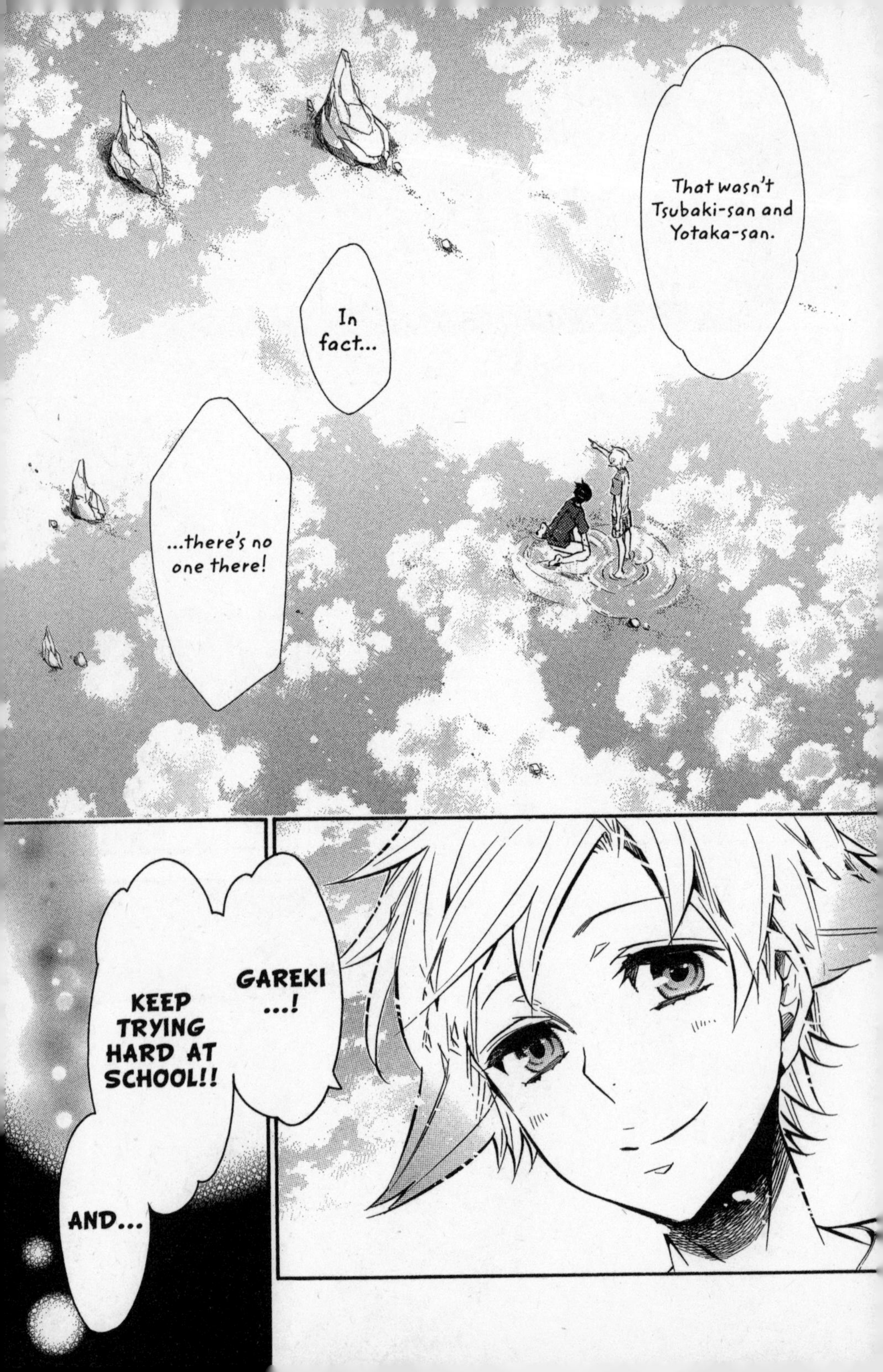

That wasn't Tsubaki-san and Yotaka-san.
In fact...
...there's no one there!
GAREKI ...!
KEEP TRYING HARD AT SCHOOL!!
AND...

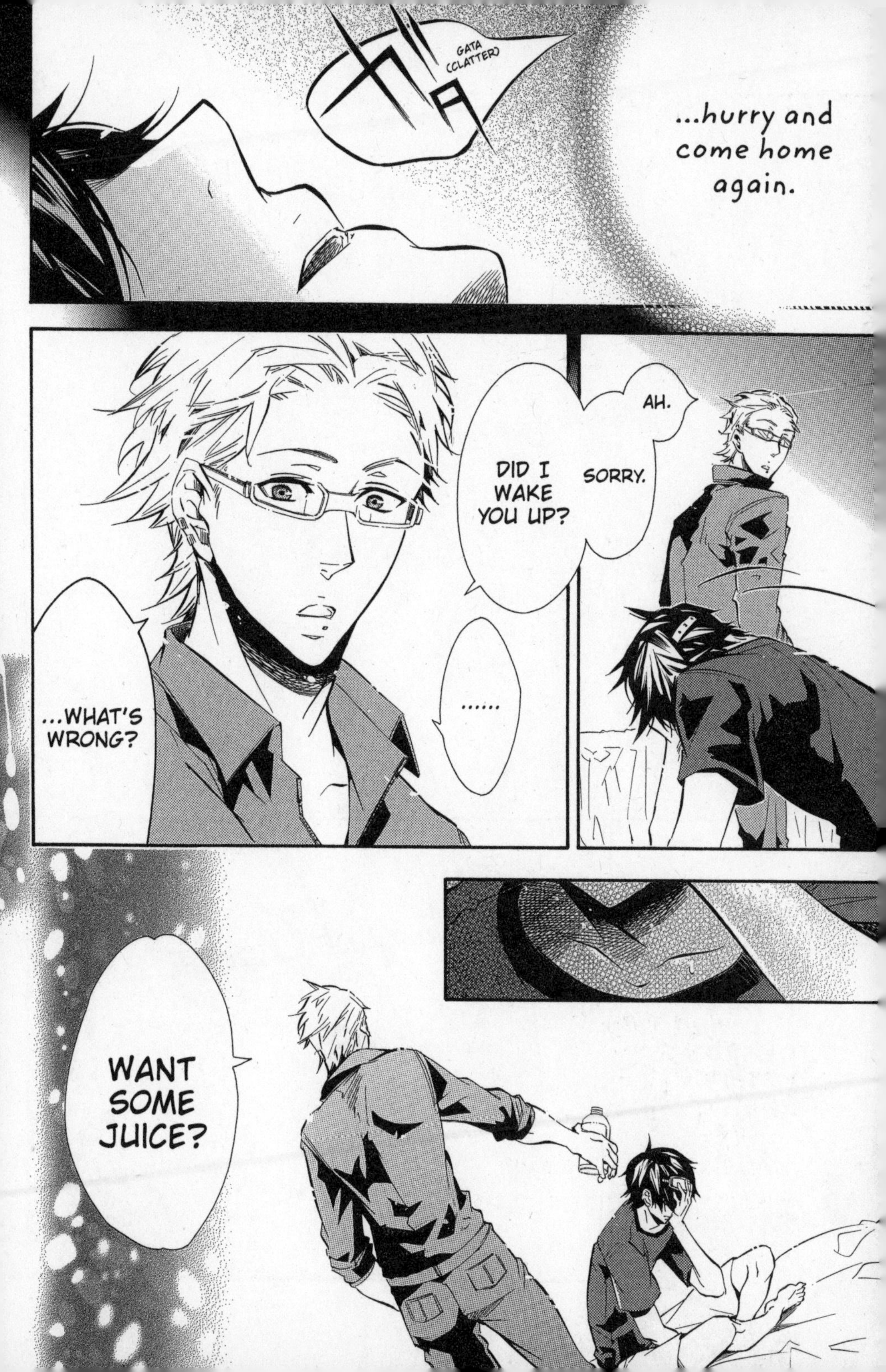
...hurry and come home again.
GATA (CLATTER)
AH.
SORRY.
DID I WAKE YOU UP?
......
...WHAT'S WRONG?
WANT SOME JUICE?

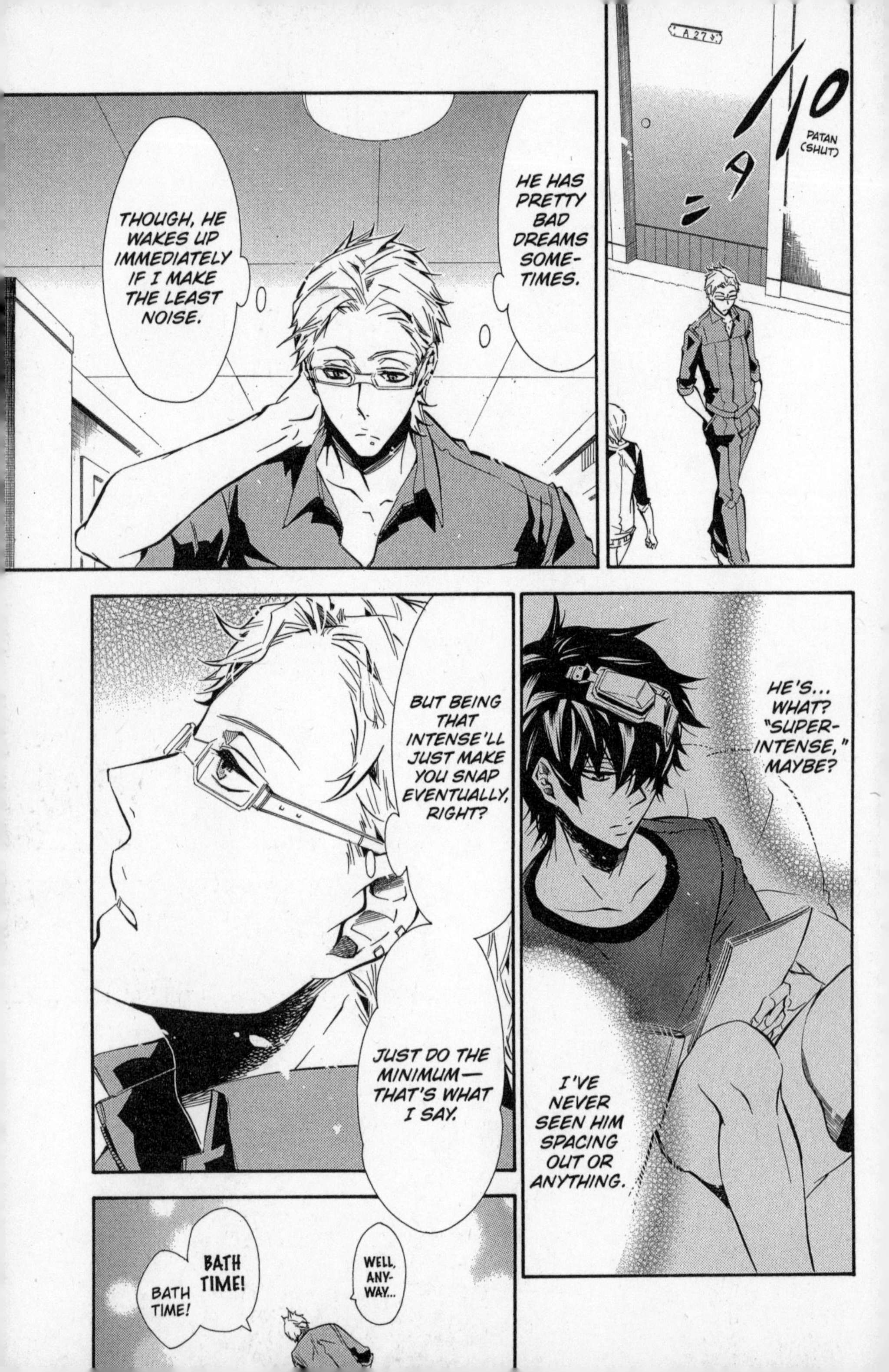
A 27
PATAN (SHUT)
HE HAS PRETTY BAD DREAMS SOME-TIMES.
THOUGH, HE WAKES UP IMMEDIATELY IF I MAKE THE LEAST NOISE.
HE'S... WHAT? "SUPER-INTENSE," MAYBE?
I'VE NEVER SEEN HIM SPACING OUT OR ANYTHING.
BUT BEING THAT INTENSE'LL JUST MAKE YOU SNAP EVENTUALLY, RIGHT?
JUST DO THE MINIMUM— THAT'S WHAT I SAY.
WELL, ANYWAY...
BATH TIME!
BATH TIME!

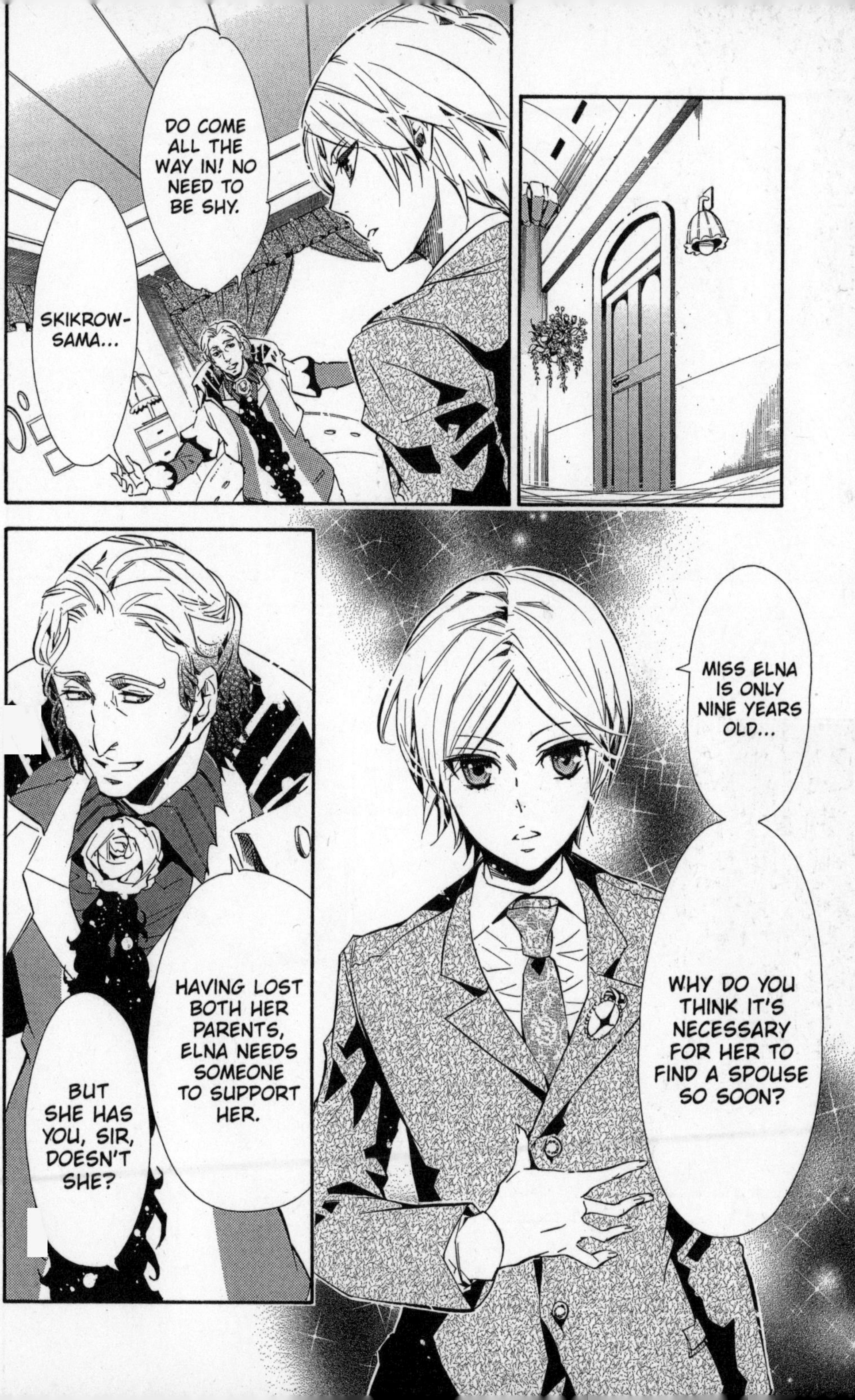
DO COME ALL THE WAY IN! NO NEED TO BE SHY.
SKIKROW-SAMA...
MISS ELNA IS ONLY NINE YEARS OLD...
WHY DO YOU THINK IT'S NECESSARY FOR HER TO FIND A SPOUSE SO SOON?
HAVING LOST BOTH HER PARENTS, ELNA NEEDS SOMEONE TO SUPPORT HER.
BUT SHE HAS YOU, SIR, DOESN'T SHE?

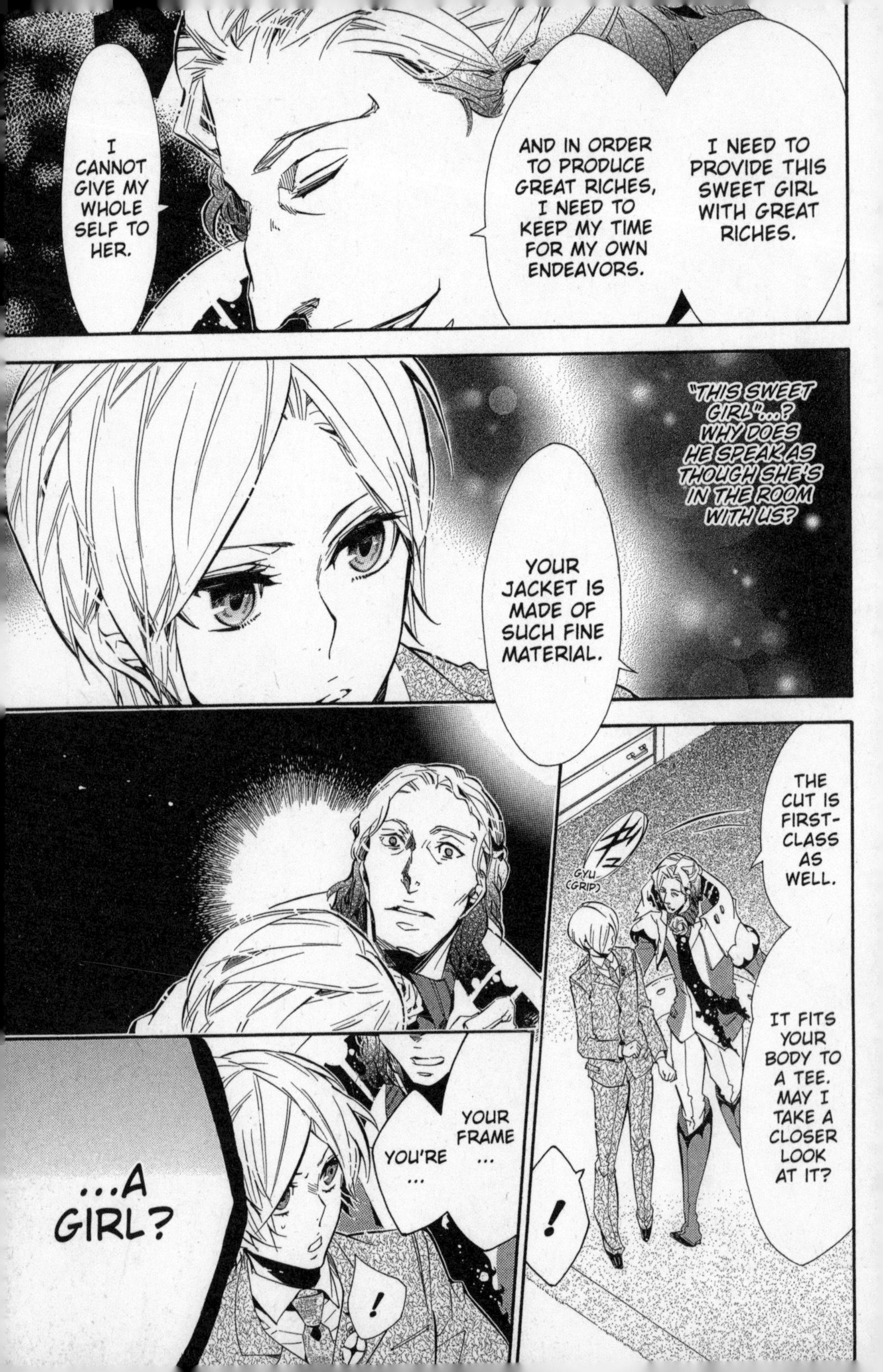
I NEED TO PROVIDE THIS SWEET GIRL WITH GREAT RICHES.
AND IN ORDER TO PRODUCE GREAT RICHES, I NEED TO KEEP MY TIME FOR MY OWN ENDEAVORS.
I CANNOT GIVE MY WHOLE SELF TO HER.
"THIS SWEET GIRL"...? WHY DOES HE SPEAK AS THOUGH SHE'S IN THE ROOM WITH US?
YOUR JACKET IS MADE OF SUCH FINE MATERIAL.
THE CUT IS FIRST-CLASS AS WELL.
GYU (GRIP)
IT FITS YOUR BODY TO A TEE. MAY I TAKE A CLOSER LOOK AT IT?
!
YOUR FRAME ...
YOU'RE ...
...A GIRL?
!

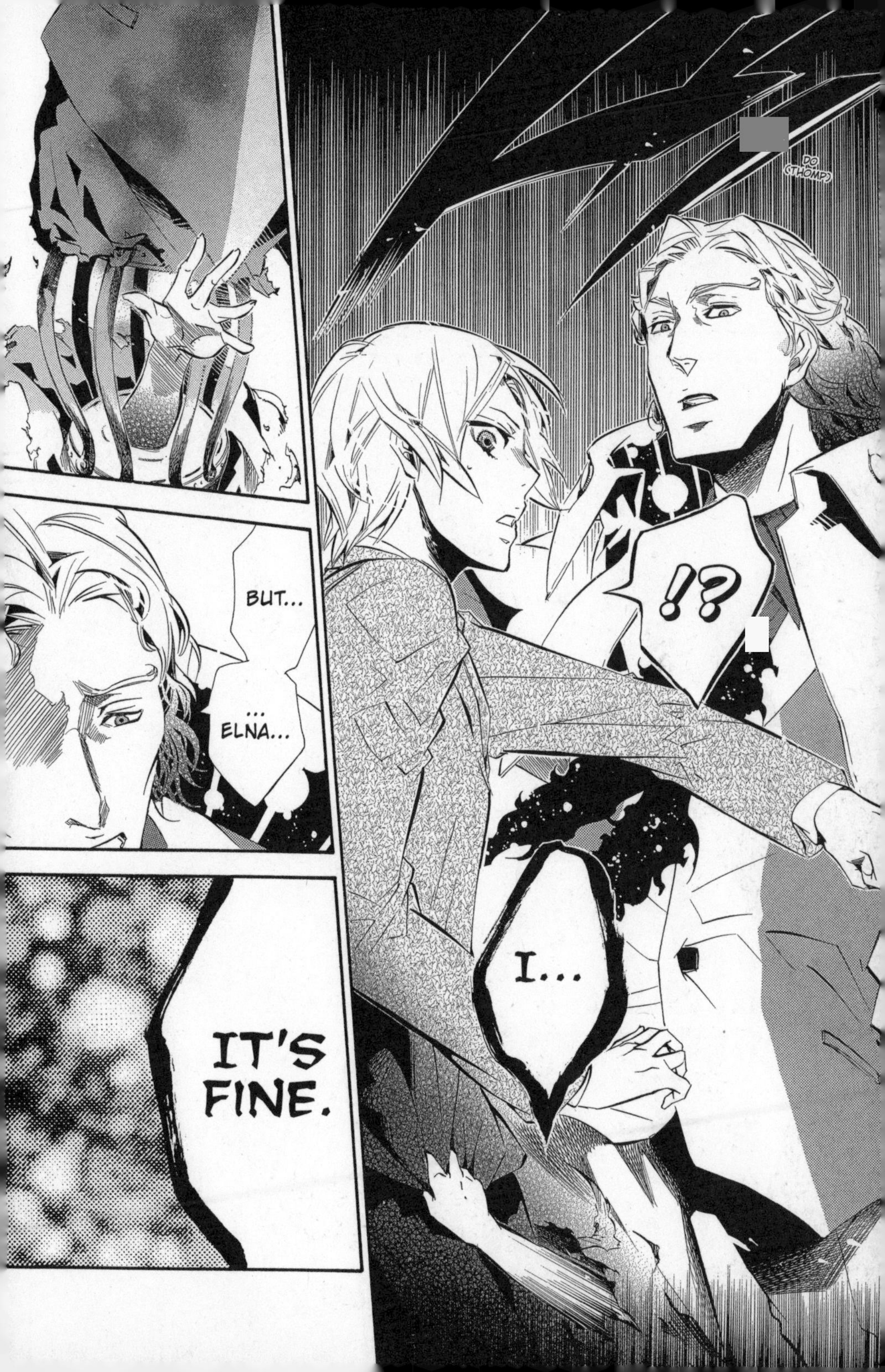
DO (THOMP)
!?
I...
BUT...
...ELNA...
IT'S FINE.

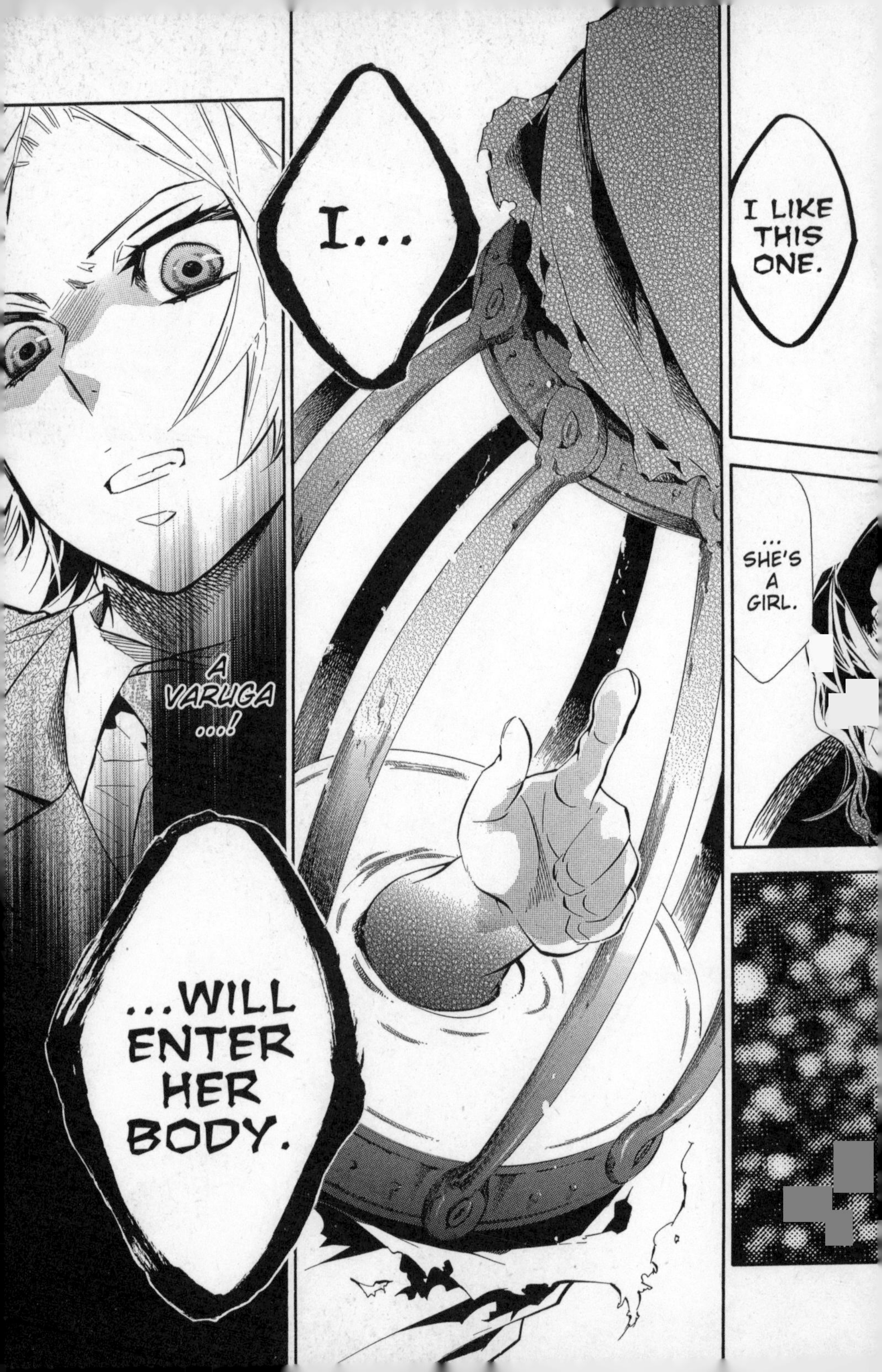
I LIKE THIS ONE.
...SHE'S A GIRL.
I...
A VARUGA...!
...WILL ENTER HER BODY.

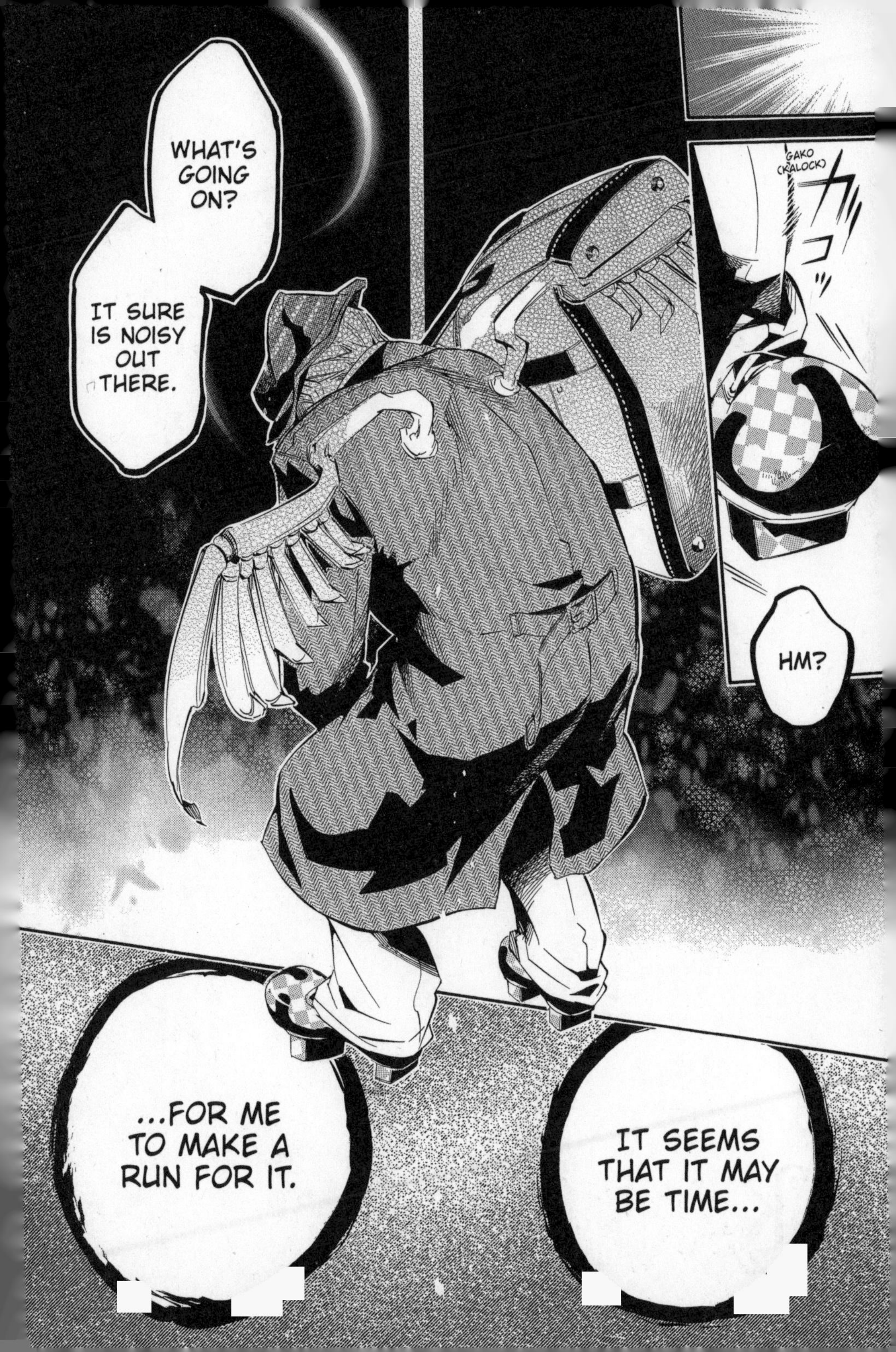
GAKO (KALOCK)
HM?
WHAT'S GOING ON?
IT SURE IS NOISY OUT THERE.
IT SEEMS THAT IT MAY BE TIME...
...FOR ME TO MAKE A RUN FOR IT.

KARNEVAL

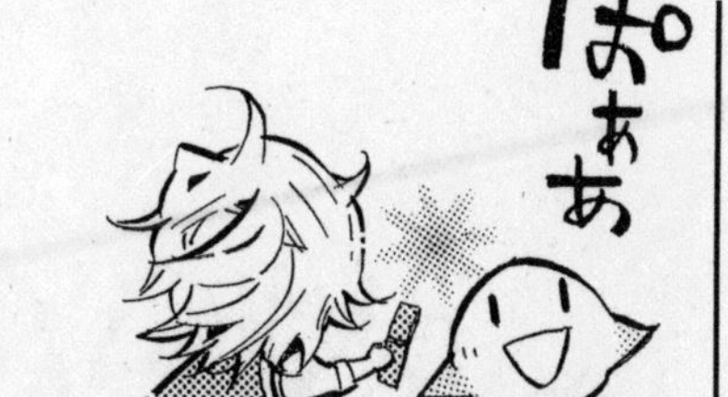
PAAA (SPARKLE)
ぱああ

KARNEVAL

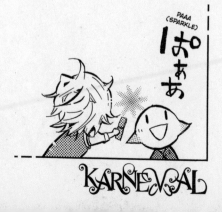

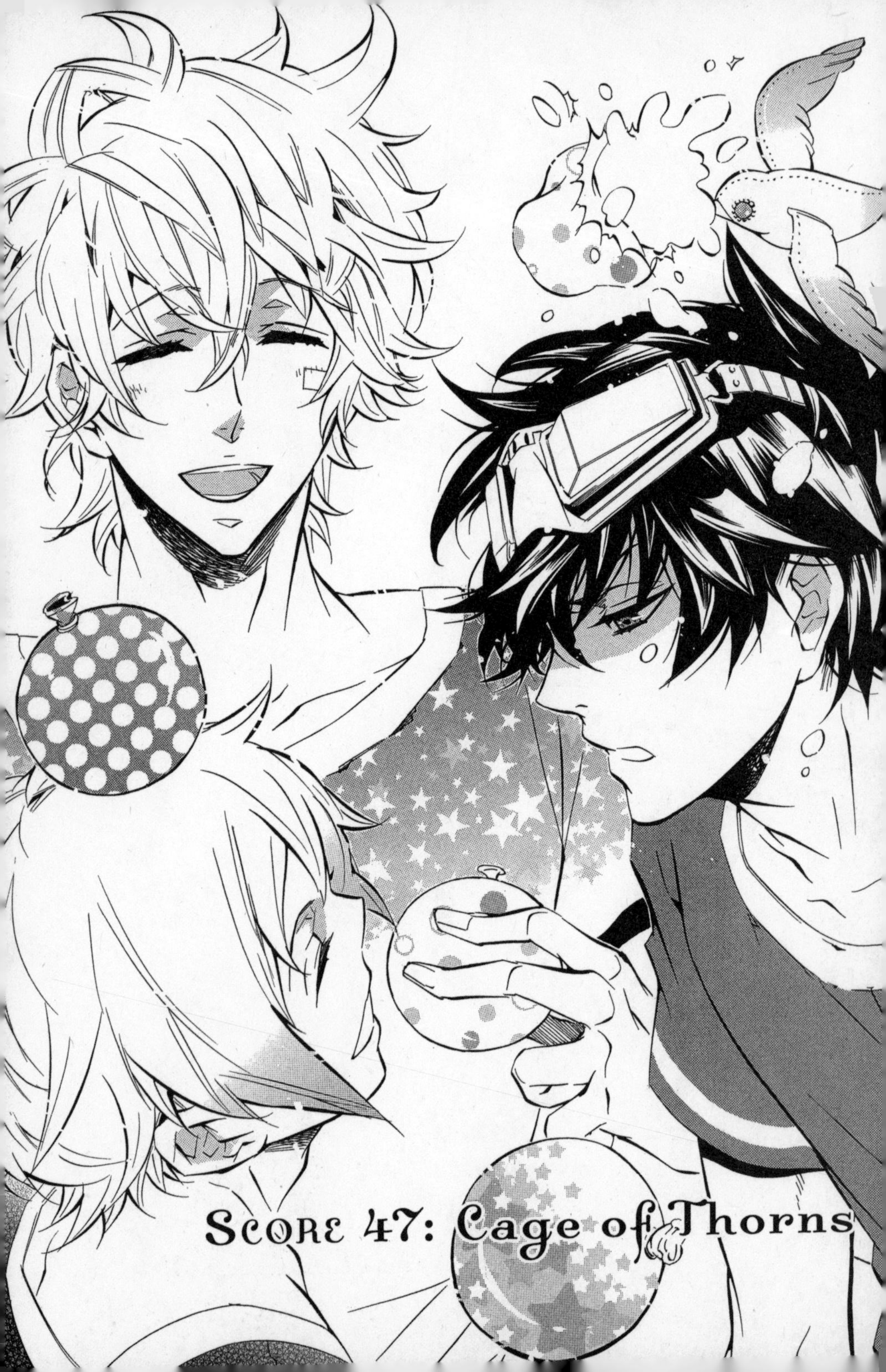

Score 47: Cage of Thorns

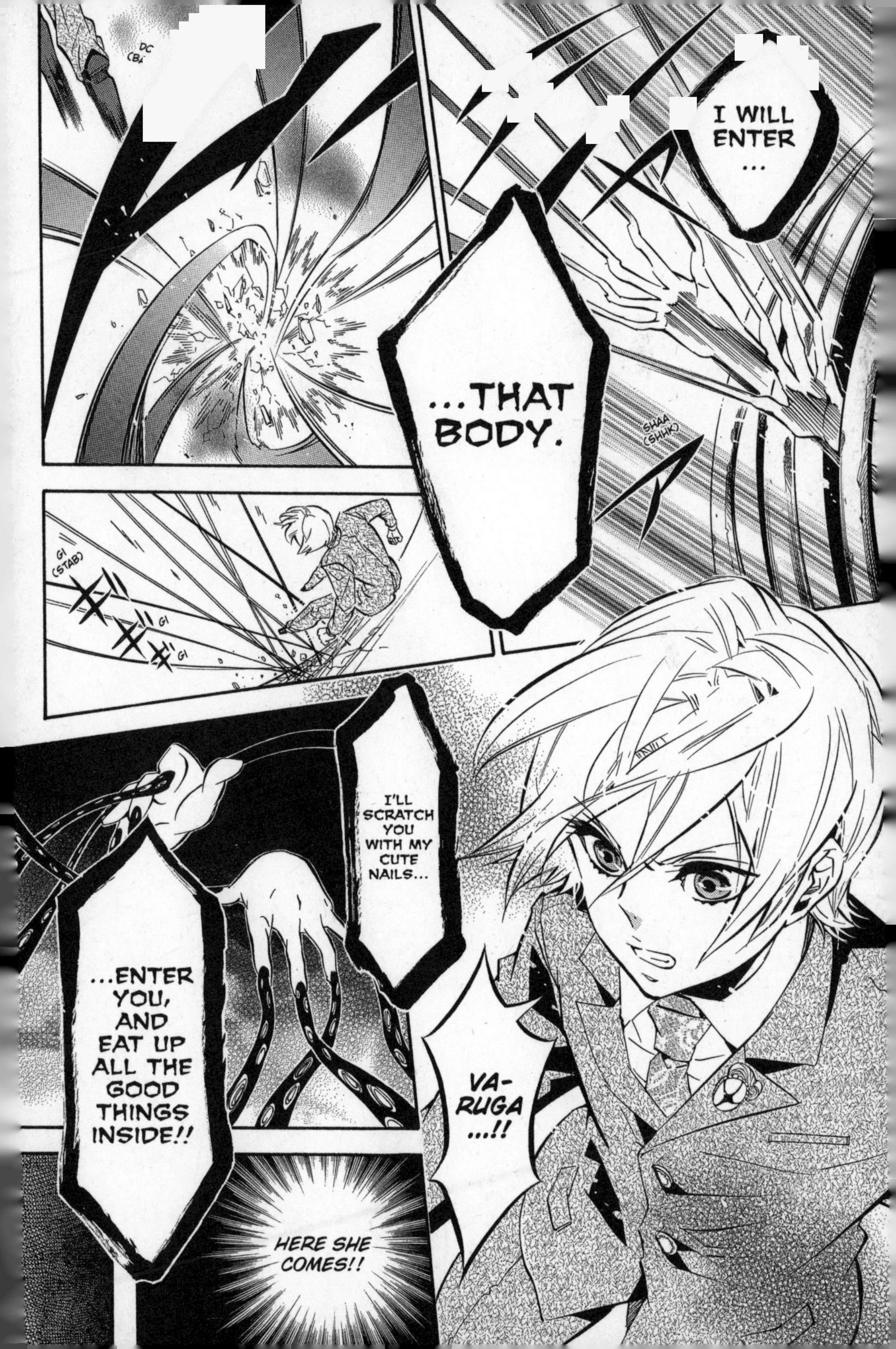
I WILL ENTER ...
...THAT BODY.
SHAA (SHHK)
DC
GI (STAB)
GI
GI
VA-RUGA ...!!
I'LL SCRATCH YOU WITH MY CUTE NAILS...
...ENTER YOU, AND EAT UP ALL THE GOOD THINGS INSIDE!!
HERE SHE COMES!!

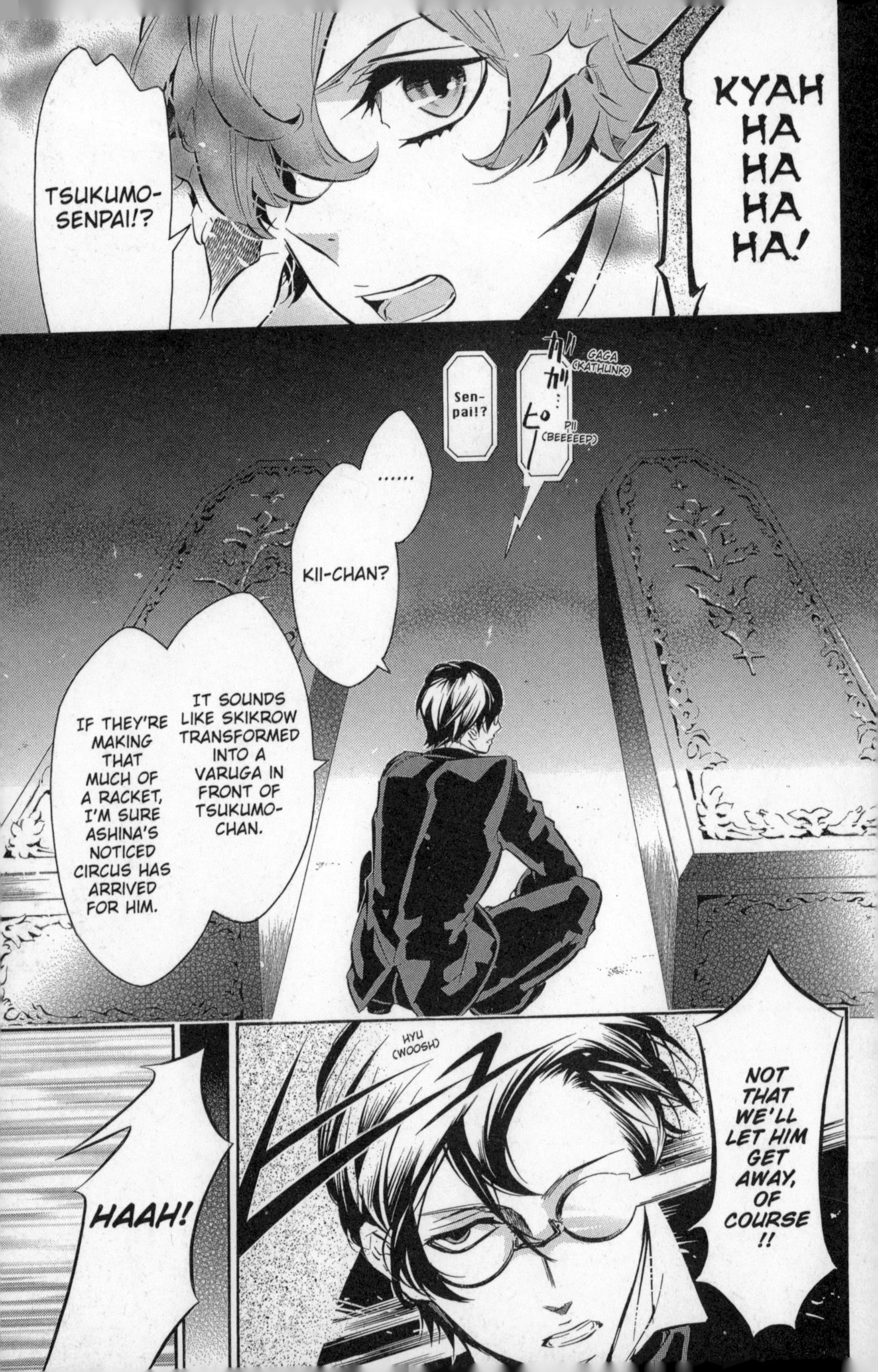
KYAH HA HA HA HA!
TSUKUMO-SENPAI!?
GAGA (KATHUNK)
PII (BEEEEEP)
Sen-pai!?
......
KII-CHAN?
IT SOUNDS LIKE SKIKROW TRANSFORMED INTO A VARUGA IN FRONT OF TSUKUMO-CHAN.
IF THEY'RE MAKING THAT MUCH OF A RACKET, I'M SURE ASHINA'S NOTICED CIRCUS HAS ARRIVED FOR HIM.
NOT THAT WE'LL LET HIM GET AWAY, OF COURSE!!
HYU (WOOSH)
HAAH!

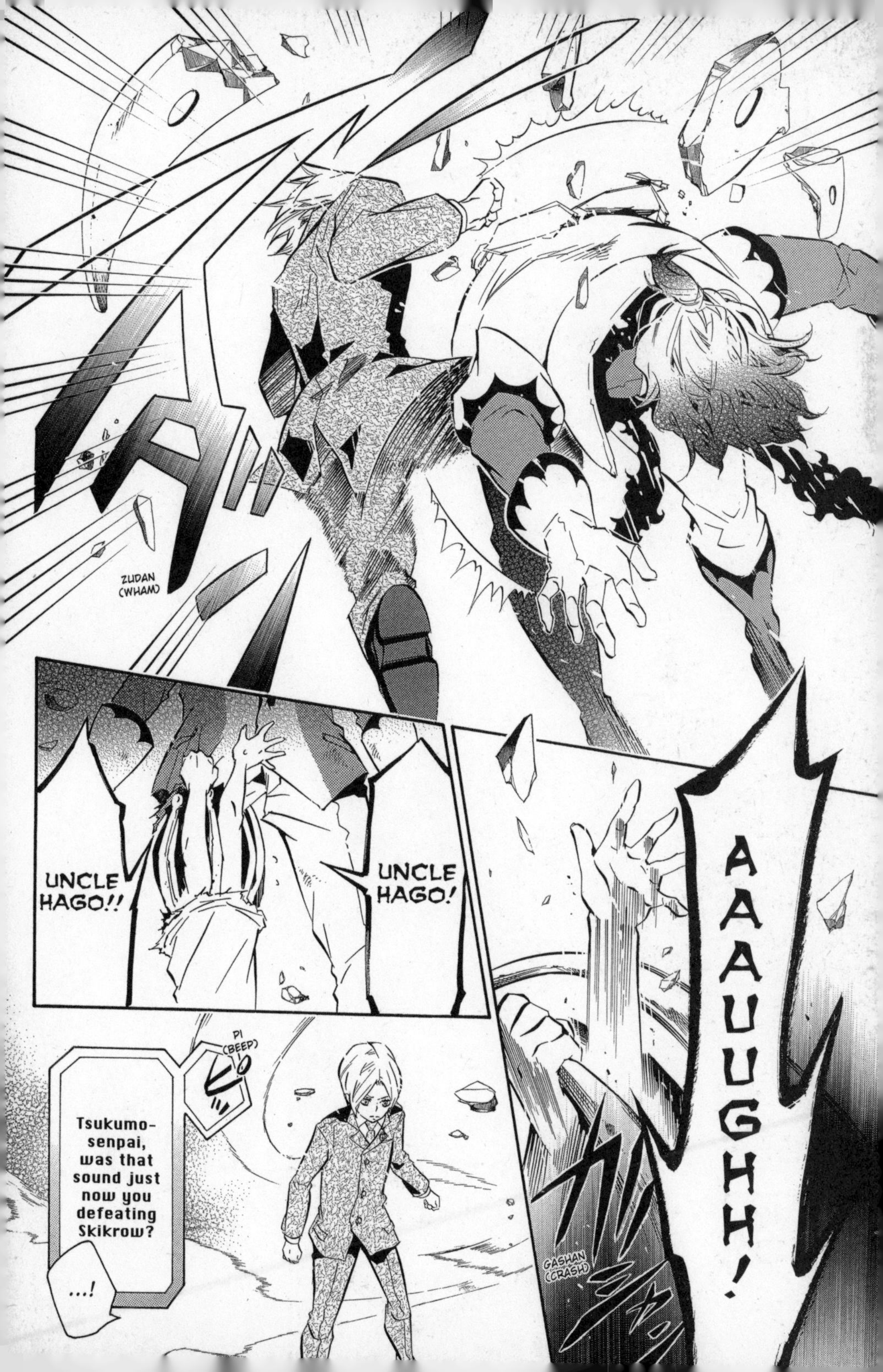
ZUDAN (WHAM)
AAAUGH!
GASHAN (CRASH)
UNCLE HAGO!
UNCLE HAGO!!
PI (BEEP)
Tsukumo-senpai, was that sound just now you defeating Skikrow?
...!

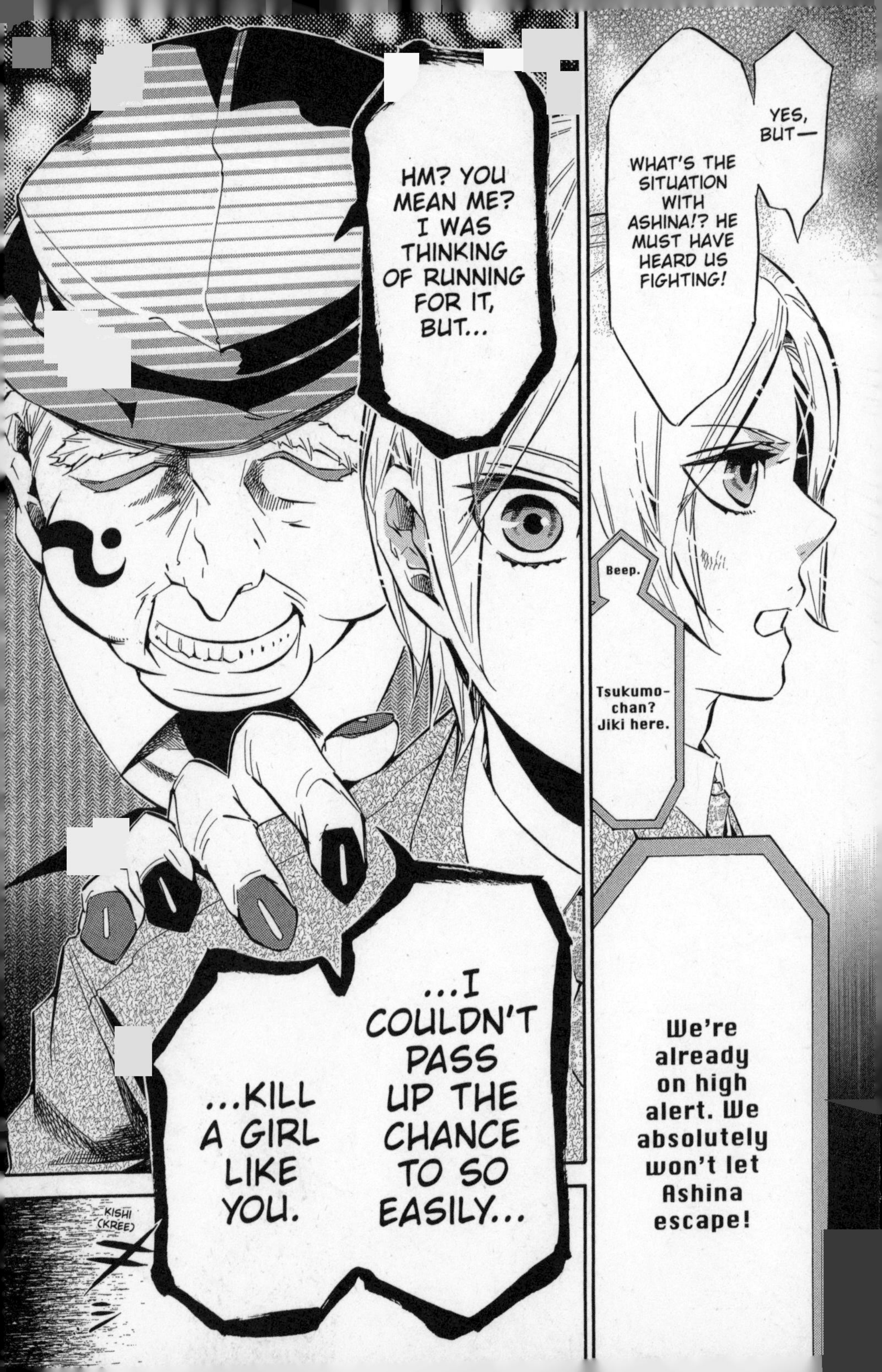
YES, BUT—
WHAT'S THE SITUATION WITH ASHINA!? HE MUST HAVE HEARD US FIGHTING!
Beep.
Tsukumo-chan? Jiki here.
We're already on high alert. We absolutely won't let Ashina escape!
HM? YOU MEAN ME? I WAS THINKING OF RUNNING FOR IT, BUT...
...I COULDN'T PASS UP THE CHANCE TO SO EASILY...
...KILL A GIRL LIKE YOU.
KISHI (KREE)

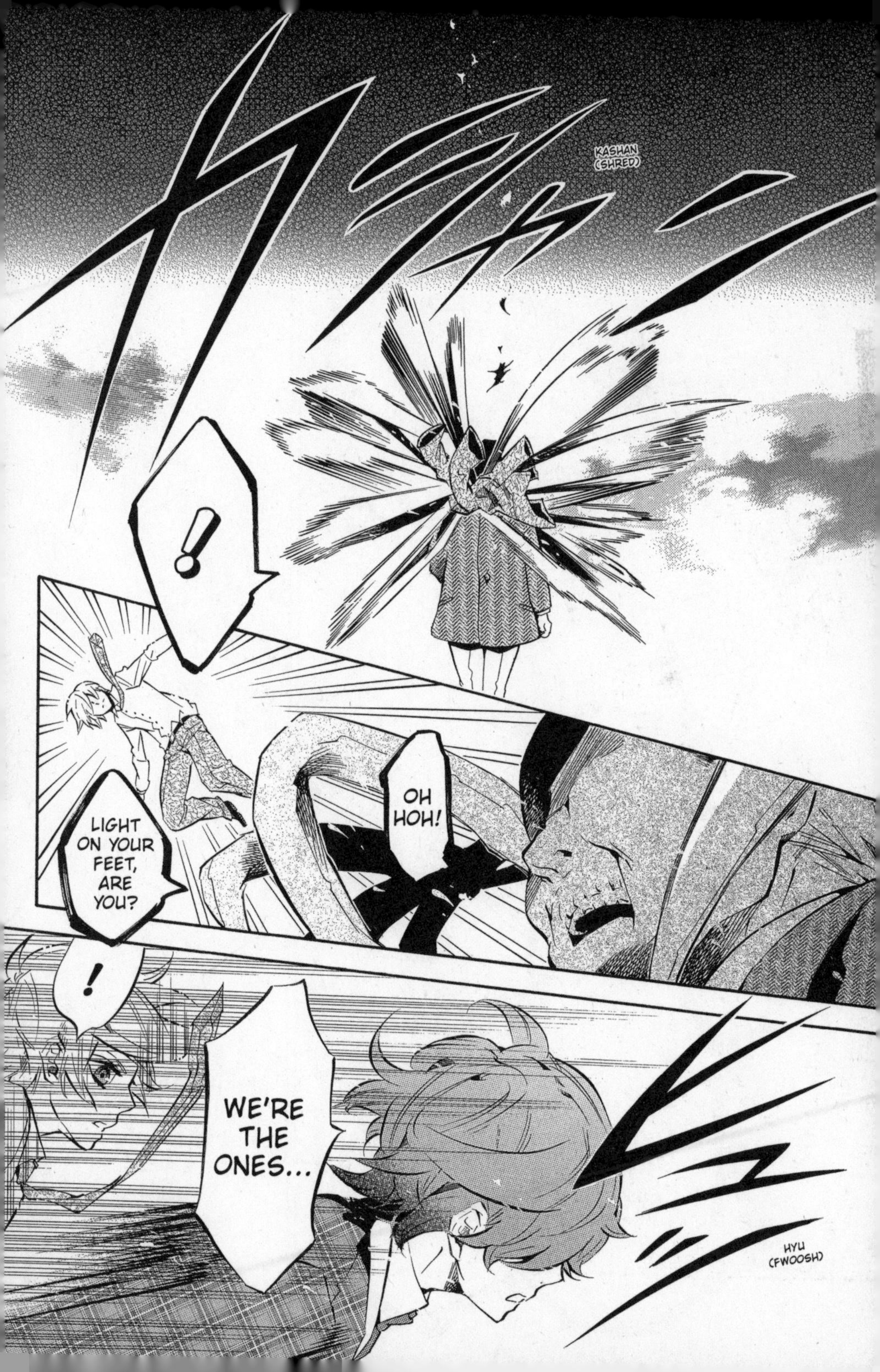
KASHAN
(SHRED)
!
OH HOH!
LIGHT ON YOUR FEET, ARE YOU?
HYU
(FWOOSH)
WE'RE THE ONES...
!

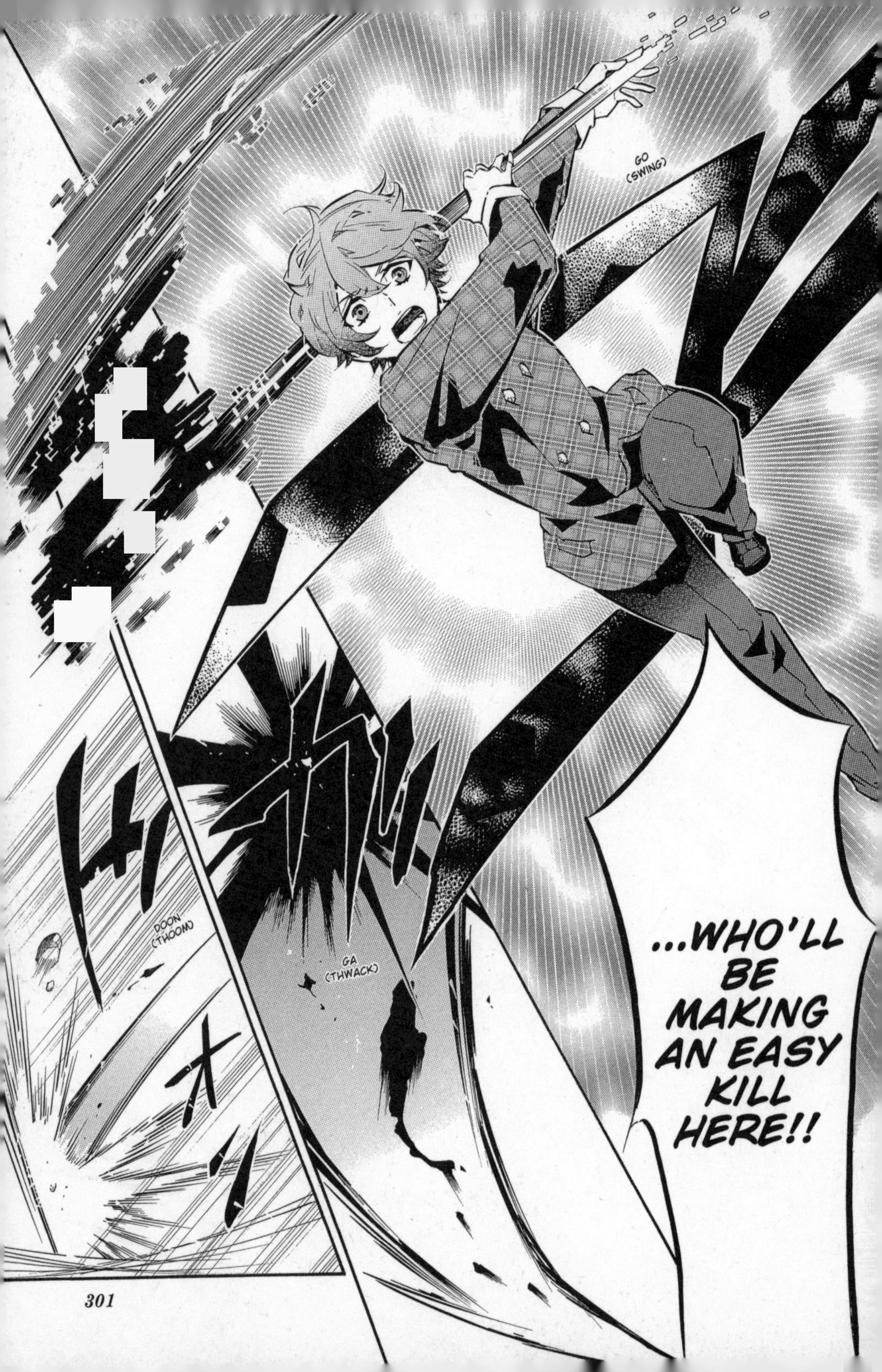
GO (SWING)
...WHO'LL BE MAKING AN EASY KILL HERE!!
GA (THWACK)
DOON (THOOM)

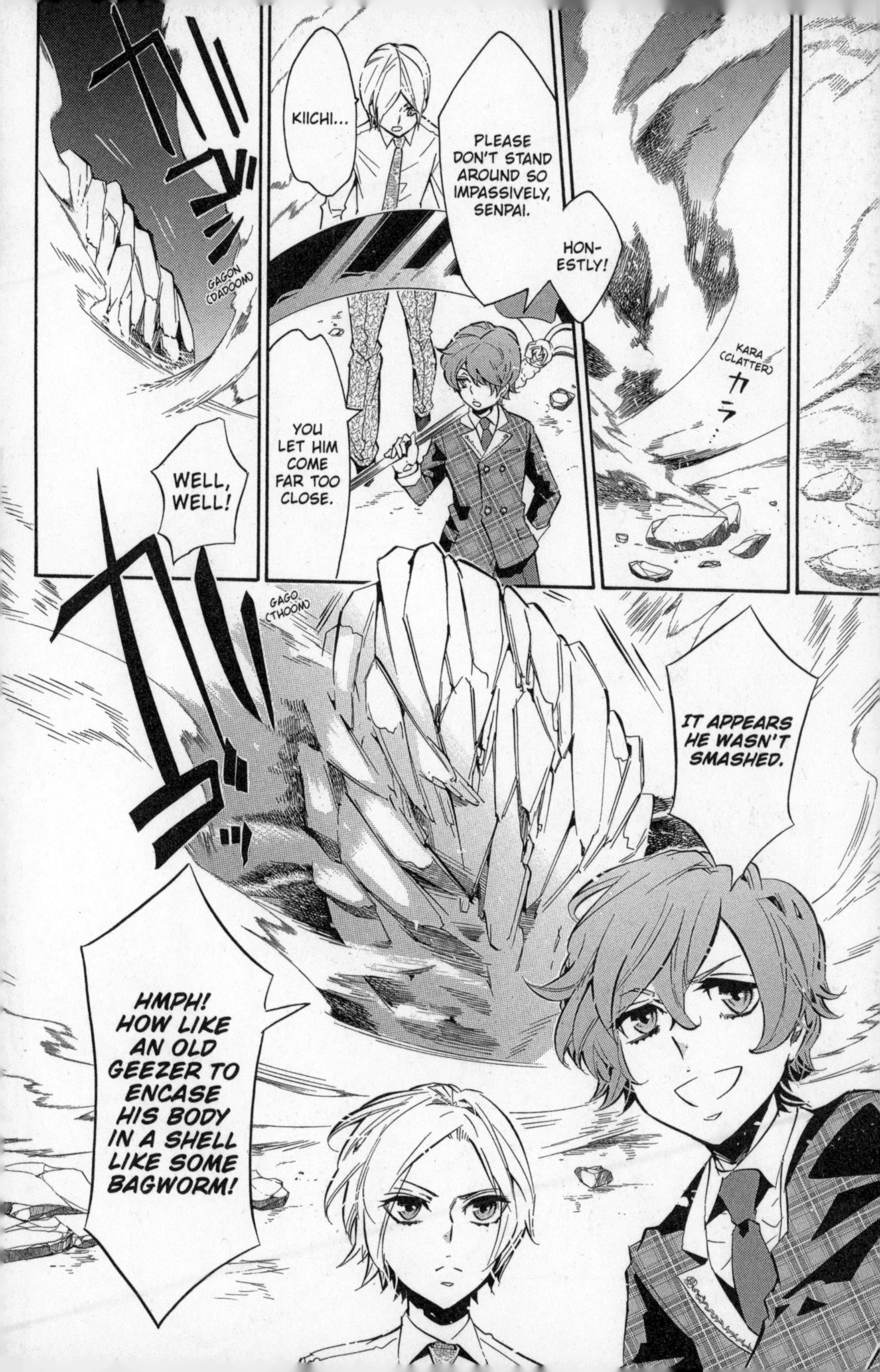
KARA (CLATTER)
カラ…
PLEASE DON'T STAND AROUND SO IMPASSIVELY, SENPAI.
HON-ESTLY!
KIICHI...
YOU LET HIM COME FAR TOO CLOSE.
GAGON (DADOOM)
WELL, WELL!
GAGO (THOOM)
IT APPEARS HE WASN'T SMASHED.
HMPH! HOW LIKE AN OLD GEEZER TO ENCASE HIS BODY IN A SHELL LIKE SOME BAGWORM!

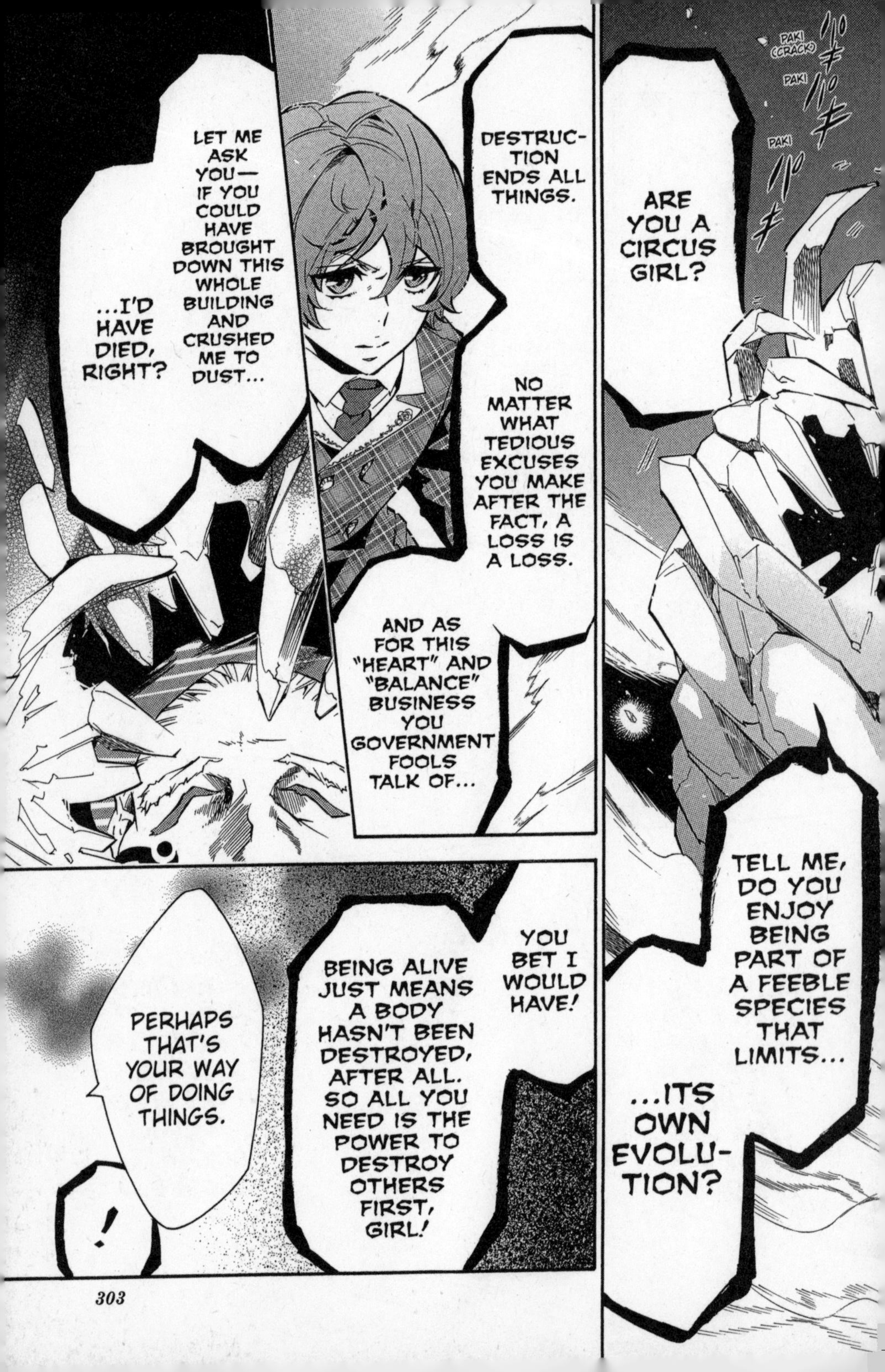
PAKI (CRACK)
PAKI
PAKI
ARE YOU A CIRCUS GIRL?
TELL ME, DO YOU ENJOY BEING PART OF A FEEBLE SPECIES THAT LIMITS...
...ITS OWN EVOLUTION?
DESTRUCTION ENDS ALL THINGS.
NO MATTER WHAT TEDIOUS EXCUSES YOU MAKE AFTER THE FACT, A LOSS IS A LOSS.
AND AS FOR THIS "HEART" AND "BALANCE" BUSINESS YOU GOVERNMENT FOOLS TALK OF...
LET ME ASK YOU—IF YOU COULD HAVE BROUGHT DOWN THIS WHOLE BUILDING AND CRUSHED ME TO DUST...
...I'D HAVE DIED, RIGHT?
YOU BET I WOULD HAVE!
BEING ALIVE JUST MEANS A BODY HASN'T BEEN DESTROYED, AFTER ALL. SO ALL YOU NEED IS THE POWER TO DESTROY OTHERS FIRST, GIRL!
PERHAPS THAT'S YOUR WAY OF DOING THINGS.
!

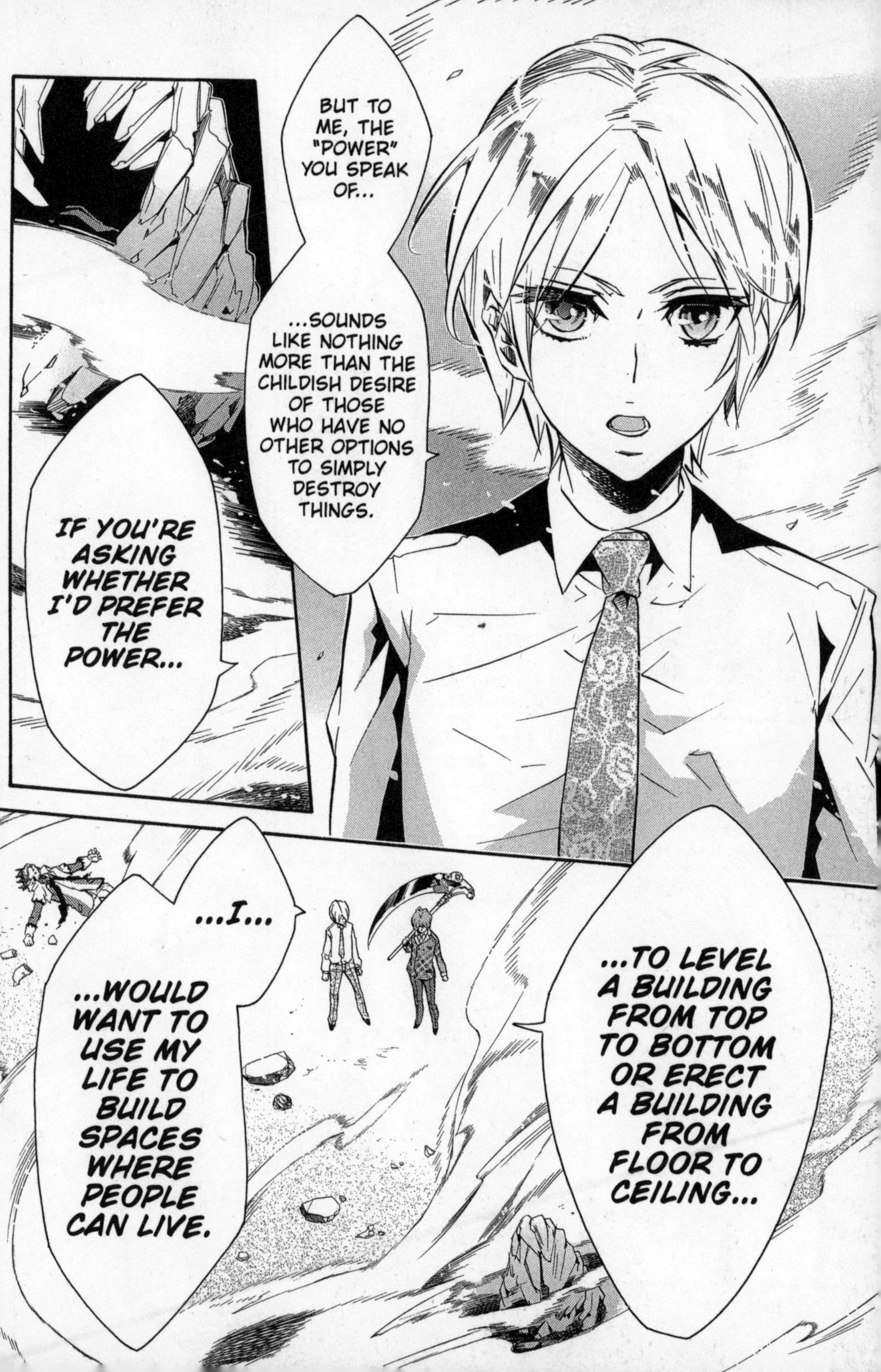
BUT TO ME, THE "POWER" YOU SPEAK OF...
...SOUNDS LIKE NOTHING MORE THAN THE CHILDISH DESIRE OF THOSE WHO HAVE NO OTHER OPTIONS TO SIMPLY DESTROY THINGS.
IF YOU'RE ASKING WHETHER I'D PREFER THE POWER...
...TO LEVEL A BUILDING FROM TOP TO BOTTOM OR ERECT A BUILDING FROM FLOOR TO CEILING...
...I...
...WOULD WANT TO USE MY LIFE TO BUILD SPACES WHERE PEOPLE CAN LIVE.

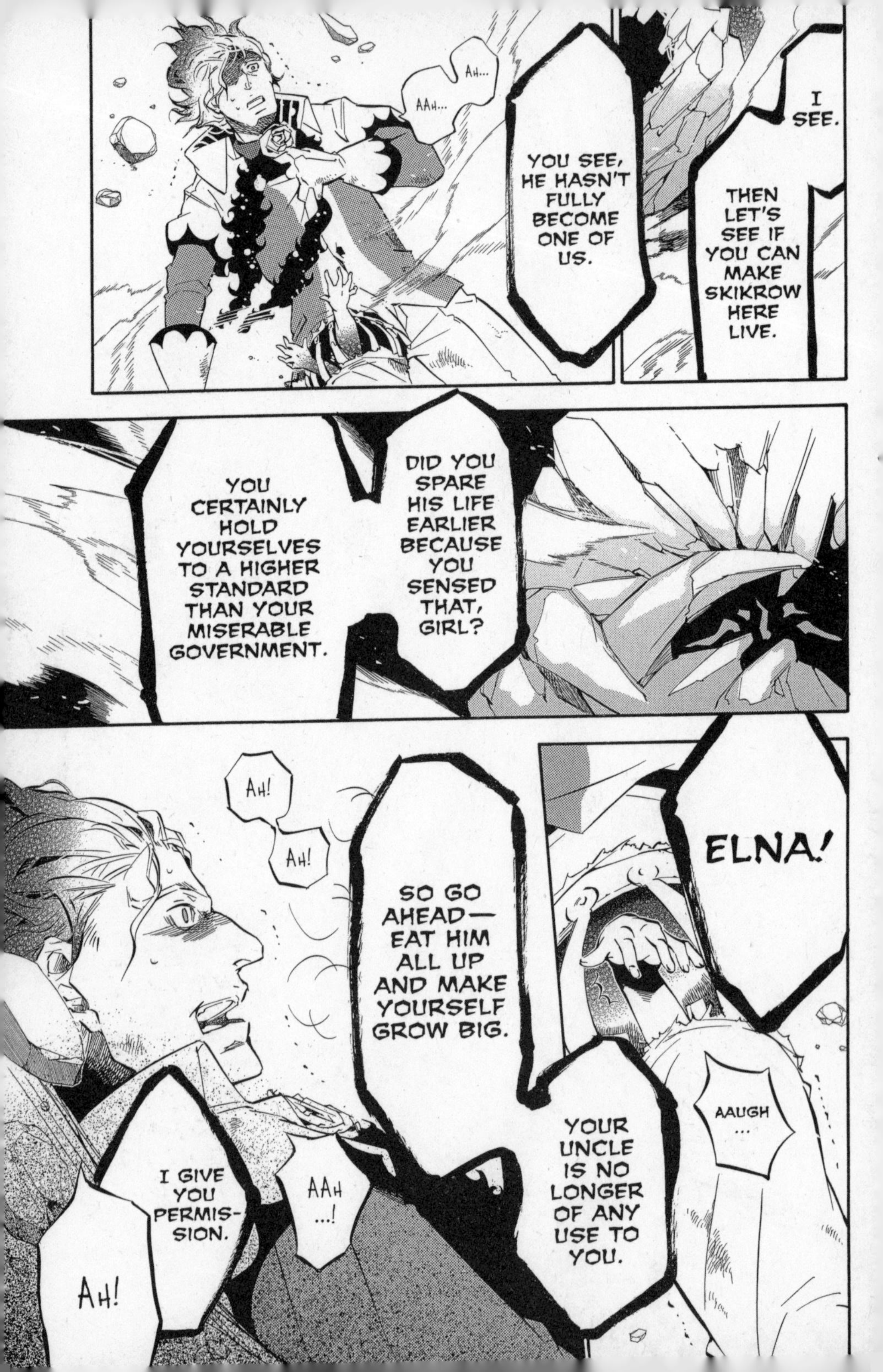
I SEE.
THEN LET'S SEE IF YOU CAN MAKE SKIKROW HERE LIVE.
YOU SEE, HE HASN'T FULLY BECOME ONE OF US.
AH...
AAH...
DID YOU SPARE HIS LIFE EARLIER BECAUSE YOU SENSED THAT, GIRL?
YOU CERTAINLY HOLD YOURSELVES TO A HIGHER STANDARD THAN YOUR MISERABLE GOVERNMENT.
ELNA!
AAUGH...
AH!
AH!
SO GO AHEAD—EAT HIM ALL UP AND MAKE YOURSELF GROW BIG.
YOUR UNCLE IS NO LONGER OF ANY USE TO YOU.
AAH...!
I GIVE YOU PERMISSION.
AH!

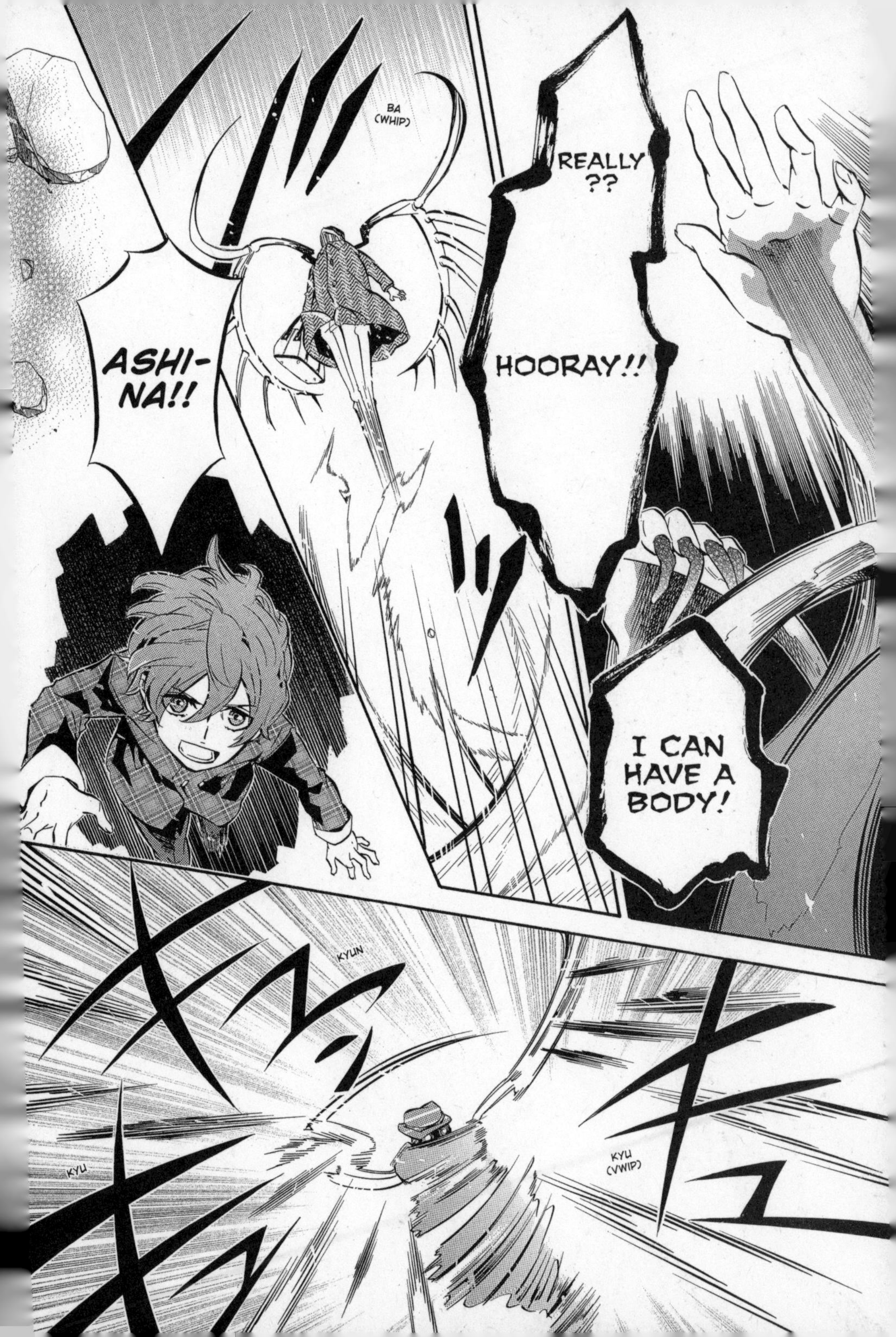
REALLY ??
HOORAY!!
I CAN HAVE A BODY!
BA (WHIP)
ASHI-NA!!
KYUN
KYU (VWIP)
KYU

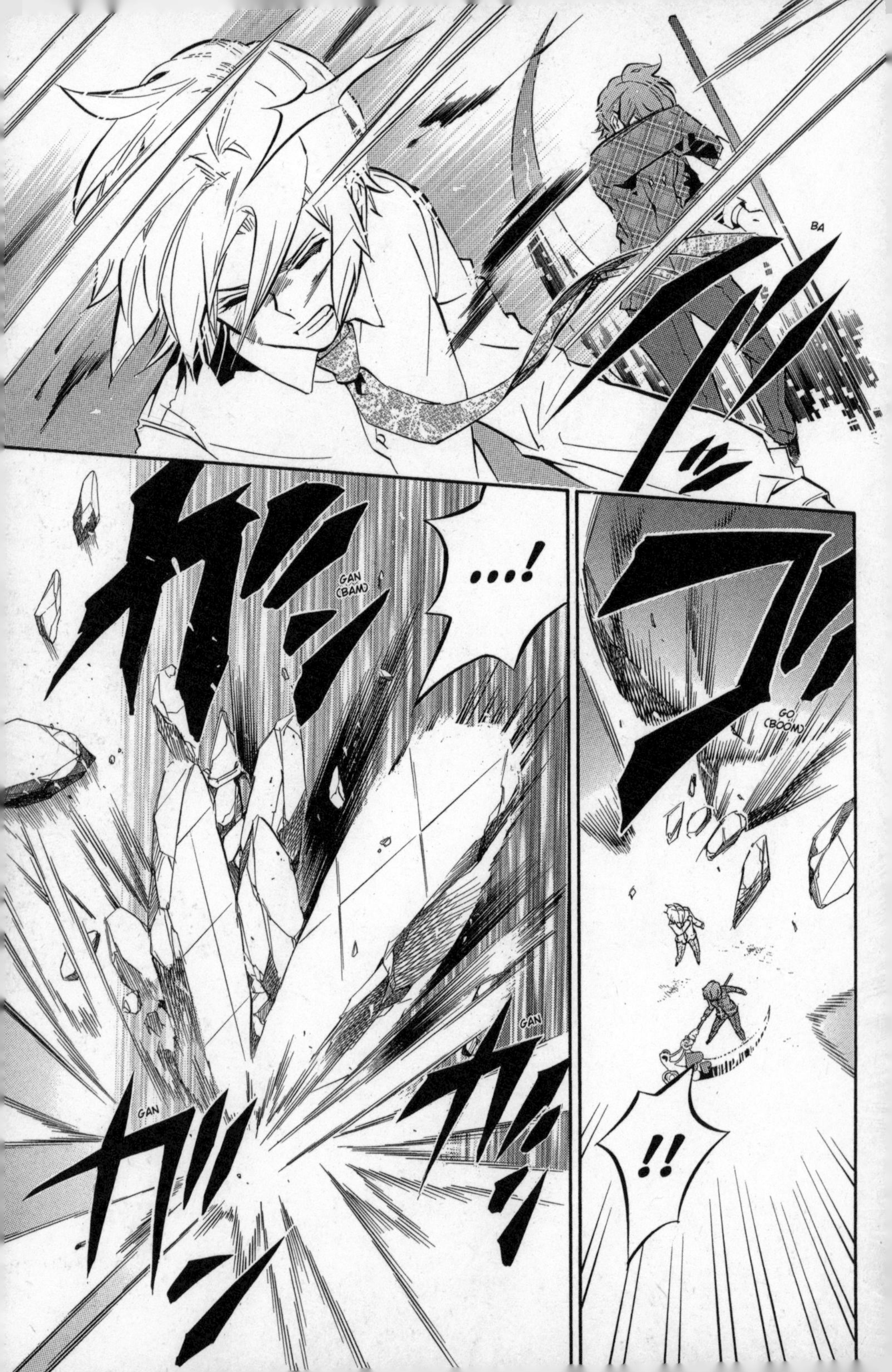
BA
GO (BOOM)
!!
...!
GAN (BAM)
GAN
GAN

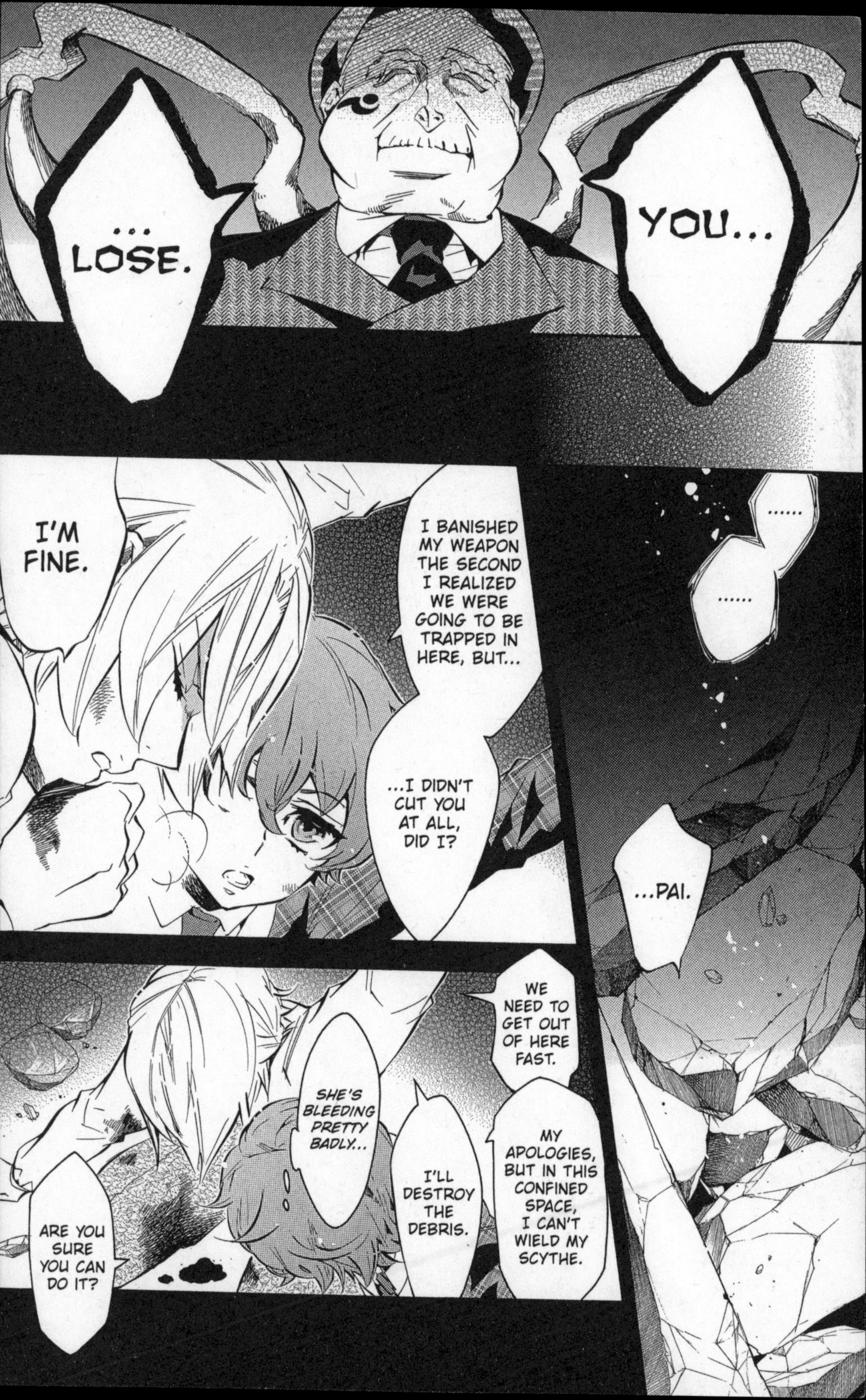
YOU...
...LOSE.
......
......
...PAI.
I BANISHED MY WEAPON THE SECOND I REALIZED WE WERE GOING TO BE TRAPPED IN HERE, BUT...
...I DIDN'T CUT YOU AT ALL, DID I?
I'M FINE.
WE NEED TO GET OUT OF HERE FAST.
SHE'S BLEEDING PRETTY BADLY...
MY APOLOGIES, BUT IN THIS CONFINED SPACE, I CAN'T WIELD MY SCYTHE.
I'LL DESTROY THE DEBRIS.
ARE YOU SURE YOU CAN DO IT?

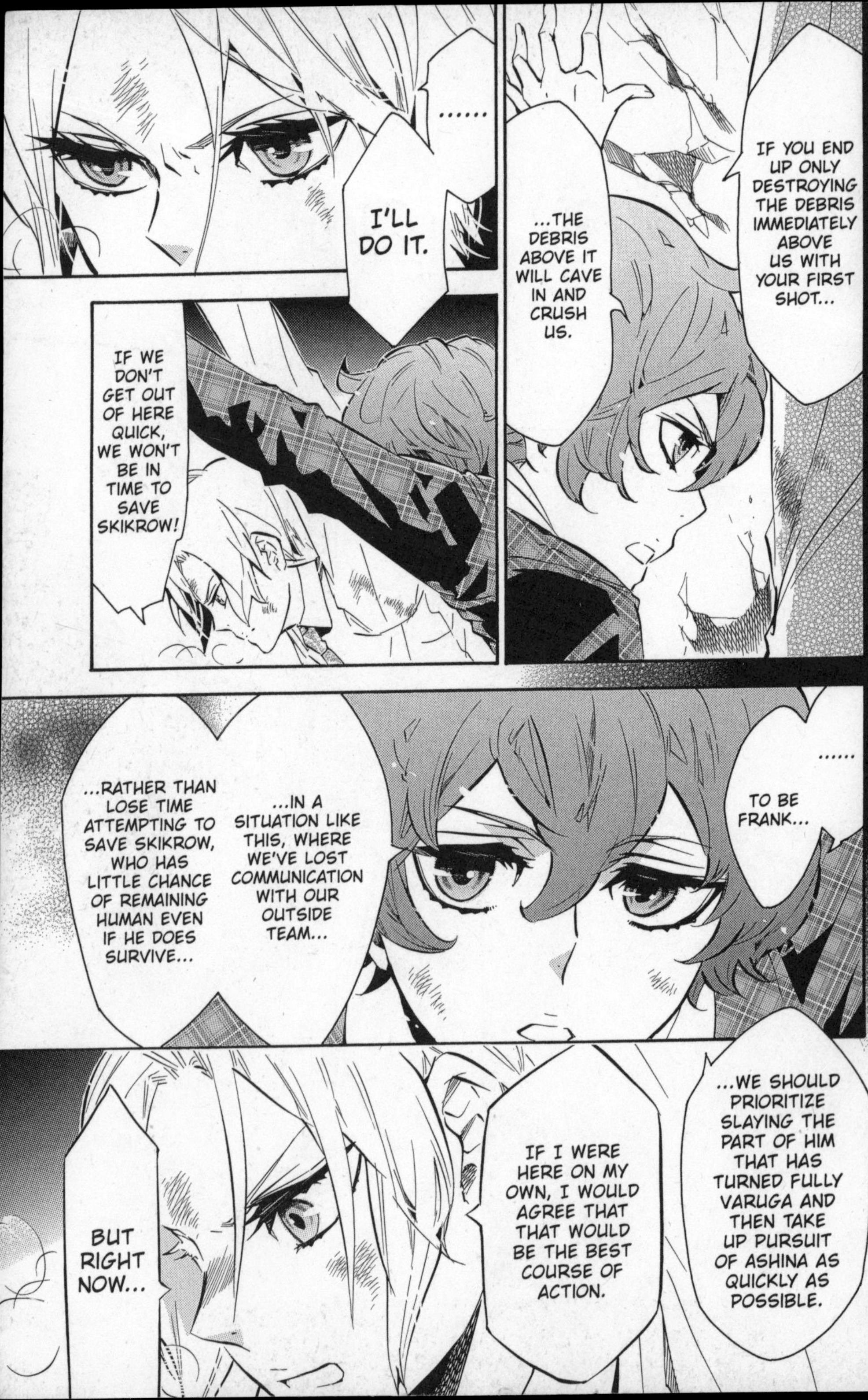
IF YOU END UP ONLY DESTROYING THE DEBRIS IMMEDIATELY ABOVE US WITH YOUR FIRST SHOT...
...THE DEBRIS ABOVE IT WILL CAVE IN AND CRUSH US.
......
I'LL DO IT.
IF WE DON'T GET OUT OF HERE QUICK, WE WON'T BE IN TIME TO SAVE SKIKROW!
......
TO BE FRANK...
...IN A SITUATION LIKE THIS, WHERE WE'VE LOST COMMUNICATION WITH OUR OUTSIDE TEAM...
...RATHER THAN LOSE TIME ATTEMPTING TO SAVE SKIKROW, WHO HAS LITTLE CHANCE OF REMAINING HUMAN EVEN IF HE DOES SURVIVE...
...WE SHOULD PRIORITIZE SLAYING THE PART OF HIM THAT HAS TURNED FULLY VARUGA AND THEN TAKE UP PURSUIT OF ASHINA AS QUICKLY AS POSSIBLE.
IF I WERE HERE ON MY OWN, I WOULD AGREE THAT THAT WOULD BE THE BEST COURSE OF ACTION.
BUT RIGHT NOW...

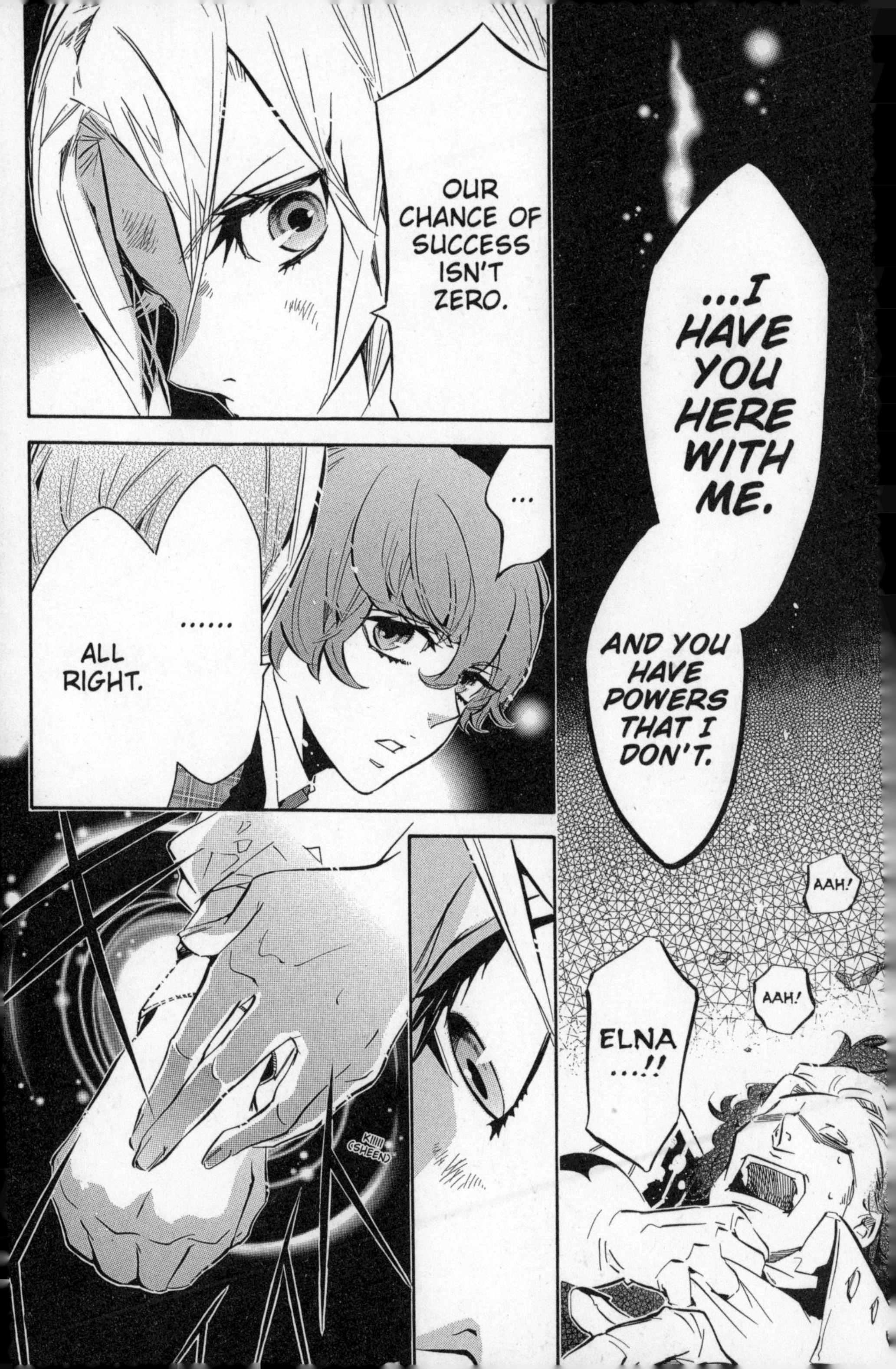
...I HAVE YOU HERE WITH ME.
AND YOU HAVE POWERS THAT I DON'T.
AAH!
AAH!
ELNA ...!!
OUR CHANCE OF SUCCESS ISN'T ZERO.
...
......
ALL RIGHT.
KIIII (SHEEN)

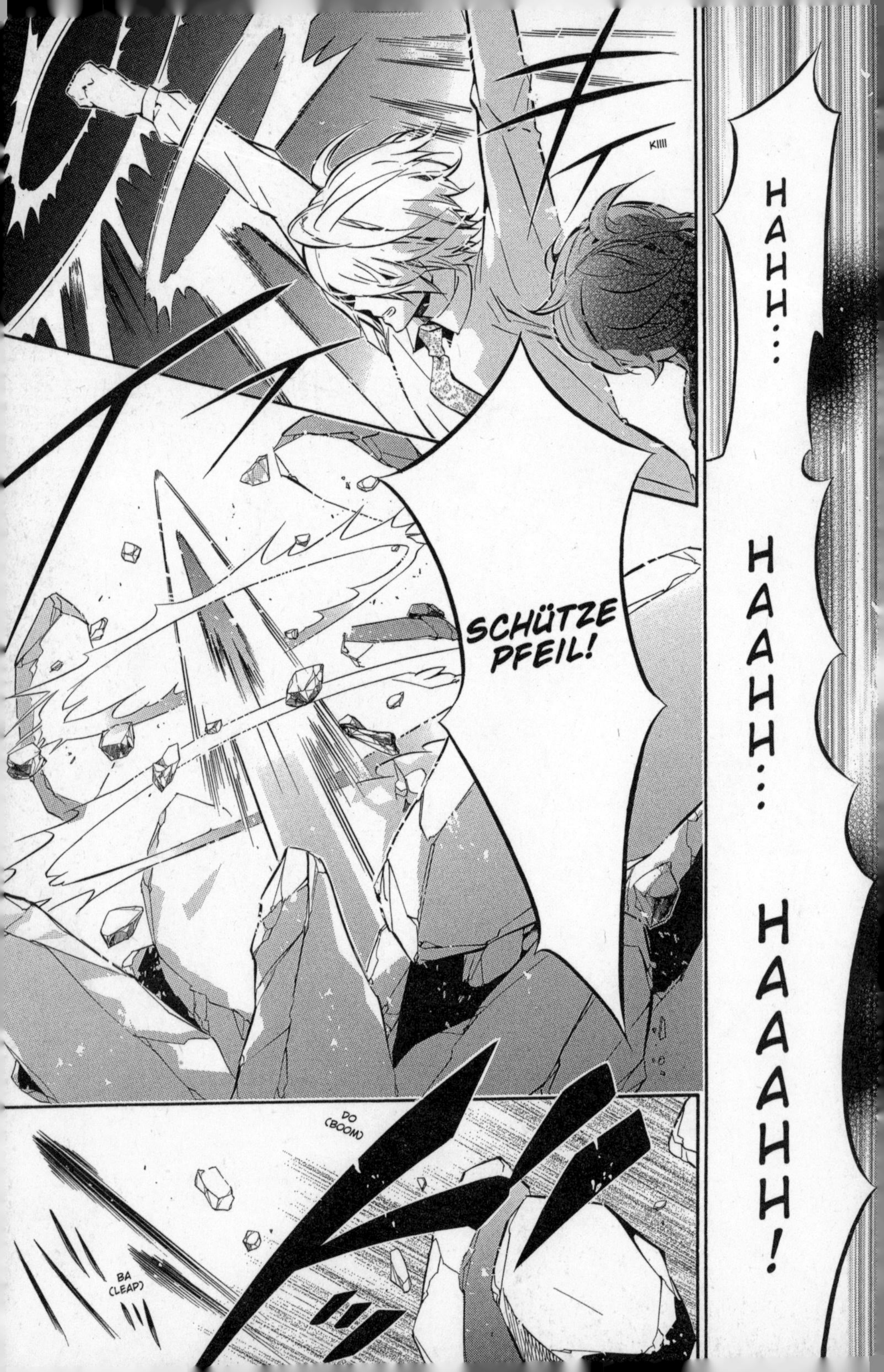
HAHH... HAAAHH... HAAAAHH!
KIIII
SCHÜTZE PFEIL!
DO (BOOM)
BA (LEAP)

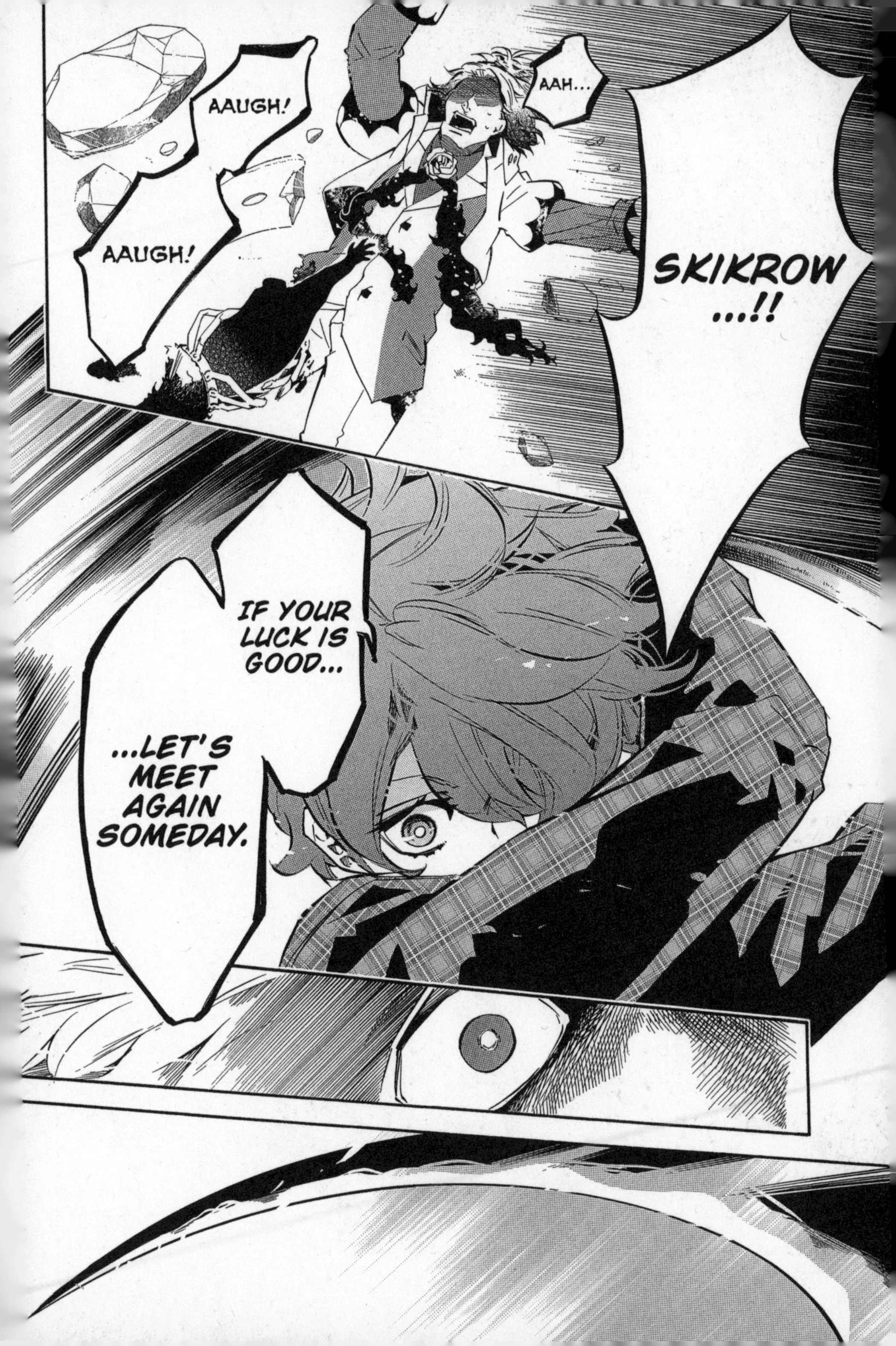
AAH...
SKIKROW...!!
AAUGH!
AAUGH!
IF YOUR LUCK IS GOOD...
...LET'S MEET AGAIN SOMEDAY.

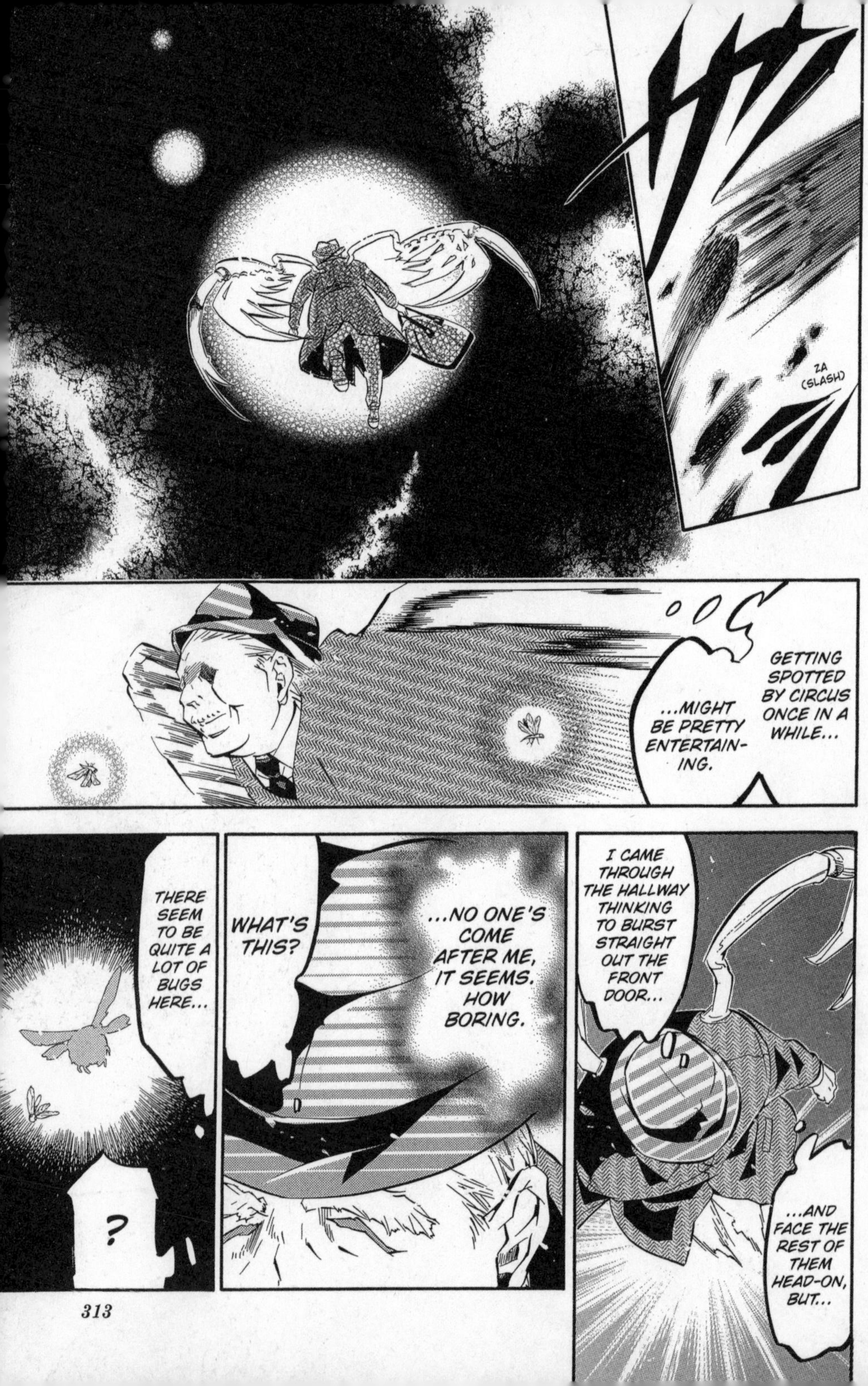
ZA (SLASH)
GETTING SPOTTED BY CIRCUS ONCE IN A WHILE...
...MIGHT BE PRETTY ENTERTAINING.
I CAME THROUGH THE HALLWAY THINKING TO BURST STRAIGHT OUT THE FRONT DOOR...
...AND FACE THE REST OF THEM HEAD-ON, BUT...
...NO ONE'S COME AFTER ME, IT SEEMS. HOW BORING.
WHAT'S THIS?
THERE SEEM TO BE QUITE A LOT OF BUGS HERE...
?

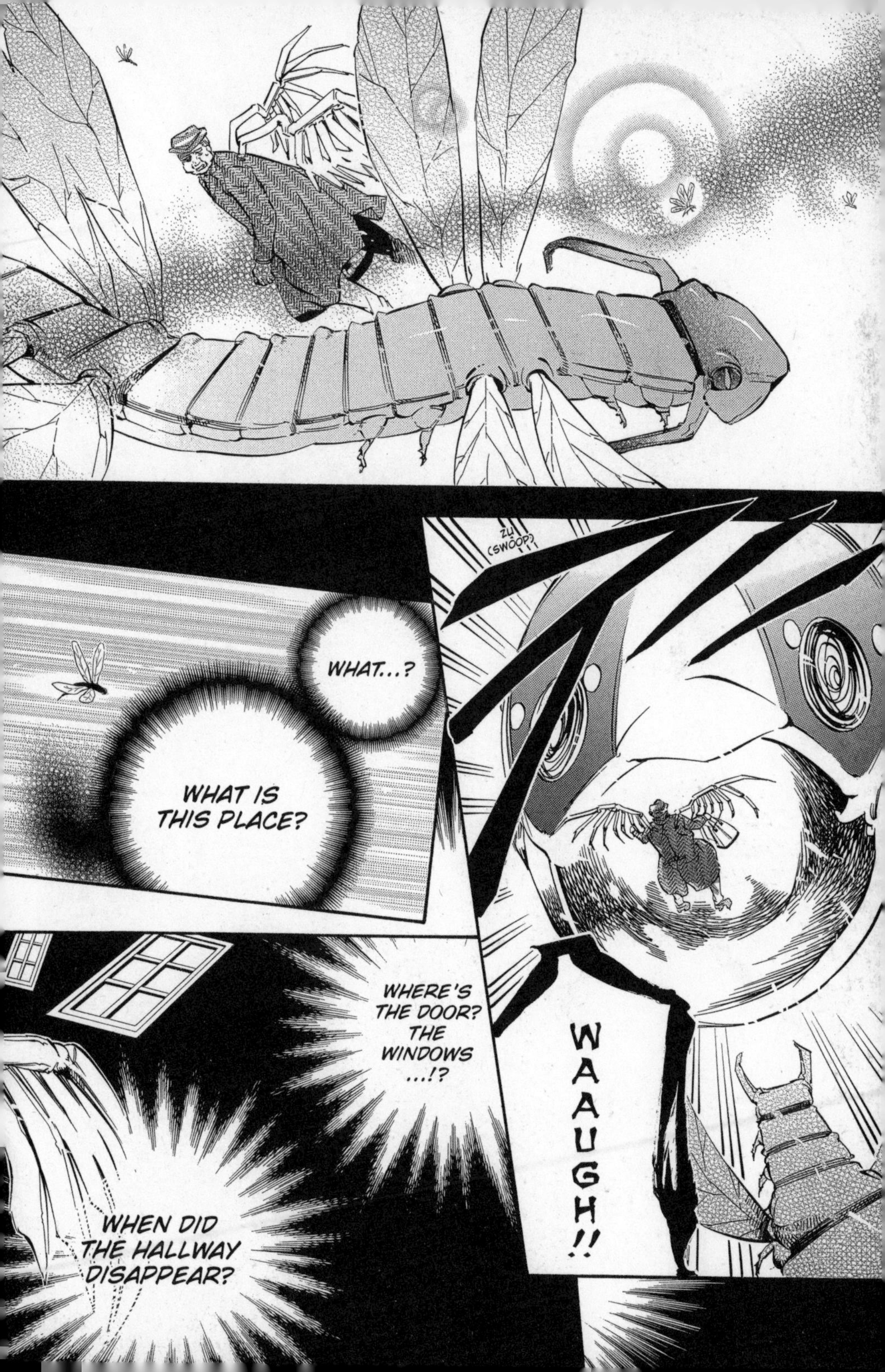
ZU (SWOOP)
WAAUGH!!
WHAT...?
WHAT IS THIS PLACE?
WHERE'S THE DOOR? THE WINDOWS ...!?
WHEN DID THE HALLWAY DISAPPEAR?

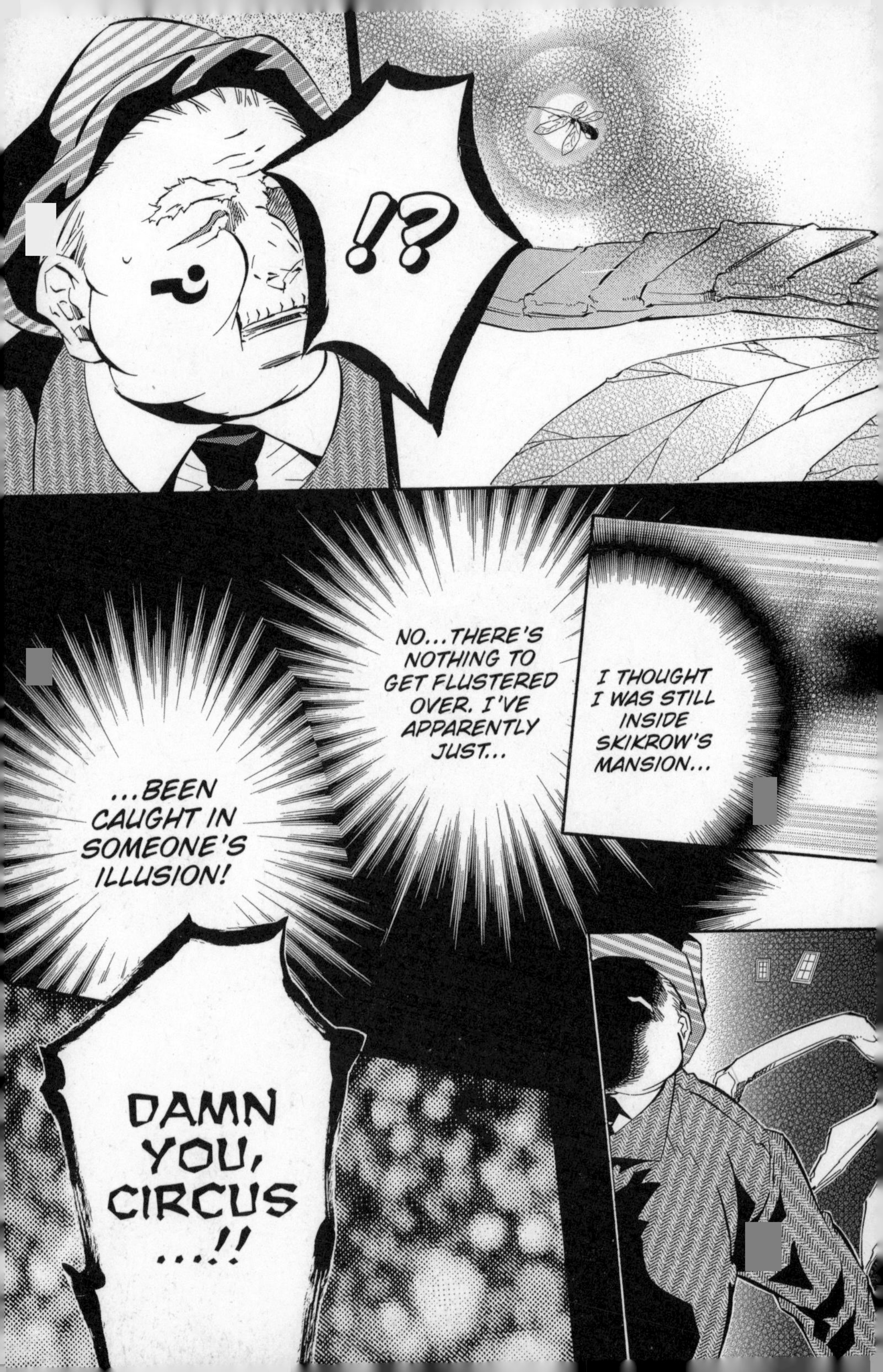
!?
I THOUGHT I WAS STILL INSIDE SKIKROW'S MANSION...
NO...THERE'S NOTHING TO GET FLUSTERED OVER. I'VE APPARENTLY JUST...
...BEEN CAUGHT IN SOMEONE'S ILLUSION!
DAMN YOU, CIRCUS ...!!

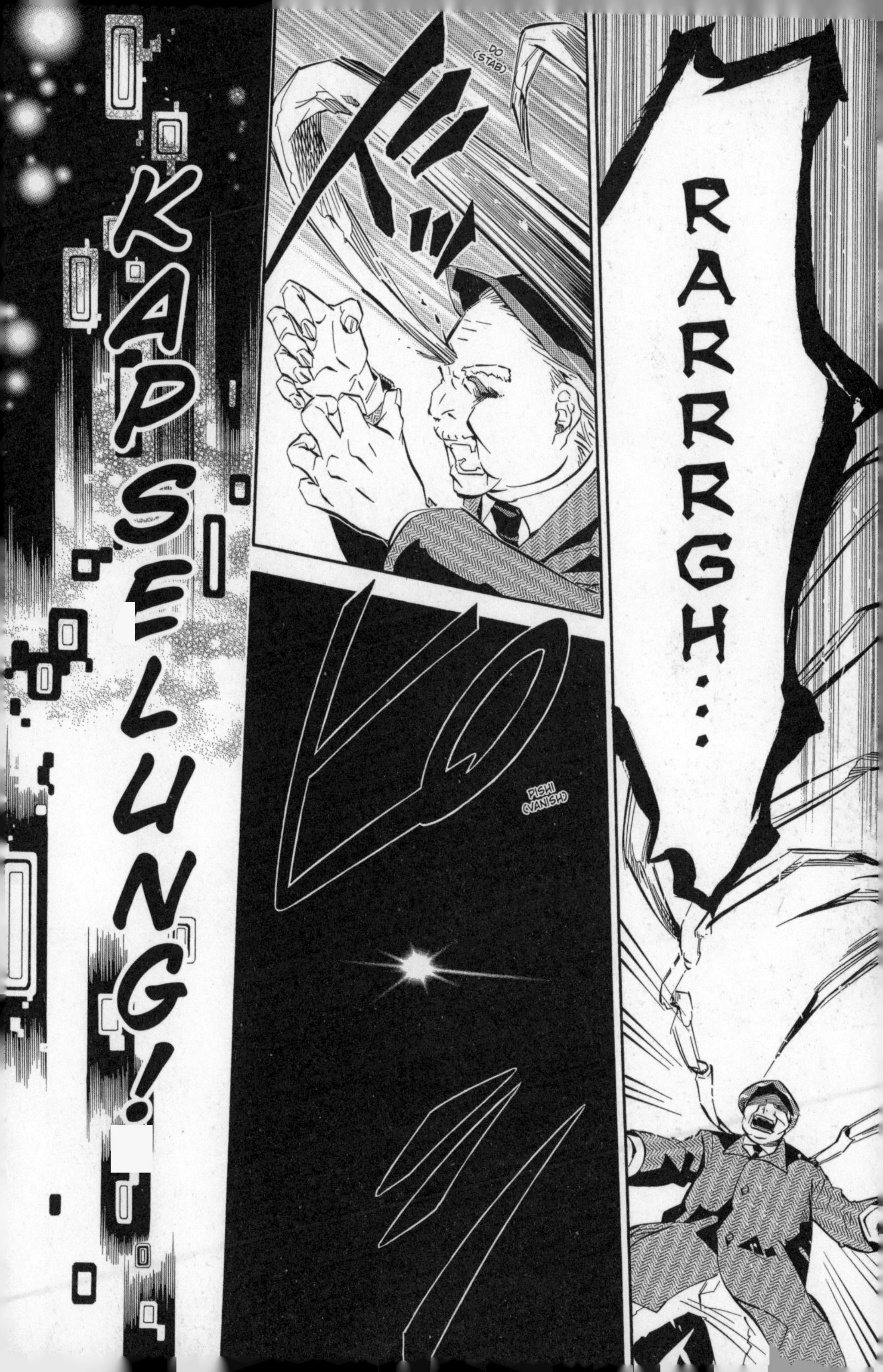
RARRRGH...
DO (STAB)
PISHI (VANISH)
KAPSELUNG!

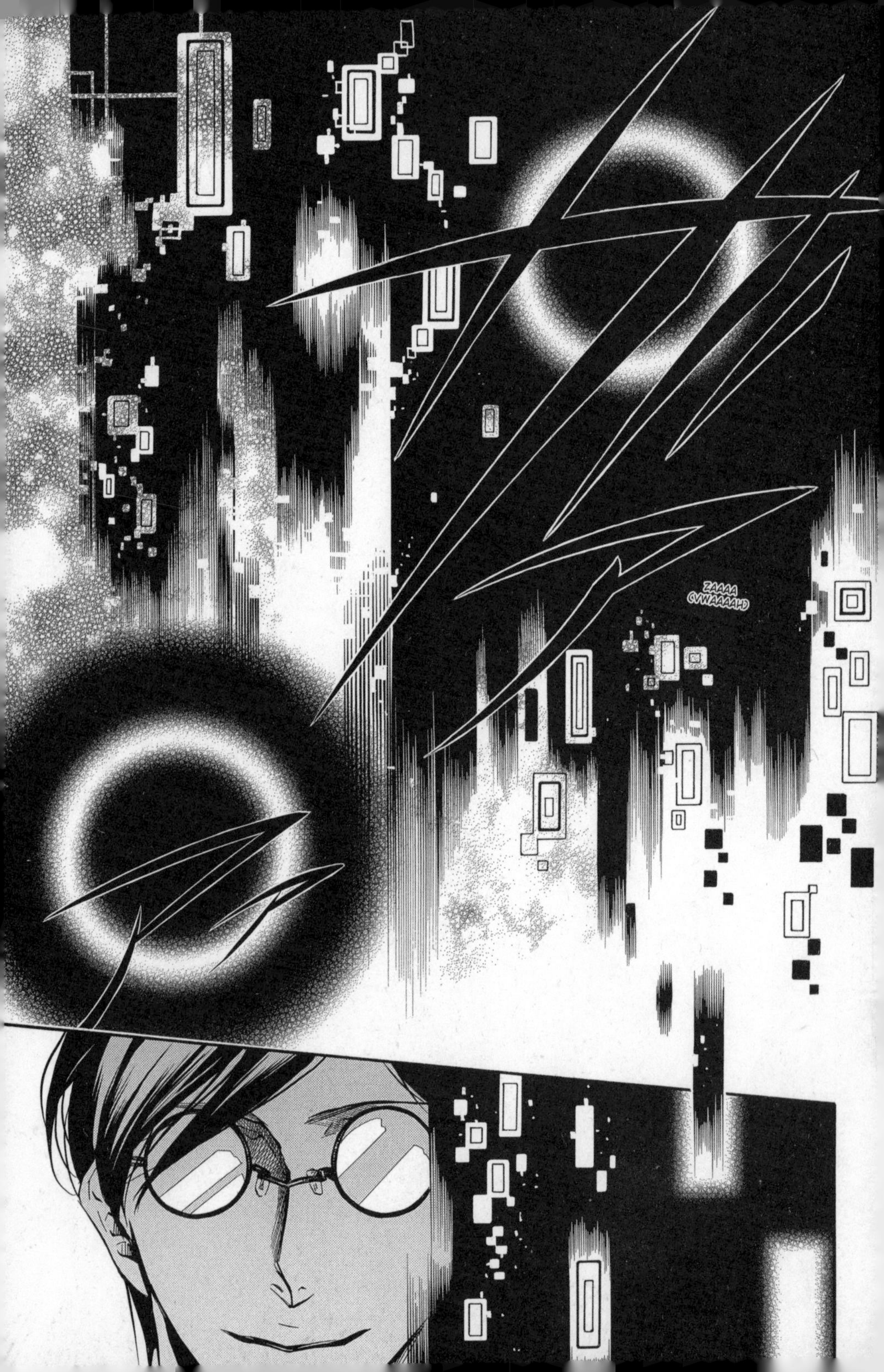
ZAAAA
(VWAAAAAH)

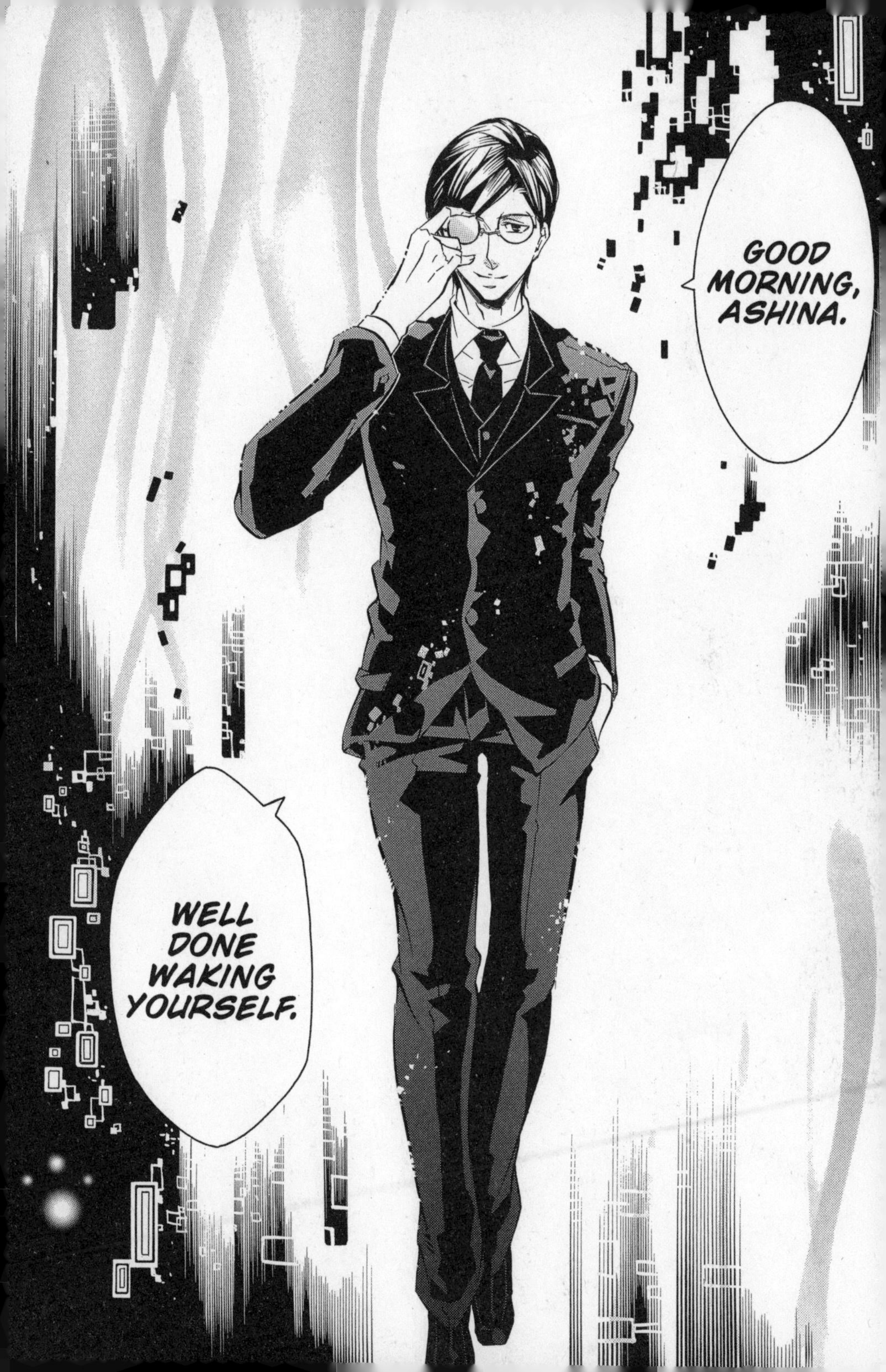
GOOD MORNING, ASHINA.
WELL DONE WAKING YOURSELF.

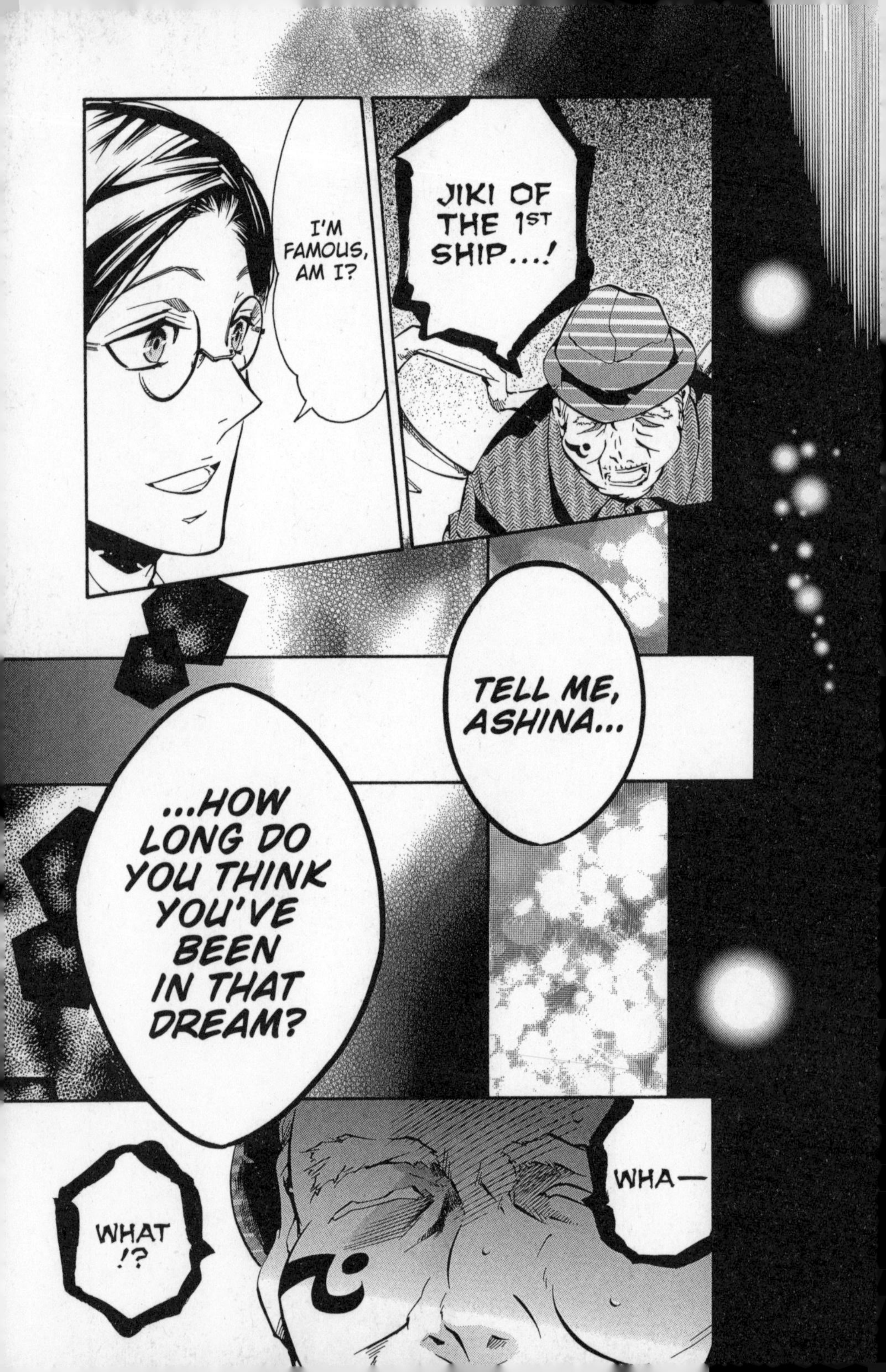
JIKI OF THE 1ST SHIP...!
I'M FAMOUS, AM I?
TELL ME, ASHINA...
...HOW LONG DO YOU THINK YOU'VE BEEN IN THAT DREAM?
WHA—
WHAT!?

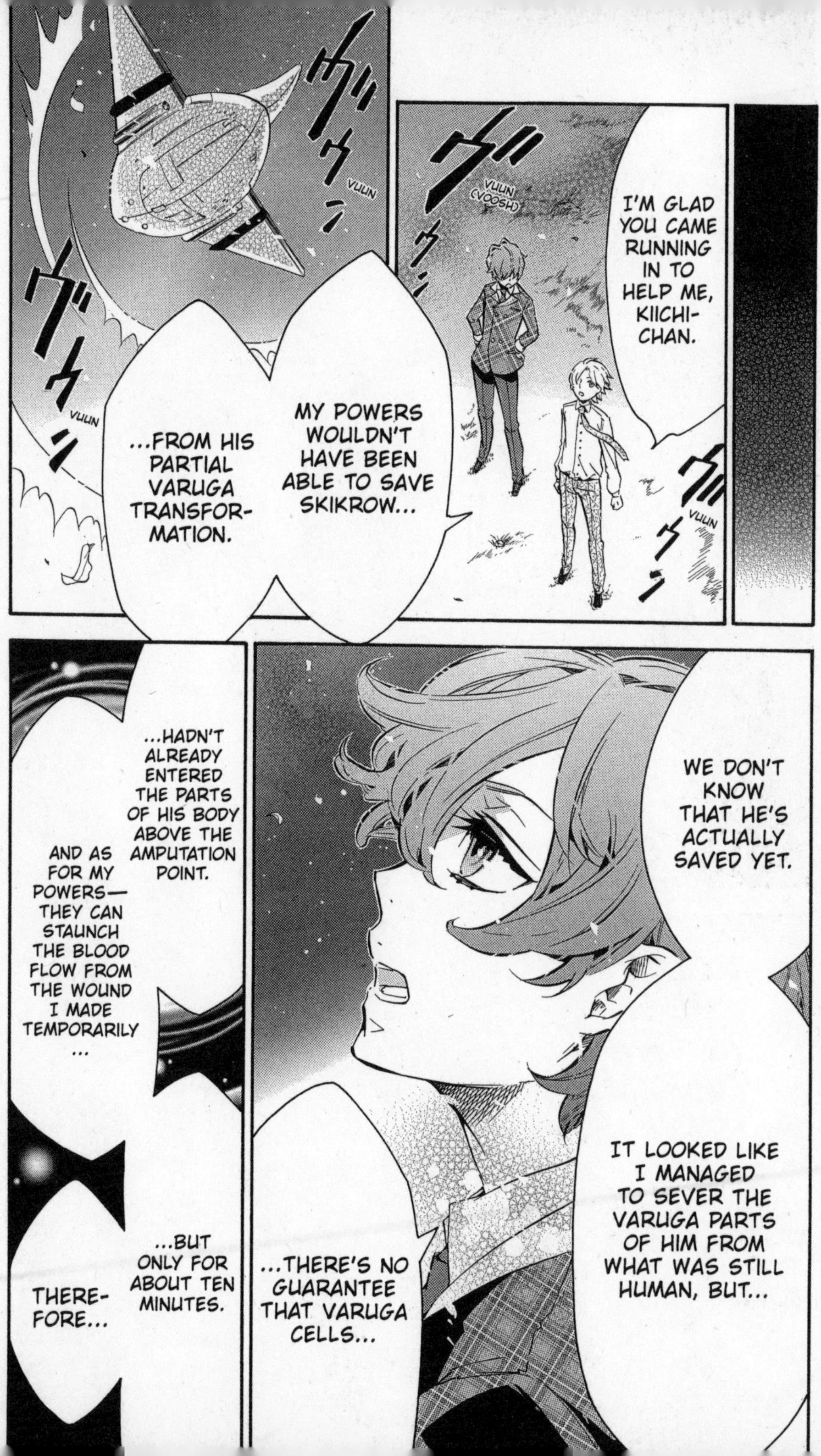
I'M GLAD YOU CAME RUNNING IN TO HELP ME, KIICHI-CHAN.
VUUN (VOOSH)
VUUN
VUUN
MY POWERS WOULDN'T HAVE BEEN ABLE TO SAVE SKIKROW...
...FROM HIS PARTIAL VARUGA TRANSFORMATION.
VUUN
WE DON'T KNOW THAT HE'S ACTUALLY SAVED YET.
IT LOOKED LIKE I MANAGED TO SEVER THE VARUGA PARTS OF HIM FROM WHAT WAS STILL HUMAN, BUT...
...THERE'S NO GUARANTEE THAT VARUGA CELLS...
...HADN'T ALREADY ENTERED THE PARTS OF HIS BODY ABOVE THE AMPUTATION POINT.
AND AS FOR MY POWERS—THEY CAN STAUNCH THE BLOOD FLOW FROM THE WOUND I MADE TEMPORARILY...
...BUT ONLY FOR ABOUT TEN MINUTES.
THEREFORE...

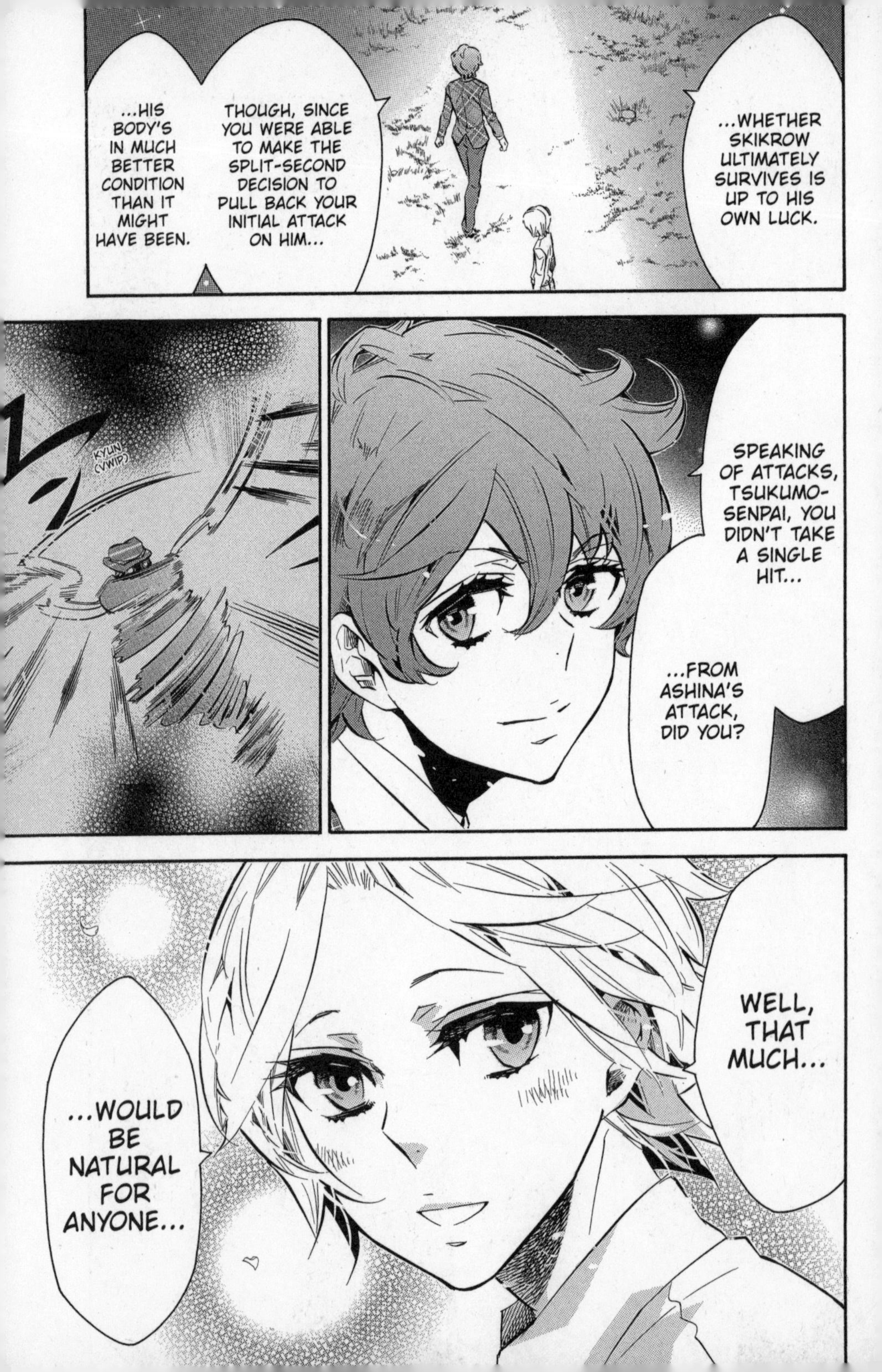
...WHETHER SKIKROW ULTIMATELY SURVIVES IS UP TO HIS OWN LUCK.
THOUGH, SINCE YOU WERE ABLE TO MAKE THE SPLIT-SECOND DECISION TO PULL BACK YOUR INITIAL ATTACK ON HIM...
...HIS BODY'S IN MUCH BETTER CONDITION THAN IT MIGHT HAVE BEEN.
SPEAKING OF ATTACKS, TSUKUMO-SENPAI, YOU DIDN'T TAKE A SINGLE HIT...
...FROM ASHINA'S ATTACK, DID YOU?
KYUN (VWIP)
WELL, THAT MUCH...
...WOULD BE NATURAL FOR ANYONE...

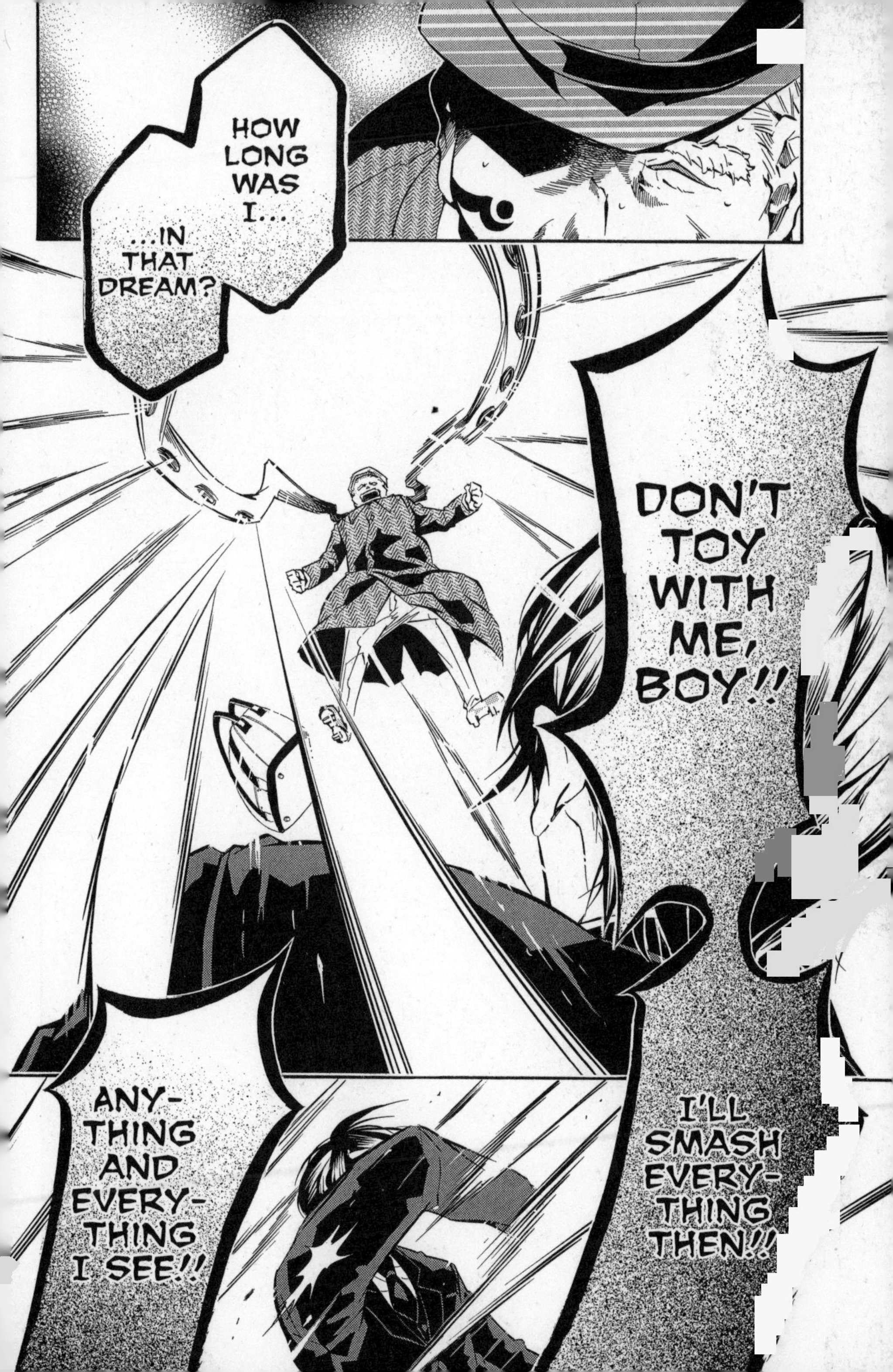
HOW LONG WAS I... ...IN THAT DREAM?
DON'T TOY WITH ME, BOY!!
I'LL SMASH EVERY-THING THEN!!
ANY-THING AND EVERY-THING I SEE!!

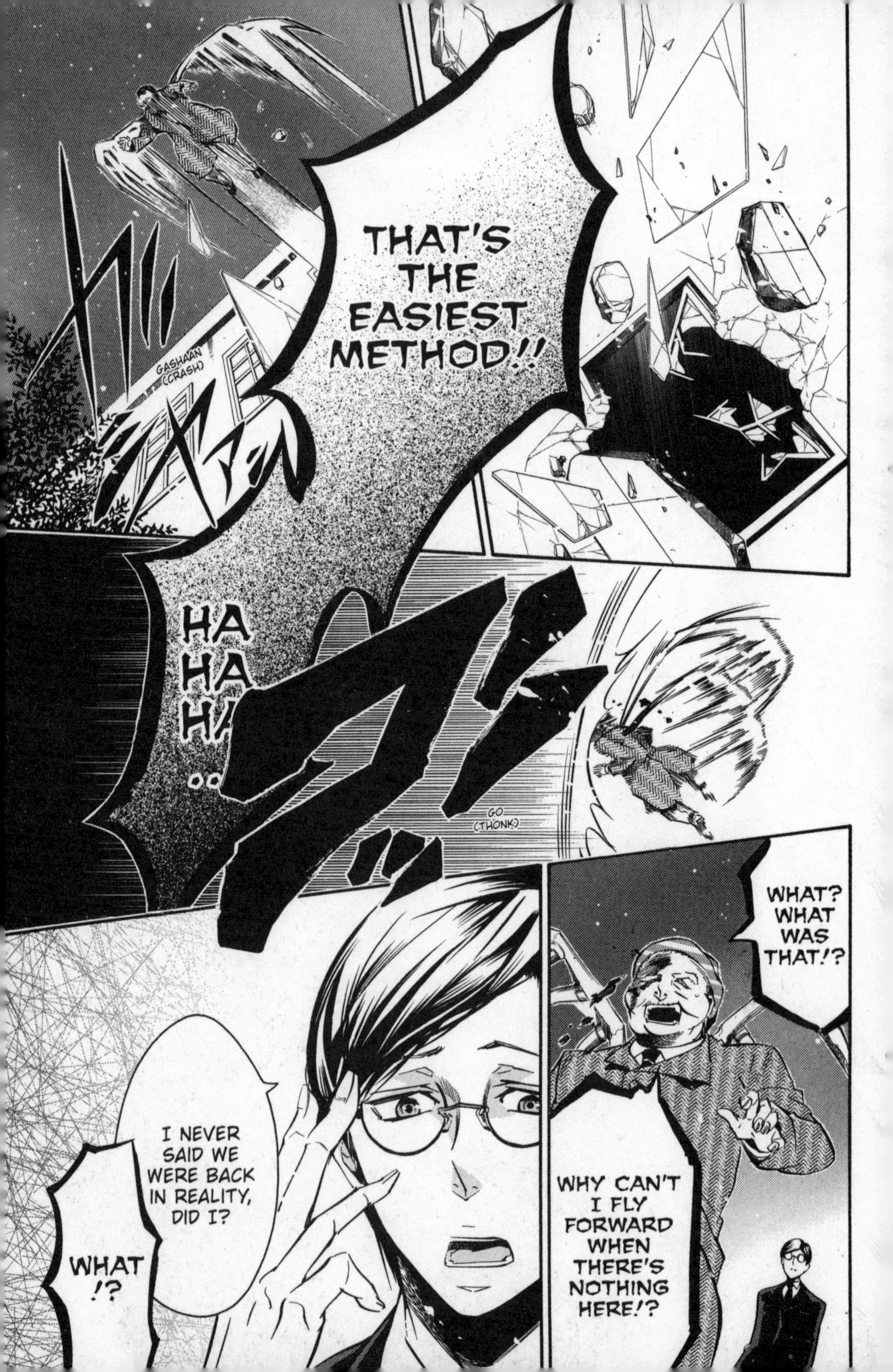
THAT'S THE EASIEST METHOD!!
GASHAAN (CRASH)
GO (THONK)
HA HA H
WHAT? WHAT WAS THAT!?
WHY CAN'T I FLY FORWARD WHEN THERE'S NOTHING HERE!?
I NEVER SAID WE WERE BACK IN REALITY, DID I?
WHAT!?

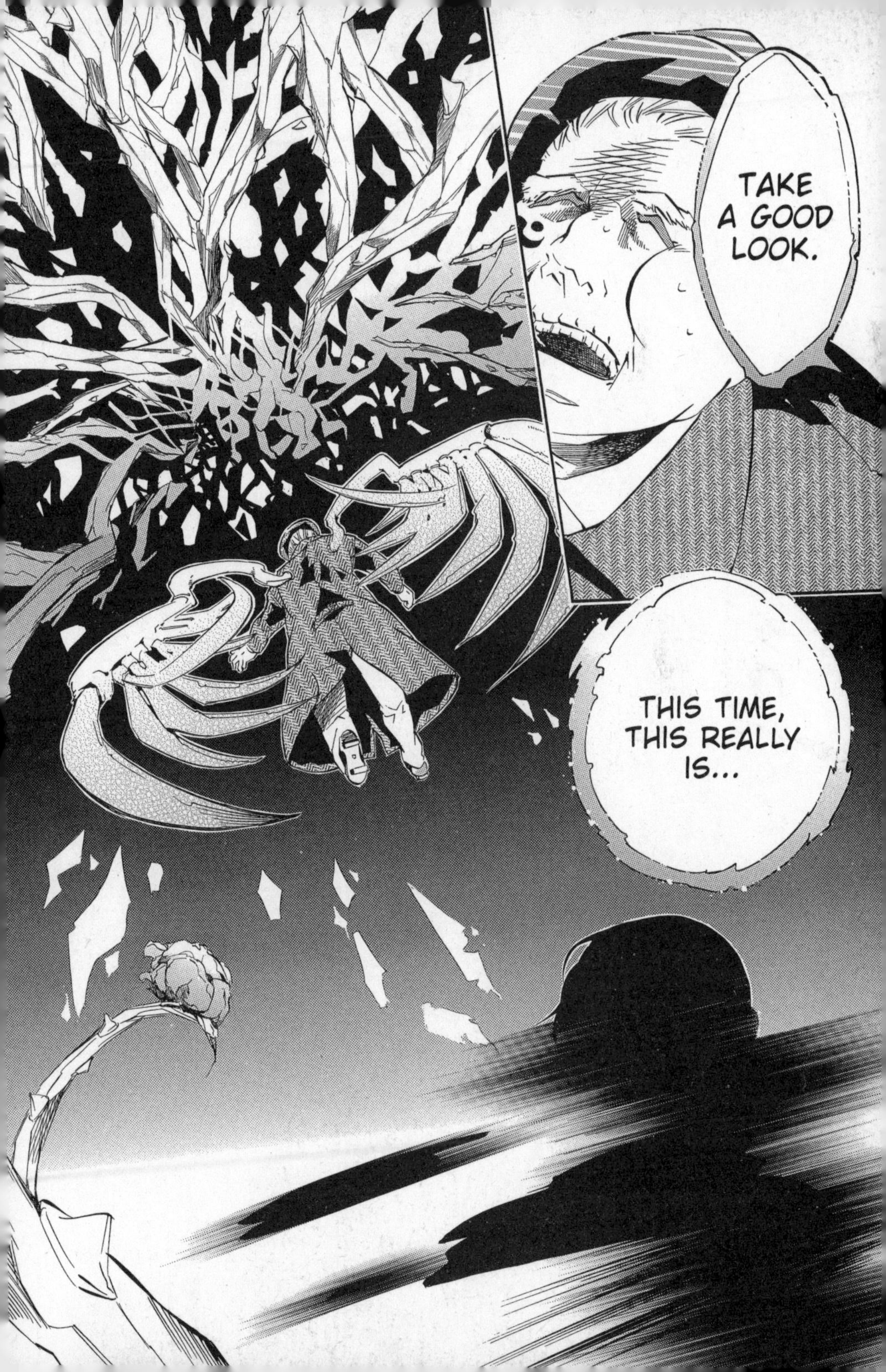
TAKE A GOOD LOOK.
THIS TIME, THIS REALLY IS...

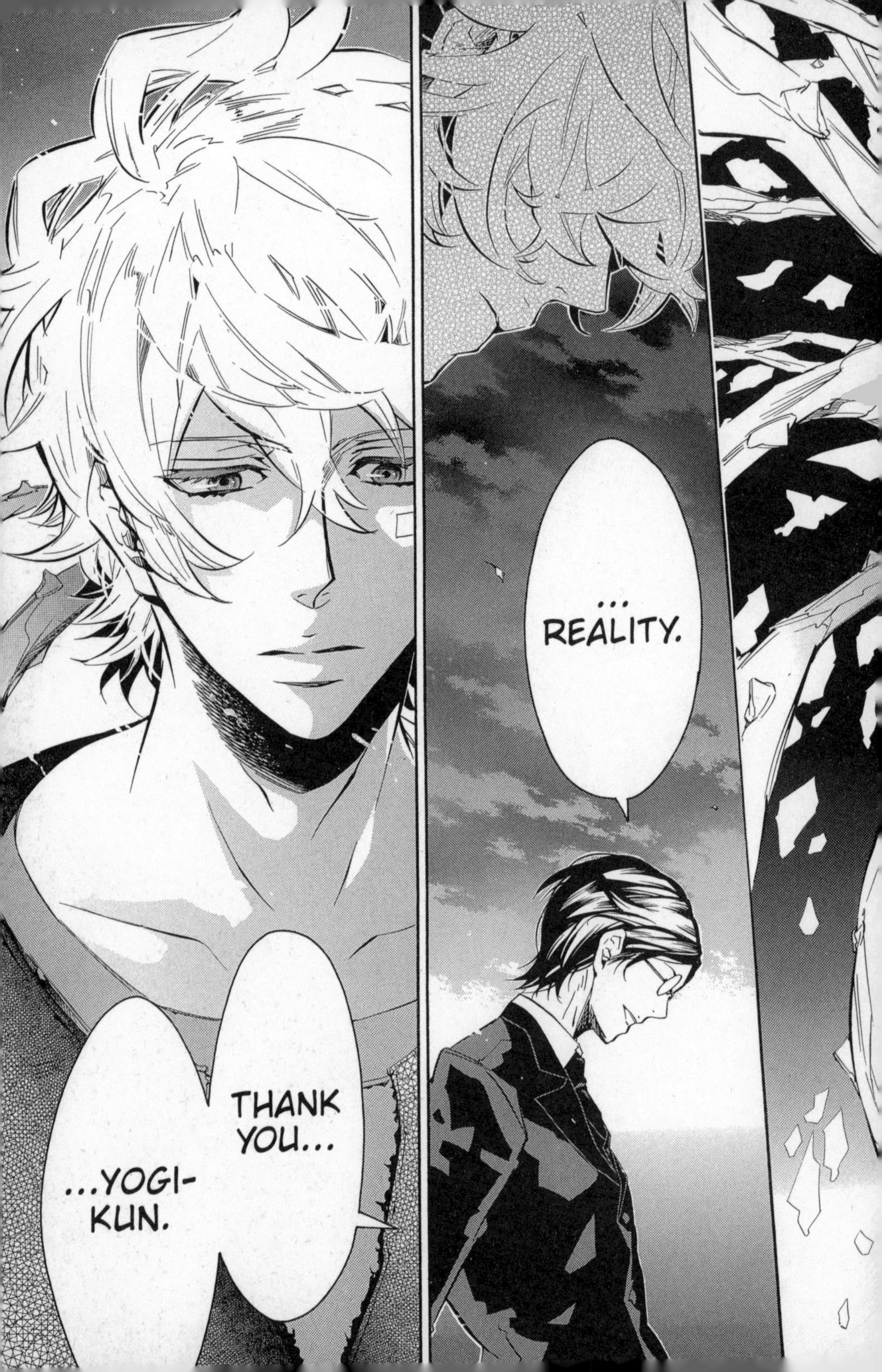
...REALITY.
THANK YOU...
...YOGI-KUN.

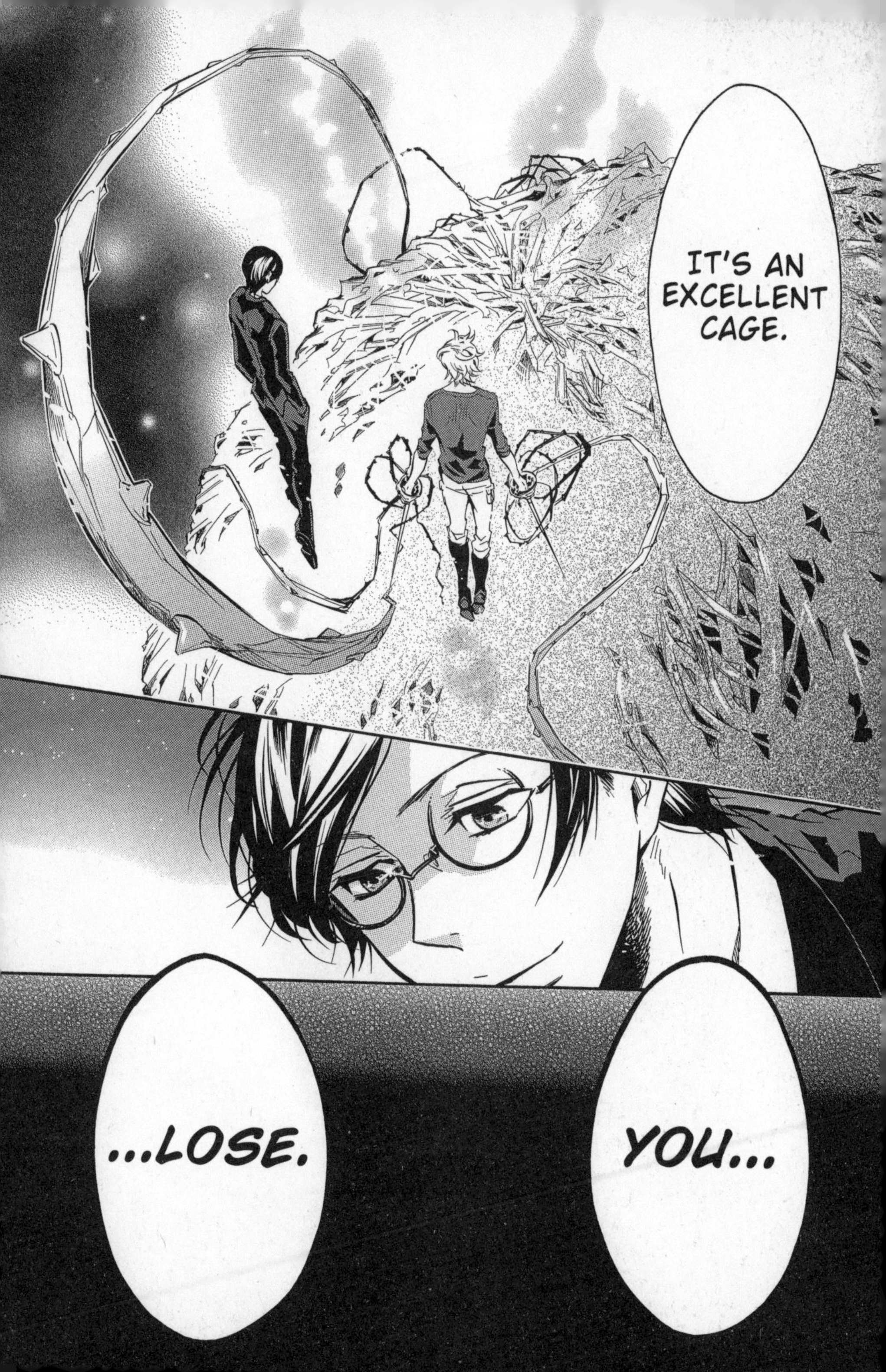
IT'S AN EXCELLENT CAGE.
YOU...
...LOSE.

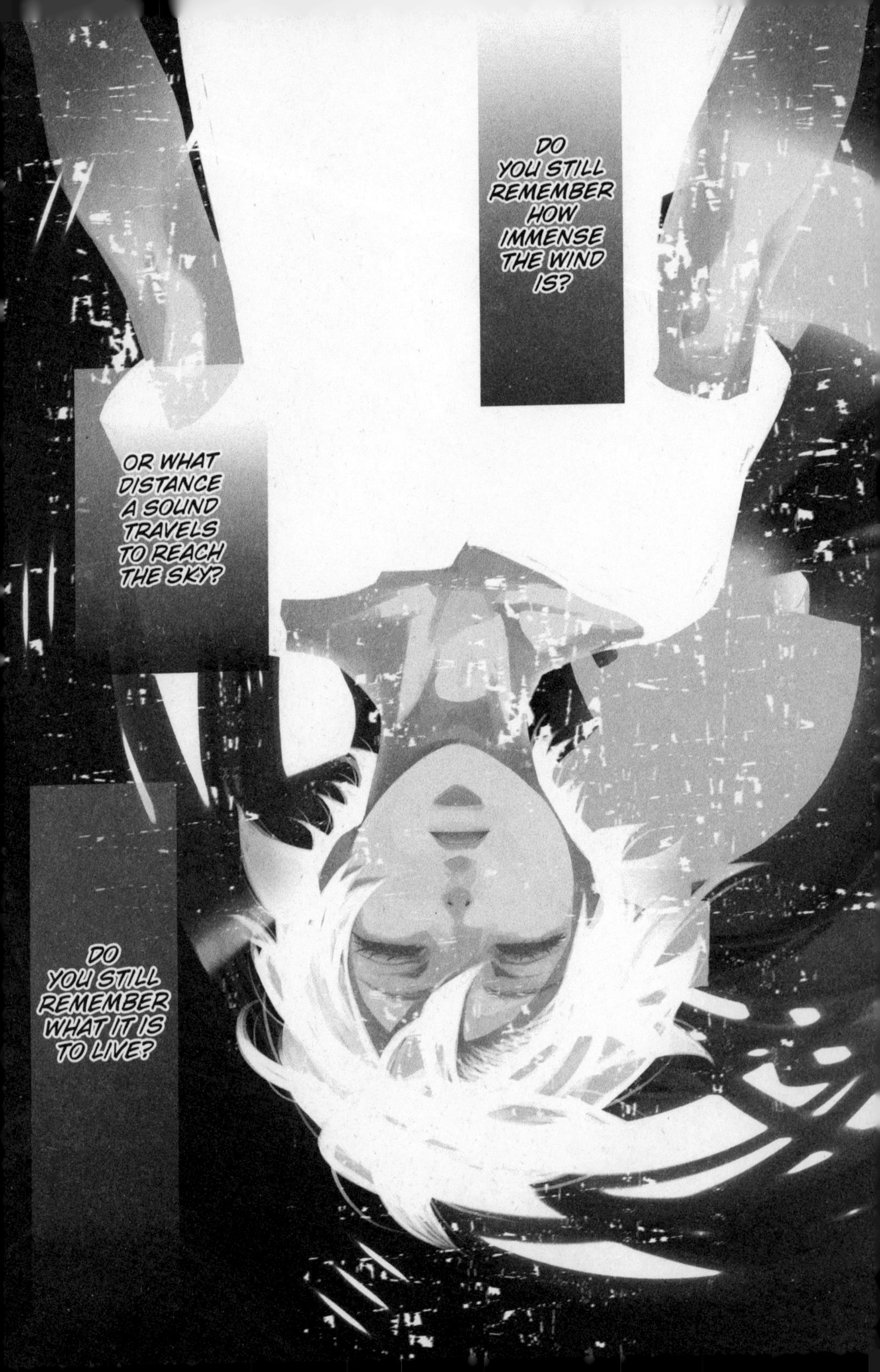
DO YOU STILL REMEMBER HOW IMMENSE THE WIND IS?
OR WHAT DISTANCE A SOUND TRAVELS TO REACH THE SKY?
DO YOU STILL REMEMBER WHAT IT IS TO LIVE?

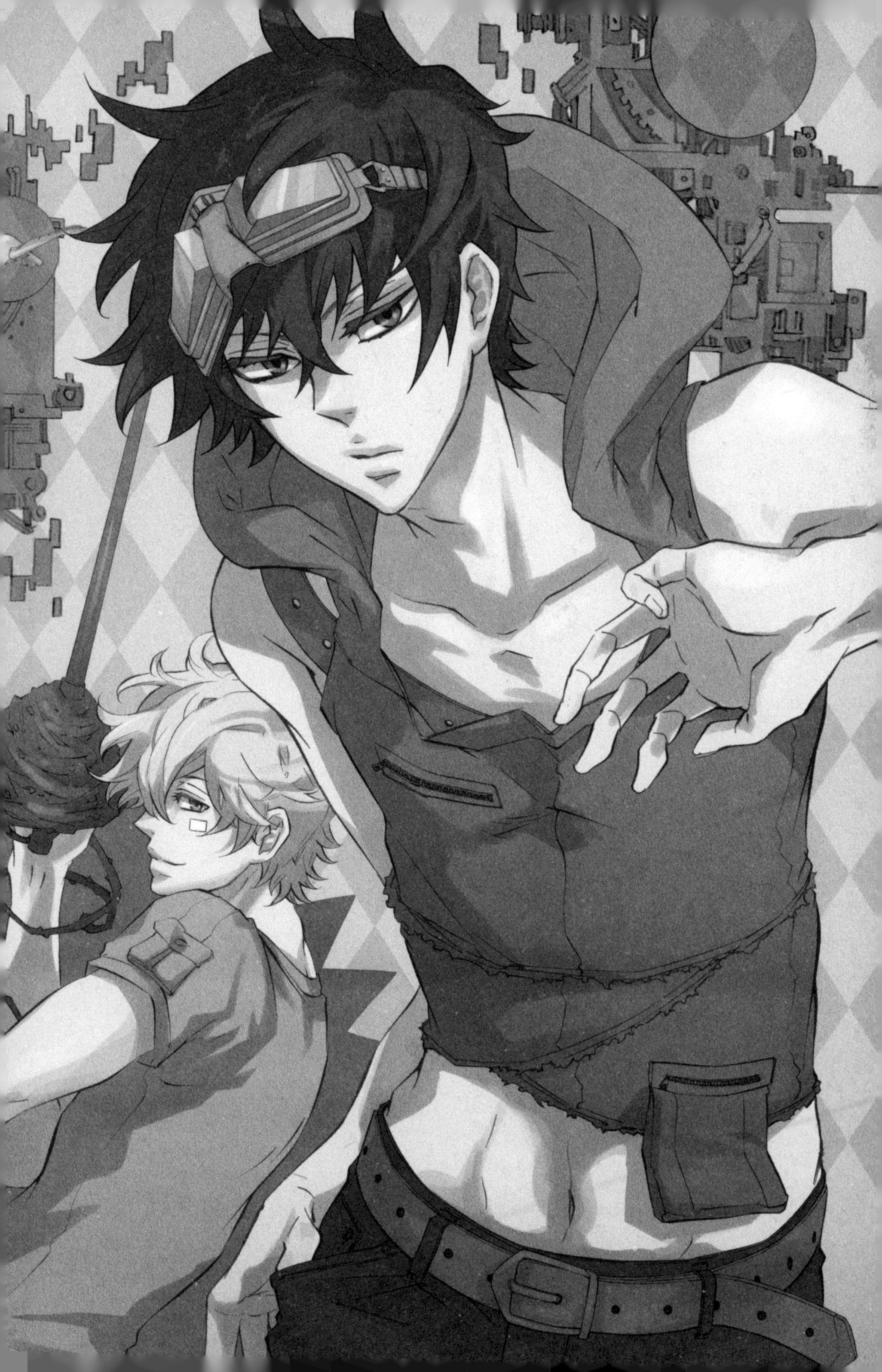

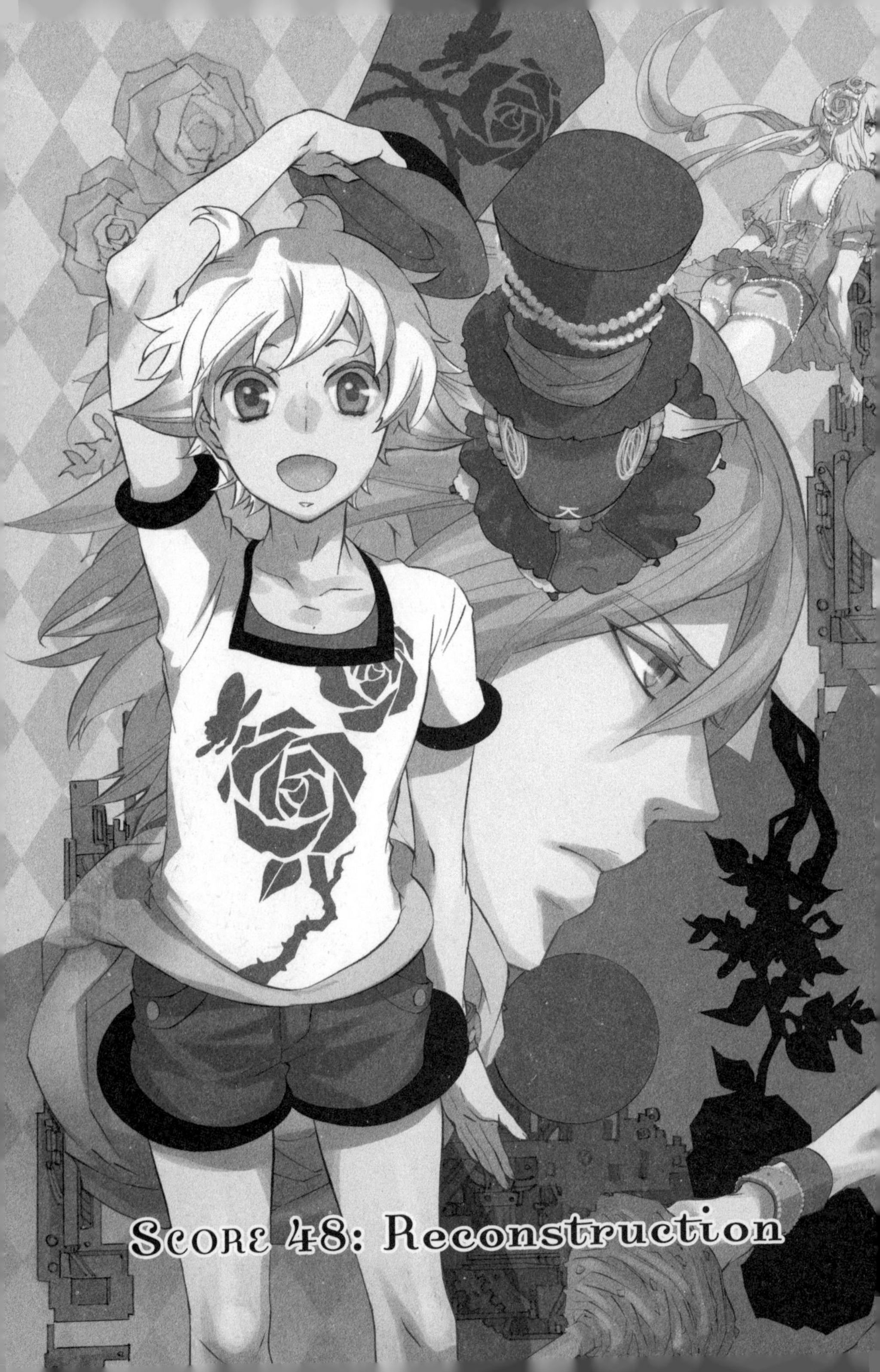
Score 48: Reconstruction

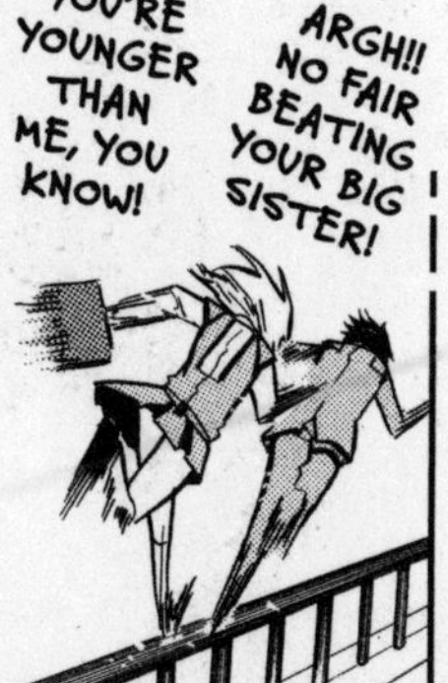
ARGH!! NO FAIR BEATING YOUR BIG SISTER!
HUH!? YOU'RE YOUNGER THAN ME, YOU KNOW!

KARNEVAL

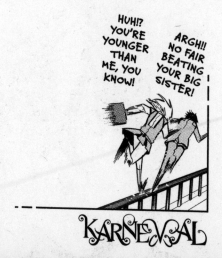

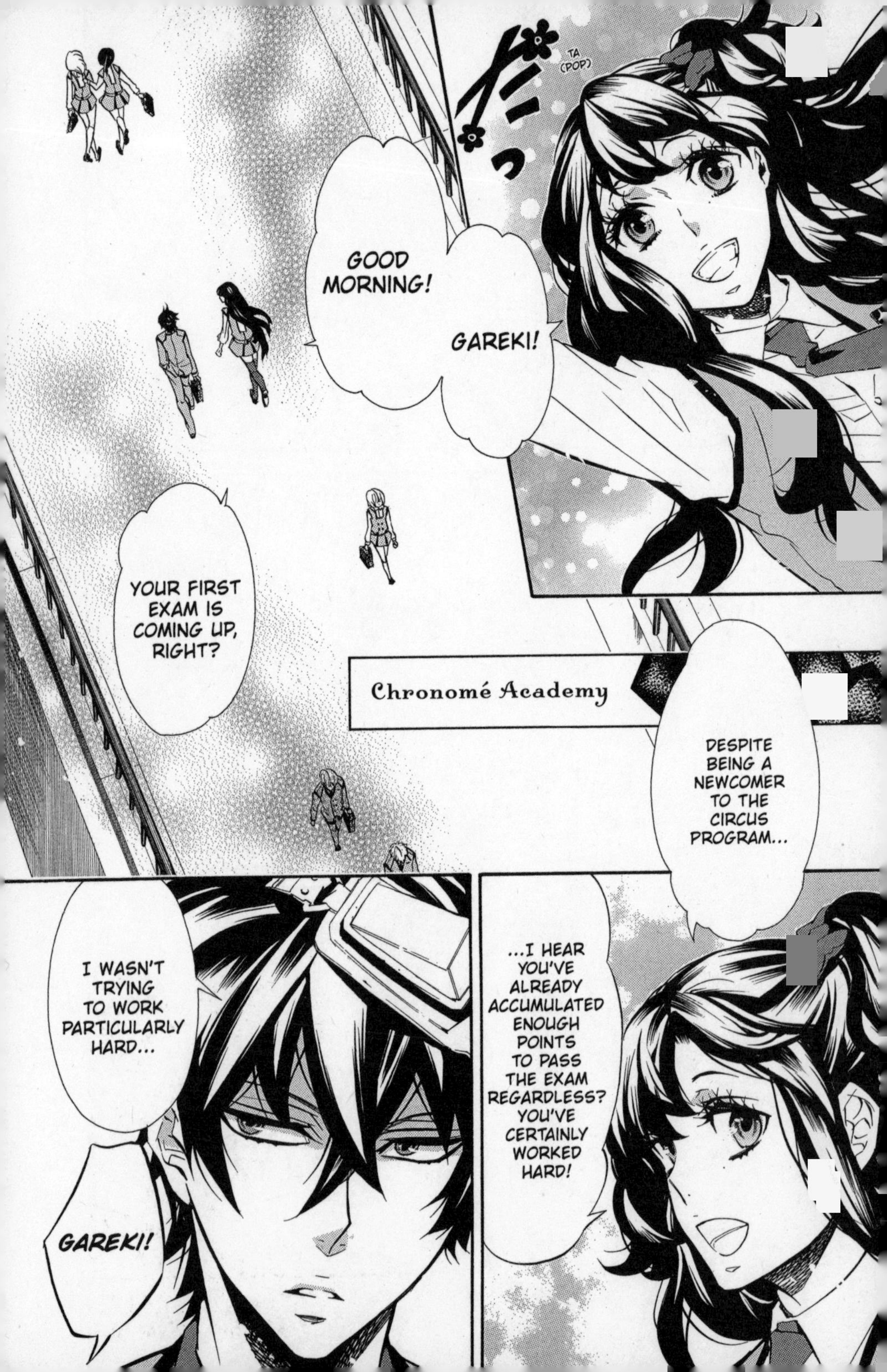
TA (POP)
GOOD MORNING!
GAREKI!
Chronomé Academy
YOUR FIRST EXAM IS COMING UP, RIGHT?
DESPITE BEING A NEWCOMER TO THE CIRCUS PROGRAM...
...I HEAR YOU'VE ALREADY ACCUMULATED ENOUGH POINTS TO PASS THE EXAM REGARDLESS? YOU'VE CERTAINLY WORKED HARD!
I WASN'T TRYING TO WORK PARTICULARLY HARD...
GAREKI!

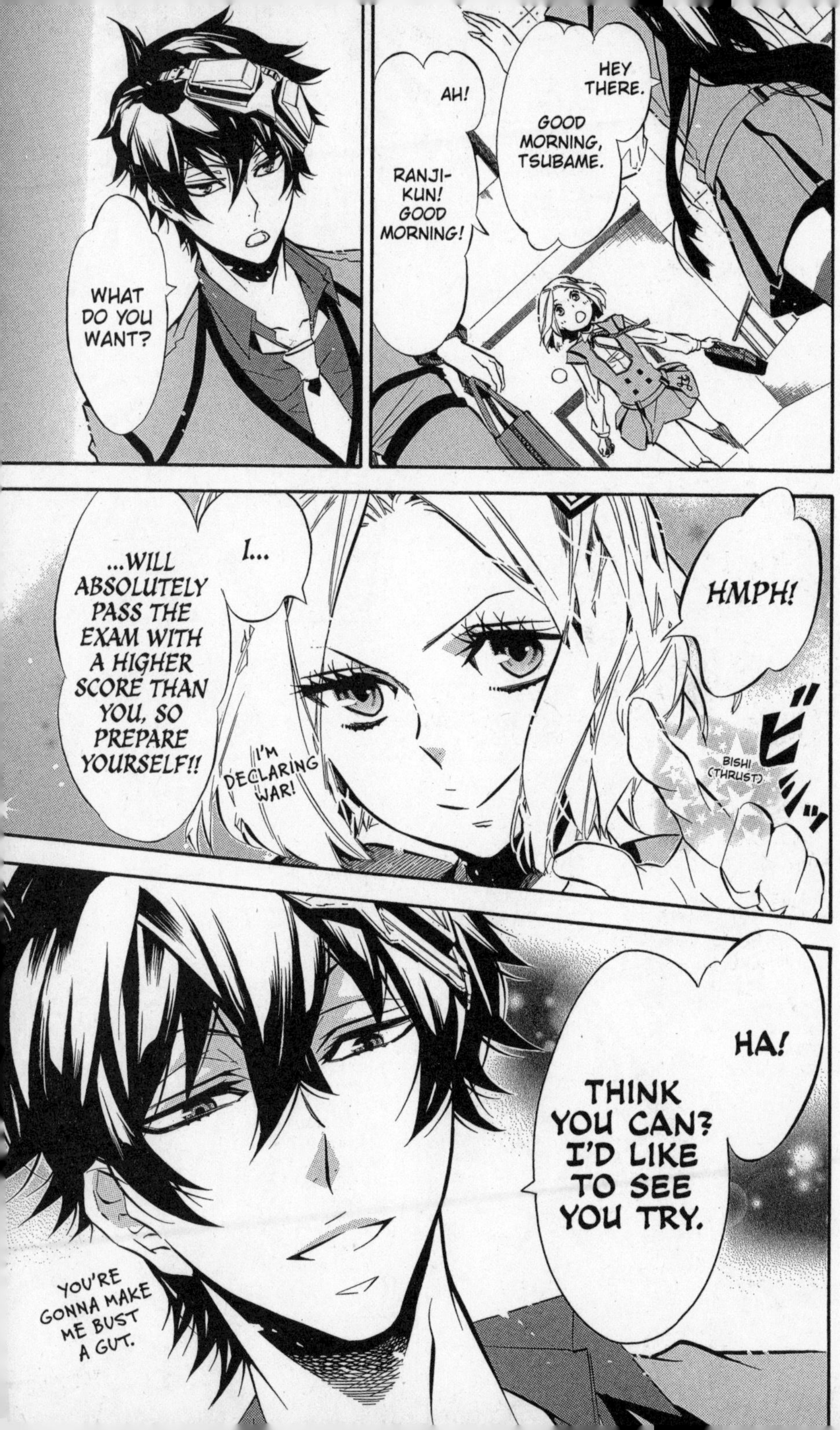
HEY THERE.
GOOD MORNING, TSUBAME.
AH!
RANJI-KUN! GOOD MORNING!
WHAT DO YOU WANT?
HMPH!
BISHI (THRUST)
I...
...WILL ABSOLUTELY PASS THE EXAM WITH A HIGHER SCORE THAN YOU, SO PREPARE YOURSELF!!
I'M DECLARING WAR!
HA!
THINK YOU CAN? I'D LIKE TO SEE YOU TRY.
YOU'RE GONNA MAKE ME BUST A GUT.

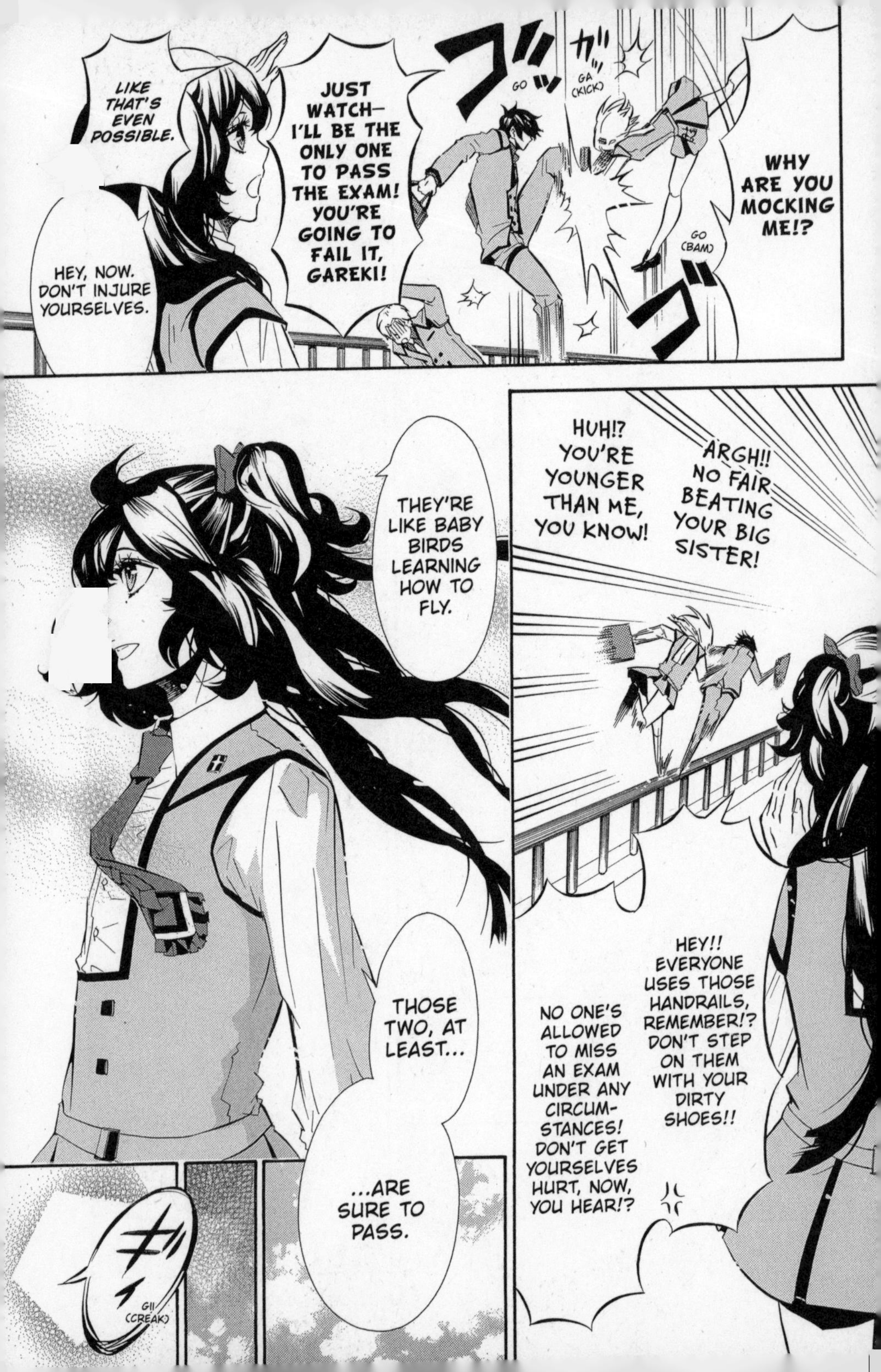
WHY ARE YOU MOCKING ME!?
GA (KICK)
GO (BAM)
GO
JUST WATCH— I'LL BE THE ONLY ONE TO PASS THE EXAM! YOU'RE GOING TO FAIL IT, GAREKI!
LIKE THAT'S EVEN POSSIBLE.
HEY, NOW. DON'T INJURE YOURSELVES.
ARGH!! NO FAIR BEATING YOUR BIG SISTER!
HUH!? YOU'RE YOUNGER THAN ME, YOU KNOW!
HEY!! EVERYONE USES THOSE HANDRAILS, REMEMBER!? DON'T STEP ON THEM WITH YOUR DIRTY SHOES!!
NO ONE'S ALLOWED TO MISS AN EXAM UNDER ANY CIRCUM-STANCES! DON'T GET YOURSELVES HURT, NOW, YOU HEAR!?
THEY'RE LIKE BABY BIRDS LEARNING HOW TO FLY.
THOSE TWO, AT LEAST...
...ARE SURE TO PASS.
GII (CREAK)

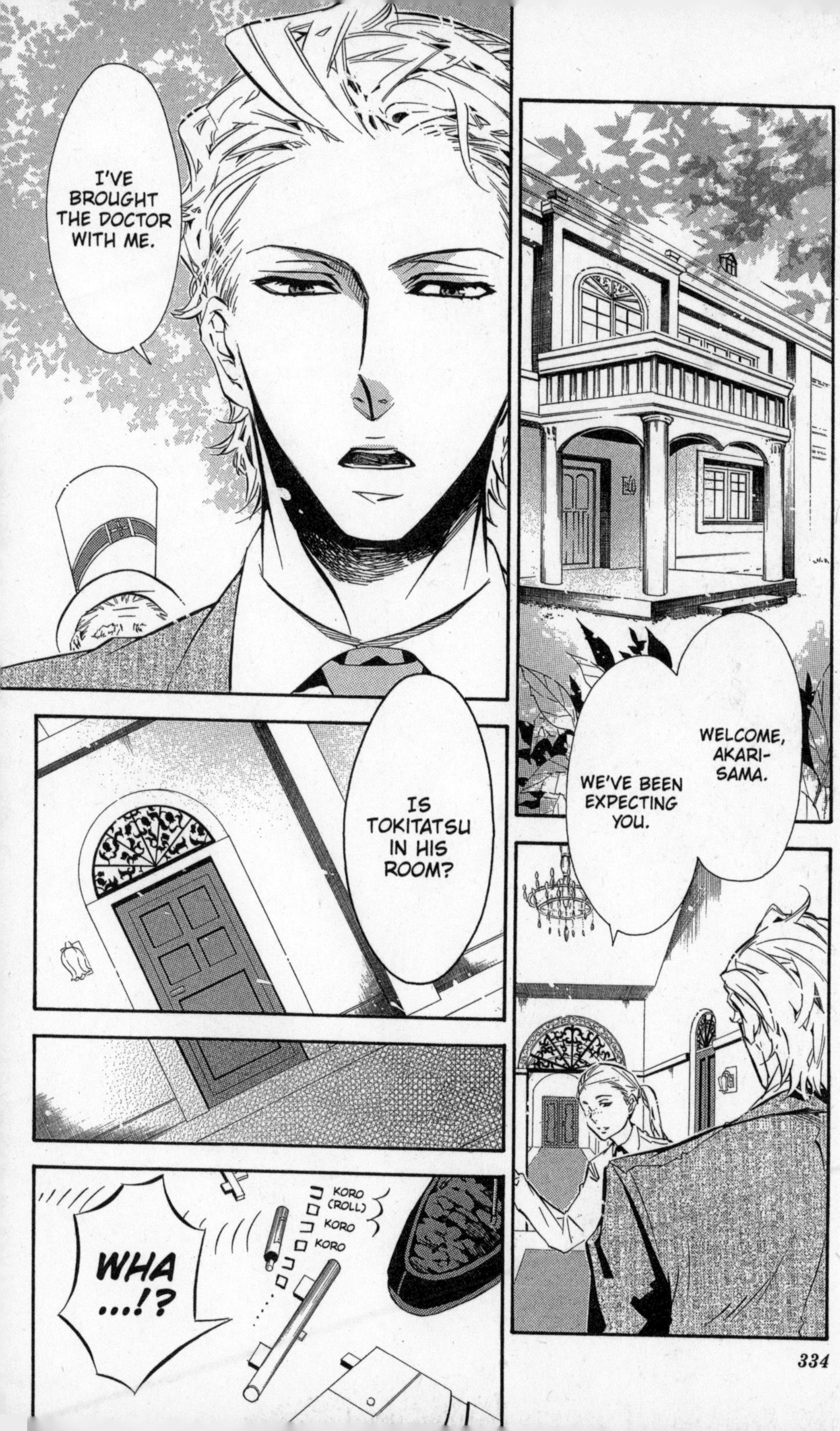
WELCOME, AKARI-SAMA.
WE'VE BEEN EXPECTING YOU.
I'VE BROUGHT THE DOCTOR WITH ME.
IS TOKITATSU IN HIS ROOM?
KORO (ROLL) KORO KORO
WHA...!?

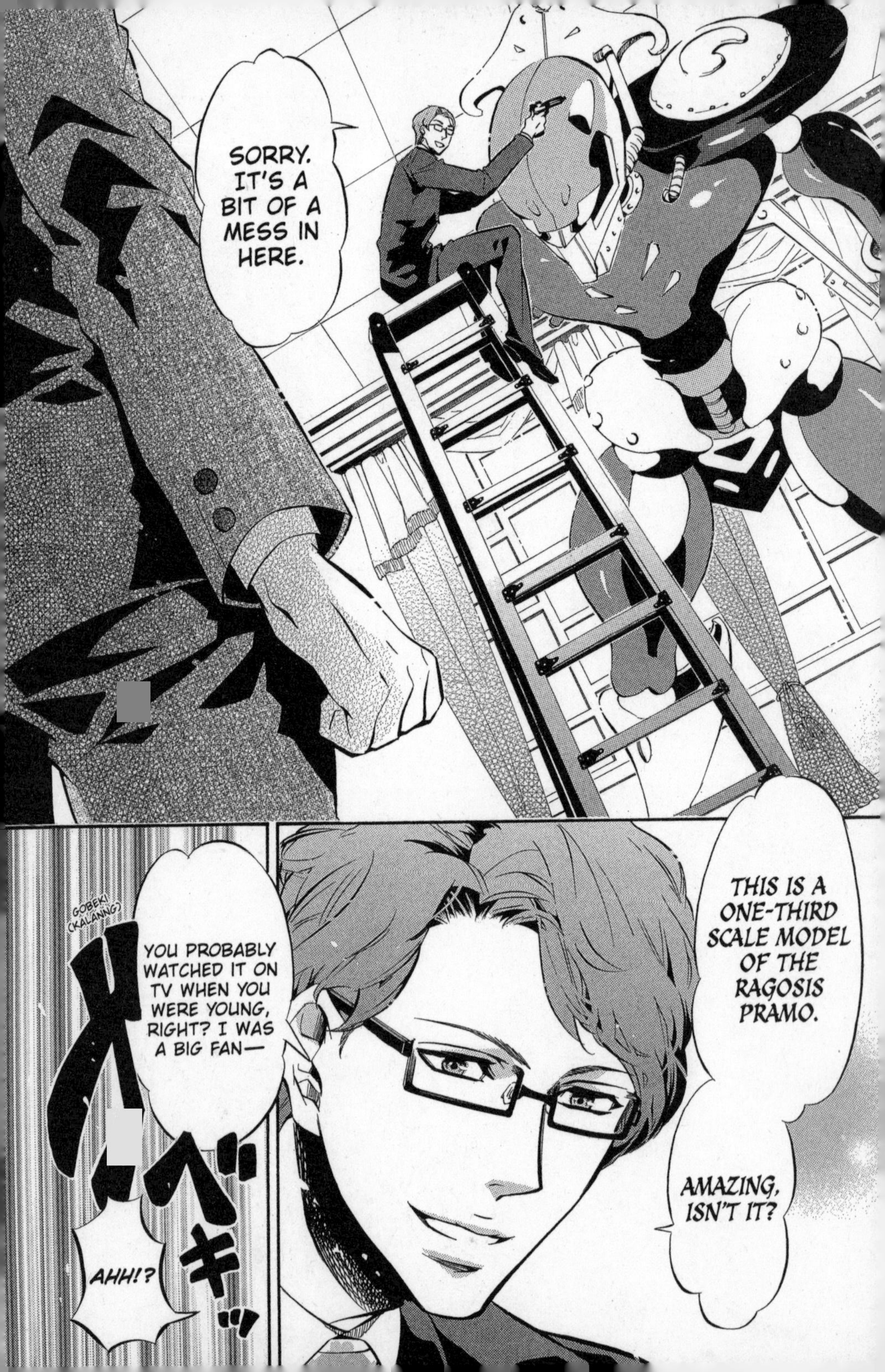
SORRY. IT'S A BIT OF A MESS IN HERE.
THIS IS A ONE-THIRD SCALE MODEL OF THE RAGOSIS PRAMO.
AMAZING, ISN'T IT?
YOU PROBABLY WATCHED IT ON TV WHEN YOU WERE YOUNG, RIGHT? I WAS A BIG FAN—
GOBEKI (KALANNG)
AHH!?

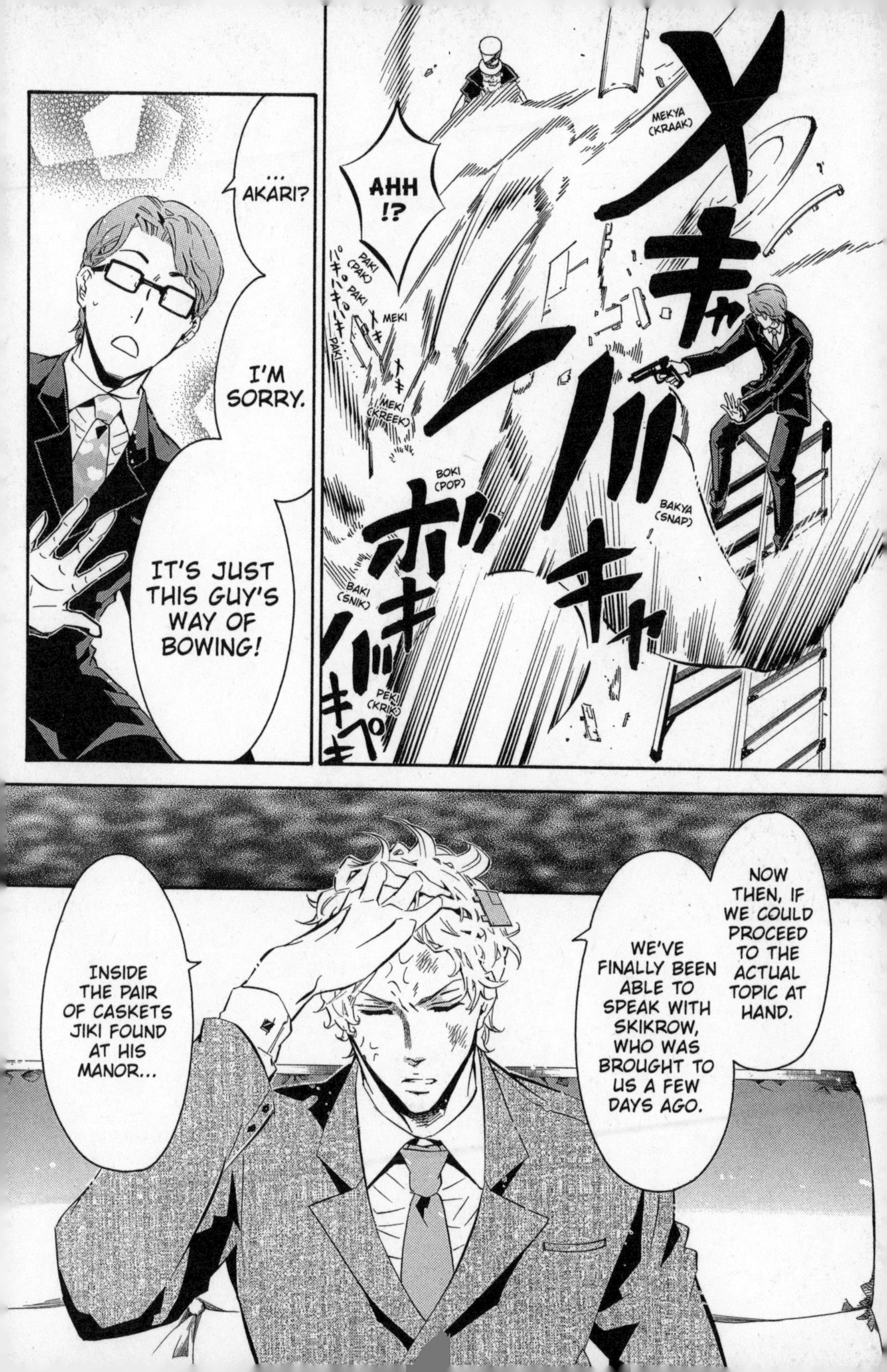
MEKYA (KRAAK)
AHH !?
PAKI (PAK) PAKI
MEKI
MEKI (KREEK)
BAKYA (SNAP)
BOKI (POP)
BAKI (SNIK)
PEKI (KRIK)
... AKARI?
I'M SORRY.
IT'S JUST THIS GUY'S WAY OF BOWING!
NOW THEN, IF WE COULD PROCEED TO THE ACTUAL TOPIC AT HAND.
WE'VE FINALLY BEEN ABLE TO SPEAK WITH SKIKROW, WHO WAS BROUGHT TO US A FEW DAYS AGO.
INSIDE THE PAIR OF CASKETS JIKI FOUND AT HIS MANOR...

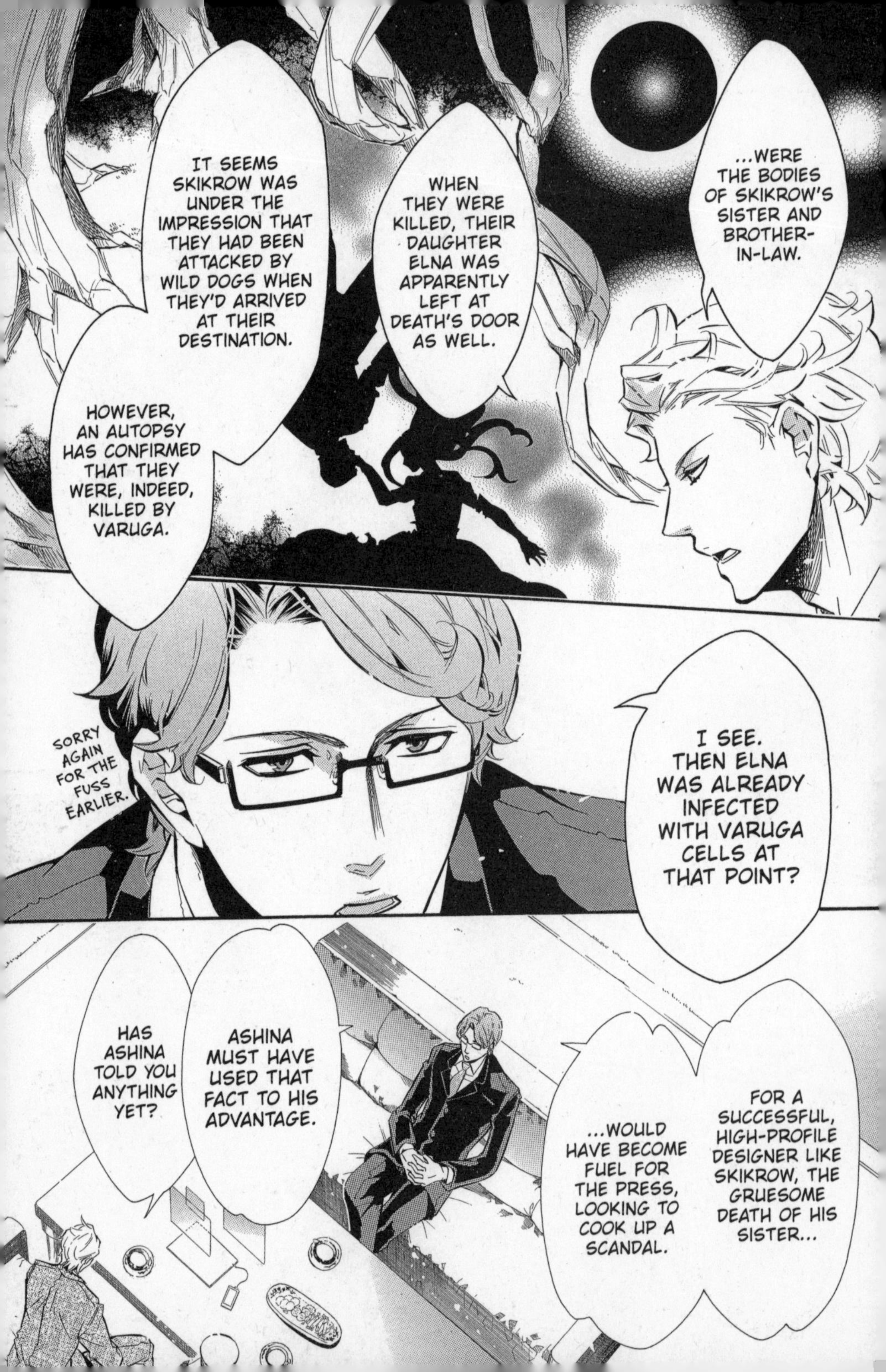
...WERE THE BODIES OF SKIKROW'S SISTER AND BROTHER-IN-LAW.
WHEN THEY WERE KILLED, THEIR DAUGHTER ELNA WAS APPARENTLY LEFT AT DEATH'S DOOR AS WELL.
IT SEEMS SKIKROW WAS UNDER THE IMPRESSION THAT THEY HAD BEEN ATTACKED BY WILD DOGS WHEN THEY'D ARRIVED AT THEIR DESTINATION.
HOWEVER, AN AUTOPSY HAS CONFIRMED THAT THEY WERE, INDEED, KILLED BY VARUGA.
I SEE. THEN ELNA WAS ALREADY INFECTED WITH VARUGA CELLS AT THAT POINT?
SORRY AGAIN FOR THE FUSS EARLIER.
FOR A SUCCESSFUL, HIGH-PROFILE DESIGNER LIKE SKIKROW, THE GRUESOME DEATH OF HIS SISTER...
...WOULD HAVE BECOME FUEL FOR THE PRESS, LOOKING TO COOK UP A SCANDAL.
ASHINA MUST HAVE USED THAT FACT TO HIS ADVANTAGE.
HAS ASHINA TOLD YOU ANYTHING YET?

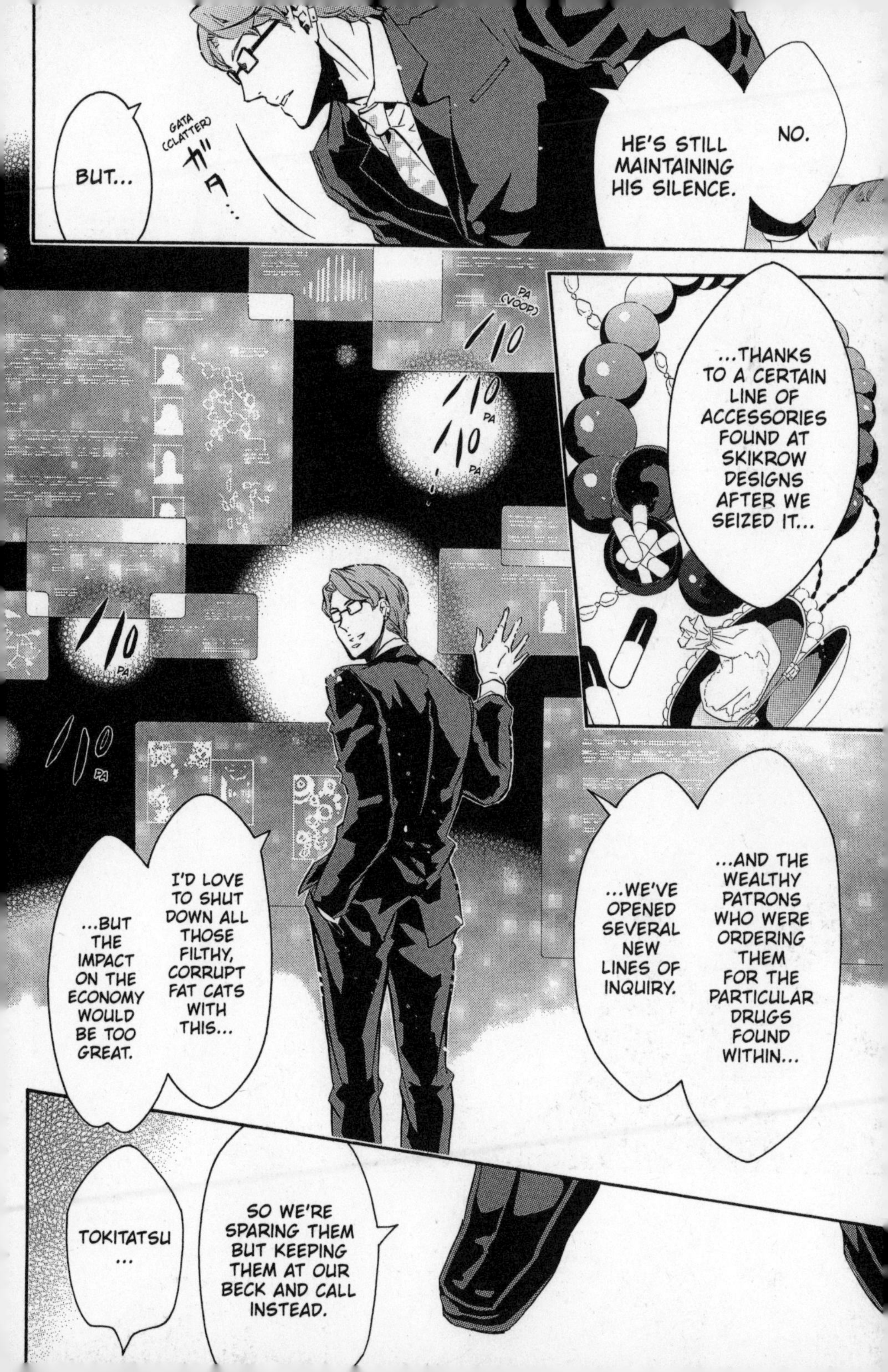
NO.
HE'S STILL MAINTAINING HIS SILENCE.
GATA (CLATTER)
BUT...
...THANKS TO A CERTAIN LINE OF ACCESSORIES FOUND AT SKIKROW DESIGNS AFTER WE SEIZED IT...
PA (VOOP)
PA
PA
PA
PA
...AND THE WEALTHY PATRONS WHO WERE ORDERING THEM FOR THE PARTICULAR DRUGS FOUND WITHIN...
...WE'VE OPENED SEVERAL NEW LINES OF INQUIRY.
I'D LOVE TO SHUT DOWN ALL THOSE FILTHY, CORRUPT FAT CATS WITH THIS...
...BUT THE IMPACT ON THE ECONOMY WOULD BE TOO GREAT.
SO WE'RE SPARING THEM BUT KEEPING THEM AT OUR BECK AND CALL INSTEAD.
TOKITATSU...

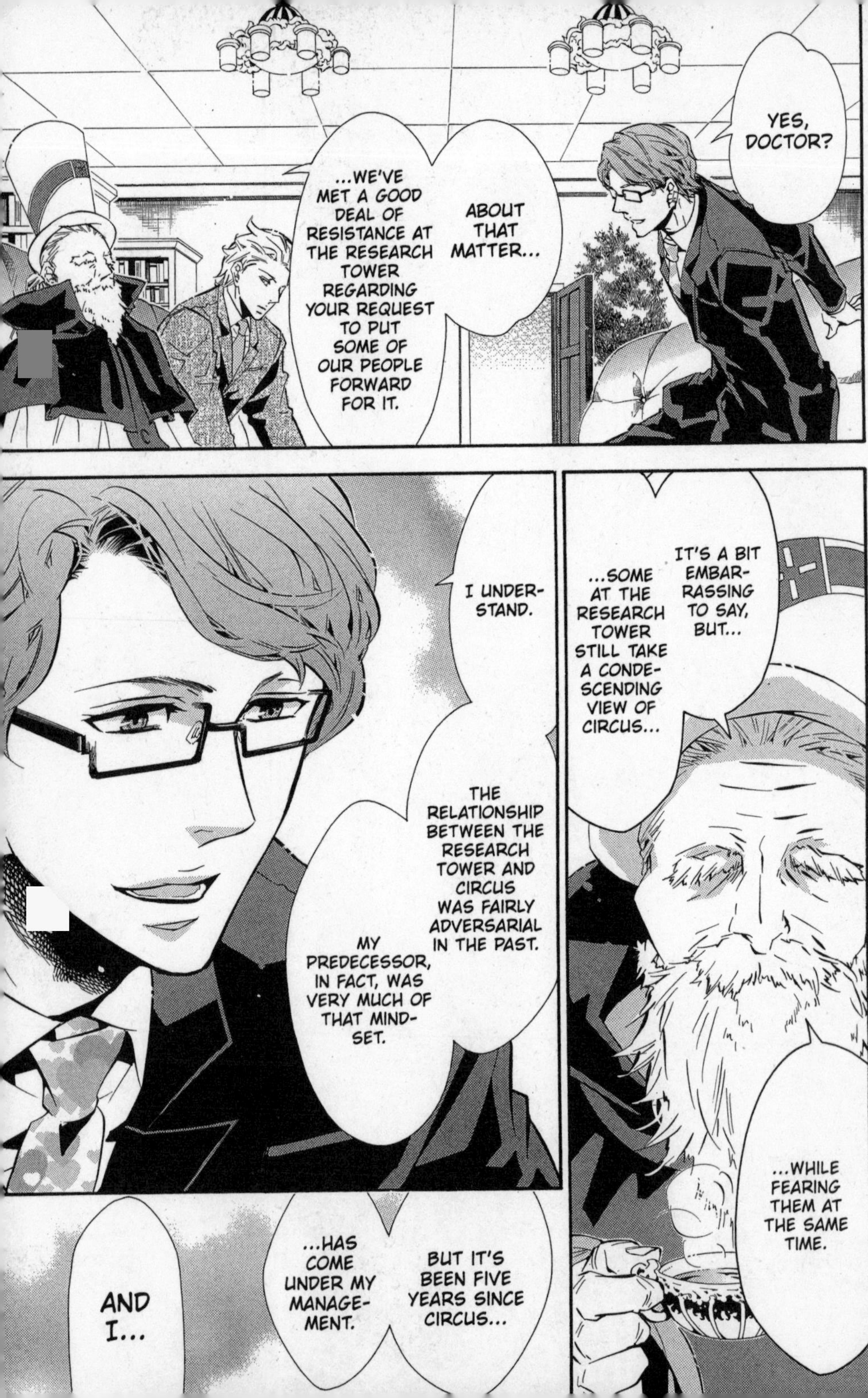
YES, DOCTOR?
ABOUT THAT MATTER...
...WE'VE MET A GOOD DEAL OF RESISTANCE AT THE RESEARCH TOWER REGARDING YOUR REQUEST TO PUT SOME OF OUR PEOPLE FORWARD FOR IT.
IT'S A BIT EMBAR-RASSING TO SAY, BUT...
...SOME AT THE RESEARCH TOWER STILL TAKE A CONDE-SCENDING VIEW OF CIRCUS...
...WHILE FEARING THEM AT THE SAME TIME.
I UNDER-STAND.
THE RELATIONSHIP BETWEEN THE RESEARCH TOWER AND CIRCUS WAS FAIRLY ADVERSARIAL IN THE PAST.
MY PREDECESSOR, IN FACT, WAS VERY MUCH OF THAT MIND-SET.
BUT IT'S BEEN FIVE YEARS SINCE CIRCUS...
...HAS COME UNDER MY MANAGE-MENT.
AND I...

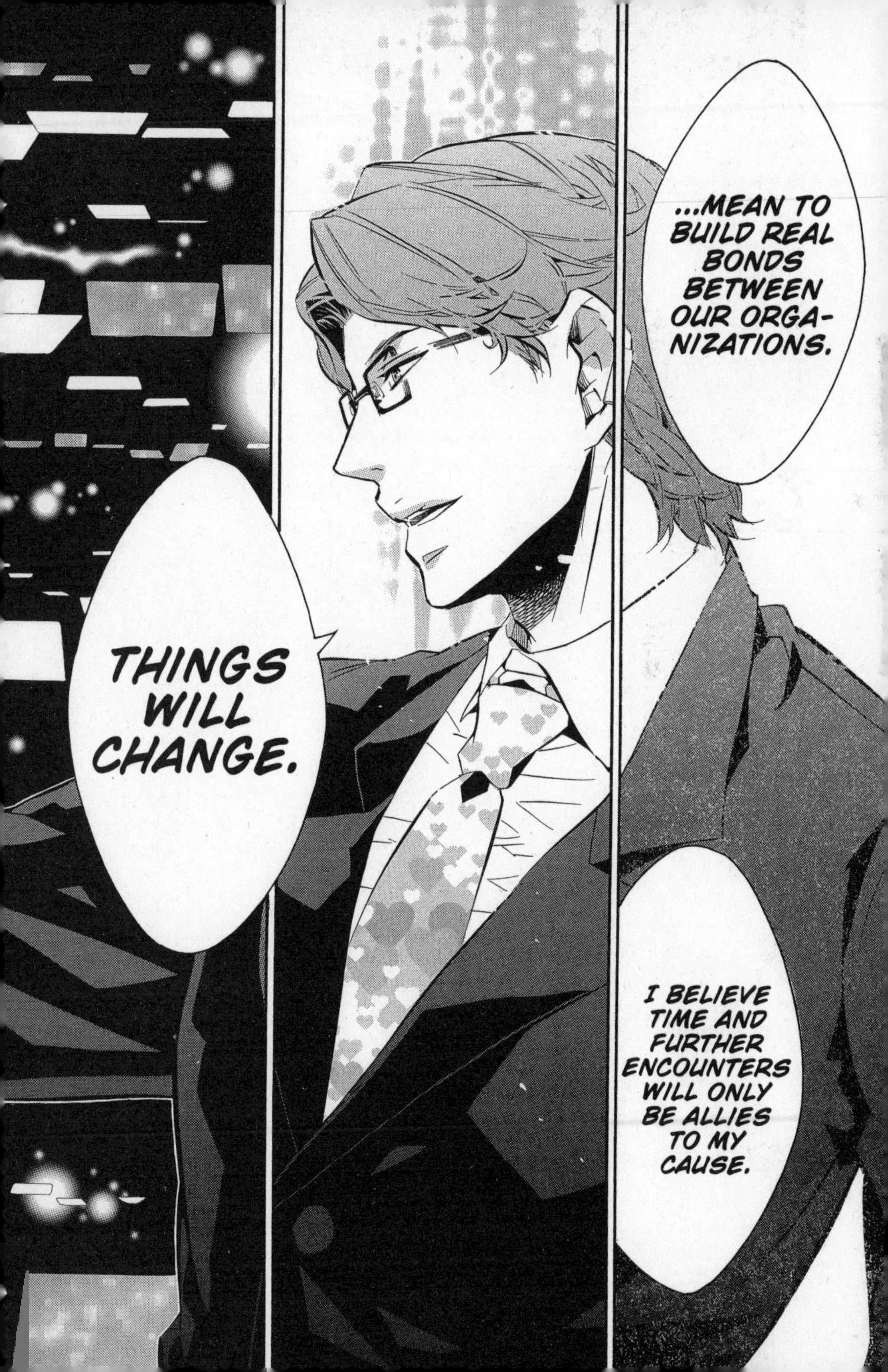
...MEAN TO BUILD REAL BONDS BETWEEN OUR ORGA-NIZATIONS.
I BELIEVE TIME AND FURTHER ENCOUNTERS WILL ONLY BE ALLIES TO MY CAUSE.
THINGS WILL CHANGE.

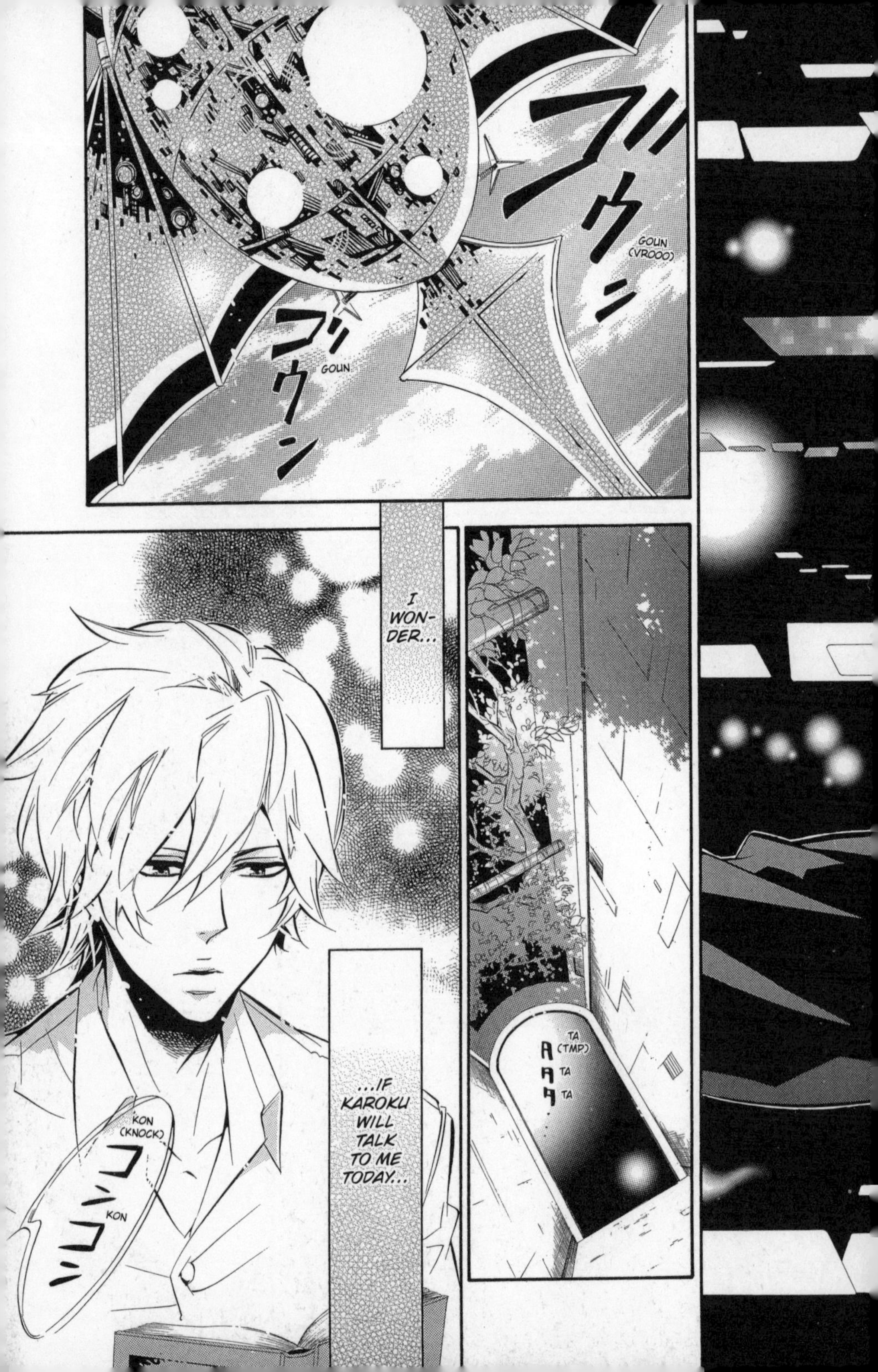
GOUN (VROOO)
GOUN
TA (TMP)
TA
TA
I WONDER...
...IF KAROKU WILL TALK TO ME TODAY...
KON (KNOCK)
KON

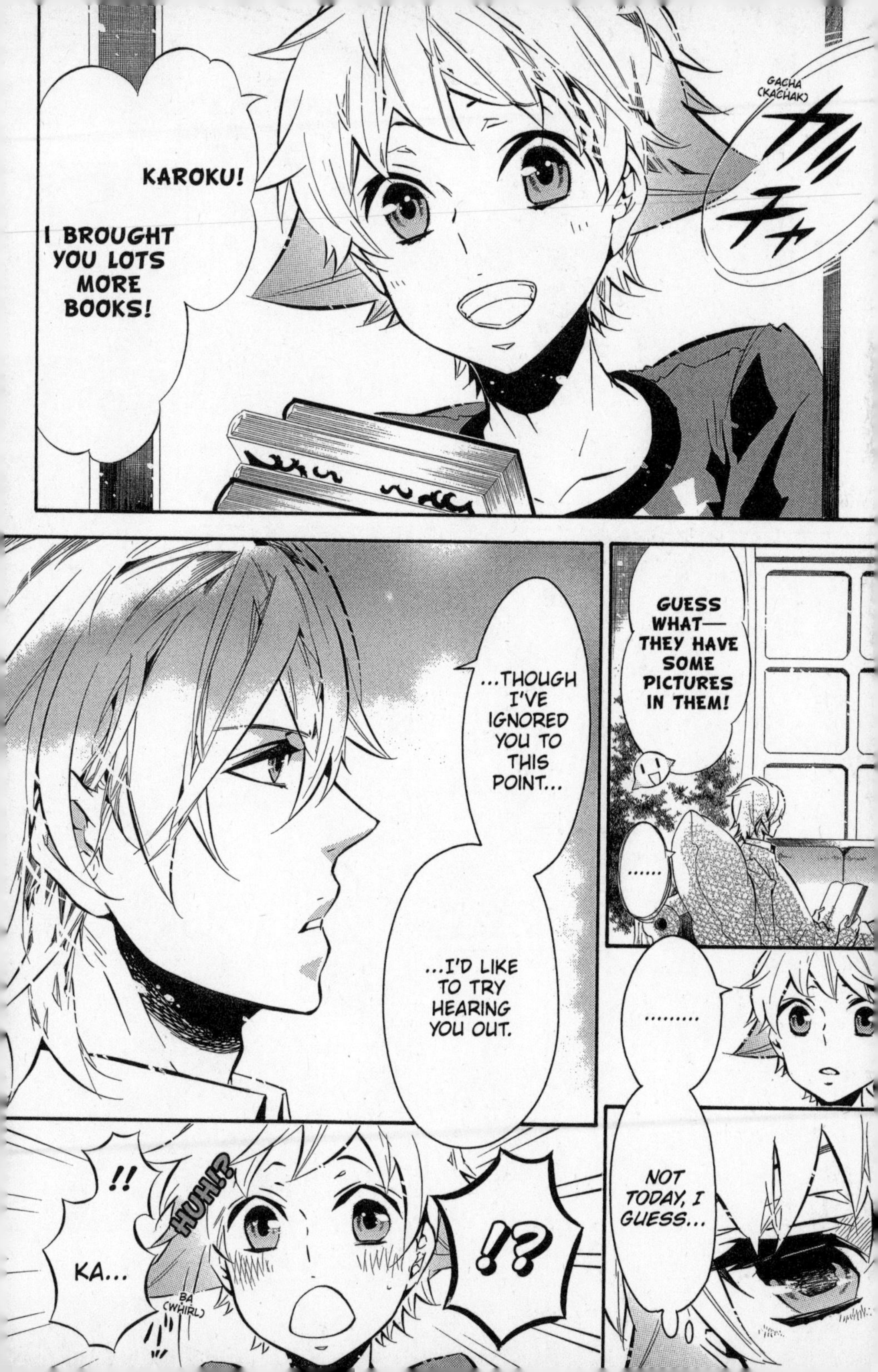
GACHA (KACHAK)
KAROKU!
I BROUGHT YOU LOTS MORE BOOKS!
GUESS WHAT—THEY HAVE SOME PICTURES IN THEM!
......
....
...THOUGH I'VE IGNORED YOU TO THIS POINT...
...I'D LIKE TO TRY HEARING YOU OUT.
NOT TODAY, I GUESS...
!?
HUH!?
!!
KA...
BA (WHIRL)

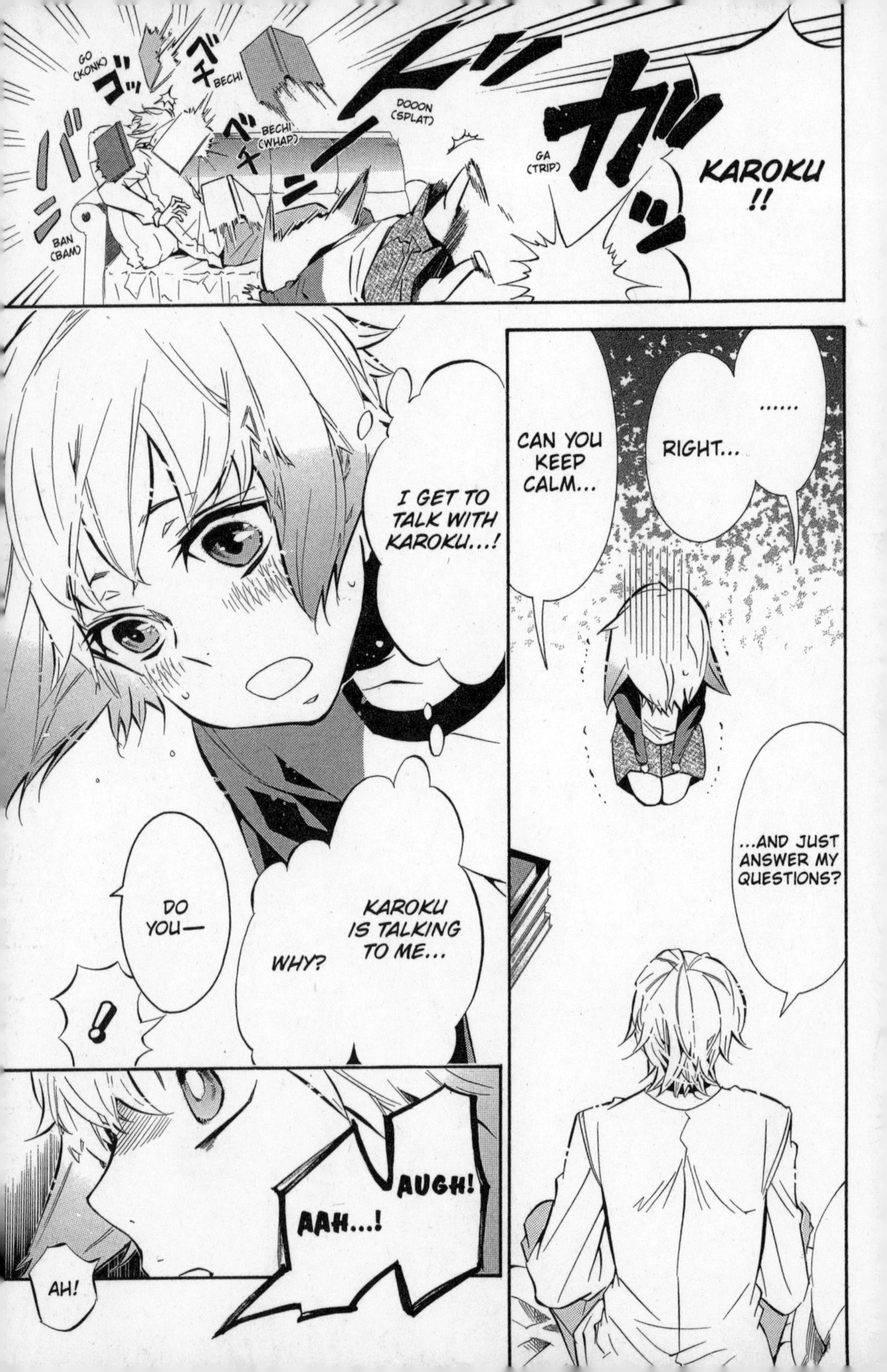
KAROKU !!
GA (TRIP)
DOOON (SPLAT)
BECHI
BECHI (WHAP)
GO (KONK)
BAN (BAM)
......
RIGHT...
CAN YOU KEEP CALM...
...AND JUST ANSWER MY QUESTIONS?
I GET TO TALK WITH KAROKU...!
KAROKU IS TALKING TO ME...
WHY?
DO YOU—
!
AUGH!
AAH...!
AH!

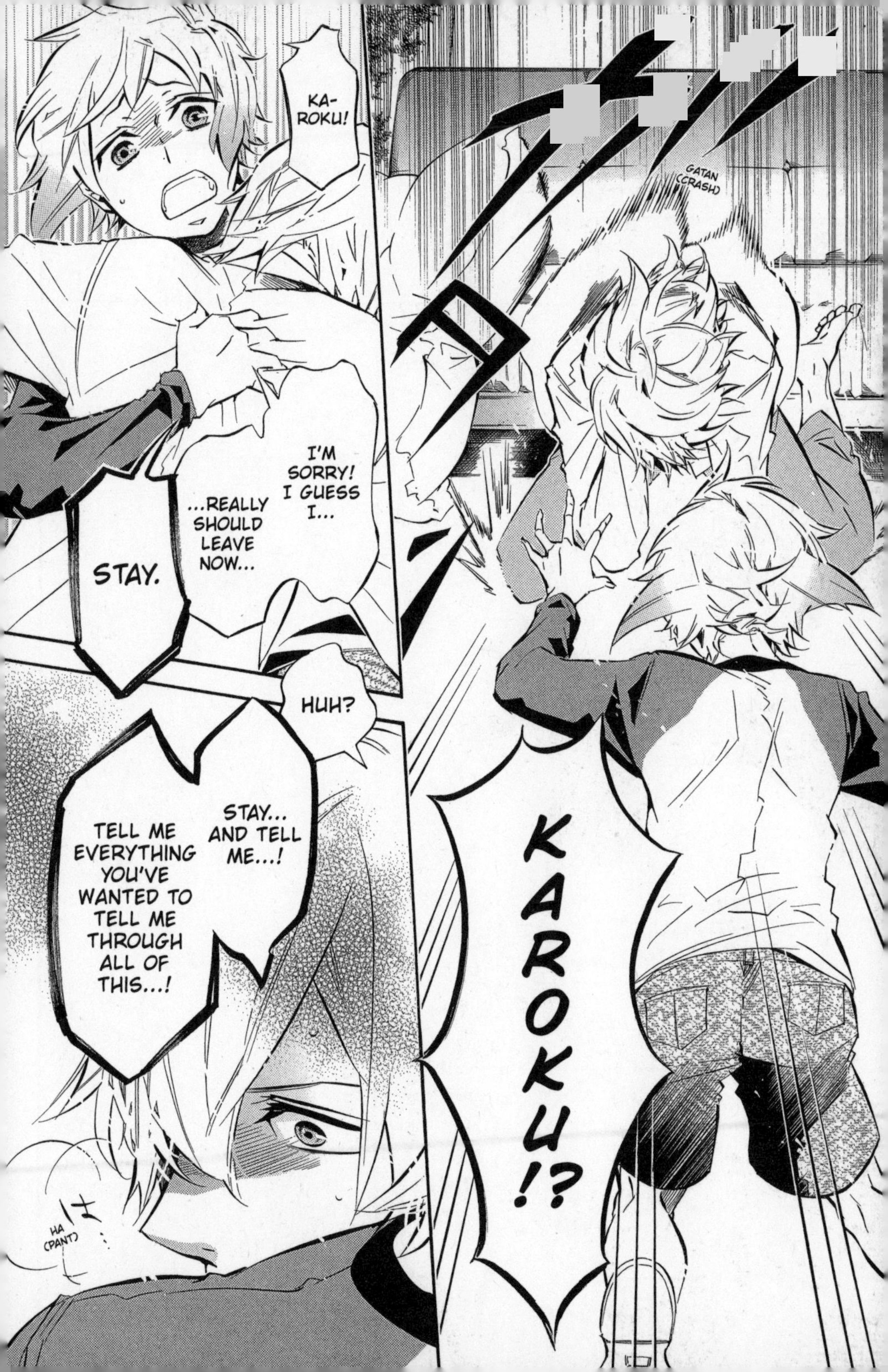
GATAN (CRASH)
KAROKU!?
KA-ROKU!
I'M SORRY! I GUESS I...
...REALLY SHOULD LEAVE NOW...
STAY.
HUH?
STAY... AND TELL ME...!
TELL ME EVERYTHING YOU'VE WANTED TO TELL ME THROUGH ALL OF THIS...!
HA (PANT)

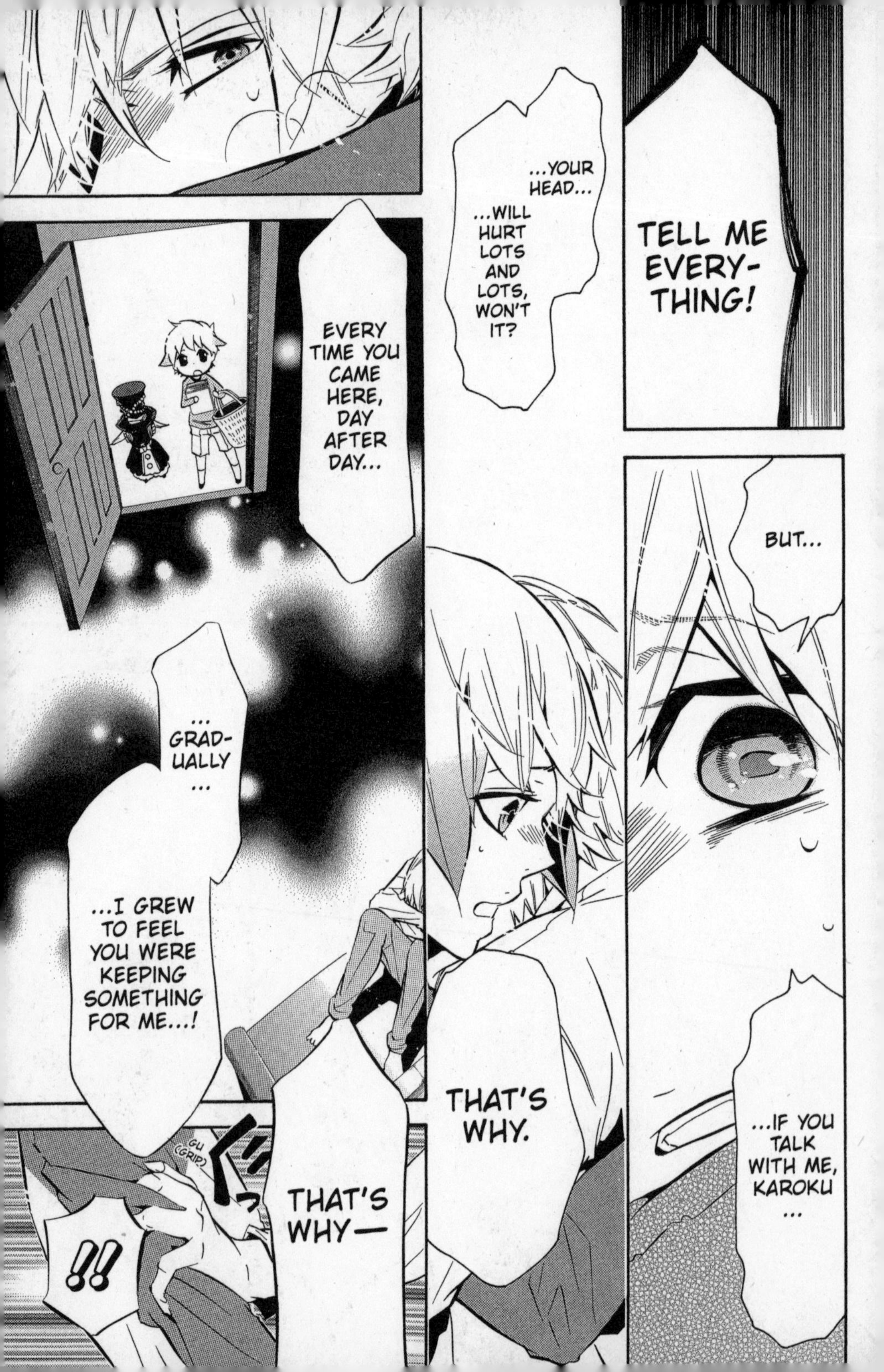
TELL ME EVERY-THING!
BUT...
...IF YOU TALK WITH ME, KAROKU...
...YOUR HEAD...
...WILL HURT LOTS AND LOTS, WON'T IT?
EVERY TIME YOU CAME HERE, DAY AFTER DAY...
...GRADUALLY...
...I GREW TO FEEL YOU WERE KEEPING SOMETHING FOR ME...!
THAT'S WHY.
THAT'S WHY—
GU (GRIP)
!!

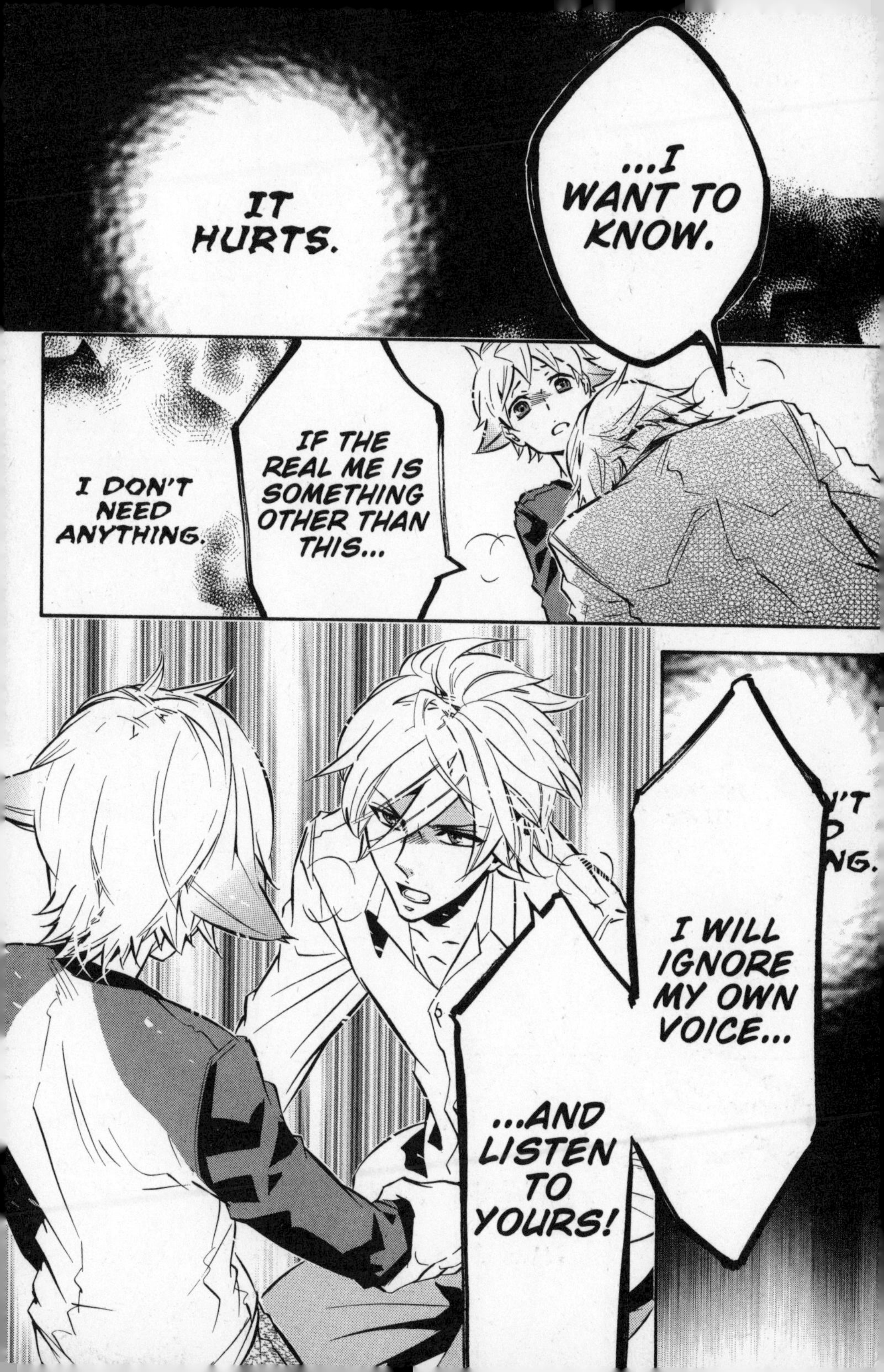
...I WANT TO KNOW.
IT HURTS.
IF THE REAL ME IS SOMETHING OTHER THAN THIS...
I DON'T NEED ANYTHING.
I WILL IGNORE MY OWN VOICE...
...AND LISTEN TO YOURS!

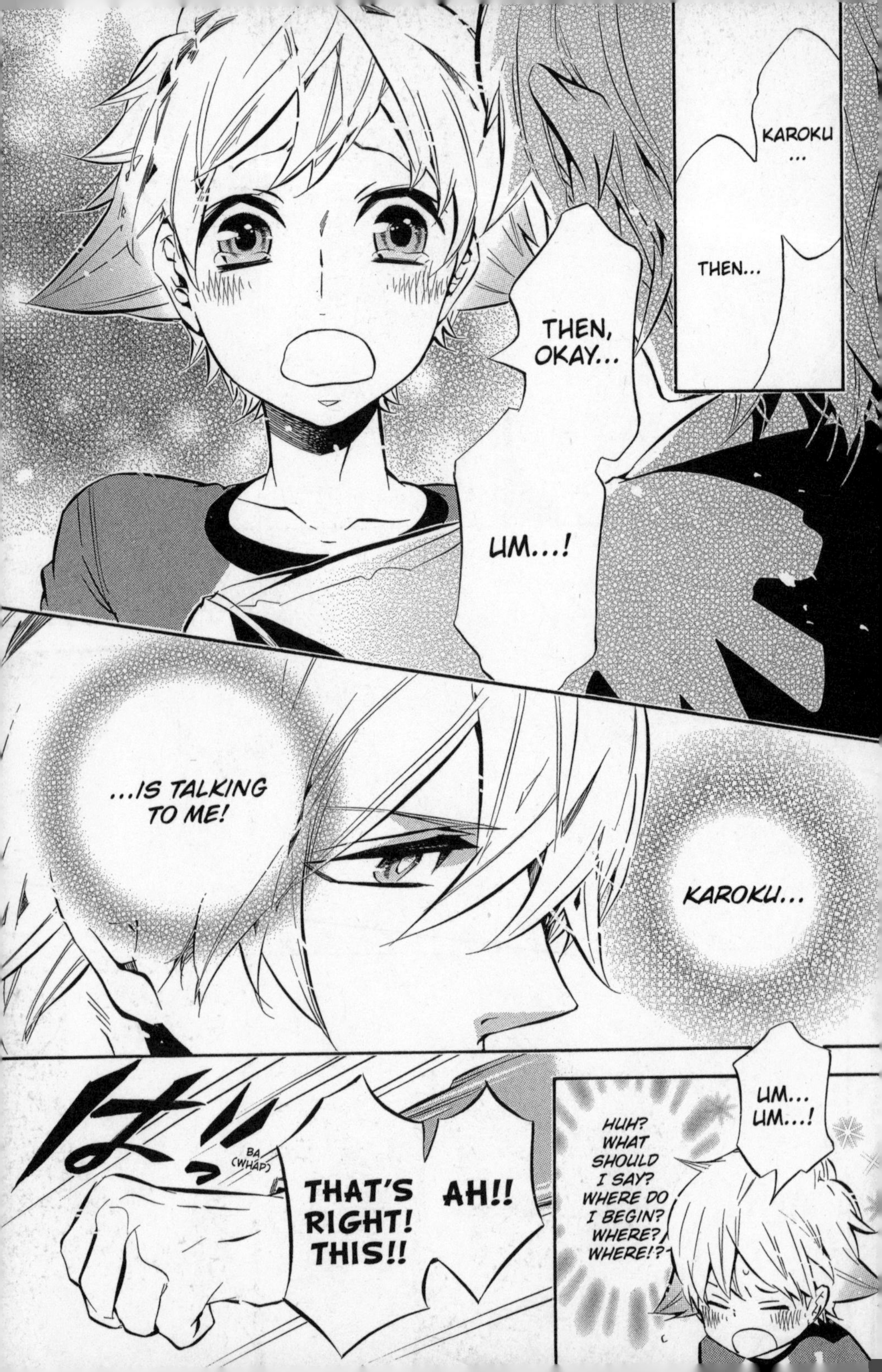
KAROKU ...
THEN...
THEN, OKAY...
UM...!
KAROKU...
...IS TALKING TO ME!
UM... UM...!
HUH? WHAT SHOULD I SAY? WHERE DO I BEGIN? WHERE? WHERE!?
AH!!
THAT'S RIGHT! THIS!!
はっ
BA (WHAP)

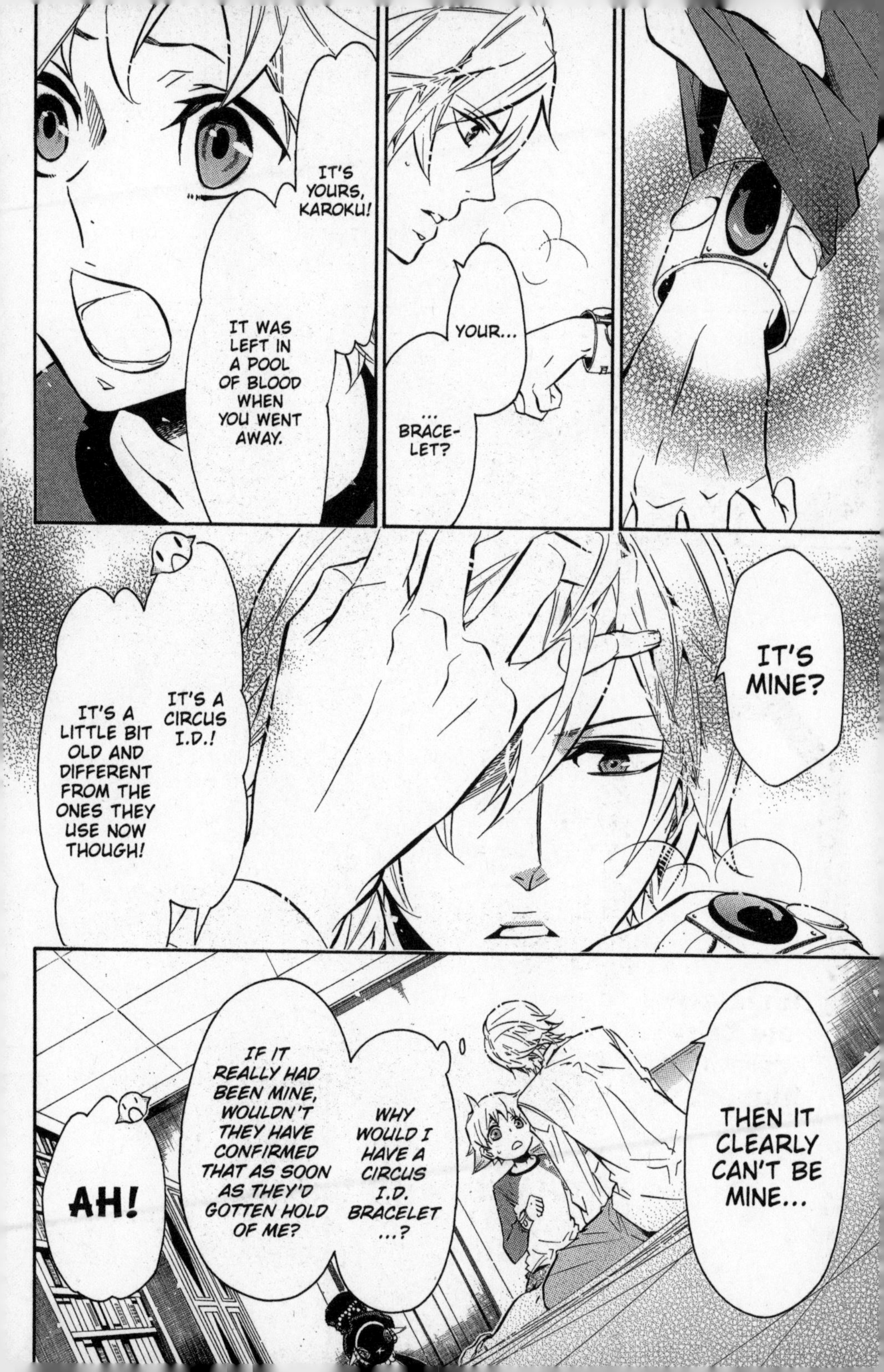
YOUR...
...BRACELET?
IT'S YOURS, KAROKU!
IT WAS LEFT IN A POOL OF BLOOD WHEN YOU WENT AWAY.
IT'S MINE?
IT'S A CIRCUS I.D.!
IT'S A LITTLE BIT OLD AND DIFFERENT FROM THE ONES THEY USE NOW THOUGH!
THEN IT CLEARLY CAN'T BE MINE...
WHY WOULD I HAVE A CIRCUS I.D. BRACELET ...?
IF IT REALLY HAD BEEN MINE, WOULDN'T THEY HAVE CONFIRMED THAT AS SOON AS THEY'D GOTTEN HOLD OF ME?
AH!

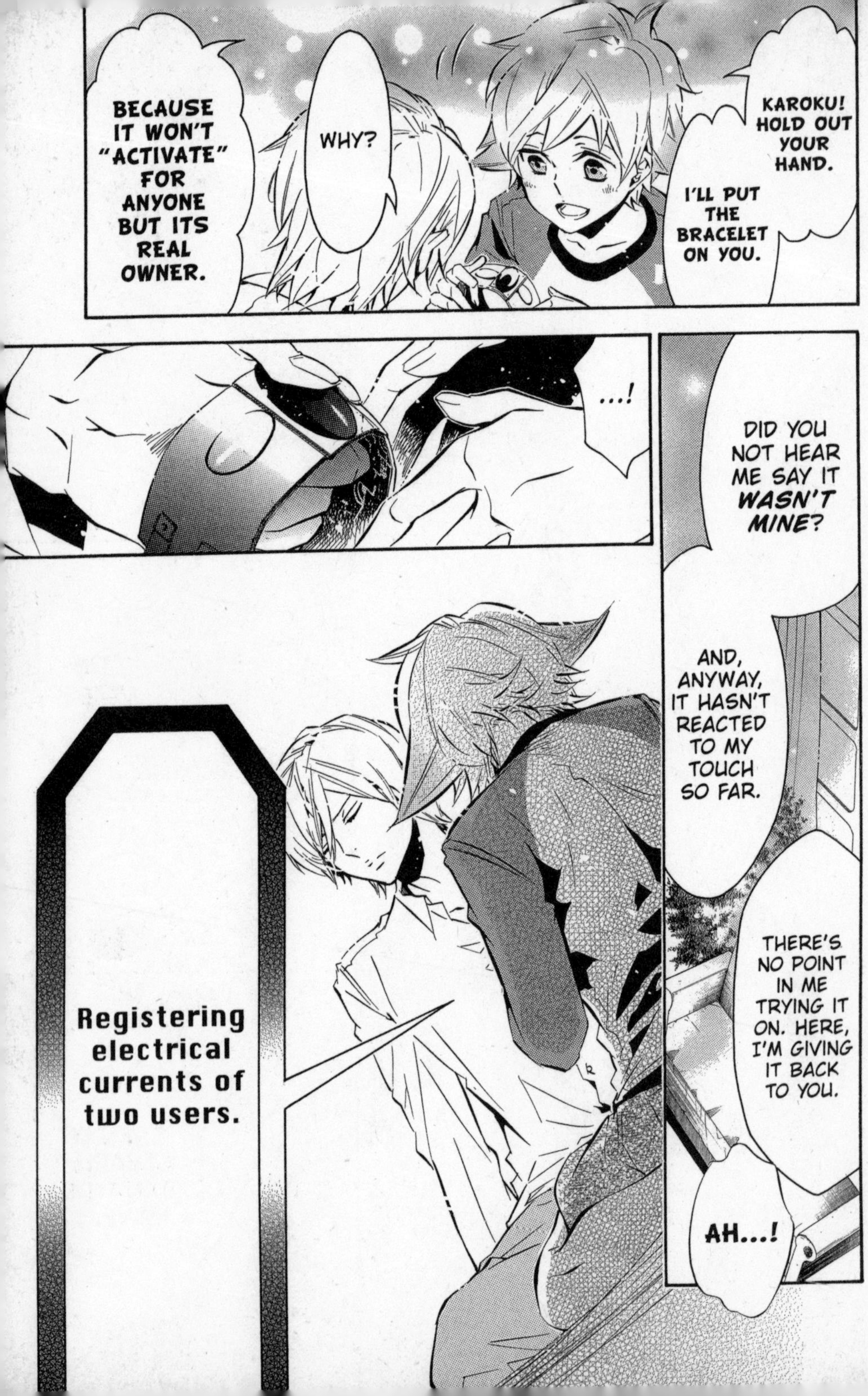
KAROKU! HOLD OUT YOUR HAND.
I'LL PUT THE BRACELET ON YOU.
WHY?
BECAUSE IT WON'T "ACTIVATE" FOR ANYONE BUT ITS REAL OWNER.
DID YOU NOT HEAR ME SAY IT *WASN'T MINE*?
AND, ANYWAY, IT HASN'T REACTED TO MY TOUCH SO FAR.
THERE'S NO POINT IN ME TRYING IT ON. HERE, I'M GIVING IT BACK TO YOU.
...!
AH...!
Registering electrical currents of two users.

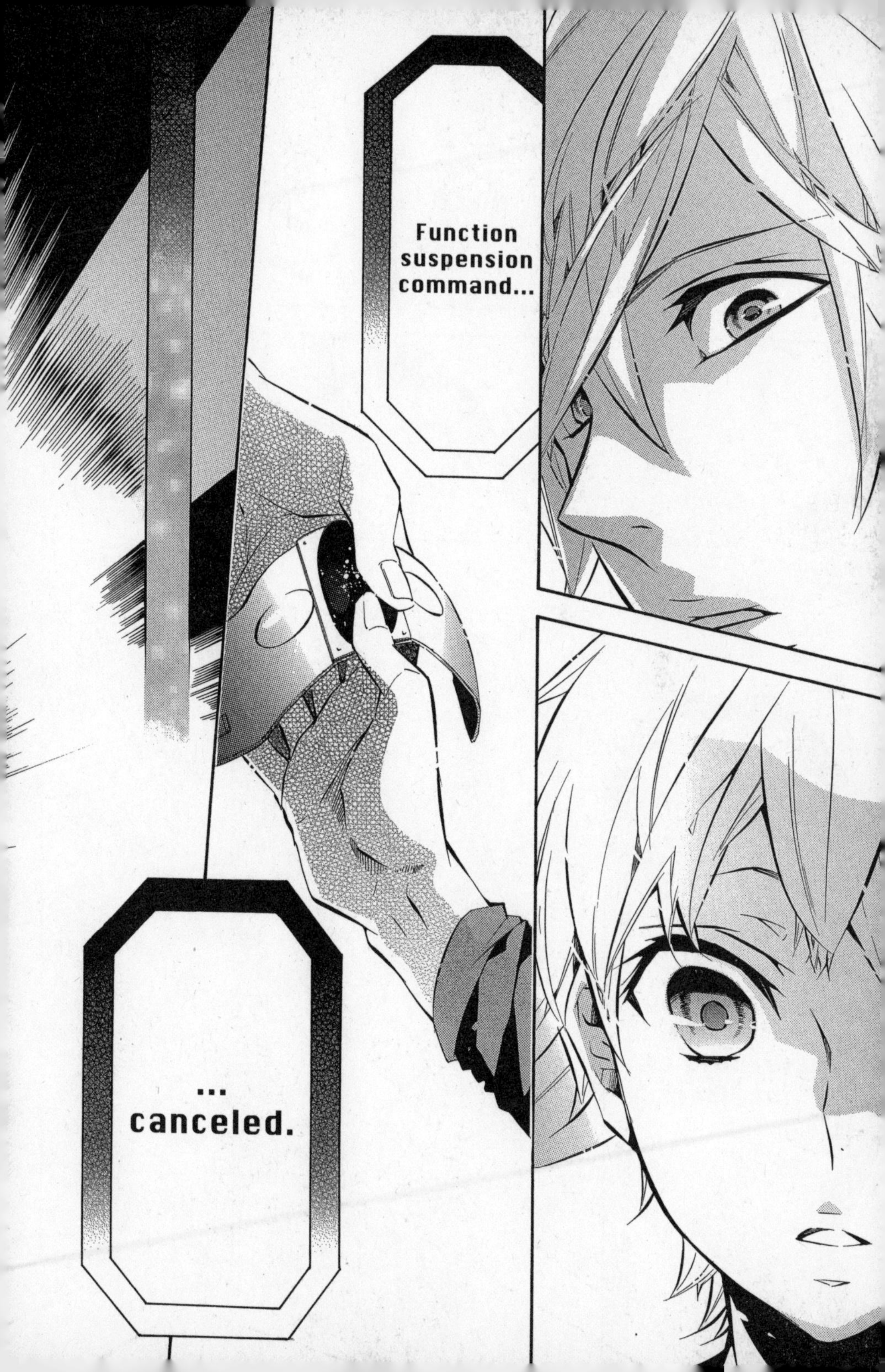
Function suspension command...
... canceled.

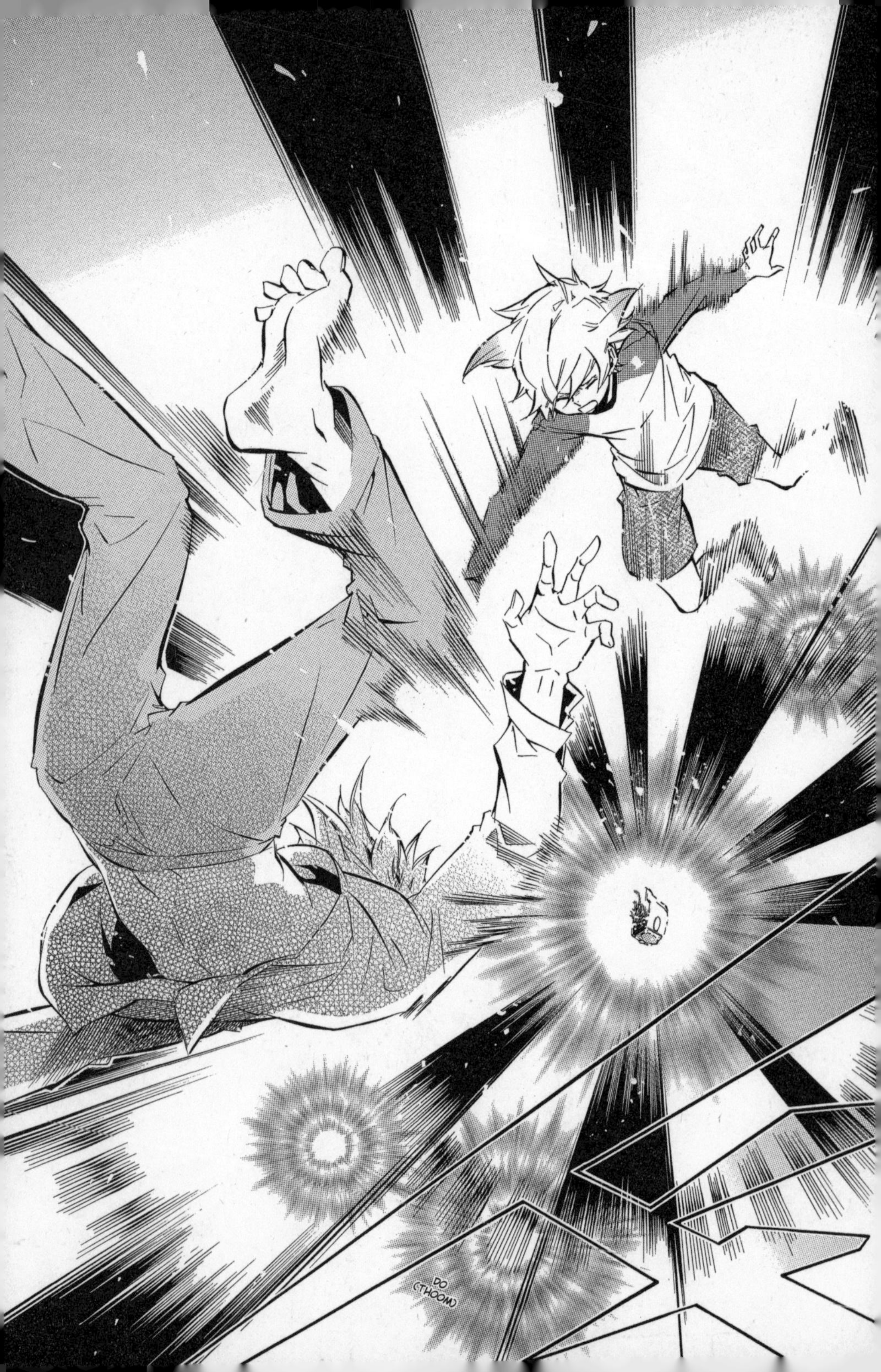
DO
(THOOM)

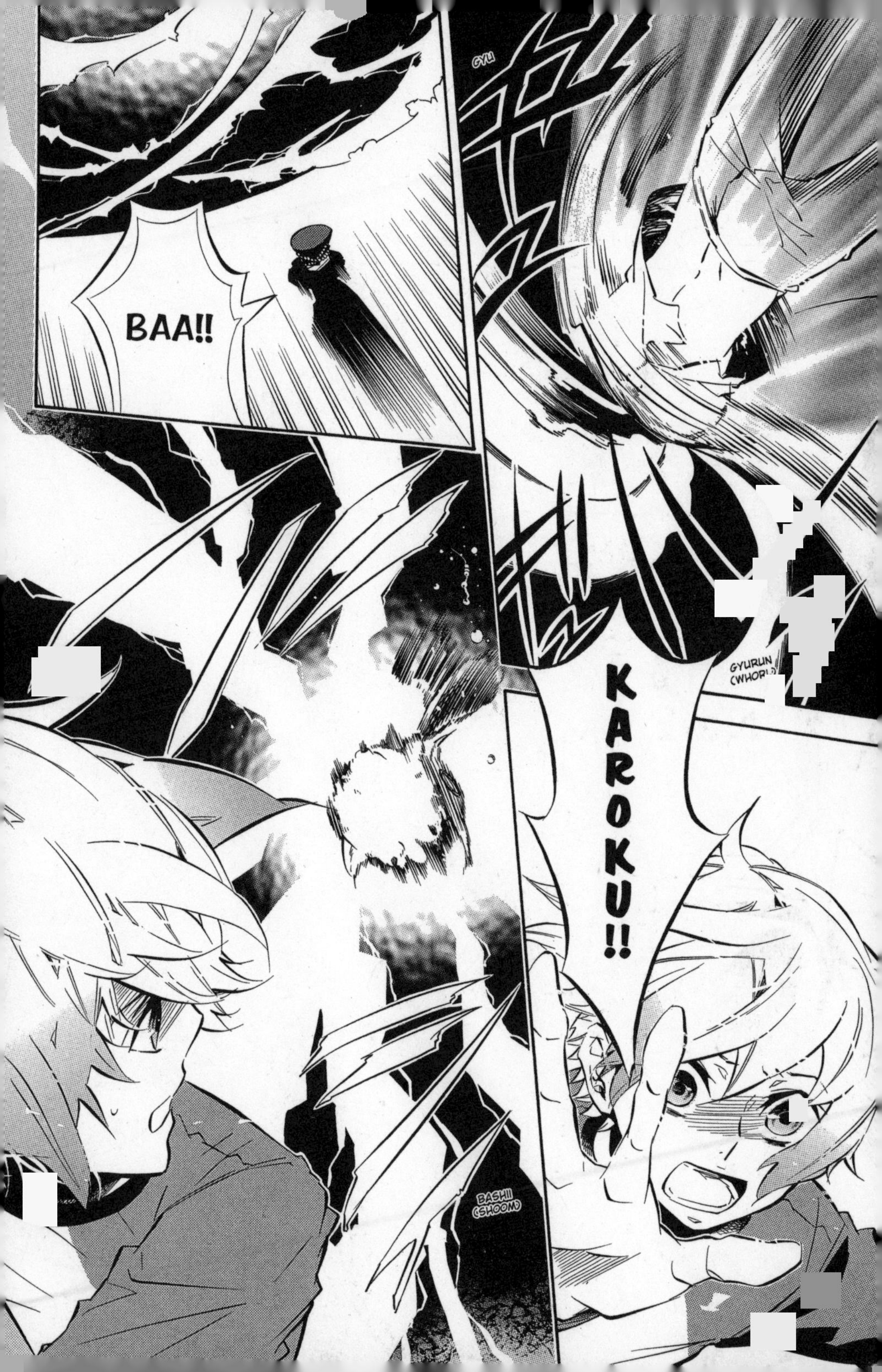
GYU
BAA!!
GYURUN
(WHOR
KAROKU!!
BASHII (SHOOM)

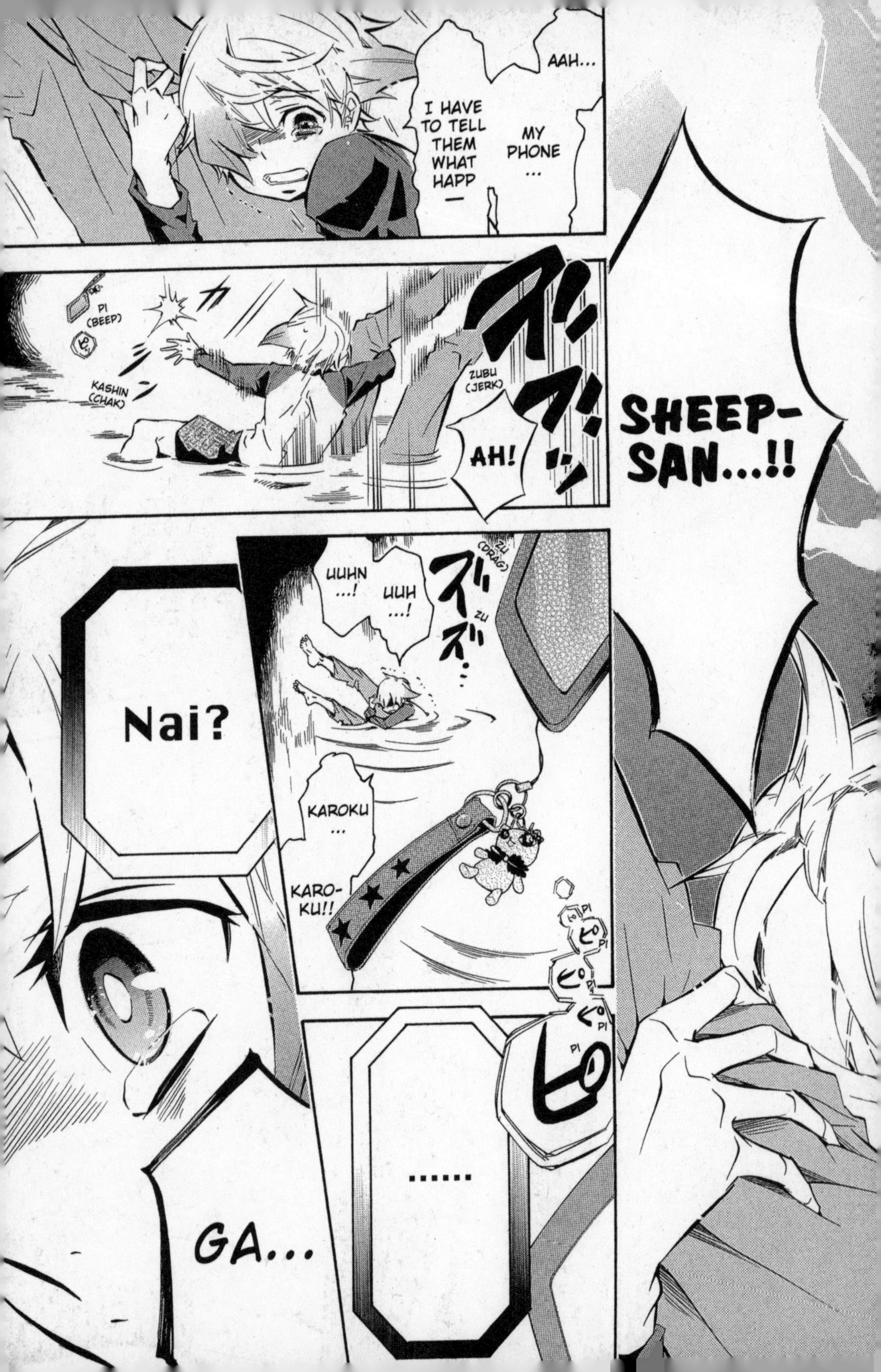
SHEEP-SAN...!!
AAH...
MY PHONE ...
I HAVE TO TELL THEM WHAT HAPP —
ZUBU (JERK)
AH!
PI (BEEP)
KASHIN (CHAK)
ZU (DRAG)
UUHN ...!
UUH ...!
ZU
KAROKU ...
KARO-KU!!
PI PI PI PI PI
Nai?
......
GA...

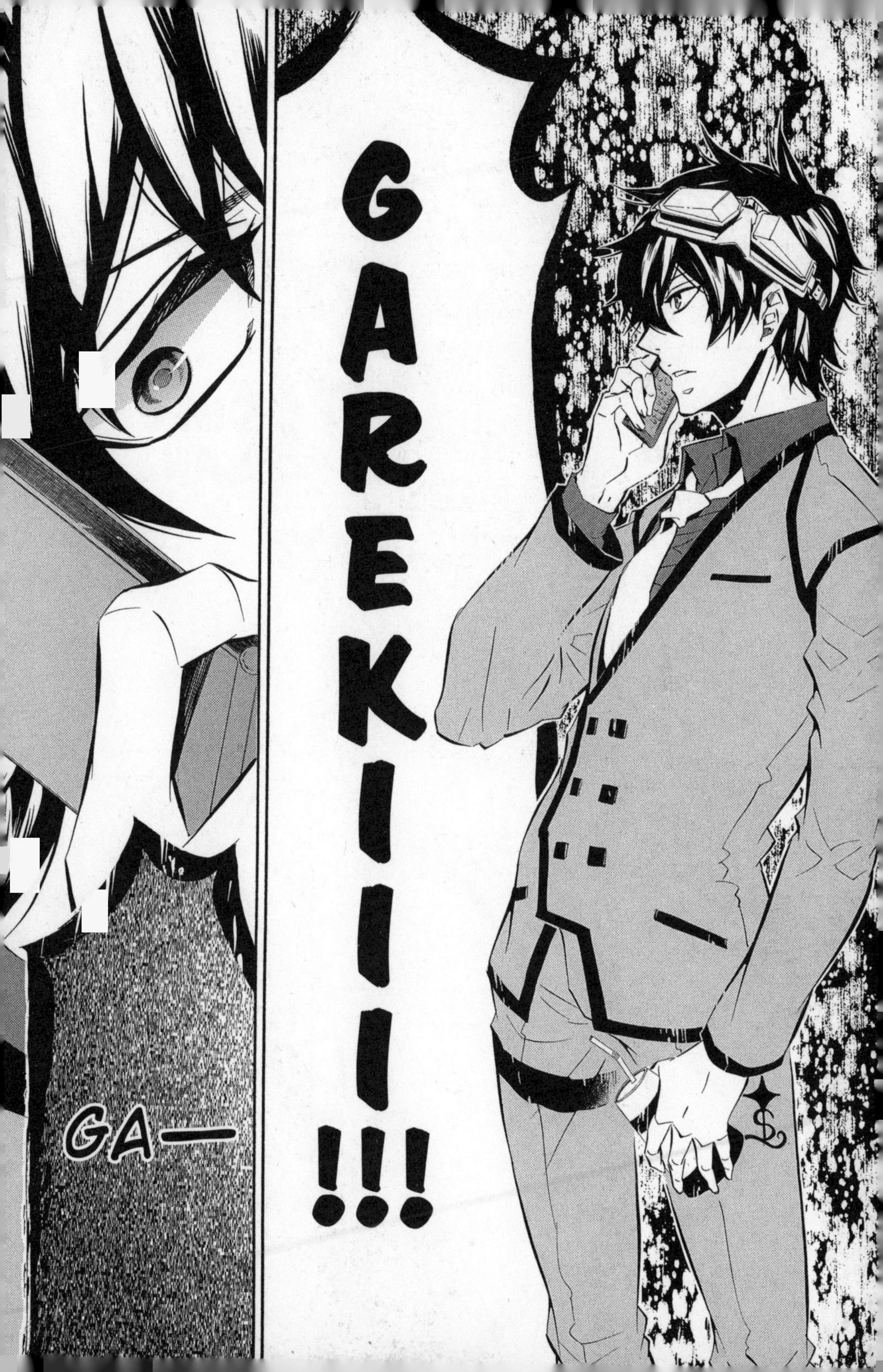
GAREKI!!!
GA—

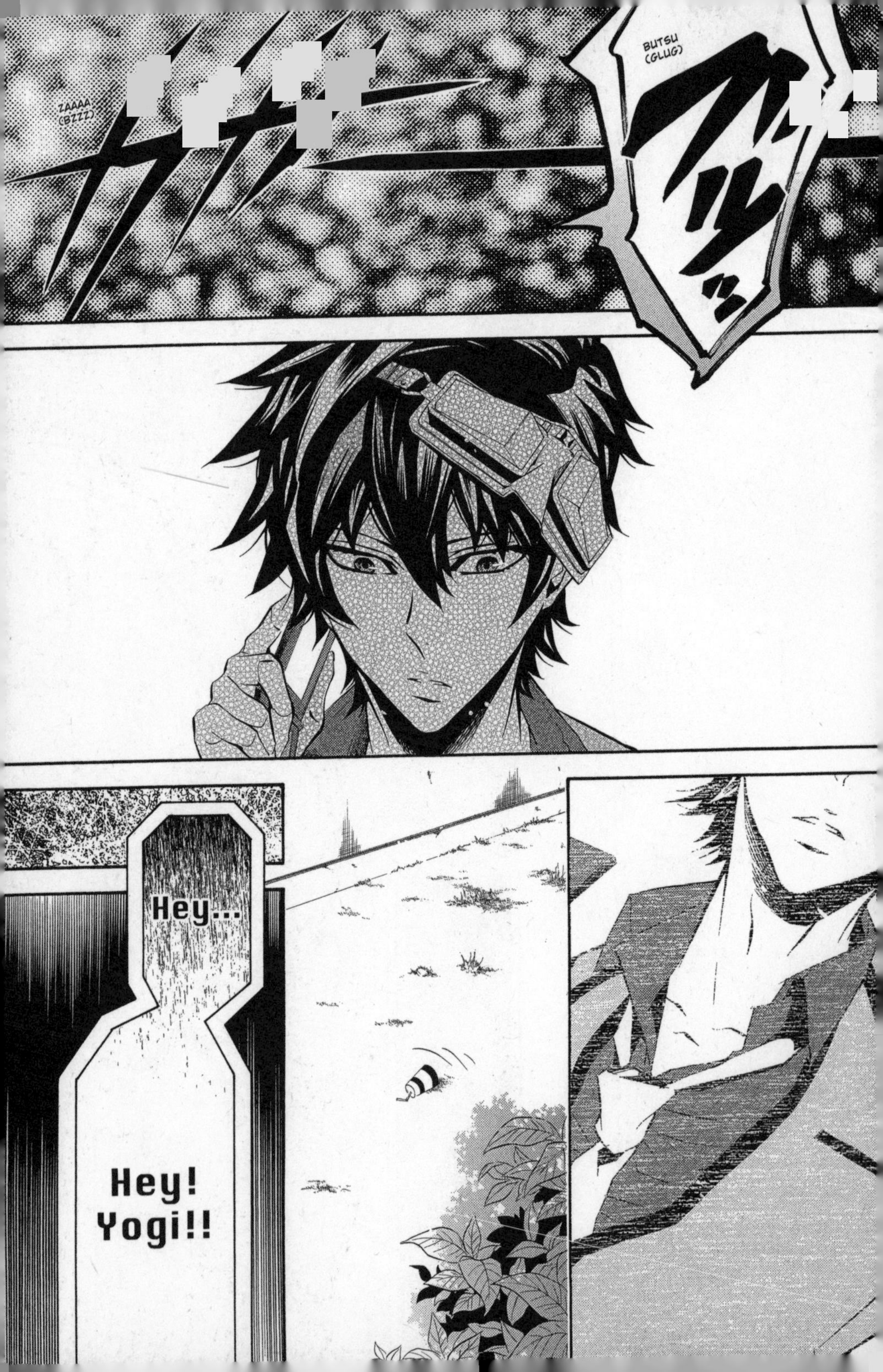
BUTSU (GLUG)
ZAAAA (BZZZ)
Hey...
Hey! Yogi!!

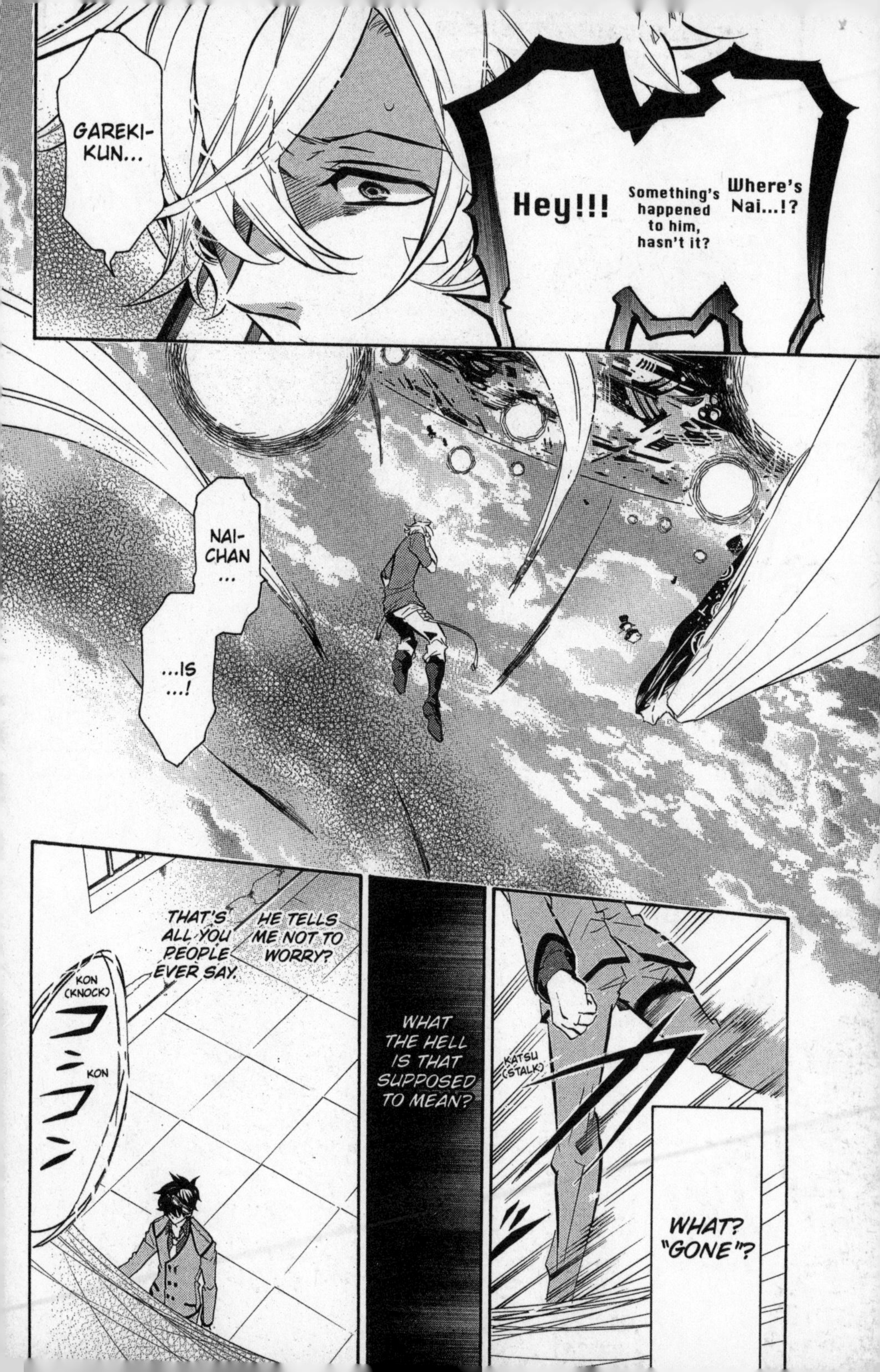
Where's Nai...!?
Something's happened to him, hasn't it?
Hey!!!
GAREKI-KUN...
NAI-CHAN ...
...IS ...!
KATSU (STALK)
WHAT? "GONE"?
WHAT THE HELL IS THAT SUPPOSED TO MEAN?
HE TELLS ME NOT TO WORRY?
THAT'S ALL YOU PEOPLE EVER SAY.
KON (KNOCK)
KON

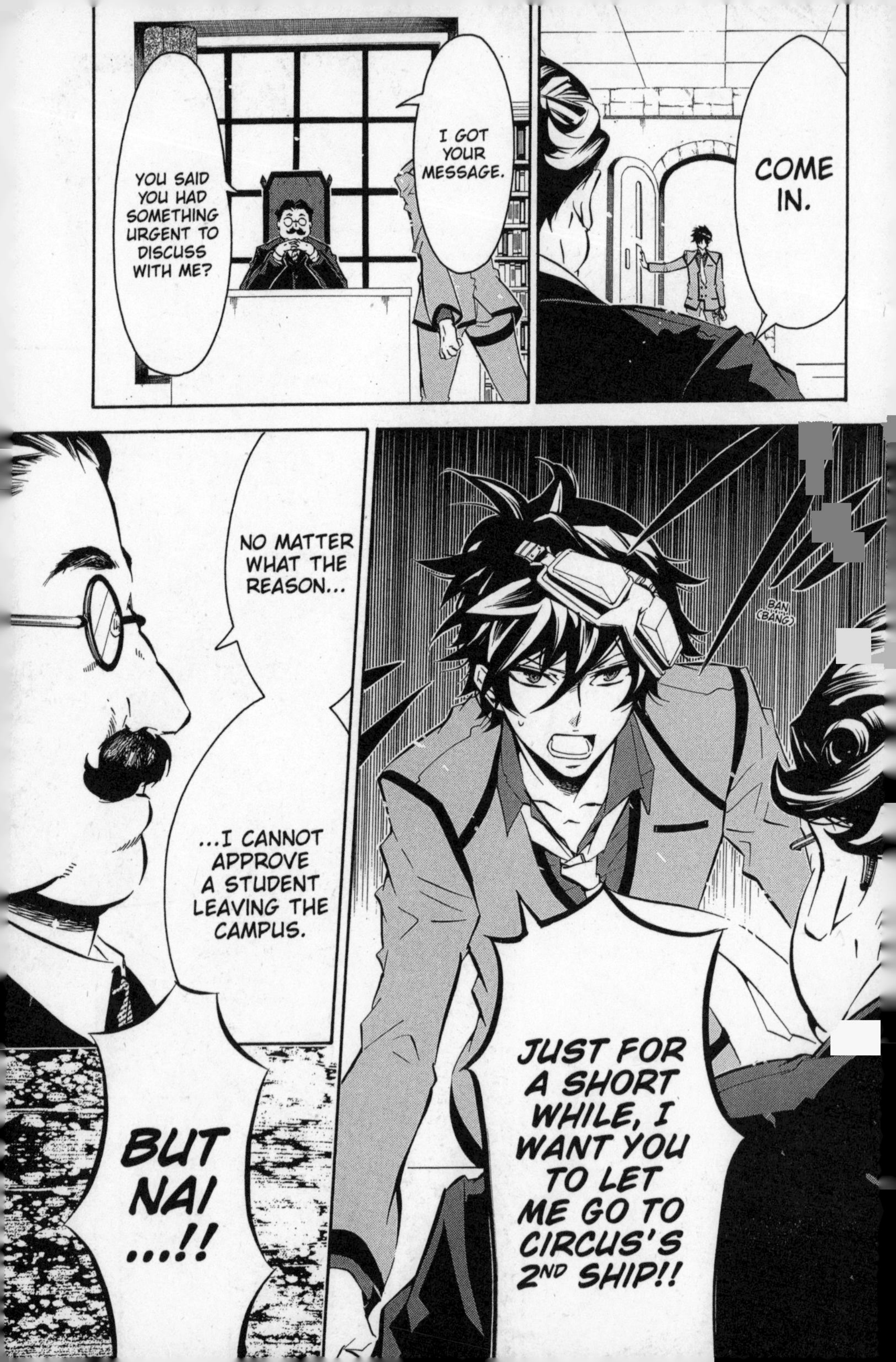
COME IN.
I GOT YOUR MESSAGE.
YOU SAID YOU HAD SOMETHING URGENT TO DISCUSS WITH ME?
BAN (BANG)
JUST FOR A SHORT WHILE, I WANT YOU TO LET ME GO TO CIRCUS'S 2ND SHIP!!
NO MATTER WHAT THE REASON...
...I CANNOT APPROVE A STUDENT LEAVING THE CAMPUS.
BUT NAI...!!

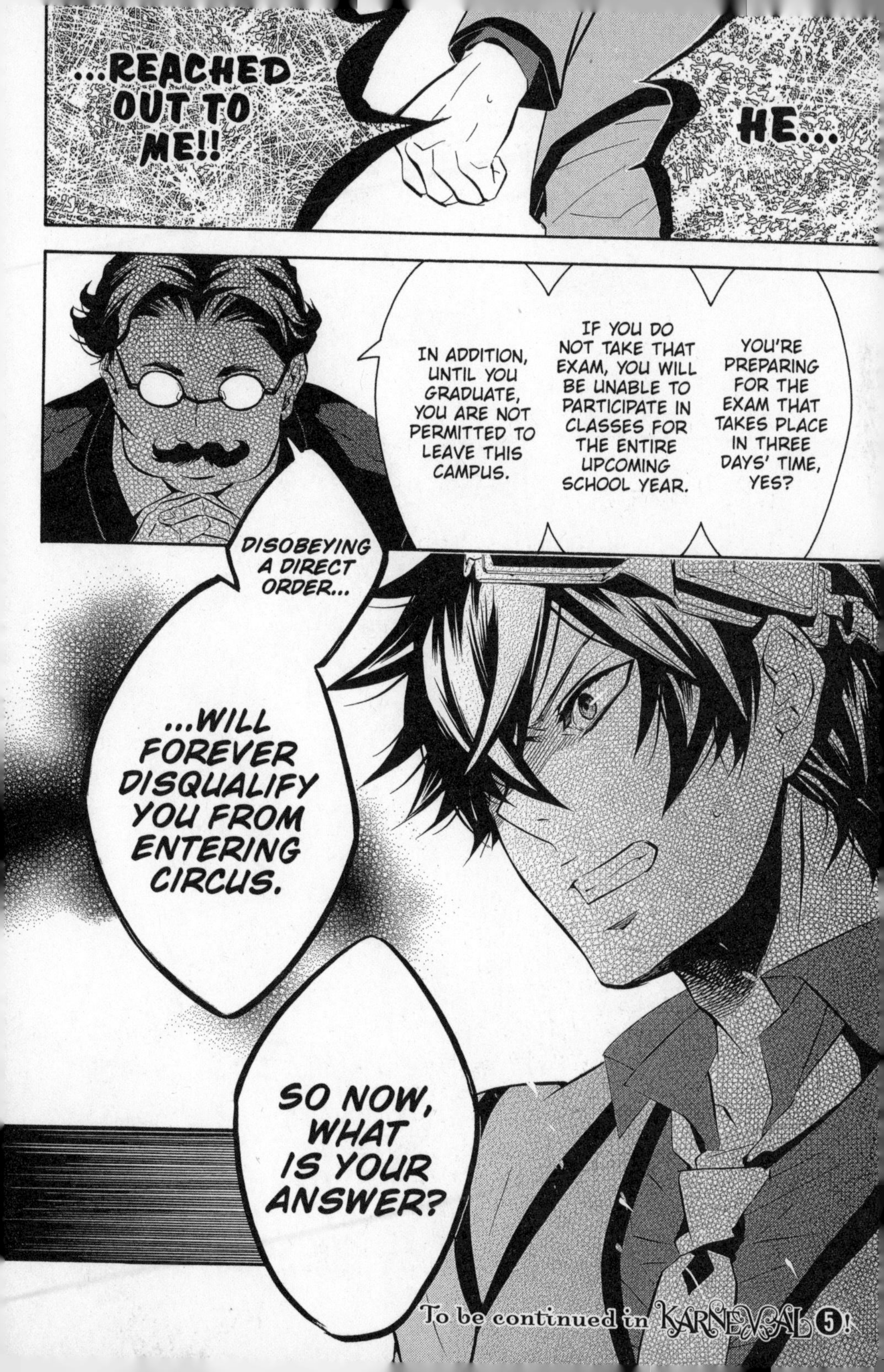
HE...
...REACHED OUT TO ME!!
YOU'RE PREPARING FOR THE EXAM THAT TAKES PLACE IN THREE DAYS' TIME, YES?
IF YOU DO NOT TAKE THAT EXAM, YOU WILL BE UNABLE TO PARTICIPATE IN CLASSES FOR THE ENTIRE UPCOMING SCHOOL YEAR.
IN ADDITION, UNTIL YOU GRADUATE, YOU ARE NOT PERMITTED TO LEAVE THIS CAMPUS.
DISOBEYING A DIRECT ORDER...
...WILL FOREVER DISQUALIFY YOU FROM ENTERING CIRCUS.
SO NOW, WHAT IS YOUR ANSWER?
To be continued in KARNEVAL 5!

KARNEVAL

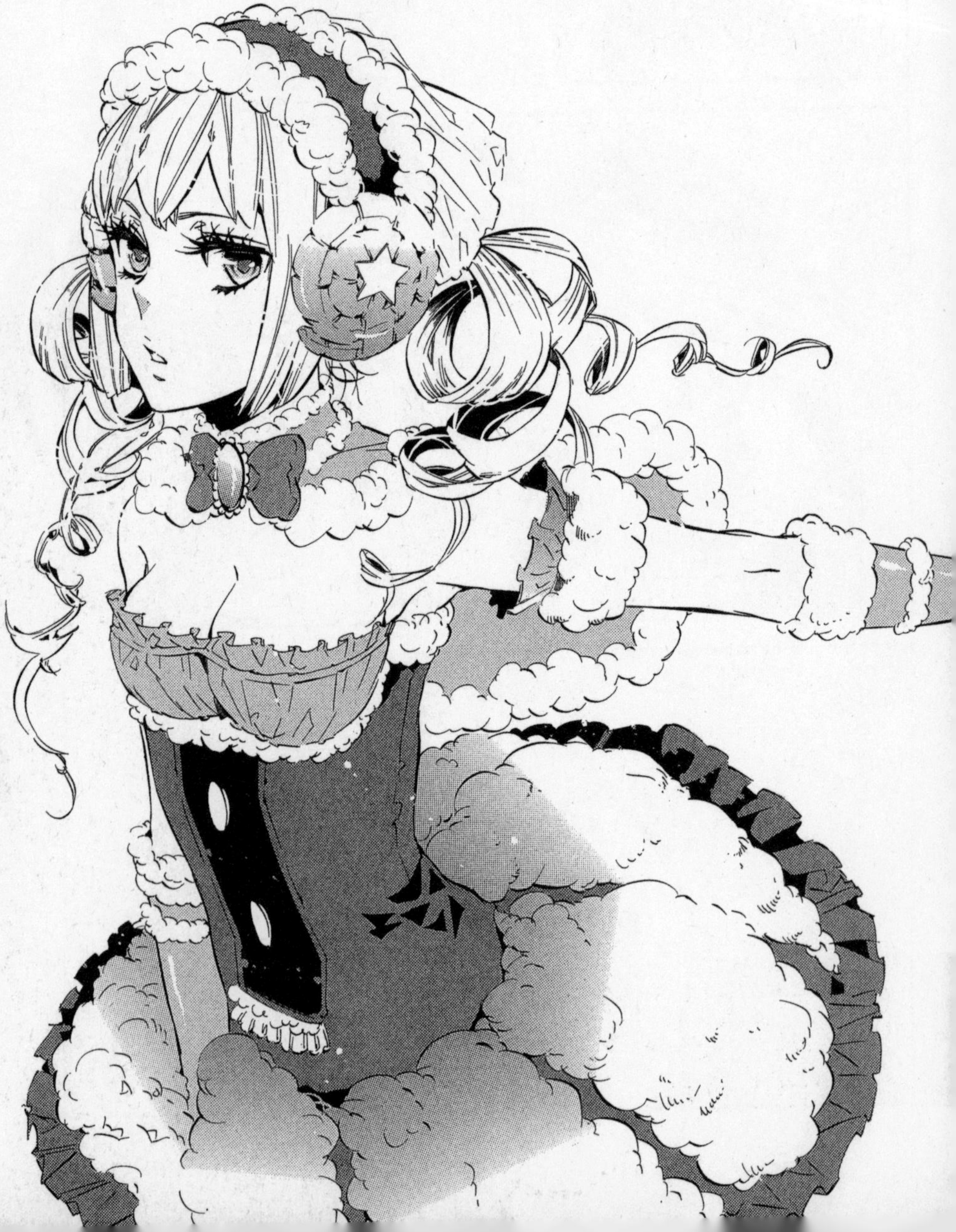

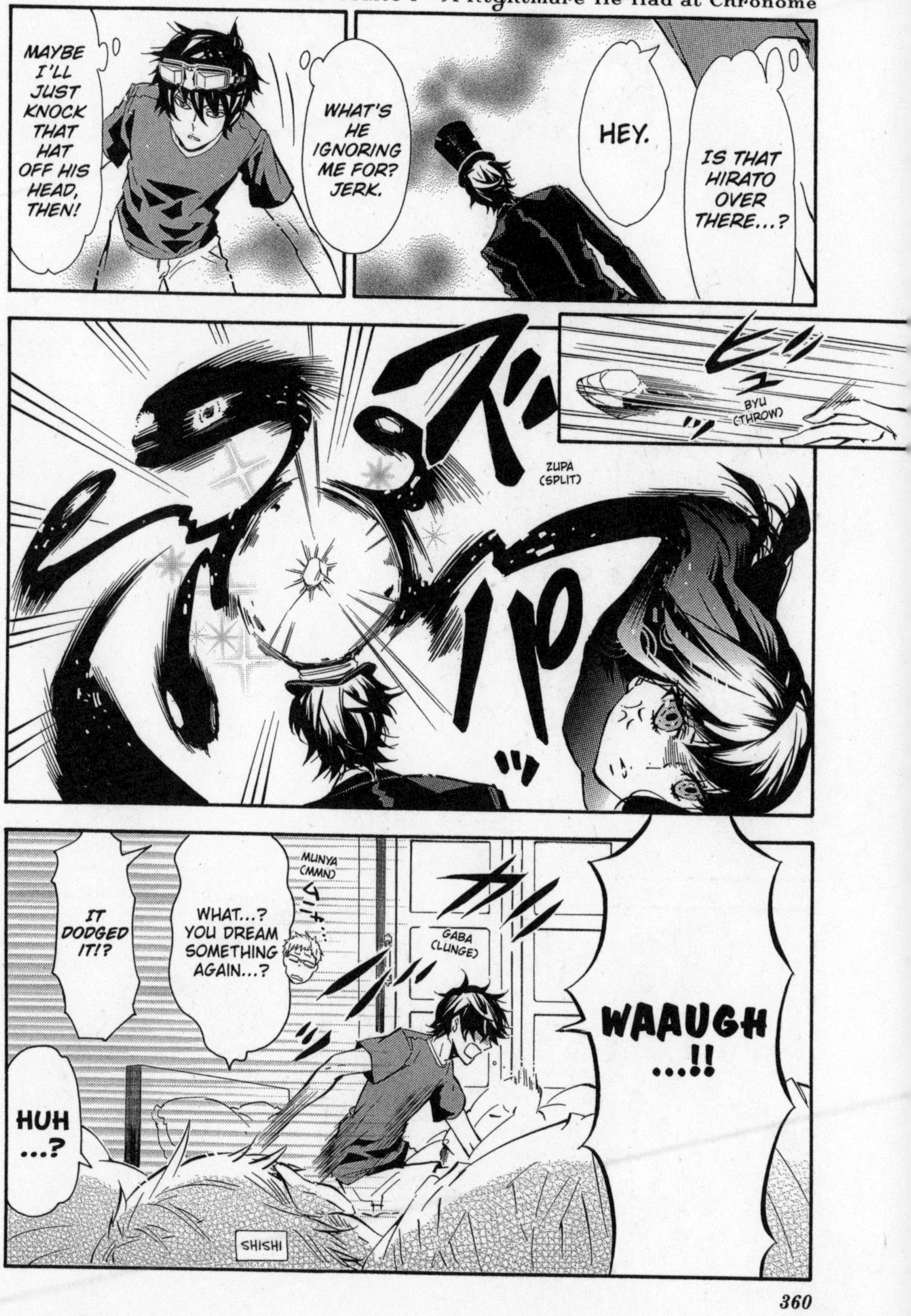
IS THAT HIRATO OVER THERE...?
HEY.
WHAT'S HE IGNORING ME FOR? JERK.
MAYBE I'LL JUST KNOCK THAT HAT OFF HIS HEAD, THEN!
BYU (THROW)
ZUPA (SPLIT)
WAAUGH ...!!
GABA (LUNGE)
MUNYA (MMN)
WHAT...? YOU DREAM SOMETHING AGAIN...?
IT DODGED IT!?
HUH ...?
SHISHI

Bonus Comic 2 - A Child's Sensibilities

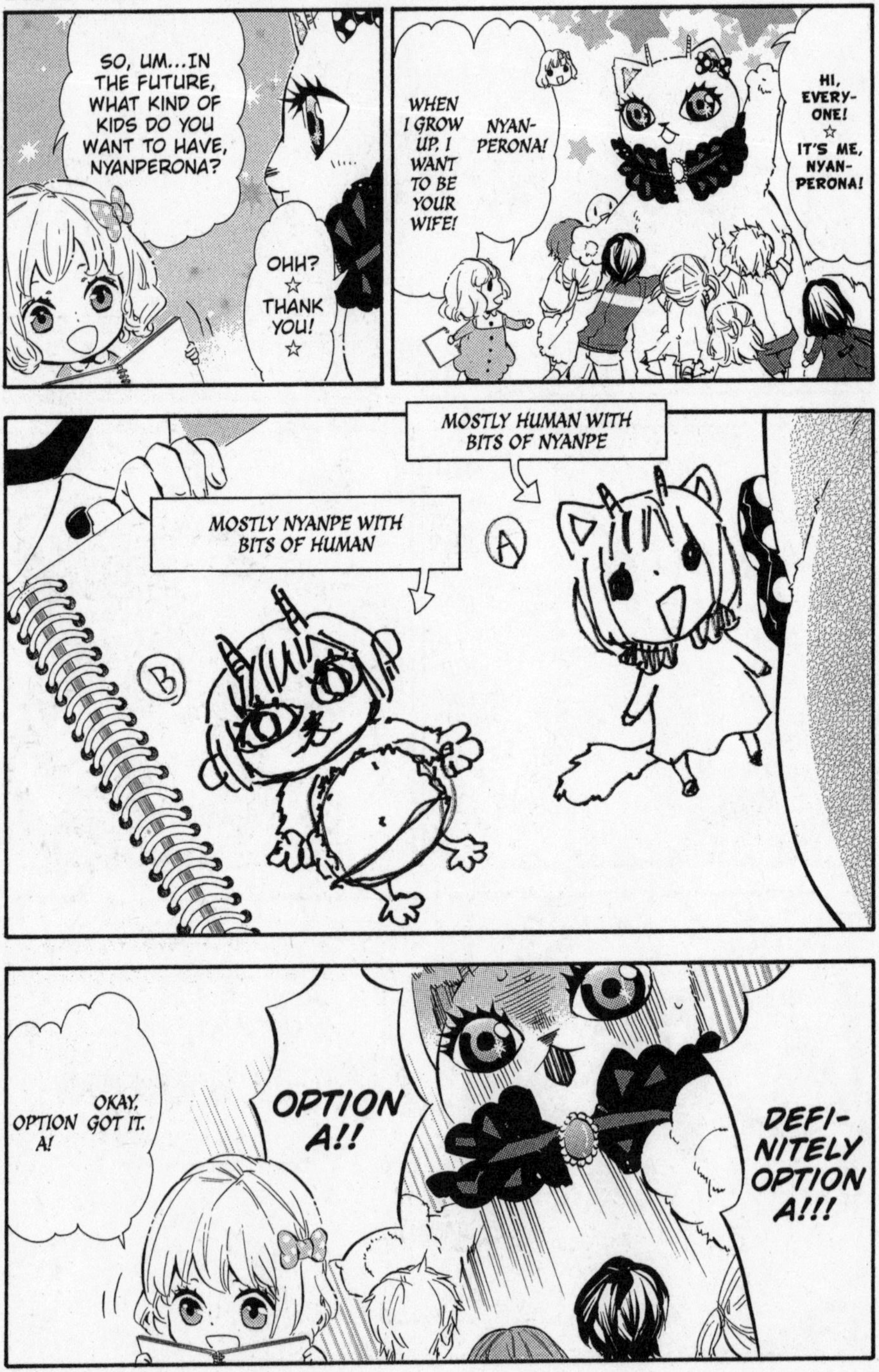
HI, EVERYONE! ☆ IT'S ME, NYANPERONA!
NYANPERONA! WHEN I GROW UP, I WANT TO BE YOUR WIFE!
SO, UM...IN THE FUTURE, WHAT KIND OF KIDS DO YOU WANT TO HAVE, NYANPERONA?
OHH? ☆ THANK YOU! ☆
MOSTLY HUMAN WITH BITS OF NYANPE
A
MOSTLY NYANPE WITH BITS OF HUMAN
B
DEFINITELY OPTION A!!!
OPTION A!!
OKAY, GOT IT. OPTION A!

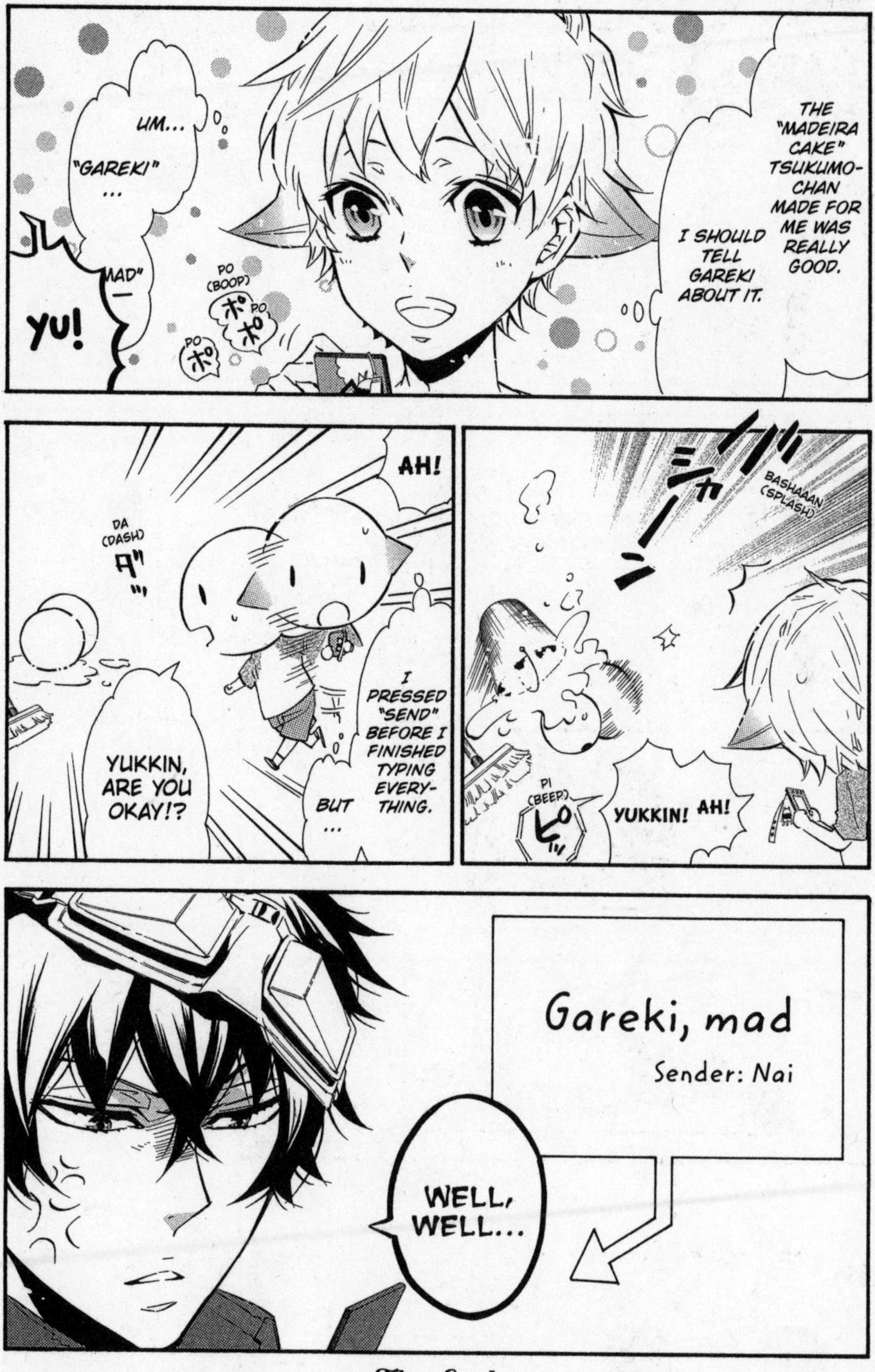
THE "MADEIRA CAKE" TSUKUMO-CHAN MADE FOR ME WAS REALLY GOOD.
I SHOULD TELL GAREKI ABOUT IT.
PO (BOOP) ポ
PO ポ
PO ポ
UM... "GAREKI" ...
"MAD" — YU!
BASHAAAN (SPLASH) バシャーン
AH!
YUKKIN!
PI (BEEP) ピッ
AH!
I PRESSED "SEND" BEFORE I FINISHED TYPING EVERYTHING.
BUT ...
DA (DASH) ダッ
YUKKIN, ARE YOU OKAY!?
Gareki, mad
Sender: Nai
WELL, WELL...

The End

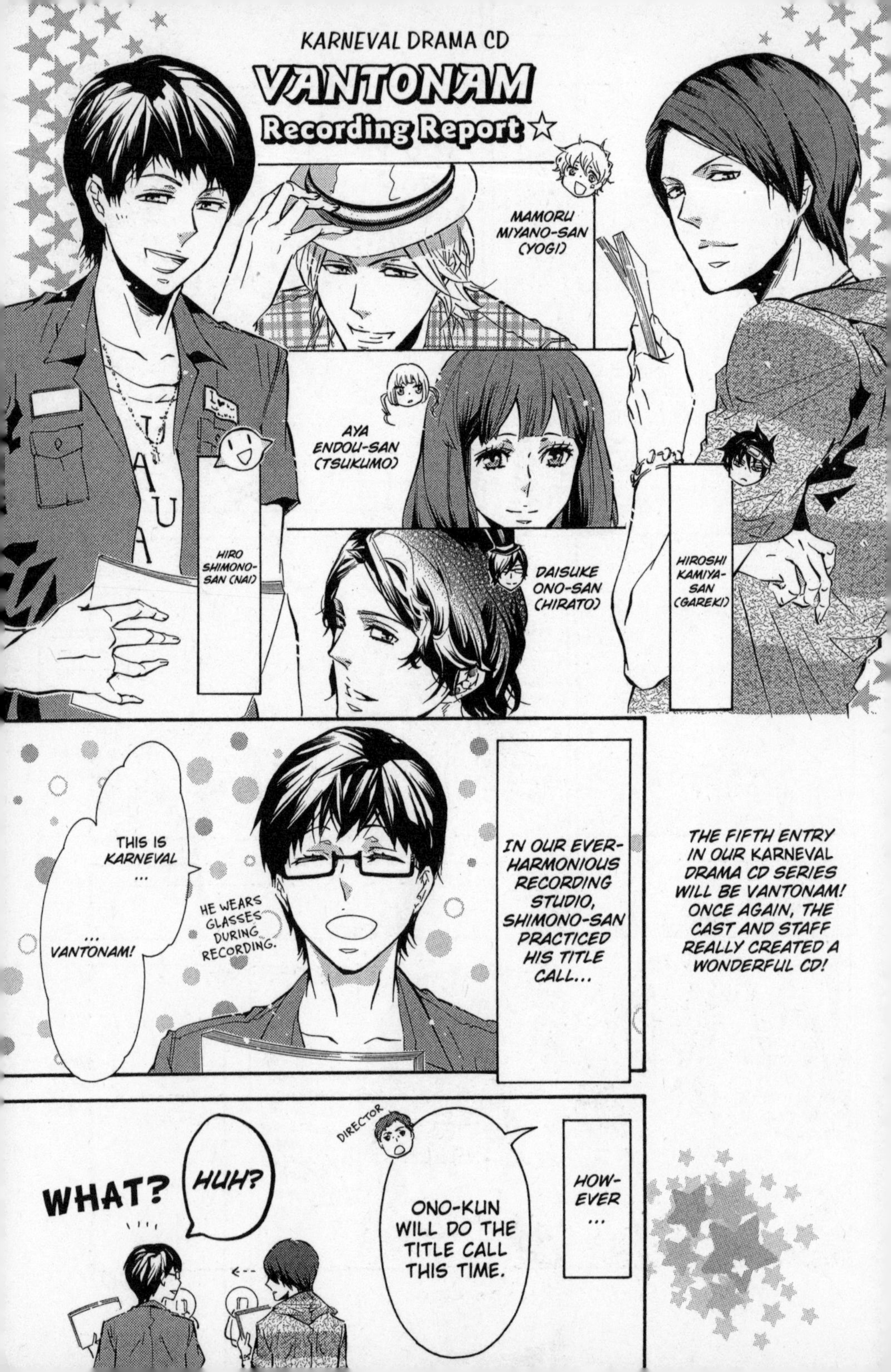
KARNEVAL DRAMA CD
VANTONAM
Recording Report ☆
MAMORU MIYANO-SAN (YOGI)
HIROSHI KAMIYA-SAN (GAREKI)
AYA ENDOU-SAN (TSUKUMO)
DAISUKE ONO-SAN (HIRATO)
HIRO SHIMONO-SAN (NAI)
THE FIFTH ENTRY IN OUR KARNEVAL DRAMA CD SERIES WILL BE VANTONAM! ONCE AGAIN, THE CAST AND STAFF REALLY CREATED A WONDERFUL CD!
IN OUR EVER-HARMONIOUS RECORDING STUDIO, SHIMONO-SAN PRACTICED HIS TITLE CALL...
HE WEARS GLASSES DURING RECORDING.
THIS IS KARNEVAL ...
... VANTONAM!
HOW-EVER ...
DIRECTOR
ONO-KUN WILL DO THE TITLE CALL THIS TIME.
HUH?
WHAT?

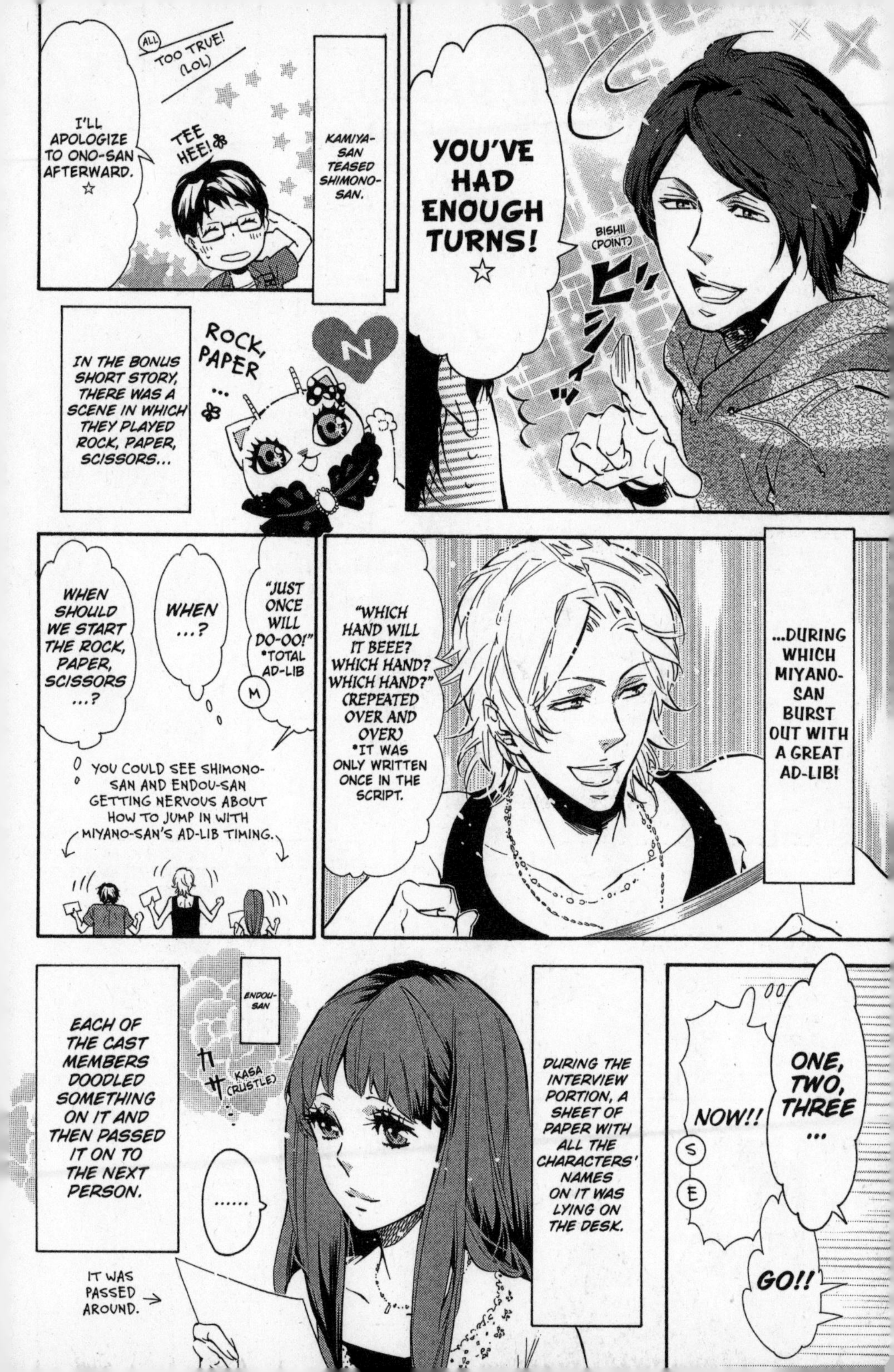

YOU'VE HAD ENOUGH TURNS! ☆
BISHII (POINT)
ビシッ
KAMIYA-SAN TEASED SHIMONO-SAN.
ALL TOO TRUE! (LOL)
I'LL APOLOGIZE TO ONO-SAN AFTERWARD. ☆
TEE HEE! ✿
IN THE BONUS SHORT STORY, THERE WAS A SCENE IN WHICH THEY PLAYED ROCK, PAPER, SCISSORS...
N
ROCK, PAPER ...
...DURING WHICH MIYANO-SAN BURST OUT WITH A GREAT AD-LIB!
"WHICH HAND WILL IT BEEE? WHICH HAND? WHICH HAND?" (REPEATED OVER AND OVER) *IT WAS ONLY WRITTEN ONCE IN THE SCRIPT.
M
"JUST ONCE WILL DO-OO!" *TOTAL AD-LIB
WHEN ...?
WHEN SHOULD WE START THE ROCK, PAPER, SCISSORS ...?
YOU COULD SEE SHIMONO-SAN AND ENDOU-SAN GETTING NERVOUS ABOUT HOW TO JUMP IN WITH MIYANO-SAN'S AD-LIB TIMING.
ONE, TWO, THREE ...
S
E
NOW!!
GO!!
DURING THE INTERVIEW PORTION, A SHEET OF PAPER WITH ALL THE CHARACTERS' NAMES ON IT WAS LYING ON THE DESK.
ENDOU-SAN
KASA (RUSTLE)
EACH OF THE CAST MEMBERS DOODLED SOMETHING ON IT AND THEN PASSED IT ON TO THE NEXT PERSON.
......
IT WAS PASSED AROUND. →

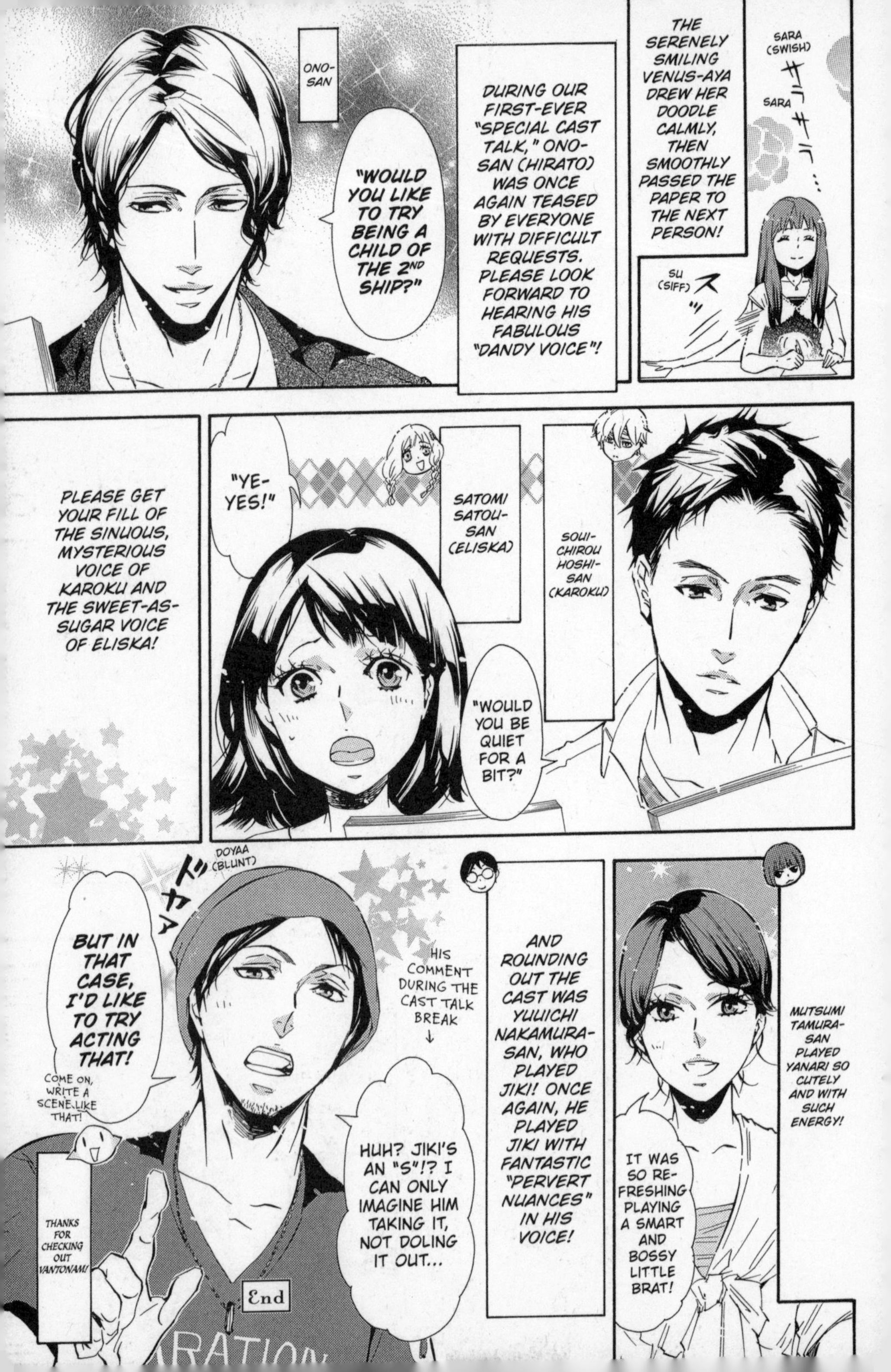
SARA (SWISH)
SARA
THE SERENELY SMILING VENUS-AYA DREW HER DOODLE CALMLY, THEN SMOOTHLY PASSED THE PAPER TO THE NEXT PERSON!
SU (SIFF)
DURING OUR FIRST-EVER "SPECIAL CAST TALK," ONO-SAN (HIRATO) WAS ONCE AGAIN TEASED BY EVERYONE WITH DIFFICULT REQUESTS. PLEASE LOOK FORWARD TO HEARING HIS FABULOUS "DANDY VOICE"!
ONO-SAN
"WOULD YOU LIKE TO TRY BEING A CHILD OF THE 2ND SHIP?"
SOUICHIROU HOSHI-SAN (KAROKU)
SATOMI SATOU-SAN (ELISKA)
"YE-YES!"
"WOULD YOU BE QUIET FOR A BIT?"
PLEASE GET YOUR FILL OF THE SINUOUS, MYSTERIOUS VOICE OF KAROKU AND THE SWEET-AS-SUGAR VOICE OF ELISKA!
MUTSUMI TAMURA-SAN PLAYED YANARI SO CUTELY AND WITH SUCH ENERGY!
IT WAS SO RE-FRESHING PLAYING A SMART AND BOSSY LITTLE BRAT!
AND ROUNDING OUT THE CAST WAS YUUICHI NAKAMURA-SAN, WHO PLAYED JIKI! ONCE AGAIN, HE PLAYED JIKI WITH FANTASTIC "PERVERT NUANCES" IN HIS VOICE!
HIS COMMENT DURING THE CAST TALK BREAK ↓
HUH? JIKI'S AN "S"!? I CAN ONLY IMAGINE HIM TAKING IT, NOT DOLING IT OUT...
DOYAA (BLUNT)
BUT IN THAT CASE, I'D LIKE TO TRY ACTING THAT!
COME ON, WRITE A SCENE LIKE THAT!
THANKS FOR CHECKING OUT VANTONAM!
End

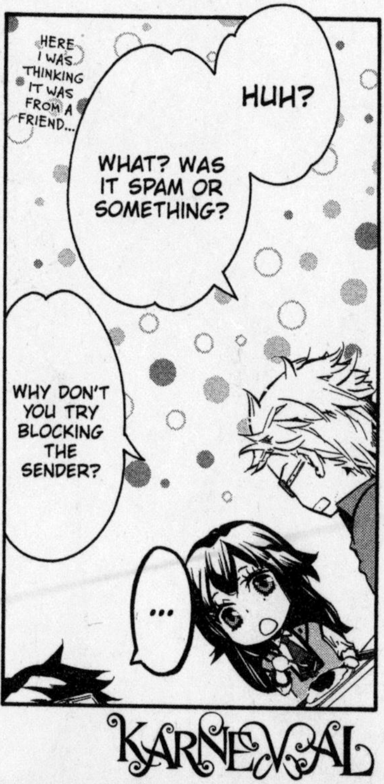
HUH?
WHAT? WAS IT SPAM OR SOMETHING?
HERE I WAS THINKING IT WAS FROM A FRIEND...
WHY DON'T YOU TRY BLOCKING THE SENDER?
...

KARNEVAL

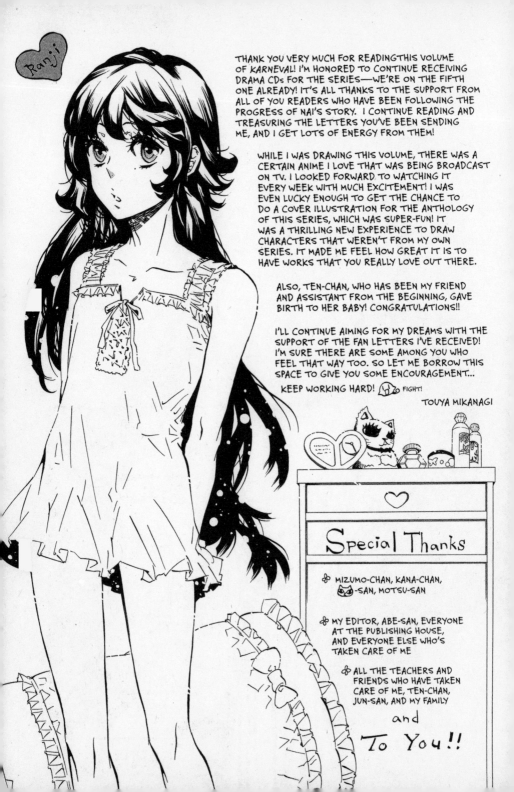

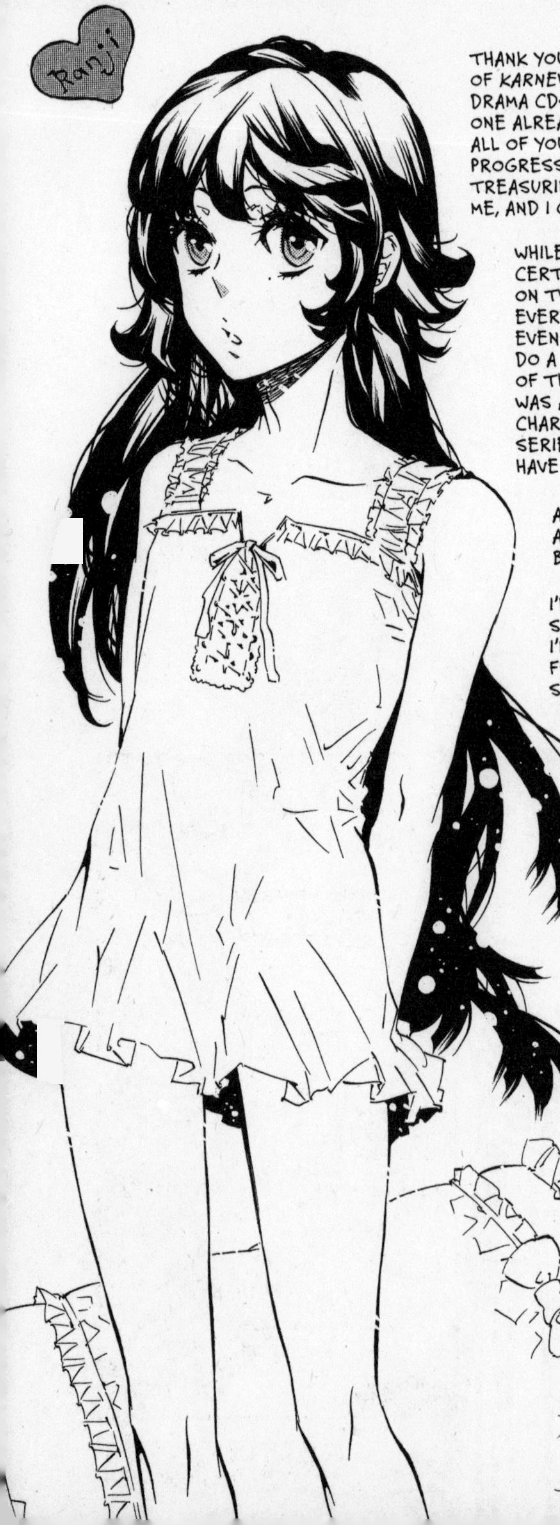
Ranji

THANK YOU VERY MUCH FOR READING THIS VOLUME OF KARNEVAL! I'M HONORED TO CONTINUE RECEIVING DRAMA CDs FOR THE SERIES—WE'RE ON THE FIFTH ONE ALREADY! IT'S ALL THANKS TO THE SUPPORT FROM ALL OF YOU READERS WHO HAVE BEEN FOLLOWING THE PROGRESS OF NAI'S STORY. I CONTINUE READING AND TREASURING THE LETTERS YOU'VE BEEN SENDING ME, AND I GET LOTS OF ENERGY FROM THEM!

WHILE I WAS DRAWING THIS VOLUME, THERE WAS A CERTAIN ANIME I LOVE THAT WAS BEING BROADCAST ON TV. I LOOKED FORWARD TO WATCHING IT EVERY WEEK WITH MUCH EXCITEMENT! I WAS EVEN LUCKY ENOUGH TO GET THE CHANCE TO DO A COVER ILLUSTRATION FOR THE ANTHOLOGY OF THIS SERIES, WHICH WAS SUPER-FUN! IT WAS A THRILLING NEW EXPERIENCE TO DRAW CHARACTERS THAT WEREN'T FROM MY OWN SERIES. IT MADE ME FEEL HOW GREAT IT IS TO HAVE WORKS THAT YOU REALLY LOVE OUT THERE.

ALSO, TEN-CHAN, WHO HAS BEEN MY FRIEND AND ASSISTANT FROM THE BEGINNING, GAVE BIRTH TO HER BABY! CONGRATULATIONS!!

I'LL CONTINUE AIMING FOR MY DREAMS WITH THE SUPPORT OF THE FAN LETTERS I'VE RECEIVED! I'M SURE THERE ARE SOME AMONG YOU WHO FEEL THAT WAY TOO. SO LET ME BORROW THIS SPACE TO GIVE YOU SOME ENCOURAGEMENT...

KEEP WORKING HARD! FIGHT!

TOUYA MIKANAGI

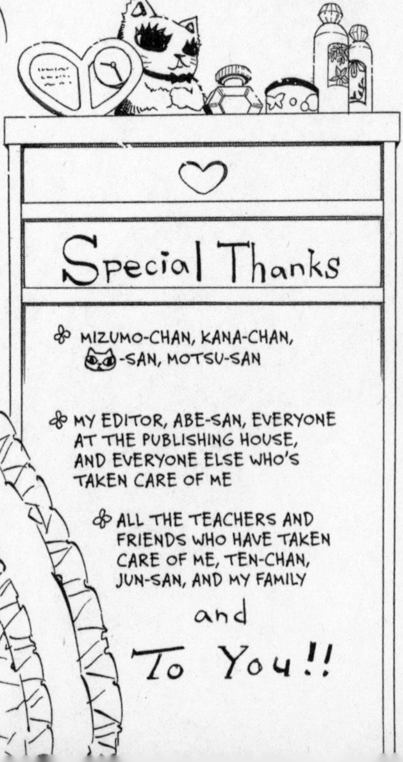

Special Thanks

- MIZUMO-CHAN, KANA-CHAN, -SAN, MOTSU-SAN
- MY EDITOR, ABE-SAN, EVERYONE AT THE PUBLISHING HOUSE, AND EVERYONE ELSE WHO'S TAKEN CARE OF ME
- ALL THE TEACHERS AND FRIENDS WHO HAVE TAKEN CARE OF ME, TEN-CHAN, JUN-SAN, AND MY FAMILY

and

To You!!

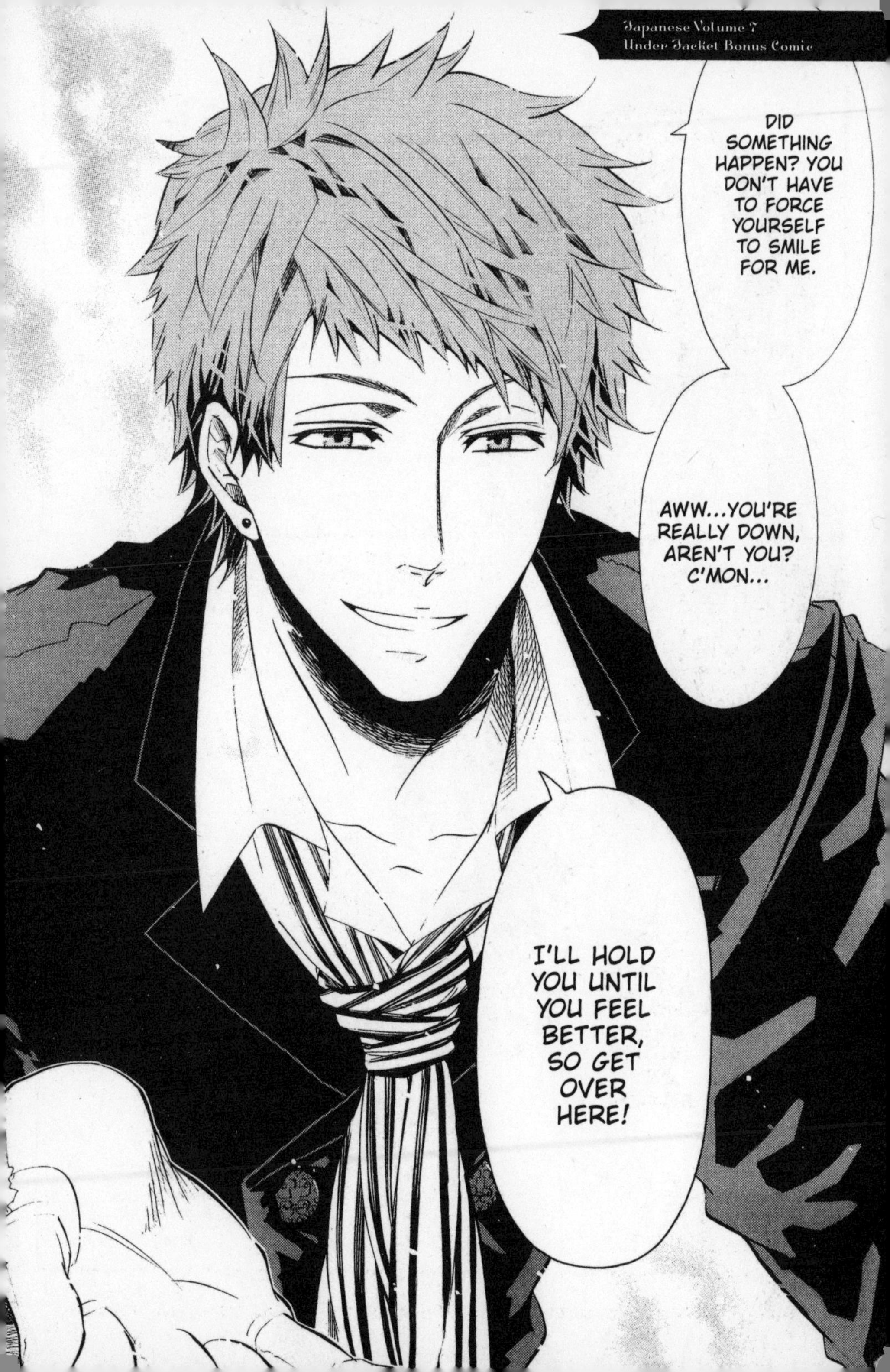
Japanese Volume 7
Under Jacket Bonus Comic
DID SOMETHING HAPPEN? YOU DON'T HAVE TO FORCE YOURSELF TO SMILE FOR ME.
AWW...YOU'RE REALLY DOWN, AREN'T YOU? C'MON...
I'LL HOLD YOU UNTIL YOU FEEL BETTER, SO GET OVER HERE!

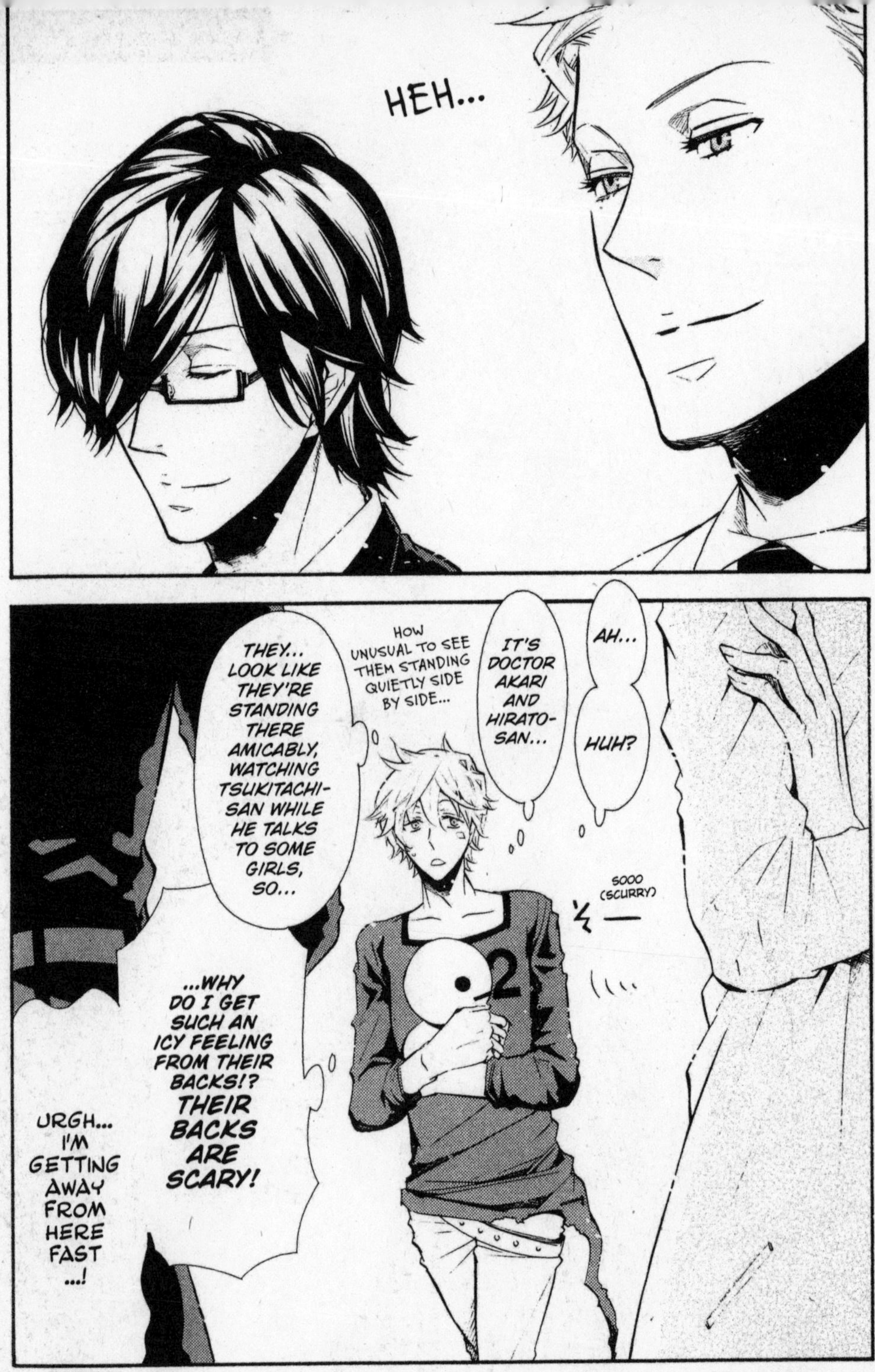
HEH...
AH... HUH?
IT'S DOCTOR AKARI AND HIRATO-SAN...
HOW UNUSUAL TO SEE THEM STANDING QUIETLY SIDE BY SIDE...
THEY... LOOK LIKE THEY'RE STANDING THERE AMICABLY, WATCHING TSUKITACHI-SAN WHILE HE TALKS TO SOME GIRLS, SO...
SOOO (SCURRY)
...WHY DO I GET SUCH AN ICY FEELING FROM THEIR BACKS!? THEIR BACKS ARE SCARY!
URGH... I'M GETTING AWAY FROM HERE FAST ...!

JIKI: ACTUALLY, YOGI-KUN, THAT'S THE TWO OF THEM RIDICULING TSUKITACHI-SAN WITH ALL THEIR MIGHT.

Japanese Volume 8
Under Jacket Bonus Comic

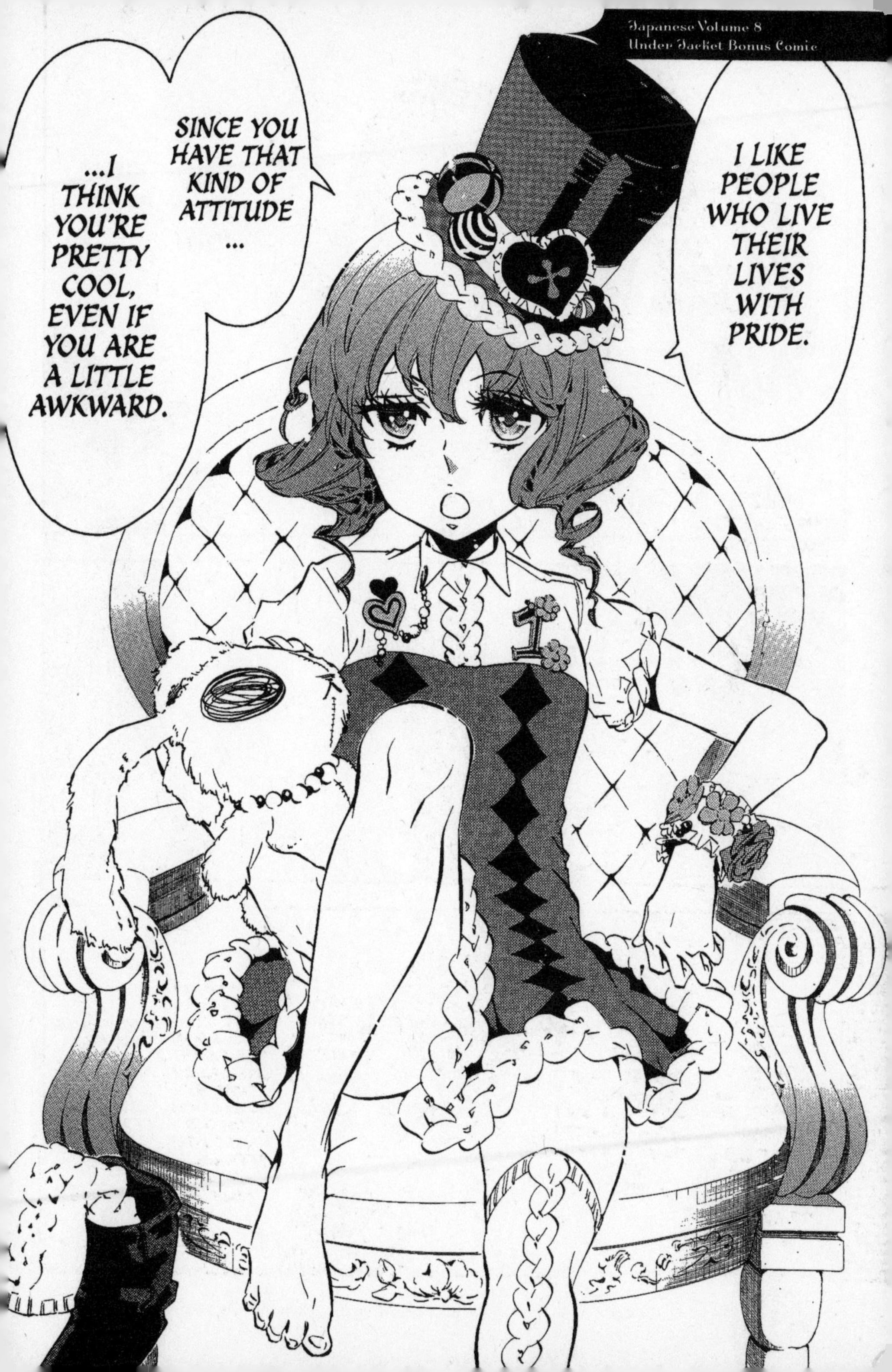
I LIKE PEOPLE WHO LIVE THEIR LIVES WITH PRIDE.
SINCE YOU HAVE THAT KIND OF ATTITUDE ...
...I THINK YOU'RE PRETTY COOL, EVEN IF YOU ARE A LITTLE AWKWARD.

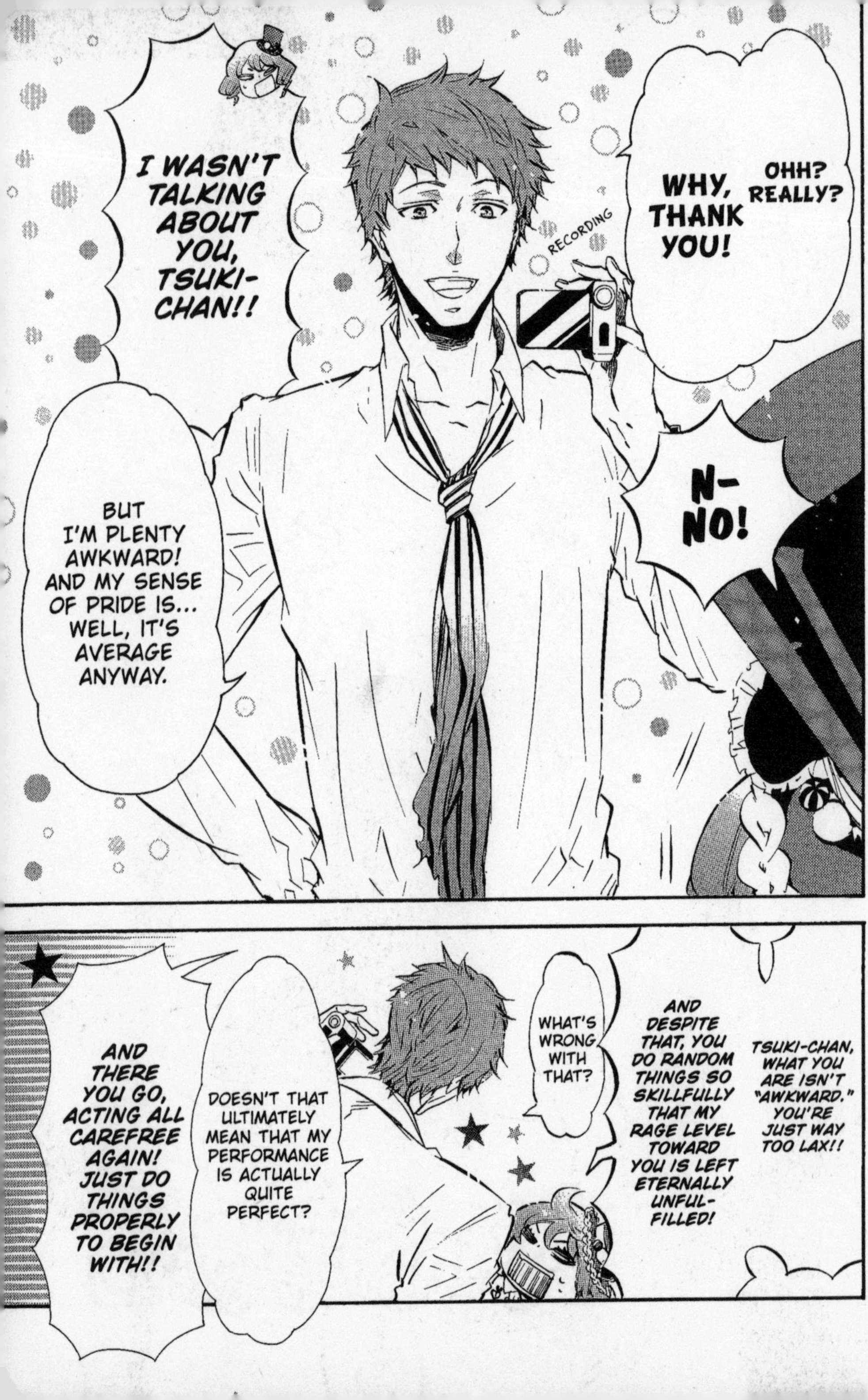
OHH? REALLY?
WHY, THANK YOU!
RECORDING
I WASN'T TALKING ABOUT YOU, TSUKI-CHAN!!
N-NO!
BUT I'M PLENTY AWKWARD! AND MY SENSE OF PRIDE IS... WELL, IT'S AVERAGE ANYWAY.
TSUKI-CHAN, WHAT YOU ARE ISN'T "AWKWARD." YOU'RE JUST WAY TOO LAX!!
AND DESPITE THAT, YOU DO RANDOM THINGS SO SKILLFULLY THAT MY RAGE LEVEL TOWARD YOU IS LEFT ETERNALLY UNFUL-FILLED!
WHAT'S WRONG WITH THAT?
DOESN'T THAT ULTIMATELY MEAN THAT MY PERFORMANCE IS ACTUALLY QUITE PERFECT?
AND THERE YOU GO, ACTING ALL CAREFREE AGAIN! JUST DO THINGS PROPERLY TO BEGIN WITH!!

KARNEVAL

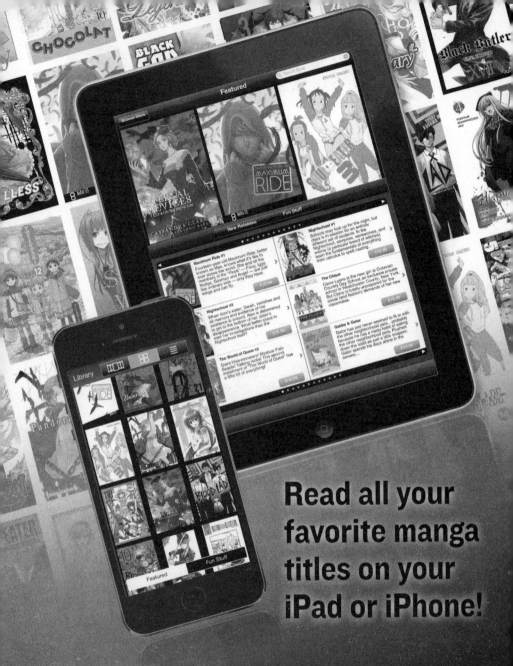

KARNEVAL 4

Touya Mikanagi

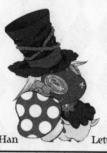

Translation: Su Mon Han   Lettering: Alexis Eckerman

Karneval vols. 7-8 © 2011 by Touya Mikanagi. All rights reserved. First published in Japan in 2011 by ICHIJINSHA. English translation rights arranged with ICHIJINSHA through Tuttle-Mori Agency, Inc., Tokyo.

Translation © 2016 by Hachette Book Group, Inc.

Yen Press
Hachette Book Group
1290 Avenue of the Americas
New York, NY 10104

www.HachetteBookGroup.com
www.YenPress.com

Yen Press is an imprint of Hachette Book Group, Inc.
The Yen Press name and logo are trademarks of Hachette Book Group, Inc.

The publisher is not responsible for websites (or their content) that are not owned by the publisher.

Library of Congress Control Number: 2015956849

First Yen Press Edition: March 2016

ISBN: 978-0-316-26349-8

10 9 8 7 6 5 4 3 2 1

BVG

Printed in the United States of America